FREUDENBERG

Carsten Knop

FREUDENBERG

A Start-up in a Revolution

With scientific assistance from
Prof. Dr. Werner Plumpe

Translated from German by Geraldine Diserens
and Elizabeth Renken

Campus Verlag
Frankfurt/New York

ISBN 978-3-593-51964-7 Print
ISBN 978-3-593-46041-3 E-Book (PDF)
ISBN 978-3-593-46040-6 E-Book (EPUB)

All rights reserved. No part of this book may be reproduced or transmitted in any form
or by any means, electronic or mechanical, including photocopying, recording, or by any
information storage and retrieval system, without permission in writing from the publishers.
Copyright © 2024 Campus Verlag GmbH, Frankfurt am Main
Cover design: Guido Klütsch, Köln
Cover illustration: above: © Christian Heyse | Profilwerkstatt GmbH;
below: © Unternehmensarchiv Freudenberg & Co. KG
Typesetting: DeinSatz Marburg UG | mg
Typeset in: Minion Pro and Avenir Next LT Pro
Printing office and bookbinder: Beltz Grafische Betriebe GmbH, Bad Langensalza
Beltz Grafische Betriebe is a climate-neutral company (ID 15985-2104-1001).
Printed in Germany

www.campus.de

CONTENTS

	Preface	9
1	**Foundation of the company**	13
	Foundation in the midst of a revolution	13
	Why Weinheim?	15
	Excursus: Leather production	17
	Application to acquire the tannery in 1828	19
	Acquisition of the tannery in 1829 and Carl Johann Freudenberg joins the firm in 1833	22
	Career success, starting a family – and rescue from insolvency	24
	New beginning on February 9, 1849 – The foundation of Heintze & Freudenberg	29
2	**Formative years, innovations and growth**	31
	From innovative patent leather to the foundation of the Carl Freudenberg company	31
	On correct behavior towards one another – the Business Principles	40
	Excursus: Social responsibility – Part 1: From foundation to the outbreak of World War I	44
	Hermann Ernst and Friedrich Carl Freudenberg: America, chrome tanning and a new patriarch	45
	Changes in the ownership structure	51
	The educational pathways of the third-generation managing directors	56
3	**From World War I to Great Depression**	61
	World War I and its impact on Freudenberg (1914–1918)	61
	Excursus: Social responsibility – Part 2: From the First to the end of the Second World War	70
	Hyperinflation and emergency money	70

	Trade unions	73
	Foundation of F&Co. (1921): Separation of the administration of the family shares from business operations	75
	Death of company patriarch Hermann Ernst Freudenberg (1923)	76
	Complete transfer of responsibility to the third generation	77
	Recapturing the markets	80
	The Great Depression and its consequences	84
	Developing technology and driving diversification	87
4	**Freudenberg in the Nazi era**	97
	Freudenberg after the Nazis came to power and the Management Board's political stance	97
	Conversion to a limited partnership	106
	"Aryanizations" and Aryanization attempts	108
	Armaments production at Freudenberg	114
	Effects of World War II on the company and its workforce	117
	Forced labor at Freudenberg	120
	The "shoe test track" in Sachsenhausen concentration camp	123
	Companies' room for maneuver between 1933 and 1945 – An essay by Werner Plumpe	127
5	**New beginning and economic miracle – Internationalization and diversification**	137
	The new beginning: The legal investigation	137
	The company under trusteeship	145
	Richard Freudenberg as a politician in the young Federal Republic of Germany	152
	Rebuilding the leather and shoe business	158
	Excursus: Social responsibility – Part 3: From the end of World War II to the end of the 1950s	169
	Nonwovens become Vileda	170
	The emergence of the first filters, innovations and the construction of the Berlin Wall	176
	The development of the seals business	178
	Entry into the vibration control technology segment	182
	The further development of the Nora segment: the first rubber floorcoverings and increasingly more rubber shoe soles	185

Environmental commitment in South America: Forestry and
timber businesses in Brazil 187
New generation on the Management Board 189
Heinz Hoppe and Freudenberg 192
Hans Freudenberg and education. 195
Era of full employment: Internationalization of the workforce
in Weinheim. 197
New partners in Japan 199
The transition from Richard to Hermann Freudenberg 203
Computing and modern business management 209
Entering the lubricants business with the takeover of Klüber 213

6 Freudenberg under the influence of economic crises, growing complexity and innovations 219

The end of the boom and the acceleration of structural change
in the markets 219
The structural crisis in the German leather industry and its effects
on Freudenberg 225
The first female executive at Freudenberg and environmental
protection. 236
The struggle to retain the shoe and synthetic leather business 238
Freudenberg and SAP. 240
Sealing and vibration control technology between oil crisis,
German reunification and López effect 247
Teething pains in China 259
Structural change? Innovation! Internationalization!
The nonwovens business from the 1960s onward 264
A new market: Freudenberg in India 276
Vileda takes households by storm 281
The rise to become a global player: The development of the
Klüber Group after being taken over by Freudenberg 289
Further development and farewell to Nora. 293
Excursus: Social responsibility – Part 4: Up to the mid-1990s 303
Managing complexity through organization: From division
organization to "**F**reudenberg **O**rganization for **Cu**stomer-Oriented
Corporate **S**tructure" (Focus). 304

7 Sustainability, mobility, digitalization – The company since the turn of the millennium 315

Euro, terrorist attacks, financial crisis, conflicts, pandemic – Freudenberg in a changing world 315

The organizational and strategic evolution: Focus 1 and its successor, Focus 2.0 325

Progression to Focus 2.0 334

Excursus: The history of the Freudenberg logo 338

Planning the future: The Odyssey project 338

The digitalization of Freudenberg 340

Digitalization in training, research and development 345

Excursus: Social Responsibility – Part 5: Since the mid-1990s 353

Freudenberg and mobility in the 21st century 356

The fuel cell – a technology for the future 368

Demographic change – a great opportunity for Freudenberg 376

Household Products, demographic change and globalization 384

Commitment to sustainability for future generations 389

Sustainability in the chemical sector 394

Sustainable solutions for the oil and gas industry 396

A systematic sustainability strategy 402

Leadership, family, values. 406

"Freudenberg will remain a family-owned enterprise" – Interviews with Mohsen Sohi and Martin Wentzler 419

A sustainable corporate culture – Freudenberg as a generational model 431

How archive treasures are revealed – The story of a traveling company and R. F.'s wardrobe trunk 435

Annotations 437

Bibliography and list of references 517

PREFACE

For the first time since it was established 175 years ago, in the middle of the 1848/49 revolution, the Freudenberg family enterprise from the southern German town of Weinheim has had a completely source-based company history compiled. The result is a book about a classic "hidden champion", written for the Freudenberg family and all Freudenberg's employees, for family enterprise owners, for history lovers, but also for people who would like to read a business novel from real life. If a company prospers through all upheavals – starting with the foundation of the German Empire, through World War I, the hyperinflation of the 1920s, the Great Depression, the Nazi dictatorship, World War II, the foundation of the Federal Republic of Germany, right up to a globalized world with a pandemic and digitalization – and if it defies all menaces, if it remains inventive and socially committed throughout, then that is a really good story.

And Freudenberg's story has been defined by the people involved, by their acumen and their talent, by setbacks and by location factors right from its foundation. Likewise, it has always been defined by competitors and amicable collaborations, as well as by the requisite modicum of luck that has constantly accompanied the internationalization efforts that were recognizable from early on.

Is Freudenberg still a classic family enterprise, given the size it has achieved on this journey? The answer is a definite "yes". There is a relationship between size and the transition to external control, but this is considerably more pronounced in the USA. In Germany, in contrast, the large family enterprises are characterized by significantly higher longevity and continuity. And Freudenberg is one of these too.

If we take a look at the lists of the 25 largest family enterprises in both countries, what stands out the most at first glance are the similarities.[1] In both countries, family enterprises top the rankings in individual sectors, and they include well-known brands and global corporations: Ford and BMW in the automotive industry, or Bertelsmann and Fox in the media sector. And then there are the companies which management consultant Hermann Simon called the "hidden champions". They are market leaders in their respective sectors and segments,

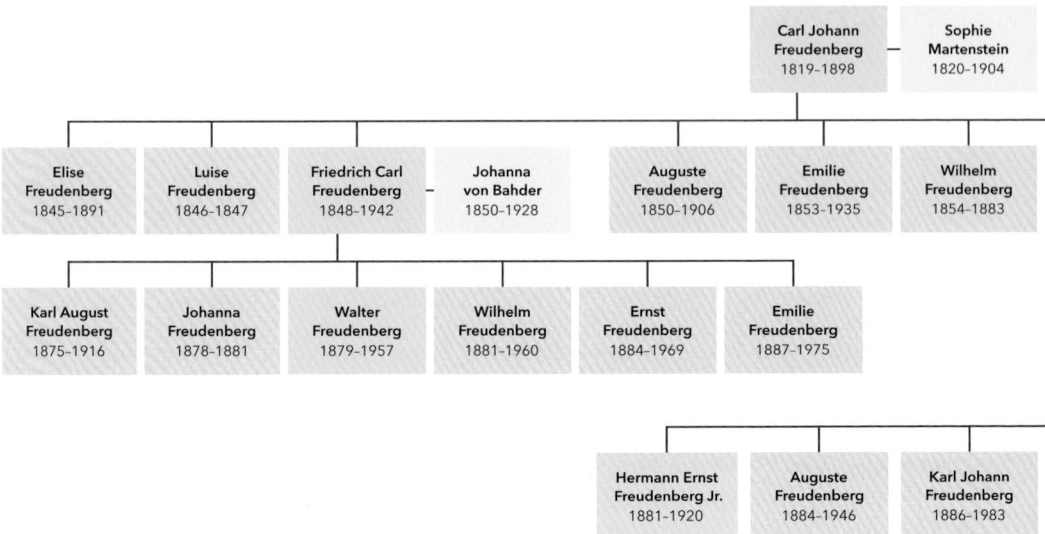

Fig. 1 Freudenberg family tree, 1st to 3rd generations
(the names in blue boxes are people who worked at the company)

or among the top three, and generate billions in turnover. However, they are virtually unknown to the general public. But particularly, they are mostly fully owned by families right up to the present day, have high equity ratios as well as a high level of vertical integration, conduct intensive research and development, and maintain close relationships with partners and customers. On the other hand, they tend to behave with reticence towards the general public. That is no different at Freudenberg.

The capital market in Germany is less efficient in contrast to the United States and the United Kingdom, a fact which leads to the low market capitalization of German companies in an international comparison. This is an advantage. For family enterprises, the incentive to list the company on the stock exchange was and is appreciably smaller. The result is that the shares, or at least the majority of them, tend to be owned more often by the respective families in Germany than in the United States, which is much more capital market-oriented. This is associated with the markedly lower importance of institutional investors, as in hedge funds, pension funds and private equity companies, who are constantly on the lookout for attractive family enterprises as candidates for a stakeholding or takeover.

Such a thing was never an issue anyway in Weinheim, the company's headquarters: Here, the family enterprise was maintained and at the same time it

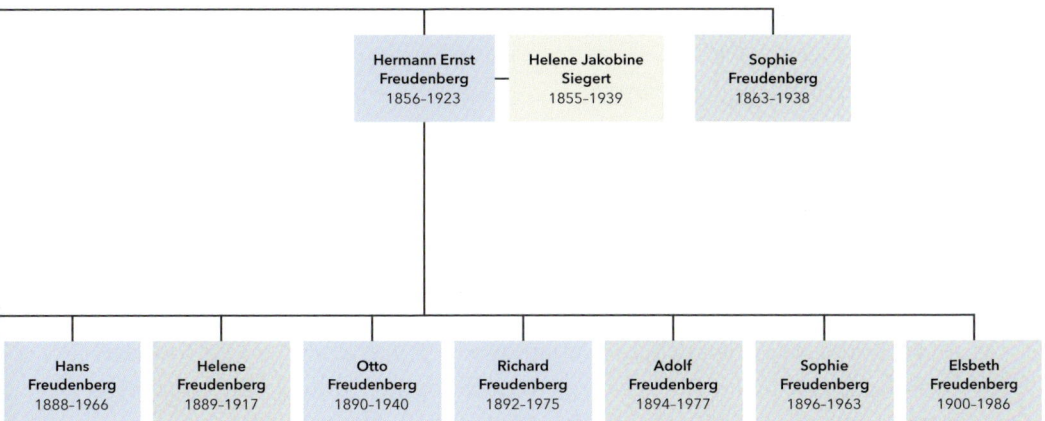

was ensured that the expertise of external managers in executive positions was used as well. Thus there was never an issue of needing a successor from within the family, something which is frequently a catalyst for the sale of a company. Because as early as 1914, Hermann Ernst Freudenberg, a son of the company's founder, was of the opinion that the company did not have to be run solely by family members. In the 1970s, the first managers from outside the family were admitted to the Management Board to promote professionalization. Guidelines for employing family members in the company guarantee equal opportunities and the achievement principle. These rules were adapted later to enable family members to maintain a special connection to the company.

In 2012, discussions about employing family members were held again and new guidelines were drawn up based on interviews and a benchmark study. These now stipulate that family members are only permitted to join the company at executive level after demonstrating external success. Overall, we see a story emerge about how the company management developed from a purely family setup right up to a professional and performance-oriented structure.

However, this book also describes the daily and strategic challenges that companies like Freudenberg face – a family enterprise that has been successful over several generations. In this context, Freudenberg benefits time and again from its collective memory and a strong corporate culture that enable it to draw the correct conclusions from previous occurrences and prepare for the future. Collective knowledge, innovation, adaptability and a long-term mindset are key to handling technological and political change. But a long-term mindset should never be confused with forbearance. That too is something which current and future managers and shareholders' representatives must communicate time and again to Freudenberg's employees.

These employees meantime come from more than 100 countries and live on an Earth that is threatened by climate change. Employees in this context naturally always means everyone in all the countries and from all nations in which Freudenberg operates. Freudenberg strives to tap the strengths of diverse cultures and create a shared value system. This is related to the objective of being a carbon-neutral company by 2045 – and helping the world to operate increasingly more sustainably itself, and various products play a role here, but especially hydrogen too as a source of energy. The coming 25 years up to the company's 200th anniversary will not be any less exciting than the time which has passed since its foundation. But in an intact family, people think in terms of generations. A culture cannot be any more sustainable, in every sense of the word and in every respect.

Carsten Knop, in spring 2024

CHAPTER 1
FOUNDATION OF THE COMPANY

Foundation in the midst of a revolution

It is February 9, 1849, a Friday. On this day, Carl Johann Freudenberg (1819–1898) and Heinrich Christian Heintze (1800–1862) establish a new firm based in Weinheim. It bears the name "Heintze & Freudenberg"[1]. 1849: It is already quite a feat for a company to have this year on its files as its founding year. And then in Baden of all places. Because this state was where the revolution in Germany had originated the previous year, and a civil war still raged here in the summer of 1849. It was in this revolutionary Baden, or more precisely, in Mannheim, that Carl Johann Freudenberg lived with his young family. There was uproar in Mannheim in the true sense of the word: "[Here, in February 1848,] a first revolutionary people's assembly took place with more than 2,500 people; countless more followed across Germany in the subsequent days and weeks."[2]

Fig. 2-3 Heinrich Christian Heintze, around 1850 ▪ Carl Johann Freudenberg, around 1875

The demands were: freedom of the press, local militias, jury courts and, as the revolution progressed, a national German state with a freely elected parliament. In Baden, the revolutionaries were divided into two camps: the liberal constitutionals and the radical democrats. Unlike in Württemberg, the liberal forces in Baden did not manage to sway public opinion. From then on, it was no longer a matter of effecting change within the existing political system there, but of achieving radical upheaval.³

Anything seemed possible in this Germany which did not even exist yet as a unified national state at that time. The country was a patchwork of independent territories, and the Grand Duchy of Baden was one of them. The ruling order that had prevailed in the German Confederation⁴ and in Europe after the end of the Napoleonic era was beginning to falter. Businesspeople, who generally tend to favor stable political conditions, followed events anxiously. This also applied to the founders of what is now the Freudenberg Group, Heinrich Christian Heintze and Carl Johann Freudenberg, and their family members.

There was an additional factor: In the midst of the revolution, Carl Johann Freudenberg's son Friedrich Carl was born in Mannheim on November 28, 1848. They were setting the course for both their professional and personal future, just wanted to have their peace – and got upheaval instead.⁵

Take over a business, even if it is with a partner – in uncertain times like these? That requires not just the right character traits, but also the right companions, in equal measure, in a person's professional and personal life. Carl Johann Freudenberg was fortunate enough to be able to combine these ingredients. But this good fortune did not run in his family. These were turbulent times, people had much less money, but more children, than nowadays. They died younger, and their surviving relatives had to start from scratch over and over again.

In Freudenberg's case, everything culminated in the events of the revolution, which was not merely a catalyst for change in European politics. It was also a key contributing factor in changing the way business worked, which in turn would enable former apprentice Carl Johann Freudenberg to gradually become a joint owner and later also sole owner of his own company. This development demonstrates how even bad news can give rise to promising new beginnings. For Heintze & Sammet, the precursor company to Heintze & Freudenberg, which we will cover in more detail further on, this bad news was the collapse of the bank through which it was financed.⁶

But up to that point, many questions still remain open: Why did the real company history start off in Weinheim of all places, when Carl Johann Freudenberg's professional roots were in Mannheim? How did the young Carl Johann Freudenberg meet his wife, Sophie? And: What sort of company was Heintze &

Sammet anyway? Why was leather so important in the region in question? To find the answers to these questions, it is time to leave the exciting revolutionary turmoil behind again – and jump back in time, back to the history preceding the newly established firm of Heintze & Freudenberg.

Why Weinheim?

Fig. 4 Johann Baptist Sammet (no year)

The history of Freudenberg is closely connected to the city of Weinheim and its leather-making tradition, although the firm started off in Mannheim. Because it was right there in Mannheim that entrepreneurs Heinrich Christian Heintze and Johann Baptist Sammet (1798–1870) established their leather business on March 1, 1823, under the name Heintze & Sammet.[7] This business was officially registered with Mannheim's business guild on August 4, 1823.[8]

Leather production, in its turn, held the "position of a key industry" in industrialization, because leather was comparable to iron in its significance as a "construction material". Hence leather was an important material that could be used in many different areas because of its unique material properties. The reasons: The tanned hide was highly elastic, supple, heat insulating, tough, and impervious to moisture, heat and friction. It was used primarily to make clothing, particularly shoes, but also as saddle leather, as leather for drive belts, for gaskets, and furthermore as bookbinding and wallet leather as well.[9]

This means that Heintze and Sammet set up their leather business at a time when leather and the associated craft of tanning played a key role. Corresponding to this, the number of artisanal businesses in the leather-producing industry rose significantly up to 1850 in Germany.[10]

The success of Heintze & Sammet's business far beyond the boundaries of Mannheim in the Grand Duchy of Baden was largely down to their trading network. For this reason, the entrepreneurs soon began to think about expansion,

Fig. 5 The beamhouse in the tannery in Müllheimer Tal (Müll plant), 1899

right up to producing their own leather. This would make the value chain deeper and they would gain better control over their own goods. These thoughts soon turned into actions: In 1828, and thus only five years after establishing the firm, they initially set up their own small boot-leg manufacturing company in Mannheim's characteristic grid of streets.[11] However, they continued to use bought-in leather for this. The desire not to merely process the leather, but also produce it themselves from then on, quickly raised the question of location. For what is needed to produce high-quality leather? The tanner's expertise and the raw materials: animal hides, good-quality running water and tanning agents – in this case, oak bark – in sufficient, meaning large, quantities.[12] None of these were available in Mannheim. There was no bark mill in Mannheim, which would have been necessary to process the tree bark into tannin. Likewise, there was no clean, running water available from a creek, and operating a tannery on Mannheim's rivers, the Rhine or the Neckar, was impossible because of the danger of flooding. Moreover, the odor-intensive leather production would have violated the police regulations that were in force at the time in the City of Mannheim, so this ruled out the establishment of tanneries in the city.[13]

For this reason, Messrs. Heintze and Sammet searched for a location for their tannery outside of Mannheim. However, this issue of location had to take additional factors into account as well: Production had to be easily accessible to Mannheim and if possible be situated within the Grand Duchy of Baden, so that they would not have to pay tariffs for transporting the finished leather to the trading house in Mannheim, where the leathers were sold on.

At this time, the Grand Duchy of Baden was part of the German Confederation which had been established at the Congress of Vienna after the end of the Napoleonic Wars in 1815. As a member state of the Confederation of the Rhine, Baden had been on Napoleon's side in the coalition wars and had grown considerably through skillful maneuvering. The end of the Napoleonic era also heralded what became known as the era of restoration in Baden. However, the state also got a constitution in 1818, which was regarded as liberal in comparison to the other states in the German Confederation.[14]

Why did tariffs have to be considered? In the 19th century, today's Germany comprised several small territories. Because of this, choosing the right location was of decisive importance in view of the duty charged in each case in cross-border trade. That means: Business relations outside Baden at that time were considered foreign trade. From a modern perspective, that sounds unimaginable, but it also shows that large internal markets without customs frontiers cannot be taken for granted.[15]

In the case of Heintze & Sammet – and thus today's Freudenberg Group – and Weinheim, at least, the ingredients all came together at the time of the firm's establishment, because Weinheim was able to fulfill all these requirements: location in the Grand Duchy of Baden, proximity and good connections to Mannheim, expertise in tanning. Leather production had a centuries-old tradition in the city. In addition, there was high-quality running water there. And there was also the oak bark required for making leather, because the city is located close to the oak woods of the Odenwald forest.

Today, Weinheim is the largest city in the Rhine-Neckar Administrative District and the headquarters of the Freudenberg Group.[16]

> **EXCURSUS:** LEATHER PRODUCTION
>
> In Weinheim, particularly the craftsmen known as bark tanners (Lohgerber) had long used the waters of Weinheim's River Weschnitz and its tributary, the Grundelbach. The "tanners made leather for saddles and tack as well as sole and shoe leather using vegetable tanning with what is known as tanbark ("Lohe", mainly oak bark, but also spruce or beech bark)." Their working method can be divided into three phases: Firstly, there is the preparation of the hides in the beamhouse, then comes the actual tanning process, and finally the finishing of the tanned hides. This precise insight is important for understanding why access to high-quality water is of such paramount significance. "In an initial step,

the raw hides were soaked in running water, which is why medieval bark tanneries were always located by running waters – as is the case in Weinheim, where the Gerberbach [tanners' creek] runs through the traditional tanning quarter of the city and where individual tanneries were located by the Grundelbach as well. After being soaked, the hides were laid out on the hide-stretching or scraping frame and the flesh and fat residue removed with the sharp, straight flesher. To remove the hairs, the hides were usually placed into the slaked lime afterwards. This involved putting the hides into vats with burnt lime or potash. The liming dissolved the top epidermal layer, which contains the hair roots. That is why the hairs could simply be scraped off with the blunt, curved moon knife, also known as a fleshing knife. Subsequently, the hides were soaked again."[17]

Anyone who reads these lines and stops to think for a minute about the smells that this must have produced will become queasy even today just thinking about it. "The work in the beamhouse was [correspondingly] exhausting: […] Initially the hides were placed or pushed into the tanning pits, which had been filled with fresh water and tanbark (oak bark that has been ground in the tan mill). The tanning pits, which were lined with oak boards, were either on the first floor or behind the workshop. At certain intervals, the hides in the tanning pits were rearranged to ensure even tanning of all the hides in the pits. After the months-long tanning process [which generally took between 15 and 18 months], the tanned hides were soaked in running water again. Afterwards, the hides were hung up to drip on frames or galleries and subsequently brought to the drying loft of the tannery. […] After the drying process, the leathers finally entered the finishing process, where they were smoothed and shaved, meaning they were given a consistent thickness, whereby shaving leather with a skiving knife must be imagined like planing wood. Lastly, the leathers were ironed to make them shine. These process steps in leather production have remained the same up to the present day. Only the processes and the processing times have changed."[18]

For a long time, the industry continued to thrive in these structures in Weinheim: "From the oldest land register of the City of Weinheim of 1588 we were able to gather that the tanners' craft flourished during the entire 16th century and was able to sell its products not just in the city and the surrounding region, but also on foreign markets via trade routes."[19]

1 Foundation of the company   19

Fig. 6-8 Depilating the skins, 1938 ▪ Tanning pits in the tannery in Müllheimer Tal, 1899 ▪ Finishing colored skins, 1899

Application to acquire the tannery in 1828

When they chose Weinheim as a location, Heintze and Sammet also decided to set up their own leather production in the town in the Bergstrasse region. Anyone who peruses the contract of sale and the land register of the City of Weinheim will discover that Heintze and Sammet initially planned to set up their leather factory in the old tanners' quarter, which was strictly subject to the guild charter. They had chosen the tannery premises of treasurer Ferdinand Hock. This included: a two-story house, courtyard, barn and tannery.[20] In addition, they wanted to acquire his share of the upstream tan mill on the Weschnitz river. So far, so good. However, a problem arose immediately: "But first the two businessmen needed permission to manufacture leather goods in Weinheim."[21] So what were they to do? In this case, the responsible office was the district authority, which was in charge of the administration of all municipalities on behalf of the government. It constituted both the lowest police authority as well as the first level of jurisdiction in all civic legal matters.[22]

Thus, Heintze and Sammet wrote a detailed application to the district authority in Weinheim, in which they clearly emphasized the economic impor-

Fig. 9-10 View of the tannery district in Weinheim, around 1890 ▪ Current view of the buildings

tance of leather production. It is dated July 12, 1828.²³ It listed various reasons why their enterprise should be approved: the advance of industry, the monopoly of foreign companies²⁴ in the leather sector, the unemployment in their own state, while at the same time the state was also imminently capable itself of producing various leather goods which it had hitherto had to procure from abroad. They did not present unsubstantiated arguments, however, because after all they had experience from Mannheim, where they produced boot legs, which had previously come from Strasbourg to the region. That had gone well: apparently so well that Heintze and Sammet stated that they had completely ousted the foreign competition – and were also already achieving sizeable sales in various foreign cities themselves. To be able to expand further, they hoped to get the go-ahead for their own leather factory in Weinheim, the place with many location advantages. However, there was also a disadvantage: Unlike Mannheim, Weinheim was not "guild-free" for tanners – meaning free of guild control. Of course, the applicants were aware of this. That is why they attempted to pre-empt this by stating to the district authority in anticipatory obedience that they did not want to sell any leather in Weinheim.²⁵

Hence the guilds called the shots in Weinheim. But what does (business) life under a guild charter²⁶ actually mean? "A guild is an association of craftsmen of the same profession who met regularly and shared not only interests but also joy and sorrow with one another."²⁷ But the guilds were primarily economic special-purpose associations. Their aim: to protect the craft and each individual craftsman. They were, so to speak, the precursors of today's employee and employer associations. Competition was regulated, which also meant that even within a guild they made sure that no master craftsman should be overly successful. Advertising was forbidden, apprentices often had a hard time, which is why journeymen's associations (*Gesellenbruderschaften*) were formed as a counterbalance, which also displeased the guilds.[28] Consequently, the guilds had good and bad times. Quality of craftsmanship was ensured, but the "rigid insistence on the traditional statutes also ultimately led to the demise of the guilds."[29]

The craftsmen in these guilds did not have it easy, even at the best of times, because for one thing the guilds bore the brunt of the cities' tax revenues. However, this critical role within the community was "crassly" disproportionate to the social standing the craftsmen held: The more important a city's craft became, the more urgent and the louder the calls to have a say in decision-making and advising, and to contribute responsibly to the common good. Time and again in the history of guilds, this led to bloody guild clashes. There were also "free" cities with no guilds, for example Nuremberg, with only one short interruption. But it was the same story everywhere: Across the centuries, various armed conflicts and later the rise of the modern factory industry in particular wreaked hardship on the craftsmen and the guilds. "The craftsman's trade was no longer a match for this competition."[30]

Thus, we can state that guilds everywhere had long been under considerable pressure when Messrs. Heintze and Sammet dared to venture into Weinheim. "In France, the Revolution had brought about the liquidation of the old guilds from 1789 onwards, and thus freedom of trade, which was also introduced into the French-occupied areas later. Prussia followed in 1810 with the introduction of free trade and only decreed the restriction of individual trades for health or security policy reasons. […] The Trade Act enacted in 1825 in Bavaria under King Max I heralded the transition from the concession system to free trade."[31] This law applied to Bavaria, whereas in the Grand Duchy of Baden, on the other hand, the "[…] Weinheim tanning masters" were "[…] incorporated into the tanners' guild right up to the 1860s. […] Trade in leather was regulated for local tanners and for foreigners, who were only allowed to offer their leather for sale at certain times on the Weinheim fairs."[32]

Others turned the signs of the times to account: These included the Mannheim-based trading company Heintze & Sammet.

What happened next with the Heintze & Sammet application is a master class in how to deal with bureaucracy in an administrative state which was now functioning quite well and which increasingly regarded the old guild rules as repugnant.[33] First of all, the district authority wanted to question the municipal council of the City of Weinheim, but it apparently regarded the whole thing as a hot potato and initially did not react at all. Then, on August 1, 1828, the Grand Duchy's district authority threatened to fine the municipal council 1 thaler.[34] This was the equivalent of about one month's pay for a simple soldier in the southern German region.[35] Based on this, it was an appreciable monetary punishment for the tanners in Weinheim. The mayor of Weinheim decided to summon his tanners' guild and the guild – not surprisingly – delivered an unfavorable statement: They did not want the rich people from Mannheim, they said, because all they wanted was to get even richer in Weinheim anyway, at the expense of the local tanners. The factory was unnecessary, as leather sales were bad already, they added, and that could be seen from the fact that the number of master tanners was already declining at that time. Their friendly alternative suggestion: Neckargemünd, Heidelberg or Wiesloch. There was simply more space there – and there were tanners there too, they said.[36] These statements were one thing above all: an expression of the local tanning craftsmen's fear of competition from industrial leather production.

And a look at the dispute at that time between the entrepreneurs from Mannheim, who were considering a resettlement, and the Weinheim guilds, who were adhering to the old traditions, is relevant from today's perspective too: Because the question of when it makes sense to give new things a chance arises at all times. Even in the very early years, Freudenberg's foundation story provides answers to this question that are still valid today. Inescapable change, fueled by technological advances, cannot be halted by regulation anyway, but at best only steered. And good ideas that displace the old order can turn into a huge benefit for everyone later – if one is just open enough to this change. That applied in the middle of the 19th century. And it still applies today.

Acquisition of the tannery in 1829 and Carl Johann Freudenberg joins the firm in 1833

Hence, the tanners' struggle turned out to be futile in this case too. On August 13, 1828, district authority official Becker approved the request of applicants Heintze and Sammet.[37] Of course, the Weinheim guild tanners did not want to give up just yet. There was still considerable toing and froing, because the Weinheim tanners' guild in its turn submitted a pleading against this resolution. They had sought assistance from a lawyer from Mannheim, whose key argument against the approval was that ultimately Heintze & Sammet would not adhere to the ban on selling leather in Weinheim.[38]

But the tanners did not prevail in this either: On March 7, 1829, the Grand Duchy's Ministry of the Interior also approved the application. Thus, Heinrich Christian Heintze and Johann Baptist Sammet were permitted to set up a leather factory in Weinheim. The only thing they were forbidden to do was conduct individual sales in Weinheim itself, which they themselves had previously offered anyway. And this was how the history of the first Weinheim leather factory began on March 7, 1829.[39]

Four years later, Carl Johann Freudenberg would start an apprenticeship with the company which had won this victory. In those days, kinship relationships were frequently essential for survival. Young people became independent very quickly, had to prove themselves, but were able and permitted to do this too, certainly in the case of Carl Johann Freudenberg. He was only nine years old when his father died, and his father had not had an easy life either. His father's early death necessitated that Carl Johann had to stand on his own feet when he was just a young teenager. In his case, it was with the help of an apprenticeship with his uncle, and thus in the Heintze & Sammet leather business in Mannheim.[40]

How this came about can be read in the memoirs of his son Friedrich Carl, who wrote this down much later, at the age of 90, in 1938: Carl Johann's father, Georg Wilhelm Freudenberg (1786–1829), had to take on responsibility at only 20 years of age himself after his own father's similarly early death. His inheritance was the "Zum Löwen" tavern in Hachenburg, which he ran from then on. But this was the era of pauperism, early industrial underemployment and the poverty crisis, and the economic situation in the country was correspondingly bad. The tavern had to be sold in early 1829 for financial reasons. A radical job change was necessary: Georg Wilhelm Freudenberg was put in charge of the customs station in Weilburg an der Lahn. He died there on March 9, 1829. Only his son Carl Johann, whom he had taken with him from Hachenburg, was living with him. It was an equally hard blow for Carl Johann's mother. She had not just lost her husband; she also had to fight for her family's economic survival now. Destitute, Catharina Elisabeth Freudenberg, née Reinhardt (1789–1843), moved with her six children to Neuwied am Rhein, because there were relatives there who would ensure the family's survival.[41] In a situation like this, a child could not simply remain a child for long. Carl Johann Freudenberg started his apprenticeship at 14 years of age. This remained common practice for a long time based on the Protestant background of Carl Johann Freudenberg's family: because after making their confirmation at the age of 14, young people were considered to be fully-fledged members of the congregation – and were accordingly treated as young adults. This also generally meant the end of their schooldays and leaving their family home. Anyone unable to enter higher education, which in this case was reserved for Carl Johann's elder brother, Wilhelm (1817–1901), began an apprenticeship or had to go into domestic service. Wherever possible, the young adults were apprenticed to a relative.[42] In this case, this was Catharina Elisabeth Freudenberg's sister, Anna Sammet. She was the wife of Johann Baptist Sammet.

With her help, Carl Johann Freudenberg got a placement in the business run by his uncle, leather merchant Sammet, in Mannheim. From all the accounts that are available, the young Freudenberg made a very good showing, because he gained not just Sammet's trust, but also that of his shareholder, Heinrich Heintze. Later, in 1844, which was also the year of his marriage to Sophie Martenstein, Freudenberg even became a silent partner in the company right at the beginning of the year. Freudenberg had already earned some money himself which he could put into the business and was thus able to acquire 20 percent of the shares in Heintze & Sammet.

Career success, starting a family – and rescue from insolvency

It was a momentous Sunday in the spring of 1843 in Mannheim when Carl Johann Freudenberg was to meet his future wife, Sophie Martenstein.[43] The best sources describing what happened back then are Sophie's own memoirs, in which she describes her family home, her childhood – and also that first meeting. Freudenberg, meanwhile, had made an impression and proven his skills during his apprenticeship and in the time thereafter – and had earned a good deal of money. So it was during this time that he met Sophie:

> "My parents lived in Worms, my father was a powerfully built man, strong, industrious and reliable, he was highly regarded, he was a businessman who ran a spice business prudently and successfully, my mother was born in Worms, her parents had a pewter business […]. I did not have much pleasure in my youth, my mother was often gravely ill, my brother could give me nothing, I was frequently permitted to travel to Wiesbaden, and also to Mannheim, for relaxation and recuperation after caring for my dear mother […]. In Mannheim I was sometimes allowed to pay visits, there was a family by the name of Krauss, Mrs. Krauss was the niece of a close friend of my parents, and she often came to visit her uncle. Once I was there for a few weeks in the spring too, there was a choral society recital which I was brought along to, and by chance we ended up sitting beside the Sammet and Reinhardt family. That was where I got to know Father [Carl Johann Freudenberg], the party left together, and we walked quite a lot of the way home together. Another day, on a Sunday, my father [Friedrich Carl Martenstein] and my mother came to collect me, and in the afternoon the young Freudenberg unexpectedly turned up, I was surprised, but was given the explanation that he often came to visit the Krauss family, it was an extremely animated

conversation and I could apprehend that he would not bid farewell very soon, he had heard that my parents had granted me permission, I was allowed to come back again in the summer, he had noted that, and when I did indeed come in June, he turned up too, my mother was with me for 2 days and we were able to see where things were leading. Mother left me there, and then I got to know Father [Carl Johann Freudenberg], because he often turned up in the evenings, after being there for a lengthy period it became clear to me that I loved him, and when he declared himself, I said yes, if my parents consent to it."[44]

If her parents consented to it – this did not just mean examining heart and character, or even appearance, but rather it was a question of economic facts, both about personal financial situation as well as career success. Sophie wrote this: "The conviction of getting a good, hardworking son-in-law, who had after all earned 5,000 guilders, prompted my father to entrust his only daughter to him." And then the wedding could be celebrated: "The engagement up to Feb. 27, 1844, was not a long one, every two weeks Father [Carl Johann Freudenberg] came to Worms, but it was a good and happy time. We celebrated a lovely big wedding, many guests were invited, relatives from Worms, my bosom friends, many of Father's [Carl Johann Freudenberg's] relatives in Mannheim, his brother, who was also engaged, Heintze, and others too."[45]

Fig. 11-12 Carl Johann Freudenberg, around 1860 ▪ Sophie Freudenberg née Martenstein, 1875

Years followed in which a young family grew. Initially two daughters were born: Elise (1845–1891), and Luise, who died young, however (1846–1847). By the time the son, Friedrich Carl (1848–1942), was born, the revolution had already broken out – the country was experiencing turmoil, in which even the bank through which the business was financed using bills of exchange collapsed.[46] Fortunately, Freudenberg's father-in-law Friedrich Carl Martenstein was at hand in this situation. It was also Martenstein's familial support that enabled his son-in-law to take advantage of the crisis as an opportunity for himself. Friedrich Carl Freudenberg, who was born in that revolutionary year, wrote this about it 90 years later in his memoirs:

> "As a result of political turbulence, the firm of Heintze & Sammet had got into financial difficulties and had to liquidate in 1848. [...] Since the liquidation necessitated the separation of the two company owners, Father could choose between the two shareholders. His choice fell to Mr. Heintze. This is how the firm of Heintze & Freudenberg, which had taken over the small calf-leather tannery since 1849, came about in Weinheim [...]. Mr. Heintze and his son Leopold, who was about 10 years younger than my father, moved to Weinheim in 1848, my parents in February 1849. We initially lived on the market square of the little town, which numbered fewer than 5,000 souls at the time [...]."[47]

Sophie Martenstein also vividly remembers this time, which obviously caused her great emotional strain at a very early stage of her marriage. She depicts in great detail the agreements that were made at the time to rescue and take over parts of the business from insolvency:

> "After long consultations with several old business associates and a lot of difficulty with the creditors, an arrangement finally came about in which it was stipulated that all the many creditors (which also included my father and my brother) shall receive their entire capital if they are willing to wait 3 years for the return of same without interest, the companies on the other hand received 60 florins [Baden guilders] instead of 100 florins and then received their money in a shorter time, in this way the hides that had been started and were included in the tannery could be prepared, the old business gradually ceased operations entirely and became defunct on liquidation. [...] Thanks to the gentlemen's considerateness, my husband received the 10,000 florins I had provided out of the liquidation assets, Mr. Heintze had to wait several years until everything was sorted, before he could get his assets back out of the previous business. Then my father was so kind that, once he saw that everything was in order, he then put me on an equal footing with my brother in his fortune, i. e., he gave me up to 30,000

florins in capital, and this formed the stock of the current business, because there was no mention of credit back then, and Father [Friedrich Carl Martenstein] still had to provide advances often for many years, which of course he rightly got back every time with interest."[48]

Let us just take out the calculator now to get a better idea of the amount of capital invested in the company: Regarding the amounts that have been passed down to us, we can say that the total assets of Carl Johann and Sophie Freudenberg came to 15,000 guilders in 1844, of which 12,000 guilders were invested in the company. Based on today's purchasing power, this would incidentally be equivalent to 275,000 euros and 220,000 euros respectively. From Carl Johann Freudenberg's capital account in the 1848 general ledger, we can determine the capital that was actually invested in the firm of Heintze & Sammet. We can read in the ledger: Investments from Carl Johann Freudenberg (November 1848): 4,300 guilders; investment from Sophie Freudenberg (November 1848): 10,000 guilders. This adds up to equity capital of 14,300 guilders in the company (without shares in the profits).[49]

We can no longer determine how high Carl Johann Freudenberg's personal assets were, apart from this amount. However, perusal of the capital account in the 1849 general ledger shows that he must have had some personal assets. Up

Fig. 13-14 The first apartment of the Carl Freudenberg family was in the house in Obertorstrasse 1 off Weinheim market square. View from around 1945 ▪ Current view

to April 1849, Carl Johann Freudenberg invests a further 3,000 guilders of equity capital into the newly established company Heintze & Freudenberg as contributions in cash. Up to July, a further 3,576.44 guilders of equity capital follow from profit shares. Thus, at the end of July 1849, Carl Johann Freudenberg holds equity of 20,876.44 guilders (which converts to around 495,000 euros) in the company.[50] This is how the course was set for a global company in the midst of the revolution.

Sophie certainly followed the commercial development of her husband's company, but she was also a caring mother. Later in her life, the two aspects would merge in a fascinating way, when she ensured that her daughters' families would also continue to retain a financial share in the company's success (see digression on donation to daughters). For the family was growing fast. Sophie Freudenberg wrote about it herself as follows: "On May 26, 1850, Auguste was born, she was the 3rd surviving child, on March 8, 1853, Emilie was born [...]. On July 15, 1854, Wilhelm was born. Shortly beforehand, in the spring, Father's sister Emilie came to help me in the house, our household in the new residence with the large courtyard and garden was bigger, I also had to go to Worms to care for my mother, so I needed someone reliable. On March 18, 1856, Hermann was born, it was a lovely time that we spent with the children [...]."[51]

Fig. 15 Hand-colored family photo, 1857, f.l.t.r.: Emilie, Hermann Ernst, Elise, Carl Johann, Sophie, Auguste, Wilhelm and Friedrich Carl Freudenberg

Hermann Ernst (1856–1923) in particular will become vitally important as the history of the company progresses. In 1863, Sophie Freudenberg, who lived until 1938, was the eighth child to be born.

New beginning on February 9, 1849 – The foundation of Heintze & Freudenberg

Thus, on February 9, 1849, the new leather factory could get going at last. The crisis caused by the failure of the bank in 1848 had turned into an opportunity. The foundation of the Heintze & Freudenberg tannery, which employed around 50 workers, was the real start of the company's history.[52] However, they did not turn their back on their old roots, and business relations between Heintze & Freudenberg on the one side and Johann Baptist Sammet on the other side continued even after the split. It is documented that Sammet's leather business in Mannheim was supplied with leather from the Heintze & Freudenberg tannery between 1849 and 1867.[53]

From a modern perspective, it is almost impossible to imagine the turbulent times in which Carl Johann Freudenberg and his partner Heinrich Christian Heintze had to keep their newly reorganized business going. More stability in politics and society would have been welcome. That is likely another reason why there was little sympathy for the revolutionary rebels, as is evident from Sophie's writings: "Heintze and bookkeeper Mansfeld, who were very unpopular with them [the rebels – ed.], fled to the Odenwald in Hesse, and also wanted to take Father [Carl Johann Freudenberg] with them. But he refused to leave the business and his family. Admittedly, it almost came to a situation where he was imprisoned like other citizens of Weinheim. It was only the intercession of butcher Odenwälder that saved him from that."[54] For a misunderstanding could easily become a substantial problem there, and this is one example of that, which cannot be connected to Carl Johann Freudenberg, however: A democratic association had formed in Weinheim which championed the republic. Reputable Weinheim citizens were involved in this association. An attack occurred on the railways, and as a result, a large number of people were indicted, including 33 from Weinheim.[55]

In this context, it is necessary to know that the revolution remained more disruptive in Baden right up to the end than in other places. "In May 1849, the republican forces called for a public assembly to convene in Offenburg in Baden. Among the forty thousand who followed the call, there were many soldiers:

Fig. 16 The site of the tannery in Müllheimer Tal in Weinheim, around 1880

They [the gathering – ed.] called for the resignation of the government and demanded the speedy convening of a constituent state assembly. Within only a few days, almost the entire military in Baden sided with the revolution. In the night of May 13–14, 1849, Grand Duke Leopold fled Baden."[56] These troops from Baden were also billeted in Weinheim. "Leopold sought the aid of the King of Prussia. This latter […] issued marching orders to 53,000 soldiers in June 1849. The Republic of Baden proclaimed on June 1 is crushed within a month."[57] The revolution remained disruptive right to the very end in Weinheim of all places: Particularly in June 1849, there was turmoil, the city changed occupying forces several times within a short time. At one stage it was the revolutionary troops, at another Prussians.[58]

At the same time, considerable investments had to be made in the company, and that at a time while troops were still billeted in their own home. Thus, the father-in-law in Worms and his money remained a key financial lifeline.

All of this made a deep impression on young mother Sophie: "The gentlemen had started the first big building job in summer [18]49, where the office was later, in the tannery, then the sound of battle came, […] building was stopped until peace and order were restored in the state again. Our finances were very low, some Saturdays a messenger went to Worms to borrow money from Father [Friedrich Carl Martenstein] for payments; it is understandable that they frequently had to contend with great worries under such conditions."[59]

CHAPTER 2
FORMATIVE YEARS, INNOVATIONS AND GROWTH

From innovative patent leather to the foundation of the Carl Freudenberg company

After the end of the revolutionary conflicts in Baden, Heintze and Freudenberg became acquainted with tanner Karl Michel and his son, Eduard, who were to become critically important to the company's early years. Because, together with his father, Eduard Michel (1830–1895)[1] brought with him a promising technique for lacquering leather which bestowed a strong boom on the company.

Sophie Freudenberg wrote about this in her memoirs:

> "Michel senior, an experienced tanner, arrived in the fall of 1849 and offered the gentlemen to set up the lacquering shop for them, saying their tannage was suitable for it; with my father's approval and support, tests were conducted in the tannery which had satisfactory results; Michel junior, 19 years old, joined the company, he had worked with his father in Paris, had the drawing of the lacquering stoves and the recipe for cooking the varnish."[2]

The courage to take a chance on the young Eduard Michel would pay off quickly. Thus, in 1850, the company was able to launch a new product, patent leather, which was in high demand at that time. It was enormously successful. After only five years, patent leather comprised 80 percent of production volume. The process was constantly refined further – and ensured the employment of 240 workers in 1855.[3] At this time, probably in 1851, Heinrich Christian Heintze's son, Leopold Heintze (1825–1874) was made a general partner in the fledgling company.[4] The circumstances at the time were also a contributing factor in the skills of the later master craftsman Michel and the development of patent leather production. In 1851, a worldwide economic boom started, in part because of the discoveries of gold in California, which gave its name to what was known as the "*Gründerzeit*" [founders' era: a time when questionably speculative companies were rashly founded in Germany – ed.] of the years 1872 to 1873. The global demand for fashionable leather boomed. To meet the high demand, Freudenberg built a lacquering shop from 1852 as a second location in Weinheim. The innovative patent leather also propelled the company's internationalization forward: Lacquered leather was desirable as a fashion item across Europe. A worldwide purchasing (raw hide imports) and sales network was set up. As early as 1850, the company had opened its first branch abroad, in Britain: Leopold Heintze

Fig. 17-18 Eduard Michel, around 1860 ▪ Leopold Heintze, around 1870

Fig. 19 The lacquering shop (later the Old Lacquering Shop plant), around 1900

settled in Liverpool to look after the shoe industry and the leather requirements of the British Empire, the largest market of all at the time.[5] In quick succession, trade relations were also set up with Italy (1851), Scandinavia (1852), Brazil (1853), Spain (1854), Russia (1855), India (1867) and with Australia (1868).[6] Business continued to thrive. The company was able to pay off the liabilities from the liquidation and founding phase. In addition, the first steam engine with a steam boiler was used in the tannery in 1855 for leather production and the business was structurally extended and thus also modernized.[7]

Friedrich Carl Freudenberg also remembers Eduard Michel and his speedy achievements:

"Eduard Michel's success during his initial 15 years (1849–1864) as manager of the lacquering shop was unusual."[8]

This is also expressed in the accolades received by the company and in its positive economic development. Heintze & Freudenberg's high-quality leather goods were exhibited at the first Expo in 1851 in London and awarded a bronze medal.[9] In 1853, the company won another bronze medal in New York, and a silver medal two years later in Paris. The awards had a major influence on business development, because the medals could be employed as a seal of quality and thus as a marketing instrument. Up to the turn of the century, there is evidence that what were known as leather tags[10] as well as embossed stamps, advertisements and posters, were used as advertising material – the company pulled out all the stops. The advertising worked; thus, the awards also made a sizeable contribution to the success of the business – in 1852, one year after the first Great Exhibition in London, the company accounts showed a sales increase of almost 34 percent. After receiving the award in New York, sales surged by more than 43 percent in 1854, while sales climbed by almost 22 percent in 1856 after the Paris Expo. The workforce continued to rise to 320 in 1856 and subsequently 420 in 1865. Sales expanded ninefold – relative to the founding year – in almost the same timeframe to nearly 800,000 Baden guilders (1856) and were already approaching the million-guilder level by 1864 at 926,176 guilders.[11]

Despite the company's financial success, the working relationship between partners Heintze and Freudenberg was difficult. Although Leopold Heintze was closer to his partner Carl Johann Freudenberg in his old age than to his own father and was even friends with him, the working relationship did not appear to be good. Heintze sen. and jun. were freemasons and held liberal views. This led to conflicts with their considerably more conservative partner. Since the elder Heintze had appointed a brother mason by the name of Otto Sexauer as an au-

Fig. 20 Leather labels made by the Carl Freudenberg company from around 1900, with prize medals from the World Expos up to 1867

thorized signatory, two camps formed in the company. The tannery – where the leather was manufactured up to the currying stage – was under the aegis of the Heintzes, while the lacquering shop was Carl Freudenberg's domain, but he gave master lacquerer Eduard Michel a free hand.[12]

The relationship between the partners Heintze and Freudenberg deteriorated increasingly following the death of Heinrich Christian Heintze in 1862, or more specifically his resignation from the company in October 1860. Various factors influenced this: Their conflicting political opinions have already been mentioned. In addition, business was no longer running particularly well in 1865, partially because of escalating technical problems in the lacquering shop. Bankhaus Rothschild bank in Frankfurt wanted to terminate the relationship with Heintze & Freudenberg – maybe for this reason, but maybe also against the backdrop of the impending war of 1866[13] – and although this was prevented, the company's dependence on other financiers increased, which also included Eduard Michel. However, Michel did not get along at all with Heintze's representative and confidant, Otto Sexauer. Michel was the manager of the lacquering shop; Sexauer was head of the tannery – at least, whenever he was there. For he could not tolerate the climate in Weinheim. In addition, he was not an expert in the business. There was also the fact that Heintze's sons were considerably younger than Freudenberg's – and in general there was a certain resistance on Heintze's part against Friedrich Carl Freudenberg joining the company.[14]

Friedrich Carl Freudenberg had been sent to his uncle in Koblenz at the age of 14, to attend a "Prussian" school there. His father's expectations were always high, but his achievements were initially unsatisfactory. Subsequently, he transitioned to high school in Karlsruhe and later to the Polytechnic University, where he completed a three-year degree course in economics and chemistry, which his father had required as preparation for his future work at the company. During semester breaks and after finishing his degree, he was sent for practical training to various tanneries in Germany, in Alsace[15] and in Denmark.[16]

It ultimately transpired that Carl Johann Freudenberg, without involving Heintze, decided to build a second tannery in 1869 in the town of Schönau, which lies to the east of Heidelberg, and then assigned its management to his son, Friedrich Carl.[17] That year, Carl Johann Freudenberg bought a disused scythe plant there.[18] Its location also fulfilled the necessary conditions for running a tannery: good water, water power, proximity to the barks required for the tanning process. On top of that, the purchase price was appealing.[19] Ultimately, the shop was run from July 1, 1869 onward – against his will and only at his father's behest – by Friedrich Carl Freudenberg.[20] Bark-tanned calfskins were tanned there by a workforce of five.[21] Later, horsehides were also processed.[22]

In this context, it is important to know that the plant in Schönau, although it was run by a member of the Freudenberg family, was not part of the Weinheim-based enterprise. And because two different tanneries do not supply the same products, the leather from Schönau was either unstamped or sold with the stamp F. W. B. (Freudenberg, Weinheim/Bergstrasse), while the leather from Weinheim was labelled as a Heintze & Freudenberg product.[23]

Incidentally, the first verifiable partnership agreement of the Heintze & Freudenberg firm likewise also dates from the year 1869, the year the Schönau plant was established. However, this agreement is a manifestation of symptoms of discord: For after the tannery was

Fig. 21 Friedrich Carl Freudenberg, 1895

built in Schönau, Leopold Heintze and Carl Johann Freudenberg initially agreed to dissolve the partnership agreement. Heintze withdrew part of his assets from the company, so Freudenberg had to take out large bank loans. But since the partners then realized the economic difficulties of a liquidation, they finally agreed on the 1869 partnership agreement – with a five-year term.[24]

In 1874, shortly before this agreement expired (and before a new agreement which had already been negotiated could come into force), Leopold Heintze died,[25] upon which his surviving relatives had their investments paid out. The disbursement was paid in accordance with the valid partnership agreement, which foresaw an inheritance regulation to this effect.[26] Since Leopold Heintze had already contracted tuberculosis when he signed the agreement, it is very likely that he deliberately included this type of settlement provision in the agreement to safeguard his family.

Looking at the overall picture, by establishing the plant in Schönau, the dissolution of the partnership agreement by the Freudenbergs had at least been tacitly accepted. However, this did not come at a small cost, either emotionally or financially. There was certainly enough demand for the products from the Schönau plant to enable the lacquering shop to grow: There were already 22 employees working in the leather factory in 1870.[27] However, the enterprise remained unprofitable for several years. Although a first small profit of 5 percent was generated in 1873, the tannery generally operated with deficits on its balance sheets up to 1881, meaning at a loss. It was only after 1881 that the tannery began to operate gainfully, meaning profitably.[28]

Thus, the company came into the sole ownership of Carl Johann Freudenberg in 1874. The firm was renamed Carl Freudenberg. The Schönau tannery was integrated into the newly established firm Carl Freudenberg. Yet the leathers from Weinheim and Schönau are still stamped differently to indicate differences in

Fig. 22 The crest of the Carl Freudenberg tannery from 1874. It shows the tools of the tanner's trade: a currier's knife, a meat knife and a hairing iron for working the skins. The tools are flanked by two lions, who together with the crown symbolize the leadership claim.

quality.²⁹ Furthermore, the economic situation in Schönau still remained fundamentally challenging. In the end, it was Hermann Ernst Freudenberg who helped his brother Friedrich Carl to steer things back onto the right track.

As already mentioned, there was a steady increase in technical problems in the patent leather manufacturing process from 1865, which led to reduced quality. Eduard Michel, the manager of the lacquering shop, was unable to tackle these problems. The patent leather manufacturing process was extremely complicated. This is a chemical process involving the gradual resinification of warmed linseed oil combined with the effects of oxygen in the presence of metal oxides as well as lampblack for blackening. "The greatest source of error lies in the upscaling of a process which has been developed on a small scale onto larger dimensions. The ratio of the vessel's content to the surface, heat economy, time periods, blending, contact with the air and other factors change fundamentally. Ultimately, Eduard Michel was no longer able to cope with this."³⁰

> "In patent leather preparation, the bottoming with linseed oil is very important, but Michel was unable to part with the dirty old residue [i. e., the burnt residue that was still in the bottom of the stove from the previous batches], 'the good oil that's still in it'. So, he heated up the sludge again and again and added freshly heated linseed oil to it, instead of operating cleanly. This went on for years. Furthermore, the bottomed surface should never be dried in the heat. For years, the hides were air-dried on the second floor. When the business was expanded, space in the attics soon became insufficient, so he hung the bottomed hides in hot drying rooms, and he boiled the lacquer fast in tall cylindrical boilers with inadequate air ingress and burnt it. The best ingredients of the linseed oil were carried in a cloud of foul-smelling fumes over Weinheim."³¹

Friedrich Carl Freudenberg remembers the turn for the worse, because alongside his technical incompetence, Michel also had poor human leadership skills:

> "[…] But the next 20 years of his service (1865–1884) delivered one failure after the other. How can this man's tragedy be explained? […] Despite the problems which Michel caused, particularly later on, we should remember him with gratitude. Our father's almost paternal affection for him emanated from this feeling. The man's core must have been better than his shell, otherwise the friendly relationship with Freudenberg would have been inexplicable. But this shell was extremely rough. He treated the workers like slaves, and that despite his principal [Carl Johann Freudenberg], whose kindly nature, as a man who had himself experienced the bitterness of poverty in his youth, was totally opposed to any harshness or unkindness."³²

During this second half of Michel's tenure at Freudenberg, which began in 1865, the political environment changed immensely as well. Under the leadership of Otto von Bismarck, the German Confederation became the German Empire in 1871. As a result, there was a unified German market for the first time. Industrialization marched on. However, there was discord at Freudenberg's top management level. On the one side the overbearing Michel, on the other, patriarch Carl Johann Freudenberg, who was esteemed by his employees for his caring nature. The company got into difficulties; the economic situation in the Empire deteriorated because of what was known as the Panic of 1873, which triggered a recession – known in Germany as the *Gründerkrise* (founders' crisis) – which lasted until 1879.[33] In addition, the quality of the company's own products also declined.[34]

Furthermore, additional conflicts quickly arose from the construction of the factory in Schönau and other building projects, which once again were related in no small part to Michel's character, and Friedrich Carl remembers this vividly later too: "I wonder where Michel got his undeniable construction skills, given that he understands nothing about structural engineering. […] A passion for building had enticed Michel into perpetrating dreadful extravagance in the completion of the Schönau factory. He even used his construction skills to

Fig. 23 The freshly lacquered leathers used to be stretched on the "Tafelacker" (panel field) wooden panels near the Old Lacquering Shop and air-dried in good weather, 1899

use costly sandstone architecture on Father's home. Above and beyond that, for 20 years he managed to gain advantages from properties and materials owned by the company and use the workers on the side. My brother Hermann used a derisory term for this procedure: 'He michelled.'"[35]

Hermann Ernst Freudenberg had spent his years of apprenticeship and peregrination in the United States and eventually returned to Germany, primarily at Friedrich Carl's[36] urgent request, in 1876:

> "In the lacquering shop, Mr. Michel reigned supreme. [...] I [Hermann Ernst Freudenberg] had access to the lacquering factory, but I did not enjoy going there, nor did anyone else, in all likelihood, because to make matters worse, Mr. M.'s [Eduard Michel] less than hospitable manners were bolstered by vicious mutts. – Once, anger got the better of me towards one of these big beasts which was skulking along behind me: I grabbed a cudgel and followed it into a corner. The incident is only worth mentioning because it gave rise to the first quarrel between Mr. Michel and myself. [...] Every working day, he went around the entire factory twice, grumbling as he went, but he repeatedly found refreshing expressions of the coarsest perspicuity. [...] Without a doubt, Mr. Michel also held a great attachment to Father, who definitely overestimated him. 'You can earn a million with Mr. Michel,' he was wont to say. However, I no more believe that Michel was responsible for the disagreements between the general partners than I do that he had initiated the acquisition of Schönau [...]. It was never possible to talk to Mr. Michel, he held forth to the whole world that his business was continually shrinking, but 'my goods are the best of the best,' and he stuck to this. So, we had to get ready for a fight. [...] I then secretly set up a small lacquering shop, which no one except for one trusted worker initially knew anything about. – I worked using my own ideas here, at first with no success, but then with good results, so that I showed the hides to Father. He was highly delighted, but the method could not be used on a large scale, such that I still experienced many difficulties later on.

Fig. 24 Hermann Ernst Freudenberg, 1879

> Nevertheless, I believed I had achieved my goal, and decided to present these new leathers to Mr. Michel. – This was on a Sunday and one of the most difficult hours that I ever experienced. – I knew, of course, that I was assuming an immense responsibility, because I knew that my move would have to lead to a break from Mr. Michel. And so it was. – In extremely furious agitation, words were uttered on his side which made it impossible for me to turn back anymore, even if I had wanted to.³⁷ – Thus the dismissal had been pronounced, but Mr. Michel continued to operate for a further year, until he handed over the keys to me. – He had thought he could straighten things out again, relying on assets of 100,000 guilders which he held in the firm and relying on Father's attachment to him. – But Father started wavering again, as Mr. Michel had correctly hoped, and in another solemn moment, I had to issue the ultimatum: 'Either Michel or me,' and he left for good. And above and beyond that, around this time, 1884, a commercial slump had also set in. Father's assets had not increased over 10 years, because Schönau mostly made losses and Weinheim only made modest earnings."³⁸

Thus, the removal of tanning master Michel was achieved by the emerging second generation. The fact that Michel had helped out the company repeatedly with major loans³⁹ was unfortunate. Michel's departure turned out to be costly and temporarily reduced the company's earnings considerably. But now the way was clear for Hermann Ernst's newly developed patent leather.⁴⁰

On correct behavior towards one another – the Business Principles

Carl Johann Freudenberg's apparently pleasant character traits and particularly in dealing with his employees as well, have already been mentioned. A good example of these is his speech to the workforce during the celebrations for his golden wedding on February 27, 1894:

> "Thank you all for the attachment which you have demonstrated towards myself and my wife through this splendid acclamation. We do not need to have a long speech, because we know each other. We share a close mutual trust. In our business, there has always been a good mutual understanding between factory owner and workers. Naturally, money has to be earned, because otherwise the head of the company has no joy in his work, and the worker far less. In this firm, it is customary for the factory owner to stand by the worker as one person to another, as one Christian to another, as brother to brother, unlike so many stock corporations, where the personal relationship has

been lost. At least 10 times already, very enticing offers have been made to me to establish my business as a stock corporation. I rejected them, because I believe in the principle that I rise and fall with my business and my workers, and I know that this is also my sons' attitude. Therefore, I raise a glass to the good mutual understanding between proprietors and workers."[41]

These were not mere words. Two decades earlier, in 1874, the entrepreneur had already established a company-financed health insurance scheme for his employees, which later developed into the Freudenberg company health insurance scheme.[42]

Carl Johann Freudenberg brought his sons Friedrich Carl and Hermann Ernst into the family enterprise to support him and made them general partners in 1887. At this time, the company already had more than 500 employees, so it already had considerable duty of care.[43]

To mark the generational change and against the backdrop of the size that the company had reached by then, Carl Johann Freudenberg wrote down his Business Principles in 1887 in his own hand now as well.[44] "Modesty, honesty, a solid financial foundation and the ability to adapt to the respective changes were his most important principles for successful entrepreneurship. The principles that were formulated back then still form the basis of the Freudenberg Group's Business Principles that are globally applicable today."[45]

Thus the company values that apply today in the form of the Business Principles and their short version, the Guiding Principles, can essentially be traced back to company founder Carl Johann Freudenberg. Carl Johann Freudenberg's trust principle played a substantial role in the development of the current Business Principles in 1994:[46] "I prefer to give my trust a hundred times and risk being taken in once; that is better than to wrongly mistrust someone once,"[47] or alternatively: "If the trust between me and my workers is disrupted, I will close up shop!"[48]

The objective of the Business Principles that were set down in writing in 1994 – in a management board which numbered increasingly fewer family members – was to define the scope of action of future members of the Management Board. The Guiding Principles dating from 1999 are an abbreviated version of these Principles. The Guiding Principles are designed to define the basic values for all employees of the Freudenberg Group: behavior towards employees, business partners, other interest groups (stakeholders) and towards third parties.[49]

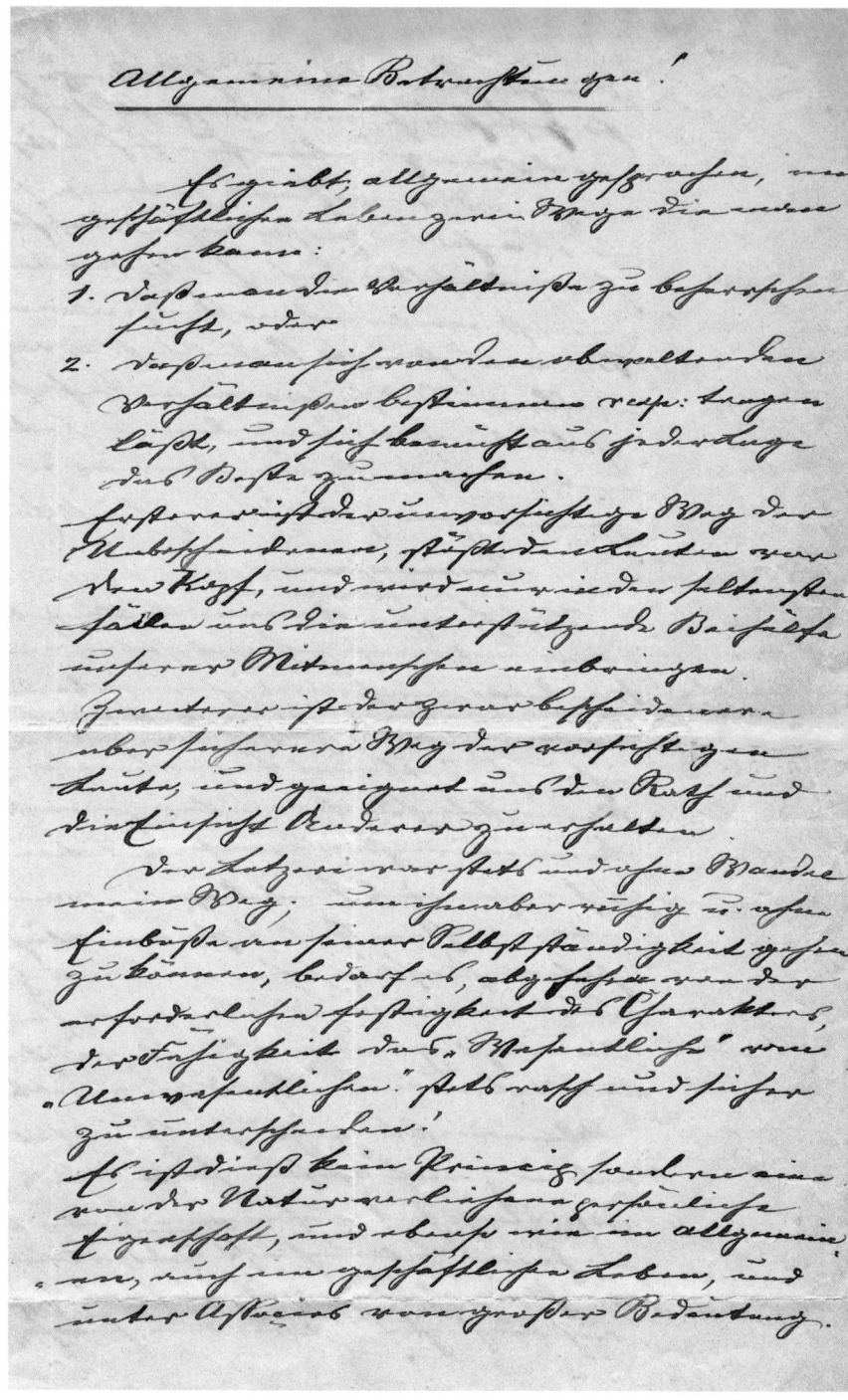

Fig. 25 First page of the 1887 Business Principles

CARL JOHANN FREUDENBERG'S BUSINESS PRINCIPLES, WRITTEN DOWN IN THEIR ORIGINAL FORM IN 1887

GENERAL OBSERVATIONS!

There are, generally speaking, two approaches to adopt in business life: 1. To seek to control events, or 2. To be governed or carried along by ongoing events, and endeavor to make the best of any situation.

The former is the incautious approach of the immodest, offends people, and only in the most infrequent of cases will procure for us the supportive assistance of our fellow men.

The latter is the more modest but safer approach of the prudent, and well suited to retaining the counsel and the insights of others.

The latter has always and unswervingly been my approach; but to pursue it calmly and without compromising your independence requires not only the necessary strength of character, but also the ability to swiftly and surely distinguish the "essential" from the "non-essential"!

This is not a principle, but a personal, nature-given characteristic, and of great importance both in general and in business, as well as between partners. The big, essential things are not so dangerous – it's easier to reach agreement because "things", of course, speak for themselves, whereas non-essential things are frequently a matter of personal views: different people see the same matter differently, with different eyes!

It is important not to have to see everything, or want to see it, and to guard against the dangerous temptations of grumbling, so as to avoid misunderstandings and discord which may propagate and multiply.

PRINCIPLES

Through all the days of my life I have labored, and am gratified, to bequeath to my children an honestly acquired fortune, I have always with almost superstitious anxiety been alert to ensure that no unjust kreuzer was included. I took the Bible's admonitions on unjust goods most literally, and have not infrequently seen how few blessings from their fortune accrue to those who were insufficiently scrupulous in their methods of acquiring money.

My principle in this regard, of taking upon myself the injustice or disadvantage in all doubtful cases, has often cost me money, sometimes a lot of money, but occasionally has benefited me, and has enabled me to always be master of the situation at the decisive moment in major business agreements, as early as 1849 and in multiple cases up to 1874, as the general partners, who were often exceedingly difficult to handle, and also their brutal advocate Grimm had to admit to me expressly and highly unwillingly.

The change in commercial businesses that occurred in the first half of our century and is still ongoing, i. e., the transformation from crafts and small businesses into factories, has affected our leather sector too, where there was once only one single leather factory, of only moderate size, Maier, Michel und Deninger, in Mainz, leather factories and large firms have now sprouted everywhere in place of the tanneries.

Naturally, our business has also been vigorously affected by these changes, and it was the detailed knowledge, which I acquired in long, arduous small business operations, and which, as I may certainly say without being immodest, none of our competitors possess in the same way, which often served me very well, and if we can say today with pride that our factory is only superior to one in terms of the size of the business, but has no superior in reputation and respectability, we are nonetheless aware that we never became unfaithful to the principles that made us big: industriousness, solidity, frugality and simplicity.

EXCURSUS: SOCIAL RESPONSIBILITY – PART 1: FROM FOUNDATION TO THE OUTBREAK OF WORLD WAR I

1874 Carl Johann Freudenberg establishes a company-financed health insurance scheme for his employees, which subsequently develops into the Freudenberg company health insurance scheme. It will be another ten years before Bismarck's social laws introduce statutory health insurance in Germany in 1884.[50]

1889 In Schönau, near Heidelberg, Sophie Freudenberg founds a social health-care center at the instigation of her daughter-in-law Johanna Freudenberg.[51]

1893 Construction of a kindergarten in Schönau and donation to the Schönau church parish by Carl Johann and Sophie Freudenberg. Friedrich Carl Freudenberg was responsible for implementing the kindergarten project.[52]

1894 To mark their golden wedding anniversary, Carl Johann and Sophie Freudenberg founded a general relief fund for employees who had fallen on hard times and their families using capital of 100,000 marks and income of 6,500 marks p.a. Carl Johann and Sophie Freudenberg put their motivation for the donation into words as follows: "In true acknowledgement of the loyal workforce of many good men and inspired by the wish to alleviate severe hardships in the lives of our workers, we are bestowing 100,000 marks in capital from our marital assets in the Carl Freudenberg company for the benefit of its workers in Weinheim and in Schönau [...]."[53]

1902 Donation of public baths to Schönau.[54]

1903   Friedrich Carl Freudenberg founds the invalids fund with capital of 100,000 marks with a yield of 4,000 marks p.a. It grants incapacitated workers a small company pension.[55]

1904   To mark their silver wedding anniversary, Hermann Ernst and Helene Freudenberg donated a widow and orphan fund with capital of 150,000 marks. Widows were to receive 200 marks p.a. and orphans 50 marks p.a.[56]

1905   The company sets up a voluntary supplementary scheme for its workers, for which the company pays all the contributions. The aim of the scheme is to supplement statutory worker insurance by adding sickness insurance, death benefits and redundancy pay.[57]

Hermann Ernst and Friedrich Carl Freudenberg: America, chrome tanning and a new patriarch

Hermann Ernst Freudenberg's professional career is the story of a new beginning. Without him, the company might not have survived the difficulties in the final stages of master lacquerer Michel's employment. Thanks to his international experience, his tenacity, his creativity and his technical expertise, he ensured that Freudenberg actually managed to emerge even stronger from the Michel crisis, when Michel's poor-quality products could only be sold by charging low prices.

Hermann Ernst modernized the production process. He expanded the product range. And even as a young man, he was already self-confident enough to stand up to the reservations of his mother, Sophie Freudenberg, who certainly struggled with her youngest son's planned sojourn in America. Self-confident assertiveness, that is a character trait which helped Hermann Ernst time and again in later life too – not just in the dispute with Michel.

The arduousness of the dismissal of the master lacquerer and the circumstances which led to it have already been described. But where had Hermann Ernst drawn the self-confidence to be able to stand up to the old veteran and guarantor of the company's early commercial success at such a young age? The answer can be found among other things in the numerous memoirs which have been compiled in the family records. Specifically, in the descriptions of the time when Hermann Ernst had argued with his parents, and particularly with his mother, about whether he would be allowed to move to the United States for two years, although he was still only 18 years old.[58]

In this context, it is important to know that Hermann Ernst had already befriended the German American Charles Mann while at school in Karlsruhe. Mann was two years older and was a member of a merchant family in Milwaukee who ran a successful timber business. It was Charles Mann who had inspired Hermann Ernst to go to America to learn the language, but also to acquire knowledge that would be important for him professionally. However: What sounds obvious from a modern perspective, meaning an overseas stay in America, seemed more like an incalculable escapade in the eyes of a caring mother back then. Why? On the one hand, people only went to America, at least as regular emigrants, if they were forced to do so for one reason or other. And the reasons in question were not generally very pleasant: economic hardship, for example, or problems with the law.[59] In this case, admittedly, it was merely an educational stay, and this form of further education abroad was definitely part of the education and training of wealthy businessmen's families. The example of his brother, Friedrich Carl, who worked in tanneries in France and Denmark to gain practical training after completing his studies in Karlsruhe, demonstrates this perfectly. Nonetheless: In Hermann Ernst's case, it was about America, after all, and not a European country. Thus, convincing his mother was no easy task.

However, Hermann Ernst was very keen to go to America and stand on his own two feet. He knew: "In Europe, he would have always remained the son of the prestigious Weinheim company, whose owner despite his deleterious business situation nonetheless knew 'how to maintain his decorum,' but also was increasingly headed for an absolutely hopeless situation."[60] Hermann Ernst got his way, spent his apprenticeship years on the other side of the Atlantic, but maintained contact with Weinheim and wrote many letters, which have been passed down to the Corporate Archives.

Ultimately it was, as already described, particularly his brother Friedrich Carl, who became increasingly nervous in those years in light of how the business was developing. Because the founders' crisis of 1873 presented the Freudenberg company with additional difficulties above and beyond the home-made technical quality problems. Stock market prices collapsed. Banks in particular got into major difficulties and loans were no longer easy to procure. On top of this, Carl Johann Freudenberg, Friedrich Carl Freudenberg and Eduard Michel simply lacked the expertise in their home country to be able to react innovatively to the company crisis and technological transformation. Michel's potential had obviously been exhausted. It was in this difficult situation that Friedrich Carl called on his brother Hermann Ernst for help.[61]

Hermann Ernst, who had long since realized that he did not want to be merely a bookkeeper, but a real entrepreneur,[62] gave in to the pressure and returned in the spring of 1876.⁶³ In this context, the fact that his father had become sole owner following the death of his partner Leopold Heintze in 1874 quickly granted him considerably more opportunities to influence his paternal company directly than would have been possible theretofore. What follows is a success story: Hermann Ernst Freudenberg did not just restructure the patent leather production process and accelerate the transition to machine work (in 1888, the first steam engine was supplied by Maschinenfabrik Chemnitz with an output of 50 hp, in the lacquering works as well now⁶⁴). He also reorganized the crucial business with the partners in Britain, whereby his English language skills, which he had meantime perfected, certainly stood him in good stead.

For at that time in Britain, actually, hundreds of boxes of leather were piling up at their most important sales partner, which was called Bevington & Sons.⁶⁵ It was Hermann Ernst who ensured that the goods bottleneck was cleared and that sales activities were handed over to George Morris, a meritorious employee of Bevington & Sons.⁶⁶ A long-standing friendship developed from this between the Morris and Freudenberg families.⁶⁷ And that is a remarkable occurrence which is typical of the culture in the Freudenberg company. Because such cases of long-standing friendships and commercial cooperation based on mutual trust were set to repeat themselves frequently across the company's history.

Fig. 26 Steam engine for hair washing in Building 1, around 1900

Incidentally, Hermann Ernst Freudenberg was married to Helene Jakobine Siegert (1855–1939). The wedding took place in Düsseldorf in 1879. Helene's father was Düsseldorf painter August Friedrich Siegert (1820–1883), a cousin of Carl Johann Freudenberg's, who came from a manufacturing family in Neuwied. And a closer look shows here, too, that these two men were bound by a lifelong friendship.[68]

In the ensuing period, Hermann Ernst continually developed new products. Particularly after Michel's removal, further decisive steps followed in quick succession: Earlier than others, Hermann Ernst realized that the upper leather manufacturing of the 19th century – flesh side out – was an aberration. From a modern perspective, this needs to be explained: Since time immemorial, people had actually prepared the hair side of the lighter hides, which was protected by the epidermis, as upper leather, like nature itself. Hermann came to appreciate this law of nature, and therefore reverted to it, and additionally decided that the upper leathers should not be sold by weight, "but should logically be sold according to the area of the surface."[69] This transition was a revolution in the market which became standard practice.

The new products, and particularly the mechanized production processes, brought the competition onto the scene, and they wanted to uncover the secrets behind Freudenberg's business success. Competitor Cornelius Heyl from

Fig. 27 View of the Hermannshof, 1899. From 1888, the house and the garden attached to it were the home of the Hermann Ernst Freudenberg family.

Worms used every possible means to close the technological gap for his company. He undertook several targeted attempts to poach Freudenberg employees who would bring their knowledge with them to Worms. And he did not even balk at industrial espionage: In 1889, Heyl offered money to an engineer who was working at Freudenberg to procure the plans of an innovative leather splitting machine that was developed by Freudenberg. But the spy was discovered. He had to leave Freudenberg without the plans, and so Heyl's attempt failed.[70]

But despite of Hermann Ernst's accomplishments, the really major reshaping of upper leather tanning at that time, which was replacing plant-based tanning agents with chromium, can be traced back to American manufacturers. They called the article that was generated after the production conversion "boxcalf".[71] There was no doubt about it: Freudenberg had to follow suit if it was to be able to continue to survive among international competition. The foreign business partners, especially the new trading partner George Morris & Sons in London,[72] were exerting pressure. Fortunately, Hermann Ernst made fast progress in this area too. He "made the [initial] attempts in 1900 in the tannery with the later master craftsman Nikolaus Schmidt".[73] "He succeeded in developing recipes for producing a chrome solution based on chromium sulfate with which he achieved respectable results in manufacturing boxcalf leather and smooth leather."[74] However, things could not be changed from one day to the next. In the end, chrome tanning was not matured and tested as a process at Freudenberg, and thus usable for industrial production, until 1904.[75] But that still meant that Freudenberg was one of the first leather manufacturers in Europe to be capable of launching a high-quality chrome-tanned calf leather on the market.[76]

The introduction of chrome tanning was "a milestone in the company's innovation history,"[77] because it could now save a great deal of time and on top of that it could stand out with markedly improved product features. Success was not long in coming: "It was not just the fact that the tanning time of around 18 months was cut down to just a few weeks. We were able to significantly improve product quality as well. The leather was waterproof, easy to care for and had a uniform surface. […] In the following years, the company became Europe's largest leather manufacturer.

That was expressed in figures too: While Freudenberg still only employed 1,400 workers in 1900, there were already 2,500 employees in 1914. Sales rose from around 12 million marks to more than 54 million marks up to before the outbreak of World War I."[78] Unfortunately, there are no sales figures available for the timeframe in between. But in the final analysis, sales rose more than fourfold within 15 years. It was not until the outbreak of World War I in 1914 that this phase of expansion came to an abrupt end.[79]

Fig. 28 Building 1, which was built in 1896, the first building on the Zwischen Dämmen site. View from 2023

The technological innovations had repercussions far beyond Freudenberg's company boundaries. An entire sector was modernized. "The chrome-tanning process that was further developed by Freudenberg fundamentally changed leather production in Europe. With the help of this leather, which was a great deal faster to produce and of higher quality, companies in the European leather industry achieved a significant increase in sales volumes and sales. Leather production developed into industrial mass production. Thus, the introduction of chrome tanning by Hermann Ernst Freudenberg [from today's perspective] is also a milestone in the history of the European leather industry."[80]

The fact that demand for Freudenberg leather continually increased in the years between 1905 and 1914 and that new production capacities were therefore required is demonstrated by the numerous structural changes during this time. Thus, at the current headquarters in Weinheim, the former "Zwischen Dämmen" plant, a new storeroom for hides with attached refrigerating chambers, a new power plant that could satisfy the company's growing energy, as well as another multistory lacquering shop all sprang up. In addition, a co-op was set up for the employees in the former bark mill in Weinheim.[81]

Work in the production areas increasingly developed away from a craft-based production process and towards industrial manufacturing, which was coupled with the constant expansion of the machinery.[82]

What applies today applied back then too: Technological stagnation was definitely not an option, even in periods of success. Because "only the grain-lacquered chrome patent leathers, which had likewise been given momentum by the Americans, were successful in the market."[83] In this area, Hermann Ernst needed a little more time to develop a viable production process. But sometime during the years 1908/09, he finally found the right ingredients here too, apparently by chance, to replace the bark-tanned patent leather, which was increasingly dwindling in importance in the years after the turn of the century, with chrome-tanned patent leather.[84]

Changes in the ownership structure

It was not only in production that a lot happened in the years around the turn of the century, but in the company's ownership structure as well. It was time for the transition to the second generation. That was why Carl Johann Freudenberg had already involved each of his sons Friedrich Carl and Hermann Ernst as equal partners in his firm, which was registered as an *offene Handelsgesellschaft* (general partnership) back in 1887,[85] and the firm thus "finally became a family enterprise."[86] Afterwards, the company's legal form continued to develop, among other things to be able to withstand the challenges of a new era: "In 1896, the *offene Handelsgesellschaft* [OHG] was transformed into a GmbH [*Gesellschaft mit beschränkter Haftung*, limited liability company]. The idea behind this was to reduce the risk of unlimited liability as the business grew, but probably also the desire to enable the two sons to continue the business as sole owners."[87] One would doubtless act no differently today.

The statutes of this new partnership agreement drawn up by Carl Johann Freudenberg in 1896 came into effect on January 1, 1897. We cannot dispense with a few unwieldy figures at this point, because they are important for realizing how the balance of power in the company gradually shifted. The shares in the equity capital of 6 million marks and thus also the voting rights were in fact determined as follows: Carl Johann Freudenberg: 2,400,000 marks (40 percent), Friedrich Carl Freudenberg: 1,740,000 marks (29 percent) and Hermann Ernst Freudenberg: 1,860,000 marks (31 percent). When the agreement was being drawn up, the three general partners concurred that Hermann Ernst's entrepreneurial achievement should be valued more highly in the distribution of profits, which was regulated accordingly in Paragraph 13 of the GmbH agreement. The profit-sharing bonuses were distributed as follows: Carl Johann Freudenberg received 11.2 percent (1/9), Friedrich Carl Freudenberg 33.2 percent (3/9), Hermann Ernst Freudenberg 55.5 percent (5/9). Taken together with Paragraph 10, through which non-distributed shares in the profit could be converted into equity capital, Hermann Ernst was thus able to constantly increase his share of the equity capital compared to his brother.[88]

In any case, things were well regulated from a commercial and entrepreneurial perspective. Ultimately, Carl Johann Freudenberg was able to look back at a highly successful life, in both his private and professional lives: "When Carl Johann Freudenberg died on August 6, 1898 in Weinheim, the workforce had increased from 50 employees to 1,293 and thus to more than twenty-five times its size at the company's foundation in 1849. During this time, sales had expanded almost sixtyfold."[89] Following the trend of the times, Carl Johann Freudenberg had not foreseen shareholdings in the company for his daughters. That is why these were paid out by their two brothers in the following years.[90]

However, it must also be explicitly noted that following the 1896 agreement and the death of Carl Johann, brothers Friedrich Carl and Hermann Ernst were in fact no longer equal partners in the company. Hermann Ernst became the new leadership figure: he became the true successor to patriarch Carl Johann. And however much they may have been guided by rational agreement, there should be no misapprehension that brothers Friedrich Carl and Hermann Ernst always saw eye to eye – despite their commercial successes, they did not have an easy time with each other in managing the company: Friedrich Carl is described as short-tempered in character, and was said to have sometimes gotten lost "in minutiae".[91] They had different political viewpoints too. Hermann Ernst evidently took little interest in politics, but Friedrich Carl was an active national liberal.[92] What is more: Since as early as his time as plant manager in Schönau, Friedrich Carl Freudenberg had been dissatisfied with his own entrepreneurial achievement, which he constantly viewed critically "with an eye to Hermann Ernst's work in Weinheim."[93]

Friedrich Carl Freudenberg's initial role during his own apprenticeship, in the management of the Schönau plant and later as a catalyst for the repatriation of his brother Hermann Ernst from America is indisputable. Friedrich Carl had received a good education, nevertheless he could not always live up to his father's high expectations – and later his brother's too – which Friedrich Carl reports vividly himself too in his memoirs, which were published in 1938, self-critically and highly reflectively.[94] And yet there are still a few things that can be attributed to Friedrich Carl, as he had decisively influenced the company's social commitment in particular. This was also due to the fact that he was married to Johanna von Bahder (1850–1928). Johanna came from a minister's family. Her father, Eduard von Bahder, was a trained theologian and became a vicar for the Badische Landeskirche (Protestant Church in Baden) in Weinheim in 1848. Johanna and Friedrich Carl, who did not live too far away from one another, became playmates when they were only children. However, the decisive factor is that her father's social commitment made an impact on Johanna too: As a result, this attitude did not just have an influence on Friedrich Carl, but also on his father, Carl Johann Freudenberg, and his father's wife, Sophie, and thus on the entire entrepreneurial family. And this very thing is reflected in the company's social commitment up to the present day.[95]

Within the company itself, however, it did not take long before Hermann Ernst and Friedrich Carl were no longer able to work together to move the operative business forward. What followed was an emotionally taxing separation of business which took several years to complete:[96] By the time Friedrich Carl retired from the Management Board, the brothers had reached an agreement regarding the business to the effect that Friedrich Carl looked after raw goods purchasing and the balance sheets. Production, technology and sales, on the other hand, were under the aegis of his brother Hermann Ernst, who was eight years younger. However, in 1902, this latter comes to the conclusion that his brother must resign from the Management Board.[97]

It is interesting that the first elements of a manager-run company are apparent in this process. Because the "1897 [1896] partnership agreement had stipulated that one of the tasks of the general meeting is also to appoint and dismiss the managing directors."[98] What emerged from this was the ground-breaking development of the legal structure in the direction of a modern corporate constitution with appointed managing directors: Ultimately, the partners in the former *Offene Handelsgesellschaft* had agreed to appoint themselves to the *Gesellschaft mit beschränkter Haftung*. By taking this step, the function of managing director was formally separated from the ownership rights. Furthermore, this legal reconfiguration was also subsequently used, in fact, to dismiss one of the company managers.[99]

In such a concise, purely fact-based compilation, this sounds a lot simpler than it was. For Friedrich Carl did not consent to this step just like that. Lawyers had to be engaged and reports drawn up. This ultimately gives rise to a new partnership agreement, and when it came into effect on February 24, 1905, Friedrich Carl Freudenberg officially resigned as managing director of Carl Freudenberg GmbH.[100] From then on, he only undertook administrative tasks, like the chairpersonships of the company health insurance scheme and the Weinheim building cooperative,[101] or he represented the company in trade organizations. When the Freudenberg & Co. holding company was founded in 1921,[102] the partners appointed him as one of the managing directors. In the end, he did not relinquish all his positions until he reached a great age. At the same time, Hermann Ernst is thus appointed sole managing director – and the payout to his sisters is finally resolved.[103] Subsequently, the allocation of shares looks like this: 74 percent of the equity capital: Hermann Ernst, 26 percent: Friedrich Carl.[104]

From a modern perspective, it is astonishing – and for the company it has remained a blessing up to the present day – that despite the differences between the brothers, the family relationship still remained intact and did not break down. Because with perspective, Friedrich Carl himself looks back very forgivingly as well: "With regard to the great boom in the business between 1887 and 1914, the incredible work which Hermann in these blessed years of peace achieved must be acknowledged."[105]

And although Hermann Ernst was the prominent figure in the company from then on, the brothers worked collaboratively to achieve the transition to the next, and thus the third family generation: Friedrich Carl's son Walter (1879–1957) and Hermann Ernst's son Hermann Ernst jun. (1881–1920) were appointed as managing directors on December 12, 1908.[106] Up until June 11, 1917 Hermann Ernst jun. officially ran the company as managing director together with his father and his cousin, Walter Freudenberg. After that point, Hermann Ernst jun. had to give up his active involvement in the company because of his worsening multiple sclerosis illness. However, he remained a member of the Management Board until his death in 1920.[107] Walter Freudenberg once wrote about his entire time on the Management Board that Hermann Ernst jun. "never, regardless of whom he was dealing with, [sought] to gain an advantage to the detriment of the others, something which made him extremely well liked, not just among his friends and closer acquaintances, but also among all business associates and employees."[108] Thus, Hermann Ernst jun. always acted like an honest businessman, as his grandfather Carl Johann Freudenberg formulated in the business statutes that were drawn up in 1887 as the standard for his successors.

Hermann Ernst jun. felt a great sense of responsibility towards the workforce. One example of this is the foundation of what was known as Automobilgesellschaft Weinheim-Trösel GmbH, which he established shortly before his death in 1920. The aim of this transport service was to make long journeys to work and back easier for the employees from Trösel and the surrounding area.[109] However, this was integrated into the local public transport system in 1922.[110] Moreover, he was interested in the education of the workers and employees, and opened up opportunities for them to receive further training. Former employee Philipp Glaser wrote about this: "He [Hermann Ernst jun.] had a great deal of appreciation, with his father's approval, for what was then known as the leather casino. Master craftsmen and foremen were united there, lectures were held in the winter months to train the listeners in trade and workmanship issues, but other topics of general education were also dealt with by a competent source."[111]

In the ten years he had worked as a member of the Management Board, Hermann Ernst jun. had helped shape the development of the company in manifold ways. For example, through his sales activities in other European countries, he helped to advance the internationalization of the company at the beginning of the 20th century.

Another one of Hermann Ernst jun.'s achievements was the drafting of a landmark partnership agreement: Together with his father, Hermann Ernst sen., his uncle, Friedrich Carl, and his cousin Walter Freudenberg, he concluded an agreement in 1917 for the general partners of the company which was designed to secure the company's ownership with an eye to the ever-increasing number of owners.[112] In the years that followed, the agreement was revised repeatedly, but the limited partnership agreement which has retained a formative influence on the company up to the present day was drawn up on this basis in 1936. This agreement will be covered in greater detail at a later juncture.

As regards the third generation joining the company, Hermann Ernst and Friedrich Carl Freudenberg had already discussed a succession rule at a very early stage for managing directors in office who were family members. In this context, Hermann Ernst wrote a letter to his brother on March 14 of 1914 which has been significant for the company's further development up to the present day. In this letter he stipulated that he by no means adhered to the viewpoint "that the managing directors must come from the family, the business is too big for this, and the family is too ramified to be able to treat it purely as a family business. The main thing is that the managing directors are experienced, diligent experts in their field, and if there are such people within the family, they should be chosen, but otherwise far more preferably outsiders."[113]

Thus, the way was already being paved here for the transition to a management model – a forward-looking deliberation.

As patriarch, Hermann Ernst Freudenberg remained the dominant member of the Management Board up to his death in 1923. However, he set great store in systematically preparing the transition to the next generation. For this reason, his son Otto joined the firm in 1910 and Hans in 1912 so that they would be prepared for later activities as managing directors.[114] Initially, however, Hermann Ernst jun. and Walter were the first members of the third generation on the Management Board of the Freudenberg firm.

The educational pathways of the third-generation managing directors

The third generation of young men who were earmarked for the company were systematically prepared for their activities as managing directors. This occurred, for example, through training periods in Germany and abroad, partially – as was already the case in the previous generations – at companies with which Freudenberg had friendly relationships, and naturally also at universities. In the case of Hermann Ernst jun., his training was aimed at him taking over responsibility for commercial management, including human resources, whereas Walter was methodically prepared for managing raw goods purchasing, Otto for managing global sales and Hans for the technical management of the company by his engineering studies. As a result, the management of the company is allocated already at an early stage into the division of tasks which is still customary today for company management boards. With one exception: Richard Freudenberg was the only one who did not pursue this educational pathway, because originally he was not planned for work in the company, or for the company at all. But how did the individual educational pathways of the third-generation managing directors take their course?

Hermann Ernst Freudenberg jun. (1881–1920)

Hermann Ernst Freudenberg jun. was born as the first of ten children of Hermann Ernst Freudenberg and his wife, Helene, on October 16, 1881 in Weinheim.[115] After taking his *Abitur* (high school leaving examination) in Frankfurt am Main in 1899, he initially completed a traineeship. He was working in the leather warehouse and the tannery at his father's business. Following on from this, he completed a two-year apprenticeship as a tanner in Switzerland. Then came a stay in England, predominantly to learn English language skills at the University of Cambridge.[116] After his one-year military service in the 14th Field Artillery Regiment in Karlsruhe,[117] Hermann Ernst jun. returned to Weinheim in the spring of 1904 at his father's suggestion for further induction. Here, his task now was to familiarize himself with the payroll office, health insurance and costings. Above and beyond this, Hermann Ernst jun. undertook numerous sales trips to Italy, Greece and Turkey, among other places.[118] Hermann Ernst jun. was not called up for military service in World War I because he suffered from multiple sclerosis. Despite his illness, however, he contributed to the company's international success. It had developed into one of the largest leather manufacturers in Europe at the beginning of the 20th century with the introduction of chrome tanning.[119]

Walter Freudenberg (1879–1957)

Walter Eduard Freudenberg, born on November 11, 1879 in Schönau near Heidelberg, was the third child of Friedrich Carl Freudenberg and his wife Johanna. In Weinheim, he initially attended the Bendersches Institut,[120] a private school which aimed to prepare scholars for the transition to the Gymnasium (high school) and university, and subsequently the Realgymnasium in Frankfurt am Main, where he took his *Abitur* (high school leaving examination) in 1898.[121] Shortly afterwards, he began an apprenticeship at Freudenberg on April 18, 1898, "to the office in the mornings, in the afternoons to what was then the storeroom for hides in the Müll [Weinheim's oldest district]."[122] He familiarized himself under his father's direction, particularly with the rawhide market. "Back then, as an apprentice […], it was my purpose to be initiated into the various types of Russian calfskins by Master Sorter Weber and Master Craftsman Schneider."[123] Walter officially completed his apprenticeship at Freudenberg in October 1899. Subsequently, he continued his training in the United States and began working at American hide trader Carroll S. Page in Hyde Park (Vermont). This trader had supplied Freudenberg with lightweight hides up to then. He undertook buying trips to New York and Canada for the firm.[124] In the last months of his stay in America, which totaled eighteen months overall, Walter was also working in shoe factories in New York, Boston and Philadelphia.[125] Between 1901 and 1902, he did his military service as a one-year volunteer in the 14th Field Artillery Regiment in Karlsruhe.[126] Directly afterwards, he tacked on a short training course in Paris, France, and in the spring of 1902 a second trip to the United States and to Canada with authorized signatory Philipp Baer.[127] When Friedrich Carl officially retired from the Management Board in 1905, the purchasing responsibilities were passed on to Walter Freudenberg.[128]

Hans Freudenberg (1888–1966)

Hans Werner Freudenberg came into the world on March 29, 1888 – he was born as the fourth of no fewer than ten children of Hermann Ernst and his wife Helene. Initially – like his cousin Walter – he attended the Bendersches Institut school in Weinheim and subsequently the Goethe-Gymnasium (high school)

in Karlsruhe.[129] After completing his school-leaving examination in July 1907,[130] he did his one-year military service from October 1907 to September 1908 in the König Wilhelm I. Uhlan [light cavalry – ed.] Regiment in Ludwigsburg.[131] Subsequently, Hans completed a degree in electrical engineering at the Technical University of Munich between 1908 and 1912. Then he joined the Institute of Electrical Engineering of the Grand Ducal Technical University of Karlsruhe as a research assistant, but this job was not destined to be of long duration: As early as 1913, Hans joined the leather factory in Weinheim. Taking his education as an engineer into account, he was initially given responsibility for the craft businesses and the power and heating supply.[132] In the First World War which soon followed, Hans was located on the Western Front as regimental aide de camp of a Landwehr (national army) infantry regiment. After the war, he returned to Weinheim in 1919 and then took on the entire gamut of technical responsibilities in the company.[133] In 1922, he was finally appointed to the Management Board as a managing director.

Otto Freudenberg (1890–1940)

Otto Helmut Freudenberg was born, shortly after Christmas, on December 28, 1890 as the sixth child of Hermann Ernst Freudenberg and his wife Helene in Weinheim, where he also went to school, which he completed in 1909 by taking the *Abitur* school-leaving examination. He too went abroad, to be precise to England and to France for his subsequent commercial education, which initially began in his father's company. There were also study trips to America. Then the army called: Between 1911 and 1912, Otto did his military service with the 4th Guard Field Artillery Regiment in Potsdam. In 1912, he joined the company again at the age of 22, to help his father in the sales area. With him, Otto under-

Fig. 29-33
Hermann Ernst Freudenberg jun., 1909 ▪ Walter Freudenberg, around 1940 ▪ Hans Freudenberg, 1938 ▪ Otto Freudenberg, 1938 ▪ Richard Freudenberg, around 1940

took a business trip to America from March 28 to June 8, 1914. However, World War I interrupted his activities for more than four years. During this time, he served as an artillery officer and was only in Weinheim on rare occasions.[134] On September 22, 1914 he was promoted to the rank of lieutenant.[135] In 1918, he returned to Weinheim a highly decorated officer[136] and was awarded the position of authorized signatory in 1919.[137] He left the military after World War I with the rank of a reserve lieutenant.[138]

Otto, who was appointed as a managing director in 1922,[139] assumed responsibility for leather sales as well as all foreign business relationships in the Freudenberg company.

Richard Freudenberg (1892–1975)

Richard Freudenberg spent his entire youth in Weinheim. Born on February 9, 1892 with ultimately nine siblings, he grew up as the seventh child of Hermann Ernst and his wife Helene, née Siegert, on the Hermannshof estate in Weinheim. He attended the Bendersches Institut school and the *Gymnasium* (high school) in Weinheim – and his father had been involved in the foundation of this school. However, the idea of becoming an entrepreneur could not have been further from his mind; Richard felt no urge to join the company. He was drawn to undertake the study of botany in Bonn, which he began in 1911. He developed a particular interest in plant genetics there. Just a short time after he moved to Bonn, in 1912, he attended the Universities of Hastings and Reading during a study trip to England. It was there that he got to know about the political culture and the democratic system of British society. After his return, Richard did not stay in the Rhineland for long; from the 1912/13 winter semester onward, he studied at the Technical University [now BHT – ed.] in Berlin, at which he also began his doctorate on crossing experiments with brassica (cabbages). But while he was preparing his dissertation, the First World War broke out. His brothers were called up to military service. As a result, his father asked him to interrupt his studies. The company in Weinheim needed his help in this situation. Richard, who was not fit for military service because he was born with a mispositioned arm, immediately joined the company on September 1, 1914.[140]

To Richard Freudenberg, this was a self-evident duty towards his family and the company. Hermann Ernst Freudenberg put this into words at the wedding of Richard and Sibille Freudenberg on September 12, 1922 as follows: "When you gave up your beloved original career [botany] without hesitation and followed the call of duty, that was a step for which we all, and especially I myself, owe you a debt of gratitude, for when the war began, I stood alone with a few faithful old workers, faced with a task that became more confusing as the days went by. You grew into your new career fast, and it completely overgrew your old love of brassica, and it was moving for your parents to follow your battle between duty and heart's desire."[141]

The fact that Richard Freudenberg did indeed initially oscillate between "duty and heart's desire" becomes evident in a letter to his mother, Helene Freudenberg, dated February 8, 1916: "The war has changed our terminology, our way of thinking and our habits so fundamentally, that through it and the daily tasks that it sets all of us to a greater or lesser degree, we are apparently losing our autonomy over the future. At least that is what I feel. In the past year, I have seen that I can stay at the factory any time for good without self-sacrifice, if I should be required there. However, if the brothers come home from the war healthy and strong enough to work, then father and the business will have their support again, and I can pursue my interests and my own goals anew. For the time being, I am grateful to have been able to do my duty as a temporary worker."[142]

Thus, he initially learned the ropes at the side of his gravely ill eldest brother, Hermann Ernst jun., in the areas of finance and human resources, the management of which he later took over. Over and above this, he systematically familiarized himself with all areas of the company.[143] At the end of the war, Richard Freudenberg, who turned out to be a very talented businessman, was so heavily embedded in the company and had become indispensable to his father to such an extent that he did not resume his botany studies.[144]

Richard was made a managing director in 1922, together with his brothers Hans and Otto, and thus appointed to the Management Board.[145]

CHAPTER 3
FROM WORLD WAR I TO GREAT DEPRESSION

"At the end of the war in 1918, we were facing a pile of rubble."
Richard Freudenberg[1]

World War I and its impact on Freudenberg (1914–1918)

A period of peace which was lengthy for that era preceded World War I. Whether this had anything to do with the fact that many European royal houses were related to each other is a moot point. In light of the economic division of labor that had become increasingly tight during the long peacetime years and the manifold contacts of numerous companies abroad, a war was neither desirable nor even really imaginable. Accordingly, in the summer of 1914, most entrepreneurs hoped that this time, too, the crisis which had erupted after the assassination of the heir to the Austrian throne in Sarajevo would be resolved peacefully. Because many exporters would have lost their most important customers.

Granted, there was an awareness that the recurrent tensions between the major powers, meaning the turbulent Balkans or the dispute about Morocco, provided for conflicts time and again. But precisely because a settlement of these crises had always been achieved, many people did not necessarily expect a major war even in the runup to August 1914.[2] For Freudenberg, at least, a war made no sense. Instead, it called the entire business model radically into question. Until World War I broke out, Freudenberg had enjoyed a steady uptick in business. In the last year of peacetime, it employed some 2,500 people.[3] The export rate was – looking back at that time from a modern perspective, almost unbelievably – more than 70 percent.[4] What we learn from this: Even back then, the business world was globalized.

The war inevitably brought about an incisive turning point. Within a short time, the conflict between the Austro-Hungarian Empire and Serbia escalated into a war between the major European powers – and with the entry of the United States in 1917 indeed became a world war which lasted more than four years. Millions of people died or suffered physical or psychological wounds.[5]

As soon as war broke out, economic conditions changed abruptly. Goods exports were initially subjected to a universal ban and were later only permitted selectively. At the same time, the English blockade directly affected those companies that were dependent on foreign deliveries. On top of this, only very shortly afterwards, state-directed raw material rationing was introduced. Ultimately, only companies that were vital to the war effort had any prospect of still procuring raw materials in sufficient quantities. Soon there was a lack of everything: raw materials, auxiliary materials, sales opportunities. And labor became a scarce commodity too. Many employees were called up for military service, large numbers of whom did not return alive. Directly after the outbreak of war, around one-third of Freudenberg's workforce was called up. In the following years, the workforce decreased because of further drafts to only around 800 employees in the end, one-third of the pre-war level.[6] More than 350 of the company's white- and blue-collar workers fell during the war.[7] Hermann Ernst's nephew Walter as well as his sons Hans and Otto, both of whom had only joined the company shortly beforehand, to be precise in 1912 and 1910 respectively, were also called up.[8]

Thus the question also had to be clarified at a very early stage as to who could replace the managing directors and senior staff who had been drafted. Walter, Otto and Hans Freudenberg had – as already mentioned – received their draft papers; Hermann Ernst Freudenberg jun.,[9] who had been a managing director since 1908, was suffering from multiple sclerosis. Since 1912, he had already been so severely impaired physically that he could only carry out his duties on the Management Board to a limited extent when war broke out.[10]

For this reason, Hermann Ernst Freudenberg – as already mentioned – recruited his second-youngest son Richard to the company in 1914. Richard familiarized himself with all areas, but particularly devoted himself to tax and financial activities, payroll and personnel management, as well as to the company's legal affairs. Despite the unhappy circumstances, this turned out to be a stroke of luck for the company, because Richard Freudenberg ended up managing his areas of responsibility successfully for almost half a century. He undoubtedly left his mark on an entire era of company history.[11]

The First World War plunged the German leather industry, which had previously been a showcase sector, even at the international level, into a crisis: Imports, exports and free trade ground to a halt. It was a disaster, at the end of which stood a pile of rubble. Although the backdrop of buildings and streets – in contrast to the end of the Second World War – remained largely intact, the outcome for companies was nonetheless catastrophic if one compares it to the development which would have been possible in the absence of war. Looking back, Richard Freudenberg (1892–1975) described the problems as follows: "There were no reserve stores available at all that went beyond the average supply, neither through official channels nor from our own initiative. […] The scarcity was exceptionally great, such that from as early as mid-1915 military requirements could hardly be met. The difficulties increased with every passing 6 months of war. Civilian shoe manufacturing as well as repair had to be more or less completely stalled as early as the end of 1915 because of a lack of sole leather."[12] While the military contracts enabled the company to survive, its future prospects worsened considerably.

In order to be able to overcome the challenges associated with the war, the state intervened heavily to steer the German economic system. Free trade was replaced by far-reaching regulation of what were known as the "war companies" (*Kriegsgesellschaften*). The objective of the more than 200 "war companies" was to ensure more efficient raw material supply through state control. To coordinate the multifarious tasks and war companies, the War Commodities Department (*Kriegsrohstoffabteilung*, KRA) had already been set up in the Prussian War Ministry in August 1914. The KRA monitored, managed and regulated the wartime economy, especially the provision of scarce raw materials, whereby the practical work was carried out by the private-sector war companies under the supervision of the military, who in some respects had the final say right up to the minutiae of daily activities. However, in practical terms, the decisive factor was the work of the private-sector specialists in buying up and distributing raw materials that were vital to the war effort, and without which it would have been unimaginable "that the war efforts could have been sustained for so long at all."[13]

War company Kriegsleder AG was responsible for the leather industry. Since the managerial staff of the "war companies" also partially came from among the ranks of industry, it is not surprising that Hermann Ernst Freudenberg was also appointed to Kriegsleder AG as a leading representative of the German leather industry. He even became deputy chairman of the company. But that was only a cold comfort: For Freudenberg, this meant one way or the other that all requisite raw materials were allocated through Kriegsleder AG. Allocation took place on the basis of processing figures from the first six months of the war. The company undertook the manufacturing of leather goods with military relevance in negotiations with the responsible departments in the Prussian War Ministry, for which Kriegsleder AG, in its turn, supplied the necessary raw materials as far as possible.[14] In this way, the area of raw materials managed by Kriegsleder AG was gradually extended. "Carl Freudenberg profited from the fact that up to the end of 1916, skins and light hides were still exempted from the 'blockages', and even exports to neutral foreign countries were still allowed."[15] When the economic situation deteriorated within the context of the Hindenburg program of the fall of 1916, in the wake of which a restructuring of the German economy took place with the aim of maximizing armaments production, room for maneuver became increasingly narrow. Although the war income partially compensated for the loss of civilian markets, Freudenberg was particularly badly affected by the cuts of the First World War because of its heavy dependence on international markets. Once it lost its traditional international markets, it was not just the company's sales that plunged steeply.[16] It was also by no means certain whether a return to world markets would be possible without any difficulty once hostilities came to an end.

As a consequence, all construction activities in the company had to be suspended, and the planned relocation of the tannery and patent leather production to new buildings in the Zwischen Dämmen plant was delayed and could not be implemented until ten years later. The building of the new headquarters, which had been planned before the war and had been designed by Heidelberg architect Albert Friedrich Speer, the father of Albert Speer, who achieved fame under the Nazis, was abandoned completely because of the war. It was not until after World War II that a solution was found for the Zwischen Dämmen central headquarters.[17]

Production was also very heavily impacted and had to be increasingly reduced. In November 1916, there were only raw goods for 14 days, which made production planning or utilization virtually impossible any more.[18] The compulsory measures imposed by Kriegsleder AG were increasingly having an effect on the company. Imports of skins as well as exports of all types of leather were forbidden. The calfskins which Freudenberg had traditionally processed were virtually no longer available at all. The 1917 business year proceeded completely under the control of the Kriegsleder AG "command economy".[19] Since the chromium salts which were indispensable for tanning could also no longer be imported, the company began to shift production to substitute tanning agents from summer 1917,[20] and even to reintroduce bark tanning, which was considered outdated.[21]

Richard Freudenberg still remembered the truly dramatic conditions in production 30 years later: "But without grease or dye, with a collection of tanning agents that are not compatible with one another, no skins can be tanned, even if they were available in sufficient quantities, into leather, not to mention into reasonably decent leather."[22] Production volume shrank to one-quarter of pre-war levels. By the end of the war, stocks of rawhides and leathers were "exceptionally low".[23] Richard Freudenberg summarized the situation unimpassionedly many years later: "At the end of the war in 1918, we were facing a pile of rubble."[24] Consequently, the *Dolchstoßlegende*, or "stab-in-the-back myth", which was widely believed after the war and which purported that the unvanquished army had been plunged into defeat by people on the home front, seemed barely credible to Richard Freudenberg: "Everyone who, like me, had held a position of responsibility in the management of a relatively large company, could only laugh about the old wives' tale of the stab in the back in the years that followed."[25]

The living conditions of the employees, and indeed of the people in Weinheim overall, were directly affected by the war, particularly because of the constantly deteriorating food supply and parallel to this the rising cost of living. For this reason, Hermann Ernst Freudenberg immediately began paying particular attention to providing for the families of his employees who had been called up to serve as soon as war broke out. Because one thing was clear from the start: The war pay would hardly be enough to live on and would be significantly lower than the wages they had previously been paid. On July 31, 1914, the day that mobilization began, Hermann Ernst Freudenberg therefore announced to the staff he had summoned to the "panel field" of the Old Lacquering Shop that he expected from those who were "joining the fight" that they would "do their part lock, stock and barrel for the Fatherland." However: "That which troubles every righteous man in this hour, the bread and support of wives and children whom they would have to leave behind, he would take care of that."[26] This occurred out of Hermann Ernst's conviction that all employees would be back home again at Christmas at the latest. His authorized signatory, Philipp Baer, on the other hand, predicted that the war would go on for at least three years.[27]

In order to ensure that employees' families were provided for, Hermann Ernst Freudenberg – fully in keeping with the tradition of care for the employees in the company – set up a relief fund for the families of the men who had immediately been drafted for military service on the day mobilization began. Per person and per day, the company paid in 1 gold mark. The employees who stayed at home could participate in the fund with a small voluntary contribution.[28] However, authorized signatory Baer was set to be proven right: the war went on far longer than expected. The consequence: The expenditure required quickly exceeded what the company could afford. In 1915, the company distributed a pamphlet to the wives with the stricture not to squander the assistance, because it was costing the company 10,000 marks a week.[29] In the following year, the fund no longer appeared on the balance sheet: The wives had been employed in the factory instead of their drafted husbands; instead of donating the assistance to them, they were now expected to replace the missing male workers and thus at the same time earn their living.[30] At the end of the war, the wives constituted more than one-third of the workforce, which had declined, as already mentioned, to only around 800 employees in 1917.[31] Alongside the women, there were also prisoners of war working there: Twelve French and eight Russian prisoners of war were employed at Carl Freudenberg during the war.[32] The war finally ended in November 1918; after that, numerous returned servicemen were reemployed immediately, with the result that at the end of 1918, the workforce had already risen again to around 1,200 employees.[33]

Despite their best efforts, the war therefore also took its toll on the company's social welfare achievements. First of all, the plant canteen, which had been run since 1892, had to be closed down as early as 1914, because disruptions to food supply to the population across the entire country had already begun in the first year of the war. As the war progressed, this led to food rationing measures in numerous cities from early 1915.[34] From then on, the employees brought their soup from home in a tin can, and every workshop had an assistant, frequently a wounded or maimed soldier, who was responsible for warming up the tin cans.[35]

The same applied to the plant co-op, which had been established in 1910 and which had been run in the tan mill: the co-op too had to shut down operations in 1914 because of the disruptions in food supply. In the co-op, employees could purchase all types of foodstuffs. These were charged to what was known as a "goods procurement account". By means of a discount system, the employees were granted a discount depending on the value of their purchases at the end of the year, which meant that the purchase was subsidized for the employees. There was a company butcher's shop and sausage factory attached to the co-op, which was run in the Zwischen Dämmen factory.[36]

As was customary across the entire Empire, gift parcels, which were known as "*Liebesgaben*", (literally: gifts of love), were also sent in Weinheim to the soldiers on the battlefield at Christmas. Accordingly, Freudenberg sent packages with chocolate, cigars, and cigarettes to its drafted employees so that those on the different fronts could thus experience at least a tiny vestige of Christmas.[37]

What did Christmas mean at the front in 1914? For several months, many millions of young men from France, England, Russia and Germany had faced each other as enemies on the German Western and Eastern Fronts. Many thousands of soldiers had already fallen by then.[38] There is a verified report that on Christmas Eve 1914, German, British and French soldiers fraternized for a few hours and celebrated Christmas together. But Christmas was celebrated despite the war at other places on the front as well: Christmas carols were sung, joint services were attended, and candles were lit.[39]

The Christmas packages were a source of great joy to the employees at the front, even if the packages frequently arrived with substantial delay. The letter of reply from V. Dielmann[40] to the company bears testament to this:

Fig. 34 Women take over men's work in leather production, around 1916

Fig. 35 Canteen in the Müll plant, 1899

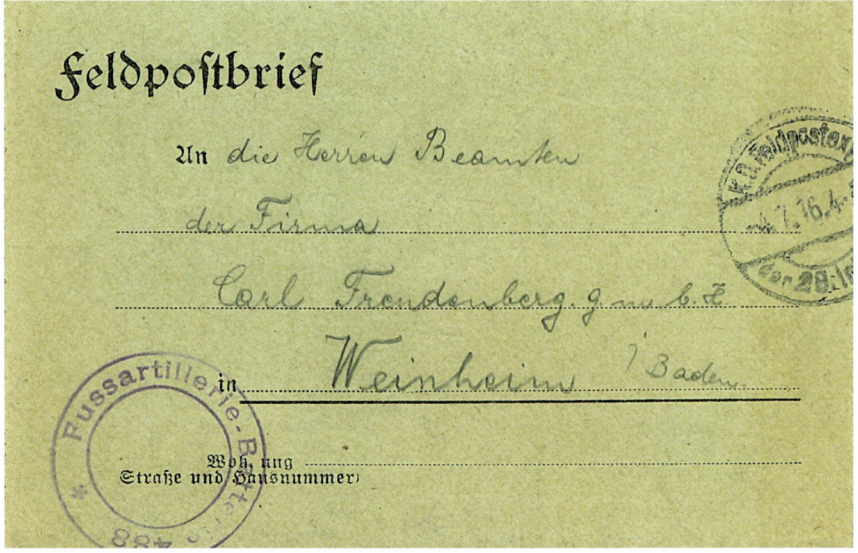

Fig. 36 Letter from the front, 1916

"Bolimów [now in Poland] May 10, 1915

My dear colleagues!

I received your Christmas package the day before yesterday, which was therefore almost six months in transit. Nevertheless, the things you sent did not suffer any hardship at all, on the contrary, cigars, cigarettes, chocolate, everything is superb & tastes magnificent. I send you many & heartfelt thanks for the lovely present, which was a real treat for me & my comrades.

I can report little news about the war to you, because you are better informed by the newspapers about all the proceedings on the battlefield than we are – Our mortar battalion was torn apart, one battery was sent to one place, the other somewhere else, we (i.e., the second one) are with the 17th Corps & are holding our position with weak forces against a much stronger adversary, while we are drawing our other troops more to the north & south & pressing the enemy together there towards the middle.

Sometimes it can happen that no shots are fired here for days & one could believe one was living in perfect peace, the weather is marvelous; day after day, the sun shines, now & again there is a thunderstorm at night, apart from that it is always very hot. Thus I am doing quite well & camp life agrees with me now too, but after all, one gets accustomed to everything in the end.

Indeed, the war has one positive aspect, one learns to be frugal & realizes that it is manageable too. We lie, for example, in the dugout on straw & sleep quite well & are also dry if it is not raining at the time. One does not need to spend much time on food & menus: rice, pearl barley, peas alternately, served with beef or pork alternately.

I would love to come home to check up on everything and also to pay my respects to you again, but there is no hope of that at the moment, on the contrary, it can go on for a very long time yet, especially if Italy also goes against us. But nous verrons to see, as the French say.

It would interest me to hear from you about what is new in Weinheim, how the business is going & the office & what my colleagues are up to. Have even more people from the office been called up since the beginning of March (that is the last time for which I have reports from it)? Yours heartily & hoping to see you again

V. Dielmann."[41]

The efforts to ensure the welfare of their employees were doubtless the result of a feeling of a moral obligation towards the soldiers, but also had a compelling reason. Freudenberg invariably had a vested interest in attracting its workers back after the war or alternatively compensating for the losses with qualified new employees. To ensure the retention of the remaining employees in the company, what was known as a service bonus agreement *(Dienstprämienvertrag)* was already being offered in the summer of 1918 to the workers who were still on the battlefield.[42] The agreement, which was drawn up by Richard Freudenberg, was an interest-bearing share held by the employees in the company's capital. Anyone who was employed for longer than five years at the company could receive an interest-bearing share of 1,200 marks in the company's capital. The aim was to bind the workforce to the company, because the sum was paid out to the heirs in the event of death. Thus, the workers always collected their interest to improve their income. The costs rose so unexpectedly that from 1929 no more agreements of this nature were entered into any more.[43] However, interest was paid out until the death of the last contracting party in 1992.[44]

> **EXCURSUS:** SOCIAL RESPONSIBILITY – PART 2: FROM THE FIRST TO THE END OF THE SECOND WORLD WAR
>
> **1914** On the day mobilization started in the First World War, Hermann Ernst Freudenberg established a relief fund for the families of men who had been called up to military service. Per man and per day, the company paid in 1 gold mark. The workforce joined in by making voluntary contributions.[45]
>
> **1918** Richard Freudenberg drew up the service bonus agreement, an interest-bearing share held by the workers in the company's capital. Workers were allowed to join the scheme until 1929. From then on, no more agreements were entered into, but the interest was paid out until the death of the last contracting party in 1992.[46]
>
> **1938** To mark Friedrich Carl Freudenberg's 90th birthday, the partners donated a fund to the City of Weinheim, the Carl Freudenberg Foundation, to support the youth of the city, who also became beneficiaries of the estate of Helene Freudenberg in 1940.[47]
>
> **1942** To mark his 50th birthday, Richard Freudenberg donated 100,000 RM, or Reichsmarks, to the City of Weinheim for the construction of an indoor swimming pool. For the same purpose, Walter and Annie Freudenberg bestowed the same amount again in 1945 to mark the 50th work anniversary of Walter Freudenberg.[48]

Hyperinflation and emergency money

Once the First World War had come to an end, there were many new challenges to overcome: The war had been financed by borrowings and bond issues, and additionally, in the wake of the Treaty of Versailles,[49] high reparation payments also had to be made now. In the dispute about the amounts and due dates, the Ruhr was finally occupied by French and Belgian soldiers in 1923, to which the German imperial government responded by proclaiming a stance of passive resistance, which had to be financed by printing money. As a result, the already battered German currency collapsed entirely; in the early summer of 1923, inflation spun out of control. While the money supply exploded, the supply of goods and services remained scarce. Furthermore, the economy's performance potential did not come even close to that of pre-war times. At the same time, the state's expenditures to stabilize the country, which was teetering on the brink of civil war, and to finance the upkeep of the passive resistance in the Ruhr, got completely out of hand.[50] The external value of the mark deteriorated dramatically:

1 dollar, which had been worth 4 marks before the outbreak of war, cost 130 billion marks on November 1, 1923. And domestic prices had developed accordingly in the same direction.[51]

The consequences of this development differed greatly for the various players in the economy. The winners of the galloping inflation were those who had debts, and thus not only the state, but also for example farmers, who got rid of their pre-war debts. But export-oriented companies which were able to sell their products abroad for hard foreign currency amid declining costs were also winners.[52] This naturally applied to Freudenberg as well, since it was traditionally a heavily export-oriented company, even though the raw material purchases, meaning the hide imports, became very expensive. On the other hand, life for the workers became exceedingly uncomfortable, since wages and prices were almost impossible to calculate any more. From today's perspective – and indeed also when viewed at the time – the development is breathtaking: Bank deposits, meaning the money held in banks, and cash in circulation, rose in June 1923 to around 524 trillion marks. The value of money declined so rapidly that in the end wages had to be paid out several times a week, and eventually on a daily basis. Municipalities and large companies – and thus also Freudenberg – additionally issued emergency money, a money substitute for the official state currency, to the value of more than 700 trillion marks. Reichsbank banknotes were issued with astronomically high face values.[53]

The effects on the income and outlay situation at Freudenberg were significant: Out of necessity, wages accounted for an increasingly small share of expenditure and net sales proceeds. The usual share of net sales proceeds accounted for by wages and salaries declined at times from 15 to 5 percent.[54] The Management Board had to find a solution to this, like other major employers too. For this reason, from August 1923 onward, what were known as Freudenberg vouchers were issued. This was a type of in-house emergency money in denominations of 1 and 2 million marks, which could be redeemed at the local banks.[55] Finally, from November 1 of crisis year 1923 onward, dollar vouchers were also issued. Their exchange value could be redeemed until midday and at the rate of that particular day at the Freudenberg main cash office or the banks.[56]

This is connected to the fact that the Carl Freudenberg company issued a 5 percent interest-bearing partial debenture for 5 million gold marks through the Rheinische Creditbank Mannheim in October 1923.[57] "With this, we were probably one of the first factories to make the move to paying part of our wages and salaries in gold marks. With the other part, backed by the trust that the company enjoyed in our immediate and wider surroundings, we committed

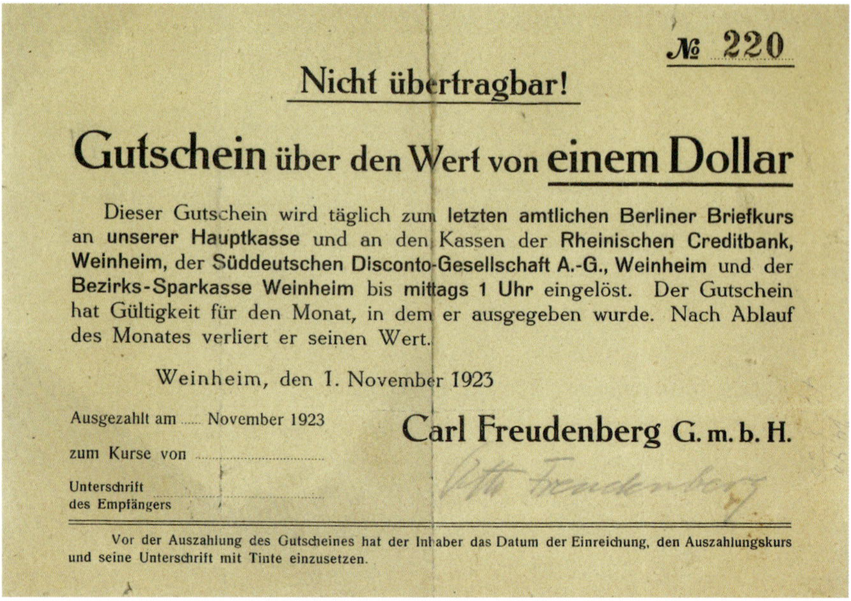
№ 220

Nicht übertragbar!

Gutschein über den Wert von einem Dollar

Dieser Gutschein wird täglich zum letzten amtlichen Berliner Briefkurs an unserer Hauptkasse und an den Kassen der Rheinischen Creditbank, Weinheim, der Süddeutschen Disconto-Gesellschaft A.-G., Weinheim und der Bezirks-Sparkasse Weinheim bis mittags 1 Uhr eingelöst. Der Gutschein hat Gültigkeit für den Monat, in dem er ausgegeben wurde. Nach Ablauf des Monates verliert er seinen Wert.

Weinheim, den 1. November 1923

Ausgezahlt am ...... November 1923

zum Kurse von ....

Unterschrift des Empfängers ....

Carl Freudenberg G. m. b. H.

Otto Freudenberg

Vor der Auszahlung des Gutscheines hat der Inhaber das Datum der Einreichung, den Auszahlungskurs und seine Unterschrift mit Tinte einzusetzen.

Fig. 37 Voucher for a dollar as emergency money for the employees, issued by Otto Freudenberg in 1923

amounts of Papiermarks and replenished our goods warehouse again," Richard Freudenberg commented on this later.[58]

For the company, the currency devaluation was a double-edged sword. The more the markets lost their function, the more difficult it was to calculate and ensure target-oriented production, not to mention the question of wages and salaries. On the other hand, Freudenberg earned foreign currency and was therefore in a position to shape the situation in its own interest too.[59] In order to counteract what was at least a potential threat of asset erosion, capital was immediately increased by 50 million marks. For this purpose, Swiss francs were deposited at the Comptoir d'Escompte de Genève bank, with the aid of Swiss shoe company and long-standing customer Bally Schuhfabriken AG.[60] The entire affair must have been a relatively good deal, because the necessary amount, as can be read in documents, was "purchased in Switzerland for a song," so obviously at extremely favorable conditions.[61]

The inflation exerted its contradictory effects on the business. As already intimated, on the one hand, products could be sold abroad at very low prices. Business boomed, but there was a problem too. Rawhides and skins had to be paid for abroad with hard currency. For this reason, the Freudenberg Management Board came up with an idea which today one would probably say was very smart: The company developed a complex system to finance its foreign business dealings. "Together with the Swiss-French tanning and banking family J. J. Mercier from Lausanne, the Externa SA financing company was established in 1921, through which the purchasing of rawhides and raw skins in France, Italy and Switzerland was processed."[62]

In point of fact, Externa was only a small office, and there were never more than ten employees working there. Only administration work was conducted, but ultimately Freudenberg held a stake of 77.5 percent. However, that alone would not have been enough. Legally, it was necessary to be able to prove an operational business, so that the entire thing did not look as if it was solely a financial vehicle. And this is where a second trick came into play: In February 1924, Freudenberg acquired a "significant [stakeholding] in the 'Tannerie de Lausanne' SA, which was in need of restructuring."[63] This tannery worked predominantly for the Swiss market. It too belonged to the J. J. Mercier group. Upper leather was produced with just under 120 employees. And the Weinheim-based company had everything under control: "The board of director positions at Tannerie de Lausanne and Externa were filled with people the Freudenbergs trusted."[64] What sort of business was conducted here? On the one hand, Tannerie de Lausanne supplied the domestic market in the normal way. That would not have been particularly remarkable in itself. However, it also sold – and this is where things get interesting – "German and Austrian leathers disguised as Swiss commodities using partially forged documents on the Polish and eastern European market."[65]

Trade unions

After the war, the Rhineland-Westphalian heavy industrialists initially succeeded in reaching an agreement with the trade unions on a new way of dealing with each other. But this came at a cost: By signing the Stinnes-Legien Agreement on November 15, 1918, which is named after the chief negotiators Hugo Stinnes, the representative of the industrialists, and union leader Carl Legien, the heavy industry sector had to accept old union demands.[66] Among other things, the agreement contained the following points: "Acknowledgement of the trade unions", "Eight-hour day without loss of earnings", "Works councils and arbitration committees with equal representation in companies with more than 50 employees", as well as "Reinstatement of demobilized soldiers". The trade unions were recognized by the companies as contracting partners on equal terms; the collective bargaining autonomy achieved then still applies today.[67]

The corresponding provisions influenced Freudenberg too, because ultimately the situation was comparable everywhere in Germany. This meant that since the end of November 1918, 40 to 50 Freudenberg workers returned to Weinheim day after day, although the company's transition to peacetime production was slow to take hold and the labor requirements could not be estimated yet. Naturally, Freudenberg too declared itself to be "fundamentally willing 'to reinstate all people standing on the battlefield again'. However, in light of the low inventory levels, it was difficult to keep even the 'current workforce busy.'"[68]

And moreover: Political developments had made the workers critical and self-assured in their attitude towards their employers. In order to recognize the workers' representation and at the same time steer it into a manageable format, the Works Council Act was passed at the beginning of 1920. From then on, in every company with at least 20 employees, an independent representative body, mostly controlled by the major trade unions, had to be elected which received rights to have a say in certain circumstances and even codetermination rights on dismissal-related issues.[69] For those family enterprises that were accustomed to patriarchal structures, this was a considerable challenge. "The relationship of top management to the Association of German Leatherworkers, in its function as the most important workers' representation in the tanning sector, was strained."[70] However, the new law was in force, and on April 18, 1920 the first

Fig. 38 The trade unions focused particularly on the production employees, like the chrome dye nailers at Freudenberg in this photo, 1920

works council meeting took place in Weinheim.[71] It appears that the mood was not particularly positive: "The Management Board complained about 'foolish socialist ideas and unfortunately also spiteful sentiments', as well as the 'socialist aberration.'"[72] "He [Hermann Ernst] regarded trade unionists 'as company externals and paid agitators'. He 'found it infernally difficult' to sit down with them at the same table after the end of the war, one of his sons recalled later."[73] Hermann Ernst Freudenberg complained about his workers: "The 'foolish people' were 'not to be dissuaded from new wage demands and persevere in their belief in good [old] days. Whatever one says against this, they see it as bias. Our nation has not attended the school of old Mistress Hardship long enough yet'."[74] "It is unbelievable how under such pitiable conditions a dispute can arise about whether working hours from 7 to 3 without a break are better than 7 to 4 with a break. But in fact, it would not have taken much for punches to have been exchanged because of this completely unimportant issue."[75] While senior director Hermann Ernst Freudenberg still found it difficult to accept the changed conditions, it was different for the younger generation on the Management Board. They were of a decidedly different opinion than their elder about dealing with the new situation. Richard and Walter Freudenberg made an effort to at least accommodate those demands of the works council which they deemed to be justified.[76]

Foundation of F&Co. (1921): Separation of the administration of the family shares from business operations

The amended tax laws in the Weimar Republic, which on the one hand comprised the conscription of wealth on what were known as "war profits" and on the other hand foresaw an increase in the top tax rate to 60 percent (1920),[77] were another serious challenge, since there was also a risk of asset erosion and the partners' income situation was deteriorating significantly. Consequently, the increased number of partners who were not active in the company brought the Management Board to a point where they fundamentally revised the existing partnership agreement dating from 1917.[78] The opportunity was taken to modernize the corporate constitution in a manner that had been indicated – as previously mentioned – in prior years: A clear separation was achieved between business operations and a holding company[79] which also assumed the administration of the family shares. The aim was, on the one hand, to finally make the

Management Board professional for the long term, and on the other hand to secure the family's influence for an equally long term. "The entire property of Carl Freudenberg GmbH was [therefore] incorporated into the Freudenberg & Co. GmbH holding company in September 1921."[80]

What was the result? "[From then on,] the holding company's limited partner rights were exercised by two managing directors with equal representation, who were elected by the two branches of the family, Friedrich Carl and Hermann Ernst Freudenberg."[81] In addition, "there were special regulations for the drawdown of capital. If one limited partner wanted to sell their shares, for example,"[82] the members of their own family initially had a right of first refusal. At the first General Meeting, Hermann Ernst and Friedrich Carl were appointed as managing directors. "After the death of Hermann Ernst in 1923, his son Richard took his place; conversely, Walter Freudenberg only acceded as successor when his father Friedrich Carl resigned from his position in 1928 at the age of 80. A three-person Board of Partners regulated those affairs that would have been impracticable and time-consuming to deal with in the larger body [of the General Meeting]. The equality of structure now prevented the arguments that had [definitely] occurred between the two branches of the family around the turn of the century."[83]

Death of company patriarch Hermann Ernst Freudenberg (1923)

1923, the last year in the life of the great patriarch Hermann Ernst, was a year of immense social uncertainty for Germany, because it was dominated by hyperinflation. Hermann Ernst's world, which had been characterized by the major successes of the pre-war years, no longer existed. While there were also those who profited from the galloping inflation, uncertainty and hardship prevailed overall, however. Creditors were just as heavily affected as those earning fixed incomes, whose livelihoods were at risk.[84] The disintegration of society was a breeding ground for radical political demands, which now became the order of the day almost everywhere, and indeed in several parts of the Empire culminated in conditions akin to a civil war. These conditions were not just fueled by the hyperinflation; the radical demands in the context and in the wake of the November Revolution also repeatedly drove the country to the brink of collapse, particularly during the Kapp putsch and the Ruhr crisis that followed it. The situation led to wildcat strikes in Baden too.[85] In Weinheim, this was additionally exacerbated by fears of a famine, and the Communist Party in particular sensed an opportunity.[86] This became a serious cause of concern for the aged Hermann Ernst Freudenberg: "He had regarded the Treaty of Versailles as an unwarranted humiliation, which he said had 'demeaned' his life's work." [87] "But for our poor Fatherland it has become much worse than the blackest picture he would have been able to paint back then. Trampled underfoot, hacked to pieces and dishonored, that is how it is lying on the ground, an object of mockery for its foes and without any joy to give it hope. And our 'loyal and strong people' in whom I had had such unerring confidence mutinied at a time of greatest need and created a revolution of envy and jealousy and thus destroyed anything the lost war had still left us," he writes in one of the last personal notes that he left behind.[88] However, the elderly patriarch was still a long way from becoming radical himself. He sympathized with the workers; indeed, they had still been the least affected by the national frenzy, he said.[89] Instead, he was doubtful about the middle classes and his ability to have any effect on them, all the more because entrepreneurs in particular should have exerted greater moderating influence before the war.[90] Therefore, unlike his father, Hermann Ernst Freudenberg – because of the consequences of the war – could only look back on his life with mixed feelings.

Hermann Ernst Freudenberg died on October 21, 1923.

Complete transfer of responsibility to the third generation

The imperial government ultimately realized that continued opposition to the occupation of the Ruhr by French troops, among others, was leading to economic ruin. Imperial Chancellor (*Reichskanzler*) Gustav Stresemann announced the end of the passive resistance on September 26, 1923 and initiated currency reform. Eventually, on November 15, 1923 the Rentenmark[91] was provisionally introduced. Subsequently, more constructive reparation negotiations could be held, and "finally, on August 30, 1924 the 'Rentenmark' was replaced by the gold-backed, fully convertible 'Reichsmark'."[92] "With the currency conversion, the hyperinflation crisis was overcome, and the business situation at Freudenberg [also] stabilized [again]."[93] The shock of the monetary devaluation ran deep – and was set to characterize the German population's attitude and their desire for a stable currency for decades to come. When monetary policy conditions returned to a sounder footing, employment statistics became more pleasing to behold as well: "In 1924, Carl Freudenberg already had a workforce of […] 2,914 employees – more than in 1913, the last peacetime year."[94]

Thus, despite everything, the older generation left their successors a business in excellent shape, buoyed by the preceding reform of the partnership agreement and the currency conversion. Now the entire responsibility lay on the shoulders of the third generation. And they could stand tall: They could hold their ground in the sector, were open to new developments and were breaking away from antiquated technologies, which on the downside did not take place entirely without friction, however. Because of course they found structures in place that had to be changed to enable them to realize their own visions. Authorized signatories, master craftsmen, clerical staff, workers – they had all established themselves in entrenched structures: "However, despite their best intentions, the young generation would initially have to be viewed as a disruptive element and also felt like that until they succeeded in asserting themselves."[95]

During these years, based on the new corporate constitution, but also in accordance with the zeitgeist, the "principle of the co-responsibility of qualified nonfamily managers" became established:[96] "A growing number of technical and commercial clerical staff, who had been hired because of the increased demand for management expertise for the expansion and rationalization of businesses as well as for administration and for the sales organization, formed a new tier between the senior staff, who were also employees, and the workers."[97] Moreover: While the currency reform of 1924 had brought stability back to the financial system again, unemployment still remained a problem, however, and not just in Baden alone. The company came up with the clever idea of investing in the future through construction activities: The lime building, the newly built wet workshop and the tannery that was newly erected between 1922 and 1924 were amalgamated into the Zwischen Dämmen plant. This had been instigated for the most part by Hans Freudenberg.[98] The amalgamation was a leap forward. Little by little, all major work processes were modernized and accommodated in new buildings.[99] This is one example: As early as "1922, the era of the draft horses was over too. From then on, 'Kruppschlepper' replaced horse-drawn transport, which brought about a significant time gain, particularly for longer routes to Schönau."[100]

In this context it is important to also get to know Hans Freudenberg, Richard's elder brother. Hans had completed his degree as an electrical engineer at TH Karlsruhe technical university in 1912, and thus shortly before the outbreak of war. Afterwards he had become a university assistant, and even after his return to the Weinheim-based company, he still maintained contact with his university. Thus, while on the one hand he initially had to familiarize himself with the field of tannery technology, which was new to him, on the other hand, however, he used his connections to the TH Karlsruhe Chair for Machine Elements

Fig. 39 Aerial photo of the Zwischen Dämmen plant, 1925. In the center of the picture, the new tannery's spacious building complex can be seen.

Fig. 40 A *Kruppschlepper* motorized towing vehicle in action, around 1930

and Powers Plants from then on to make the chemical processes in Weinheim more scientific.[101] He "devised [important] technical improvements and innovations to the machines, all the while assisted by young engineer Walther Simmer, who oversaw the leather machines and had been successful in constructing a better design of band knife splitting machine."[102] We will have considerably more to chronicle about Walther Simmer (1888–1986) at a later juncture.

In addition, the possibility of borrowing at favorable conditions enabled the company to take over the Hessische Lederwerke Neckaria leather factory in Neckarsteinach, which had gotten into financial difficulties in June 1924. It was a strategic gambit to prevent the competition from snapping up Neckaria: "The deciding factor was the concern that one of the rivals in upper leather manufacturing – potential candidates first and foremost were Doerr & Reinhart, Adler & Oppenheimer or Cornelius Heyl – could have acquired Neckaria and become a troublemaker."[103]

Recapturing the markets

"At Carl Freudenberg [in the second half of the 1920s] two-thirds of production was exported, a proportion that was set to remain stable up to the Great Depression in 1930. However, extraordinary factors like the favorable mark rate [a mark which inflated away in value, which had been favorable to business during the inflation era as described] no longer played a role now. When 'dumping abroad [had] suddenly ceased,' as Richard Freudenberg wrote, the company was confronted with a totally different situation: 'Somehow we were now in a situation of free competition.'"[104]

Rawhide and leather prices continued to rise. Soon they were actually one-fifth higher than prewar levels. "The upper leather factories' first balance sheets in gold marks revealed a high level of indebtedness. From 1924 to 1929, as Richard Freudenberg stated after 1945, these were all virtually living 'off their assets.'"[105] However, as already mentioned in the case of the takeover of Neckaria, the currency reform brought with it new opportunities for borrowing. "Carl Freudenberg took out loans too, to stimulate the business. The large loan from Rheinische Creditbank already mentioned was converted to 3.5 million RM and prolonged multiple times," meaning that its term was extended.[106]

And the company was looking at the American market again. Business trips of several months' duration by Richard and Otto Freudenberg were the foundation for ensuring that at the end of the 1920s the company's American business with boxcalf leather was stimulated, "which in light of the demanding clientele was by no means a simple undertaking."[107] Otto's activities are worth taking a closer look at too. He was the person on the Management Board who was responsible for sales and thus also for exports. Accordingly, Otto resumed his foreign trips, which he had begun in 1914, with a business trip to the USA – at that time still with his father, Hermann Ernst.[108]

One intention of this first major foreign trip was to regain trust after World War I. For this reason, Otto Freudenberg visited many former business partners and potential new customers to resurrect former business relationships as well as generate new business. Accompanied by his brother, Adolf Freudenberg, Otto traveled to the USA, Canada, Japan, Korea, China, Hong Kong, Indonesia, Singapore and Sri Lanka between September 1924 and March 1925. From July to October 1929, his travels took him to South America, more precisely to Brazil, Argentina, Bolivia, Peru and Chile. A further trip to North America, which was already affected by the Great Depression, followed between June and August 1932.[109]

"Because of his obliging and agreeable nature, he found it easy to gain the confidence of foreign customers. Looking back, his cousin Walter Freudenberg, noted that while Otto was 'not a difficult character,' he had set great store 'in having clear authority as well in the field of work which he had acquired with great patience.'"[110] However, Otto did not just travel; branches were also established or alternatively foreign stakeholdings acquired to stabilize the foreign business activities. Thus Carl Freudenberg Inc. was established in Boston in 1929, "to mitigate the negative effects of the currency fluctuations with the help of this representative office."[111] The company proceeded in a similar way in Italy too. Because in the late 1920s and early 1930s, high duties were imposed everywhere which made it almost impossible to export up-

Fig. 41 Otto and Hermann Ernst Freudenberg (from left) on their passage to America, 1914

per leathers to Italy. To overcome this hurdle, "Freudenberg acquired half of the Industria Lombarda Pelli al Cromo tannery in Lambrate near Milan in 1933. The other half of the shares were owned by the Alberto Rollier & Co. company in Milan, which had been Freudenberg's sole agent for Italy since 1930."[112]

At that time, the Management Board had several issues to contend with in the area of export financing. For this purpose, many more organizations were established, like for example Exportvereinigung von deutschen Lederwerken GmbH" ('Exled') with headquarters in Hamburg, which was set up in January 1928. The organization "aims to facilitate the leather exports of the Carl Freudenberg, Carl Simon Söhne (Kirn) and Fritz Häuser AG (Backnang) companies to Central America."[113] The takeover of Bankvereeniging Kralingen bank in Rotterdam in 1927 also pursued this objective. "When the banking institute had to be liquidated in spring of 1934 because of the currency regulations, Freudenberg & Co. GmbH took over all assets."[114] A look at the bank in Rotterdam is interesting for another reason as well: Because from 1928 onward, the Dutch bank held a majority stakeholding in the Hanseatische Reederei Emil Offen shipping company, which had eight oceangoing vessels that were thus transferred into Freudenberg's direct ownership.[115] And with an eye to the uncertain currency situation, spreading the risk in this area too appeared to make sense to the Management Board in order not to have to rely solely on the core leather business any more.[116] The diversification of the company and thus the spreading of risk had begun in 1929 with the production of the first leather seals, which will be described in greater detail at a later juncture.

Currency reform, foreign loans and an improvement in the relationships with the allied victors of World War I led to an economic recovery in 1924, which lasted until 1929, with an interruption in 1925/26. All industry branches, including new ones, were able to significantly increase their production. In 1928/29, industrial production and wages overall returned to the level of the prewar era. However, the Reich's budget had been in a difficult situation again since the middle of the 1920s. In addition, the trade balance was in deficit. Above and beyond this, the current account was heavily burdened by the ongoing reparation payments, to the extent that the balance of payments could only be kept in equilibrium with considerable capital imports, through which the Reich got into an exceedingly unfavorable debt situation which would significantly contribute to the worsening of the Great Depression in 1931.[117] Because of these difficult circumstances, the Reich was unable to set the necessary reform of financial and taxation policy in motion. At the beginning of 1930, the Reich was unable to implement almost any fiscal policy. As a result, the Weimar Republic's last parliamentary government resigned in the spring of 1930 and was replaced by Heinrich Brüning's presidential cabinet, which would then set about trying to restore the Reich's capacity to act.

Despite increases in sales and exports, many companies were in a difficult situation.[118] In the years from 1925 to 1929, wage trends far outpaced improvements in productivity. That is bad for employers at any time, since ultimately the difference negatively impacts companies' profit-and-loss accounts. Thus that also applied at that time.[119] Many companies therefore attempted to improve their cost structures on their own initiative, particularly through extensive technological rationalization and the reorganization of corporate structures (trust formation), which admittedly was not possible everywhere. Far-reaching restructuring occurred particularly in heavy industry, and in the chemical and electrotechnical industries, while other areas like agriculture, which was still large, were in a constant state of crisis. Additionally, in the wake of the war, the domestic market was weak, and the savings rate among the impoverished population was low. Numerous banks pursued an extremely risky business policy. They issued loans with long repayment terms on the basis of short-term refinancing – with incalculable consequences. All of these factors were not good omens, especially since international economic relations were extremely unstable following the devastations of the war and the prevailing monetary regime, the gold standard, was proving to be increasingly unsuitable to secure global integration. A crisis could assume dramatic proportions.[120] And this crisis was going to come.

"In the 'phase of expansive rationalization strategies', the catchwords circulating everywhere were typification, harmonization, standardization, synchronization of process organization as well as mass production, which were meant to be achieved using the magic ingredient of 'rationalization' of the entire economic process."[121] In Weinheim, however, as with other leather manufacturers as well, the question was more complex. It was a question of whether income really could be increased by formalizing the long and complex work processes of tanning, and also whether the workers would go along with these steps. Answers were found to these questions very quickly: A transition from individual to conveyor belt manufacturing was not very attractive for leather manufacturers. "In addition, the numerous small and medium-sized manufacturers in particular anticipated that the limitation of articles required for conveyor belt production would constitute a sales risk."[122] Hermann Ernst Freudenberg had already been anything but impressed back in 1914 after a visit to the Ford plants in Detroit, who were leaders in conveyor belt production with their Model T.[123] From his perspective, "rationalization and conveyor belt manufacturing, as they were conducted in the mechanical engineering and automobile industry, were 'unthinkable in the leather industry.'"[124] "For the topic of rationalization measures barely played a role in the meetings of the works council either in the interwar years. However, the Freudenbergs' numerous trips to the 'New World' showed how fascinated these latter nonetheless were by the undeniably impressive mass-production shoe factories and the tanneries supplying them."[125]

The Great Depression and its consequences

The reasons for the economic upheavals that were emerging in 1929 and which ultimately reached the entire world were – as already indicated – a long chain of unfavorable circumstances: "The 'combination of speculation crash, recession, crisis in the international currency and financial system, structural weaknesses as well as an increasingly protectionist economic and trade policy' brought about a crisis of hitherto unknown dimensions."[126] The result was fast-rising mass unemployment in Germany too. The crisis was long lasting, especially since countries sought their salvation among other things with the protective tariffs we already mentioned, which further curbed economic activity.[127]

During this phase, Heinrich Brüning, Chancellor of the German Reich, pursued a strict deflationary policy in Berlin: Taxes were increased, social spending was slashed, and wages and salaries in the public sector were cut. By doing this, Brüning wanted to absorb the crisis-related reduction in tax receipts. Brüning's aim was to balance the Reich budget by means of stringent austerity measures and, in doing so, at the same time to make it clear that Germany would not be in a position to service the reparation obligations even with the greatest austerity efforts. One effect of the strict austerity policy was that Germany's international competitiveness improved.[128]

"This led to a hitherto unknown decline in prices [deflation], but at the same time contributed to insolvencies and credit defaults and [in this way] further heated the social crisis. Brüning's rigorous plan aimed to utilize the export industry as an engine of economic recovery."[129] Initially, this strategy was comparatively successful too. Exports had a stabilizing effect and the balance of trade deficit disappeared, though admittedly at the price of a significant deterioration in living standards in the country. But then the financial and banking crisis of 1931 thwarted the strategy through and through. The collapse of the global economy rendered Brüning's policy totally ineffective. From early fall 1931, all parameters deteriorated dramatically. In winter 1931/32, the crisis reached its unimaginable apogee.[130]

The impending recession was already becoming apparent in Weinheim as early as 1928 – and thus even before the outbreak of the worldwide economic crisis: The second-largest company in the town, agricultural machinery factory Badenia, had to file for insolvency. Very soon afterwards, the Freudenbergs watched the foreign business which was so important to the company become a cause for concern.[131] As early as from "the start of July 1930, the USA levied duties of 15 percent on leather; in 1931, state currency control was introduced in Germany and the free convertibility of the Reichsmark was repealed; in March/April 1932, Great Britain," which had given up the gold standard in September 1931 and had withdrawn behind what were known as 'imperial preferences', "decreed" a duty on leather. That meant that Great Britain, "the main sales market for Freudenberg leathers, likewise imposed duty of 15 percent, which was raised shortly thereafter to 30 percent." In addition to the crash of the sterling exchange rate after the gold standard was abandoned, that also led to a drastic deterioration in sales. "To make matters worse, the dollar" – which had likewise given up its pegging to gold in 1933 – "also devalued" sharply. "Up to 1936, Freudenberg's foreign sales declined to 25 percent because of this. Leather exports suffered a blow due to this development from which they would never again recover. [...] Whereas in 1931, one-third of Freudenberg goods were still being exported to England, this share had shrunk to one-fifth two years later."[132]

Under the conditions of protective tariffs and currency manipulations such as were commonplace after the summer of 1931, German exports could scarcely be maintained any longer. Not even a radicalization of Brüning's policy of domestic devaluation could have overcome hurdles such as these. Freudenberg's export share plummeted. "A further compounding factor was the dependence on the capricious shoe fashions: Patent leather, which up to now had been a lucrative Freudenberg specialty, went out of fashion and became a 'problem child'. While Freudenberg was still able to charge 1.73 RM per square meter for this in 1928, it only received 0.70 RM for it in July 1932."[133] The Management Board reacted to this: In Neckarsteinach, production was switched to Chevreau leather. This was smooth, chrome-tanned goatskin leather which better satisfied fashion demands. In Schönau, on the other hand, production was switched to chrome side leather made from native hides. However, competitors came up with this idea too, meaning that this did not really enable the company to extricate itself from the pressure of competition. "Richard Freudenberg assessed the sales situation in September 1930 to be so difficult that they should be very happy 'if we are spared short-time working and dismissals.'"[134] Nevertheless, considerable downward adjustments of working hours and hourly wages could not be avoided: "Weekly working hours for the around 3,500 employees declined from 42 hours in 1930 to 34 hours in 1932. At the same time, hourly wages in the same time period were gradually reduced from 1.31 RM to 0.86 RM. As early as the fall of 1930, Richard Freudenberg spoke of the "horrific unemployment in the city."[135]

And although these measures were undoubtedly serious, ultimately the company was still not spared from introducing a short-time working model as well, despite Richard Freudenberg's hopes. It remained his goal to avoid dismissals, but the employees had to pay a very high price for this. "The employees were now only working half the time, but were also only getting half the wages." There was a changeover every two weeks: one-half of the employees stayed at home, while the others kept production going. The measure yielded only minimal success. "At the end of 1932, the Management Board was faced with the alternative of either letting 600 to 700 employees go, or reducing weekly working hours to 32 or even only 24 hours. A few years later, the Management Board regretted not having cut back production already in 1930. However, they felt it was their obligation to maintain the workforce 'in difficult times too.'"[136]

At Freudenberg, exchange rate gains from their export business prevented the absolute worst. Above and beyond this, the company was helped by new financial instruments which are no longer even vaguely familiar to us today and which were created as a reaction to the Great Depression.[137] "The best known is likely what is known as the *Stillhaltemark* ["standstill" mark – ed.]: A considerable share of the Freudenberg debt was covered by what was known as the 'standstill agreement' that was inked in the summer of 1931 in Basel between the representatives of foreign creditors and German debtor banks. The loans granted to German banks in foreign currencies, particularly by British financial institutions, prevented British and American banks from withdrawing their monies unexpectedly. However, these agreements did not apply to the Swiss firm Externa, and its liquidity slumped dramatically. In the previous years, Freudenberg had taken out high short-term loans in France worth 25 million French francs and 11 million Swiss francs respectively. However, the excess capacities on the leather market led to a situation where raw materials were weighing down the warehouses in Weinheim like lead."[138]

Thus, by the turn of the year 1932/33, Externa's reserves were fully depleted. It was no longer able to repay the loans it had taken out. For Freudenberg, this was a serious problem: "A liquidation of the Swiss company would have meant the loss of up to one-third of the receivables as well as payment obligations worth over 1 million Swiss francs for Carl Freudenberg. Therefore, the company was provisionally kept afloat, but without any prospect of getting back into the black."[139]

However, the company was able to rely on its network once again. Several bridging loans were granted, also from foreign partners right up to Alfred

Morris Sons & Co. in London: "Without this 'altruistic assistance,' as Richard Freudenberg explained with hindsight, 'I do not know how we would have survived these crisis years so apparently naturally to the outside observer.'"[140]

When there is no longer any demand, prices fall drastically. This mechanism is one of the fundamentals of doing business in free market economies – and this is what happened here too. "Richard Freudenberg described the dramatic situation in hindsight as follows: 'Just how difficult this price crash was can be seen from the fact that, for example, the unit price per calfskin had fallen from its peak of RM 15.65 in March 1928 to RM 2.73 in July 1932. With the large inventories of around 1 1/2 million units which we had and had to have in stock, everyone can calculate for themselves how this repercussion affected us. The leather trade and the shoe industry both domestically and abroad passed on the entire devaluation resulting from the competition without exception to the upper leather factories and ourselves, such that we suffered asset losses of around 850,000 RM from 1929 to 1932.'"[141]

However, there was also a light at the end of the tunnel for Freudenberg and its major competitors. Because in a situation such as this, the fittest generally survive, and in this case, these were the large manufacturers, which had greater staying power than the small and medium-sized plants. In addition, business was not catastrophic everywhere in the world; South America constituted a pleasant exception.[142]

Developing technology and driving diversification

The fact that the sales price for leathers at the height of the Great Depression fell to 20 percent of the purchase price for rawhides posed considerable challenges for Richard, Hans, Otto and Walter Freudenberg. However, it also gave the four men some good ideas, because they decided to expand the product portfolio – and to do this through both horizontal and later also through vertical diversification. This was a direct reaction to the abovementioned slump in the price of leathers: Therefore, in 1929, the company began the "manufacture of sleeve seals made of leather for the growing automobile industry," to tap new sales markets.[143] This step into the market for supplier products in the car industry can in turn be described as horizontal diversification, and thus as a broadening of the established product range.

The entry into the market for sealing technology is regarded as the "moment when Freudenberg's Schumpeterian diversification was born."[144] Although the

Fig. 42 Production of sealing sleeves on a spindle press, around 1930

term "diversification strategy" did not exist yet back then, it was very clear to the Freudenbergs that even as the leading upper leather tannery, the company was too vulnerable in a difficult economic situation since it had a relatively narrow product range but more than 3,000 employees. Ultimately, the company only had one product (in different variations), only operated in the consumer goods sector and was dependent both on the constantly fast-changing fashion industry as well as on exports: after all, 66 percent of leathers had gone to export before the outbreak of the Great Depression. Thus, horizontal diversification was driven forward despite major financial problems. For the company's development in the decades that followed, right up to the present day, they could not have taken a better decision. In the years between 1929 and 1933, a solid foundation was laid for the future of the company.[145]

But how did the idea come about to manufacture leather seals of all things? Egon Elöd, Head of the Textile Institute at the Technical University in Karlsruhe and advisor to Hans Freudenberg, who was the director responsible for technology on the Management Board, returned from the United States in 1929 and showed Hans a seal made of leather that he had brought back with him from America. Up to then, German companies did not have a product like this in their product ranges. Anyone who needed the sleeves had to pay for expensive imported goods. Hence the market was there, but the domestic products were lacking. Hans Freudenberg was quite obviously very receptive to the idea of producing sleeves like these themselves and initially to use leather offcuts productively to do this. The company had always paid a great deal of attention to making profitable use of waste materials. The waste materials were sorted carefully and sold if prospective buyers could be found for them. One example of this profitable use of waste materials from leather production is the processing of the hairs removed from the hides. These had already been sorted by color, cleaned, and subsequently sold on as a raw material to the felt industry back in the 19th century at Freudenberg.[146] Nowadays, this would be described as sustainable development, but it was practiced at an early stage at Freudenberg.

Thus, an employee was now required who had the expertise to develop sealing sleeves made of chrome leather. The company chose engineer Walther Simmer (1888–1986). Up to then, Simmer had been responsible for the tannery machines, but definitely had time on his hands because of the shrinking leather production. Then everything happened very fast. As early as mid-1929, Simmer conducted the first tests, with initially one employee, then with two: "First, the chrome-tanned leather was given the right thickness through splitting, then it was impregnated with wax, cut round, molded into the required shape on [a hand spindle and] pendulum foot presses with embossing tools, subsequently cut off on the outside and finally pressed round on the inside."[147]

The first serial production order came in shortly. It was for a cap collar with a 15-millimeter diameter for the centralized lubrication system developed by the Willy Vogel company for automobiles. The company was based in Berlin, had purchased in America up to then, could now save the high customs surcharge and purchased at one-third of the price from Freudenberg. However, the price was still high enough, at least from the perspective of Freudenberg's Management Board, who were pleased about the high margins and accommodated the seal manufacturing of the small Technical Leather department in rooms belonging to the shrinking patent leather production. Soon, "the first folding bellows and cardan shaft seals in the shape of folding bellows were manufactured" for the front-wheel drive Adler Triumph car.[148] This is how Freudenberg unexpectedly became a supplier to the automotive industry.

Three years after the work on the first leather seals started, something eventually began with the "Simmerring" in 1932 which can be described as the era of sealing technology at Freudenberg.[149] Because the Simmerring, a radial shaft sealing ring for sealing rotating shafts, replaced the felt seals that had been used up to then. The ring was a technological innovation from Freudenberg's development department, probably inspired by a sample of a radial shaft sealing ring from the United States. The Simmerring comprised a sheet metal casing, into which a leather sleeve is mounted. Its outstanding feature: By using a worm spring, the radial force is additionally increased, and with it the sealing performance as well. The product name was attributed to the aforementioned Freudenberg developer, Walther Simmer, who designed the innovative shaft sealing ring together with his team.[150] This was a veritable leap forward for the associated applications. Why? The previous seals had the disadvantage that they frequently tended to overheat, which led to bearing damage in engines and axle box bearings. The Simmerring, on the other hand, delivered considerably better results right from the start.¹⁵¹ And the name was set to become very well known in the decades to come. "The fundamentally new idea was to mount a leather sleeve in a sheet metal casing and offer it as a complete module."¹⁵²

The first serial production of the shaft sealing rings was already given to the Wanderer factory in Zwickau in 1932. Time and again, the "Simmerring"¹⁵³ name had always led to Walther Simmer being personally considered the inventor. He himself made it quite clear that this was not the case in correspondence with the Carl Freudenberg company in April 1951.

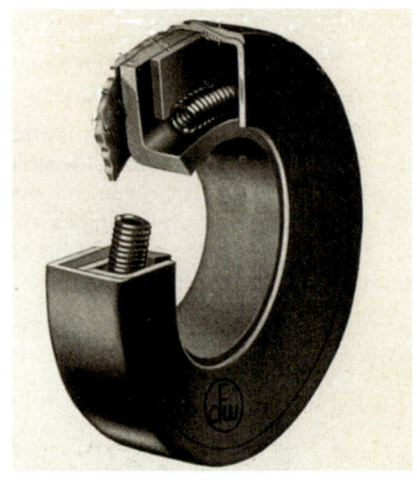

Fig. 43 Advertising image showing the interior of a Simmerring, 1932

However, in a letter to Georg Boysen, the head of seal sales at Freudenberg at the time, Walther Simmer also added:¹⁵⁴ "But there is one thing you cannot challenge me on: that I have provided my entire expertise and knowledge for around 20 years in the development of the sealing department and the Simmerring, and made the name Simmerring into a term that is synonymous with shaft seals."¹⁵⁵

It was already evident at an early stage that Simmer and Freudenberg had only achieved their successes because a lot of confidence had been placed in the inventor, the – from a modern perspective cutting-edge – working environment had promoted the developers' creativity and the entire project had additionally been paired with the patience and the staying power of the Management Board.¹⁵⁶ Moreover, the innovative sealing technology "was the main reason that Freudenberg came out of the Great Depression more successfully than most other German leather factories."¹⁵⁷

But even after overcoming the Great Depression, the business environment remained difficult for Freudenberg. Therefore, the company made every effort to expand its portfolio. From 1933 onward, this also occurred through vertical diversification. By entering the shoe manufacturing segment with the takeover of the Conrad Tack company, the value chain within the core product of leather was extended. However, this entailed an "Aryanization" which was strongly connected to the Nazi era and is therefore extremely morally charged.

After the takeover of Tack, the shoe division was expanded further: Freudenberg gradually acquired the Gustav Hoffmann children's shoe factory in Kleve

Fig. 44-45 Advertisement for Tack ladies' shoes, 1940 ▪ Letterhead of the Gustav Hoffmann firm with the logo of the Elefanten brand, 1934

and its *Elefanten* brand between 1933 and 1936. Additionally, Freudenberg expanded its shoe activities between 1937 and 1938 through the "Aryanization" of the companies J. Kern & Co. GmbH in Pirmasens, a manufacturer of heel counters, and C. Fisch & Co. in Heidelberg, a baby shoe producer, which will be elaborated on at a later juncture.[158]

Since the Nazis' economic policy was geared towards becoming independent of supplies from abroad (self-sufficiency), it quickly became more difficult to import sufficient rawhides for leather production in the original core business after the Nazis rose to power in 1933. From 1934 onward, leather became scarce in Germany. The Freudenberg Management Board's response to this was to attempt to launch an innovation campaign above and beyond the Simmerring. For this reason, what was known as the Main Laboratory was set up. Management of the laboratory was entrusted to chemist Ernst Demme (1900–1984). This latter's first experiments were centered on the profitable use of hide and leather offcuts from the tannery (collagen products) and – naturally – the search for leather substitute materials.[159] Thus, very soon, elastomer research on the modification and further development of *Buna* synthetic rubber was now the focus of Demme's research work. This resulted in the first elastomer compounds based on the nitrile butadiene rubber Buna N, which was sold by the I. G. Farben company under the brand name "Perbunan". This was a material that was set to form the basis for numerous Freudenberg products in the coming years.[160]

With the help of Perbunan, Freudenberg replaced leather with rubber as a sealing material: In 1936, a seal made of Perbunan was developed that had outstandingly high temperature and swelling resistance to petroleum, because petroleum in its turn was used as a lubricant for engines. Therefore, the Simmerring made of Perbunan was the next major evolutionary step for sealing technology – and better opportunities opened up to give the body of the seal the shape desired by the respective customer. Now the basic form could already be shaped in the vulcanizing tool and the sealing lip was adjusted precisely to the specific application purpose in a special postprocessing step. With this innovation, Freudenberg ultimately became the leading seal specialist.[161]

Fig. 46 View of the main laboratory, around 1938

"Entering the elastomer processing [segment] had considerable impact on the company's international orientation. In 1936, the first licensing contracts were completed with foreign partners to set up Simmerring production plants. In Italy, manufacturing of Simmerrings began together with the Corte & Cosso company in Turin and in Great Britain in Newcastle upon Tyne with George Angus Co. Limited."[162] Freudenberg maintained intensive and long-standing partnerships with both companies. The British company, for example, was extremely appreciative of the fact that this was a very high-quality product: Thus after the war (WWII), Angus was interested in resuming business relations with Freudenberg at a very early stage,[163] and before the war, the Royal Air Force in Great Britain was highly enamored with the quality of the Simmerring.[164] On the other hand, the history of the decades-long collaboration with Corte & Cosso demonstrates how greatly Freudenberg valued long-standing, amicable relationships with business partners.[165]

The elastomer research, coupled with the search for leather substitute materials, led the company to yet another significant development of a new product: the *Nora* sole.[166] In 1935, chemist Walter Nürnberger (1899–1986) had been hired to conduct further development of the elastomer materials. Under his direction, successes were rapidly achieved in the development of elastomer compounds, since he categorized *Buna* – from a modern perspective – correctly as a suitable leather substitute material. Apart from the seals – an existing business – he already broached the idea in 1936 to replace leather shoe soles with *Buna*. The first *Nora* shoe soles were developed as early as 1936. However, several technical problems needed to be solved first. Specifically, unlike classic leather soles, the soles could not be sewn or nailed on, but instead had to be glued, which required time-consuming tests.[167] The slip resistance of the outsole was initially a problem as well.[168] However, the *Nora* sole was already considered "the best replacement sole on the market" at the start of 1938.[169] As a result, a new raw materials mixing plant was set up in Weinheim under the management of Walter Nürnberger.[170] At the end of 1938, large-scale *Nora* production started in the Zwischen Dämmen Freudenberg works with processing capacity of 300 tons of *Buna* per month.[171]

The name *Nora,* under which the sole products were marketed and became known, is also derived from an abbreviation of Norimberga, the Latin name for Nuremberg [German: Nürnberg], and is thus a homage to the developer of the product, Walter Nürnberger.[172]

Walter Nürnberger's rapid successes in the area of elastomer compounds led to tensions with his development colleague, Walther Simmer. Eventually, this led to Nürnberger's departure from the company on January 15, 1940.[173]

The first shoe sole worldwide to be made from synthetic rubber, sold under the brand name *Nora*,[174] was an innovation milestone for Freudenberg from a technical perspective. Nevertheless, this product also led to involvement in one of the darkest chapters of company history, which will be expanded on in even greater detail at a later juncture.

It was not just the development of the *Nora* sole that was based on the search for leather substitute materials, but also the portfolio expansion into nonwovens in 1936, which has had a formative impact on the company up to the present day: "When young chemist Dr. Carl Ludwig Nottebohm came to Weinheim in 1936 and offered Hans Freudenberg the latex synthetic leather with a nonwoven backing which he had developed, the Management Board seized the opportunity that was proffered at once."[175] Nottebohm was hired. A synthetic leather production line was set up that went into large-scale production in 1938. "However, the synthetic leather was a very stiff material which was only suitable for bags and cases."[176] Thus the market was always extremely small, and after the currency reform of 1948 demand for this type of replacement product consequently collapsed, since people wanted to buy real leather products again. The product had failed. But not entirely, however. Because at Freudenberg, people had already been mulling over ideas since the start of the 1940s on how to make alternative use of the nonwoven material which up to now had only been used as a backing material for the synthetic leather.

It was manufactured on what are known as carders (carding machines) which originally came from thread manufacturing, where they were used for teasing out cotton. The fibers that were teased in this way[177] for the nonwoven material, which was initially made of cotton mixed with a little rayon, was rendered into a surface and compressed in several layers into a fleece, which gave the nonwoven material the quality of a textile fabric. This process is still used today in nonwoven material production.

And after World War II, there was a prevailing lack of support material that was required to give clothing its shape. This was taken as an opportunity to develop the nonwoven materials in this direction from 1946.[178]

As soon as the diversification began, the Freudenberg Management Board started looking for new possibilities for using the glue stock, which was generated in large amounts as a waste product during leather manufacture. For this reason, at the beginning of the 1930s, Hans Freudenberg showed a great interest in a synthetic sausage skin developed by Hamburg-born engineer Walter Becker which was based on glue stock. In 1930, the associated patent was registered and two years later, production of the *Naturin* artificial sausage skins began in the Becker, Schulze & Co. firm in Hamburg-Altona based on the process Becker had developed. Freudenberg entered into negotiations with Becker, and it became clear very soon that a collaboration would be a good idea for both partners.[179] As

Fig. 47 Production of nonwovens using a carding machine, around 1938

early as 1933, what was known as the "mass", meaning collagen fibers from processed glue stock, entered into production at Freudenberg in Weinheim for the manufacture of artificial sausage skins for the Naturin joint venture.[180]

Then, in 1933, when part of the site of the former Badenia machinery factory in Weinheim was up for sale, the business partners decided to relocate production of the artificial sausage skins from Hamburg to Weinheim because the factory in Hamburg offered no opportunities for expansion.[181] Finally, the Naturin GmbH company was established on May 15, 1933, and Freudenberg acquired a 49 percent shareholding in the joint venture.[182] In 1934, the Naturin factory commenced production on the site of the former Badenia machinery factory in Weinheim.[183] Subsequently, Naturin developed into the leading manufacturer of artificial sausage skins in Europe.[184] In 1990, Freudenberg sold its share in Naturin to Spanish company Viscofan.[185]

Yet another interesting synthetic product was developed from the collaboration with Naturin. In 1934, Walter Becker conducted the first experiment in the Naturin factory to manufacture a thin fiber for textile uses from collagen fiber mass. This experiment was continued in 1935 at the behest of Hans Freudenberg in the Old Lacquering Shop factory. In the process, it emerged that no fiber could be produced from this material which was thin, could be spun and was similar to artificial silk. At the same time, however, it was discovered that a "synthetic horsehair" could be manufactured from the mass if it was blackened by soot, pressed through metal nozzles and subsequently tanned. As a result, a "Marena" production department was set up. Textile engineer Hellmut Dobler was tasked with the production and marketing of the "*Marena* fiber" for the brush industry and for horsehair spinning mills. Annual production before the outbreak of World War II had already reached 530 tonnes. However, the *Marena* fiber was ultimately unable to compete against the benefits of the synthetic fibers (nylon) which had meantime come onto the market: Operations were discontinued in 1959.[186]

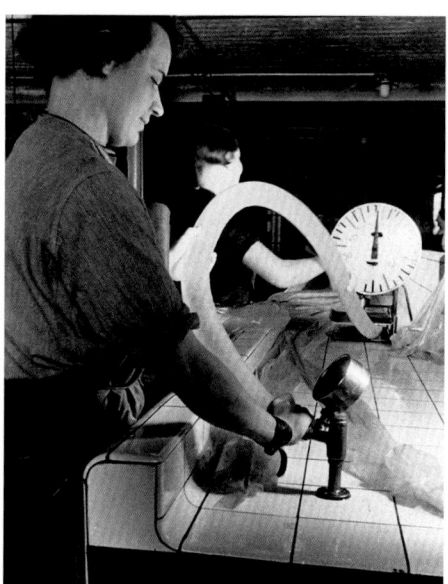

Fig. 48 Quality control of the Naturin firm's sausage skins, 1938

The horizontal and vertical expansion of the product portfolio led the company onto a path of scientizing and thus turned it into an industrial company with a modern character which increasingly developed away from being a traditional tannery business.[187] The diversification into the areas of sealing technology and nonwovens (synthetic leather) and the shareholding in the Naturin company is – unlike shoes – significant right up to the present day. Undoubtedly, the leather supply shortfall brought about by the Nazi policy of self-sufficiency was the motivation for many diversification measures. However, it should not be overlooked that the portfolio expansion that contributed considerably to the company's success after 1933 had already partially begun before the Nazis rose to power. The company development problems in the years of the Weimar Republic, incidentally not just at Freudenberg, encouraged such measures, and the outcome of these measures fundamentally changed the technological nature of many businesses.

CHAPTER 4
FREUDENBERG IN THE NAZI ERA

Freudenberg after the Nazis came to power and the Management Board's political stance[1]

On January 30, 1933 President Paul von Hindenburg appointed Adolf Hitler as Chancellor, although he opposed Hitler. However, certain political circles had managed to convince Hindenburg that the social, economic and political crises of the Weimar Republic could only be tackled with the participation of the Nazi Party (NSDAP). These politicians, who were led by Franz von Papen, were convinced that they could keep Hitler in check. They were completely wrong – because the dissolution of the Reichstag and setting the date for new elections for March 5, 1933 was exactly what Hitler had actually intended. His objective had always been the destruction of democracy. And he knew that he would be able to make use of instruments which had now become commonplace in the Weimar Republic, and these were emergency decrees. These gave him immense room for maneuver in the run-up to the new elections.[2]

Just one day after the Reichstag fire of February 27, 1933 the emergency decree "For the Protection of People and State" was issued. It constituted the formal basis for the abrogation of civil rights and the persecution of political opponents as well as of other groups which the Nazis termed "enemies of the people" (*Volksfeinde*).[3] In addition, the emergency decree "For the Protection of the German People" had already been passed on February 4, 1933. Under the pretext of warding off danger, it was now permissible to ban newspapers and public assemblies as well as to suppress public criticism.[4]

Amid these conditions, state-sanctioned terror ran rampant during the election campaign period. Almost all communist candidates were arrested if they had not managed to escape underground beforehand. Numerous social democrats also went underground, and the party executive emigrated to Prague.[5] In light of all of this, it was extremely surprising that the NSDAP did not succeed in garnering an absolute majority in the elections on March 5, 1933: Although almost all Germans who were eligible to vote cast their vote, only 43.9 percent of them voted – with a voter turnout of 88.8 percent, which would be considered incredibly high today – for Hitler and his party. However, together with the remnants of the German national party (DNVP), that was enough for a parliamentary majority and the continuation of Hitler's rule.[6]

The Enabling Act (*Ermächtigungsgesetz*) of March 23, 1933, against which only the remaining members of the SPD parliamentary party voted, formed the pseudo-legal foundation for the subsequent and increasingly more comprehensive dictatorship. Exercising resistance against this dictatorship became extremely risky, because since the Reichstag fire, the suppression of any and every political opposition was already being brutally imposed using what was known as "protective custody" and the establishment of concentration camps. The trade unions were disempowered on May 2, 1933, when the regime forcibly amalgamated them, together with the employer associations, into the German Labor Front (DAF). In mid-July 1933, only the NSDAP remained as the one and only permitted party. The states in the German Reich as well as social associations, radio and the press were controlled and synchronized. No more than the business associations, the German armed forces (*Reichswehr*) had let themselves be captivated by Hitler's political offers. The Reichswehr was relieved of its worries about competition from the SA particularly because of the murder of the entire SA leadership, including its leader Ernst Röhm, on June 30, 1934, which was organized by the SS and the Gestapo. The German Protestant church (*Evan-*

Fig. 49 Nazi demonstration during the dedication of the memorial for the citizens of Weinheim who fell in World War I, on October 18, 1936. Source: Stadtarchiv Weinheim

gelische Kirche) was split. The Catholic Church tried to at least secure its rights within the new state by signing a treaty with the regime, the *Reichskonkordat*.[7] Any political opposition was heavily suppressed. However, the Hitler government actually met with a positive reception too following the experiences of the Great Depression. Large parts of the economy hoped for an end to the economic crisis at last, precisely because the government was strong. Therefore, irrespective of their political convictions, many entrepreneurs pinned their hopes on the new government, and its obvious brutalities were to a large extent overlooked.[8]

What was the outcome of the March 5, 2023 election in Weinheim? A glance at the election results shows that the NSDAP was as strong here as it was in the entire German Reich. The party gained 46.44 percent overall, the SPD 15.55 percent, the Communist Party (KPD) 19.2 percent and the German State Party (Deutsche Staatspartei), a pitiful remnant of the liberal German Democratic Party (DDP), only 1.84 percent of the votes.[9] The mood was such that Hitler was already made an honorary citizen of Weinheim on March 21, 1933. This was also the day of the opening session of the new "Reichstag" parliament in the Garrison Church in Potsdam, at which Hindenburg and with him many representatives of the old elite abandoned their opposition to Hitler. On this day too, a "ceremonial meeting" of the city council in Weinheim took place, at which the city council unanimously awarded honorary citizenship to Hitler, Hindenburg and two other citizens of Weinheim.[10]

Before long, life became unbearable for the Jews who lived in Weinheim. At the time the Nazis acceded to power, 170 Jewish citizens lived in Weinheim. Only shortly after the Reichstag elections in March 1933, the NSDAP in Weinheim participated in the boycott of Jewish businesses organized across the Reich on April 1, 1933:[11] "SA

Fig. 50 The Weinheim synagogue after its destruction during the November pogroms in 1938. Source: Stadtarchiv Weinheim

people positioned themselves in front of each of the 32 boycotted shops to prevent citizens from shopping in the stores. In addition, the SA and SS people stood before buildings where Jewish lawyers and doctors lived and worked holding a placard on which was written: 'The Jews are our misfortune!'"[12] A perpetual wave of obstructions, discriminations and persecutions followed, and when the November pogroms took place in 1938, the Jewish community in Weinheim was permanently disbanded: On November 8, SA men destroyed the interior of the synagogue, and two days later, it was blown up. In the city center, the windows of Jewish shops were smashed, Jewish dwellings searched, and Jewish citizens arrested.[13] Finally, in October 1940, the local authorities deported the last remaining Jews in the city to the Gurs internment camp in France as part of what was known as the Wagner-Bürckel operation.[14]

For the Freudenberg Management Board, the Nazis' accession to power became a moral and ethical challenge. Firstly, it should be noted that Richard, Hans, Otto as well as Walter Freudenberg were bourgeois economic supporters of the Weimar Republic. This can be proven particularly by Richard Freudenberg's intensive political involvement in the left-wing liberal German Democratic Party (DDP).[15] Between 1919 and 1925, Richard Freudenberg was a DDP MP in the Baden State Parliament (*Landtag*).[16] Up to 1933, a "liberal and anti-totalitarian fundamental attitude"[17] can be clearly determined among the members of the Freudenberg Management Board. As early as February 1933, there was a dispute in the press which clearly demonstrates the attitude of Richard and Walter Freudenberg to Nazi politics. Thus an article in Mannheim-based Nazi newspaper *Volksstimme* dated February 18, 1933 states that Richard Freudenberg had declared a year earlier that "Hitler [...] in every respect [was] suitable to occupy the position of a spa hotel manager or a ringmaster; he could never be eligible to be a head of state."[18] And likewise in 1933 there were also election announcements from Walter Freudenberg in local daily newspapers, in which he clearly spoke out in favor of the "liberal center of the German middle classes." The Nazi district leadership commented on this by saying that Walter Freudenberg was positioning himself "protectively in front of the Social Democrats."[19] Although the members of the Management Board increasingly adopted a collaborative stance towards the Nazi dictatorship in the years that followed, as will be elaborated on at a later juncture, these examples show Richard and Walter Freudenberg right into 1933 as "upstanding and staunch defenders of democracy."[20]

Undoubtedly, the aspect that some members of the Freudenberg family were married to Jewish wives played an important role too. The result was that these parts of the family very soon felt compelled to leave Germany. Thus, one of these, Friedrich Carl Freudenberg's youngest son, Ernst Freudenberg (1884–1967),

Fig. 51-52 Ernst Freudenberg, 1932 ▪ Ida Freudenberg, 1932

emigrated from Germany. At the time of the Nazi accession to power, he was a Professor of Pediatrics in Marburg. His wife, Ida Siegheim (1887–1951), was of Jewish descent. For this reason, Ernst Freudenberg was banned from his profession in 1937.[21] The situation of Ernst and Ida Freudenberg was summarized very succinctly by the Kassel District Court in the 1952 compensation procedures: "There cannot be any doubt that the wife of the applicant, [Ernst Freudenberg], being Jewish, was among the racially persecuted […]. However, the applicant must also be counted among this group of persons, because he, although non-Jewish himself, had stuck by his Jewish spouse. […] There can be no doubt about the fact that the applicant was subjected to persecution measures. […] Taking all these circumstances into consideration, he was therefore compelled to emigrate."[22] Thus Ernst Freudenberg accepted the offer of a position as Chair of Pediatrics at the Medical Faculty in Basle in February 1938 and hence emigrated to Switzerland in 1938. In order to be able to pay the "Reich flight tax"[23] which then became due, he was forced to dispose of half of his company shares, which were taken over by the incumbent managing directors. Then, in 1939, he sold the remainder of his shares to various family members and thereby retired from the company as a general partner.[24]

Adolf Freudenberg (1894–1977), the younger brother of Hans, Otto and Richard Freudenberg, suffered a similar fate. Because his wife was also of Jewish descent, he had already resigned from his position as a diplomat at the Foreign Office in Berlin in the mid-1930s.²⁵ He subsequently studied theology and became a Protestant pastor in Brandenburg.²⁶ In October 1938, the Berlin-Zehlendorf tax office imposed a writ of seizure on part of his Limited Partnership contribution as a security for a potential Reich flight tax payment in the event that Adolf Freudenberg were to emigrate.²⁷ Even at the start of November 1938, he did not harbor any "emigration intentions,"²⁸ as evidenced by a letter to his brother Richard dated November 10. Initially, the writ of seizure did not appear to have any effect on his status as a partner. However, due to the effects of the November pogroms and the intensification of the repressive measures towards the Jewish population that followed immediately afterwards, this changed very quickly. Elsa Freudenberg still recalled many years later: "Thus it was clear to us that we had to leave Germany, at the very least for our children's sake."²⁹ Adolf Freudenberg took "the dangers that have emerged recently"³⁰ very seriously. They prompted him to submit an emigration application to the Berlin authorities for himself and his family. In order to be able to pay the Reich flight tax which then became due and – presumably – to be able to pay living expenses for himself and his family during their emigration, he offered all his shares for sale to the general partners as well as to many Limited Partners in December 1938.³¹ Why he, unlike Ernst Freudenberg, disposed of all his shares immediately cannot be determined on the basis of the surviving sources. When the sale was

Fig. 53 Elsa and Adolf Freudenberg on their wedding day, 1920

completed in early 1939, Adolf Freudenberg likewise resigned from the company as a partner.[32] He relocated to England at the end of March 1939 under the terms of an agreement between the church leadership of the German Protestant Church and the ecumenical representative of the British churches.[33] In the same month, he was tasked with looking after German refugees by the Ecumenical Council of Churches in Switzerland. In summer 1939, Adolf Freudenberg went to Geneva to set up a refugee agency which he ran himself on behalf of the Confessing Church, among others, and which set up an alliance with the London-based Office for International Refugee Aid. Adolf Freudenberg's apartment in Geneva served as a transit station for numerous refugees and as a place of refuge for oppositionists.[34]

In 1951, Adolf and Ernst Freudenberg's company shares were transferred back to them. This restitution "was intended from the outset [...], as soon as the political circumstances would permit it."[35] At the same time, the re-entry of Adolf and Ernst as partners was backdated to July 1, 1950.[36] However, when Adolf and Ernst Freudenberg returned as partners, their percentage of the shares was reduced. This was because during the period after their resignations, two capital increases had taken place in the company in which they were unable to participate. As part of the restitution, they were compensated for profits they had missed out on wherever possible with extraordinary payments from the partners' shares.[37]

Thus the shares, compared to the reimbursements for the most diverse restitution entitlements in the Federal Republic of Germany overall, were returned relatively early. Hence the restitution did not occur on the basis of the laws of the Federal Republic of Germany either – the German Restitution Act (*Bundesrückerstattungsgesetz*) only came into effect in 1957 – but instead on the basis of the restitution laws of the military governments of the Allied Occupation Zones. These laws were enacted between 1947 and 1949 and only incorporated into German law later.[38]

There was also the fact that the company was under trusteeship from 1945 to 1948 and for this reason a restitution of the shares was initially impossible.[39] Throughout this time, no general meetings could take place, and a resolution of the general meeting was required to enable Adolf and Ernst Freudenberg to rejoin the company. During the general meeting of September 25, 1948 – the first after the end of World War II – the process of reparations was indeed initiated: "Richard Freudenberg furthermore declared unopposed that it was self-evident that the company and the partners are honor-bound to reach an agreement with the retired former partners Adolf and Ernst Freudenberg, or rather their families, irrespective of the current status of legal requirements, in a fair manner that conforms to the nature of our family company."⁴⁰ The readmittance to the shareholder group then occurred during the general meeting of June 24, 1951.⁴¹ The Reich flight tax was also reimbursed to Adolf and Ernst Freudenberg by the Federal Republic of Germany between 1957 and 1958.⁴²

Looking back, the emigrations that were forced by the Nazi regime's repressive measures are the main reason why a relatively high number of Freudenberg partners are domiciled outside Germany up to the present day. Since then, this has always had to be taken into account very thoroughly time and again by the company, among other things for tax reasons – including the choice of legal form.⁴³

In contrast, Richard, Hans and Walter Freudenberg joined the Nazi party (NSDAP), but not until January 1943, however. One of the reasons for this was likely to have been the "worry about the consequences of ongoing political attacks […] which were being directed against the company."⁴⁴ Thus Richard Freudenberg, for example, found himself subjected to constant investigation proceedings by the *Reichssicherheitshauptamt*, and thus by the SS. Among other things, he was confronted with accusations that he was in constant communication with contacts abroad whom the Nazis considered to be suspect.⁴⁵ Nevertheless, a pragmatic approach to the new political circumstances can be swiftly identified at Freudenberg too, however. These circumstances had to be accepted as the fundamental conditions for conducting business anyway, especially in a market environment that was becoming increasingly driven by politics. Since at the same time private ownership rights were still respected, open conflicts did not arise: "One came to terms with the circumstances all the more so in view of the fact that in the 'Third Reich' ownership circumstances – at least of non-Jews – were not touched despite all the threats, and the pursuit of profit as a production incentive remained unchanged. Carl Freudenberg acted as one of the most important companies in the leather industry, showed a certain rebelliousness on occasion towards the new leaders, but ultimately adapted after all and paradoxically even profited from the policy of self-sufficiency which one [it – ed.] actually rejected."⁴⁶ This also included the fact that they acted generously, at least to insistent "requests": Accordingly, Freudenberg acquiesced to various demands to support the Nazi party financially, for example through the annual amounts paid to the "Adolf Hitler Fund of Trade and Industry," donations for the Winter Relief, or a donation for the construction of an airplane for the *Luftwaffe*. The Management Board were not the only people participating in these "gestures"; white- and blue-collar workers were also forced to make various payments. However, one could not say there was any real enthusiasm for these. The introduction of the "German salute", which was passed by resolution of the works council in January 1934 for everyday factory use, proved difficult to implement at any rate, which was due on the one hand to a lack of "political enthusiasm" on the part of the workforce and on the other hand to the reluctance of the Management Board to enforce this.[47]

Apart from the political circumstances, the background to the ultimately pragmatic arrangement was the difficult economic conditions during the Great Depression, which were also reflected in Weinheim.[48] There was a lack of orders, and the working hours for a normal worker were only 36 hours.[49] At the works council meeting of January 10, 1933 Richard Freudenberg spoke openly to the workers' representatives about the "bad trend in business"[50] and announced layoffs. Then on March 4, 1933 150 employees were actually laid off. However, despite the depressing situation, the Nazi party had remained irrelevant within the company up to then, but efforts to set up a cell of the National Socialist Factory Cell Organization (NSBO) at Freudenberg soon began. The NSBO "regarded itself as a company combat troop of Adolf Hitler and attempted […] to increase its following among the Freudenberg employees."[51]

Thus on March 27, 1933 "the first official NSBO meeting [took] place [at Freudenberg], at which the local group leader Kurt Niceus and Nazi Philipp Oswald, who was employed at the company, committed their followers to the party line." Finally, on April 22, Fritz Plattner, the local state chairman of the NSBO, introduced himself at Freudenberg. Immediately, he arbitrarily ordered the removal and dismissal of Works Council Chairman Philipp Vetter as well as of three further opposing works council members. In addition, the dismissal of eight politically undesirable Freudenberg employees was demanded. Only a few days later, on April 28, 1933, Plattner installed a works council that had been forced to toe the Nazi party line with corresponding new members. Richard Freudenberg did not necessarily let himself be intimidated by all of this, as a look at the Vetter case shows, because he recommended to Vetter "to stay at home for two weeks and then return to his workplace."[52] Vetter was re-employed in May 1933.[53] However, at the same time, it was perfectly clear to Richard Freudenberg that his room for maneuver was being constantly reduced by the new ruling powers, which he expressed to a business partner as follows: "Not for one moment do I believe that the factory is still our property."[54] That was also evident in the increasingly extensive interference in company culture and day-to-day operations. Through the enactment of the "Work Order Act" (*Arbeitsordnungsgesetz*) in January 1934, the "*Führerprinzip*" [leadership principle – basically a dictatorship ethos – ed.] also entered into Freudenberg culture. What followed thereafter was an ideological loading of the company's organization on the basis of Nazism: Entrepreneurs became "*Betriebsführer*" (company leaders) and the workforce became a "following" (*Gefolgschaft*) who had pledged their loyalty to their "*Betriebsführer*".[55] By constructing a leader-follower relationship, the aim was to defuse the dichotomy between capital and work, and in fact harmonize it.

Alongside the NSBO, the German Labor Front (DAF) also increasingly exerted its power in the years that followed. From 1938 onwards, DAF membership was obligatory for all "following members". However, only the outbreak of war made very harshly clear where all of this was meant to lead: "When the war started, call-ups and emergency drills became part of everyday operations." In the factory roll calls, it became increasingly common to remember those employees who had lost their lives in the war.[56]

Overall, it can be said that the Freudenberg Management Board "tried to keep the Nazi ideology out of everyday operations as much as they could and adhere to the family and company traditions." Freudenberg, "as one of the most important companies in the leather industry, showed a certain rebelliousness on occasion towards the new leaders [ruling powers], but ultimately adapted after all and paradoxically even profited from the policy of self-sufficiency which one actually rejected [as an export-oriented company]. [...] Despite all the Management Board's personal aversion to the Nazis and despite all the quarrels with the Nazi authorities, the company ultimately acted cooperatively and profited from Nazi economic policy up to the end of the 'Third Reich.'"[57]

Conversion to a limited partnership

Hitler was of the opinion "that the anonymous stock corporations belonged in the hands of the state." The result was a Nazi financial and economic policy that increasingly discriminated against stock corporations and constrained them in their room for maneuver. For example, the Loan Fund Act limited the possibilities for dividend payouts by legal entities and thus by stock corporations. After this came limitations on dividends and an "increase in corporate tax on stock corporations from 20 to 30 percent." This had a direct impact on Freudenberg too, because for example the equity capital of the Freudenberg & Co. holding company could no longer be increased.[58] Thus, in 1936, the Management Board decided to convert the Carl Freudenberg and Freudenberg & Co. companies, which had both been previously operated with the legal form of a GmbH (limited liability company), into limited partnerships and therefore into unincorporated companies, since this had the associated advantage of considerable tax benefits.[59]

Freudenberg was by no means an exception in doing this: "In light of these developments, numerous middle-sized companies changed their ownership structures: The number of *GmbHs* fell from 1934 to 1936 from 55,000 to below 26,000!"[60]

Although the previous system of separating rights of disposal and property had proven worthwhile,[61] the Freudenberg & Co. GmbH holding company, which had been created in 1921, and also most of the subsidiaries, were converted from the legal form of GmbH or *Aktiengesellschaft* (stock company) into *Kommanditgesellschaften* (limited partnerships, KG) in 1936.[62] The limited partnership contract was drawn up at that time by Frankfurt-based lawyer and specialist for company law Ernst Boesebeck. The contract turned out to be an exceedingly effective solution. It initially secured the company's survival interests, which were given priority over the shareholders' individual interests. In addition, it ensured considerable stability in company financing and in the work of the Management Board.[63] Quite apart from the conditions of its origin, it proved to be a trailblazing measure. In essence, it forms the basis for the partnership agreement of Freudenberg & Co. KG as the holding company of the Freudenberg Group right up to the present day.[64]

The aim of the limited partnership contract was to amalgamate the benefits of the two legal forms together. The result was what is known as a "capital limited partnership", meaning a limited partnership which has the organizational structure of a stock corporation.[65] The retention of the family enterprise remained the primary objective. It was therefore explicitly expressed in the new partnership agreement that it "is a company which is already in the hands of the third generation of the Freudenberg family, was kept going through good times and bad by the family and which should remain unchanged as a family enterprise in accordance with the wishes of its founder and the current owners."[66] Thus the contract could not be canceled even in the event that "the company [should become] temporarily unprofitable"[67] "or if individual shareholders should be interested in realizing the assets they have invested in the company."[68] Should "differences occur between the shareholders,"[69] these had to take a back seat "behind the overall interest in safeguarding the family enterprise."[70][71]

"The conversion was agreed upon in individual discussions with the 18 shareholders. At an extraordinary general meeting in Frankfurt, Richard Freudenberg declared that one was acquiescing to the government's wishes 'despite one's own reservations.'"[72] He expressed these reservations as follows: "We are departing reluctantly from the legally stricter G. m. b. H. form, since from the beginning our understanding of responsibility was never connected to our external form. I am more worried about the thought that despite the greatest possible legal precautions, property and income will move in much greater proximity to the shareholders than was the case with the G. m. b. H., and that at least one point, and that is the right to terminate [the agreement] for cause, gives the individual shareholders a much greater opportunity to set aside company interests some time and terminate the association of companies for personal or arbitrary reasons. Those were also the reasons why the G. m. b. H. form was chosen for our management company in 1921 and not that of a limited partnership."[73]

The limited partnership contract was signed by the 18 partners on November 28, 1936. "All shares of Freudenberg & Co. were transferred to the personal ownership of the general partners within the family. The admission of a partner who did not belong to the family required a three-quarter majority of the general partners. Apart from a fixed salary, the four general partners with personal liability received a profit-related bonus and were responsible for running the business." The previous Management Board members Walter, Hans, Otto and Richard Freudenberg, all of them fulfilling the same function, acted with immediate effect as general managers and general partners of the Freudenberg & Co. KG family holding company and of "subsidiary Carl Freudenberg, which had likewise been converted into a limited partnership, whose sole Limited Partner was Freudenberg & Co."[74]

This was how the definition of a limited partnership[75] was turned into a reality: Because a limited partnership comprises one or several partners with unlimited and personal liability (the general partners) and at least one partner whose liability is limited to their capital contribution (limited partner). Legal entities can also be general or limited partners, as was the case at Freudenberg.

"Aryanizations" and Aryanization attempts

Between 1933 and 1945, Freudenberg took over several Jewish companies in Germany in the course of what were known as "Aryanizations", meaning the squeezing out of Jews from business life, which was aggressively promoted politically.[76] While the transactions were formally processed like purchases, the balance of power was so unequal between the negotiating parties that in reality most Jewish businesspeople were robbed of their businesses by the purchasers. Looking at Freudenberg, it can likewise be said regarding these transactions that there was a progressively greater involvement in the regime's policy of systematic violation of human rights. Initially, the company behaved passively and reacted to the initiatives of Jewish company owners who had come under pressure.

However, after the first takeovers, a certain routine increasingly became evident, and ultimately the initiatives were actively launched by the company as a means of business expansion as well. Among others, the "Aryanizations" by Freudenberg described below took place during the Nazi era.

The takeover of shoe factory and retail chain Conrad Tack & Cie., which had been established in 1883, is currently considered by researchers to be one of the first "Aryanizations" in Germany. It took place in the fall of 1933 – and it likely also took place so early because the initiative came from Tack itself. As "Europe's oldest shoe corporation" the company had already achieved record sales of almost 38 million Reichsmarks in 1929.[77]

However, the existential crisis of the German leather industry – triggered by the Great Depression – was a crisis of the shoe industry at the same time, since demand for shoes shrank dramatically as a consequence of the crisis. And this had also hit Tack very hard economically. Thus initial takeover negotiations already took place between Tack and Carl Freudenberg in 1932, and hence before Adolf Hitler was elected Chancellor of the Reich. The two companies knew each other well, and had close connections. Freudenberg was Tack's largest leather supplier. However, these initial negotiations failed.[78]

Then, in the spring of 1933, Tack's major shareholder and general manager, Hermann Krojanker, tried to prevent the takeover of his company by the Nazis through adhering to "*Gleichschaltung*" (Nazi-enforced conformity), which was, however, only a formality.[79] After this too failed, Krojanker resumed the takeover negotiations with Freudenberg. Then, in the fall of 1933, the two parties reached a contractual agreement and the "Aryanization" of the Tack company took place.[80] The motives for and the basic attitudes about the takeover negotiations can be described as follows: "The Freudenberg company, and particularly Richard Freudenberg, who was primarily in charge, would certainly not have become involved in it if they had not seen prospects for the further development

Fig. 54-55 Tack retail outlet in Mannheim-Plankenhof, which opened on April 1, 1936 ▪ Exhibition stand for Tack shoes at the "Deutschland" exhibition in Berlin, 1936

of the Tack business. But at the same time they believed they were able to help a Jewish business partner in an extraordinary predicament. For those immediately involved, the takeover still proceeded to a large extent in the same manner as traditional sales negotiations, although the ugly attendant circumstances [like for example the boycott of the Tack branches by the Nazis] already showed the total aggressiveness of the Nazi regime which had only just been established."[81]

After 1945, Freudenberg was able to agree on a restitution settlement with the former Tack shareholders and heirs, and the shoe company and its branches remained in the Weinheim company's ownership.[82]

The J. Kern & Co. GmbH company in Pirmasens was also active in the shoe manufacturing industry. This factory, which had only been established in 1929 and specialized in heel counters,[83] was offered for purchase by one of its partners to Tack and thus to Freudenberg in April 1937.

In May 1937, the company was initially signed over to Freudenberg in a "memorandum of understanding". Nevertheless, the negotiations continued for some time. Finally, in May 1938, the little company was integrated into Freudenberg[84] and deleted from the company register at the end of 1938. Although the purchase price agreed between the parties was paid, the lion's share of the money did not go to the Jewish owners, but to the Nazi state because of tax arrears and Reich flight tax.[85] In 1939, the business was moved to Weinheim, since Pirmasens was vacated for military reasons.[86]

A settlement was also reached after the war with the former Jewish owners of the Kern company. However, after a restitution settlement was agreed in 1950,[87] "business relations [were] resumed again very soon" with the family of the former owners.[88]

Eventually, "Aryanizations" began to become "normal" – although particularly when it comes to Freudenberg, each individual case must be considered separately: In the case of "Baby" shoe factory C. Fisch & Co. oHG in Heidelberg, which was "Aryanized" in 1938, the initiative stemmed from the management board of shoe manufacturer Gustav Hoffmann AG, a company which – as explained already – had been gradually taken over by Freudenberg from 1933 onward.[89] Particularly Hoffmann board member Walther Siegert, a cousin of Richard Freudenberg, was instrumental in pushing forward with the takeover of C. Fisch & Co. After 1945, the owners were paid compensation as part of the restitution negotiations.[90]

In the summer of 1938, the Sigmund Hirsch oHG and Sigmund Hirsch KG[91] companies, which had been based in Weinheim since they were established in 1868, were also transferred to Freudenberg with their factory buildings and their real estate.[92] Hirsch was a long-standing competitor of Freudenberg, they knew

Fig. 56 Sigmund Hirsch leather factory in Weinheim, 1913

each other well – and therefore their dealings with one another were likewise anything but cold and businesslike. Specializing in horse hide leather, which was rougher and less expensive than calf or goat leather, the Hirsch company had been managed since the end of the 1920s by the third generation of the family, Arthur and Fritz Hirsch.[93] The "Aryanization" of Hirsch was conducted through Deutsche Bank Mannheim,[94] which transferred the Freudenberg purchase price between July and December 1938.

The fact that the "Aryanization" of Hirsch took place in restrained conditions is demonstrated by the aspect that even after the takeover, the Hirsch family did not sever contacts with the Freudenbergs. "Although the family had been forced to sell by the Nazi regime, the negotiations were fair and decent and an appropriate amount was paid, which was subsequently collected almost in its entirety by the Nazi authorities, however."[95] Max Hirsch, one of the general managers, wrote this about it in 1940 while in exile: "After deduction of the 25 % for the Reich flight tax, the initial 20 % for the Jewish levy (which was soon followed by a further 5 %) and the other regular ongoing taxes, our assets were initially reduced by half. The remaining amount became blocked mark assets, which at the time of our emigration was converted into foreign currency by the Golddiskontbank on a case-by-case basis in not very large amounts at only 6 %, so that in reality, my assets came to only 3 % of my last recorded statement of assets."[96] Following the November pogroms, Max Hirsch, along with Julius, Fritz and Arthur

Hirsch, were arrested in November 1938 and transported to Dachau concentration camp. Richard Freudenberg used his direct contact with Baden's Minister President Walther Köhler to achieve their release. At the end of 1938, the Hirsch families emigrated to the United States and received support from the Freudenbergs in their preparations to leave the country and their exile.[97]

In 1944, Arthur Hirsch was questioned by the FBI during his American exile about the "Aryanization" of his company by Freudenberg. He described Richard Freudenberg as a "shrewd, calculating, and thoroughly dependable business man. He is definitely the type that would be anti-Nazi, but enough of a realist to continue his operations under the regime and remain on friendly terms with the persons in power."[98] Richard Freudenberg still remained friends with the Hirsch family, he said, even "when it was dangerous to be friendly with Jews."[99] "Eventually, a restitution settlement agreed in June 1949 led to payments amounting to 1.8 million deutschmarks onto a joint account owned by the Hirsch family. The Hirsch family continued to stay in occasional contact with the Freudenbergs."[100]

Outside Germany and in the occupied territories, many German companies pursued their "Aryanization plans" in a "considerably more unrestrained" manner than in Germany. Freudenberg's behavior must be viewed critically in this context too. There were two motives for this: On the one hand, the opportunity for a takeover arose, and the company wanted to take advantage of it – as was the case with French shoe manufacturer Chaussures André, which had a similar company and sales structure to Tack and thus fitted into Freudenberg's overall strategy. On the other hand, there was considerable competitive pressure in the sector, because there were already legitimate fears that competitors like Salamander or Bata could seize the opportunity for a takeover faster.[101]

After what is known as the annexation ("*Anschluss*") of Austria to the German Reich in 1938, Freudenberg attempted to take advantage of the possibility of "Aryanization" in Austria too. Thus Freudenberg planned the takeover of Del-Ka Schuhindustrie und Handels AG, one of the most important companies in the Austrian shoe industry. The aim was to affiliate the Del-Ka branches into the Tack outlet chain.[102] After the authorized bank, Österreichische Creditanstalt,[103] had indicated its approval, Tack presented a purchase offer for Del-Ka on March 30, 1938. But because interested parties from the former Austrian region were given precedence over the large German companies, the takeover attempt failed.[104] Nevertheless, Freudenberg stuck to its plan for expansion into the newly accessible Austrian market. In the spring of 1940, Creditanstalt endeavored to sell its shareholdings in Del-Ka and Aeterna, a shoe factory which was likewise in Jewish ownership and in severe business difficulties.[105] As a consequence of this, Freudenberg submitted another purchase offer, this time using mediation by Deutsche Bank. But this time too, the attempts failed because of the Vienna authorities, who did not want to hand over Del-Ka to a company from the "Altreich".[106]

In order to be able to expand its own market position as a shoe manufacturer in France too, Freudenberg attempted to acquire a significant minority shareholding in the largest French shoe producer, Chaussures André, which was based in Nancy, from its Jewish owner from 1941 onward. However, Freudenberg met with considerable resistance from French authorities, industrialists and banks, who would have preferred to divide up the Jewish company among French interests and therefore prevented a takeover by Freudenberg.[107]

The only takeover of a foreign company that verifiably occurred based on existing sources was that of Société Chromex. This company had already been a licensee for the production of Freudenberg Simmerrings in France, which was also the overriding reason for the takeover initiative. Ultimately, the objective was to protect Freudenberg patents and technological expertise. Since 1934, Freudenberg had already held a 75 percent shareholding in Chromex anyway through Swiss business associate Jacques Keller.[108] The eventual takeover by Freudenberg, which the Reich's Economic Ministry confirmed in the summer of 1941, was facilitated by this shareholding.[109]

From a research perspective, the Freudenberg "Aryanizations" can be described in summary as follows:

"If one reviews the 'Aryanizations' of the Carl Freudenberg company that took place in the years from 1933 to 1938, then a few characteristics are noticeable. In general, it was Richard Freudenberg himself who conducted the negotiations. Walter Freudenberg was only involved in exceptional cases; Hans and Otto Freudenberg appear only marginally in the sources. Richard Freudenberg, and this is particularly evident in the comparatively large-scale 'Aryanizations' of Tack and Hirsch, made every effort not to take advantage of the Jewish owners, and despite the mandatory nature of the negotiations, of which all participants were naturally aware, to pay a reasonable price, which in general was determined by an arbitrator who was mutually agreed by both parties. He was only prepared in exceptional cases to conduct 'Aryanizations' – as in the Hirsch case – by the parent company in Weinheim. He was more unscrupulous in the case of 'Aryanizations' that took place in the name of Tack or Gustav Hoffmann. With the passage of time, a certain routine crept into the 'Aryanizations', which had been processed in a more businesslike manner since 1937 and in which callousness was sometimes mingled in the prosaic inflection of correspondence. [...] The attempt to maintain commercial integrity and human decency was no longer kept up consistently at Carl Freudenberg from then on. [...] The behavior of the Weinheim-based company confirms the finding that many, if not even most German companies conducted 'Aryanization projects' considerably more unrestrainedly outside German borders than they did in the Reich. […]. The company in Weinheim, or alternatively its subsidiary, Tack, which often acted as a player, would not have been obliged to participate in most of the 'Aryanizations.'"110

Armaments production at Freudenberg

Freudenberg was a supplier of the armaments industry in World War II. The significance of the company is also evident from the fact that Richard Freudenberg was appointed "*Wehrwirtschaftsführer*" for the leather sector by the Reich's Economic Ministry on July 5, 1938. The aim of appointments such as these, which often occurred at the suggestion of the *Wehrmacht*, was to honor "*Betriebsführer*" [managers – ed.] of companies categorized as vital to the war effort. Membership of the Nazi party (NSDAP) was not decisively important for this. Richard Freudenberg used the title particularly whenever he required "faster access to authorities," or wanted to safeguard "civilian shoe manufacturing against the demands of the *Wehrmacht*" or prevent "the removal of workers." "The pompous honor could also be used on local party bigwigs."111

Freudenberg's inclusion in the war economy organization can also be seen from the job that Walter Freudenberg accepted in occupied Poland. Following the invasion of the *Wehrmacht*, the *Haupttreuhandstelle Ost* (HTO, Main Trustee Office for the East) was established in mid-October 1939. It had the objective of documenting Polish property and administering it "up to the transfer into German hands." On the orders of Major General Robert Bührmann, the "authorized representative for recording raw materials in the former Pol-

Fig. 57 Advertisement for the use of Simmerrings in civil and military vehicles, 1942

ish territories," Walter Freudenberg was in charge of the HTO department IV 5 "Leather, Skins, Hides (including furs)" from October 1939 as *Hauptmann* [captain – ed.] and as a leather industry specialist. In the districts of Warsaw, Radom, Lublin, Kraków and Lodz, he was "formally responsible under military orders for the seizure, allocation and the outward transportation of the requisitioned raw materials, mostly hides from overseas, skins, leathers and furs, which were transported out immediately by the wagonful. The goods assessed by Walter Freudenberg as an expert were sent to various tanneries in Germany. He also offered price proposals to the Wifo [*Wirtschaftliche Forschungsgesellschaft*] or to the exploitation company for seized material which was passed on for example to 'ethnic German' firms, in accordance with Bührmann's instructions."[112]

Outside the traditional leather business, Freudenberg had developed into a market leader in seals for the civilian automotive industry in Germany before 1939, particularly because of the Simmerring that had been developed in 1932. The civilian business collapsed with the outbreak of war. The "destruction of the foreign network, the decline in exports as well as the effective discontinuation of private car manufacturing"[113] also contributed to this. Instead, military requirements came to the forefront. Additionally, the company increasingly received orders from the development departments of the *Luftwaffe*, the army and the navy. These orders were placed, for example, by the OKH army high command, the Reichsbahn central office, but also by companies like Ago Flugzeug-

Fig. 58 Car show in Berlin in 1938: Reich Chancellor Adolf Hitler (2nd from left) also visited the Simmerwerk stand. In the photo on the right: Hans Freudenberg

Fig. 59 Forced laborers in the Simmerring factory in Schopfheim, 1943

werke, Daimler-Benz, Zahnradfabrik Friedrichshafen and Auto-Union.[114] Freudenberg supplied these customers with products including seals for all possible types of applications, for example for use in military vehicles or devices, and moreover shoes and shoe materials, as well as synthetic leather for motorbike bags and ammunition boxes.[115]

Part of the seal production in Weinheim was moved to alternative factories in 1939 – this occurred either by order of the Reich Air Ministry or the *Wehrmacht*. In Schriesheim, among other things sealing sleeves were produced for struts for the aircraft industry, axle bearing seals for the Reichsbahn and crawler track seals for tracked vehicles.[116] In addition, an alternative factory was set up for the manufacture of seals and molded rubber components in Schopfheim near the Swiss border in the southern Black Forest, which was estimated to be less vulnerable to air strikes. Production began there in 1941: From May 1942, rubber heels and rubber outsoles made of *Buna* as well as accessories for tank tracks and other vehicles were supplied to various customers. Most of the employees working in Schopfheim were women, among them also forced laborers from the Soviet Union.[117]

After the end of the war, Richard Freudenberg explained that Freudenberg had not been an arms factory, saying that at most they had manufactured "feeder line items". However, following the academic reappraisal of the surviving sources, a differentiated picture emerges from a modern perspective: "Nonetheless, this constitutes an inadmissible abridgement of the overall situation. Particularly the Simmerwerk, but also the seal factories in Schriesheim and Schopfheim, belonged in the context of armaments production with their supply material."[118]

Effects of World War II on the company and its workforce

Even though the involvement in the armaments industry stabilized the company economically, the hardships caused by the war were enormous. Not only was a large portion of the civilian market lost, but the war was soon felt directly in Weinheim too. Yet again, many employees were called up to military service – and many lost their lives. From Richard Freudenberg's report on business development which he gave at the 1952 Christmas party in the Müll factory,[119] a number of 934 war dead[120] and 244 missing can initially be derived. It was not until 1955, after most prisoners of war had returned, that it became clear that around 1,000 employees had not come home from the war.[121] Thus, as a proportion of the employee figures in 1939 – overall 4,198 employees were working in the Carl Freudenberg company's factories in Weinheim, Schönau, Neckarsteinach and Schopfheim[122] – around a quarter of the workforce died in World War II.

On September 9, 1944, 380 employees were drafted to Alsace to dig anti-tank trenches in the town of Buc. That led to production cutbacks and thus met with resistance at Freudenberg. The outcome: "When the redoubt deployment was not finished on time as agreed after three weeks, Richard Freudenberg ran the risk of a conflict with deputy *Gauleiter* Hermann Röhn and achieved that the workers were finally able to return to Weinheim on October 4."[123]

Nine Freudenberg family members fell during deployments at the front, including managing director Otto Freudenberg. At the beginning of World War II, he had reported for active duty. On June 19, 1940 he died of the wounds he had sustained as captain and commander of an artillery battery during battles outside Paris.[124] Although he could have easily been exempted from military service because of his position in the company, Otto Freudenberg reported voluntarily for active service in 1939, and this requires an explanation. Probably because of his trustworthy, reliable and punctual character, a fact which emerges from the sources, he felt obliged to join the many employees of the company who had been called up to military service and become a soldier himself again when war broke out. In addition, it was self-evident that as a reserve officer from the ranks of the Management Board, he would take on this "obligatory deployment […] for the firm."[125] [126] Whether he also took this step because of his own convictions, his honor as an officer or the feeling of still having a score to settle following the loss of World War I, cannot be ascertained from the surviving sources.

As they had already done in World War I, the Management Board attempted to maintain contact with the employees who had been called up and took charge of ensuring that the families who were affected were provided for. Thus it

Fig. 60 Hauptmann Otto Freudenberg during the French Campaign, 1940

was decided in 1940 to support the families of the front-line soldiers financially. "In addition to the state support, voluntary allowances were paid to the families of the workers and employees who had been drafted for military service which was calculated according to the number of children; however, unmarried employees were excluded from this."[127] In addition, in January 1945, the Freudenberg Management Board decided to set up a savings book for the children of the fallen Freudenberg employees backdated to when the war broke out.[128]

In contrast to the large German cities, which lay in ruins for the most part at the end of World War II, there were no major bombing raids on the city of Weinheim in the war years from 1939 to 1945.[129] When the Americans marched into Weinheim in March 1945, the city was surrendered without almost any fighting, which also enabled the damage to property to be kept to a minimum. Richard, but also Hans Freudenberg made a significant contribution to this, since they advocated for a peaceful withdrawal of the lion's share of the *Wehrmacht* from Weinheim.[130]

Only one airstrike on the Weinheim-based plants of the Freudenberg company which caused damage has been documented, and this was in early August 1941 on the Zwischen Dämmen plant premises. In a report to the partners of the Freudenberg company, Hans Freudenberg and authorized signatory Paul Vogler described the aftermath of this attack:

> "In the night of August 6 to 7, the alarm was sounded at half past midnight. [...] At 1.15 am, light demolition bombs fell onto the factory premises at track 2, which struck the fields near the sewage plant without causing any damage. The airplane involved came from a northeasterly direction, and soon turned around and headed for the factory again. This time, around 100 incendiary bombs were dropped, which in some cases struck very nearly directly beside or on the factory premises. The fire watches distributed throughout the buildings as well as the standby units immediately began extinguishing the bombs with the aid of the firefighting equipment provided. They were

completely successful at numerous locations. [...] However, they did not manage to smother all incendiary bombs which had hit the wooden storage depots on both sides of the entrance. [...] Initially, the factory fire brigade began fighting the fires with hoses with all their might, supported before long by the city fire brigade, which rushed to the scene, and by the Naturin company's own fire brigade. Moreover, the fire brigades from Hemsbach, Birkenau, Lützelsachsen and Heddesheim also turned up, in some cases very quickly. [...] At around 2.30 am, they had gotten the fire under control to such an extent that they were able to pull out some of the brigades again. [...] However, no new raid took place. [...] Luckily, no injuries occurred. At a preliminary estimate, the damages come to about 60,000 RM in building damage and around 250,000 RM in damage to stocks and machines. [...] Operations were hardly interrupted at all."[131]

In summary, it can be said that in this respect Freudenberg was largely spared any damage during the war and no production buildings were destroyed. Although the boilerhouse, which was very important for electricity supply, was one of the buildings affected, it was only damaged on the outside and could soon be put back into operation again.[132] Consequently, the air raid only had a minimal impact on the continuation of production at the Zwischen Dämmen plant.

The Freudenberg company's stand-alone plants in Schönau, Neckarsteinach, Schopfheim and Schriesheim had no war damage whatsoever to report. In contrast to this, branches of Freudenberg subsidiaries outside Weinheim in some cases saw considerable destruction. For example, the Gustav Hoffmann

Fig. 61 Damage to the Zwischen Dämmen factory site after the air raid in August 1941

children's shoe factory in Kleve, which produced the "Elefanten" shoe brand, suffered heavy damage in air raids. For this reason, the Management Board in Weinheim relocated part of the functional machinery to Weinheim as a backup in 1944 so that they could set up a new shoe production facility there.[133] Some of the machinery from the heavily damaged Conrad Tack & Cie. AG shoe factory in Burg near Magdeburg also came to Weinheim.[134] The Tack headquarters in Berlin, and thus the administration and the shoe warehouse, were completely destroyed by an air raid in the early hours of March 1, 1943. Many of the Tack retail shops in city centers had been heavily damaged by air strikes.[135]

While the war was ongoing, no one could foresee that Weinheim would ultimately remain unscathed from heavy air raids. On the contrary: The Management Board was extremely worried. Therefore, against the backdrop of the heavy bomb attacks on Mannheim, Hans Freudenberg launched an initiative in 1944 to set up protection measures for the workforce and the population. Together with the head of the Freudenberg construction department, Fritz Käpernick, he had the idea of building air raid tunnels. Thus Freudenberg constructed three large air raid tunnels in Weinheim, which together were designed to accommodate around 6,000 people.[136]

Forced labor at Freudenberg

The first foreign (forced) laborers at Freudenberg were French prisoners of war. They were followed by recruited civilian workers from Italy and occupied France, then Belgians (Flemish) and Dutch people, and finally forcibly recruited Poles, Ukrainians and Russian women. Between 1940 and 1945, a total of 1,845 foreign workers were employed at Carl Freudenberg in Weinheim, Schönau and Schopfheim.[137] These figures can be broken down as follows based on surviving sources:[138]

Country/Origin	Year	Number
Alsace	from 1943	1
Estonia	from 1942	3
Finland	from 1943	1
Belgium	from 1942	165
France (civilian workers)	from 1942	311
Netherlands	from 1942	37
Italy	from 1941	287

Country/Origin	Year	Number
Prisoners of war (France/Alsace)[139]	1940-1943	213
Latvia	from 1945	1
Poland	from 1942	451
Russia (Russian women)	from 1942	348
Stateless people (probably Russian women)	from 1943	2
Czechs	from 1942	2
Ukrainians	from 1945	1
Unknown (probably from: Netherlands (9), Belgium (6), Italy (3), Poland (2), Russia (1), France (1))	from 1942	22
		1,845

Fig. 62 Number of foreign workers at Carl Freudenberg, 1940–1945

What can be discerned from the surviving figures is the fact that as the Second World War continued on, there was an increased lack of labor in the German economy – and thus also at Freudenberg.[140] Companies reacted to this by asking for workers from the Reich's labor office, the *Reichsanstalt für Arbeitsvermittlung*, or at their local employment offices. These latter then allocated available workers to the companies according to their production output. The longer the war continued, the more frequently these workers were forced laborers.[141] This is also reflected in the annual averages of the foreign workers employed at Freudenberg between 1940 and 1945:[142]

Year	Forced laborers (FL) as of 12/31	Employees (EMP) CF[143]	FLs' share of EMP [in %]
1940	197*	4,398	4.5
1941	194*	4,150	4.7
1942	1,080	4,994	21.6
1943	1,044	5,028	20.8
1944	794	4,213	18.8
1945	711**	3,974	17.9

* These are French prisoners of war.
** Date of analysis: March 31, 1945.

Fig. 63 Foreign workers and total workforce at Carl Freudenberg, 1940–1945

"Carl Freudenberg had to bow to the seemingly unavoidable circumstances with regard to employing forced laborers too, unwillingly at the outset, certainly, but then with a certain routine, however. The fact that human decency had not been entirely lost is demonstrated by the circumstance that Richard Freudenberg occasionally obtained an impression of the conditions of the forced laborers' quarters himself and attempted to improve the situation."[144] Nevertheless, Richard Freudenberg was thoroughly aware of the forced nature of the employment of the foreign workers, as contemporary sources corroborate.[145]

However, forced laborers from western and eastern countries were certainly treated differently. This is reflected, for example, in their accommodation. Whereas the "western workers" were initially accommodated in Weinheim hotels and inns, and later in production buildings renovated for them on the factory premises, the company built wooden barracks for the "eastern workers" to standard specifications stipulated by the paramilitary Reich labor service, the *Reichsarbeitsdienst*. The "western workers" could move about relatively freely – with the agreement of the local authorities – in their free time within a radius of 30 kilometers around Weinheim. Thus they were able, for example, to go to the hairdresser or the cinema, and even go on excursions, like to Heidelberg. In contrast, the freedom of movement afforded to the "eastern workers" was significantly more limited.[146]

Although the company attempted to ensure that all "foreigners [were] also fed and sated sufficiently"[147] by purchasing food, nevertheless there were differences between "western workers" and "eastern workers" regarding their food as well. After the end of the war, Richard Freudenberg gave a statement on this, saying that the provision of potatoes and vegetables had been above average. "The daily ration had been 2,000 calories, and above this for strenuous physical work." In the "eastern workers'" camp housing the Ukrainian women, a sick bay had been set up which was run by a Russian nurse. Independently of this, the forced laborers were entitled to medical care.[148] According to later statements of company physician Dr. Hans Bayer, who had been working at the company since 1945, a total of four forced laborers had died at Freudenberg between 1942 and 1945: two Flemish workers from tuberculosis, one Pole, also from tuberculosis, and a Russian woman from peritonitis.[149] "Thus the death rate was – taking the war conditions into account as well – comparatively very low at 0.2 percent."[150]

US Lieutenant Guy W. Wharton, who investigated the living conditions of the forced laborers in Weinheim after the end of the war, assessed the treatment of the forced laborers at Freudenberg as follows: "Our investigation disclosed that the Displaced Persons there received fair treatment, their living conditions were above the average and no evidence was presented to us at any time that they had ever been mistreated."[151]

Fig. 64 Serving food to the forced laborers in Schopfheim in the wooden barracks constructed specially for the purpose, 1943

Even if the sources on forced labor at Freudenberg show "that treatment was indeed better than at many other companies of comparable size,"[152] the fact nonetheless remains that the foreign workers were forcibly working for the Freudenberg company in Germany, far away from their homelands and their families.

In February 2000, Freudenberg participated with a sum of 10 million deutschmarks, and thus within the normal range, in the Foundation Initiative of the German Industry "Remembrance, Responsibility and Future" (EVZ) to provide restitution to former forced laborers, for the formation of which around 6,500 German companies had ultimately banded together.[153]

The "shoe test track" in Sachsenhausen concentration camp

During the war, a shortage economy prevailed, and that also applied to the availability of footwear. Supplying the *Wehrmacht* was given priority in shoe production too. At the same time, shoes continued to be required for private use. Ultimately, the scarcity of raw materials led to the use of leather substitute materials which had not been tested up to then in shoe and sole manufacturing. This material had to be tested for its suitability first before it could be used in production. It was planned to solve this problem by setting up a "shoe test track".[154] Since 1937, employees and pensioners in Weinheim had been testing the Freudenberg *Nora* soles, whose development has already been described, by conducting systematic wearing tests.[155] On the basis of this experience as well as in his position as an important representative of the German leather and shoe industry, Richard Freudenberg made a proposal to his colleagues in the association in November 1939 to intensify the existing testing procedure. The idea was to set up a centralized shoe test track for the German shoe and leather industry modeled on the shoe test track that was operated at Freudenberg in Weinheim. It was Richard Freudenberg's opinion that the young men from the *Reichsarbeitsdienst*, who had been completing obligatory paramilitary training there since the mid-1930s, should be deployed as shoe testers for the shoe test track that was to be newly established.[156] The Nazi authorities picked up this idea but implemented it in a totally different, criminal manner.

The result was the construction of the "shoe test track" in the Sachsenhausen concentration camp. This occurred on the orders of the "Reich Office for Economic Expansion" from May 1940 onward: For this, a test track was set up around the roll call square of the concentration camp which was 700 meters long and was made of seven different road surfaces – concrete, clinker, sand, paths graveled with lime, grit and rough grit, and paving stones. The management of the Sachsenhausen concentration camp and thus direct responsibility for operating the "shoe test track" lay with the SS and the camp administration, to be precise the head of the *Schuhprüfstelle* in the concentration camp.[157] For the inmates, walking on the new shoe materials quickly became torture, and ultimately the track was then used accordingly by the camp's SS too: as a punishment order. The "shoe test track" was operated until the spring of 1945. While the prisoners initially walked average daily distances of up to 35 kilometers, this figure increased in the years that followed to more than 40 kilometers. In addition, some inmates had to carry sacks filled with sand or tiles on their backs. Harassment by the SS and employees of the *Schuhprüfstelle* was not uncommon. Many prisoners collapsed and died. The number of fatalities is unknown.[158]

From June 1940 onwards, testing was conducted there for at least 79 companies, among them also for Freudenberg.[159] From the fall of 1943 onwards, the *Wehrmacht* also had the materials for the standardized lace-up boot it was planning for all troops tested on the test track.[160] Freudenberg did not initiate or operate the "shoe test track" in the Sachsenhausen concentration camp. However,

Fig. 65 Preserved remains of the "shoe test track" run by the SS, in the Sachsenhausen concentration camp memorial site, 2014

the company did participate in the centralized material tests for the German shoe industry along with at least 78 other firms.

Apart from shoes and shoe soles, tests were also conducted on shoe care products, glues, textiles as well as new types of leather from unfamiliar animal hides. From the sources, Freudenberg's participation in two joint tests can be determined for the period from 1940 to 1941. The sources show that Freudenberg had had materials tested for shoe soles (outsole, middle sole and slipper sole material). There is no unambiguous evidence of participation in further tests. However, joint tests on the "shoe test track" in the Sachsenhausen concentration camp became compulsory in 1941 by order of the Reich Office for the Leather Industry (*Reichsstelle für Lederwirtschaft*).[161] Thus it can be assumed that Freudenberg participated in further tests too.

Richard Freudenberg was informed about the main administrative and financial matters pertaining to the "shoe test track" in his function as an important representative of the German shoe and leather industry. Although it is unlikely that he saw the shoe testers in the concentration camp, four managers from Freudenberg, or to be precise, from Tack, maintained contact with the shoe test officers in the Sachsenhausen concentration camp: Wilhelm Braunss, Head of the Shoe Division at Freudenberg and an employee at *Gemeinschaft Schuhe*;[162] Ernst Demme, the chemist and founder of the main laboratory at Freudenberg; Josef Weber, the technical director at the Tack shoe factory; and Florenz Brockmeyer, the divisional head of production and technical development at *Gemeinschaft Schuhe*. Among these people, Wilhelm Braunss is particularly significant. He joined Freudenberg in the spring of 1939 as a specialist advisor for the shoe industry. His tasks included technical consulting on "shoe supply issues" as well as on synthetic materials. In this function he attended German leather and shoe industry trade conferences. Thus he became "his company's contact for the shoe test track" when the "Reich Office for the Leather Industry set up expert groups on 'gluing issues' in the fall of 1940." He was regularly involved in the discussion about the results of the "wearing tests in Oranienburg" at consultations of the shoe industry's expert group.[163] No investigations were conducted on these circumstances at his Denazification Trial, which took place after 1945.[164] Despite intensive source research, it cannot be ascertained whether the abovementioned managers were aware of the circumstances of the shoe tests. However, since they were involved in some cases in the measurement of the shoes, it is possible that they knew the inhumane conditions under which the wearing tests were being conducted.

Companies' room for maneuver between 1933 and 1945
An essay by Werner Plumpe

Right up to the present day, the role that private companies played in the "Third Reich" has been the subject of considerable attention which has, if anything, increased rather than decreased in recent years. While in the years immediately following the war many companies were regarded very critically, their managements subjected to an intensive denazification process and frequently stripped of their positions – certain companies like the I. G. Farben corporation, the large companies on the Ruhr or the major banks were actually broken up completely because of their willingness to cooperate with the Nazi regime and its crimes – there was very little to be heard in the 1950s and 1960s about what were known as the "dark years" of many companies. In public debates, numerous companies were able to rehabilitate themselves through their readiness to side clearly with the West in the Cold War. In any case, there were hardly any probing inquiries any more, and when there were, these originated from the GDR and were unable to claim much legitimacy in the West. During this time, many companies came to terms with their history, and while it was not necessarily forgotten, it was nevertheless not generally talked about or was portrayed in a very abbreviated form.

There were very different reasons for this. Frequently, there were indeed findings which the companies preferred to keep under wraps. There was also the fact that several of the protagonists of that time were still alive and a younger generation which had been brought up by this older one simply did not dare to ask probing questions. Many sources had also fallen victim to the war themselves. Additionally, numerous German companies had previously had their headquarters in Berlin, the eastern regions [i. e., that were no longer German – ed.] or the subsequent GDR, meaning that the relevant documents were not available at all. To that extent, it was not solely a case of shameful concealment; frequently, it was also a matter of ignorance. And finally, it is likely that many companies were simply afraid of being called to account legally because of their past or at least because of individual occurrences in their history.

This milieu of "not asking" was not restricted to companies: it was typical for West German society overall. The critical appraisal of a Tübingen University lecture series in 1967 about the Nazi era carried the revealing title: "The helpless anti-Fascism." This formulation described the situation in which Nazism may have been condemned, but where a tough confrontation with the surviving protagonists of the era, unless they had been directly involved in the criminal machinations, was nonetheless lacking. There was frequently also a lack of the necessary detailed knowledge, which has only been furnished since the 1970s by the upsurge in relevant research into the era and into companies.

In this context, it was initially the records in state archives that helped to make the history of certain companies transparent. It would still take some time before these companies themselves would open up their archives to independent research. However, the documents, specifically about forced labor in numerous companies, were nonetheless prolific enough to put these topics prominently onto companies' agendas, and by no means in Germany alone. Since the courts in Germany did not accept pertinent claims for damages, the claimants moved their claims to the USA and were able to put many companies under pressure effectively from there.

At the latest at that point, it became clear that the tradition of not talking about it could no longer be upheld and that it was becoming downright dangerous for companies to conceal or whitewash their own past. The case of Daimler-Benz marked a turning point in this respect, since an initial study on forced labor at the southern German automotive manufacturer revealed considerable deficiencies and clearly recorded the extent and practice of forced labor. After fierce criticism, another academic study became necessary which turned out to be significantly more adequate to the subject matter. In the years that followed, companies initially faced the public cautiously, until the willingness of Deutsche Bank to have its history in the Nazi era appraised independently and without any reservation to mark its 125th anniversary in 1995 heralded a turning point. Now the issue of forced labor which had long dominated the discourse was joined by the entire complex of "Aryanization", company expansion in the shadow of the *Wehrmacht* into the occupied territories, or the participation in individual criminal complexes such as the utilization of the property of concentration camp prisoners or participation in trade with stolen goods like gold or art works.

Little by little, numerous company histories have been appraised since the 1990s – initially the histories of prominent corporations in particular, for which dealing honestly with their history became almost a necessity within the context of globalization. But also increasingly, little by little, the histories of small and medium-sized, mostly family enterprises, for whom the fears of an unreserved appraisal of their company history frequently entailed a painful personal aspect as well, since after all it was parents and grandparents who could potentially become the focus of accusations.

That has led to a density of corporate history portrayals about the Nazi era which is likely unprecedented worldwide up to the present day, although there are still individual companies whose history has not been researched, especially if the firms no longer exist today and their archive material has been scattered to the four winds. However, that does not change the picture that is valid today. Even though they are not complete, the findings are unequivocal and so robust that new research will at best only marginally change this picture. Firstly, one will have to conclude that the people who were members of management boards differed very little from the average of the German population in their political relationship to Nazism and to the dictatorship.

While the number of entrepreneurs who were active supporters of Nazism was low – that of its opponents most likely even lower – the relationship of the vast majority can be qualified as a type of "opportunism", which is not in itself surprising among management boards who have to get along with every political environment that their company is subjected to. How are companies supposed to react when the political environment changes radically? They are accustomed to accepting political change. Discerning the proportions of this change in their various aspects and assessing them correctly is probably too much to expect of most management boards, who generally come to terms with it in the first instance – and they did this with Hitler's government too when he ascended to power in 1933. And even if they had thought the new government was a disaster: What options for action existed in a political world which made its nature as a dictatorship immediately visible?

People can join the resistance or emigrate; companies cannot do that. They can refuse to continue to function economically. However, this only comes at the cost of their own existence and the livelihoods of their employees. In the vast majority of cases, the management boards did not view Hitler's government as a disaster, but instead had positive expectations of it following the experiences with the supposedly incapacitated last governments of the Weimar Republic, which was indicative of a certain degree of adaptive behavior.

Incidentally, this everyday opportunism had little to do with the political opinions demonstrated by management boards in the days of the Weimar Republic. Right-wing opponents of the republic, like the head of Gutehoffnungshütte mining company, Paul Reusch, or Fritz Thyssen from steel company Vereinigte Stahlwerke, were able to become explicit opponents of Nazism later; liberal entrepreneurial families like the Reemtsmas in Hamburg or the Freudenbergs in Weinheim were able to adapt more or less smoothly. Noticeable critics of the regime like Robert Bosch nonetheless contributed to rearmament and the wartime economy through their company; and even though self-assured chemical industrialists like Carl Bosch or Carl Duisberg grumbled, they nonetheless knew how to adapt after it emerged that the new government made concessions to the company on important issues [petrol agreement – an agreement between I. G. Farben and the German Reich for the supply of synthetic petrol – ed.].

There were died-in-the-wool Nazi entrepreneurs, like for example Paul Pleiger, Hans Kehrl or Ernst Tengelmann, but they were the exception rather than the rule. In addition, the academic study on the history of Dr. Oetker demonstrates that an evaluation of the head of the company at the time, Richard Kaselowsky, who supported Nazism very consciously as a movement promoting social integration among the workforce, is by no means easy. Even actually being a member of the "*Freundeskreis des Reichsführers SS*" [a group of German industrialists that aimed to strengthen connections to the Nazis – ed.] means very little, even though it can be an indication; a close look is required. And this close look will particularly find among the prominent Nazis those entrepreneurial personalities who expected to gain commercial and upward mobility advantages from their involvement in the regime, like for example Fritz Kiehn, and probably also Ferdinand Porsche – an aspect that hardly carried any weight at all among established management boards.

This cooperation came as a result of down-to-earth considerations. The fact that in their division of labor, one of the Reemtsma brothers was a member of the mounted SS brigade, the *Reiter-SS*, was strategy. While the company sponsored Hermann Göring, in order to immunize itself against criticism from other companies which were obviously more influential politically, the company management attempted to establish good contacts itself which could pay off symbolically and maybe even in practice as well. This was also how Karl Ritter von Halt, being a leading sports official and co-organizer of the 1936 Olympic Games, managed to get onto the management board of Deutsche Bank.

Just the extreme willingness of numerous companies to participate in the Adolf Hitler Fund of German Trade and Industry in the spring of 1933 demonstrated the will to literally buy the favor of the new government – a favor which they certainly would be right in assuming they would not gain automatically, since after all Nazism was considered to be rather suspicious of socialist tendencies, at least among those companies who had supported Hindenburg's candidacy against Hitler in 1932. To this extent, the increasing alignment of the Freudenberg company – which indeed had initially been extremely suspect politically and regarded critically, and whose owners had previously been aligned at least partially to left-wing liberalism – to the political framework of the armaments and war economy also fits into this pattern. They could hardly evade cooperation, but they could at least maintain their influence as they saw fit: a fatal logic in every respect that seemed to the management board – which was considered politically unreliable because of its political stance during the Weimar Republic era – to be unavoidable. When the company leadership collectively joined the Nazi Party in 1943, this was only the final expression of this logic of conflict avoidance through adaptation.

Hence, although a close political relationship with the regime was more the exception than the rule, the willingness to participate in the armaments and war industry, and indeed to really make an effort to seize corresponding business opportunities, was pronounced. After the severe crisis of the early 1930s, which had constituted an existential threat to numerous businesses, it was hardly surprising that they would seize "new opportunities". In any case, there are hardly any traces of companies that would have waived commercial advantages to evade the regime and its armaments and war policy. In this respect, not all were as unscrupulous as Friedrich Flick, who specifically participated in "Aryanizations" and – being aware of his wrongdoing – endeavored to cover his tracks right from the start.

The extremely bad experiences of the armaments industry in World War I and its at best sluggish conversion after 1918 were still raw memories in the minds of the heavy industry on the Ruhr. After being heavily battered by the Great Depression, these companies nonetheless welcomed the elimination of the workers' movement by Hitler's government, just as they participated in the rearmament and its back-door financing right from the outset, though not necessarily enthusiastically. However, in 1936, when the regime, which was suffering from a chronic shortage of foreign currency, pushed the mining companies to smelt inferior German ores, the companies on the Rhine and the Ruhr reacted reticently, since this was obviously not economically justifiable. At that, the regime basically confiscated the mining corporations' ore mine properties and established a state-owned company, Reichswerke Hermann Göring, which then implemented what German heavy industry did not want to do voluntarily and developed it to sizeable dimensions.

Hugo Junkers met with a similar fate. His aircraft factories were designated to become a key component of Nazi air armament, something which Junkers, who calculated rationally, did not like. A military aircraft market was not sustainable independently, but would always be dependent on the state. Above and beyond this, the one-sided fixation on military aircraft bothered Junkers, who was interested in a modern fleet of commercial airplanes. The regime did not hesitate to oust him from his own company and replace him with a manager who was loyal to the regime. The message was clear: Cooperation was rewarded, resistance sanctioned. In most cases, drastic measures were unnecessary. The regime lured companies with attractive (admittedly dubiously financed) armaments contracts which many industrial companies accepted without serious misgivings after the hard years of the Great Depression.

And even those companies which were barely suitable for armaments contracts because of their production focus attempted to attain the status of being vital to rearmament, in order to be able to benefit from state contracts – because the associated sectors boomed as a result of the massive rearmament, while the recovery bypassed those areas of the German economy which were not vital to the war effort. Importance to the war effort increasingly became a factor for corporate success – and sometimes for sheer survival.

In this way, companies' room for maneuver became increasingly narrow, and actually not because the state had fundamentally called companies' decision-making autonomy into question, but because it gradually restricted the opportunities for successful commercial actions and oriented the remaining action corridors clearly in the direction of the rearmament requirements. Through the distribution of raw materials, semi-finished goods, energy and auxiliary materials, and particularly workers, which had been in short supply since the mid-1930s, the state equally had the means to directly utilize incentives by awarding armaments contracts. Thus, while switching to armaments production did not necessarily occur by force, it nonetheless increasingly became the only alternative for many companies, even though numerous companies made every effort to at least maintain the potential for the requisite civil capacity, in order not to be completely unable to operate after the end of the rearmament and war economy. In light of the fact that ultimately two-thirds of domestic production was soon utilized for rearmament and the military, the dimensions of this de facto "predicament" are clear.

This also explains why a company like Freudenberg, even if it was only as part of rearmament and war economy measures and in association with numerous other firms, was even prepared to avail of the "services" of concentration camp inmates to check the quality of its products (the "shoe test track" at the Sachsenhausen concentration camp), and not because of political convictions: The dependence on the state's willingness to continue to supply the company with raw materials and auxiliary materials ultimately necessitated almost boundless cooperation. Nazism gradually drew all participants involved, who like the companies could not entirely refuse the state's demands, into its modus operandi of escalation, which eventually made them no longer even shrink from obvious crimes as well. The acclimatization into a state-run distribution economy began at an early stage. The willingness to participate in economic administration in so-called self-governing bodies, namely in economic groups and trade associations, was almost a "matter of course", at least in pre-war times. The participation of numerous industrialists, who initially found it quite appealing to advance to the rank of *Wehrwirtschaftsführer* [a title bestowed by the Nazis on the executives of companies vital to rearmament – ed.], was not particularly remarkable in itself, but definitely had far-reaching consequences, because the expansion of the raw materials procurement and management into plunder during the war also followed this logic. Participating in this seemed obvious, even though this, as in the case of Walter Freudenberg in Poland, still took place in a restrained form and he disapproved of the flagrant crimes. However, he was just as much involved in the procurement and utilization of raw materials in Poland as the entire company was in the expansion of the armaments industry into the occupied areas of western Europe. Other entrepreneurs had much fewer scruples in this regard.

While companies' ability to be able to decide about their own production program gradually diminished in this way, until it dried up down to the last dregs in the war economy, room for maneuver was nonetheless retained in setting up production vital to rearmament, which most companies also exploited very creatively to influence the contract parameters when hammering out the content of production and supply contracts. Since the Nazi state operated on the principle of a "self-administrating economy" under none other than the later Rearmament Minister, Albert Speer, based on the reasoning that direct state management of companies was neither feasible in practice nor more efficient overall than their private management, the opportunities for doing this certainly existed. On the issue of employing forced laborers, research has meantime clearly identified the connections.

In light of the millions of German workers who had been drafted to military service, the vast majority of companies were only able to continue to participate in the armaments and war production at all because they were gradually allocated forced laborers (particularly prisoners of war, deportees, forced foreign laborers and eventually prisoners and camp inmates), which the companies could not do without during the war without risking their very survival – because following the de-Judaization and shutdown campaigns, companies that did not conform to the performance requirements were closed down and their raw materials and workforces utilized elsewhere. If a company wanted to secure its survival and potentially build up reserves for the post-war period, it had to be and remain vital to the war effort; that meant it had to positively endeavor to gain a rating to this effect. In this respect, the almost ubiquitous use of forced labor in industry was not just a result of the labor shortage. It can also be easily explained by the behavior of many companies, less so however the respective treatment of the forced laborers, which could differ vastly from company to company.

There are certainly examples of comparatively humane treatment of forced labor; Freudenberg is among them. However, in the majority of cases, the companies adhered relatively strictly to the state guidelines on the payment, board and lodgings of the forced laborers, which was how racist classification right up to the inhumane treatment of prisoners and camp inmates moved into day-to-day working life. Wherever the SS ran the forced labor camps themselves and maintained control over them, there was little room for maneuver within business operations; where this access was lacking, room for maneuver was greater, but even there the racist harassment remained the order of the day, especially since any friendly contact with forced laborers was in some cases severely punished. In any case, examples of humane exploitation of room for maneuver are rare; frequently, such developments depended on the individual bravery of superiors and work colleagues, who were taking a considerable risk themselves in doing so. Freudenberg was one such example. Directly after the Americans marched into Weinheim, an American officer spoke of the "fair treatment"[165] of forced labor at Freudenberg; that does not change the facts about the nature of the forced labor, but it does shed light on the Management Board.

Although not necessarily on their own initiative, the willingness of many companies to cooperate did not even stop at obvious atrocities. While I. G. Farbenindustrie AG built its factory in Auschwitz under political pressure, it had no problems using the prisoners in the concentration camp there as workers afterwards. And the "shoe test track" at the Sachsenhausen concentration camp, on which replacement materials were tested for their suitability, would probably not have existed either without the war and the leather supply shortages. Furthermore, the fact that the shoe test track was set up in a concentration camp did not deter the participating companies from having their materials tested there either.

Another example of the use of politically facilitated opportunities for action is the entire complex of "Aryanization", which ranged from unscrupulous enrichment at the expense of Jewish former owners through indifferent ignorance right up to honest attempts to help Jewish entrepreneurs to at least sell their property at a reasonably equitable price or secure it through name changes. Ultimately, the German occupation of large parts of Europe offered considerable opportunities for action; many companies recognized opportunities for expansion, which they also seized whenever they were allowed. Freudenberg participated in various "Aryanizations" both in Germany and later in the occupied territories as well, whereas its success in the Netherlands and France was not particularly extensive, although the company certainly pursued its goals to gain influence over relevant companies or keep out the competition with vigor, since there was no interest in France to grant German companies significant influence. In any case, the company did not leave "scorched earth" behind; even at an early stage after the war, regular business contacts with France were resumed.

It is hardly surprising that companies "joined in" during a dictatorship and a war; the functional imperatives of commercial companies in an increasingly totalitarian rearmament and war economy make that sufficiently transparent. Thus in this respect it is not the "whether" that needs to be explained, but rather the "how", and there are telling differences here that show that room for maneuver did exist and how it was used in individual cases. The regime increasingly implemented its goals and its visions using terrorist means; it definitely required courage to take advantage of any room for maneuver that existed, for example to maintain civil production lines, to treat forced laborers humanely or to protect Jewish employees and colleagues – bravery that from a modern perspective occurred much too seldom. However, it was particularly the circumstances that determined everyday life within companies.

When the war was over in the spring of 1945 and the armaments industry had to be abandoned, there were hardly any companies that mourned the loss of the war economy at all or even would have wanted to continue the practices that were customary up to 1945. Meanwhile, companies did not like to face reality, but disavowed their own previous behavior or saw themselves as victims of dictatorial measures: They did not want to do it, but could not do anything else. Even if this is visibly a case of deflection of guilt, and although the companies wanted to avoid a looming punishment, the dissociation from their own past was comprehensive. These were not heroic acts that they were keeping quiet. This was clear to most company management boards, who were now endeavoring to gain denazification certificates or other forms of exoneration. They just did not want to take the rap for something that others were responsible for – most entrepreneurs were convinced of this.

This rejection of responsibility, initially as a protective mechanism, subsequently ended up becoming established, until eventually, in the 1970s and 1980s, it could no longer be upheld. Incidentally, that did not help them much in the early days. Most company management boards, meaning those in the American occupation zone, by no means evaded the denazification, or rather the reparations, for example for unlawfully appropriated assets, in the initial post-war period. More contemporary research has clearly shown that the years between 1945 and 1949 brought about the most comprehensive replacement of business elites in Germany's recent economic history – a disruption that only came to an end as part of the emerging Cold War. However, most but by no means all companies were able to safeguard their existence, at least as long as they were in the West. Many of them began the journey towards the *Wirtschaftswunder*, Germany's economic miracle, under new management. These new or changed managements did not want to go back to Nazism, but it would take time and – by no means infrequently – public pressure as well for them to finally accept personal responsibility or accept their company's responsibility for the years leading up to 1945.

CHAPTER 5
NEW BEGINNING AND ECONOMIC MIRACLE
INTERNATIONALIZATION AND DIVERSIFICATION

The new beginning: The legal investigation

In 1945 in Weinheim, people did not have to wait until May came and the war ended when the German *Wehrmacht* capitulated. As early as February and throughout the month of March, British and American armed forces had conquered the regions on the left bank of the Rhine. "On March 7, they crossed the Rhine at Remagen, and a few weeks later at Nierstein. Weinheim lay directly in the Allies' path [...]. The anticipated Nazi 'defensive battle' was expected to take place along a line to the south of Heidelberg. Orders given from Berlin to render the machines at Freudenberg unusable before the Allied invasion were circumvented through clever pseudo-dismantlement." On March 28 around 9 am, the first commando units of the 44th American Infantry Division reached the Freudenberg Zwischen Dämmen plant in Weinheim, over which the white flag was already flying. "Shortly afterwards, the white flag was flying on the town hall too [...]. In contrast, battles were still being fought around the Müll plant and in Lützelsachsen to the south up to the morning of March 30."[1]

After Richard Freudenberg had been appointed provisional mayor by the American Military Government,[2] he negotiated the regulations for the transition to the occupation very shortly afterwards with the American city commander.[3] On April 3, 1945 he addressed inhabitants of the city of Weinheim by leaflet.[4]

On May 10, 1945 and thus directly after the capitulation of the *Wehrmacht* in Reims and in Berlin, Richard Freudenberg was appointed provisional head of the administrative district by the American occupying forces, above and beyond his role of provisional mayor, but this "post-war career" came to a swift end. He only held both of his offices as provisional mayor and as head of the administrative district for a short time, because directly after the organized denazification measures began, Richard Freudenberg was also targeted by the occupying force.[5] Probably because of a denunciation and because of his job as *Abwehrbeauftragter*, or rather *Wehrwirtschaftsführer*, he was arrested by American Mil-

An die Einwohner der Stadt Weinheim!

Am Ende der Woche, in der die letzten Reste der deutschen Wehrmacht sich der überwältigenden Macht der Alliierten ergeben haben, drängt es mich, der ich die nicht gesuchte Verantwortung als Bürgermeister trage, einiges zu sagen.

Zunächst gehen meine Gedanken zu den vielen Millionen Gefallenen, zu den Verwundeten und Kranken dieses Krieges und zu den Gefangenen.

Bei allem Leid, das wir und insbesondere die, die unmittelbar getroffen sind, zu tragen haben, dürfen wir unserem Herrgott danken, daß unsere Stadt nicht zerstört worden ist. Dadurch ist der Wiederanfang für uns unendlich viel leichter als z. B. für unsere Nachbarstadt Mannheim.

Wir müssen uns aber klar darüber sein, daß unsere Armut viel größer ist als sie uns in unserer unzerstörten Stadt erscheint. Wir leben aus Vorräten an Nahrungsmitteln, wir arbeiten aus Vorräten an Rohstoffen, und wir leben aus unserem Vermögen an Geld. Mit all diesen Dingen gilt es hauszuhalten, bis es gelingt, wieder eine bescheidene, in sich ausgeglichene Wirtschaft zu treiben.

Hilfe von außen ist nicht zu erwarten. Ich kann der Bevölkerung schwere Opfer nicht ersparen. Die Nahrungsmittelzuteilungen müssen den allgemein möglichen Sätzen in Kürze voll angeglichen werden. Die Unterstützungen aller Art, auch die Pensionen und Gehälter, müssen auf ein kaum tragbares Minimum gesenkt werden. Unterstützungen müssen und dürfen nur denen gewährt werden, die wegen Alter und Krankheit oder aus sonstigen Gründen, die auf das genaueste überprüft werden müssen, nicht arbeiten können. Ich weiß, daß diese Umstellung von vielen als hart und undankbar empfunden wird; aber es hat keinen Zweck, die Politik der Selbsttäuschung weiter zu treiben.

Die aufgerichteten Kartenhäuser sind zusammengestürzt. Wir müssen uns auf den Boden der harten Tatsachen stellen, d. h. ganz klein, mit innerem Anstand und Wahrhaftigkeit von neuem anfangen.

Unser Zusammenbruch ist in einem selten schönen Frühling offenbar geworden. Lassen Sie es uns als gutes Omen nehmen, daß auf dunkle Zeiten auch wieder lichtere kommen. Diese fallen uns aber nicht in den Schoß. Sie müssen erarbeitet werden, daß unsere Arbeit uns hinstellt. Sie müssen aber auch erarbeitet werden durch eine starke, innere, anständige Gesinnung. Ich ermahne die Erwachsenen, ein wachsames Auge auf die Jugend zu haben. In einer freien Welt, der wir dienen wollen, gilt der Mensch auf Grund seines inneren Anstandes, nicht nach äußerem Getue, das uns so geblendet und verführt hat. Nicht die Schlechtesten unter uns atmen im Innersten auf, daß der Schein dem Sein gewichen ist. Laßt uns fleißig sein, denn nur so bannen wir die Not. Laßt uns demütig sein, denn nur so werden wir nicht unterwürfig. Laßt uns einander dienen, denn nur so können wir Ruhe halten und in Jahren das tiefe Tal überwinden. Laßt uns mit unserem ganzen Willen das entsetzliche Wort Lügen strafen, daß mit Hitler's Ende nur Zersetzung Trumpf sein wird.

In diesem Sinne laßt uns an die Arbeit gehen. In diesem Sinne bitte ich, mir zu helfen.

Richard Freudenberg
Bürgermeister

Fig. 66 Leaflet "To the inhabitants of Weinheim!" dated April 3, 1945

itary's secret service as early as the end of May 1945 and subsequently taken to a prison in Mannheim.[6]

In the summer of 1945, Richard Freudenberg realized that the investigations had to be taken very seriously. On July 2, 1945 he wrote to his wife, Sibille:

> "After the interrogation which I had today at noon, I am taking things very seriously; they are going into the fundamentals. I feel free from guilt, insofar as one can do at all as a German and a human being. I am asking God to give me the strength to get

through this ordeal. I had hoped so much to be able to write something different to you. I do not know where my path will next take me, how long we will be torn apart. Be prepared for a long time, and likewise till we hear from each other again. Farewell … Richard."⁷

Thus evidently his state of mind was predominantly one of grave concern.

Therefore, only one day later, his brothers Adolf and Hans Freudenberg buoyed him up: "As I already said to you, there is really no reason for pessimism. Hold your head up high and try to rise above it and see the bigger picture. Just be patient and stay calm," Adolf Freudenberg wrote. And Hans added: "I too do not take the situation so seriously. You have done nothing that you could not justify. […] The business is running. The men are all right. If a business can survive, it is ours. Courage, please."⁸

But Richard Freudenberg was severely depressed, as is evident yet another day later in a letter to Weinheim-based pastor Hermann Brecht: "I am suffering from embarrassment that, with my entire internal attitude, I am considered to be politically ensnared and from now on am being put on a par with people whom I thoroughly reject. I am afraid of the circle into which I am coming."⁹ Brecht himself had written a letter to the American investigators on July 1, 1945, in which he advocated for Richard Freudenberg:

> "It was and is generally known here that Mr. Freudenberg has never been a friend of Nazism and that he had always rejected the evil excesses of the same. Although he nevertheless became a party member and also accepted some important office or other – this was the general opinion – he only ever did this in order to be able to prevent worse things in this way and thus also for the benefit of all. […] Also, in a time where it did not appear advisable to profess one's faith in the church, Mr. Freudenberg nonetheless did not shy away from doing this repeatedly."¹⁰

Further statements made for the benefit of Richard Freudenberg, among them from Social Democrat workers, subsequently led to his initially being released in mid-September 1945. However, any joy about this occurrence was not set to last for long. Only a short time afterwards, Richard Freudenberg was placed under house arrest. Now his activities as a member of the Deutsche Bank supervisory board were also a focal point of the investigations. "On October 27, 1945 [Richard] Freudenberg was dismissed as a general partner of Carl Freudenberg on the basis of the 'Directive to Commanding Generals Military Districts, 7 July 1945.'"

"While still under house arrest, Richard Freudenberg explained his role at Deutsche Bank to the responsible officer of the Military Government for the

Mannheim administrative district, Lieutenant Joseph H. Bernfeld: He said he had been appointed to the supervisory board as an important industrialist from Baden and he had neither worked in business operations nor on the working committee (*Arbeitsausschuss*). He had only attended seven of the total of 12 supervisory board meetings during the time of his membership – and these had been so uneventful that he could no longer even remember the subject matter, he said. He had only taken cognizance of the annual and half-yearly accounts, he said. As proof, as it were, he submitted the low compensation he had received as expenses for his work, between 4,100 RM and 5,700 RM annually." Together with his superior, Major Barney Barnes, Joseph Bernfeld actually became convinced that in the case of the entrepreneur from Weinheim "the wrong person had indeed been arrested."[11] He recommended terminating the hearings against Richard Freudenberg. However, this was initially prevented at the discussion before the Sub-Committee of the Military Affairs Committee of the United States Senate for politically motivated reasons.[12]

Initially, all objections were fruitless. In fact, the situation deteriorated yet again. In mid-November 1945, Richard Freudenberg's house arrest was converted into imprisonment, which he spent in various internment camps up to the spring of 1947. The background to these measures was the strict attitude of the American Military Government in all denazification issues. In the US capital city of Washington, the widespread opinion at the end of the war was that "the industrialists working in leading positions would also have to be […] held criminally liable as accessories." At the outset, this approach was in line with the British and Soviet expectations about the prosecution of Nazi criminals. But the American authorities were much more forceful than their British and Russian counterparts in their daily routine.[13]

However, the unity among the occupying forces was set to come to an end very quickly; relations between the former Allies in the West on the one side and in the East on the other increasingly degenerated in the nascent Cold War. At the beginning, this did not have much effect on the day-to-day treatment of incriminated people. Rather, in Washington, behind "the scenes […], vigorous policy clashes" were being fought about the denazification policy; and the American investigators' collaboration among each another was also anything but harmonious. "The Americans had an immense administrative apparatus on both sides of the Atlantic at their disposal, whose offices did not always complement each other in practice, however, but frequently worked side by side, and indeed sometimes even hindered each other. At times, seven bodies were working on the complex material of denazification and criminal prosecution […]." In contrast, interrogations of the accused themselves rarely took place. Richard Freudenberg too was moved from camp to camp, but hardly any progress was made at all in the matter itself. Meanwhile, in Washington, a political dispute raged in which ultimately those people won who were of the opinion that the interests of the United States as a world power must be taken into account to a greater extent. This was also connected to the fact that the Soviet war allies were increasingly turning into adversaries, which caused the Americans to have a greater interest in rebuilding western Germany.[14] Thus the long uncertainty about the fate of Richard Freudenberg and his internment period were also brought to an end.

Finally, the Denazification Panel hearing against Richard Freudenberg took place in early June 1947. The hearings were terminated with his classification into the "Exonerated" category. Walter Freudenberg, who had likewise been part of the Management Board, had had to leave the company at the end of October 1945; like Richard Freudenberg, he had been dismissed as a general partner of Carl Freudenberg.[15] One year later, the hearings initiated against Walter Freudenberg before the Denazification Panel in Weinheim were also terminated with his classification into the "Exonerated" category.[16] In 1948, Walter Freudenberg went into retirement after having worked at the company for 50 years. With his departure, Freudenberg lost a specialist in raw skins and rawhides – and thus in the basis for high-quality leather – of worldwide renown from active managerial responsibility at that time. His scientific studies on the leather industry, like the "International Dictionary of the Leather and Allied Trades" which he first published in 1936, or his four-volume work on the global skin and hide market dating from 1954, bear testimony to his in-depth expert knowledge and earned him an honorary doctorate from the University of Leeds in the UK in 1956.[17]

The Denazification Panel hearings against Hans Freudenberg, the third member of the Management Board, were initiated in late summer of 1945 when he filled out the Military Government of Germany's questionnaire himself.[18] In contrast to Richard and Walter Freudenberg, he was able to resume his activities as technical director of the company and thus his previous tasks on the Management Board after an interruption of only three days – despite the ongoing Denazification Panel hearings.[19] These were not terminated until November 28, 1946 with a denazification certificate which assigned him to the category of "Followers".[20]

Most Freudenberg employees who had initially been dismissed, including executive employees and technicians as well, were re-employed a short time after the end of their Denazification Panel hearing, if the judgment permitted it. That was important too, because: "Academic employees like […] Demme and Nottebohm were mainly responsible for our fast reconnection to global technical standards. Georg Boysen, who was initially a purchaser for a department store in Mannheim for a short time, returned to Weinheim and eventually became head of Simrit sales at Carl Freudenberg. [...] Josef Weber took over as head of the Simmerwerk, the seal manufacturing plant, as well as the *Igelit* and *Nora* divisions. Wilhelm Braunss too was retained as a key worker. [...] It was not much different in the companies affiliated to Carl Freudenberg. [...] Walther Siegert was arrested by the British in May 1946 and only returned to Tack after eight months of imprisonment at the beginning of 1947."[21] Thus it is worth taking a short look at the Denazification Panel hearings of the individuals involved, since – as elsewhere in the German economy too – continuity of personnel was ultimately of extreme importance.

Chemist Ernst Demme, who joined the Freudenberg company in 1934 as the first head of the Central Development Division,[22] was not a member of the Nazi Party (NSDAP); he was a member of the German Labor Front (DAF) from 1935 to 1945 – membership of which, as described earlier, had become obligatory for all employees from 1938 – and was a member of the National Socialist People's Welfare (NSV) from 1934/35 to 1945. The Denazification Panel hearings against Demme were closed because he was classified as "not incriminated" by the Weinheim Denazification Panel.[23] As can be derived from the lists of personnel for denazification, Carl Ludwig Nottebohm was not a member of the Nazi Party either. He worked from 1936 to 1969 at Freudenberg.[24] No Denazification Panel hearings were initiated against him, since he received the classification of "not affected" on October 15, 1946.[25]

Georg Boysen, on the other hand, who was the commercial manager of the Simrit division at Freudenberg, was dismissed from Freudenberg on October 5, 1945 on the basis of Law No. 8 of the Military Government in the American Occupation Zone.[26] It can be seen from the registration form which had been filled out by Boysen in May 1946 that he had been a member of the Nazi Party from 1933 to 1945 as well as a member of the DAF from 1935 to 1945 and of the NSV from 1938 to 1945. However, in all organizations mentioned, he had held neither office nor rank. On September 1, 1947 the Denazification Panel in Mannheim, where he had last lived, submitted a request to classify Boysen among the incriminated, "because he was a member of the Nazi Party since January 15, 1933 [...]. Moreover, he was a member of the DAF and the NSV." Some statements and attestations in his favor from people who had worked with Boysen or had been acquainted with him between 1933 and 1945 caused him to receive classification into the "Followers" category on December 11, 1947. However, the Mannheim Denazification Panel imposed a financial atonement sum amounting to 2,000 Reichsmarks (RM) on him. In addition, Boysen had to defray the costs of the hearings.[27]

The Head of the Shoe Division, Wilhelm Braunss, had been employed at the Freudenberg company as a master shoemaker since 1939. At the same time, he was also an employee at *Gemeinschaft Schuhe*.[28] Similarly, the registration form that Braunss filled out on April 29, 1946 for the American authorities shows that he had been a member of the Nazi Party since 1938 and a member of the DAF from 1937 to 1945. And, like Boysen, he had held no office – according to the registration form – in either organization. Braunss was assigned to the "Followers" category on September 26, 1946. A financial atonement sum of 500 RM was imposed on him. Furthermore, like Boysen, Braunss had to defray the costs of the hearings.[29]

Walther Simmer, the developer of the Simmerring which bears his name, who had joined Freudenberg in 1918 as a tannery engineer and the Nazi Party in 1933,[30] was dismissed from the company on October 20, 1945 on the basis of Law No. 8 of the Military Government in the American Occupation Zone. On September 24, 1946 Hans Freudenberg and Simmer met to discuss the possibility of further collaboration. At this meeting, Simmer already expressed the wish for a "freelance activity."[31] Although no clear understanding was reached between the two parties at this meeting, lawyer Carl Hans Barz drew up a draft contract on the basis of Freudenberg's notes on the meeting. The draft states the following:

> "I. Now that Mr. Simmer has been categorized as a Follower by the Denazification Panel, the Carl Freudenberg company is prepared to revive the previous contractual relationship with Mr. Simmer, which was dissolved by Law No. 8 and dismissal by the American Military Government, at any time by mutual agreement as soon as Mr. Simmer's employability is legally binding. [...] II. For the time being, Mr. Simmer does not wish to avail of the opportunity which is open to him pursuant to Section I, but instead to establish his own technical consultancy office, whose location he reserves for himself. [...] Mr. Simmer will also make himself available to the Carl Freudenberg company in future too on all matters pertaining to the Simmerwerk. [...] Mr. Simmer cedes the use of the 'Simmer' name, as heretofore, to the Carl Freudenberg company to label their products to the same extent as before as well as the utilization of all patents and other property rights belonging to him."[32]

Consequently, it can be determined that the company was indeed interested in continuing to employ Walther Simmer. This was especially due to the fact that the rights to the name for the Simmerring were held by Simmer himself and thus Freudenberg found itself in a dependent relationship to him.

Simmer explained to Hans Freudenberg in a further meeting on February 3, 1947 that he planned to build his own Simmerring factory in Austria and for this reason required some machines from Freudenberg. In August 1947, after the conclusion of the Denazification Panel hearings, Simmer was categorized into Group IV: Followers. He had to pay a one-off atonement sum of 2,000 RM into a restitution fund.[33]

The negotiations between Simmer and the Freudenberg company were probably concluded in September 1947. When he returned to Austria, Walther Simmer left the company for good. Because the rights to the name and the patent rights were still valid, the Simmerwerk plant in Weinheim was renamed the Simrit-Werk. Freudenberg continued to use the Simmerring brand name and trademark. However, because the company had been under trusteeship since November 1, 1945, it first had to apply for authorization to the Finance Ministry in Stuttgart "for the transfer of fixtures and fittings to third parties." This request to transfer the machines to Simmer by the beginning of July 1948 was approved first by the President of the Federal State District of Baden, Department of Business and Transport at the State Business Office, and then also the Finance Ministry in Stuttgart.[34] In 1948, Simmer returned to his homeland of Austria, where he established the Simmerwerke firm in Kufstein in 1949. In 1983, Freudenberg acquired 50 percent of the shares of the Simmerwerke factory W. Simmer GesmbH & Co. KG there.[35] Finally, in 1992, all shares in the Simmerwerke firm were transferred to Freudenberg. The son of company founder Walther Simmer, Kommerzienrat Eberhard Simmer, went into retirement in 1992 and therefore transferred all his shares to Freudenberg.[36] Since 1994, the company has operated under the name Freudenberg Simrit Kufstein.[37]

Two further senior employees had been exonerated in the course of their Denazification Panel hearings, a fact which was set to become very important in the years that followed with regard to the management of Freudenberg: Paul Vogler (1890–1968), head of accounting, and Carl Gustav Müller (1896–1968). Neither was a member of the Nazi party, but they had been members of the DAF and NSV from the mid-1930s onward. However, they had held no offices. Paul Vogler was categorized as "not affected" by Law No. 104, the Law for the Liberation from National Socialism and Militarism, on November 5, 1946 by the Denazification Panel in Weinheim. The hearings against Müller were likewise closed because he was not incriminated, as the Denazification Panel explained in the writ of *nolle prosequi*.[38]

In light of the uncertainties which the Denazification Panel hearings initially entailed, it was therefore of decisive importance to the company that even before his arrest at the end of May 1945, Richard Freudenberg succeeded in getting the Military Government to grant "that while retaining my brother, Hans, our authorized signatories Paul Vogler and C. G. Müller were appointed as custodians of the company."³⁹ Thus during the time of the trusteeship, Hans Freudenberg was the only member of the management board to assume responsibility for part of business operations as technical director.⁴⁰

The period of trusteeship under Vogler and Müller in particular deserves a closer look.

The company under trusteeship

After the invasion of the Americans, the company attempted to resume production as quickly as possible. In Weinheim, there was still a lack of coal in the months following the end of the war, and travel, or more precisely transportation options, were poor. However, demand for leather and shoes among the population, but also among the occupying forces, was high. "The occupation forces [therefore already] approved a limited resumption of civil production […] on April 3, 1945" – and thus at a time in which the war was not yet over at all in other parts of Germany. "Only the Simmerwerk [plant] had to initially close because of its armaments production. Richard Freudenberg reassured the workers in the Zwischen Dämmen plant in a speech [directly after the end of the war] and even promised future weekly working time of 20 hours."⁴¹ As described, however, Richard Freudenberg was practically unable to attend to the progress of business affairs himself at all any more from then on.

Finally, on November 1, 1945, the American military authorities placed the company under trusteeship on the basis of Law No. 52. Thus it was under Allied Property Control by the Military Government from that time onward. As already mentioned, authorized signatories Vogler and Müller were appointed as custodians. Initially, they had managed the company temporarily, and then from the end of February 1946 officially as custodians as well.⁴² That was a good choice, as it very quickly emerged, because Vogler had the commercial side under control, Müller on the other hand the technical matters. "Both men represent the rights and interests of Freudenberg's entire assets towards third parties."⁴³ They administered the company's asset holdings and were obliged to submit monthly reports to the Military Government on aggregate balances and trial balances.⁴⁴ However, according to the stipulations of the American Military Government, the fiduciary asset management did not merely include the preservation of property. Over and above this, it was incumbent on the custodians to maintain the property and ensure that it did not deteriorate either in value or in usefulness. This ultimately meant managing the company and thus running

Fig. 67-68 Carl Gustav Müller, around 1962 ▪ Paul Vogler, 1955

the company's business operations.⁴⁵ Although Vogler and Müller had now officially taken over responsibility for the company, Hans Freudenberg was also involved in management tasks again following the conclusion of his Denazification Panel hearing in November 1946. Evidently the military authorities tolerated this despite the trusteeship.⁴⁶

Paul Vogler, who was born in Weinheim, had already spent his entire schooldays with Richard Freudenberg, who was only two years his junior.⁴⁷ He completed commercial studies at the Handelshochschule Mannheim and subsequently underwent further training as an accountant in Leipzig and London. At the end of March 1920, Vogler returned to his native city of Weinheim and was appointed Head of Accounting at Freudenberg. From then on, he was responsible, among other things, for dealing with tax issues.⁴⁸

Carl Gustav Müller, in his turn, came from Bremen. After completing his degree as an engineer at the Technische Hochschule [technical university, now KIT – ed.] in Karlsruhe, he joined the company in 1922. Initially he was responsible for the Heat and Energy Management area, then he took over responsibility for the Metalworking Departments and after 1930 worked closely alongside Walther Simmer, who at that time was responsible for engineering. The sources show clearly that both Vogler and Müller were key confidants of Richard and Hans Freudenberg. Vogler was a close associate of Richard Freudenberg's, having been head of bookkeeping for many years. Müller was one of Hans Freudenberg's closest colleagues in all matters pertaining to the technical design of production processes.⁴⁹

Richard Freudenberg later described the trusteeship period as follows in an address: "We must be immensely grateful to fate that the Military Government accepted my proposal and appointed Messrs. Vogler and Müller as custodians of the company assets and the company's affairs. Both gentlemen knew how to count the pennies. Both carried out their duties as true custodians without any ambitions of their own. For this commitment alone we owe them […] lasting gratitude."[50]

In 1955, Paul Vogler entered retirement after having worked for the company for 35 years; Carl Gustav Müller followed his example in 1961 after working for almost 40 years for Freudenberg.[51]

During the trusteeship period, Hans Freudenberg assumed key management tasks too. However, his real passion continued to be for technology, which is why he too hoped that his brother Richard would return soon. He expressed this wish in a letter to Richard Freudenberg in 1946 as follows: "It is really high time that you returned to the head [of the company] again so that I could dedicate myself to operations as in the past. I honestly have no aspirations to play the big shot."[52]

As early as the fall of 1945 – and thus at the time at which Freudenberg was placed under trusteeship – around 3,200 employees worked in Weinheim with working time of 40 hours per week. Including the stand-alone plants in Schönau, Schriesheim and Schopfheim, the workforce actually numbered 3,677 employees.[53] The fact that this was feasible so quickly again was on the one hand because the Freudenberg plants in Weinheim were spared all major air raids. In addition, on the one hand because of the exertions of Richard and Hans Freudenberg, the city could be handed over to the Americans almost entirely without a fight, something which likewise prevented any major damage. On the other hand, the company in Weinheim was in a position to build up extensive inventories of skins and rawhides during the last two years of the war – that was a good basis for jump-starting business operations.[54]

Fundamentally, however, the importance of the leather industry had now declined significantly as compared to its position before the war. There were several reasons for this: Rawhide is a byproduct of livestock slaughtering, and thus its production is dependent on livestock numbers and on meat consumption. In the initial years after the war, the consequences of the war were clearly discernible here, since raw material supply from within Germany was very challenging. In addition, many European countries restricted their skin and hide exports after the war. Furthermore, because of the separation of the occupation zones and exclusion from global markets, production capacity of leather manufacturing in West Germany remained too high overall. But that was not all: Because of the increased use of rubber in the shoe industry, sales volumes of bottom leather declined. There was less demand for harness and saddler's leather because of the discontinuation of orders from the military and the mechanization of agriculture. Moreover, drive-belt leather was increasingly being replaced by rubber and plastics. Even the rising sales volumes of upper leather for the shoe industry could not compensate for this.[55]

Nevertheless, "Freudenberg [...] became – even if only for a transition period – predominantly a tannery again: Two-thirds of turnover came from the leather segments, whose shares [of turnover] had declined in the last year of the war to below one-third. However, because of a lack of raw materials, production came to only one-quarter of pre-war levels. In the case of rubber, this proportion was actually only 15 percent in the fall of 1945. When the resin required for sole manufacturing, which had to be mixed with the synthetic rubber, ran out at the *Nora* plant, a troop of 60 men was put together to extract resin in the Odenwald forest: Trees were tapped, the sap that leaked out was collected and subsequently boiled at the *Nora* plant – a Stone Age method that was used until raw materials from abroad could be purchased again in 1949."[56]

As early as the fall of 1945, the company was producing 30,000 pairs of shoes per month again, which was a sizeable number, but significantly below 1944 manufacturing levels.[57] The lion's share of shoe production took place in the shoe manufacturing plant which had been set up at the end of the war in Weinheim. The machines which had been relocated to Weinheim from the plants in Kleve and Burg in 1944 to 1945 – as already mentioned – formed the basis for this plant.[58] Alongside this, the company endeavored to also get the partially destroyed factories at Gustav Hoffmann in Kleve and Conrad Tack in Burg back up and running again, which they succeeded in doing as well.[59] However, the "struggle for the allocation of skins, hides and other raw materials [remained] [...] an ongoing theme up to this time"[60] at Freudenberg. The shoes that were produced were also "frequently exchanged for skins and hides as a 'barter transaction.'"[61]

Then, in the fall of 1945, the Simmerwerk plant resumed production of seals again too. These were supplied to the US Army and to suppliers to the US Army, like for example Opel in Rüsselsheim and Daimler-Benz in Mannheim.[62]

But what was particularly fascinating: Most of the products manufactured by Freudenberg directly after the end of the war were for the needs of the population. These improvised emergency products, or "hawker's tray products", as Hans Freudenberg called them, included for example fiberboards, underlay shingles for roofs, *Lederhosen* (traditional leather trousers), rubber caps, spoons and metal roof tiles.[63]

Hans Freudenberg summarized the situation in the company in the months after the invasion of the Americans as follows:

"The plant and Weinheim itself were undamaged. Raw materials were sufficient to be able to work for several months initially. The sudden interruption of leather and collagen fiber [or "mass"] production urged us to begin operations quickly if the spoilage of raw goods and semi-finished products was to be prevented. The workforce in Weinheim and the surrounding hamlets were within the authorized 6-km border, and almost all were within the 15-km border which was soon stipulated. This fact made it our duty to get operations up and running again as quickly as possible and we soon received verbal permission to start work too. We started working across a broad front by not just manufacturing the current products, but by manufacturing all possible products whose production had been partially prepared in the months before the collapse [...]. Above and beyond that, we made it our task to give as much outward stimulus as possible. Thus we already purchased an exhaust steam turbine on May 10, 1945 from BBC and ordered a second one with greater contact pressure as a replacement for the turbine that was built in 1913. We rebuilt the railway bridge to Birkenau that had been destroyed and later supported the restoration efforts on the tunnel near Waldmichelbach. Soon, barter transactions, which were subsequently so maligned, began. One of the first was an order for small motors from a small factory that had been totally destroyed, in order to trade these motors with Pfaff for sewing machines for the shoe factory."[64]

This illustrates how the company immediately endeavored to make something out of the situation that prevailed after the war as quickly as possible. The decision to make an investment in an exhaust steam turbine as early as May 1945 is particularly surprising from today's perspective. Thus the situation cannot be described as a "total collapse" or a "zero hour", as this detail alone shows.

However, during this era of new beginnings, the Allied Control Council's plans for dismantlement also had to be warded off. One year after the end of the war, in the spring of 1946, Hans Freudenberg feared the worst, even as far as the end of the business: "The situation in German industry will be desperate in a few months. Nothing has happened to crank up the base materials producing industry."[65] Numerous documentations were submitted with the aim of proving how important the company was for the Allies as well. It worked: "In the fall of 1946, the Allied plans for dismantlement were off the table."[66]

But things were different for the Conrad Tack shoe factory in Burg, which was in the Soviet occupation zone. In March 1946, this factory was completely dismantled by resolution of the Soviet Military Government. As early as September 30 of the same year, Freudenberg's expropriation occurred pursuant to Order No. 124 of the Soviet Military Administration.[67] For that reason, the construction and start-up of a new, but much smaller, shoe manufacturing facility for Tack shoes took place in the fall of 1946 in Mühlheim am Main, near Offenbach.[68]

At this juncture, the *Marena* and *Naturin* plant resumed production again too. At the same time, the resumption of *Nora* production was also planned.[69]

Thus things continued to improve: Then, in 1947, for the first time in its existence, Freudenberg employed more than 5,000 workers. "Upper leather manufacturing remained the mainstay of business for some time, and with money from the Marshall Plan [the huge US recovery plan for Europe], raw skins and hides could be purchased from abroad."[70]

As for Richard Freudenberg, whose private assets had been frozen during the period of his imprisonment and had been released again at the end of 1947,[71] continuing to work at the company was a matter of course after his personal post-war turmoil had been resolved. After the accusations against him had been clarified, he immediately started working actively for the family enterprise again.

Finally, in 1948, the trusteeship was lifted. Walter Freudenberg resigned from the Management Board and from business operations. Thus the Management Board initially only comprised Richard and Hans Freudenberg. At the same time, however, the fourth generation was given responsibility at the company. Helmut Fabricius and Hans Erich Freudenberg became members of the Management Board and general partners in 1949 – for both of them, their path into the company had already been mapped out before World War II.

Hans Erich Freudenberg (1911–1981), the youngest son of Hermann Ernst Freudenberg jun., who had died back in 1920, was the first family member from the fourth generation to join the company back in 1933. However, World War II initially interrupted his work. After his return from captivity as a prisoner of war of the Americans, the Weinheim Denazification Panel brought an action against Hans Erich Freudenberg on January 15, 1947 because of his membership in the Nazi Party (NSDAP) and the SA, and submitted an application to have him classified in the "Lesser Offenders'" category.[72] On January 24, 1947 Hans Erich Freudenberg wrote to the Weinheim Denazification Panel: "In the SA, my position was always characterized by the fact that as a 'capitalist' I was always treated more or less as if I did not belong."[73] Several attestations that were submitted in his favor – particularly pertaining to his activities as a squad leader (*Scharführer*) in the SA – caused the Weinheim Denazification Panel to classify Hans Erich Freudenberg into the "Followers" category on October 24, 1947.[74]

When he rejoined the family enterprise, Hans Erich Freudenberg dedicated himself from 1947 onward to tasks related to the reorganization of the company, for example setting up materials management, cost accounting and a cost estimation system.[75] Later, too, he dealt with the organization of the company time and again.

In 1949, he assumed responsibility for shoe manufacturing in Weinheim and Offenbach.[76] At a very early stage, Hans Erich Freudenberg realized the significance of close collaboration with Japan and a technology exchange between Freudenberg and Japanese business. During numerous trips, he established contact with important Japanese companies,[77] who are still closely associated with Freudenberg either in the business area of seals or alternatively who operate in the area of nonwovens as a Freudenberg Business Group today.[78] "It is his undisputed achievement to have laid the foundations for our [referring to the Freudenberg company] strong industrial activities in Japan."[79]

Helmut Fabricius (1909–1991), the son of Emilie Freudenberg, the youngest daughter of Friedrich Carl Freudenberg, had joined the company in 1937, where he had initially familiarized himself with international skin and hide procurement. In 1939, the war interrupted his work at the company for the time being. He returned midyear in 1946 from American imprisonment.[80] On October 18, 1946 Helmut Fabricius submitted a voluntary declaration to the Weinheim Denazification Panel. Although Helmut Fabricius was a member of both the Nazi Party (NSDAP) and the SS, it is clear from the surviving sources that no charges were brought against him by the Denazification Panel.[81]

Then, in 1949, as a general partner, he assumed responsibility for legal, tax, financial and Limited Partner affairs. In addition, he looked after the administration of shareholdings and, as a successor to Walter Freudenberg, hide procurement. He set up the shareholding administration system, which coordinated the foreign subsidiaries in matters pertaining to external accounting, taxation and finance.[82] After the end of World War II, Helmut Fabricius was "the only lawyer in the company up to 1955, in all those years an individual [who was] for all intents and purposes the legal department of the growing firm. There was no time left for purchasing hides."[83]

However, there was continuity in another area as well, because contacts were soon renewed abroad again and a network of partnerships was quickly established.[84] This is also evident from the fact that Richard Freudenberg undertook a trip to the United States very soon after the Denazification Panel hearing was over, in which he was particularly interested in re-establishing relationships with American tanners and business partners.[85] In a letter to his brother Hans, Richard Freudenberg wrote the following on June 15, 1948 about his acceptance into the circle of American partners: "Time and again I can emphasize that our name and our reputation here in this country is respected and considerable. People have no idea at all how much they are overestimating us, because no one is getting any idea of the difficulties we have to overcome."[86]

In June 1948, "the currency reform created a solid basis for calculation for sales and procurement again."[87] An address given by Hans Freudenberg in connection with the currency reform also shows clearly the immensely important role that leather played at Freudenberg at that time: "It would probably be wrong to venture into completely new production areas; instead, we basically want to stay on our track, serve the leather and shoe area and then, besides that, the seals division with its tasks."[88]

The currency reform marked a turning point for post-war Germany: The public had not found out about the details until the evening of June 18, 1948. With the expiration of the Reichsmark on June 20, 1948, all the debts of the Reich had also expired. Private liabilities and all bank and savings balances were devalued at a ratio of 100 to 6.5. For each resident of the three Western occupation zones, 60 deutschmarks in cash were foreseen in exchange for 60 Reichsmarks.[89]

"The date of 'Day X' had been kept a secret for as long as possible, even from German politicians. Nevertheless, because everyone suspected what was coming, nothing was on sale in the shops in the days before June 20. While the businesspeople were hoarding their goods, everyone was trying to negotiate anything at all for their worthless Reichsmarks. After June 20, 1948 the situation changed abruptly. Warehouses were opened, the shop windows were full. Prices rose. The black market collapsed. The currency reform unilaterally benefited the owners of material assets and was tantamount to a virtual expropriation of owners of monetary assets, because ownership of land, of means of production and of goods remained unaffected by the new order."[90] At Freudenberg, the nominal value of the equity capital was converted from Reichsmarks to deutschmarks at a ratio of 10 to 9.[91]

Richard Freudenberg as a politician in the young Federal Republic of Germany

The currency reform was an important step on the way to the foundation of the Federal Republic of Germany, in which Richard Freudenberg was also politically active again. His political career, which he had pursued alongside his commercial activities, had begun back in 1919 when he was elected to Weinheim

Fig. 69-70 Richard Freudenberg's election placard for the city and municipal council, 1947 ▪ Theodor Heuss and Richard Freudenberg having a discussion, 1962

municipal council. A short time afterwards, he was additionally elected as a member of parliament for the German Democratic Party (DDP) to the Baden State Parliament in Karlsruhe. He held this seat up to 1929. As a member of the Budget Committee, he advocated, not surprisingly for an entrepreneur, particularly for economic and fiscal policy topics. The points on his agenda are still topical today too: He was concerned with the reorganization of tax legislation, free trade, the interests of his sector, of course, but also school education, funding for Handelshochschule Mannheim and additionally, as should be a matter of course for every member of parliament, the interests of his constituency.[92]

Since he was elected to the State Parliament, Richard Freudenberg was active in the executive committee of the DDP in Baden, which as a result garnered him greater influence on the party's state policies. Following his resignation from the State Parliament after the dissolution of the DDP, or more precisely, of its successor organization, the German State Party (Deutsche Staatspartei) in 1933, he was additionally executive chairman of the state association for Baden.[93] Richard – like all members of the Management Board at the time – was a proponent of the Weimar Republic. During the Nazi era, the Freudenbergs, as already described, held no political offices, apart from their activities in the "self-administration of the economy." However, in Richard Freudenberg's case, this was set to change rapidly after the end of the war.

Richard relied particularly on the power of his name in this context – and held office from 1947 onward as city and district councilor of the PWV (Parteilose Wählervereinigung), a non-party voters' association which he had founded and which later became the Freie Wählervereinigung.[94] In 1949, he stood as a non-party and independent candidate in the constituency of Mannheim-Land for the first *Bundestag*, the new West German parliament. Before his candidacy, he had refused the offer of the Democratic People's Party (DVP) to stand for them as a candidate for the *Bundestag* in the Mannheim-Land constituency. That was a decision against a candidacy with a safety net: Because the FDP/DVP candidacy had strategic advantages in the constituency, Richard would have been elected very safely to the *Bundestag* because he ranked second on the FDP/DVP state list. In addition, this was certainly an honor, because his second place on the list was behind the later German Federal President Theodor Heuss. Heuss was a friend of Richard Freudenberg's; they had known each other for a long time from their joint work in the DDP. Heuss had already written a letter to the investigating Americans during the difficult time of Richard Freudenberg's arrest in which he advocated strongly for Freudenberg. Freudenberg had warned him, the former member of parliament of the DDP in the Reichstag, at an early stage about political persecution by the Nazis and was urgently needed at the company in Weinheim, Heuss wrote.[95]

Freudenberg turned down the DVP's offer for two reasons: He was a proponent of the simple majority vote. Losing the election in his constituency should not open up the opportunity to enter parliament after all through a place on the party list, he believed. This consideration was based on his historical experiences, because as he saw it, the Weimar Republic had collapsed due to the quarrels of the far too numerous parties. For this reason, Freudenberg advocated the majority vote system, which should lead to a stable two-party, or at most three-party system. Moreover, he hoped to be closer to his own voters by standing for election as a non-party candidate. He wanted to make the right political decision – but not one that had to obey party or parliamentary party requirements. He was concerned with personal responsibility: towards his voters and his conscience.

Richard Freudenberg did not actually need the safety net – and thus provided an interesting footnote in German history: He was the first and also the only member of the German *Bundestag* up to the present day to be elected without the support of a party organization.[96] Richard Freudenberg won the election in his Mannheim-Land constituency as a direct candidate with 43.69 percent of the votes. Thus he was significantly ahead of the CDU candidate, who achieved 25.54 percent. However, his affiliation with political liberalism remained: Richard Freudenberg joined the FDP parliamentary party as a guest. He also worked on the committees on foreign trade issues and local reorganization for the FDP parliamentary party. He continued to remain true to himself. As he had done during his earlier time in the Baden State Parliament, he endorsed the creation of a European economic area in combination with the removal of tariffs, on the committees.[97]

At this juncture, it is time for an overview of the new political beginnings in the Federal Republic of Germany. For this, one must know that in the immediate post-war period, there was an "antifascist" consensus which gave rise to the structural principles of the party and association landscape in post-war Germany:[98] the interdenominational CDU and CSU, for example, "the opening up of the SPD towards new classes and the amalgamation of the nationalist-liberal and leftist-liberal traditional lines in the FDP."[99]

During the Berlin Blockade by the Soviet Union in 1948/49, this attitude was extended to include an anti-Communist consensus: As a result, the minister presidents of the West German federal states also accepted the offer of the Western forces to set up a state comprising the Western zones[100] – initially as a temporary measure or "transitory measure" ("*Transitorium*" was the term used by Theodor Heuss) to eventually become a pan-German solution. Up to "the summer of 1948, the French occupation zone had led a segregated life of its own, the Military Government there did not like to see connections beyond the borders of its area of influence, quite in contrast to the Americans and British," who had amalgamated their zones into the "Bizone" in January 1947, in which the contours of a new state gradually began to emerge.[101] After the Bizone became a Trizone when the French zone joined, it was then only a short step to the foundation of the Federal Republic of Germany in 1949.[102]

The underlying socialist sentiment which was also widespread in the West in the post-war era finally gave way to the social market economy in the 1950s, which was championed by the first Economics Minister, Ludwig Erhard.[103] It was accompanied by a development which was termed the "economic miracle" (*Wirtschaftswunder*). After three decades of wars and crises, the new order brought back a feeling of security and normality again for the first time. Another interesting fact: The state redistribution rate in the founding years of the Federal Republic of Germany exceeded that of all other Western countries. In the constant competition between the two major parties, stable patterns of a social and distributive state formed, and all participants became accustomed to rising income and state benefits. After gaining pride in their own economic performance, known as "economic patriotism", trust developed in the welfare state.[104]

Even before the establishment of the Federal Republic of Germany, the Western occupation zones had been included in the Marshall Plan and the European trade structures based on it.¹⁰⁵ Western integration was at the core of the foreign policy of the first German Chancellor, Konrad Adenauer (CDU). He believed the Federal Republic should be firmly anchored in a Western European and Atlantic context and in this way secured and protected from national solo efforts. Adenauer was prepared to make far-reaching compromises towards the West.¹⁰⁶

In the Petersberg Agreement of 1949, Adenauer achieved the end of Western dismantling. In 1952, the foundation of the European Coal and Steel Community (ECSC), often called the "*Montanunion*" (Mining and Metallurgy Union) in German, brought about the emergence of a supranational European structure with which on the one hand German heavy industry was controlled, but on the other hand the Federal Republic of Germany cooperated as an equal partner with France, Italy and the Benelux states.¹⁰⁷

Richard Freudenberg's political work is closely connected to these major decisions. Moreover, he can even be called one of "Baden-Württemberg's trailblazers,"¹⁰⁸ because one of the focal points of his political activity was his commitment to the foundation of this southwestern federal state. Due to economic policy considerations as well, Richard Freudenberg advocated the merger of the three post-war federal states of (South) Baden, Württemberg-Baden and Württemberg-Hohenzollern into a "southwestern state". The proceedings up to that point were rather exhausting, because initially the negotiations of the three "southwestern German states" about a merger had failed in 1950. The result: Now the federal government had to take charge of the situation and Richard Freuden-

Fig. 71 Richard Freudenberg holding a speech in the German Bundestag, 1950

berg sat on the Committee for Internal Reorganization in Bonn. On that committee, he proposed subdividing the three states for the upcoming referendum on the "southwestern state" into four constituencies. This idea was incorporated into the voting law for the referendum on December 9, 1951. And this in turn led to the foundation of today's federal state of Baden-Württemberg in 1952.[109]

However, he also continued to champion the majority voting right in his function as a member of the *Bundestag*. Not surprisingly, his position in the discussions about electoral law for the German *Bundestag* was based on his convictions about voting rights which have already been described. Only those who had received a simple majority, but at least one-third of all votes cast, should be allowed to enter parliament as members. In a second step, and thus if none of the candidates had exceeded the relevant thresholds, he believed there should be a run-off between the two front-running candidates. That was by no means opportunistic, because this attitude was detrimental to Richard Freudenberg. The FDP parliamentary party disapproved of his ideas, they voted for the plurality vote.[110]

In fact, in general, Richard Freudenberg did not allow his opinion to be swayed by tactical considerations to his own personal benefit – and in doing so did not shrink from the major federal policy issues either. This was evident on December 5, 1952, when Freudenberg voted in the *Bundestag* against Germany's plans to join the European Defence Community, whose formation was to ultimately founder in 1954 on France's resistance,[111] and which would have meant a rearmament of the Federal Republic. Richard Freudenberg campaigned passionately against raising armies again in a divided country – because one day these might potentially have to fight against each other.[112] This deviated fundamentally from the majority of the FDP parliamentary party; the result was the end of his collaboration with the FDP parliamentary party.[113]

It must be noted in this context that the Korean War had begun in June 1950, which "reignited the discussion about the defense of Western Europe. In a security memorandum, Konrad Adenauer requested in August 1950 that the military presence of the Western Allies in the Federal Republic be strengthened and pledged a contingent of German troops in the event that it should come to the formation of a European army."[114] Many discussions followed on from this, including Richard Freudenberg's speech. Ultimately, it was decided that the Federal Republic of Germany would join the Western defense alliance, NATO, which occurred in 1955.[115] On January 2, 1956 the first 1,000 volunteer soldiers reported for duty. Two months later, compulsory military service was introduced.[116]

However, Richard Freudenberg was already no longer involved in these decisions in Bonn, because in the elections to the second *Bundestag* on September 6, 1953 he lost out with 20.8 percent of the votes to the CDU candidate, who achieved 38.13 percent of the votes. He had lost the support of the FDP and they had put forward their own candidate.[117] For Richard Freudenberg, this meant the end of his commitment in federal politics, but not in local politics, however. On the contrary: he helped shape local politics for a very long time – right up to 1970. Additionally, he held important honorary positions in the business world, for example as President of the Mannheim Chamber of Commerce and Industry from 1957 to 1971. Furthermore, he sat on the board of the umbrella Association of German Chambers of Commerce and Industry, DIHT.[118]

Rebuilding the leather and shoe business

With the currency reform of June 1948 and the subsequent cessation of economic regulation and government control of the economy to a large extent, particularly in the area of consumer and non-durable goods, free market conditions returned almost immediately. However, since West German foreign trade had not been liberalized at the same time, prices shot up, in some cases exorbitantly, in light of the widespread shortages of raw materials, auxiliaries and goods. It goes without saying that the leather business, specifically shoe manufacturing, was also affected. In November 1948, the first and hitherto only general strike in post-war history occurred, in which protests against alleged price gouging erupted.[119] Under pressure from the protests, the combined economic administration of the American and British occupied zones under the leadership of Ludwig Erhard introduced "government control of textiles and shoes again, by launching what was known as the *Jedermann* [everyone – ed.] program. Then, clothing and shoes were produced in standardized and cheap – state-controlled – serial production. There were fixed prices and an official seal. The mechanism was simple: Companies only received coveted raw materials like leather if they were willing to make parts of their production capacities available for the *Jedermann* program. In November 1948, 750,000 pairs of *Jedermann* shoes were already delivered in West Germany."[120]

This led to an exciting episode in the company's history: It is about the rapid rise and fall of the *Jedermann* shoe, which was well received by consumers because of the shortage situation, but nonetheless was not really popular. However, the *Jedermann* program did achieve its goal of securing raw material supply.

In Freudenberg's case, the establishment of the Vital shoe company on October 22, 1949, which occurred officially under the name Vital-Schuh-Gesellschaft

Hartwig & Co., also belongs in this context.¹²¹ It was based on the shoe manufacturing which had been instigated in Weinheim in the Müll plant after the end of the war. Richard Freudenberg expressed the reasons for setting up the factory in a speech to the workforce:

> "You know [...] that we began shoe production here in Weinheim in 1945, when everything had collapsed. When I realized that the war was lost and even before Hofmann, the shoe factory we were acquainted with, was burning, I had the shoe machines brought from Kleve to Weinheim, so that, when the moment of collapse came, we could set up civilian production. Some of you have worked on this from the very beginning. The idea at the time was that we give work to the workers returning from the front, as I have seen all my life by my father's example and as those who manage the company after Hans and I have to see, will see and do see as well: being an employer means providing work. We were right to begin shoe manufacturing in Weinheim in 1945 in competition against old, established shoe factories, despite the difficulties, I can remember as if it was yesterday, when I was mayor of this city at the time, how happy I was that I quickly received authorization to begin work in our factories in general, on the basis of shoe manufacturing."¹²²

At first, production of shoes began in the Müll factory in Weinheim for subsidiaries Tack and Gustav Hoffmann. But then, from 1948 onward, the initially very successful shoes for the *Jedermann* program were produced, which were sold under the name *Noraflex* shoes and were fitted with the *Nora* molded soles which were considered to be indestructible.¹²³

The later Management Board Member Werner Kumpf (1915–2009) summarized the development of the *Jedermann* shoe at Freudenberg as follows:

> "Then [at the time of the currency reform in the shoe factory in Weinheim] we made a shoe [...], it was what was known as a '*Jedermann*' shoe [...], which had very good wearing properties. For the first time, we had slightly better leather again [...], we could put a rubber sole underneath again, we heat-sealed both. That was an outstanding [shoe], it could not be killed at all [...]. Everyone thought: With this [shoe] we can keep our Vital shoe factory going for the next ten years. Especially since the Freudenbergs were never very interested in fashion, this was something solid, we made one in brown and black, a similar one each for ladies and gentlemen, and this shoe initially sold fabulously well and then about – I would say after one and a half years – [...] it was unsellable. Then people wanted more fashionable [products] again."¹²⁴

It can happen that quickly in the consumer goods business if one banks too much on the customers' heads and too little on their hearts: July 1950 is the last time there is a record of a "Noraflex" collection in the sources, which corresponds to Werner Kumpf's statements.[125]

However, the entire *Jedermann* program must be viewed primarily in the context of the issue of raw material supply. Because in November 1948, Richard Freudenberg was still plagued by "worries about developments in the shoe and leather area," as he expressed in a letter to Ludwig Erhard: "Since I am very well aware of the political consequences of any failure of the free market economy in the area of shoes in particular and believe that the overall direction of your economic policy is right, I would ask you to be convinced that I have done everything to help minimize the difficulties. […] I will ease up all the less because I want to avoid decisions being taken in 'momentary hysteria' – to use your words as a native of Mannheim – that would have to have disastrous effects for the entire German economy in the future."[126]

The currency reform on June 20, 1948 had "hit [the German] leather industry at a low point in the supply [of raw skins] and even any hoarded stocks of skins, hides, leather and shoes were unable to change this overall picture in any way." This was due, on the one hand, to the insufficient availability of foreign currency for raw skin procurement – in the wake of the government control of the leather industry – and a lack of domestic supply.[127]

The release of leather and raw hides from government controls and the associated free pricing in the wake of the currency reform appeared to have come too soon for the leather industry, "because the conditions for a free market economy and free pricing in the leather sector were lacking, meaning sufficient stocks and sufficient replenishment."[128] And only the agreements on delivery and price commitments between the leather and shoe industry required as part of the "*Jedermann*" program finally brought some relief with regard to price increases for raw skins. Richard Freudenberg expressed this as follows: "The mistake that was made on June 20 [meaning the premature release of supply and demand in a completely free economy], to which despite our warning the really major mistake was also added that the domestic hides were sold at auction, appeared to have been corrected."[129]

However, the tanners' association agreement, which was meant to counteract the price increases, was undermined time and again at auctions for domestic hides. The result: More and more tanners exited the agreement again. The fear of being driven out of the market was too great. Thus, the massive price hike for hides could not be slowed down.[130] Because of the strong influence of skin prices on the price of leather, this was also accordingly high. As early as August 1949,

Fig. 72 Richard Freudenberg and Ludwig Erhard (right) at a gathering of the Association of German Chambers of Industry and Commerce (DIHT), 1969

in his function as Director of Economic Administration of the combined American and British occupied zones, Ludwig Erhard assessed "the current prices for domestic leather, when viewed as an average, [as] still too high."[131]

Yet, at the end of 1948, the situation had certainly eased somewhat: The leather manufacturing industry's hide supply was secured again because of raw material purchases in the United States under the terms of the Marshall Plan, which caused prices to decline. However, Richard Freudenberg viewed the procurement of finished leather above and beyond this one-off import system very critically. In a letter to Ludwig Erhard in December 1948, he felt it important to emphasize "that under the terms of Marshall Plan we must import raw materials and not semi-finished and finished products in order for our economy to recover."[132] Thus it is not surprising that he attempted to prevent the purchase of finished leather from the United States and the United Kingdom for the Bizone with a value of 6 million dollars to be repeated in February 1949. In a letter to this effect to Ludwig Erhard, he explained his reasons, in this case in his function as Chairman of the Working Group of Tanners' Associations of the Combined Economic Area:

> "The repeated import of leather must result in raw hide imports and thus the basis of employment of German leather production being dampened again. [...] What is hap-

pening to us today in leather will be demanded by the American and English textile industry, rubber industry or shoe industry based on the same considerations. The problems that German leather manufacturing faces, now that it cannot purchase the raw goods that it wants, but instead must purchase the raw goods that it is enjoined to do, are understandably infinitely more difficult from a technical and economic perspective than the problems that our American and English colleagues are facing. [...] However, if we do not succeed in keeping our domestic leather production going in a reasonably viable way at all despite all these difficulties, then all hope must fade as well that we can develop direct or indirect export with German leather production again."[133]

Based on these considerations, it can also be understood why Richard Freudenberg, as a liberal economic politician, advocated a continuation of the government control of the German leather industry to Ludwig Erhard in March 1949 – and how difficult it was to get back to "normal" conditions:

"I fear that conditions in the leather manufacturing and leather processing industry are still too raw to give away the last opportunities for state intervention now already. Every interruption of a reasonably orderly raw material supply from abroad can very quickly disrupt the economic consolidation, and particularly pricing policy consolidation, in leather and shoes, and cause an unwanted new upward movement in domestic skin and hide prices. [...] The fact that I, of all people, and you know my attitude towards a free and independent economy, must take this position should show you how seriously I regard the consequences."[134]

Nevertheless, finished leathers – predominantly from the United States – continued to be imported to Germany.[135] On the other hand, the government control of the leather industry also led to raw hides being imported which, although they could be processed into high-quality types of leather by the tanneries, they did not meet the needs of the main customer segment, the shoe industry. In this context, Richard Freudenberg pointed out in a letter to Ludwig Erhard in August 1949 that "the Trizone's overall production of both upper as well as bottom leather at least fully meets the needs of the shoe industry. [...] Since demand from the leather goods industry is still insignificant, we definitely have an overproduction of upper leather, but in many cases of types and ranges that are not accepted given the current requirements of the shoe trade and the shoe industry. [...] However, as I already wrote to you in my letter of July 7, imports are inevitable and often are not subject to the will of the donors."[136]

Richard Freudenberg summarizes the numerous problems in a letter to Ludwig Erhard dated December 22, 1949 as follows: "One can hardly imagine that the second half century which will soon be dawning will present us with greater problems than the waning first half century has done."¹³⁷

Thus, leather continued to play a dominant role in the Freudenberg company's product portfolio. But that was not without its problems, for in this era of government control, which lasted until 1952, the first signs of a fundamental structural crisis in the German leather industry were also emerging.

The German leather industry's main problem after the end of World War II was the considerable dependence on imports of raw skins.¹³⁸ This resulted in extreme price increases, which the German leather industry was virtually unable to pass on to its customers at all. As a consequence, significant cost increases remained, with the associated negative effects on the company's earnings position. This can be proved pertaining to Freudenberg specifically by the example of how hide prices developed: Purchase prices for cow hides in the years from 1948 until 1960 were on average around 300 percent higher than the purchase prices before World War II; in 1951 they were actually almost 450 percent above the reference values before 1945. In the case of calf hides, the development was even more dramatic: For these, the average purchase price in the same time span was around 550 percent above the level before World War II, and at their peak actually 700 percent above pre-1945 prices.¹³⁹

The reasons for the increase in purchase prices were that hide and skin demand from the German leather industry could not be met by domestic supply, the traditional eastern European sourcing markets were gone, and other countries in some cases imposed quotas on their exports. One example of the last case is France, where the imposition of quotas was meant to also ensure that the French leather industry could meet its demand domestically and in doing so was much more independent of price developments on the world market.¹⁴⁰

The problem of dependence on expensive hide imports remained an ongoing issue at Freudenberg. As late as 1960, 60 percent of calf skins and around 80 percent of cow hides had to be imported – meaning that raw materials accounted for 70 percent of the cost of the finished leather.¹⁴¹ Another structural problem the leather industry had was the ever-increasing penetration of plastic and replacement materials into the traditional markets for leather. This was a process which – beginning in the 1930s – put the leather industry under constantly rising pressure from the 1950s onward.¹⁴² Through their own development of leather replacement products like shoe soles, seals, or later synthetic leather under the brand name *Helia* in the 1960s, Freudenberg was on the one hand very farsighted to develop into other areas, but in doing so the company at the same time entered into direct competition with its own traditional product, leather, as well.

The structural problems of the German leather industry were particularly evident in a comparison of the industry's development with the growth of German industry in the years of the German economic miracle. West German industry profited from the Korean War in particular as well: Because Western countries had to expand their armaments production, and civilian business areas suffered because of this. Since it was not permitted to manufacture any defense equipment in Germany at this juncture, it only made sense to concentrate on jumping into the emerging gap and satisfy the demand for capital and consumer goods. There was also the fact that German products did not have to be paid for with scarce dollars. Hence export volumes increased significantly in the years between 1952 and 1958.[143]

The Federal Republic of Germany could also afford the strong growth because the numerous displaced persons and refugees meant that there were enough workers available who could be deployed to build up the economy.[144]

Up to 1956, German industry as a whole was able to increase production volumes by 213 percent in comparison to 1936, whereas in the leather industry, the comparable increase was only 87 percent. This led to a situation where a total of 177 leather manufacturing firms had to shut down between 1949 and 1956 and the actual profits generated were growing increasingly smaller.[145]

Freudenberg attempted to counteract this development, among other things with the expansion of its portfolio by adding velours leather to its product range in 1949 as well as with the takeover of the Tannerie de Varces tannery near Grenoble in France in 1956. The expansion into France occurred against the backdrop of the imposition of export quotas for calf skins described above. In order to ensure access to the French raw skin market, which was important to Freudenberg, the Management Board decided that Freudenberg would set up its own production in France. In addition to this, Freudenberg acquired the Teneria Temola in Cuautla in Mexico in 1961, a tannery with a shoe factory attached, to expedite its own technological development and gain better access to the American market.[146]

Market developments accordingly had an effect on the turnover that Freudenberg was able to achieve in the leather business: While other parts of the group grew fast, leather's share – despite the targeted acquisitions – declined continually. Leather's share of corporate turnover fell from 43 percent in 1951 through 37 percent (1954) to 33 percent in 1957. In 1962 it was down to only one-fifth for the first time, but then rose slightly once again because of the acquisition in Mexico, however. But ultimately, the position of the founding product, leather, remained heavily under pressure at Freudenberg.[147]

The difficulties in the legacy leather business, with which nonetheless money was still earned over many years, also offered opportunities for new managers:

Thus Hermann Freudenberg (1924–2010) joined the company on August 1, 1950, with responsibility for the tannery. Hermann, a son of Adolf Freudenberg's – the latter a brother of Hans and Richard Freudenberg's – had initially completed a traineeship as a tanner in Switzerland and directly afterwards a chemistry degree in Geneva. He assumed technical responsibility for the leather division.[148]

The fact that Hermann Freudenberg was undoubtedly aware of the problems in the leather segment when he joined the company is evident from a letter to his uncle Hans, which he wrote during a summer traineeship at the company in August 1948:

> "On beginning practical work in this company, one can easily be overcome with fear and dread in the face of the multifariousness and wealth of technical problems, which appear to be almost boundless. […] It is certainly hardly possible to master the different areas down to all the last details. For that reason, I was very pleased about your formulation of the apprenticeship on a broad front. Uncle Richard initiated me into the *Nora* factory, where I would likely have had the best possibility of showing that I will not shy away from any dirt. In these 2 months, I want to try to work through production systematically and particularly also to spend some time working with Dr. Demme in the mechanical testing room. It is a new and very interesting area, and I will have ample opportunity to learn chemistry there. Tomorrow I will travel with Dr. Siegert and Mr. Schäfer to the Swiss border, where we will meet Mr. Recht, who will travel to America at the beginning of September. It will be instructional for me to be present, because there will be talk of the changes and the new problems in the tannery there."[149]

Since responsibilities under the very personal management of Hans and Richard Freudenberg were evidently not clearly demarcated at that time, "there was a lot of scope for one's own initiative, of which Hermann Freudenberg took advantage."[150] Thus he always endeavored to improve the productivity of leather manufacturing and the quality of the leather with technological innovations.[151] In April 1959, Hermann Freudenberg became a general partner and was thus appointed to the Management Board, where he now assumed responsibility for the entire leather business.[152]

Dieter Freudenberg (1926–2010), the youngest son of Otto Freudenberg, also took on responsibility in the leather division already at an early age and despite other personal interests at this time. He had joined the company after returning from captivity as a prisoner of war of the British in October 1945. Hermann Freudenberg put on record how this came to pass when he gave his speech to mark Dieter's 60th birthday: "Hans and Richard Freudenberg insisted that you make yourself available to the company without any long career detours. You saw the necessity of the times and subordinated your own personal interests to those of the company, because you would have dearly loved to attend university." Since he had been unable to complete any training after taking his high school leaving examination (*Abitur*) and doing military service immediately afterwards, he initially familiarized himself with the leather business from October 1945 to September 1947 as part of an internship, during which he went through all the "stages of tanning from the hide magazine right up to finishing, and this through integration into the daily work process right up to piecework."[153]

Subsequently, he expanded continually on his existing knowledge up to the fall of 1952 through commercial training in Germany and abroad as well as further practical experience in the area of the shoe and leather business. His career path led him from France through England and South Africa as far as Argentina.[154] During the time from the fall of 1952 until June 1953, Dieter Freudenberg traveled through several South American countries as a leather salesman on behalf of Freudenberg.[155]

It can be stated that the "early, intensive encounters with other cultures"[156] had a lasting impact on Dieter Freudenberg. As Hermann Freudenberg in his speech to mark Dieter's 60th birthday in 1986 explained, he was "the first [one] after the war whom the company sent to these countries, which indeed were of great significance to the company both for the import of hides as well as for the purchase of our products."[157] After his return in the summer of 1953, Dieter Freudenberg took on management tasks in Weinheim in leather sales for Germany and abroad.[158] Dieter Freudenberg also joined the Management Board likewise in 1959 as a general partner.[159] In the years that followed, he managed leather sales and the *Nora* division.[160]

As was already apparent from the history concerning the "*Jedermann*" shoe, leather and the shoe business are closely interconnected, which is why a brief look at the development of the shoe division at Freudenberg in the years of Germany's economic recovery is also worthwhile.

Apart from the *Vital* shoe factory that has already been mentioned, Freudenberg also had two further shoe production facilities. At Gustav Hoffmann in Kleve, the leading manufacturer of children's shoes in Germany at the time, production volumes of the *Elefanten* brand had already reached the level of 4.1 million pairs of shoes in 1949, which was still around 11 percent below the pre-war level in 1938.[161] Conrad Tack relocated his production from Mühlheim to Offenbach, where a modern shoe factory began operations in 1951.[162] In the entire group, the shoe division had a 34.7 percent share of turnover. Together with leather, this came to 77.9 percent of turnover, while the other business areas at that juncture "only" stood for 22.1 percent of the company's total turnover.[163] However, the coming decades were set to become difficult in the shoe and – as already intimated – in the leather business. The fate of Tack's shoe production was like a portent of this: Despite the most intensive efforts, the Tack shoe brand could no longer become established in West Germany, which is why Tack shoe production in Offenbach was discontinued as early as in October 1952. In the following years, another production line of the Vital shoe company moved into the plant.[164] However, the Tack shop branches were retained, and Tack became purely a shoe retailing company.[165] Hans Erich Freudenberg summarized the necessity of this step very succinctly several years later: "It was not until the release of the Tack firm from manufacturing responsibility that […] the trading side of the company, which had been revived on a small scale, was able to recover."[166] Thus from 1952 the shoe division at Freudenberg was divided into the Gustav Hoffmann manufacturing companies – with the main factory in Kleve and smaller stand-alone plants – and Vital – with shoe factories in Weinheim and Offenbach – as well as shoe retailing through the Conrad Tack network of stores.

At Gustav Hoffmann in Kleve, production volumes in children's and adolescents' shoes reached 6.4 million pairs of shoes in 1959, which corresponded to a 56 percent increase in production as compared to 1949 and was already 39 percent above the pre-war level. Turnover was at 72.8 million deutschmarks and had thus achieved a 51 percent increase within ten years.[167]

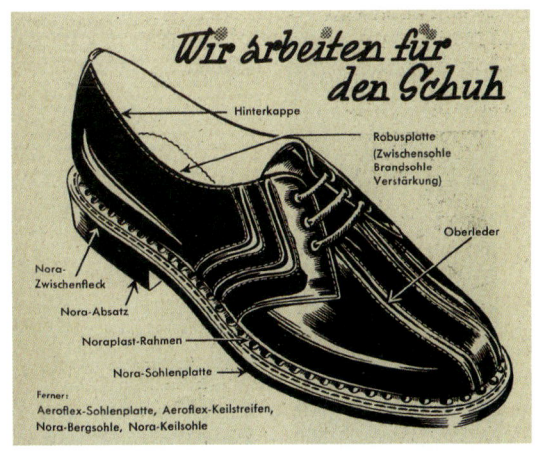

Fig. 73 Freudenberg shoe components, 1953

Shoe materials from other business divisions also found their way into the shoes which were produced at Freudenberg in the various factories. Figure 73 shows an overview from 1953.[168]

In 1954, Freudenberg was one of West Germany's biggest shoe manufacturers. Of the 810 shoe factories with more than 10 employees, only 12 had a workforce of more than 1,000 employees.[169] Freudenberg belonged to this group, with no fewer than two production facilities: the Vital shoe factory in Weinheim and the Elefanten children's and adolescents' shoe factory in Kleve.[170] There was also a lot to lose. At that time, shoes had reached a 28.3 percent share of the overall group's turnover, and together with leather actually accounted for a 65.3 percent share. The remaining business divisions had already grown to a 34.6 percent share.[171] 1956 – because of the ongoing rise in the standard of living – turned out to be the most successful postwar year to date in the West German shoe industry. However, the yields of most shoe manufacturers in West Germany were unsatisfactory.[172]

The yield issue also hit the Vital shoe factory, which slipped into the red, from which it could only be gotten out again "with the greatest effort". Then, in the years 1958 to 1961, "in the average of these four years annually around 500,000 deutschmarks" were earned again.[173] One reason for this was that the Curator sales department, which was part of Freudenberg & Co., took over the shoe factory in Offenbach in April 1958. Thus a program change that had already been initiated in 1957 took place, away from orthopedic utility shoes and towards comfortable, fashionable ladies' shoes, which were sold under the Curator brand name.[174]

Nevertheless, this business remained challenging.[175] Consequently, the Vital shoe factory in Weinheim ceased production at the end of 1964.[176] Thus Freudenberg was reacting to market developments in which "large enterprises with a mixed, standard range" steadily lost market shares to "small and medium-sized enterprises that had specialized in the relevant subsegments." From then on, Freudenberg concentrated on the specialized production of brand-named shoes of the Curator and Elefanten brands, as well as shoe retailing through the network of Conrad Tack stores. Hans Erich Freudenberg summarized the reasons for this in a study on the company's challenges from 1968: "The impossibility of specialized technological developments and the uniformity of the machines that were offered and used everywhere limits special advantages of a brand to characteristics that cannot be trademarked, which make the consumer benefit (fit, lightness, relative durability) or the prestige utility ('look', fashion, material) stand out. However, since everything in shoe manufacturing can be copied immediately, specific benefits only last for a very short time. The necessity of having to conquer one's market share completely from scratch again twice a year proves once again the advantage of a specialty that is shielded by a brand, has a profile and is versatile. If the satisfied or interested consumer demands such brands, which really mean something, then the retailer will have to or want to carry them."[177] Twice a year from scratch – that shows clearly that they were active in the fashion industry here, because of course a new collection is required both for spring/summer as well as for fall/winter.

However, there is another important issue too: Despite all the difficulties, leather and shoes together still remained the most important business in Freudenberg's portfolio for many years. And, with the money earned in this, later diversification and internationalization steps and their – in some cases considerable – teething troubles could also be financed, which was accompanied by a significant expansion in the product range. This included, among other things, the development of the nonwovens area with the start of production of *Vileda* cleaning cloths and *Vlieseline* interlinings for the textile industry in 1948.

> **EXCURSUS:** SOCIAL RESPONSIBILITY – PART 3: FROM THE END OF WORLD WAR II TO THE END OF THE 1950S
>
> **1948** Beginning of involvement in aid to the disabled with the establishment of the disabled workshop in Schloss Werneck near Schweinfurt, in which predominantly disabled war veterans found employment.[178] In 1988, in collaboration with the Verein für Gemeindediakonie und Rehabilitation e.V., an aid organization run by the German Protestant (*Evangelische*) church, a workshop was set up for 26 multiply and mentally disabled people in the Müllheimer Tal plant.[179] The company won many awards for inclusivity, for example the Special Award of the Rhineland-Palatinate state award for the inclusion of severely disabled people in 2016.[180]
>
> **1949** To mark the company's 100th anniversary, the partners donated money to promote home ownership.[181] Additionally, two foundations, each with 10-year terms, are set up for the cities of Weinheim and Schönau to support needy citizens.
>
> **1951** The first free meal program (*Freitisch*) for older needy people is organized using donations from members of the workforce at Christmas.[182]
>
> **1957** To mark the 100th birthday of master craftsman Meister Georg Böhler,[183] the sum of 5,000 deutschmarks is provided annually for 10 years to support particularly gifted young craftspeople of good character who had attended the Weinheim vocational school until they completed their apprenticeship. The aim was to support between two and five apprentices every year. In 1967, the foundation is extended by a further three years up to 1970.[184]
>
> **1958** To mark his 70th birthday, Hans Freudenberg founded the Heiner and Walter Freudenberg Foundation to support gifted adolescents. It existed from 1960 to 1978.[185]

Nonwovens become Vileda

The expansion of the portfolio in 1936 to include nonwovens, which has been a defining moment to the company up to the present day, has already been mentioned. Chemist Carl Ludwig Nottebohm had brought this innovation to Weinheim at that time. The synthetic leather, which was based on a nonwoven backing, was initially only suitable for bags and cases; the sales market was small – and following the currency reform there was no demand for substitute materials any more. Yet, since the beginning of the 1940s, the company had already been giving some thought to how the nonwoven backing material could otherwise be used. Nottebohm himself reports on this in an anecdote: "Professor Mechels had a suit made from the first lengths of nonwoven which proved to have sufficient strength. He showed it to me and then declared that he was going to play skittles that evening and would show the suit to his fellow skittle players. A little later, he called me in a state of great agitation: 'Mr. Nottebohm, the nonwoven material is useless after all. My pants burst while I was playing skittles!'"[186] Ultimately, another track appeared to be more promising: After World War II, there was also a shortage of support material, which was needed to give shape to clothing. This was used as an opportunity to develop the nonwovens further in this direction from 1946.[187] Near the end of 1947, decisive progress was achieved in the production technique. An improvement in the structure of the fiber that was produced offered benefits for manufacturing lighter nonwoven materials in particular. In the end, this also led to soft, flexible products. This was one of the prerequisites for the transition to new and more appealing nonwovens. With an eye to the changes that had occurred in consumer behavior after the currency reform, it was indeed a fortunate coincidence that precisely at this time two new product groups were actually emerging: the household articles with the name *Vileda* and the interlinings under the brand name "*Vlieseline*".[188] This chapter will deal with both product lines.

In Weinheim, production began of a new isoelastic nonwoven interlining for clothing in 1948, with the name *Vlieseline*, a textile which is only connected at the intersection of the overlying fibers and gains its specific characteristics, like stability, porosity and elasticity because of this.[189] The myth of the Golden Fleece [*Vlies* in German – ed.] was the inspiration for the name. Between 1948 and 1954, black, cream and gray interlinings for clothing come onto the market – it is the beginning of a Freudenberg success story which has continued up to the present day. As early as 1952, the first fashion shows with external models made on *Vlieseline* were held, initially in West German cities, and abroad as well later, for circles of experts from the clothing trade and for industry.[190] These models from the Frankfurt School of Fashion were then followed in 1953 onward by the company's own models from the "*Vlieseline Studio*". The studio developed because new collections had to be assembled regularly and the versatile processing possibilities of the Freudenberg nonwovens had to be demonstrated using models. Additionally, from 1953 the *vlieseline-Modedienst* fashion trade magazine was published. And even today, *Vlieseline* is still an established brand in the tailoring industry.[191] Distribution of these interlinings in Germany was initially conducted successfully together with the Franz Pfaff commercial agency, which was based in Heidelberg and with whom a sales company was established for this purpose.[192] Pfaff went into retirement in 1975 and his company was dissolved, upon which Freudenberg took over the sales activities on its own account.[193]

Interlinings, as the name suggests, are usually not visible, however. Thus Freudenberg's activities in the household products segment have always been better known to the general public. Furthermore, the path to *Vileda* household articles also branched off from the base material, synthetic leather, which was known as the *Viledon* semi-finished material. Cotton, which had become so scarce during the war and the post-war period, became available for production again with the aid of barter transactions. Cotton was set to become a deciding factor, because during the production process for the *Vileda* cloth, the observation skills of two employees played a decisive role in this context. They noticed that cleaning ladies used the cutoffs from the *Viledon* semi-finished material, which was composed of this cotton, to mop up while they were working.[194]

Why? The pieces of cloth became soft in water, pliant, absorbing the cleaning water while still retaining a respectable stability. This observation inspired the developers: Window cloths and the entire series of household cloths were set to be developed based on this usage. As early as 1947, Carl Ludwig Nottebohm

Fig. 74–75 The "Vlieseline Studio" winter collection, 1959 ▪ "Vlieseline Studio" fashion show in Amsterdam, 1955

Fig. 76 Advertising poster for the Vileda window cloth, 1950

developed the *Vileda* window cloth from this idea.[195] Nottebohm's comments on the development of the window cloth are also interesting: "I recall that I had already had the idea much earlier to produce a porous material for battery switches. The soft material that came out as a result then actually led to the window leather, to *Vileda* and the household cloths segment. […] I worked on this for quite a long time. The process consisted of introducing salt into the nonwoven mixture and dissolving it out again afterwards. Depending on the grain size of the salt, fine or larger pores formed. […] I immediately demonstrated my new window leather to him [Richard Freudenberg]. Richard was excited. He immediately began cleaning windows." And it was not just the head of the group who was excited: On June 23, 1948, and thus shortly after the currency reform, the company was surprised by a major contract with a volume worth 300,000 deutschmarks. "I myself was almost a little alarmed and worried as to whether such a large order could also be completed smoothly," Nottebohm later recalled.[196]

The well-known product, or rather brand name, *Vileda*, which was highly successful in the following decades and was initially only used for the window cloth, is a modification of the German "*wie Leder*" ["like leather" – the two words sounded like "Vileda" when pronounced in the local German dialect – ed.], for the nonwoven cloth really does feel like a washleather, or "chamois". Thus the name *Vileda* was originally meant to be used for the synthetic leather. However, Otto Freudenberg felt the term did not sound technical enough and therefore suggested the name *Viledon*, which would provide better sales opportunities. Although the inventor, Carl Ludwig Nottebohm, thought that *Viledon* sounded "more like a medicinal product," Otto Freudenberg's name for the artificial leather remained. However, this meant that the name *Vileda* was available for the new postwar product line and was just as suitable for the window cloth.[197]

After the currency reform and the introduction of the deutschmark, consumers' wishes also began to become increasingly more important. In a ration economy during and in the first years after the war, consumers accepted what was allocated to them. Now they could decide, and with rising incomes, their latitude for decision-making became larger. Companies had to take this into consideration if they were to be successful during the economic miracle. Thus the expansion of the product portfolio came at the right time.

Suddenly, procuring raw materials and technology were no longer the only problems either. Totally different business skills were required: selling and adapting the products to market requirements. Virtually from one day to the next, as was the case with shoes, customer interest now played a much greater role. In the household series, this interest was directed particularly at the floor cloth with the brand name *Vlieser*, which had likewise been developed in 1948. There was huge demand for this cloth. One of the sales representatives had picked up the floor cloths by the truckload and sold the load directly from the truck in a matter of hours, according to a report from that time.[198]

In 1948, the company also exhibited at the first Frankfurt Trade Fair. "Exhibitors from 33 industries set up their stands. 300,000 prospective buyers attended the first 'deutschmark fair', the first comprehensive fair after currency reform."[199] The 1948 fair was an important impetus for the strong growth in the *Vlieser* floor cloth business – an initial spark, as it were.[200]

However, very strong growth also harbors unexpected difficulties, and that applies in this case too. Once again, there are fascinating comments on this in Wilhelm Lauppe's report: In order to meet the fibrous material requirements quickly, "large amounts of cotton waste containing lubricating oil from the cotton mills" were now also processed. "Thus, oily fibers were brought into extremely close contact with natural latex through the impregnation." However, this was breaking new ground: "In warehouses with piles of floor cloths – in packets of 50 cloths piled up on top of each other – strange fires occurred. The fire always broke out at the weekend, frequently during the night from Saturday to Sunday or on Sunday morning." Was this arson? "'The cleaning rag factory at Freudenberg is burning,' was a call that prompted malicious satisfaction among some people, but caused deep alarm to those directly affected."[201]

The building insurers assailed Freudenberg with questions, as Lauppe recalls: "The Feuersocietät Berlin [a fire insurance company – ed.] conducted correspondence right up to 1951 with the aim of bringing the person responsible for production to justice. Measurements of the temperature progression in the piles showed that when the pile was left undisturbed, the temperature rose very slowly and then increasingly fast – until it reached the point of spontaneous ignition." Finally, an explanation was found. During the week, the pile was turned constantly, so nothing happened. Neither any individual piece nor a package of 50 pieces was able to store the heat that had developed strongly enough to trigger a spontaneous ignition. But then the weekend came. The piles were left untouched. And the escalation up to the point of ignition became possible. "It is a case of warming up through autoxidation," which caused the disaster. "The rubber experts which the Management Board had called in from Leverkusen were surprised at the event. When components were mixed in the rolling mill using the technique known back then and a thick sheet was manufactured, an escalation of heating like this was never observed. Thus it was the extremely fine distribution of the rubber binding agents with the ingredients which were dangerous because of the abnormally large interior surface [...] which ultimately led to the fires."[202]

At the beginning of July 1949, the Management Board was extremely worried about this development: The figures show how serious the problems in the nonwovens business were. In May 1949, at Freudenberg's 100-year anniversary party, there were 350 employees working in the area of nonwovens. As early as July, this figure dropped down to 20 again, like in the time before the floorcloth boom. After this critical month, business continued at the lowest level. It was saved by the business of interlinings for clothing: When an order for 20,000 meters of *Vlieseline* came in from the *Vlieseline* sales representative in Essen in August, this was viewed as a new beginning and helped to boost morale again among the employees working in nonwovens production.[203] The fast onset of success in *Vlieseline* interlining was reflected in rapidly rising turnover, which rose sixteenfold from 1950 to 1955.[204]

Soon, methods were developed to test the finished products. An entire series of tests led to products of a much more homogenous quality. The time was also used to expand the household product group to include other types of cloths, namely *Vlextil* (wiping or household cloth) and *Vlik* (washing-up cloth). It can be seen in the balance sheets that initially small, but definitely constantly rising, profits were reported from as early as 1949 onward.[205]

Additionally, the first spin-off also took place during the time of the currency reform: In the summer of 1948, what was known as the Frema contract was signed with textile finishing company Martini in Augsburg. The word Frema stood for an abbreviation of Freudenberg-Martini. Both partners each held a 50 percent share in the joint venture for the production of cleaning cloths and later also of nonwovens, the second nonwovens product line which was still important alongside *Vileda*. Production of the *Vileda* window cloth as well as of the *Vlextil* wiping or household cloth began in 1949 in the Fremawerk plant in Augsburg. Freudenberg had had contact with Martini as early as the end of the 1930s, but the greater collaboration that had been planned had not materialized because of a lack of cooperation from the Reich Economics Ministry. Both parties were pleased to resume discussions on collaboration again after the war. Martini was interested in active involvement in a second industrial area; Freudenberg could expand the requisite production capacities faster.[206] The partnership with Martini can also be seen as a further example of a good relationship at eye level with a third party, which worked well over a very long period and was cultivated by the Freudenbergs beforehand and afterwards.

In the years that followed, the *Viledon* nonwovens segment in Weinheim collaborated together with a growing number of affiliated factories in a group which for its part further developed the technology through its own findings. An important point had been included in the Frema contract and the subsequent later agreements with further partners, like for example the American company Pellon: All advances were available to all members of the group as well. Thus isolation and secretiveness were counteracted from the very start.[207] Today, something like this would probably be called "open source". In any case, it was a successful model.

The establishment of the first foreign production company in 1950 in the United States can also be regarded in connection with the uptick in the new nonwoven products. It was of paramount importance to the further development of Freudenberg's business, not just commercially, but also symbolically. Together with US partners David Morgenstern and Alexander Westreich, Freudenberg set up the aforementioned Pellon Corporation in the city of Lowell in the US state of Massachusetts to produce interlinings. Both the machines required for setting up production as well as the technological expertise came from Freudenberg.[208] The Americans assumed the task of foreign currency procurement, which was not so easy for the Weinheim-based company.[209] Incidentally, the name "Pellon" is derived from the Latin word "*pellis*" (meaning pelt or hide), to recall Freudenberg's traditional leather trade. As a result, Pellon also became the brand name for Freudenberg nonwovens on the important US market.[210] However, the collaboration with the partners, particularly with David Morgenstern, was not without friction from the beginning, which increasingly led to tensions. This ultimately resulted in Freudenberg buying out the two partners, Morgenstern and Westreich, between 1956 and 1957, because it was essential to Freudenberg to be represented strongly and independently in this important business line in the United States.[211]

Nevertheless, the creation of new nonwovens production capacity did not remain restricted to America. Thus the establishment of the Bondina Ltd. nonwovens joint venture took place in 1956 in the United Kingdom.[212] As was already the case in the United States, Freudenberg relied on regional partners who contributed an understanding of regional market conditions. Thus Freudenberg and British company Bradford Dyers' Association Ltd. each held a 50 percent stake in Bondina Ltd. That same year, Bondina started up a new nonwovens factory in the village of Greetland, which was intended to serve the British and Irish markets. The boom in the petticoat business in particular provided Bondina's interlinings with strong growth in the UK. The plant already had to be extended after only two years. When the British partner was acquired by textile company Viyella International Ltd. in 1967, Freudenberg exercised the option right it had required to be stipulated in the joint-venture contract for precisely this eventuality and acquired all the shares in Bondina Ltd.[213]

Freudenberg's development in the 1950s was characterized by two significant strategic approaches which ran in parallel: further diversification and the associated expansion of the product range, as well as the internationalization of its own production. Its internationalization was driven by the idea of producing within the regions for the regions, and doing this together with regional partners who contributed an understanding of regional peculiarities. This form of internationalization has been characteristic of Freudenberg up to the present day and is part of its formula for success.

In this context, the company's economic development, its diversification and its further internationalization are so closely interconnected that it is sometimes difficult to distinguish between them. This successful development will be elucidated more understandably in the following chapters using some examples.

The emergence of the first filters, innovations and the construction of the Berlin Wall

Exploring new market opportunities also led to a diversification step in nonwovens at Freudenberg which remains significant up to the present day: the development of the first nonwoven filters. Strictly speaking, the impetus for the development of the filters came from Hans Freudenberg's driver,[214] who got his trouser cuffs dirty time and again from the dust and dirt sucked in from the streets through the ventilation system. To avoid this, he got himself a piece of nonwoven fabric from the Viledon production facility and attached it to the engine intake air pipe. Hans Freudenberg passed on this observation from his daily life to the team of nonwoven developers led by Carl Ludwig Nottebohm, who was also responsible for nonwovens production.[215] This good idea was adopted, and initial efforts to develop filter nonwovens for air filtration were begun around 1950. As early as December 1954, a patent for a "filter cloth made of porous randomly oriented fiber nonwoven, impregnated with a binding agent, for dust collectors, gas filters and air purifiers" was registered.²¹⁶ However, the breakthrough was not achieved until the development of filter mats in 1956. The patent for a "self-supporting gas filter mat and process for its manufacture" dated September 1956 constitutes the foundation for the first fully developed *Viledon* filter mats,²¹⁷ which were launched on the market in 1957.²¹⁸ These were initially utilized for medical purposes, like for example for air purification in hospitals and laboratories, and for demanding industrial applications like for paint booths in the automotive industry.²¹⁹ Above and beyond this, they were used everywhere air had to be purified, and thus in the ventilation systems of factories, high-rise buildings, restaurants or movie theaters. Thus the foundation stone had been laid for the business field of technical nonwovens for industrial applications. Demand was high: Just two years after market launch, *Viledon* industrial filter mats were being exported to 13 countries.²²⁰

Fig. 77 Filter mat production, 1967

The division continued to grow steadily, partly due to the development of new products in the 1960s. One example of this is the engine intake air filter for the automotive industry, sold from 1963 onward, with which the air drawn into the engine compartment is purified – a technology which is applied in the same way right up to the present day. This growth was reflected in sales and turnover figures – thus sales volume was raised by 30 percent in 1963.²²¹ A large part of this surge was achieved by the *Viledon* filter distribution company that was established specifically for this purpose by Kurt Huber (1919–2016) at the end of the 1950s and also managed by him.²²² The growth also led to a further expansion in production capacity. Thus as early as 1963, premises had to be rented outside the factory premises in Weinheim for the storage, the finishing process – meaning for cutting to size, sorting and packaging – as well as for the dispatch of the *Viledon* filter mats. In Weinheim itself, the shortage of space for the expanding *Viledon* production steadily increased. This did not apply to the filters alone, but also to the entire nonwovens production. For that reason, Freudenberg built new production halls in the Zwischen Dämmen plant from 1961 onward – and began operating further modern production plants there.²²³

The year 1957 was not just associated with the launch of the Freudenberg filter mats, but was additionally the year of the "Sputnik shock": With the successful entry of the then Soviet Union into unmanned space flight, the West's feeling of technological superiority dissipated very quickly. Within a very short time, West German backwardness in high technology entered the public spotlight, and efforts to catch up were accelerated accordingly. From 1950 to 1955, the private sector's expenditure on research and development grew by 400 million deutschmarks to a total of 600 million deutschmarks, and actually reached 1.6 billion deutschmarks in the year 1960. Public expenditure reached a similarly high level.[224] Although state and private research funding had nothing to do with Freudenberg directly, it was clear to the public that economic success and technological advances were closely interlinked, and stiff competition prevailed. Anyone who wanted to be successful in this area had to invest in it. That was clear to those responsible at Freudenberg too. Their technological orientation was obviously fully in line with current trends. Looking at the other business areas, that is also evident time and again.

The development of the seals business

In the postwar era, in view of the difficulties associated with leather, not just the nonwovens business, but also sealing technology became increasingly important to Freudenberg: Production of seals had already been resumed in 1946 in Weinheim. Initially, only replacement supplies for the US Army were manufactured after receiving authorization from the Allies. "In addition, production of cup seals for bicycle pumps was allowed and, on a small scale, seals for repairing farm machinery and trucks." Since automotive production in Germany had not yet started up again, Freudenberg concentrated at first on the production of seals for agricultural machinery, which were allowed to be manufactured again. At the end of 1948, the Simrit-Werk plant already employed 580 workers again.[225]

Then, from the early 1950s, the effects of the economic miracle, the immense reconstruction efforts and the rapid return of the German economy to the world markets were the determining factors for the burgeoning challenges. The successful expansion of the automotive industry was the prime factor in this context. Consequently, the high demand for industrial products in general had an impact not just in the new business area of nonwovens, but also had an enormous effect on Freudenberg's sealing business, since Simrit seals were also fitted in many vehicles and machines. During the 1950s, the automotive industry increased its production fivefold.²²⁶ The prime example of this is the VW Beetle: In 1955, the one millionth Beetle rolled off the assembly line in Wolfsburg.²²⁷ At Freudenberg, the automotive boom from 1949 had been accompanied by the modernization of manufacturing technology and the systematic expansion of the Buna plant to enable new types of rubber to be processed. Thus the plant was able to produce the first silicon compounds as early as 1953.²²⁸ This was also expressed in figures: On January 3, 1953, the 100 millionth Simmerring was manufactured.²²⁹ At the end of the same year, the plant was able to produce 40,000 Simmerrings a day. In this phase of building the sealing business, "Georg Boysen, with a high level of technical expertise, proved to be the man of the hour for Simrit as head of sales."²³⁰ Under his management, turnover increased almost fivefold within only six years, until his retirement in 1954: from 7.5 million deutschmarks in 1948 to 32.7 million deutschmarks in 1954.²³¹ Thus the share of the Freudenberg Group's overall turnover contributed by the sealing business constituted 11.4 percent.²³²

At the same time, further products were developed, in some cases in direct collaboration with customers: Seals for hydraulic pit props in mining, shock absorber seals and seals for the newly developed air brakes. And a further market segment was added in the form of the newly invented *Vulkollan* hydraulic seals. *Vulkollan* is a polyurethane (PU) developed by Bayer. Under Simrit's brand name Hydrofit, the hydraulic seals found a major sales market in the hydraulics industry and in mining in the countries of northern Europe, particularly in Sweden.²³³

In 1953, the new material also aroused the interest of US company Greer Hydraulics, which was headquartered in New York. Greer Hydraulics was a manufacturer of patented accumulator bladders for hydraulic aggregates. Freudenberg in its turn was interested in manufacturing rubber bladders for the European market. Thus a licensing agreement was signed to manufacture the bladders – and a production facility was set up in the Old Lacquering Shop in the Buna plant in Weinheim.²³⁴ A more intensive exchange of technical expertise developed from this collaboration, which eventually culminated in the establishment of the Greer Industries Inc. joint venture in New York in 1954, in which both partners participated with equal shares, for the manufacture of *Vulkollan* polyurethane products. Initially, these consisted predominantly of hydraulic bladders, seals and molded parts for the automotive industry. The first production plant began operations in the same year, and the new product line was given the name *Disogrin*.²³⁵ That was the beginning of the development of the company's own seal production in North America, which however did not go as smoothly as had been envisaged. There were high reject rates in production because of technical difficulties in processing the polyurethane. The losses accumulated to such an extent that Greer soon lost interest in the joint venture. Freudenberg on the other hand was convinced of the prospects for success and acquired all the shares in 1957. The company was renamed Disogrin Industries Corp.[236] This demonstrates Freudenberg's strong long-term orientation – what is known as family enterprises' long-haul focus.

However, the company initially continued to have technical difficulties. As a result, Disogrin was legally integrated into the Pellon Corporation, Freudenberg's American nonwovens subsidiary, in 1961, to make Disogrin financially secure. Then success finally came: In 1964, US corporation Caterpillar, the leading manufacturer of large construction machinery on the world market, fitted Disogrin hydraulic seals for the first time, evidently to their greatest satisfaction. Within a short time, Caterpillar became their principal customer. Disogrin also gradually developed to become the leading seals supplier to other hydraulic customers too. In addition, the product portfolio was expanded, so that in 1968 it comprised polyurethane seals, predominantly for the hydraulic and pneumatic sector, highly abrasion-resistant molded parts and PU wheels for industrial trucks.[237]

The growing sealing business – turnover had climbed above the 50 million deutschmarks level for the first time in 1957 – soon required expansion investments to be made. Capacities in the rubber mixing plant (mixing plant) in the Buna plant of the Old Lacquering Factory were doubled up to 1959. In addition, production of fluororubbers had begun, and while these displayed high temperature resistance, they were nonetheless difficult to process.[238]

Meanwhile, for Freudenberg, expansion also continued in other European countries as well. This had been intrinsically facilitated by the 1957 Treaty of Rome, the foundation of the European Economic Community and the simplification of European collaboration.[239] In Italy, there had been a partnership already anyway since 1936 with the Corte & Cosso company. The joint venture with the Cosso family was expanded rapidly under the name Corcos and can be regarded today virtually as a blueprint for subsequent internationalization activities, because it was based on a long-term collaboration – and a really friendly partnership in difficult times.

It is worth taking a separate look at this. In 1936, a licensing agreement was signed with the Corte & Cosso company in Turin for the production of Simmerrings in Italy.[240] The collaboration was interrupted for a short time towards the end of World War II, but it revived again quickly after the end of the war in 1945. Italian co-owner Francesco Corte died in 1955. This led to a change in responsibilities. Ludovico Cosso became the sole General Manager of the Corte & Cosso firm. His son Mario took over the technical management of the plant in Pinerolo. Giuseppe Corte (1930–1970), son of the late Francesco Corte, on the other hand managed the commercial business in Turin.[241]

Fig. 78 The management of the Corcos firm on a visit to Weinheim, 1985: Dario Debernardi, Maria Cosso-Eynard, Siegfried Hinz (Freudenberg Management Board), Franz Vogel (from left)

In 1957, Freudenberg and Corte & Cosso intensified their collaboration and established the Corcos S. A. S. joint venture, headquartered in Turin, on July 15 of the same year, for the manufacture of seals for the Italian market. At the same time, a new production building was erected in the city of Pinerolo. Corte & Cosso contributed the lion's share of the financial resources to the joint venture, Freudenberg provided the machinery, tools and the expertise in return. Corcos took on sole representation for Freudenberg seals throughout Italy. Ludovico Cosso became the sole General Manager of Corcos.[242] Turnover and profits developed positively.[243]

However, this spirit of optimism was marred by a tragedy in Italy: On their return trip from a trade fair in Milan in 1960, Ludovico and Mario Cosso were killed in an accident. This necessarily caused consequences under company law: Thus Ludovico Cosso's shares in the business were transferred to the Corte & Cosso company. As a result, Freudenberg and Corte & Cosso each held 50 percent of the shares in the Corcos joint venture now. Giuseppe Corte and Hans Pekar took over the management board. Hans Pekar had already been seconded by Freudenberg to Italy as an engineer in 1957 and was responsible for technology from then on.[244]

Maria Luisa Cosso, Ludovico Cosso's daughter, became sole heiress of the Cosso family's shares. At that time, she was 22 years old and studying to be a teacher, and had no intention of joining her father's business. Nonetheless, she felt a strong duty towards her heritage and took on commercial responsibility.[245] "However, she had great reservations as to whether she – being unfamiliar with business and technical issues – should and could take such immense responsibility for the company upon herself. In the meantime, the company was coming under additional stress from the fact that other companies were attempting to poach the trained workers, and rumors were being spread in Pinerolo that after the tragic death of the general manager and his son, the company could probably no longer be retained. Thus it was important for Maria Luisa Cosso to join the company and document the continuity outwardly."[246]

During this phase, Richard Freudenberg – influenced by his own experiences when he joined his father's company during World War I – became her mentor. Since he believed that she could rise to the challenge, he encouraged Maria Luisa Cosso to assume responsibility for the company. And she did, by initially letting herself be trained by her employees in the factory at every workstation, to learn the technology. The side-effect was that the workforce developed confidence in her management qualities and not one employee left the company. Afterwards, the management board of the joint venture was reorganized. Giuseppe Corte took over sales and customer support, Maria Luisa Cosso procurement, personnel, marketing as well as business management, and Hans Pekar management of production.[247]

The company continued to thrive, and employee numbers rose significantly – from 16 employees in 1957 to 213 in 1970. Turnover climbed from 200 million lira [the Italian currency at the time – ed.] in 1959 to 1.1 billion lira in 1970.[248]

Entry into the vibration control technology segment

The intensive economic and technological structural change of the postwar era, with the weaknesses in the leather industry and the booming sealing technology, prompted the Management Board to keep a very close eye on the changing markets as well as to rapidly examine technological business opportunities and seize them where appropriate. Consequently, the potential of a field of application closely related to sealing technology, vibration control technology, grabbed Hans and Richard Freudenberg's attention as early as the mid-1950s. This technology evidently showed great promise, since technological development in automotive and mechanical engineering was increasingly determined by striving for greater performance and higher speeds. This was also accompanied by higher revolutions and lighter machine design, which led to increased vibration behavior in motors and machines, which could ultimately result in the failure of important components. The solution to this problem was and is fitting vibration control technology components.[249] Thus initial talks began in 1955 about a potential collaboration between Freudenberg and Metalastik Limited, a British vibration control technology manufacturer based in Leicester (England).[250] Its general manager, engineer Mac Goldsmith, who had worked in vibration technology at Phoenix in Hamburg until he emigrated in 1937, had built up a company of this type in Leicester. He got to know Richard Freudenberg through Professor Nallinger, the head of technical development at Daimler-Benz, and, as he wrote to Hans Freudenberg, was highly interested in a collaboration:[251]

> "Dear Mr. Freudenberg, two weeks ago I had the pleasure of meeting your brother, Richard in Vulpera through our mutual friend Professor Nallinger. As we are being requested by various Motor Car Manufacturers to extend our activities to Germany, I discussed this matter with your brother and he suggested to send you some literature of our products. [...] It is quite possible that we might be interested in some of your developments in other fields, such as rubber soles and Vulkollan components, for our other Companies [...]."[252]

Mac Goldsmith was obviously interested in collaborating with Freudenberg, and the people in Weinheim listened to him attentively. And Freudenberg did indeed acquire a license for vibration control technology components from Metalastik Limited in 1957. The agreement initially ran for a five-year term. Different percentage rates of licensing fees were stipulated in the licensing agreement for the products' various areas of application (in automotive engineering, rail vehicles or in general mechanical engineering). In Weinheim, the Metalastik department was established.[253] And shock absorbers, vibration dampers and ultrabrushings were now being manufactured under the name Metalastik.[254] Peter Wentzler (1924–2001), a member of the Management Board and son-in-law of Richard Freudenberg, was responsible for the management of Metalastik from 1959 up to 1972.[255] In the same year, the long-standing Simrit employee Heinz Stober (1913–2003)[256] took over management of operations in the Metalastik department, and he was responsible for this up to 1977.[257]

At the beginning, there were difficulties in setting up the Metalastik production process. "Since no one had experience, the production plants were purchased and set up following the English instructions to the letter. [...] Initially,

Fig. 79 Production of ultra bushings, 1979

because of our own lack of experience with rubber-metal elements for vibration insulation and dampening, English prospectuses were translated and potential customers were approached. It thereby emerged very quickly that despite the immense preliminary work and encouragement from the automotive industry, it was by no means easy to gain a foothold in the market. On the contrary, Metalastik was immediately faced with a full barrage of competitive pressure and had to first prove its capability."[258]

It was not until 1962 that a specialized development department was set up. Under the management of Klaus Kurr (1931–2022), the technical problems were solved. With the ensuing development of vulcanized torsional vibration dampers, initially for truck engines and a little later for car engines, and the start of production shortly afterwards, business was now booming.[259] In 1967, turnover was 10 million deutschmarks and profits were thus – ten years after the licensing agreement was inked – at break-even point for the first time.[260]

The further development of the Nora segment: the first rubber floorcoverings and more and more rubber shoe soles

The constant search for expansion and improvement opportunities in the area of rubber processing did not just affect the sealing and vibration technology sector at Freudenberg, but also the *Nora* plant.[261] After large-scale manufacturing of *Nora* soles had already been running since 1938,[262] production of "Noraplast" shoes made of pressed soft PVC began in 1948.[263] Then, two years later, the "Noraplan" rubber floorcovering came onto the market, and Freudenberg had entered the floorcoverings business. The first *Nora* floors were laid in schools, public buildings, hospitals, hotels, movie theaters, theaters, but also in private homes.[264] However, the novel rubber floorcovering, although well received in the market, was not spared from teething problems. The technical problems were only solved for good in 1952 by the close collaboration of laboratory and sales departments coordinated by the head of the *Nora* plant, Heinz Hoppe (1917–1994).[265] From 1955 onward, *Nora* press-molded soft PVC boots were manufactured.[266]

However, the rubber technology repeatedly presented the company with new challenges. In this context, one occurrence from the early years of the *Nora* plant has left a lasting impression: that of November 1, 1957. On that day, at noon, the plant fire alarm was initially set off,[267] then, because of the very strong formation of smoke in the rubber warehouse concerned (building 51) – which burned down completely as a result – the major alarm was sounded. Since the plant fire brigade was unable to get the fire under control, despite its very rapidly initiated action, the fire brigade in Weinheim and the plant fire brigade in the *Naturin* plant were initially called in to help. Soon afterwards, the Heppenheim city fire brigade, the Mannheim professional fire brigade and the plant fire brigade of the Total company in Ladenburg were additionally called in for support. The fire very quickly spread to the adjacent building 44a, which was also completely destroyed. Because of the strong heat and flying sparks, the roof of a further building on the opposite side of the street caught fire (building 42) and its top floor was completely gutted. In total, around 1,000 square meters of the plant premises was ablaze.[268] During the fire-fighting offensive, which was conducted from all directions, water was predominantly used – initially from the water supply on the plant premises, later by extraction from the Weschnitz river. After the building 51 warehouse collapsed, the Total plant fire brigade started using foam to extinguish the building fires. At 2.30 pm, the major fire, which had intermittently threatened to spread to numerous neighboring buildings, was under control. The main laboratory at the time and parts of the leather factory were particularly endangered.[269]

Building 51 was particularly badly affected. It burned down completely. This was the *Nora* plant's raw material warehouse for shoe sole manufacturing.[270] Additionally, buildings 44a (completely gutted) and 42 (top floor burned out) were affected.[271] Despite prosecutorial and criminal investigations, the cause of the fire could not be determined. However, it is very likely that the fire was triggered by the self-ignition of what were known as batch dolls (batch = the premix of rubber and various filler materials) which were manufactured by the night shift (shift ended at 6 am) in the adjacent regeneration plant building.[272]

An interesting secondary aspect of the prosecutorial investigations of the cause of the fire comes from the circumstance that the public prosecutors first of all had initiated investigation proceedings against the plant manager of the *Nora* plant, Helmut Stepf (1912–1962)[273] and the safety engineer who was in charge, Platz, for allegedly neglecting their duty of care. When Hans and Richard Freudenberg found out about the investigation, their reaction was clear: They declared to the public prosecutors, "that it is not acceptable to indict Mr. Stepf as operations manager of the *Nora* plant and Mr. Platz as safety engineer, because the responsibility for it lies solely with Messrs. Hans Freudenberg and Richard Freudenberg."[274] The proceedings were dropped in March 1958, since the allegations of the public prosecutor's office were refuted or rather proved to be untenable.[275] Despite the considerable damage – apart from the buildings, an entire month's production supply of rubber for the *Nora* plant had also fallen victim to the flames – production could start up again already the next day, since only a few of the machines had been damaged. The loss amount came to 4 million deutschmarks, which would correspond to around 10.6 million euros today.[276]

Then, in 1960, production began of *Nora* PVC shoes and PVC boots using an injection molding technique developed by Freudenberg.[277] Finally, the Norament flooring with a pastille surface was developed and launched on the market in 1967.[278] The first major project was the new airport in Frankfurt am Main, where around 80,000 square meters of Norament flooring were laid between the years 1969 and 1972.[279]

Nora was also able to benefit from a significant shift in demand in the area of shoe manufacturing. From the 1950s onward, the bottom leather for shoe soles was increasingly replaced by rubber or alternatively rubber materials. The displacement process took place at breakneck speed: By the end of the 1960s, the leather sole had largely been squeezed out of the market. This can be accordingly seen from the figures: Of the entire production of shoe soles in Germany, the

Fig. 80 Calender line for Nora floorcoverings, 1964

share accounted for by rubber soles changed from 54.4 percent in 1952 through 77.6 percent in 1960 to 80.5 percent in 1968. The reasons for the triumph of the rubber sole are easy to comprehend: They were easier to adapt to fashion developments, and they were very suitable for light footwear as well as particularly for sports, children's and adolescents' shoes. There was also the fact of the higher cost-effectiveness in producing the soles. During the same timeframe, the *Nora* sole's market-leading position expanded accordingly: The market share of German rubber sole sales volume held by *Nora* soles grew from 19.4 percent in 1954 through 30.3 percent in 1960 to 37.5 percent in 1968.[280]

Environmental commitment in South America: Forestry and timber businesses in Brazil

At the end of the 1950s, Freudenberg directed its attention again to the American continent: this time to South America. The next stage of internationalization took place in Brazil in 1958, which at the same time also expanded the product portfolio and thus constituted a further step in diversification for Freudenberg: In Brazil, Freudenberg set up its first production plant. In Agudos, a former coffee plantation was acquired and reforested. Subsequently, a timber-processing plant was set up to manufacture chipboard and veneers. The key trigger for Freudenberg's unusual forestry investment can be found the previous year: On a flight to the United States, Richard Freudenberg made the acquaintance of the previous head of the UNO Forestry Commission for South America, Graf von der Recke. This latter aroused Richard Freudenberg's interest in Brazil's new, ecologically oriented reforestation program and recommended contacting forester Horst Schuckar in São Paulo.[281] When deciding in favor of a financial commitment in Brazil, one of the factors that played a role for Richard Freudenberg was the fact that he wanted to spread the business risk further geographically too and was searching for an investment far away from the East-West conflict. In the following year, Freudenberg already purchased a fallow coffee plantation in Agudos in the state of São Paulo at Schuckar's suggestion. The site, which was only reachable on unpaved roads, was situated 325 kilometers from the state capital and was expanded to include further reforestation areas up to 11,000 hectares in the following years.[282]

The project had a pioneering character for Brazil in two aspects: While the native Brazilian timber industry up to now had generally practiced the overexploitation of naturally growing araucaria trees, Freudenberg's investment already aimed at that time at an ecologically sustainable and long-term usable reforestation which is highly modern today. Just how unusual this approach was is evident from a later report from Richard Freudenberg:

> "When we intimated to the 'Instituto Nacional do Pinho' that we planned to conduct the first clear cuttings of 30–50 cm strong trees [...] at 17-year intervals, they shook their heads incredulously, since they had no experience at all regarding the quality of the wood and during our discussion had assumed that we wanted to practice overexploitation after a 17-year turnaround time to make money quickly."[283]

The settlement, which was established under the name Companhia Agro Florestal Monte Alegre Ltd. (CAFMA) also received an exemplary infrastructure, with company housing, a school, an outpatient medical clinic, a company kitchen, a chapel and a small zoological museum for the schoolchildren. The workers and their families received information about the flora and fauna of the region through the plant's own newspaper, *Cafmanchete,* and they could use this medium to discuss their own concerns as well.[284]

Around 1965, the forested areas had grown sufficiently to enable the first logging to begin. This was linked to considerations about how the anticipated volumes should be further processed, for example for manufacturing furniture or paper.²⁸⁵ Some tests that had been commissioned demonstrated the suitability of the Freudenberg timbers as a basis for paper pulps too.²⁸⁶ Nevertheless, Richard Freudenberg decided to use the chips and waste wood to manufacture chipboard, which was still relatively unknown in Brazil. Freudenberg Industrias Madeireiras (FIM) was established in 1965 for processing the timber, initially with a sawmill, then a chipboard factory followed. To celebrate the expansion of this plant, Richard Freudenberg and Helmut Fabricius traveled there in person in 1972 and were received in a highly official capacity by the local authorities.²⁸⁷ As the diameter of the trunks increased, they were also able to begin production of veneers. "Thus a company developed in Agudos that was regarded for good reason by the sector as a model for forestry and processing technology."²⁸⁸

The forestry and timber factories remained in the Freudenberg portfolio right up to the end of the 1980s, but were also considered rather an anomaly, however. A change in corporate strategy in the form of concentration on Freudenberg's core competencies and at the same time the increasing pressure to consolidate in the Brazilian timber business finally led to the sale of both companies in 1988. The companies were sold to Brazil's largest timber processing company, Duratex S. A.²⁸⁹

In a message to the management executives dated September 1988, the step was explained by the lack of connection to Freudenberg's other business and general market developments: The forestry and timber businesses in Brazil "only played a limited role in the Group's global strategy up to now; there were no synergies with other Freudenberg divisions. On the other hand, despite our high capital investment, our two timber firms are too small to be able to conduct an independent market policy in the long term in light of the trend towards concentration that has been observable for several years in the Brazilian timber processing industry. Under the current circumstances, it appears to make sense to give up our commitment in the timber industry and instead boost the Group's other Brazilian companies […] in their activities and finance them accordingly in their future tasks."²⁹⁰

New generation on the Management Board

Up to 1959, the Management Board was heavily oriented towards the senior managers Richard and Hans Freudenberg, but particularly to Richard Freudenberg. Hans Erich Freudenberg, who had moved up to the Management Board in 1949 along with Helmut Fabricius, had himself pointed out "the informal hierarchization between the generations;" he described "the time on the Management

Board up to the retirement"²⁹¹ of "Hans Freudenberg and the joining of five further successors from the fourth generation as the 'era of the two', although there were actually four."²⁹²

The situation was comparable to "the previous entrepreneurial succession."²⁹³ "Even back then, as long as the patriarchal senior was in the company, the relevant decisions were dependent on him. Even if the various generations shared the Management Board positions, the entrepreneurial control had not really been passed on to the successors."²⁹⁴

However, in light of the advancing diversification and internationalization, because of the strong growth of the company and the associated complexity as well as the scientizing of research and company management, this could not continue like this. Therefore, things changed with the simultaneous admission of five further family members to the Management Board in 1959. After the "era of the two", the "era of the seven" now began.²⁹⁵ To make things just a little more complicated, however, there were actually eight initially: Richard Freudenberg only left the company three years later, in 1962.

Alongside Helmut Fabricius and Hans Erich Freudenberg, who were already active on the Management Board, these were Dieter and Hermann Freudenberg, the sons of Otto and Adolf Freudenberg, who have been introduced here already; Kurt Kraft (1907–1996), Karl Johann Freudenberg's son-in-law; Otto Schildhauer (1912–1987), Hans Freudenberg's son-in-law; and Peter Wentzler, Richard Freudenberg's son-in-law, who has also been mentioned already.²⁹⁶ Thus it was no longer only members of the family from a direct line of descent who now assumed responsibility, but also family members' husbands who had the relevant suitability. At that time, non-family members were not foreseen for positions on the Management Board.

Dieter Freudenberg was the first member of the fourth generation to join the company for the first time after World War II. He was appointed as a general partner together with the other new appointees in 1959. From that time, his main responsibilities were leather procurement and the *Nora* division.²⁹⁷

Hermann Freudenberg was likewise appointed as a general partner in 1959. As a result, he then assumed responsibility for the entire leather business.²⁹⁸

Otto Schildhauer had joined the company in 1945 as a tanner's apprentice. He worked from 1947 onward in the Schönau factory, whose management he took over two years later as plant manager.²⁹⁹ In 1956, he became the successor to Heinz Hoppe, who had left the company in 1954, as head of the *Nora* plant in Weinheim. At the same time, he took over management of the plant and fire protection, and then later also the entire logistics area and central technology. In the sources, Schildhauer is described as a man with great technical talent. Af-

Fig. 81 The Management Board, 1962: Helmut Fabricius, Hermann Freudenberg, Kurt Kraft, Dieter Freudenberg, Peter Wentzler with his son Henrik, Hans Erich Freudenberg and Otto Schildhauer (from left)

ter taking his high school leaving examination (*Abitur*) he completed a bank apprenticeship[300] and contributed management experience as a former officer in the *Wehrmacht*. "The fact that he, in contrast to Dieter Freudenberg, was able to assume an executive function so soon after joining the company can likely also be explained by his advanced age. After all, Hans Erich Freudenberg and Helmut Fabricius, who were approximately the same age, were already appointed as general partners in the same year, while Dieter Freudenberg, who was only just 23 years old, was still sent around the world for further training."[301]

They were also joined by Kurt Kraft, as well as by the likewise previously mentioned Peter Wentzler. Closer contact had developed between the Freudenberg and Wentzler families through Dieter Freudenberg. Peter Wentzler himself came from a family of tanners and had joined the company in 1949, where he initially took over responsibility for raw material procurement in the leather business after Walter Freudenberg's retirement. In 1950, he married Ursula Sibille Freudenberg, Richard Freudenberg's daughter. "Thus the young Wentzler soon received great responsibility when he joined the company."[302] In 1959, he was appointed to the Management Board as a general partner.[303]

Kurt Kraft was a "lateral entrant": Kraft, who had grown up in Nuremberg, had completed various stages of his chemistry studies in Heidelberg, Berlin and

Munich.³⁰⁴ He obtained his doctorate and qualified as a professor. His first employer was the Knoll AG pharmaceutical company in Ludwigshafen. There, his field of activity was research; however, Kraft had also been working since 1942 as a lecturer at the University of Heidelberg. This aspect of his resume is decisive, because this enabled Kraft to become a colleague of Karl Johann Freudenberg, who had held a chair there since 1926. Thus it transpired that Kraft met Karl Johann Freudenberg's daughter in the midst of the war; it was not long before the wedding followed. But he was also making progress in his career: He had had the opportunity to gain management experience on the management board of Knoll AG since 1947. In addition, Kraft received a full professorship in Heidelberg in 1953.³⁰⁵

"In the 1950s […], when […] the diversification of the company continued successfully and particularly the nonwovens technology became a promising business area," members of the Management Board had obviously already regarded the experienced manager and chemist as the right person for the expansion and further development of the nonwovens business. He initially familiarized himself for one year by working in various technical departments of the company before he took over management of the nonwovens division within the Management Board in 1959.³⁰⁶

Thus Dieter Freudenberg, Hermann Freudenberg, Otto Schildhauer, Peter Wentzler and Kurt Kraft were the ones who were newly appointed as general partners and directors in 1959.³⁰⁷ Indeed, Hans Erich Freudenberg and Helmut Fabricius had already been active on the Management Board since 1949 – in total, therefore, seven sons and sons-in-law from the fourth generation of the owner family had moved up to the top management.

In the previous year, Hans Freudenberg had turned 70. "He retired from the company in accordance with the statutes and took over as chairman of the Board of Partners, until finally Richard Freudenberg also retired from the Management Board in accordance with the statutes in 1962, likewise moved to the supervisory body and took over its management."³⁰⁸

Heinz Hoppe and Freudenberg

The appointment of non-family members to the Management Board was not yet foreseen. This makes it interesting to take a look at Heinz Hoppe – who has only been mentioned in passing up to now – who left the company for this reason, made a career at Daimler-Benz, and later returned to Weinheim in a key position. Hoppe, who was born in East Prussia [now Russian and Polish territories – ed.], had come to Heidelberg with his family after the end of World War II. In Heidelberg the former officer, who was looking for a job, met Hans Freudenberg through his parents-in-law. During a walk together, Hans Freudenberg asked him about his career to date and what he could do. Hoppe's response: "I cannot do anything. The only thing that I can do, or so I believe is this: I can learn something."[309] This answer had evidently impressed Hans Freudenberg, because he immediately offered him a job at Freudenberg in Weinheim, where Hoppe began working on January 2, 1946.[310]

Fig. 82 Heinz Hoppe, 1973. Source: Mercedes-Archiv

This led him initially for three months to the bookkeeping department, and afterwards he gained some insight into the various production areas – as a normal production employee. His path led him through the tannery, the Simrit-Werk plant and the shoe factory to the *Nora* plant. There he got to know all the *Nora* production areas as well as the associated laboratory, and all aspects of them at that, within one year. Because at the start, he was working as a so-called "*Rußnickel*" (sooty nickel – a 10 Pfennig coin), where he took on the job of weighing in the soot for the rubber mixtures in the mixing plant – an extremely dirty activity, hence the "term of endearment". Two of Heinz Hoppe's "*Rußnickel*" colleagues back then were Hermann and Dieter Freudenberg. Thus they had got to know and appreciate each other at an early stage.

After this basic practical training in the *Nora* plant, Hoppe was posted by Hans Freudenberg, who had become his mentor, for six months to the "Bayer (Leverkusen) company's central rubber laboratory," to learn the basics of rubber chemistry there and to prepare him for his future management task. After he returned to Weinheim, he was then assigned the management of the *Nora* plant at the end of 1947. In his new function, he visited the leading rubber processing companies in the United States and from this trip he brought back with him the impetus for a fundamental modernization of the *Nora* plant at the beginning of the 1950s, which considerably improves productivity and quality following its implementation.[311] Hermann Freudenberg acknowledged this in his obituary for

Heinz Hoppe in 1994 as follows: "Thus he laid the foundation for the modern plant we have today."[312]

But despite his successes and considerable esteem within the Freudenberg family, he did not see the right chances for advancement for himself within the company. This was mainly due to the fact that "qualified family members were just joining the company, such that the chances for managerial positions were inevitably slim." The managerial position that Heinz Hoppe had in mind was appointment to the Management Board. In the 1950s, this path still remained closed to him. When a corresponding career opportunity was then offered to him at Daimler-Benz, Heinz Hoppe decided to leave Freudenberg and take up his job at Daimler-Benz, where he ultimately rose up the ranks as far as the management board. Heinz Hoppe's memories of this time demonstrate that he did this with a heavy heart: "The departure from Freudenberg at that time was one of my most difficult and for me personally one of the most momentous decisions."[313]

However, he still kept up contact with Weinheim.[314] Hermann and Dieter Freudenberg described their relationship to Heinz Hoppe as follows at the celebration to mark his 65th birthday: "We would [...] also like to express that we count you among the good friends of our family. We know that both Hans and Richard Freudenberg felt very attached to you."[315] Thus it was also no problem to select Heinz Hoppe to participate on the Board of Partners of the Freudenberg Group in 1982, of which he was a member until 1990.[316]

After he was elected to the Board of Partners on April 24, 1982 he contributed "his immense industrial experience and manifold contacts."[317] This also explains why Heinz Hoppe up to now has been the first and only non-family member to hold the post of Chairman of the Board of Partners. He took over the position in 1983 as successor to Helmut Fabricius and retained the chairmanship up to 1988. When Hermann Freudenberg moved from the Management Board to the Board of Partners, Hoppe passed on the chairmanship to Hermann Freudenberg.[318] This was a matter of course for him, not least because of his close relationship with the Freudenberg family, and precisely also because he had "successfully executed [this office] supported by the absolute trust of all the partners."[319]

Hans Freudenberg and education

Hans Freudenberg, the person who "discovered" Hoppe, realized at a very early stage that for many young people, the transition from school to working life – whether as an apprentice or as a so-called "young worker" – was not easy, since at the age of usually 14 years old, they were frequently not mature enough for working life. For that reason, he set up what was known as the transition school for apprentices and young workers at Freudenberg in 1950. Freudenberg thus adopted a pioneering role in postwar Germany with regard to the vocational preparation of adolescents. Thus the adolescents already received a few weeks of special lessons before their real entry into working life, which were designed to make the transition from school to job easier for them. Like the apprentices' workshop, the transition school at Freudenberg also exists up to the present day.[320] After the end of World War II, many young people were faced with the problem that their fathers had fallen in the war or were missing in action and their families were therefore dependent on their additional earnings. Thus many of these adolescents did not try to find an apprenticeship, but joined Freudenberg as untrained young workers, and thus as job entrants who were not doing a traineeship but were integrated directly into the production process. Hans Freudenberg therefore developed the idea of systematic support for the young workers. They were sent to the transition school with the apprentices, and they received basic training in a craft in the apprentices' workshop. On top of this, they were assigned a supervisor within the company. These supervisors were trained to recognize the adolescents' hidden talents. Frequently, the young workers could be offered apprenticeship contracts after a probation period, of which many young workers took advantage: Of those who finished school

Fig. 83 Hans Freudenberg with apprentices, 1955

in 1957, 30 percent switched to an apprenticeship, which significantly improved their career prospects. Driven by this idea and the positive experience from it, Hans Freudenberg developed the idea of a gifted youth program in 1954.[321] The question that was driving him was: "Why does our education system not provide for more gifted young people to be able to attend high school or university?"[322]

Initially, four apprentices were selected who had distinguished themselves through particularly good performance in the apprentices' workshop. They were set to take their high school leaving examination (*Abitur*) that qualifies for university as Freudenberg scholarship recipients. After all four had passed this successfully, a systematic support program for gifted youths was launched. Through financial support, this enabled gifted Freudenberg apprentices with primary or secondary school leaving certificates to go through to general matriculation standard (*Abitur*) and beyond this to study at university. In 1958, the gifted youth support was transferred to the Heiner and Walter Freudenberg Foundation,[323] which was established by Hans Freudenberg to mark his 70th birthday.[324]

Various secondary schools from the region participated in providing education up to *Abitur*.[325] The gifted youth support was not discontinued until 1978 when the Federal Training Assistance Act (BaföG) came into effect.[326] Throughout the entire lifetime of the foundation, 145 people were supported. Thus 110 young workers and apprentices as well as 35 scholarship recipients outside the company were able to achieve a better school-leaving qualification and in some cases complete a course of study.[327]

Over and above this, Hans Freudenberg's talent support ultimately led to his involvement in education policy. On his initiative, the Ettlingen Circle was founded in 1957.[328] The Ettlingen Circle, in which Hans Freudenberg was the driving force, constituted an association of German industrialists and leading educationalists and educational reformers, to whom alongside Hans Freudenberg further renowned entrepreneurs belonged, like Robert Bosch, Ernst Böhringer and Hanns Voith.[329] In the Ettlingen Circle the educational reforms that were needed were discussed and demands formulated accordingly to politicians. The most important demands of the Ettlingen Circle, which were implemented by politicians and already formulated in May 1957 as "proposals to ameliorate the emergencies in education and training," were:[330]

1. Introduction of a 9th obligatory school year.
2. Introduction of a 10th school year in middle school (*Realschule*).
3. Offering a foreign language from the 5th school year.
4. Inclusion of craft workers' activities.
5. Interchangeability of the types of schools among each other.

6. Establishment of countrywide gifted student support which was not restricted to universities.
7. Promotion of the so-called second-chance education (*Zweiter Bildungsweg*), which allowed people already working to gain access to attain general matriculation standard (*Abitur*).[331]

As an engineer, Hans Freudenberg was always open to innovation. This openness, combined with his efforts to promote young talent in the company, make him a pioneer of today's talent promotion and talent management – and not just at Freudenberg.[332]

In 1964, Hans Freudenberg retired from the *Ettlingen Circle* and handed over the organization of the meetings to his nephew, Hermann Freudenberg, for whom educating youth was also a main concern. Finally, the *Ettlingen Circle* was dissolved in 1977. It was integrated into the *Ettlinger Gespräche Foundation* in the Stifterverband der Deutschen Wirtschaft, to which Hermann Freudenberg continued to belong as a member.[333]

From the start, the work of the *Ettlingen Circle* was determined by two leading questions. Firstly: Are the existing educational reserves being utilized sufficiently by the education system? Secondly: What contribution does the education system make to the process of social differentiation? These were also the formative questions of the later educational reforms in Germany. The *Ettlingen Circle* always pursued the objective "of social modernization." This focused equally on both the economic concerns as well as the social and societal dimension. That made it an important source of inspiration for German education policy.[334]

Era of full employment: Internationalization of the workforce in Weinheim

At the end of the 1950s, the German economy was experiencing a new spring in the wake of the economic miracle. After the many periods of unemployment which people had had to get through between 1918 and 1953, for the first time in the 20th century, there were now too few workers. It was the era of full employment. Everywhere in the Federal Republic, people were looking for workers from the rest of Europe. At Freudenberg the plan was to initially only recruit employees from one single country, and it chose Spain. The first recruitment campaign took place in 1960 in the province of Alicante. On September 4, 1960, 104 Spaniards with job

Fig. 84 Spanish guest workers on their way home for Christmas, 1966

contracts joined the company; in October 110 more arrived, and in December a further 62 Spanish employees.³³⁵

The company built a hostel at the northern end of the Zwischen Dämmen plant site, on Langmaasweg, where initially 260 workers could live at modest cost. Soon, this accommodation was no longer adequate. The Gasthaus zum Storchen inn was converted into a hostel in 1963 (65 beds). In Birkenau, the Cornelius-Heim building was converted for the workers.³³⁶ The men soon moved their families to be with them; many remained in Weinheim. Hence the hostels disappeared again after around ten years, because the families found accommodation in regular apartments and houses. In some cases, they settled in so well that many no longer want to return home, and are meantime living in Weinheim in the second and third generation.

The new foreign workers were initially deployed in all production areas of Carl Freudenberg. Employment contracts did not follow until much later. To overcome the language barrier, an interpreter, Eduardo Forgass del Rio, was hired who carried out both interpreting activities as well as creating written notices (announcements, instructions) in Spanish in the hostels and in the production halls.³³⁷ The first workers from Spain were followed by others from Italy and then from Spain again: In 1961, a further 50 workers were recruited in the provinces of Badajoz and Caceres. At the end of 1961, there were 500 male and 114 female employees from Spain and Italy. In the same year, systematic foreign language lessons began for employees. At the same time, free German lessons were set up for the "guest workers" ("*Gastarbeiter*") who had been working at Freudenberg since 1960.³³⁸

In 1963, the first two Turkish employees arrived. At the beginning of 1963, Freudenberg employed a total of 814 foreign female (141) and male (673) workers. Among these, 654 came from Spain (108 women and 546 men).³³⁹ In 1970, foreign employees comprised a 22 percent share of the total workforce at Carl Freudenberg, which corresponded to 3,150 foreign workers. Among these,

1,600 came from Spain and 651 from Turkey. Gradually, the proportions among the nations began to shift.[340]

New partners in Japan

But Germany was not the only country experiencing a boom at the end of the 1950s and in the first half of the 1960s, Japan also underwent a true economic miracle after losing the war. The success of Japanese industry was based among other things on the accurate observation of new developments and trends around the globe. The effects this had on optics, consumer electronics and automotive engineering are well documented. It would therefore be astonishing if Japanese companies had not already given their full attention to the emerging nonwovens industry already in the 1950s.[341] On the other hand, Japanese industry was increasingly becoming an example that could be learned from with its peculiarities, especially in the areas of production organization, quality control and industrial relations. The transformation in Japanese industry from laggard to cooperation partner can also be observed from Freudenberg's virtually classic example.[342]

The unusual growth in Japanese industry after World War II prompted the Freudenberg management to develop the contacts that had only existed up to then as trade relations for leather. Hans Erich Freudenberg, the then Head of the Economics Department,[343] undertook a trip to Japan for several months in 1959 to examine the possibility of further contacts with Japanese industry.[344]

How this came to pass is also fascinating: The trigger for Hans Erich Freudenberg's trip to Japan for several months had been Shozo Iwakuma, a young chemist at Japan Reichold Co. This company was a joint venture for the production of finishing chemicals for the textiles industry. The shareholders were on the one hand Dainippon Ink Co., a company owned by the Kawamura family for the manufacture of printing inks, and on the other hand the American Reichold chemical corporation. Chemist Shozo Iwakuma had drawn Dainippon CEO Katsumi Kawamura's attention to nonwovens, and he also traveled to Germany in 1958 to forge contacts in this sector. Freudenberg was renowned as a manufacturer of high-quality nonwovens; thus Weinheim was naturally on the list of places to visit. Subsequently, Iwakuma urged Kawamura to propose to Freudenberg a partnership in Japan to manufacture nonwovens. This was how contact was established between Kawamura on the one side and Freudenberg on the other side. Katsumi Kawamura then visited Freudenberg in Weinheim himself in 1959. As a result of the negotiations, a preliminary contract was formulated which was signed in the same year in Zurich.[345]

The fleshed out preliminary contract was finalized in 1960 and approved by the responsible Japanese ministry (the M. I. T. I.). The company that was established in this way was called Japan Vilene Co. Ltd.,[346] and was headquartered in Tokyo. The partners were Dainippon Ink Co. with 38 percent, Freudenberg with 33 percent, Toyo Rayon Co. (later renamed Toray Co.) with 25 percent and K. Brasch & Co. with 4 percent of the shares.[347] Kurt Brasch, who gave his name to K. Brasch & Co., in his turn was a German-Japanese national and a major expert in Japan and its culture. All Freudenberg's contacts with the Japanese leather and shoe industry were already going through him and his company. He acted as a translator and contact between Freudenberg and the Japanese partners.[348]

The ministerial approval did not just authorize the transfer of future licensing payments; it also facilitated the import of goods manufactured in Germany to prepare the future business in Japan. In 1960, the Japanese market was virtually closed due to strict import controls on nonwovens. However, through the establishment of the Japan Vilene Company, it was opened up for Freudenberg nonwovens through the authorized licensing and shareholding agreement. The volume of goods set in motion in this way until the Japan Vilene Company's

Fig. 85 Opening of the Japan Vilene plant in Tokyo, 1972

own production was up and running amounted to several million square meters, which would never have reached the Japanese market in another way.³⁴⁹

Freudenberg took on the planning of the Japan Vilene Company factory in Shiga from Weinheim and the procurement of the machinery; the Kawamura Group provided the staff. The senior executives of the newly established Japan Vilene Company were trained in Weinheim from December 1960 to May 1961. The factory was built in the city of Moriyama on Lake Biwa in Shiga Prefecture, near Kyoto. Its new building was built on a concrete grate from the fall of 1960, to protect the building from earthquake damage. Assembly and start-up took place in accordance with the agreement under management from Weinheim, meaning that production of interlinings could already begin in Factory One in 1961.³⁵⁰

But nonwovens were not the only business that was doing well, because a very interesting collaboration opportunity emerged in Japan for Freudenberg and its partners in the area of seals too. On his 1959 trip, Hans Erich Freudenberg also became aware of the Nippon Oil Seal Industry Co. Ltd. (NOK), which already covered 80 percent of the Japanese automobile and machinery industry's seal requirements with a product portfolio similar to Freudenberg's.³⁵¹ Shogo Tsuru, the then Vice President of NOK,³⁵² displayed great interest in collaborating³⁵³ with Freudenberg and met with Hans Erich Freudenberg in the factory in Haneda near Tokyo.³⁵⁴

Fig. 86 Signing the partnership agreement between Freudenberg and NOK in Weinheim, 1960: Helmut Fabricius, Richard Freudenberg, Hans Erich Freudenberg, Shogo Tsuru, Kurt Brasch (from left)

Hans Erich Freudenberg described the meeting with Shogo Tsuru in retrospect as pleasant, noting that despite needing help from translators "we understood each other very well."[355] In a later travel report, he wrote: "The experiences with the companies associated with us show that personal contacts and a relationship of mutual trust are the cornerstones of collaboration. Human reliability and good will are everywhere. […] The assets and the sales volume in which we have a shareholding require an extraordinary degree of contact maintenance and constant interest. […] They don't just expect technical processes and investments from us, but also friendship, interest and constructive criticism which should characterize this close partnership."[356] The friendly relationships, particularly also between Richard Freudenberg and Shogo Tsuru, played a major role in the trusting collaboration.[357] It also says in the introductory sentence of the agreement: "A collaboration in a spirit of mutual sincerity and mutual trust has been established between the Carl Freudenberg company […] and the Nippon Oil Seal company […]."[358]

On his first visit, Hans Erich Freudenberg received an insight into the plant in Haneda and described the company's high standard for performance, but also the difficult production conditions with old machines and old buildings, however.[359] It was clear that both companies could profit from the collaboration. Before an agreement was reached, two top NOK technicians visited the plant in Weinheim to get to know the current technological status and the opportunities for NOK.[360]

The talks with the Japanese authorities continued for several months,[361] such that the Shogo Tsuru agreement was not signed in Weinheim until March 15, 1960. This agreement gave Freudenberg a 25 percent stake in NOK's share capital, and both companies pledged a constant exchange of experiences, technical processes and expertise for the manufacture of sealing elements.[362]

During a second visit in 1961, Hans Erich Freudenberg took part in one of the shareholders' meetings at NOK with around 80 shareholders, at which among other things the purpose of the association with a foreign partner was discussed. Shogo Tsuru's arguments in favor of the agreement were concentrated on three points: "ongoing consultation in the area of plastics and manufacturing development," "financing aid" and "development of new production lines apart from 'packings.'" These were expected to begin in three to five years. During this period, the aim was to double production to at least around 100 million deutschmarks in annual turnover and a certain degree of market saturation was expected up to this juncture.[363] Above and beyond the area of technology, topics like organization, leadership and quality systems were also included in the ongoing exchange of experience. Furthermore, a constant exchange of personnel already began in 1961 with a two-year training course for 20 Japanese employees from NOK in Weinheim.[364]

The partnership with the Japan Vilene Company also developed exceedingly positively, and because the Japanese clothing industry was going through a complete development phase at the time, the Japan Vilene Company quickly expanded into larger dimensions too. Factory One was followed by Factory Two on the same site in 1965, and was already supplemented by a third factory unit in 1967 on the same property, which was extended by land purchase. In Moriyama, 16 conventional plants, alongside specialized production plants, had now been built. In 1967, the hitherto unusual rapid growth, which the Japan Vilene Company incidentally shared with many areas of Japanese industry, particularly the textile sector, was extrapolated into the future, meaning that further expansion of production capacity was planned. Simply extending the manufacturing site in Moriyama was not considered advisable, thus the plan was for an additional factory in another province. This was based on various considerations, among other things the wish to have two production sites which were independent from one another. A large site was acquired in a new industrial zone in the Koga district, 60 kilometers north of Tokyo. The new factory, which was planned with generous proportions and equipped with abundant company apartments, was set to be used particularly for the manufacture of synthetic leather, a product that was seeing high levels of demand at that time.[365]

However, during the construction phase, the emerging economic stagnation was already becoming apparent which actually culminated in a recession in the Japanese textile industry that lasted for many years. This occurred precisely at a time when the capital expenditure of around 25 million deutschmarks could no longer be reduced significantly. Some machine orders were cancelled; however, the Japan Vilene Company could not be prevented from getting into a position where it was no longer able to earn back the sharply increased fixed costs, and it got into difficulties which lasted into the 1970s.[366]

The transition from Richard to Hermann Freudenberg

Richard Freudenberg's lifetime achievements are impressive: For 48 years, he played an active role in business operations at the company, and most of the time – across a total of four decades – he held the position of Speaker of the Management Board. This is continuity which has become unimaginable in the present day, at least in the vast majority of large companies. But even after he had resigned as a general partner and Speaker of the Management Board in 1962, after his 70th birthday, this did not constitute a final farewell. Instead, Richard Freudenberg still continued to help shape the development of the company even afterwards in his function of Chairman of the Board of Partners. One example of this is the acquisition of specialty lubricant manufacturer Klüber Lubrication, which will be elaborated on in greater detail at a later juncture. The special role which Richard Freudenberg played then is a development that remains remarkable to this day.

At Richard Freudenberg's birthday party on February 9, 1962 his brother Hans Freudenberg gave a speech in which he initially acknowledged his long years of service at the company. Then Hans went into more detail about Richard's forthcoming tasks on the Board of Partners: "As we have agreed, you will remain connected to the active management of the company by virtue of the fact that you will continue to chair the meetings of the general partners and various responsibilities, whether in Weinheim or companies affiliated with us, will remain directly within your purview. Above and beyond this, you will assume chairmanship of the Board of Partners of Freudenberg & Co."[367] As Hans Freudenberg likewise stated in his speech, it was stipulated in the version of the Freudenberg & Co. KG partnership agreement that was valid at the time, that as soon as "a general partner has reached the age of 65 years," he can then decide "whether he feels capable and is willing to continue to remain in the company as a general partner. Without the need for a separate declaration or a resolution of the general meeting, the general partners leave the company at the beginning of the financial year that follows the year they reached the age of 70." Since the financial year still ended on June 30 at that time, Richard Freudenberg therefore resigned as Speaker of the Management Board on June 30, 1962 and became Chairman of the Board of Partners as of July 1, 1962.[368]

However, in Richard Freudenberg's case, the company expressly wanted to ensure it continued to retain his expertise: Therefore, the general partners[369] and the Board of Partners[370] with its Chairman, Hans Freudenberg, resolved that the "senior boss" Richard Freudenberg should stay in the top echelon of the company, among other things through attendance at the meetings of the Management Board and taking on responsibility for business operations in specific areas of responsibility. This resolution is unusual. No other member of the Board of Partners – neither before nor after Richard Freudenberg's term of office – was ever granted such rights.[371] It can be determined from the surviving Management Board minutes[372] that Richard Freudenberg had indeed attended the monthly meetings of the Management Board, even after he had resigned as Chairman of the Board of Partners in 1972, up to the end of May 1975 – and therefore up to a short time before his death.[373]

After Richard Freudenberg had resigned from the Management Board in 1962, his nephew Hermann assumed the function of Speaker of the Board. His areas of operational responsibility additionally included: leather manufacturing, raw material procurement, plastics factory, *Helia* synthetic leather, human resources and staff welfare, cost distribution and computing.[374] In a document for the Management Board dated September 18, 1964 Richard described that Hermann Freudenberg had been appointed "as Speaker" to the workforce at his suggestion.[375]

Up to this transition, Richard himself had assumed a dominant role in the management of the company as Speaker of the Management Board because of his strong personality, but afterwards he drew back at the Management Board meetings to assume a more reserved and advisory function, as Hermann Freudenberg's report on the key outcomes of the Management Board meeting on July 12, 1972, for example, illustrates. This meeting dealt primarily with the situation in the leather division, which was increasingly coming under pressure: "Reinhart [Freudenberg] attended for the first time and was greeted by Uncle Richard as a new G. P. [general partner]. [...] Dieter [Freudenberg] began his fundamental remarks with an explanation of the income that could be expected in the Carl Freudenberg leather business for 1972, which he estimated, calculated by procurement, as a loss of between 9 and 9.5 mill. deutschmarks. [...] Errors which were made at the company in the past include the excessively strong focus on the shoe industry, the very limited activity in the direction of the leather goods industry, the complete exclusion of garment and furniture leather; overestimation of earnings opportunities in exports [...], the hectic pace of the market caused a hectic pace in sales (collection design!), too little contact with the business, many complaints because of defective production, poor use or lack of documents, excessively high total production costs, unsatisfactory supply capability." Directly afterwards, the measures already taken by Hermann Freudenberg were listed. At the end of the report, Hermann Freudenberg points out that Richard Freudenberg warned them "to be careful during the process conversions."[376]

Additionally, the Management Board minutes show that Richard was referred to time and again as "Uncle Richard" – because at this time, it was no longer only brothers and cousins on the Management Board who were directing the company, but also first and second cousins, as well as the cousins' husbands. And facing them alone stood their uncle, Richard Freudenberg – a family member from the third generation. Richard Freudenberg explained how he himself perceived the generational change in the Management Board in a speech at the general meeting on June 16, 1962 in Heidelberg:

"Both in 1961 and in particular in the first half of 1962, we continued to adjust the management of the company to the generational change. See how much better prepared and familiarized with their responsibilities the next generation is than we were on the sudden death of our father in 1923. I hope that the resolutions we have adopted prove to be good. We can be pleased that a well-trained team is standing ready that understands the concept of integration and that knows that everyone has to pull together. Since Hans and I have been placed at the center of attention so much in the past years, we know full well that we would have been unable to get our work done for a long time now without the circumspect and good cooperation of the men of the coming generation. You can really rest assured that even when Hans and I increasingly withdraw from the company because of age, nothing will change in the firm's line management. This certainty is another reason why we are envied by many."[377]

A further and visually more striking indication of Richard Freudenberg's special role can be found in the brochure *Carl Freudenberg – Informationen über das Unternehmen* from 1969, which gives an overview of the group. As Chairman of the Board of Partners, together with the seven members of the Management Board, Richard Freudenberg is still portrayed in the brochure as part of the company management – and in a clearly highlighted position (Fig. 87).[378]

Then, as Speaker of the Management Board, Hermann Freudenberg – under Richard's watchful eye – initiated remarkable change processes at the company. A professionalization in management style was accompanied at the same time by the introduction of transparent organizational structures and the early uptake of electronic data processing."[379]

After his 80th birthday, Richard Freudenberg then also resigned as Chairman of the Board of Partners at the end of the 1972 financial year on June 30. Kurt Kraft became his successor as of July 1, 1972.[380] However, Richard remained a member of the Board of Partners up to his death – but without a vote.[381] In this context, it is interesting to look at the speeches given by Kurt Kraft and Richard Freudenberg at the general meeting on April 15, 1972, at which the relevant changes were announced:

"Dear Uncle Richard, after you relinquish the chairmanship of the Board of Partners at the end of June, I would like to thank you [...] with all my heart for everything [...] that you have done for all of us, for the company and for the family during those long years. You took on a huge responsibility at a difficult time, while you were still very young, and you played a significant role in helping the factory, that was still more or less limited to leather in the [19]20s, to grow [...] into a global corporation today, and which has moreover also expanded into the most diverse areas. You yourself contrib-

Fig. 87 The Management Board, 1969[382]

uted a number of initiatives for this expansion. You always supported what had been suggested by others, and we are exceptionally grateful that you did not just go into great detail in all technical things, but also never forgot the company's direction overriding all this. Above and beyond this, you personally committed yourself for the company – I would almost like to say – day and night, for its concerns, but also for the people in the company, and collaborated up to now time and again, when key new appointments had to be made. Particularly at a time where the replacement of the older generation is being played out in front of us, the younger generation, you have set the course in an exemplary manner and achieved a smooth transition, and we would like to thank you sincerely for this, especially the general partners [...]."[383]

Richard found it hard to bid farewell, even though it was not a final farewell yet. He took the opportunity to make his stance very clear once again that concern about the company must always be placed above one's own interests:

"You will understand that after what will soon be 60 years, it is not easy for one to recede into the background completely. Because of the statutes, I will remain a member of the Board of Partners – as a guest, or however one wishes to put it. I hope that I will nonetheless still be able to help the further development of the company to a certain extent then. And I may say to you, the general partners and the members of the Board of Partners, [...] like in the past, for all the decisions that must be made, and I would like to ask you all to do this and [I would ask you] time and again for all time in the future: to think of the company first, and then of the company again, and only at intervals of yourselves."[384]

This was the end of the era of the third generation of the family in the management of the company. Hermann Freudenberg was now definitively the "first among equals" on the Management Board. Through the diversification it had initiated and the associated internationalization of production, the third generation had laid the foundation for today's global group of companies. The transition to the fourth generation that had now been finally completed occurred at a time of upheaval for the company: The traditional leather business was undergoing its most severe crisis since the foundation of the company. Above and beyond this, the sealing business was likewise coming under pressure because of the oil price crisis. This resulted in an interesting parallel: The third generation had also had to take over responsibility for the company in challenging times which were characterized by hyperinflation and the Great Depression. Now the crises and the complexity of the company required new management approaches and methods, for example in electronic data processing and organization, which were implemented rigorously by the fourth generation under Hermann Freudenberg's management.

Computing and modern business management

As mentioned, when Hermann Freudenberg joined the Management Board, one of the areas he assumed responsibility for was computing, which was set to become increasingly important for the company's success in the following decades. However, it would be erroneous to assume that Freudenberg was not using computing at all at the end of the 1950s – on the contrary: Freudenberg had actually addressed the issue at a very early stage. Thus punch card systems were introduced into the accounting department at Freudenberg at the turn of the year 1941/42 under Paul Vogler's management.[385] They had actually already been used in the 1930s at Tack, a subsidiary Freudenberg had acquired. Freudenberg's first contact, or rather that of subsidiary Tack, to the Deutsche Hollerith-Maschinen Gesellschaft mbH (Dehomag) can be traced back to 1933. Dehomag, which would later be subsumed into American company International Business Machines (IBM), was the manufacturer and lessor of electromechanical machines for handling and processing punch cards at the time. Based

Fig. 88 Computer center with IBM 7070 system in Weinheim, 1963

on surviving correspondence, it can be assumed that the punch card process was introduced at Tack in 1934.[386]

At the beginning of the 1950s, there was agreement among the Management Board at Freudenberg that the use of punch card systems needed to be expanded even further. Hans Erich Freudenberg could see the benefits clearly: The aim was to be able to put the working capital that was tied up to better use and more profitably in another area and for more valuable purposes; because the new machines contributed to being able to control inventory levels better – and accordingly reduce them to the bare minimum. Evidently Hans Erich Freudenberg regarded the greatest risk to be a lack of acceptance of the new opportunities in computing among his senior executives. He therefore urged them to utilize the numerical data that was made available to them profitably too.[387]

Thus the technology was highly interesting to the company. It could be used to increase transparency at a time where Freudenberg was experiencing strong growth – which would have been a much greater challenge still without taking advantage of the opportunities offered by technological progress in company management too.[388] Heinrich Karrer (1912–2000), who was largely responsible for the introduction of the computing systems at Freudenberg, likewise recalled the reasons for the further expansion of the department in a speech he held in 1967:

> "The driving force behind the leasing of the first data processing system was primarily the wish to separate the costs of the tannery from those costs that were produced by […] newly added businesses. The task comprised of recognizing these businesses in their cost structure and laying the foundation for a proper calculation. The speed and the new possibilities afforded by the punch card process accommodated these extensive tasks. In 1939, the first preparations were made and in 1942 the first system was leased."[389]

Karrer also explained what happened in the following 25 years: "Today, we look after 39 independent divisions with 440 cost units. Additional organizational tasks were passed on to us which become comprehensible because of growth in turnover from 179 mill. in 1952 to 563 mill. in 1966. It became necessary to penetrate increasingly deeper into the processes of our administration and our businesses and to utilize the new technologies to do this."[390] Karrer was, so to speak, a doyen of data processing, because he had already been responsible for the punch card systems even before the outbreak of World War II.[391] For him, this was about a lot more than just technology. Indeed, the introduction of these systems had considerable effects on operational processes right from the start. That is a phenomenon which has been retained regarding the introduction of new hardware or software at the company up to the present day: The right structures for the effective deployment of modern technology always had to be created first. Hans Freudenberg was a great help to Karrer in those days.[392]

Eventually, the punch cards were replaced from 1956 onward. They were followed by vacuum-tube computers which had considerably greater performance capability, for the punch-card machines only mastered addition and subtraction. Then all that changed: "The first-generation computers made it possible to carry out more complex calculations like multiplication and division." With the expansion of the character set, the computers' evaluations became more readable, which enabled the cash flows of the fast-growing business to be controlled.[393] Vacuum-tube computers – also known as valve computers or electronic computers – constituted an interim technology between the analog punch card systems and modern computer systems. These first-generation computers, as they are now known, worked with electron tubes as switching elements. They were very big and consumed a lot of electricity. The conversion at Freudenberg followed the business management zeitgeist, since vacuum-tube computers had already been operating since the mid-1940s and became standard in the course of the 1950s in the world of large companies and of science. The first vacuum-tube computer – known back then as electronic brain – went into operation in Germany for the first time on October 6, 1951, and then only temporarily too – for three weeks at the Berlin Radio Exhibition [Berliner Funkausstellung, now IFA – ed.]. The first permanently installed vacuum-tube computer was probably put into operation at the end of 1952 at Göttingen University.[394]

Thus when Hans Freudenberg went into retirement in 1958, his nephew Hermann could build on this state of technology. At that time, it was to take only four years until the first transistor computers began to replace the vacuum-tube systems. "This was the start of a trend towards increasingly smaller components in electrical engineering and in computer manufacturing that has lasted up to the present day. Transistors replaced the electronic tube for the first time in 1955 as a switching, control, storage and amplifier element in computer systems: at Bell Laboratories, USA, the first transistor digital computer emerged that was fitted with 800 transistors […] – built for the US Air Force." Many additional benefits militated in favor of the transistor's triumph over the electronic tube: The dimensions were significantly smaller, and because of this and the completely different design, the weight declined too. In addition, the circuits – and thus also the calculations – became faster. After switching the system on, it functioned without any further delay. The life span, which in the case of valve computers tended to be modest, was now virtually unlimited.[395]

Production of larger circuits also became significantly easier: "The individual switching elements like transistors, diodes, resistors and capacitors were mounted on what are known as circuit cards and then soldered together. This technology later led to the development of printed circuit boards, [...] in whose holes the individual components were inserted and then soldered at the back. This made the second-generation computers considerably more reliable, more powerful, easier to maintain and cheaper to manufacture – the foundations were laid for their widespread usage."[396]

It was a similar story at Freudenberg: "Initially, individual transistors mounted on cards were used. At the same time, the ongoing miniaturization of the circuit boards began." The development led to Hermann Freudenberg's assignment of Wolfgang Hock, the Head of Business Management in the leather division, whom he greatly esteemed, to set up a central administration department in 1964. "At first, the computing department regarded this as an assignment in the area of office organization, to optimize the typical office tasks – like writing and calculating, or rather transporting, filing and retrieving documents. It would not become apparent until later that this was not quite correct." [397]

In 1964, IBM began development of a new generation of mainframe computers; the system was called the IBM/360. In doing so, the company revolutionized the IT sector and thus paved the way for its own success story in the decades that followed. The decisive issue from a modern viewpoint: For the first time, it was possible to use the same program on different types of computer. In IT jargon, this characteristic is still known today as compatibility. That means that customers "could expand their computing capacity as needed when more was required,"[398] without having to adapt the software itself. That was a revolution in the sector. In addition, the computers were extremely reliable; a reputation which has remained intact for the mainframes category right up to the present day.[399] For IBM, this development was a real breakthrough: A new era in information technology had begun.[400]

For a company like Freudenberg, this progress was significant too. Now the conversion costs shifted predominantly to introducing new software systems, whether at the level of operating systems, for databases, office software or standard programs for business management, which are also known as enterprise resource planning (ERP) systems – and today mostly come from the German SAP group. As to the question of which software systems had the best cost-benefit ratio, Freudenberg had to constantly take new decisions back then. That is a challenge in information technology which all decision-makers regularly face even now, as will become evident in the further course of Freudenberg's history too.[401]

Entering the lubricants business with the takeover of Klüber

This episode in Freudenberg's company history also shows what entrepreneurs can achieve through the power of their own ideas. At the same time, it proves how important trust, and the long-standing relationships that are built on it, are in a successful business – and how much considerations based on this can shape a company's advancement. The story in question begins on April 1, 1929. On that day, Theodor Klüber (1905–1982), a young pharmacist from an established company in the petroleum sector, who was 24 years old at the time, established his own small company. The company, that was called Theodor Klüber, was entered into the commercial register as a retail company for petroleum products. The foundation was based on a good business idea, and he had the right timing: Developments in technology, particularly in the automotive and mechanical engineering industry, offered the opportunity of expansion and international development in the following decades.[402]

However, Theodor did not get the idea out of the blue; it too had a long tradition at its basis: because his grandfather, who bore the same name, had already laid the foundations when he established a drugstore in 1869 in Schweinfurt.[403] In a letter to business associates on the transformation of the company's legal form dated March 31, 1959 the grandson Theodor Klüber elaborated as follows: "My grandfather, Theodor Klüber, was one of the first to recognize the future of petroleum at the beginning of the [18]70s and procured this product from the first ships that brought petroleum to Germany and introduced it into his business area. Thanks to the boom in Schweinfurt's industry, my father, Fritz Klüber, was able to expand the sale of petroleum products considerably. He was also the first to supply […] Schweinfurt's emerging industry with lubricants."[404]

In 1938, the young Theodor Klüber then built a proper petroleum factory that bore his name. Production began of oil blends that were marketed under the brand names Univis, Penreco and Permalub. In 1950, development of specialty lubricants began. Because of the rapid success achieved with these new products, Klüber then concentrated on their development, production and sales from 1955 onward. In 1959, the establishment took place of the Klüber Lubrication GmbH München KG company as successor company to the Theodor Klüber petroleum factory.[405] And this was ultimately the company that was set to become an important Freudenberg subsidiary because of its lubricants as well as the synergies with the Simrit-Werk plant's sealing products.

A few years later, because Theodor Klüber – following several operations – was no longer in good health, he sought out a company that would continue running his own firm the way he would have wanted. His acquaintance with Richard Freudenberg would become the point of departure for his considerations to offer his company for sale to Freudenberg.[406] Thus he wrote to Richard Freudenberg on December 2, 1965:

> "Dear Mr. Freudenberg, we have not heard from one another for a long time, and thus I hope this letter finds you in the best of health. […] My own health has not been particularly good; I had to go into hospital in August for my tenth operation and have only been back from hospital for a few days. The reason I am writing to you today is in a completely different field from the matter for which I have hitherto had the pleasure of meeting you. As is evident from the above remarks, my general state of health is not the best, and when one is over 60, one understandably has to deal with the question: how will one's enterprises fare in the future, if death takes you one day. My wife has a severe war disability and was not permitted to have any children for that reason, and thus my companies – there are eight in total – will one day be orphaned. None of our relatives are suitable as potential successors. Thus I must transfer ownership of the firms into other hands and this should take place while I can still remain active myself. Our two companies have been in contact with each other for years. It is not so much that we do business together, but rather that we advise a common clientele. My companies are renowned internationally as specialists for extremely robust lubricants, and we deliver to around 60 industrialized countries. […] It is my opinion that my enterprises would fit very well with yours and our area of expertise could complement your products excellently. A considerable expansion in turnover through a collaboration of this type would be no problem at all. Thus I must and wish to gradually disengage from my enterprises and would like to be sure that they are passing into the right hands […] US companies would be interested in my firms, but I refuse to sell my firms to the US on grounds of conviction. Europe is already flooded with US capital anyway, and I don't want to encourage the further selloff of Europe. […] Now I would like to ask you: Would you be interested in taking over my firms while retaining our name? My request for 95 % of all shares lies far below the abovementioned figure. A cash amount would have to be paid and a life annuity as long as my wife and I are alive. […] 5 % of all shares will remain inalienable and will later be transferred to the ownership of the Theodor and Helen Klüber Peace Foundation in Salzburg so that the Klüber name will always remain in some way associated with the company."[407]

It is also interesting to learn why Klüber and Freudenberg knew each other at all: As already described in the chapter on his political activities, Richard Freudenberg had held a speech in the *Bundestag* on December 5, 1952 against the Federal

Republic of Germany joining the European Defence Community, which attracted a great deal of public interest. At that time, Freudenberg, while being interrupted by much heckling, had said among other things:

> "I ask the worrying question: In striving for our protection in the agitated weeks after the outbreak of the Korean conflict, have we given sufficient consideration to the 18 million Germans who are spending their lives in bondage in the Soviet sector? Would it not have been truer internally to bring their fate to the forefront during the treaty negotiations and not discuss the deployment of German soldiers for defense purposes until the point when we can determine our political future together with those 18 million? [...] That as a people torn into two camps, we can run the risk that Germans will have to fight against Germans. Just because the Soviets are arming Germans, we have no justification to do the same."[408]

Klüber had understood this rejection of the rearmament of the Federal Republic as a sign of a true pacifist attitude. He himself also held this basic pacifist philosophy. He documented it in 1976, together with his wife Helen Klüber (1910–1986), in a political testament that was part of their later foundation: Both were dedicated idealists in the sense of classical socialism, but particularly anti-militarism.[409] Klüber got in contact with Richard Freudenberg after the *Bundestag* speech to "let [him] know that he was of exactly the same opinion."[410] And for this reason, he saw in Richard several years later the "right hands" into which he wished to hand his company.[411]

In any case, Richard Freudenberg submitted Klüber's offer to the Management Board on January 5, 1966 in the form of an explanatory memorandum.[412] He wrote: "Mr. Theodor Klüber, whom I know through my political activity, informed me in a letter dated December 2, 1965 that he and his wife, who are the sole owners of his company, or rather companies, are concerned about the continuation of their company in the event of his demise." Furthermore, Richard explained why Klüber had set up a complicated – in his view – company organization and structure.[413]

For this juncture, the Klüber group comprised nine companies, of

Fig. 89 Theodor Klüber, around 1970

which five were production and sales companies and four were holding, or more precisely consulting or purchasing companies.[414]

On January 18, 1966 Richard Freudenberg and Ernst Demme[415] visited Theodor Klüber in Munich. Richard Freudenberg described his impressions of this visit in his memorandum to Hermann Freudenberg dated January 24, 1966:

> "During our visit, I too was very positively impressed. In particular, he seems to me to have a very good workforce of young employees who are technically adept in all aspects of the business. […] Most of the gentlemen have been with the company for many years." In a letter to the Management Board, Richard Freudenberg came to the following conclusion: "After much deliberation, he [Theodor Klüber] would greatly appreciate it if we would decide to buy and at the same time were able to name someone whom he could then familiarize with the entire business, whereby I would like to point out once again that his employees appear to work quite independently. Mr. Klüber hopes, both for his company but also for our Simrit division, that they will be able to help each other mutually in many areas in working on sealing and lubrication problems. Mr. Klüber has few dealings with the automotive industry. Mr. and Mrs. Klüber ask that we fundamentally decide whether we are prepared to acquire the 95 % that has been offered. Given the large volume of hidden reserves and the value of their know-how, I do not believe that we will be able to bargain them down much from the 3.5 million deutschmarks and the annual life annuity of 100,000 deutschmarks. On the other hand, we can almost certainly get the properties that Mrs. Klüber owns and that are associated with the manufacturing plants promised to us at a relatively favorable preemption price."[416]

In the end, however, the issue of the preemption price became the subject of intense negotiations and research after all, including by third parties like for example business information services[417] – which just goes to show how laborious transactions can become in day-to-day business, even when there is fundamental mutual agreement. In any case, Helmut Fabricius and Günter Balbach, the Head of the Finance Department at Freudenberg, visited the Klüber firm in Munich at the end of June 1966.[418] Theodor Klüber's offer for sale dated January 10, 1966, which was fleshed out later, was amended and finalized after numerous joint meetings on June 28, 1966 to the effect that "alongside the 3.5 mill. deutschmarks for the assets tied up in the nine companies and the life annuity of the part of the property in Munich, which is not part of the company assets, has been offered for 2,060,000.00 deutschmarks and alongside that an option on the factory premises in Salzburg has been promised for the price of 1 mill. deutschmarks."[419]

On the basis of this altered offer for sale dated June 28, 1966 the basic resolution was adopted by the general partners on July 1, 1966 to take over Klüber Lubrication, "whereby an optimum improvement of conditions should be achieved."[420]

Hermann Freudenberg summarized the Management Board meeting of July 1, 1966 and the consultations on accepting Klüber's offer for sale clearly and succinctly: "The only unanimous opinion was that the purchase price was much too high. Uncle Richard spoke on the phone with Mr. Klüber while we were all present to announce Helmut's [Fabricius] visit on July 4 and to inform Mr. Klüber that his notion of a sales price seemed to us to be at least 1 million, if not 1.5 million, too high. The main arguments that were to be put forward to Mr. Klüber, who was considered to be sensitive and difficult, were the complicated corporate structure which we would not be able to maintain and then higher taxes which would result in lower profit expectations for us."[421]

The fact that Richard Freudenberg in his function of Chairman of the Board of Partners had attended this Management Board meeting and had been involved in the sale negotiations clearly shows – as already described – that even after he resigned from the Management Board, he still played a key role in the top echelon of the company.

Thus the negotiations between Freudenberg and Klüber proved difficult and lasted for a total of nine months – from December 1965 to August 1966. But on August 9, the Klüber Group was then officially taken over by Freudenberg with a turnover of a little less than 10 million deutschmarks. This occurred with the entry of Klüber Lubrication Verwaltungsgesellschaft KG, whose shares were fully owned by Freudenberg & Co., into the company register.[422] The transfer of the remaining shares from Theodor and Helen Klüber to Freudenberg occurred on August 12, 1966 and was regulated within the framework of complex contractual structures.[423] Among other things, these contracts also included a consulting contract with Theodor Klüber.[424] Peter Wentzler became the Management Board member responsible for Klüber.[425] Through his consultancy activities, Theodor Klüber continued to play an pivotal role in the development and marketing of the products, advised the Management Board and the development department, influenced new areas of activity, maintained contact with trade associations and retained his function as a lubricants expert up to only a few years before his death.[426]

Günter Balbach, who was responsible for handling the acquisition of Klüber, summarized in a 1979 report why Freudenberg stuck with the purchase of Klüber – despite the difficult negotiations with Theodor Klüber – for so long: "Freudenberg was extremely interested in the acquisition of the KL Group for several reasons: a) Klüber was a profitable company, b) Klüber had prospects for the future, c) There was potential to combine it with Simrit (cross-fertilization)." According to Balbach, the room for negotiation with regard to both the purchase price as well as other aspects of the arrangement was limited. Theodor Klüber "knew that Freudenberg was interested and 'dictated' his conditions. We had to accept these conditions or forego the acquisition."[427]

CHAPTER 6
FREUDENBERG UNDER THE INFLUENCE OF ECONOMIC CRISES, GROWING COMPLEXITY AND INNOVATIONS

The end of the boom and the acceleration of structural change in the markets

After almost two decades of high economic growth rates, rising incomes and low unemployment, which were only interrupted briefly by the 1966/67 recession, there were indications in the first half of the 1970s that the reconstruction boom was coming to an end. The high growth rates that had defined everyday business life in the 1950s and 1960s were giving way to the return of a tangible economic cycle with its upswings, and of course also downturns: economic crises, stiffer competition and a sharp increase in global competition now dominated the picture and thus also shaped the challenges that the Freudenberg company was faced with. And these were not just a matter of the changes in macroeconomic conditions.

An economic downturn occurred in 1966 which "result[ed] in wage cuts and layoffs. In 1967, there is 'negative economic growth' for the first time. Gross national product is declining by 0.2 percent, while the unemployment rate is rising from 0.7 to [an at that time exceedingly remarkable] 2.2 percent."[1] In 1966/67, the Federal Republic of Germany entered its first recession since the early 1950s, which led to considerable uncertainty among the population.[2] Ludwig Erhard, who had only replaced Konrad Adenauer as German Chancellor in 1963, proved to be helpless in the face of this crisis and additionally acted extremely ineptly. His standing as the "Father of the Economic Miracle" crumbled within a short time; at the end of 1966, Erhard had already been pushed out of office as Chancellor, especially since the government seemed to be losing control of the most visible moment of the crisis, the Ruhr pit closures.[3]

Therefore the transition to a grand coalition of CDU/CSU and SPD under the new Chancellor, Kurt-Georg Kiesinger (CDU), relied right from the start on greater state involvement in economic policy and on a new economic policy concept that was closely associated with the name of the new Economics Minister, Karl Schiller (SPD).[4] Its most obvious expression was the passing of the Stability and Growth Act on May 10, 1967. From then on, a comprehensive instrument was available for what was known as global control of the economy and finances with which to combat economic fluctuations better.[5] Whether the speed that the crisis was overcome can be attributed to this anticyclical economic policy is open to debate; however, to the general public, Karl Schiller appeared to be the man of the moment: under his policy, the boom evidently returned. In fact, the speed with which the recession was overcome was not solely the result of the new economic policy, to which it was naturally ascribed. Many companies contributed to the upturn under their own steam.

At the start of the 1970s, the political and monetary conditions of entrepreneurial activity also began to slip, and initially the loss of fixed exchange rates under the Bretton Woods system particularly played a major role. In August 1971, the US Administration at first decided not to back the dollar against gold any longer. This caused the collapse of the international monetary system that had been agreed in the US village of Bretton Woods in 1944. Two years later, the fixed currency parities were also abandoned, which caused a steep devaluation in the dollar and some other currencies, whereas the deutschmark increased sharply in value. This generated considerable turbulence in German exports, which became significantly more expensive. The fact that more or less simultaneously the Club of Rome, an informal association of scientists and industrialists, presented an extremely pessimistic forecast for the future of the world economy in its report on "The Limits to Growth" did not just bring about a first environmental discussion that had to be taken seriously, but also unnerved the public deeply.[6]

Then the steep rise in oil prices in October 1973 came as a shock. It made it clear to Germany that the country was dependent on imported energy. The oil-exporting Arab countries used the "Yom Kippur War", which had broken out after Egypt and Syria had attacked Israel, as an opportunity to raise the price of oil drastically and reduce output. However, they did not take part in the war themselves, but some of the countries which had come together to form the cartel of oil-exporting states which is known as OPEC today supported the aggressors. The price of a barrel of crude oil quadrupled within three months to 11.60 US dollars from 2.70. That was a blow to the Federal Republic of Germany, which covered 55 percent of its energy requirements from imported oil, and 75 percent of that came from Arab states.[7]

The Federal Republic under German Chancellor Willy Brandt (SPD), who held the office from 1969 to 1974, decided on "drastic forms of energy-saving."[8]

Thus driving bans and speed limits were enacted, among other things, using the catchphrase "carfree Sundays" which is still common today.[9] "At the end of 1973, the situation is easing in the Middle East. [...] However, the oil-producing countries are still maintaining the drastic price increases."[10] Meanwhile, the German economy was feeling the effects of the oil crisis: car manufacturers ordained short-time work in their factories after car sales plummeted, which in turn affected Freudenberg too as an automotive supplier. The simultaneous increases in steel prices additionally weighed down on Freudenberg because of the exceedingly high use of steel in sealing and vibration control technology. The situation was similarly grim among construction materials manufacturers, in the chemical industry and in iron and steel production.[11] Moreover, the leather industry, which was already in the midst of a structural crisis anyway, was hit hard by the 1973/74 oil crisis as well.

Only a short time later, the oil crisis, in whose wake inflation and unemployment also rose, culminated in the first really serious post-war economic crisis, which emerged in 1974. In 1975, unemployment figures, which had only been around 273,000 as recently as 1973, and were equivalent to full employment, exceeded one million.[12] Economic output dropped by more than 2 percent; and the high growth rates of the 1950s and 1960s would not return later either. In the last quarter of the 20th century, average economic growth was only around 1.9 percent and the unemployment rate rose to more than 10 percent.[13] In light of the mass unemployment, the Federal Republic enacted a recruitment freeze for foreign workers early as 1973.[14]

From a modern perspective, the "particular intensity" of the economic crisis in West Germany can be explained, according to experts, "on the one hand by a temporary saturation in demand for consumer goods, on the other hand by structural problems in former growth sectors like the construction industry, the steel industry, mechanical engineering and the automotive industry. The crisis was exacerbated not only by high wage agreements and the resulting efforts of employers to lower wage costs by cutting jobs, but also by the concurrent economic downturn in almost all Western industrialized countries, which prevented any compensation for the dwindling domestic demand in the Federal Republic by increasing exports."[15]

The events made a lasting impression on Hermann Freudenberg too, as can be seen from a speech he held in December 1974:

> "A year ago, we were all feeling the effects of the oil crisis, whose repercussions were not foreseeable. Today we can determine that it marked the start of a phase in the economic development of industrialized nations which is setting tasks for politicians and

economists for which there is simply no recipe yet, but whose problems are having a major impact on all our lives. The realization of the vulnerability of our growth-oriented economic system, of the dependence on new centers of power which has only now been apprehended, has given us all pause for thought and governed our economic behavior, whether consciously or unconsciously."[16]

Looking back, however, the Management Board also described the difficult years of 1974 and 1975 as an opportunity "to be able to identify the problems more clearly and implement solutions that would have been met with unsurmountable resistance in good years. Positive effects arising from this can be discerned in our company too; corporate and central divisions have been heavily streamlined and product development is also making valuable progress. [...] However, the fundamental problem remains that costs and charges in Germany are still so high that numerous sectors – including many of our customers – are increasingly being forced to relocate abroad to retain their market position."[17] Thus the pressure to go international persisted simply due to the migrating customers. This could be seen in the relocation of production by many sectors to low-wage countries, initially in southern Europe and later in Asia and South America. For Freudenberg as a supplier, this meant that it had to follow its customers around the world to the new production regions.[18]

Against this backdrop, it is particularly interesting to take a closer look at the Partners' Report on the Business for 1975, since the triggers of the recession from Freudenberg's perspective are stated precisely here. According to the report, reasons had included the "running down of the overstocked inventories that industry and trade had accumulated during the commodity crisis in the first half of 1974," the reticence of unsettled consumers because of rising unemployment figures, the restriction of private and state investments and the negative impact on world trade. This last point was the result of the increased deficits in the balance of payments of the customer countries, which originated from the increased crude oil prices and the strong exchange rate fluctuations. Above and beyond this, difficulties emerged for large swathes of the German export industry, and thus also for Freudenberg, from the steady increase in wages as well as in other costs and taxes. These costs could not be passed on through sales prices, which were already high because of the strong appreciation of the deutschmark. This ultimately led to a deterioration in Freudenberg's international competitiveness.[19]

And so Freudenberg too had to eventually resort to the instrument of short-time work in Germany, for example in the Schwalmstadt plant.[20] However, the first signs of a return to normality were already emerging in the fall of 1975. "Inventories had been run down to normal levels, meaning that retail and the processing industry had to stock up again for their day-to-day requirements. The recovery set in fastest and most visibly in the USA, from which our American shareholdings also profited. The other industrialized countries, whose economic and social systems are not as adaptable as those of the United States, followed on at a significantly slower rate."[21]

This was correspondingly reflected in the figures for the entire Freudenberg Group at the end of the year: "Turnover declined by 5.8 percent in 1975 compared to 1974, falling from 1.631 million deutschmarks to 1.536 million deutschmarks, and this decrease stemmed almost entirely from our German companies' export business, which was 21 percent below the previous year, whereas domestic turnover only fell by 1.5 percent and turnover of our foreign plants by 0.9 percent."[22] This is in certain respects remarkable, because in a macroeconomic context it tended to be export demand that helped Germany to overcome the economic crisis.[23] In this context, the German economy overall profited from the consequences of the abandonment of the Bretton Woods exchange rate regulation too. After it was unpegged, the deutschmark appreciated strongly, on the one hand to the detriment of the export industry, but which meant on the other hand that a considerable portion of the higher oil costs, which after all were incurred in devalued dollars, could be compensated for. Furthermore, the German export industry proved to be flexible enough to react to the changed "terms of trade", which developed to the benefit of German exports again as early as 1978.[24] Unemployment levels also declined again to just below one million in 1978.[25] However, overall conditions remained complicated, because inflation figures fell only marginally despite the economic slowdown.[26] The term "stagflation", an amalgamation of "stagnation" and "inflation", became established for this concurrence of rising prices, high unemployment and only sluggish economic development.[27] The last years in office of Helmut Schmidt (SPD), who had replaced Willy Brandt as Chancellor in 1974, were overshadowed by this and by the simultaneously strongly growing national debt.

In the Partners' Report on the Business for financial year 1976, the Management Board drew a cautious conclusion again: "The quite positive picture that is emerging for the development of our group in 1976 should not disguise the fact that the era of regular growth is over for most of the sectors in which we operate. Because of international competition, it will often not be possible to pass on unavoidable cost increases in our prices in the future too. To counteract the danger of a long-term downward trend, we have focused more strongly on the possibilities for diversification again, giving preference to related sectors. [...] Alongside this, we are working on new developments for our traditional markets and on further improving our performance; the reserves to do this will become smaller, but of course they will never be exhausted entirely."[28]

The early 1980s brought a new setback. In 1979, oil prices rose sharply again. That heated up inflation not just in the USA, meaning that finally the new Chairman of the U.S. Federal Reserve, Paul Volcker, felt compelled to take a drastic measure: In 1979 he hiked the leading interest rate to almost 20 percent, which brought a halt to inflation, but also to the global economy, which buckled in 1980/81. The economic downturn also cost US President Jimmy Carter his re-election. The new president, Ronald Reagan, implemented a drastic change in economic policy, just like Margaret Thatcher had already tackled in the United Kingdom: The era of Keynesian economics came to an end. That also cost German Social Democrat Chancellor Helmut Schmidt his office, and he had to make way for Helmut Kohl (CDU) in 1982. However, despite the serious crisis at the beginning of the 1980s, the global economy rapidly picked up momentum again. In the end, oil prices declined by almost half. This and the opening up of China brought about a decisive step towards globalization. Thus, although the 1980s might have begun very turbulently, they seemed to end very quietly.[29]

The most remarkable event of the late 1980s, which otherwise seemed to pass relatively unspectacularly, was undoubtedly the fall of the Berlin Wall in 1989. In the period of reunification that followed, the two German states faced a task of unprecedented proportions from 1989 onward. This involved the preparation and implementation not only of the political unification, but also of the transformation of the socialist planned economy into a modern market economy.[30] Then, in July 1990, the State Treaty [between the Federal Republic of Germany and the German Democratic Republic – ed.] establishing a monetary, economic and social union heralded the real economic reunification of Germany. The foundation for the introduction of a social market economy in the new German Länder was laid with the acceptance of the Federal Republic's economic and social order and the introduction of the deutschmark as the official currency.[31] While the introduction of the deutschmark was joyfully received, it also unsparingly revealed the weaknesses in the economy of the German Democratic Republic (GDR), which had seen no structural movement for many years. Consequently, in the 1990s, the East German economy underwent a profound structural change, in the course of which unemployment and government debt continued to rise.[32]

Economic and social integration generated extreme pressure to adapt among East German companies. The newly established *Treuhandanstalt* was a public agency tasked with privatizing the more than 12,000 state-owned East German companies. The majority of these were sold to private owners. In some cases, this was preceded by extensive restructuring measures. Around 3,000 companies were closed down. The *Treuhandanstalt* was responsible for a total of almost four million employees. The "Gemeinschaftswerk Aufschwung Ost" was a stimulus package designed to tackle the economic crisis in the five new Länder. In addition, what was known as a "solidarity surcharge" was introduced, which was basically an increase in income tax. At the same time, an eastward enlargement of the European Union occurred, and a resolution was passed to introduce the new European currency – the euro. Thus the framework conditions of German economic policy changed significantly.[33] Freudenberg too endeavored to find a way to become established in the new Länder after the fall of the Berlin Wall and the implementation of German unification.[34] In addition, new markets were emerging in the eastern European countries, and at the same time opportunities for more cost-efficient production plants – based on the Freudenberg maxim of producing in the region for the region.[35] Thus, the market conditions were changing yet again there too.

The structural crisis in the German leather industry and its effects on Freudenberg

Since the beginning of the 1960s, the entire German leather industry had already been under pressure. The economic miracle had accelerated structural change in the various sectors, which caused leather manufacturing in Germany to become less and less important. As early as 1960, production had declined by almost 12 percent compared to the previous year, and likewise the following years up to 1963, with declines of between 3 percent and 5 percent, show a shrinking sector, which had now fallen to the bottom of the league of West German industries.[36] The structural problems of the leather industry were clearly reflected here. They had already set in at the end of World War II; finally, at the start of the 1970s, they culminated in a real sectoral crisis, against the background of which it is remarkable how long Freudenberg continued to hang on to its traditional business – and how much was undertaken to stabilize it time and again. The causes of the crisis were manifold, and some influential factors had an effect over the years:[37] Back as far as the 1950s, the constantly rising rawhide prices had been a strain on the business. This led to considerable cost pressure, which was additionally fueled by the industrial catch-up process in developing countries, particularly in South America. Those states account for approximately 70 percent of the total stocks of cattle and calves in the world, right up to today. And the rawhides that were produced directly in the countries of origin were increasingly processed in those countries into leather or semi-finished goods themselves, in order to occupy more high-margin business areas in the value chain. This commercial development, which is in itself perfectly normal, was increasingly boosted by state protectionism. Frequently, this process was accompanied by export restrictions on skins and hides, through which the respective states wanted to secure privileged access to raw materials for their own constantly developing leather industries. In this way, the cost pressure on the German leather industry continued to increase on both the international as well as the domestic market.[38]

An additional difficulty emanated from the gradual relocation of leather processing to low-wage countries, which was predominantly the result of the immense cost pressure both in the shoe industry and in leather production. Production relocations in the German shoe industry began at the end of the 1960s, particularly to southern Europe and to Yugoslavia. Since the relocated shoe manufacturers procured "their leather directly in the new shoe manufacturing locations now,"[39] the German leather industry lost its most important customer for upper leathers.[40] The logical consequence was that the leather industry itself gradually relocated to these countries, which not only had "cost and competition advantages over German leather producers [because of] their market proximity to the shoe industry that was located there."[41] There were also more lax requirements regarding all aspects of wastewater disposal. Thus, for example, in the newly created tannery centers in Italy and Spain, up to 300 tanneries shared one wastewater treatment plant. Not so in Germany: There, the industrial leather manufacturers generally operated their own wastewater treatment plants.[42] The higher German wage levels further fanned the flames of relocation. At the beginning of the 1970s, the pressure on the German leather industry increased even more because of tanneries in South America.[43] Thus massive price pressure was generated, particularly in the area of standard and mass-produced goods. A particularly disagreeable fact for the industry: This pressure could not be compensated by raising end customer prices.[44]

Add to this the constantly tightening environmental protection requirements which burdened the German leather producers with rising environmental protection costs. In other countries, these requirements either did not exist at all, or only to a significantly more limited extent, and additionally were not consistently implemented by the authorities. Thus producers from these countries gained a cost advantage that enabled them to offer their leather at low prices on the market. To the detriment of the German factories, a type of environmental dumping came about.[45]

None of this made the already complicated situation any easier, since during this time more and more synthetic products were muscling in on the market, which increased the competitive pressure to a hitherto unknown degree.[46] A veritable crowding-out process began, in which leather was being replaced to an increasingly greater extent by high-quality synthetic leather in its traditional areas of application. In 1966, this development was already at an advanced stage in countries like the United States and Japan. Leather, and particularly high-quality calf leather, was really only granted any long-term prospects at all as upper leather in the premium segment.[47] As if that were not enough, further challenges arose on top of those, which made things difficult for the traditional sector in Germany. Fashions were changing increasingly rapidly, production times of the individual products were becoming shorter to be able to adapt "even faster to market requirements,"[48] [49] and lastly, the strong deutschmark exerted additional price pressure on the German leather industry's export business as well.[50]

The outcome of these developments was a dramatic process of adaptation. Thus, the number of leather-producing factories in Germany declined from 223 in 1964 to only 115 in 1980. And twenty years later, there were actually only 25 leather producers left.[51]

These changes did not leave Freudenberg unscathed, even though the challenges were initially overcome successfully. By expanding the production of high-quality calf leather and increasing exports, turnover in the leather business division was actually improved slightly.[52] In 1966, the leather division again achieved a 21.5 percent share of group sales. However, that was no longer reflected in the operating result: The share of net income generated by leather was only 5.2 percent.[53]

It was clear to the Management Board that structural changes were taking place here. The cutthroat competition with substitute products was already described by Hans Erich Freudenberg as a disruptive factor for the leather business in 1967:

> "Today, the former 'leather market' has now been significantly expanded by a multitude of products which are being used alongside real leather and increasingly replacing it. Synthetic leathers have meantime broken into even the last bastions that natural leather had been able to hold up to now, and they have the same appearance and also the same physical properties – and indeed in some cases even better ones – than natural leather. [...] With the incursion of the large-scale chemical industry and many new specialized plastics processing companies into the leather market, an entirely new world has emerged for us structurally. We are no longer competing with the small and medium-sized, labor-intensive tanneries that are plying their mechanical trade as they have done since time immemorial; instead, we are competing specifically with the sector that develops, plans and invests most generously. The chemical indus-

try has totally different and much more highly developed marketing methods than the tanners. It supports its products much more intensively and expensively. We are standing right in the middle of dramatic events. [...] I would like to claim that the only fact that can calm us down as tanners is that we have long since been more than just tanners!"[54]

Simply waiting patiently, or even sitting out the changes, was not an option; Freudenberg had to react, particularly to the substitution pressure. What emerged from that is the story of a steep rise – and an equally breathtaking business downturn. In 1963, production of PVC foamed synthetic leather under the brand name "Helia" began in Weinheim. At this time – as already mentioned – the market for synthetic leather was constantly expanding. More and more large firms, frequently not from the leather sector, were entering the market with synthetic leather and foamed synthetic leather and competing with classical upper leather producers. In this context, Freudenberg further developed a technology that was already in use. As early as the 1950s, Freudenberg had produced PVC foam for molded foam parts or alternatively PVC foil and foam combinations in the form of armrests or later dashboards for the automotive industry. Above and beyond this, PVC was also used as material for shoes and boots. However, Rudolf Wassermann (1913–1976), one of the first Management Board members from outside the family from 1971 to 1976, who joined the company in 1958 as

Fig. 90 Helia production, 1975

Head of the Plastics Division and was thus responsible for Helia later, saw little expansion potential in this application, which is why he endeavored to find other areas of application for the PVC foam.[55] Instead, because of the extensive experience and the large customer base that Freudenberg had in the leather market, Wassermann regarded foamed synthetic leather as a good opportunity to complement the leather business. In 1959, planning kicked off for the development of a dedicated production plant, which began operations in 1963.[56]

The Helia foamed synthetic leather was manufactured in what is known as reverse process production. By printing, embossing or lacquering the surface, foamed synthetic leather with a multitude of surface structures and colors could be produced. The volume and different textile carriers enabled variable tactile sensation options, which meant that a large range of applications could be covered. This meant that customer demand for innovative optics could be easily met, particularly in the fashion industry.[57] As early as 1970, Helia was produced in approximately 3,000 different articles and colors. In contrast to leather, synthetic leather was often easier to process, was simpler to clean and considerably more cost-effective. However, the Management Board always regarded synthetic leather as a complement to leather, particularly in a significantly lower price class. It was never their aim to produce a fully-fledged leather substitute.[58]

Time and again in the initial years, production volumes were increased enormously. Between 1963 and 1973, turnover increased by almost 50 percent on average each year. The machinery and production halls were also continually expanded: Production of Helia began in a new production hall with a coating machine. Further production buildings for the operation of additional production machines were built in quick succession. As early as 1971, the sixth coating machine was commissioned and a new production record of 40 million square meters was achieved for Helia. Two years later, turnover was at 180 million deutschmarks and generating 11.8 percent of group sales, and thus almost 20 million deutschmarks higher than leather turnover. Within 10 years, Freudenberg had become Europe's largest synthetic leather manufacturer.[59]

The leather division, in contrast, continued to face a difficult market situation. In a study dating from 1968 about the company's challenges, Hans Erich Freudenberg again issued a stern warning about the emerging problems in the leather business: The Freudenberg leather business was too big and too sluggish to have the flexibility that was urgently needed, in Hans Erich Freudenberg's opinion – something which he described as the "burden of size." At the end, he summarized: "In our tanneries at CF [Carl Freudenberg], we are not prepared for the events of the coming 3–5 years on the leather market agility and ingenuity as well as a willingness to break away from antiquated market [...]. Only the most outstanding exertion of all our strengths, ideas and methods in all areas of the leather business will get us through the coming years, if we don't want to wither away in [the] leather [business] – to all intents and purposes subsidized by the other divisions."[60] He would be proved right.

Despite the evident difficulties, leather's share of turnover – as pertaining to the entire group – could initially be maintained; in 1968, it was still at 20 percent.[61] However, profits fell markedly, which was mainly because the three German tanneries in Weinheim, Schönau and Neckarsteinach were operating at a loss.[62] The steep price increases for calfskins and the associated high prices for finished calf leather led to a situation in the shoe industry where calf leather was increasingly being replaced by more cost-effective types of leather for the shoes' upper leathers, which put the Freudenberg leather business under pressure too.[63] Nevertheless, Freudenberg commanded a 33 percent market share of upper leather production within the German leather industry in 1969, producing 73 million square feet. This corresponded to the leather requirements for approximately 40 million pairs of leather shoes.[64]

The immense structural change in the leather trade had still been cushioned by the high growth rates in the reconstruction and economic miracle years, but at the end of the 1960s, a change in the macroeconomic environment was gradually becoming evident. Despite the problems in the leather division, Freudenberg actually managed to come through the 1967 recession almost completely unscathed: turnover and profits rose. However, the structural burden of the loss-making leather business was by no means lifted. In 1970, net income fell sharply, not least because of the losses in the European leather business in particular.[65] Consequently, it was obvious that a real crisis would inevitably emerge sooner or later from the structural problems in the leather business. Then the German leather industry also posted a decline of 13 percent in production volume in 1970. Freudenberg too suffered a decline in production and turnover because of sharply falling demand for high-quality calf leather, smooth side leathers and velours leather. Major changeovers to new types of leather became necessary to stabilize the situation.[66] This worked too in the short term: In financial year 1971, the leather division achieved its nominally highest turnover in company history, posting 252 million deutschmarks, which corresponded to an 18.9 percent share of group sales. Nevertheless, Freudenberg's German tanneries continued to operate at a loss.[67]

Then, in the following year, Freudenberg felt the full impact of the structural crisis in the German leather industry, when the hide prices on the world market, which were already high anyway, doubled again. The reasons for the astronomical price increases were on the one hand a scarcity of rawhides[68] and on the other hand rising demand for leather for shoes, clothing, furniture, bags and accessories. As had already happened in the 1950s, these price hikes could not be passed on to customers.[69] This was a huge problem for Freudenberg, since the hide accounted for 50 percent of the cost of the net sales price of a leather.[70] Consequently, turnover in the leather division slumped by 27 percent compared to the previous year.[71] This also led to a significant deterioration in income, which could not be offset – because of the lower wage levels – by the tanneries in Varces and the Teneria Temola in Mexico, which were operating profitably.[72] The bitter realization: Freudenberg was no longer competitive in an international comparison.[73]

Initially, the Management Board combined the necessary structural adaptations with a commitment to leather – out of strategic conviction, but likely also to assuage the workforce: "Resolutions to this effect were taken this week within the Management Board. The result is a clear 'yes' to leather. Our company needs leather – not just because it is our traditional product – in our product range for our customers; a key strength of our company lies precisely in having a complement to synthetic leather, nonwovens, etc., for example as supplier to the shoe industry," Hermann Freudenberg said in a speech to employees in 1972. As operational measures, production of side leather in Schönau, that of calf and patent leather in Weinheim and chrome tanning – because of the better wastewater treatment plant – were all concentrated in Weinheim. Above and beyond this, investments were made in new technologies and a decision was taken to reduce dependence on the shoe industry, which purchased 90 percent of Freudenberg's leather.[74]

Nevertheless, it was clear to all involved, particularly to the Management Board and the trade unions, that the loss-making area could not be maintained in its current size indefinitely, but instead had to shrink. Due to the effects of the structural crisis in leather, a rationalization protection agreement came into effect on January 1, 1973 which had been agreed between the Gewerkschaft Leder leatherworkers union and the leather industry in November 1972. This agreement granted special social protection to manual workers in the German leather industry (from the age of 45 and with 10 years of service at the company).[75]

In addition, the developments that followed on from the oil crisis were a further major challenge for Freudenberg's leather business in a situation that was already difficult. Price pressure was high, particularly against the competition from southern Europe and South America, because the tanneries that were located there could produce their leather more cost-effectively and sell it at lower prices without endangering their profits in the process, due to their relatively weak currencies.[76] Alongside a slump in demand for certain types of leather, there was also a sharp decline in incoming orders in 1973, which led to extremely low employment. One measure used to combat this was the continuation of the concentration and modernization process in leather production that had already been initiated in Weinheim in 1972.[77] The order situation deteriorated rapidly.[78] At the end of the financial year, there was a loss of 32.6 million deutschmarks in the leather division.[79] The ratio to group income, which was approximately 51 million deutschmarks[80] in 1973, illustrates the dramatic situation which the Freudenberg leather division faced.

Now the Management Board was seriously questioning whether it should continue to produce leather: "The question is whether we can cut our costs to such an extent that we can compete with European competitors. If we keep going, a speedy decision will be required, because of the unrest that is prevailing everywhere, about what order of magnitude we should cut down to and where we will manufacture."[81] Despite the catastrophic market situation in the leather segment, which did not augur any prospect of improvement in the long term either, the Management Board initially decided to only undertake an adjustment of production to the sales opportunities.[82]

But that was an inadequate step. Because of the persistently critical situation, the Management Board was ultimately compelled to terminate leather production in the Neckarsteinach plant in 1973 and in the Schönau plant in 1974.[83] A total of 455 employees were affected by the plant closures.[84]

In 1974, the repercussions of the oil crisis were an additional aggravating factor which led to a significant decline in consumption, which hugely affected the leather business.[85] As a result, turnover from leather shrank dramatically yet again: by approximately 43 percent. Thus its share of group sales declined within three years from almost 20 percent to only 5.6 percent.[86] Therefore, the Management Board decided to convert leather production from mass production to high-quality specialty leather, which led to a further drastic reduction of the plant to only a few hundred employees. Hence, approximately 80 percent of the jobs in the leather factories in Weinheim, Schönau and Neckarsteinach were cut overall from 1969 to 1974. This corresponded to a reduction of 1,534 employees. Part of the workforce found a new home in other Freudenberg plants.[87] Alongside similar implementations in other business areas, the job cuts that were required for the structural adaptation of the leather division also necessitated early retirements and layoffs. Turnover declined to around 50 million deutschmarks, a level that remained relatively stable into the 1990s; but its share of group sales plummeted to only 0.5 percent.[88] The shrinking of the leather division and the concentration on high-quality calfskins – a process in which the owner family was also involved through the Board of Partners[89] – led to a certain stabilization in the traditional division, even though the persistently high rawhide prices still negatively impacted business.[90] While other major producers like for example Heyl AG, Adler & Oppenheimer and Lederwerke Backnang – all of them tanneries that produced standard side leather on an industrial scale – had to close down their factories completely, Freudenberg was nonetheless able to maintain continuity. However, one result of the process of "downsizing" the leather division was also that 25,000 square meters of production area in Weinheim was freed up which could then be used by other business divisions.[91]

Hans Erich Freudenberg explained why the Management Board had hung on to traditional businesses for a long time – despite the structural problems that had been identified at an early stage – particularly in the leather and shoe business, and later in the synthetic leather business too, in his speech to the partners to mark his departure from the company in 1976: In the Management Board "we were still governed by an 'it cannot be, because it must not be!'"[92] Ultimately, on the part of the Management Board, "the driving factor for the readiness to accept losses temporarily"[93] and delay structural adjustments in the leather division that had been necessary for a long time was the "sense of responsibility for the jobs and an attachment to traditions."[94]

In mid-1976, a perceptible improvement set in due to falling rawhide prices in the United States and healthy order intake levels.[95] This was evident from profit figures: For the first time after seven years of losses, the leather division was able to achieve a small profit of 300,000 deutschmarks in 1976. However, this was not a lasting recovery. The division posted a loss again the very next year.[96] In order to survive in the market, semi-finished goods from tanneries in "developing countries" were increasingly bought in. Their quality was increasingly improving because of the provision of technical expertise. These bought-in products were then processed further in the leather factories in Weinheim and Varces. The company's own leather production in Weinheim continued to concentrate on high-quality specialty leathers, like for example the "world-renowned boxcalf". The workforce in the leather factory had to be adjusted further to the market situation in 1979. Now, only approximately 300 employees were working in Weinheim, and in Varces only 50.[97] Finally, leather production in Varces was closed down completely in 1980 and the factory site was sold in 1981.[98] In the same year, Freudenberg also sold off 24.5 percent of its shares in Teneria Temola in Mexico to its long-standing joint venture partner, the Irurita family, which subsequently owned a majority shareholding in Teneria Temola.[99]

The remaining 45 percent of the shares was sold to the Irurita family in 1992. Thus Freudenberg concentrated its leather production completely at the Weinheim headquarters.[100]

Because of the persistent problems which offered no prospects for the future, particularly for the side leather segment, the Management Board decided to shut down side leather production at the end of 1983 and to focus the leather division exclusively on the classical calf leather product line in future. In this market segment, after all, Freudenberg still held a market share of between 60 and 70 percent in Germany at this time.[101] However, even this measure did not initially appear to bring about a turnaround in the downward trend in the traditional product. Between 1978 and 1986, the leather division stayed consistently loss-making.[102] In this situation, an internal company study on the profitability of the leather division reached the conclusion that "continuation" was no longer possible "from an economic perspective."[103]

Therefore, by 1986 if not before, the complete cessation of the traditional business was discussed within the Management Board. A letter was even drafted to the partners which was intended to inform them about the closure. Then, however, this measure was not implemented after all and therefore the letter was not sent either.[104]

Instead, because of the positive market signals for the luxury segment, in which Freudenberg had specialized in the leather business with its calf leathers, cost optimization potential was sought again and the business was kept running with a further reduction in production capacity.[105]

A stabilization of profits was indeed achieved by the measures that were implemented to adjust capacity. In 1987, the leather division was able to post a small profit again, of approximately 100,000 deutschmarks.[106] In the following year, this actually exceeded one million deutschmarks.[107] After 17 difficult and at times very dramatic years, the company had finally succeeded in getting its traditional business on the road to success again by concentrating on the "high-quality leather for the luxury segment" market niche. The heavily export-oriented leather division supplied manufacturers of high-quality shoes and leather goods on all continents and was the leading company in this luxury segment.[108] In 1989, profits even rose to 4.1 million deutschmarks.[109] Even US President George Bush Sr. ordered three pairs of shoes made of Freudenberg leather from Freudenberg customer Allen Edmonds Shoe Corporation in that financial year.[110]

However, this success did not last long: In 1997, the business division that was now trading under the name Freudenberg Leder KG posted a loss again, which rose fast because of the economic crisis in Southeast Asia and the BSE crisis which erupted shortly afterwards. In addition, the terror attacks of September 11,

2001 exacerbated an economic downturn which impaired demand, particularly in the luxury segment, and thus led to further declines in sales.[111] Even at the beginning of 2002, there was no end in sight to the catastrophic order situation in the leather division – and no prospects for improvement.[112]

Therefore, Freudenberg's Management Board passed a resolution in February to cease leather production as of September 30, 2002.[113] This was the company's response to the persistently high losses in the division for many years.[114]

"Clinging on to the leather business in its former magnitude" at that time, as Peter Bettermann (1947–2021), the Speaker of the Management Board back then, formulated in the same year in a Partners' Report on the Business, "would have led to the demise of this company […]. Luckily, there were always people in management positions at Freudenberg who had realized at an early stage that the losses in [the] leather [division] and later in the shoe shops that were derived from it were a warning sign and taken action accordingly. […] And it is to this well-established tradition that we feel committed. And all the more so because we know from our own experience how laborious and painful it is to combat sources of loss. […] Upholding this basic virtue, and living by the principles prescribed by the family in the way we combat the losses: this is the truly valuable tradition to which every management board of our company feels and must feel committed."[115]

Bettermann had joined the Management Board in 1994. He initially took over management of the Focus project and took over responsibility for business administration (Group controlling) and computing from Rudolf Fischer (1933–1997). Later, he also took over responsibility for finance and legal affairs from Reinhart Freudenberg, and from 1997 assumed the role of Speaker of the Management Board, which he held up to 2012.[116] Fischer was a member of the Management Board from 1987 to 1995. He was responsible for the business administration area with the functions of corporate planning, financial accounting Carl Freudenberg, cost accounting and income statement, organization/computing and structural organization. In addition, from January 1988 onward he took over management of the company's shoe division, which had previously been in Hermann Freudenberg's remit.[117]

On December 31, 2002 Freudenberg Leder KG ceased operations permanently. The era of Freudenberg leather came to a close after 153 years. However, it lives on in Weinheimer Leder GmbH, which was newly established by the former directors of Leder KG in 2002. This distribution company also took over part of the former customer base as well as Freudenberg's expertise. Thus it continued production with partner company Kegar in Poland with the designation: "Manufactured using traditional Freudenberg-methods."[118]

"It was a lugubrious dismantling, which fortunately did not have an extensive effect on the workforce, because other divisions were growing at the same time. That was [...] a crisis, and it was only ended in [the] leather [division] because one day we said, now we're going to finally call it a day, there is hardly anything left any more. Looking back, we would have saved an insane amount of money if we had closed it down a lot faster, but that wasn't an option emotionally," Reinhart Freudenberg said later, looking back at the end of the leather business.[119]

The first female executive at Freudenberg and environmental protection

The leather business is not the only thing that has a long-standing tradition at Freudenberg: environmental protection does too. Investments were made in environmental protection because of statutory requirements, but also because it was evident to Freudenberg right from the start that a clean environment is a key prerequisite for corporate success. This was based particularly on the realization at an early stage that a clean environment is important for the quality of life of present and future generations. And specifically the waters surrounding Weinheim had to be protected from contamination, which was a threat arising from leather production in particular. For this reason, a first wastewater treatment plant had been put into operation in Weinheim as early as 1898, which is thus one of the German prototypes for wastewater treatment plants.[120] Lieselotte Feikes (1923–2008) was inordinately committed to environmental protection, and later she was Freudenberg's first environmental protection officer for many years.

After she joined the company in 1953, Lieselotte Feikes first task initially comprised "to conduct a review of the wastewater from our tanneries in Weinheim and Schönau."[121] Deriving from this, she developed an innovative process for treating wastewater from tanneries through the precipitation of iron sulfate – known as the "CF process".[122] On the basis of these new insights, she developed a concept for wastewater treatment in the Schönau plant.[123] In 1956, the first three-stage pilot wastewater treatment plant was put into operation in Schönau according to her plans, which "constituted an absolute novelty in the area of treating tannery wastewaters."[124]

This was considered to be a forerunner for the planned wastewater treatment plant in the Zwischen Dämmen plant in Weinheim, which was set to be five

Fig. 91 Lieselotte Feikes gives a school group a tour through the wastewater treatment plant, 1976

times as large. Construction began in 1964. Three years later, the first mechanical clarifying stage was completed and began its work. In 1975, second stage of the treatment plant, based on the "CF process", became the chemical operational – construction had begun two years earlier.[125]

The third biological purification stage of the wastewater treatment plant began operations on May 31, 1976 – building work had begun in 1975.[126] During this stage, the organic compounds that still remain in the water after the chemical purification are transformed by active bacteria and microbes into new bacterial substances, which can be easily separated from the water.[127] Now the three-stage (mechanical, chemical, biological) wastewater treatment plant in Weinheim was complete.[128] Further structurally identical company wastewater treatment plants followed in France, Brazil and Mexico.[129]

In 1969, Lieselotte Feikes was assigned responsibility for the leather laboratory, which meant she advanced to become the first female executive at Freudenberg. Her appointment as Freudenberg's first environmental protection officer followed in 1972.[130] A year later, Feikes took over management of the newly established central area of Environmental Protection.[131] Feikes left the company as of January 31, 1984, but was still connected to it in an advisory capacity until 1991 and thus almost eight years after her retirement.[132] She remained environmental protection officer and Chairwoman of the Environmental Protection Committee until 1987.[133] These functions are still an important part of the Health, Safety and Environment corporate function today.

The struggle to retain the shoe and synthetic leather business

The speedy positive development of the Helia division which has already been described and which prevailed until the start of the 1970s did not last long. As early as 1972, Hermann Freudenberg reported the first difficulties. Synthetic leather was being used in increasingly lower price categories in the area spanning the shoe industry and leather goods.[134] The price pressure also increased because of the growing competition, which was offering synthetic leather at lower prices. At the same time, production costs were rising: Because of the oil crisis in 1973, the price of petrochemical raw materials rose by 10 to 40 percent, and in the case of cotton, the price increase was even up to 80 percent.[135] Additionally, measures were becoming necessary for environmental protection, which – as in the leather industry – often played a tangential role among foreign competitors.[136] On top of this, demand had been falling since 1974 as a result of the recession that had been triggered by the oil crisis. This occasionally led to short-time working in the Helia division in 1975 and led the Management Board to the assessment that the volume of synthetic leather sold in 1973 constituted an upper limit.[137]

In order to counteract the rising costs, a restructuring of production took place towards cheaper materials.[138] Despite all endeavors, the Helia division posted a loss for the first time in 1978.[139]

The synthetic leather business continued to decline in the coming years too, meaning that production volumes had to be constantly reduced.[140] Above and beyond this, the product range was streamlined, but this only temporarily led to an improvement.[141] The Helia division made losses up to 1985.[142] Since the ruinous competition in the shoe and leather goods industry still continued, synthetic leather battled against a shrinking market and a persistently negative profit situation in the following years too. This finally led to the decision in 2000 to close down the Helia division.[143] The synthetic leather division of the "Helia" product group was sold to Konrad Hornschuch AG at the end of February 2001 and this was the end of Freudenberg's synthetic leather business.[144]

As was the case with leather and synthetic leather, the further development of the Freudenberg shoe division turned out to be difficult as well. The structural problems in the leather industry weighed on the German shoe industry too in a similar fashion. Nevertheless, the Freudenberg shoe division was still doing well at the end of the 1960s, especially in the children's and adolescents' shoe business. In 1968, more than 4,100 workers were employed in total at Gustav Hoffmann, the most important manufacturer of children's and adolescents' shoes at that time. This corresponded to approximately 20 percent of Freudenberg's total workforce.¹⁴⁵ A year later, production volume of children's and adolescents' shoes reached the figure of 8.8 million pairs of shoes, meaning that production volume had more than doubled within 20 years.¹⁴⁶ And shoe wholesaling firm Conrad Tack sold approximately 1.1 million pairs of shoes that year through its 30 outlets in West Germany.¹⁴⁷

But competition was getting stiffer in the market segment for children's and adolescents' shoes as well: In order to continue to successfully hold its own, from 1970 onward Gustav Gustav Hoffmann increasingly relied on targeted advertising for the Elefanten brand, which was subdivided into different categories: learn to walk shoes, kindergarten shoes, good weather shoes, wind and weather shoes, and party shoes. In order to achieve a broad distribution of the promotional messages, a total of 188 color television commercial spots were taken out in 1970 on all ARD public broadcasting channels, as well as 40 full-page "four-color advertisements in high-circulation general interest magazines."¹⁴⁸

In 1973, the workforce at the Elefanten Group comprised approximately 4,150 employees. Daily production of all Elefanten plants came to 45,000 pairs of shoes. Finally, in 1979, Gustav Hoffmann GmbH became Elefanten-Schuh GmbH.¹⁴⁹

In 1987, Freudenberg's shoe division generated sales of approximately 300 million deutschmarks.¹⁵⁰ But Elefanten shoes were meantime seeing persistently high cost pressure, since production took place exclusively in Germany. This led to the decision to close the plant in Walldorf and relocate production to Portugal. Hence Elefanten-Schuh GmbH too was following the trend of relocating production to countries with lower wage levels. The relocation had a positive effect on Elefanten-Schuh GmbH's cost structure as early as 1988. With total turnover of approximately 304 million deutschmarks, the entire shoe business division, comprising shoe manufacturing and shoe retailing, was now able to achieve an 8.6 percent share of Group sales.¹⁵¹

In 1989, the shoe factory in Offenbach, which was under severe pressure, was closed down. Continuing production – despite considerable restructuring measures in the preceding years – was no longer econom-

Fig. 92 Advertisement for Elefanten children's shoes, 1989

ically justifiable.[152] In 1990, Elefanten-Schuh GmbH established a joint venture with Allen Edmonds of Port Washington (USA) for the sale and the production of children's shoes.[153] However, things were continuing to develop in the wrong direction overall.[154] In 1995, the shoe division achieved a 6.7 percent share of Group turnover with turnover of approximately 337 million deutschmarks.[155] To make production cheaper, the shoe division opened another factory in Partisanske in Slovakia in 1997.[156]

In 1999, shoe retail chain Tack Schuh GmbH in Offenbach, with 48 outlets and 731 employees, was sold to Suez Industrie S. A., Paris. With the divestment of Tack, Freudenberg concentrated from then on solely on the production of brand-name children's shoes with high quality standards (Elefanten) and of children's shoes in the mid-price segment (Jela).[157] Meantime, the shoe division could only achieve a 2.8 percent share of group turnover with turnover of 200.8 million deutschmarks.[158]

Finally, in 2001, Freudenberg decided to close down its old-established shoe business entirely. This decision was taken against the backdrop of the Freudenberg Group's business principle to play a leading role in its markets.[159] The last remaining shoe company, Freudenberg Kleve GmbH (and thus formerly Elefanten-Schuh GmbH) was sold to the British firm Clarks Group as of March 1, 2001 along with the entire business assets including the shareholdings in Portugal, the United States and Slovakia.[160]

Freudenberg and SAP

At the beginning of the 1960s, IBM commanded a hefty market share in information technology. It was not only Freudenberg that relied on this technology. The logo of "Big Blue", as IBM was also known because of its blue corporate color, could be found on nine out of ten mainframe computers that were built.[161] Maybe a comparison will help understand how important IBM was back then from today's perspective: The name resonated in the same way that the names Google, Apple or Amazon do today. All larger companies relied on IBM's computer technology in issues of automation and digitalization. The later founders of SAP, who initially all worked for the German subsidiary of American technological pioneer IBM, were also enticed from these companies. The foundation history of SAP, the largest German software corporation right up to the present day, is closely associated with an order from Freudenberg in Weinheim; SAP was even established in Weinheim.

From 1967 onward, there was a key account management team which was responsible for Freudenberg, at the IBM Germany branch office in Mannheim. This team, which was headed by Rolf Müller, included the subsequent SAP founders Claus Wellenreuther, Klaus Tschira (1940–2015), Dietmar Hopp and Hasso Plattner, as well as the later Head of IT at Freudenberg, Karl Sinz. And the fifth co-founder of SAP, Hans-Werner Hector, was also an employee at IBM in Mannheim. Wellenreuther was one of the few people with a degree in business whom IBM had employed at that time. "Most of the younger employees had degrees in engineering, physics or mathematics: They were supposed to make technical and scientific data processing accessible to their customers in companies. However, when the new, third generation of computers came along, there were many interesting tasks in the area of commercial applications. That meant that IBM's technical and scientific employees would soon have to complete commercial training too and be deployed in commercial data processing projects." These commercial applications were predominantly supporting the accounts department, but also production planning and distribution.[162]

This new orientation bothered a few of the technologically oriented IBM employees. One example of this is the resource planning for the two IBM employees Eberhard Kilgus and Karl Sinz. Both had studied electrical engineering at the Technical University in Stuttgart and preferred to be deployed at IBM's customer BBC (now ABB), an electrical engineering corporation in which the two men expected to see technical and scientific applications. They could not agree, so they drew lots.[163] Sinz looked back at the situation in an interview in 2003: "We were a team with several young consultants – and renowned customers. We drew lots with matches for allocation to our customers, and I lost – or at least, that is what I thought at the time. Initially, I could not really relate to Freudenberg. But that was set to change very soon."[164] From October 1965 onward, he advised his customer, Freudenberg, in his role as IBM systems consultant. It turned out to be a long-term relationship: Sinz, who was born in 1939, ultimately worked for Freudenberg as a senior executive from 1977 to 2003. He was a long-standing head of the functional area Organization/IT and up to his retirement General Manager of Freudenberg Informatik KG.[165]

It fits in with this new epoch in the sector that the later SAP co-founder Hopp and his colleagues at IBM dealt with software at all. "In the very early years of the computer industry, the computers were the only thing that counted, programs were considered to be worthless, generally, you simply got them with the computers. An independent sector focusing on computer programming did not develop until the start of the 1970s. The reasons for this were manifold: technological innovations, expanding demand for such products, economic change.

However, the trigger is considered to be the great "unbundling" at IBM. In 1969, in order to avoid a looming antitrust lawsuit, the computer corporation decided to sell hardware and software separately from then on."[166]

On the initiative of Sales Director Rolf Müller, an accounting system was set to be developed for small and medium-sized customers for the IBM/360-20 system, which was selling well at that time. He chose accounting as an application area because every customer needed this application and the rules governing it applied and still apply uniformly to all companies because of centuries-old practices and legal regulations.[167]

Wellenreuther was assigned the task and developed this accounting system for his customer, Naturin, in Weinheim, which belonged to his major customer, Freudenberg. In the 1970s, the system became known, at least among experts, as the "Wellenreuther bookkeeping system". However, after various organizational changes, there was a stronger new development from IBM in this area, Fibu (financial bookkeeping), which was stepping into the limelight as an official IBM product – and Wellenreuther had been passed over during this development. Annoyed by his employer IBM's lack of interest in "his" product, Wellenreuther handed in his notice at the end of September 1970 and then marketed the system he had created himself. Six months later, Hopp, Plattner, Hector and Tschira joined him. Most likely the bookkeeping system played a decisive role in the initial difficult period for SAP, which was then founded on April 1, 1972.[168] However, "SAP – known back then under the name 'Systemanalyse – Programmentwicklung Hector, Hopp, Plattner, Tschira, Dr. Wellenreuther' and domiciled in Stettiner Strasse in Weinheim – worked"[169] initially not predominantly for Freudenberg, but for British chemical corporation Imperial Chemical Industries (ICI) in its nylon fiber factory in Östringen. There, "SAP [had been] given an order for an integrated software package for financial accounting, materials management and order processing [...]. This was set to become the foundation for a 'standard software' which was then also used in other companies."[170]

"The SAP founders benefited from another leap in technological development. Compared to today, monitors were still wickedly expensive, but just under 40 years ago, monitors became affordable, at least for companies, for the first time. Together with a keyboard and data cable, they made something possible which is considered a matter of course today: to communicate directly and in real time with a computer, meaning to press a key and at the same second to see a letter on the screen and. At that time stack processing, also known as batch processing, dominated. Before a computer could process data at all and could only spit them out again on a printer, they had to be punched laboriously onto punch cards with which the computer then had to be fed."[171]

"At that time, SAP was […] not the only start-up company that wanted to sell standard software. And like many others, it might have also [fallen into oblivion] again very quickly" – if Hopp and Plattner had not been granted interesting freedoms at ICI in Östringen. Because the managers of the factory did not hesitate when the SAP founders proposed that they would develop the programs further for ICI at their own expense: "As the start-up's first customer, ICI immediately ordered software for 638,000 deutschmarks. The order was a stroke of good fortune in other ways too: The fiber factory was one of the most modern in its sector, not just technologically, but also commercially."[172]

The cooperative relationship with its first customers was very important for SAP at the beginning for another reason too: "A mainframe of its own was simply unaffordable to SAP at that time, it would have cost multiple times the value of the order. So the SAP people used the ICI mainframe to test their programs – at night, when the computer had nothing else to do. During the day, they programmed their real-time applications, which is why they later called their first software package 'System R' (the names for the R/1, R/2 and R/3 product generations that are familiar today – came about later)."[173] Both of these, meaning the use of the computer center as well as the resale of the software, were also set to play an important role later with respect to SAP's relationship with Freudenberg, because in 1974, Freudenberg was looking for a solution for the implementation of a new accounting concept. SAP in its turn was on the lookout for new customers for their corresponding system. "Parts of it – primarily bookkeeping – were meantime being tested outside ICI, in development or alternatively in use, for example at 3K-Möbel, Knoll, John Deere and other customers. IBM [meantime] was very interested in the spread of the SAP system, since this required a relatively large amount of hardware – IBM's main focus at that time." The main problem with respect to Freudenberg, however, was the system software that was installed there, which was not compatible with the current SAP system.[174]

The "IBM employee responsible [for Freudenberg], Karl Sinz, endeavored to convince his former colleagues at SAP that a […] viable solution […] for CF [Carl Freudenberg] would have to be of great interest to SAP, because many of the major potential customers likewise ran their computer centers on the system basis" which was used by Freudenberg. "Dietmar Hopp and Claus Tschira were interested, Hasso Plattner was against making a system conversion at this time, since he […] feared performance problems. However, after CF [Carl Freudenberg] demonstrated added interest as a result of a visit to ICI and as well as the business – described in a contract on six DIN A4 pages […] – offered a good development environment in the CF computer center, SAP agreed to a system conversion." In 1976, the project was sealed accordingly. "The task consisted of two parts. On the one hand, the system basis had to be converted. Tschira looked after that with two assistants, supported by Georg Hirt and Jürgen Kratzer from CF [Carl Freudenberg], who contributed the […] [company-specific software] expertise. On the other hand, the application had to be amended and extended. Plattner was mainly working […] on this with his employees."[175] It can be seen from the lists of the monthly rental costs for such a system how important the use of the existing computer centers was to the SAP founders. Thus the monthly rent for the use of the IBM System 370 at Freudenberg in 1971 was calculated by IBM at almost 312,000 deutschmarks.[176]

"Then SAP also used the version of the SAP software" that emerged at Freudenberg" at other companies like Grundig, Philips and Jacobs. Thus the decision in favor of the work turned into a benefit for both sides: […] Freudenberg got very good applications for its systems from this project and SAP was able to use this solution to develop its customer base in the area of major customers."[177]

There is an interesting anecdote from the time when the programs were being developed at Freudenberg: "Plattner still programmed using punch cards, because he could use this process for all customers. In addition, he maintained […] that it was the better process. He had his big programs, the 'PGs', in card form in big cases. Whenever changes had to be made, the changes were not made in the source program and then compiled. Often, large programs could only be compiled overnight, because they ran for hours. For this reason, a technique developed by which changes or additions ('patches') were laboriously worked into the machine program and tested further. If the change was successful, it was also added to the stack of punch cards for the source program. Mr. Plattner did this expertly with colored punch cards in his mouth and hands in order to maintain an overview of the changes. After a hard day's work, the source program then looked quite colorful and tattered. Once, one of the CF programmers wanted to contribute to keeping order in Plattner's work and duplicated the source program onto fresh punch cards. When Mr. Plattner returned to the firm again and saw that his entire color history had been destroyed, he left again immediately. He left the message that he would not continue with his work until the program was available again in the form in which he had generated it. This caused a great commotion. However, they were able to put the program back together again in its original form from the card waste container."[178]

In the years that followed, Freudenberg also worked closely with the IBM consultants led by Sinz and his former colleagues and current SAP protagonists. Heinrich Karrer, who was responsible for the functional area of Business Administration with the departments Central Business Administration and Organization/IT (OD) at Freudenberg, commissioned Karl Sinz with the selection of a suitable candidate for the position of head of the OD department because of his expertise in the computing area in 1976. He then applied for the position himself and was hired by Freudenberg as of January 1, 1977. In the years that followed, Sinz led the department into autonomy, or rather independence, in the form of Freudenberg Informatik KG, which was established in 1995.[179]

In a chronological overview, it becomes clear when Freudenberg had passed through which development stages with SAP up to then: The start of the adaptation of the SAP software to Freudenberg's database system in 1975 was followed by upgrades in the financial accounting software and finally, in 1978, its introduction, initially at Simrit. In 1981, the next stage was the introduction of a standard software in materials management; plant accounting followed in 1983; an in-house development for processing approvals within the SAP system in 1984; and production planning and control for special purpose engineering in 1991.[180]

Parallel to the introduction of the SAP software solutions, the computer systems that had been installed were also developed further. At the end of the 1970s, Freudenberg initially purchased computers that could be used in a decentralized setup, like the IBM 8100 system. The company used these computers at Megulastik in Neuenburg as well as in materials management. What was new about these systems was that they could work as a network with the mainframe. However, the most important milestone in the history of IT at that time was the rise of personal computers from the middle of the 1980s onward, to be precise, the rise of the IBM PC or alternatively IBM-compatible personal computers. Because the personal computer, known in abbreviation as "PC", enabled the universal availability of information technology, ultimately, it found its way onto almost every desk. The "computer", as it was commonly known, became the industry standard, since it could be used for the most varied applications in the most diverse situations. The use of PCs grew exponentially – at Freudenberg too.[181]

This resulted in the data processing department at Freudenberg gaining a new task: advising about PC use and controlling PC deployment. This was also connected to the objective of preventing an uncontrolled and uneconomic proliferation of PC applications as well as to improve efficiency and productivity in handling software solutions like Lotus, Excel, Text4 and Word. This went hand in hand with the early – and, from today's perspective, right – decision at Freudenberg in favor of Microsoft software and against the comparable IBM products at the time. That meant using Microsoft DOS and Windows instead of the IBM operating system PS/2, Word instead of Text4 and Excel instead of the alternative spreadsheet software Lotus.[182]

Fig. 93 Early computer-aided design (CAD) programming on a PC, 1989

Computer centers, which had to be reachable seven days a week, around the clock, because they supported production facilities that worked in multiple shifts, led to the need to automate. The challenge consisted particularly in the need to constantly replace the magnetic storage tapes. These had to be inserted or removed manually by the employees at the magnetic tape console, whenever this was indicated by the system. In order to be able to implement this around the clock and permanently, the idea was posited at Freudenberg at an early stage to deploy a robot to do this. This should carry out the replacement of the magnetic storage tapes independently in the computer center, meaning that the manual replacement that was used up to then would be eliminated. Queries to all leading manufacturers – including to market leader IBM – soon presented the realization that no solution for automated magnetic tape cassette processing existed on the market in the mid-1980s and that no one was working on a system such as this either. Freudenberg made a virtue of this necessity and now began its own development of a robot system that was suitable for the purpose. The mechanical part was built by an external service provider according to Freudenberg's specifications, the software integration into the computer center was programmed by the in-house IT department. Thus the first automated magnetic tape cassette robot was likely developed at Freudenberg, which was put into operation from 1987 onward.[183]

When the further development of the SAP R/2 applications became visible and the new R/3 version was announced at the beginning of the 1990s, Freudenberg's IT department succeeded in adapting to the transition at an early stage. The new SAP R/3 software became usable on a client-server architecture, in which personal computers were connected to network computers (servers). This architecture continued to push the mainframe computers increasingly into the background. It was more economic and enabled working with graphic interfaces as well as incorporation of the internet, which likewise became increasingly widespread in the course of the following years.[184]

Sealing and vibration control technology between oil crisis, German reunification and López effect

In the 1960s, the sealing technology division undertook important, but also urgently necessary steps towards internationalization: Production was expanded in North America; various distribution companies were set up in Europe. And because the division was constantly being confronted with a significant shortage of labor at the established production facilities, new plants were opened in rural regions to move closer to a workforce potential that was still untapped. This occurred in Reichelsheim, Schwalmstadt and Oberwihl, among other places. At that time, however, the shortage of labor was not the only problem. The machines were so old that in some cases the sealing business had to contend with quality difficulties and as a result with delivery backlogs. The result was an unpleasant drop in orders. The situation was made even more critical by the recession in 1967.

But with regard to the starting situation: At the end of 1959, sales in the sealing business were at 66.6 million deutschmarks, and the Simrit-Werk plant employed 2,278 workers.[185] That year, the issue of internationalization already played a role with the establishment of Simrit S. A. as a distribution company in Paris.[186] Further investments were made at the Weinheim headquarters as well: In 1961, construction began of an extended mixing plant in the Zwischen Dämmen plant, whereupon the mixing plant in the Old Lacquering Plant could be decommissioned and relocated completely. Capacity initially comprised 500 tons per month. Thus, as a result – with the exception of the Schopfheim plant – all European elastomer processing plants were supplied with rubber compounds by Freudenberg.[187]

However, things did not constantly improve; on the contrary: After the strong growth of the 1950s with rising sales figures (1959: 66.6 million deutschmarks, 1960: 86.5 million deutschmarks, 1961: 95.9 million deutschmarks), a significant business decline set in from 1962 onward in the sealing division. The reasons for this, apart from rising scrap production, which was a sign of extensive quality problems, also included a slight economic downturn at the beginning of the 1960s. However, the main problem was undoubtedly the significant order processing times of three to six months for orders which could not be processed directly off the shelf. This led to a 20 percent decline in sales to 78.1 million deutschmarks in 1962. Although turnover rose again from 1963 onward, deadline and quality problems continued to dominate daily business.[188]

Initially, however, the division was able to celebrate a record. In 1964, sales in the sealing division exceeded the 100 million deutschmarks level for the first time, at 102.1 million deutschmarks – with a return on sales of almost 15 percent.[189] Meanwhile, this renewed strong growth exacerbated the existing capacity bottlenecks. Since a labor shortage already prevailed in Weinheim, Freudenberg followed the general trend in German industry to invest in rural areas. Plant openings followed up to 1966 in Treysa (now Schwalmstadt) and Reichelsheim.[190]

The short recession with which the German economy was directly confronted in 1967 also impacted Freudenberg's Simrit sealing division, since the production restrictions in the automotive and automotive supply industry had corresponding effects. Sales slumped by 10 percent to 105.5 million deutschmarks. This led to declining capacity utilization, which is why staff had to be let go, by means of natural attrition and through transfers to other Freudenberg companies which were less severely affected by the downturn. The workforce in the sealing division was reduced by 266 employees. However, this development was set to be over soon. As early as the following year, more than 500 new employees were hired. Alongside this, further investments were made in expanding capacity in the sealing division – both in Weinheim and in the German stand-alone plants. Then, in 1968, sales also rose by more than 40 percent. The export quota had now reached almost 20 percent already.[191]

Wilhelm Schmitt, who was a member of the Management Board from 1983 to 1993, played a pivotal role in the reorganization of this area. As the new Head of Technical Development, he now initiated the systematic development of a quality assurance system to get the quality problems that still persisted under control.[192] Schmitt also gathered suggestions from staying for many weeks at NOK in Japan in 1964. The insights into NOK's quality-oriented, highly modern production technology influenced the reorganization of quality assurance at Freudenberg.[193] Looking back, the member of the Management Board responsible for the division, Peter Wentzler, acknowledged the success of these measures: "The quality standard of our products can be described as good. It is likely that Simrit still ranks among the top class of the producer group."[194]

The efforts to internationalize the business were also continued, this time in the United States: In 1968, Freudenberg acquired a 25 percent shareholding in International Packings Corp. Ltd. (IPC) in Bristol, New Hampshire, which had been established in 1949. This expanded Freudenberg's independent seal production in America considerably. As a result, Freudenberg acquired all the shares in IPC up to the year 1984, and the company thus gradually became a full subsidiary of the Freudenberg Group.[195] The president of IPC, David S. Williams,[196] was on the lookout for a partner that operated independently of the American competition, because he was extremely worried about this in particular, as well as about the rising development costs. Through the mediation of Rolf Merton, Freudenberg's representative in America, who was located in New York, first contact ensued in 1964 between Freudenberg and IPC, which was followed in 1966 by the first mutual visits and the start of an exchange of technological experience. Collaboration with IPC was likewise of interest to Freudenberg, since access to the major American automotive manufacturers was improved because of the already established, and on top of that quality-oriented, automotive supplier. Its product portfolio was oriented particularly towards the requirements of the three large automotive manufacturers General Motors, Ford and Chrysler, and the associated large-scale production.[197]

However, the takeover of IPC led to an increasingly stiff competitive situation between Freudenberg and NOK on the American market from the 1970s onward. This also negatively impacted the relationship between Freudenberg and NOK outside America, since Freudenberg and NOK practiced a close exchange of expertise. This problem was not solved until the merger of Freudenberg and NOK's American business to form the Freudenberg-NOK General Partnership joint venture.[198]

Freudenberg also profited from the long-lasting – apart from the short dip in 1967 – boom of the 1960s in its other business areas. In vibration control technology, for example – which was still operated separately at that time – sales had almost doubled in 1968 compared to the previous year, at more than 19 million deutschmarks. After that, however, progress was no longer so straightforward as this increase would suggest: Sales were increased to 32 million deutschmarks by 1970. Nevertheless, despite these successes, the operating result in vibration control technology was not always positive, since – for good reason – a lot of money flowed into development and capacity expansion. It was a constant struggle to reach high quality standards: The reject level remained a major cost factor, at approximately 10 percent. Exports only accounted for 1.2 percent of sales; thus there was still a lot to do in this area too, which was so important for the permanent stabilization of this extremely important business.[199] In 1970, against this backdrop, but also with an eye to the possibility of gaining workers from rural regions and even from France at the new site, a modern plant was opened in Neuenburg am Rhein. Production there initially comprised torsional vibration dampers, chassis parts and engine mounts, as well as small-batch production of parts for rail vehicles and mechanical engineering.[200] By 1974, the entire production of rubber metal parts had been relocated from Weinheim to Neuenburg.[201] In Weinheim, all that remained was the Management Board, technical development, distribution and administration, as well as production preparation.[202]

The original licensing agreement with Metalastik Limited from 1957 expired in 1973. From then on, Freudenberg operated independently in vibration control technology and the name of the business division and unit was initially changed to Megulastik and subsequently to Freudenberg-Megulastik.[203] Sound insulation was also included as a new field of activity in 1975, in accordance with Freudenberg's strategy of diversifying into related product areas. This was a fast-growing field of activity, particularly because of the Sound Insulation Act: "The dampening of structure-borne sound [meaning the sound of mechanical bodies and components] and its emission to machines and automobiles was related to Megulastik's field of activity. The market for sound protection products was undergoing substantial growth [...]." From then on, both noise protection cabins for the encapsulation of machines as well as elements for sound absorption were developed and manufactured.[204]

Even under Siegfried Hinz (1927–2001), the Management Board member who had been responsible for sealing and vibration control technology since 1973, the company did not lose sight of the expansion of its foreign business despite the effects of the oil crisis – the decline in automobile production in particular had led to significant order slumps in the sealing business in 1974.[205] In 1975, Simrit de Mexico was established with partner Irurita. The company's headquarters were in Cuautla, where a seal factory was also built.[206] In France, Simrit S. A. moved to Mâcon and saw the construction of a seal production facility, which began operations the following year.[207] In 1976, further foreign investments were made: In Spain, Hiscasa, a seal manufacturer, was acquired. It operated from 1988 onward as Freudenberg Compoñentes and after 1993 as Freudenberg Ibérica.[208] Since 1977, production had taken place in Parets del Vallès.[209]

Seal production underwent an important innovation in 1976 with the introduction of the Q76 quality assurance program. Wilhelm Schmitt had adjusted the Japanese Kaizen method for Q76, as it was practiced at Toyota, but also at NOK, for German production. The program was a reaction to the stagnating markets, the increasingly stiff competition situation – especially in international competition – and rising quality requirements from customers. It had the objective of identifying individual weak points, but was primarily to improve the quality of individuals' work and of collaboration within the team overall. To do this, Freudenberg introduced a concept that was totally new for that time in Germany involving quality circles and project groups: small working groups who analyze upcoming issues and elaborate proposals for solutions. Identifying and eliminating sources of errors became the task of the new "Error source notification program". This led not only to quality improvements on the product side, but also to significant improvements in production processes and thus to an increase in productivity and a reduction in production costs. Only five years after the initiative had begun, more than 10,000 notifications and suggestions for improvement had been received for seal manufacturing.[210] A look at the broad portfolio of the seal division shows how important quality management was. In 1979, this comprised approximately 70,000 different products. In one month, up to 32,000 were processed, for approximately 6,000 customers from around the world.[211]

Fig. 94 Billboard with the Q76 mascot, Simmi, 1980

Pursuing the innovation and diversification idea further, Freudenberg turned its attention to the increasingly important area of electronics in 1977: The company acquired 75 percent of the shares of the small firm F & O Electronic Systems GmbH & Co. in Neckargemünd, a manufacturer of microprocessors for specialty areas, like for example computer printers and programmed learning systems.[212] Then, in 1981, this business was shifted to the area of flexible printed circuit boards. Under the brand name Simflex, Freudenberg began production of printed circuit boards and printed circuits, which are used for example in mobile phones, together with NOK.[213] From 1996 onward, the joint venture operated under the name Freudenberg Mektec GmbH & Co. KG, but then, in 2010, Freudenberg passed on its shareholding in Freudenberg Mektec to its long-standing joint venture partner NOK.[214]

Fig. 95 Simflex printed circuit board production, 1992

The late 1970s and the 1980s were years of internationalization, but also of constant adaptation to changing business conditions – in vibration control technology too. In 1978, a joint venture was established with NOK, and NOK-Megulastik Co. Ltd. was born.[215] The most important customer was still the automotive industry.[216]

Finally, in 1985 and in the years that followed on directly from it, significant new products came onto the market, for example adaptive dampers, flexural vibration dampers, improved vibration absorbers, hydraulic bushings, along with bearings for German rail company Deutsche Bahn's ICE high-speed train. In sealing technology, the 1980s were initially characterized by a technological innovation: the Simmerring with a sealing lip made from the raw material PTFE came onto the market. The novel Simmerring soon found widespread use in the internal combustion engines of the European and American engine and vehicle manufacturers. Because of its technologically superior material properties, it replaced the elastomer sealing edge which had been used up to then – and paved the way for new applications for the Simmerring: PTFE material is outstanding because of its chemical resistance to almost all aggressive mediums, like for example oils, fats, acids, lyes, solvents and gases. Added to this are its retained flexibility, even at the lowest temperatures of below minus 40 degrees Celsius, and high-temperature resistance up to above plus 200 degrees Celsius.[217]

Organizational progress was also set in motion in production too: From 1985 a complete conversion of production from the traditional, monotonous block production with constant repetition of the same hand movements to production in what are known as "industrial cells" took place within three years. At Freudenberg, an "industrial cell" was to be regarded like a small "factory within a factory", in which an employee assembled "their" product completely – from picking up the blank, right up to packaging. In this way, the work not only becomes more varied, but the quality of the finished products rises significantly too. A markedly lower scrap rate was a confirmation of the success of this measure: Whereas this had still been previously measured in percent, it was only a matter of per thousand after the conversion of production.[218] From then on, the employees acted independently as far as possible, and motivation improved as well because there was more variety in the job.

As a result, a reduction in production costs and shorter delivery times could be achieved.[219] The new production philosophy – based on the idle zero (IZ) principle, meaning "avoiding the unnecessary" – developed from the Q76 quality assurance program that was introduced ten years earlier and additionally took into account Kanban as well as just-in-time methods that Freudenberg had learned know from its Japanese partner NOK. Therefore, as preparation, numerous Freudenberg employees were familiarized with IZ production on-site at NOK in Japan.[220] Kanban comes from Japan originally: automotive corporation Toyota had invented it back in 1947. The name is composed of the two Japanese syllables "kan" and "ban", which mean "signal card". Initially it was designed to optimize material flow: tasks are divided into small steps and worked through one after the other.[221]

Reinhart Freudenberg later recalled the "implacable quality criteria of the Japanese" with their zero-error tolerance. "The processes in the factories, perfect logistics, no stocks, just-in-time delivery, those were also things that we learned in Japan, and this Kaizen principle too, that you basically endeavor to solve problems in small working groups on all levels. Therefore, that was probably very important even then and gave us a head start in Europe."[222]

The entire business revived significantly in the course of the 1980s: "The auspicious climate that prevailed in Germany and internationally in the motor vehicle and investment goods industry also benefited the development of the seals and molded parts division. With an above-average increase in sales of 11.3 percent to 820.4 million deutschmarks [in 1988], the division was able to cement its position in the most important markets."[223]

During this time, an important development for the division was the serial production of innovative engine components made from fiber-reinforced plastics in the expanded Reichelsheim plant. Innovations like this had a positive effect on profitability.[224] However, the technology from Reichelsheim did not just make cars fast: On February 15, 1984 German duo Hans Stanggassinger and Franz Wembacher from Berchtesgaden won the gold medal in the double luge at the Winter Olympics in Sarajevo. With them was a Freudenberg product: a thermoplastic molded part developed and produced in Reichelsheim for the steering suspension ensured temperature-independent maneuverability of the luge.[225]

In 1989, Freudenberg began the process of merging the American subisidiaries IPC, Disogrin, Escan (vibration control technology), Simrit Corp. (distribution) and Simrit de Mexico into one single company headquartered in Detroit, and thus in the immediate vicinity of the US automotive industry – deliberations on this move had already begun two years earlier. The reason: The individual companies worked independently of each other and even developed different strategies. Nevertheless, they supplied the same customers, sometimes with competing products. At that time, Freudenberg lacked an identity of its own on the North American continent. Thus the aim of the merger was to achieve a unified presence in sealing and vibration control technology in North America.[226] However, the reorganization process in these businesses was not finished yet. As already mentioned, the Freudenberg companies in the United States – especially IPC – found themselves in a competitive situation with their Japanese partner NOK from the 1970s onward. This latter's US subsidiary, NOK Inc., had opened its own sealing plant in La Grange in Georgia in 1982 in the wake of the growing number of sales of Japanese vehicles in the United States, which further exacerbated the competitive situation. This was increasingly impacting the relationship of the partners in Tokyo and Weinheim and finally led to talks between the Management Boards about the possibility of working the North American market jointly from 1988 onward. In the spirit of the long-standing, trusting collaboration, the partners agreed on a joint-venture solution.[227]

As of July 1, 1989, Freudenberg-NOK General Partnership (FNGP) was then established in Plymouth, Michigan. This brought about the merger of all North American companies belonging to the two partners in the sealing and vibration control technology area. It was an important milestone for both companies, since the newly established firm rose to become the most important seal producer in North America. In Freudenberg's case, this concerned IPC Ltd., Disogrin Industries, Escan Corporation, Simrit Corporation and Simrit de Mexico.[228] The distribution of shares was calculated from the balance of the individual sales of all the companies integrated into the joint venture: The Freudenberg companies together accounted for 75 percent and NOK Inc. 25 percent of total sales. This ratio was also reflected in the companies' assets.[229]

Fig. 96 Establishment of FNGP, 1989: Masato Tsuru (left) and Reinhart Freudenberg (right) are pictured planting a tree. In the center of the photo: Joe Day, the first President of FNGP

Because of German reunification, Freudenberg was also able to find a way to enter the market in the new Länder. In 1992, Freudenberg ultimately took over a total of 600 employees and three factories belonging to Polymant Kautschuk- and Kunststoffverarbeitung GmbH in Berlin, Velten near Berlin and Triptis.[230] The factories' economic situation was rated as difficult. In urgent need of modernization, the markets had to be developed completely from scratch again, since the previous customers in Eastern Germany and Eastern Europe had been lost without any replacements. However, the qualified personnel working there and the long-term positive future of these traditional industrial regions of Germany led Freudenberg to believe the efforts were justified. Economically, the situation continued to be unsatisfactory, since a significant business slowdown quickly followed on from the reunification boom. Results in the division and in the company overall deteriorated across the board and were negative overall. External pressure came from the poor automotive business as well as declines in the mechanical engineering industry and trade in technical goods.[231]

Finally, in 1992, Freudenberg was confronted with a serious sales and structural crisis in the sealing and vibration control technology area. This led to considerable need for adaptation. Under the aegis of Peter Stehle, the Management Board member who had been responsible for these divisions since 1990, and who also became a general partner a year later and took over responsibility from Hinz for seals and molded parts, as well as for the vibration control technology and Freudenberg-NOK divisions,[232] and of Jörg Sost, head of the sealing division and from 2005 until 2010 a member of the Management Board, drastic measures were taken. The objective was to restore competitiveness under market conditions that had changed completely.[233]

The result: In 1993, the vibration control technology division was merged with the seals and molded parts division to form the sealing and vibration control technology division (DS), and the "Megulastik" brand name disappeared.[234] The Partners' Report on the Business from 1992 described the reasons for this and also the future corporate structure: The measure made sense, it stated, since both divisions "by and large serve the same customer base, the automotive industry and general mechanical engineering, and are also related when it comes to their technology. The DS division is sub-divided into seven business areas according to its product groups. The individual European production sites belonging to DS will concentrate on specific product groups, in order to be able to take advantage of the benefits of larger production volumes, more profound specialized knowledge and a simpler organization."[235] The seven business units each had a lead center with Europe-wide responsibility for the areas of development, production, quality assurance, logistics, marketing and controlling. The lead centers were complemented by satellite production facilities.[236]

At Freudenberg, the introduction of these lead centers came at a time when the so-called "López effect" had become a wake-up call for automotive suppliers. In the 1990s, the effects of the new procurement policy of the General Motors, and later Volkswagen, head of purchasing José Ignacio López were deeply perceptible in the automotive supply sector. Like everywhere else, they led to extensive adjustment efforts at Freudenberg too. These were changes which would later become notorious across the entire automotive supply sector under the name López effect. What was it all about? When Ferdinand Piëch became chairman of the board of management at Volkswagen in 1993, a loss of almost 2 billion deutschmarks was posted in the company's accounts. The reason: excessively high production costs, which were significantly above the sector average. Therefore Piëch headhunted José Ignacio López, who was renowned as a "cost killer"[237] from competitor Opel. As purchasing manager there, López had pushed down prices by exerting immense pressure on the respective suppliers. Opel and its then parent company, General Motors, and Volkswagen would fight a pitched legal battle in the coming years. The accusation: López allegedly took boxfuls of internal documents with him from Opel. Ultimately, the legal battle would cost López his job on the management board at Volkswagen (VW) in 1996. In the meantime, López nonetheless got down to work there, from his perspective successfully: VW posted a profit again already in 1994. Not all of VW's suppliers survived.[238] Freudenberg too had to address this challenge in the respective business units.

Jörg Sost, who was division head of sealing and vibration control technology, informed the Management Board about the negotiating situation with VW with drastic words: "We currently have a price differential of 25 percent compared to VW's expectations. It is essential that this gap is closed. Basically, additional volumes can only be gained via price; the reaction was very good; at VW, they had not expected that CF [Carl Freudenberg] would prove to be so flexible in this way; the proposals we made are currently being processed; it is certain that without such a reaction from VW, we would have been cut back bit by bit."[239] Sost also discovered in this context that one can never pull back from any customer, not even from VW. He was convinced that Freudenberg would have to fundamentally adapt to a lower price level in the future too. In case they would be unable to achieve an adequate return on the new price basis, the fundamental question would have to be asked as to whether they should continue to pursue the business at all. This much was clear: Prices could no longer be calculated autonomously. Freudenberg too would have to accept that they were made by the market.[240]

Later Sost described the challenge in somewhat greater detail: The most diverse technologies and manufacturing processes were being used at Freudenberg in sealing technology. In order to remain competitive, they had to identify the best technology and then roll this out comprehensively throughout the company. In this respect, "López [… was] a gift", because "the German automotive industry was no longer competitive, neither technologically nor cost-wise," Sost recalls. When López demanded of the suppliers that they lower their prices by 30 percent with immediate effect, he had "woken up the industry." In Sost's opinion, a great many incentives to change and improve occurred at Freudenberg and in the entire automotive industry because of this. At Freudenberg it became evident, with respect to the technology problem described above, "that the positioning that the sealing division had back then 'was totally wrong,'" according to Sost.[241]

In fact, the entire sealing and vibration control technology division was only able to maintain its market position in 1994 through high price concessions, which led to a negative result. In the Partners' Report on the Business, the situation was described quite soberly and unsparingly: "The past year showed clearly that far-reaching restructuring is still required for the German sites in Neuenburg and Velten because of high costs. The business – although it is technologically demanding – can only be operated successfully if we have cost leadership. The concepts required for this have been developed and are now being implemented systematically."[242] Thus the problem that caused returns to collapse because of the high price concessions could only be tackled with a significant increase in productivity in order to be able to continue operating the sealing and vibration control technology business in the long term. As a consequence of this, the cost-cutting was expedited through the productivity increases that had already been initiated under the Europe-wide lead center concept and the adoption of further Japanese methods and technologies.[243]

The López effect was set to remain perceptible in the following year too. There were still reports about price pressure and far-reaching concessions. However, there were hopeful aspects mixed in with the situation report: "At the Neuenburg and Weinheim sites, however, the restructuring in the key divisions is starting to take hold."[244] Step by step, the rigorous restructuring of the business was having an impact, the concentration of individual product groups in specialized sites – the lead center concept – was increasingly paying off. Freudenberg-NOK in the United States was also able to increase sales and income considerably against the backdrop of the revival in the automotive sector.[245] "What was achieved by the division there is remarkable, because after only a few years, it had absorbed these price cuts. And then things continued on well again and we then actually felt somehow stronger than the competition," Reinhart Freudenberg recalled later.[246]

During this time, the development of the Q76 program, which had meantime proven itself, was also progressed: In 1994, the division introduced the important and rapidly successful GROWTTH program as a significant design element of corporate culture – the acronym stood for "Get Rid of Waste Through Team Harmony" and was based on Q76. The same methods were used as for Kaizen; thus Japanese management methods were adopted around the entire world, all as a result of the López effect. Freudenberg had already been gathering initial experience with GROWTTH since 1992 at Freudenberg-NOK General Partnership in the USA. Two years later, it became standard within the division around the world. The concept of actively processing cross-hierarchical projects and implementing improvements immediately, as well as learning about a specific task across the entire value chain, worked.

In the mid-1990s, sealing and vibration control technology had overcome a significant challenge: Far-reaching measures, the lion's share of which, at least with regard to the management methods, were adopted from Japan, restored the company's competitiveness again under completely altered market conditions.²⁴⁷ In the wake of this, the divisions had been merged, and there was additionally a new organizational concept (lead centers). During those years, the repercussions of the López effect on the automotive supply sector were tremendous, and Freudenberg and its experiences are a prime example of this.

Teething pains in China

Just one year after Chinese head of state Deng Xiaoping initiated the economic opening of China²⁴⁸ in 1978, Freudenberg took the first steps towards tapping the Chinese market – but initially only indirectly, in distribution. This occurred, as so often happened in Freudenberg's company history, with the aid of reliable partners: Bremen-based company C. Melchers & Co. had already been a distribution partner of Freudenberg's in China since 1923 for leather goods and later also for shoe products. Then, from 1979 onward, Melchers additionally took over sole agency for Freudenberg leather and shoe products in the region.²⁴⁹

Additionally, that same year, activities to set up proprietary production facilities in the country began. Although these were set to remain fruitless to a large extent for a long time, they nevertheless provide a fascinating insight into the difficulties that prevailed back then in entering this foreign market which is so important today. Since NOK had also set its sights on the Chinese market, Freudenberg joined forces with its Japanese partner in 1979 to initiate direct contact with the Chinese First Ministry of Machine Building of Guangdong Province in Shanghai. The objective was the establishment of a joint venture for the production of seals. Distribution partner Melchers mediated in this regard and discovered in advance that the Chinese would decide themselves whether NOK or Freudenberg would be the main joint venture partner. This would depend on what conditions were offered, particularly for export quotas, which was important to the Chinese side because of the associated procurement of foreign currency. The negotiations dragged on into the following year.²⁵⁰

On the invitation of the First Ministry of Machine Building and the Ministry for Agricultural Machine Building, representatives from the Freudenberg sealing division Simrit visited Beijing and Guangzhou in September 1979. In their travel report, they summarized that a "technological backwardness on the part of the Chinese" was discernible. Freudenberg had presented the Chinese delegation with a list of questions, "which comprised the Chinese market, the infrastructure, including energy supply and environmental problems, as well as basic questions on attitude to property, on licenses and patents and financing issues." The answers to these questions were intended to form the basis for further discussions. Above and beyond this, the "shockingly low productivity" of the factories visited, the "unusually low salary and wage costs" (30 to 80 yuan/month; a bicycle cost 180 yuan) as well as "around 20 million 'work seekers' (the Chinese expression)" were topics of the discussions.[251]

Just one month later, Freudenberg and NOK reached an agreement about how they would proceed jointly in China. At this meeting, the NOK management particularly emphasized "the necessity for the NOK cooperation." Shogo Tsuru, at that time Chairman of NOK, warned that cooperation agreements with Chinese partners had to be "handled with extreme caution," but "are useful and expedient. However, we should not rush anything in how we proceed, and be aware of the political structure and also its potential for change."[252]

The discussions on a joint venture for sealing production in China were continued at the beginning of 1980. The First Ministry of Machine Building approved a joint venture under certain conditions. For example, the wages of all Chinese as well as foreign employees should be agreed in advance with the ministry, meaning with a government authority, beforehand.[253] At the end of 1980, the discussions came to a standstill, however. Although the Chinese side still showed an interest in a joint venture, it was ultimately unable to answer decisive questions from Freudenberg and NOK. Dieter Freudenberg, who was participating in the discussions, explained this inability predominately as a "total lack of understanding for the simplest business contexts as well as [...] the total ignorance of macroeconomic contexts." Freudenberg delivered a corresponding conclusion following a visit to China in October 1980: "My impression has been intensified in the course of the trip that the time for joint ventures has not yet come."[254]

Following Dieter Freudenberg's recommendation, the company attempted to strive for other forms of cooperation with the First Ministry of Machine Building in December 1980, as can be derived from a letter from the Simrit division management: "Negotiations up to now have revealed the manifold difficulties in the agreement of joint ventures. Other Western companies interested in joint venture agreements report about similar experiences too. Furthermore, the Joint Venture Law of the People's Republic of China that was passed in the past year also requires further implementation laws, which have been announced on the part of your government, but have not been adopted yet. We therefore come to the conclusion that we should also consider different forms of cooperation on both sides."[255] This was an assessment that the NOK management shared too.[256]

Subsequently, a cooperation agreement in the form of countertrade was proposed by the Chinese side before year-end. However, because of the transfer of knowledge required, countertrade was not an option for Freudenberg at that time.[257]

NOK and Freudenberg reached an agreement – with an eye to competitors too – to address all joint venture projects in China together. With this in mind, the way forward was planned: Thus NOK should be the main partner first, and then Freudenberg. Both parties planned to attend meetings jointly, if possible. Representative offices were set up in Beijing and Guangzhou.[258] There had been disagreements between NOK and Freudenberg about how to proceed in China prior to this, so that both sides believed it to be necessary to contractually stipulate a joint approach for tapping the Chinese market.[259]

Despite these joint efforts, all negotiations on setting up a production facility for seals in China finally came to a standstill in 1982. Nevertheless, they planned to continue observing the market, particularly because it was common knowledge that their important customer, Volkswagen, was planning to set up its own production facility in China.[260]

A new attempt was made in 1985, but in the nonwovens business. In 1985, after a trip to China, Norbert Dahlström (1936–2014) – who had been the Management Board member responsible for the nonwovens division since 1978[261] – proposed a joint venture with China National Textiles (CNT) as well as plans for a production facility for nonwovens in Nantong. Freudenberg was supported in this by the government organization CITIC, the China International Trust and Investment Corporation. It had the task of promoting industrial cooperation with Western firms. Protecting Freudenberg technologies played an important role in these negotiations too.[262] The discussions about a joint venture in Nantong, which was planned to be set up together with Japan Vilene Company, initially led, up to August, to a positive feasibility study of the project as a prerequisite for a subsequent joint venture.[263] However, the Chinese negotiating partners subsequently rejected the compromise proposals tabled by Freudenberg (and Japan Vilene Company) and retreated to their original demands, which were not acceptable to Freudenberg. While Freudenberg – as it generally did when conducting its activities in the various regions of the world – was focused primarily on the domestic market, the Chinese side insisted on a high export quota to earn foreign currency. Thus the negotiations finally came to a complete standstill in the fall, after the licensing and technical support offers had also been rejected.[264]

Nevertheless, Dahlström was not discouraged and formulated his assessment of the Chinese market very forcefully:

"My conclusion from these observations and initial impressions, which are definitely still incomplete and subjective, is by no means negative, on the contrary, I am more convinced than ever that Freudenberg must participate at an early stage in China's industrial development and can make real contributions here too. We cannot and must not wait until the most serious difficulties have been overcome and then fling ourselves onto the moving train. […] Just as we cannot let ourselves be blinded by the current euphoric and optimistic mood, it is equally irresponsible to ignore the enormous market and human potential in China and, biding our time, let the impending boom pass without our active and creative participation."[265]

At the start of the 7th Five-Year Plan in 1986, the Chinese government encouraged foreign investors to invest in certain focus areas: energy exploitation, electrical engineering industry, plant engineering, construction material industry and infrastructure construction, and modernization of existing factories. In this context, the authorities clearly granted companies with foreign capital interests (equity joint ventures) priority over cooperative companies (contractual/cooperative joint ventures).[266] Just for this reason alone, this did nothing to change the difficulties of gaining a foothold in China.

Overall, the Freudenberg Management Board still had rather a wait-and-see attitude in 1988: Although the Chinese market was not interesting in the short term, it said, it nonetheless offered possibilities in the long term.[267] However, this reserved assessment was revised quickly when the market developed dynamically after Deng Xiaoping's forced economic opening of China in 1990.[268]

In the wake of this open-door policy, establishing joint ventures was also made easier, to enable the development of local production facilities for high-quality technological products for the growing Chinese economy. The prerequisites for commercial involvement in China had clearly improved, and the automobile market, which was so relevant to Freudenberg, was undergoing "speedy development". The division management at Freudenberg sealing and vibration control technology estimated annual growth rates of 20 percent for the Chinese automobile market. What made it particularly urgent for Freudenberg was the fact that the two major automobile customers, Volkswagen and the French PSA Group (Peugeot and Citroën), were already operating their own factories in China and were very interested in being supplied by the Freudenberg Group from local production facilities. Hence the Management Board decided in November 1992 – together with NOK – to follow its customers and start setting up their own seal production facility in China.[269]

In order to be able to meet the needs of its customers in China as quickly as possible, Freudenberg bought into an existing joint venture in the automotive city

Fig. 97 Opening ceremony for the nonwovens factory in Suzhou, China, with representatives from the Chinese authorities, 1996

of Changchun at the end of 1992. To do this, it acquired French seal manufacturer Procal S. A. in Langres, which had a production facility in China through this joint venture. This acquisition was a "jump-start in China"[270] for Freudenberg and also helped to improve Freudenberg's position on the French market.[271] Then, when it took over the joint venture agreement from Procal, the actual development of its own first production facility in China began in 1993 in Changchun.[272] The company was renamed Changchun NOK-Freudenberg Oilseal Co., Ltd.[273] NOK and Freudenberg subsequently acquired all the remaining shares in the joint venture.[274] As early as September 1994, the Management Board decided to build a further seal plant together with NOK in China in the city of Wuxi, and for this purpose established Wuxi NOK-Freudenberg Oilseal Co. Ltd. in 1995.[275] The company was established without any Chinese participation as a completely German-Japanese joint venture – a possibility that had only existed since the beginning of the 1990s in the wake of China's new "open-door" under Deng Xiaoping.[276] Production in the seal factory in Changchun began in 1995 and in Wuxi in 1996.

The nonwovens were also finally able to implement their first production facility in China. Together with Japan Vilene Company, a production company was built for interlinings in Suzhou: Freudenberg & Vilene Nonwovens (Suzhou) Co. Ltd. It started production in 1996 and was established – like the company in Wuxi – as a so-called wholly foreign owned company, meaning without any participation of Chinese partners.[277]

Moreover, NOK-Freudenberg Asia Holding Co. Pte. Ltd. was established as a holding company for the activities of sealing and vibration control technology in China and India. The headquarters are in Singapore and the companies hold equal shares.[278] In the following years, China developed into one of the most important growth markets for the company.

Structural change? Innovation! Internationalization! The nonwovens business from the 1960s onward

The nonwovens business is a further example of the pressure to adapt, to which even a seemingly established area of the company can be subjected because of external changes: While interlinings for the clothing industry contributed 95 percent of sales at the end of the 1950s, at the beginning of the 1970s – with increased sales – nonwoven products already accounted for 70 percent.[279] The reason for this lay in the far-reaching structural change to which the German textile and clothing industry had been subjected since the beginning of the 1960s.[280]

The textile and clothing industry in Germany was confronted "at a very early stage and almost simultaneously"[281] with decisive difficulties. At the end of the 1950s, the textile crisis ended the era of catch-up requirements for clothing in the Federal Republic of Germany. Production stagnated, and the company reacted to the crisis with short-time working and a reduction in employee numbers. The textile crisis was triggered particularly by a rise in raw material prices and sales declines, which led to overproduction. Alongside these, the unpegging of exchange rates caused disadvantages for the German clothing industry, which could not keep up because of its high wage costs compared to the cheap competition abroad – particularly from eastern and southern Europe and East Asia.[282]

There was a constant decline in competitiveness: "Under the pressure of the domestic and foreign competition, the clothing industry was only able to pass on a third of the cost increase in material and wages in its prices."[283] In addition, changes in consumer behavior also had a negative impact on the development of the clothing industry from the 1960s onward. Customers were increasingly spending their money on consumer durables like televisions and automobiles. Furthermore, the tourism sector was also gaining in importance. This led to an acceleration in the sales decline in the clothing industry in Germany. As a result of this, many companies relocated their production abroad. Initially, German clothing companies built their production facilities in southern and eastern Europe, for example in Italy, Poland or Hungary. From the 1970s, an increasing concentration on Asian countries like Hong Kong and South Korea took place. As a result of this sectoral crisis, the number of German factories in the textile and clothing industry shrank by more than 60 percent between 1960 and 1990.[284]

From the 1960s, the Freudenberg nonwovens division, as a supplier to the clothing industry, was accordingly under constant pressure to adapt. As will become evident, the company contended with the challenge of the sectoral crisis in the clothing industry in two ways. On the one hand, internationalization was expedited through the development of numerous factories and newly established companies abroad, in order to take the developments in the clothing market into account. On the other hand, a diverse range of new, innovative products was developed. In this regard, the company pursued two different approaches. Firstly, it worked specifically on interlining innovations for the clothing industry, in order to secure or even expand its own market position in the traditional nonwovens market. Subsequently, product innovations for other areas of application enabled it to enter new markets, which meant that the dependence on the clothing industry could be reduced. Both the internationalization and the development of new products prospered with remarkable success.

The first step towards internationalization during this timeframe took place in 1962 in Spain. Nontex S. A., whose name stood for the company product range of **non**-woven **tex**tiles, was established in 1958 by a group of Spanish textile industrialists. It produced nonwoven interlinings in Santander using a process developed in-house.[285] When the Spanish market was opened up, Nontex increasingly came under pressure from competing foreign products. For that reason, the company started looking for a cooperation partner with suitable expertise in nonwovens. Discussions with Freudenberg ultimately led to Freudenberg acquiring a 25.7 percent share in Nontex S. A. on September 21, 1962. As so often happened in the history of the family enterprise, this succeeded through the supported of an acquainted entrepreneur, in this case Géza Tolnai (1909–1989),[286] with whom Freudenberg remained associated for a long time. Freudenberg granted Nontex the right to Freudenberg nonwovens for the clothing sector in Santander and to distribute them in its home country. In addition, Freudenberg said it was prepared to provide Nontex with its own expertise in the production of nonwovens. In return, Nontex pledged to use Freudenberg's registered trademarks.[287]

After the agreement was concluded, production was converted to the Freudenberg process and Nontex was assigned the right to sell its products under the brand name Flieselina. Then Nontex also took over Freudenberg's distribution methods. This led to faster positive business development of the fledgling company, which moved to Parets del Vallès in 1968. In 1987, Nontex S. A. was renamed Freudenberg Telas sin Tejer S. A.[288] By 1993, Freudenberg had taken over all the shares in the company.[289]

The systematic development of international nonwovens production, which had already begun in the 1950s with Pellon in North America and Bondina in the United Kingdom was accelerated again at the end of the 1960s – among other things as a reaction to developments in the clothing sector, where many customers were shifting their production abroad, out of Germany.[290] The establishment of Vilene Argentina S. R. L. in Buenos Aires in 1969 was an important step in the expansion. Only a year later, Freudenberg took the first steps towards South Africa – initially with the distribution of interlinings and once again two years later with the establishment of the production company Vilene South Africa (Pty.) Ltd. in Cape Town. Thus Freudenberg was now producing nonwovens in South America and in Africa from the beginning of the 1970s.[291]

Apart from this international expansion, the first reaction to the difficult situation in the German clothing sector on Freudenberg's part, however, was particularly in a specific innovation strategy in the nonwovens division. As a response to the trend among customers to replace sewing with labor-saving processes, such as for example welding or gluing, Freudenberg had already developed iron-on nonwovens at the beginning of the 1960s. These already comprised almost one-third of production in 1963. At that time, interlinings still comprised the lion's share of nonwoven production at Freudenberg. In total, the company had more than 70 types of nonwovens in its product range, to be able to fulfill all the requirements and purposes for the most diverse types of cloth that existed among industry and in tailoring.[292]

Further new developments followed. They helped customers to improve their products and at the same time solve factory problems. One example was the successful introduction of what was known as the computer dot in the fall of 1972. At the beginning of the 1970s, 70 percent of all the interlinings that were to be found in articles of clothing were attached without sewing. This technique turned the development and manufacturing of modern plants into a relatively complicated affair. The interlinings were joined to the outer fabrics with overprinted artificial resin dots, which became sticky when they were exposed to heat. After they cooled down, both materials were joined together, and this bond was resistant to washing or dry cleaning. At the beginning of the 1970s, most of the producers of attachable interlinings had these dots arranged in rows and columns. This made sense, because the weave of knitted and woven outer fabrics for clothing is arranged in a regular pattern. "However, this geometrically identical or similar composition can be dangerous. If outer fabrics are particularly heavily structured, the lines of the dot-shaped overprinted adhesive interfacings can align with the outer fabric weave. Then moiré-like waves occur on the surface of the outer fabric. Then the resulting article of clothing is unsellable, because its appearance cannot be repaired." To prevent this, the resourceful Freudenberg experts invented a printing layout for this dot print in which the sticky dots are randomly distributed, but are still regularly spread. This was able to prevent the printing layout from mirroring the weave of an outer fabric and the outer surface of an article of clothing always remained smooth from then on as a result.[293]

In order to be less dependent on the high-risk clothing industry, which was subject to constantly changing fashion influences, the use of the nonwovens was systematically expanded into other areas of application. This occurred particularly through the development of new nonwovens, the use of other raw materials or other production processes.[294] The result was strong growth in technical nonwovens. These included predominantly filter mats for air purification and filter materials for dust extraction in the area of industry, as well as separators which were used in storage batteries as separators and filters between anodes and cathodes.[295] The development of these specially impregnated nonwovens for batteries had already begun at the end of the 1950s; distribution started in 1961.[296] Nonwoven separators became an important product area at Freudenberg, later among other things also used for applications in electro mobility.

The importance of the function that Freudenberg filter mats assumed in the automotive sector at the end of the 1960s can be seen from the company's presence at the IAA automobile trade fair in Frankfurt in 1967: The finest nonwoven fiber filter mats were displayed there, which were used in the paint spray booths in automobile factories and car repair shops. The task of the Viledon filter mats comprised making the incoming air in the paint spray booths dust-free and distributing it evenly. Above and beyond this, filter mats were also used for the purification of fresh air in the heating and ventilation unit – in some cases already as standard.[297]

The search for alternative nonwoven applications finally led Freudenberg developer Ludwig Hartmann (1925–2010) to the completely new spunbonded process. Initially, Hartmann worked on nonwovens which were bonded with bonding fibers and thus did so without affixing them with foam or dispersion as was usual at the time. Since the fibers required for this were very difficult to procure, Hartmann began to investigate fiber polymers. He came up with the idea that he could spin out the fibers himself, and developed a special nozzle for this. This was the beginning of the development of spunbonded nonwovens, because

Fig. 98 Testing facility for spunbonded nonwovens with developer Ludwig Hartmann (left) and his employee Gerhard Müller, 1961

in this way – by using swivel channels underneath the nozzle – the resulting endless fiber could be maintained and deposited to form a fleece. In 1961, he succeeded in combining the fiber production and fleece formation processes into one single, almost simultaneous production stage for the first time on an industrial scale. He described the resulting product as spunbonded nonwovens. And with that, the spunbonded nonwovens division at Freudenberg was born.[298] Building on these initial successes, a first small spunbonded nonwoven production facility was built in Weinheim and the technical expertise for it was expanded systematically. The new development was provided with patent protection rights and initial market experience was gained with the new product domestically and abroad.[299]

Chemical corporation BASF also had technical expertise and experience in this specialized area of nonwovens manufacturing.[300] As early as January 1970, Freudenberg and BASF therefore decided "to collaborate in the area of 'manufacturing spunbonded fabrics and spunbonded nonwovens by continuously spinning polymers and suitable deposition and bonding of the spun endless fibers' […]"[301]. In future, development, production and distribution were to be conducted via the Lutravil Spinnvlies GmbH & Co. firm, which was headquartered in Kaiserslautern and newly established for this purpose. Both companies held a 50 percent share in this joint venture.³⁰² At the groundbreaking ceremony on June 24, 1970 at the factory site in Kaiserslautern, the responsible Management Board member, Kurt Kraft, said: "The groundbreaking ceremony for this plant is the conclusion and the crowning glory of long years of development work, but at the same time it is also an important new beginning." In 1975, Freudenberg took over BASF's shares, and Ludwig Hartmann became the technical head of the new spunbonded nonwovens division. He subsequently expedited the internationalization of the division.³⁰³

In 1970, the division also began operating the modernized and expanded ready-to-wear technical center – the "Vlieseline Studio" – in the nonwovens factory in Weinheim. In this way, services to the ready-to-wear industry could be boosted.³⁰⁴

With the Vlieseline Studio, Freudenberg had risked taking a step into the fashion industry which was unique at the time: It began – as already mentioned – in March 1953 at a small table measuring 60 × 90 centimeters in a small corner of the Vlieseline production facility. The first so-called half pieces were produced. "Undoubtedly not a really appropriate atmosphere for creations that should please the eye. Initially it was only half dresses whose *Vlieseline* framework served to provide information about the use and processing of *Vlieseline*. It was a success. We therefore decided to expand this facility." Initially, the sewing workshop was moved to a separate room, later on to a wooden barrack which had been built in the yard of the nonwoven plant in Weinheim. The studio approached leading weavers and printers and began – using the latest fabrics – producing collections, for the spring and summer as well as for the fall and winter season. The idea of presenting an interlining fabric that had been sown onto this material and showing the dresses in fashion shows was a brand-new thing

Fig. 99 Sewing interlinings into the Vlieseline Studio fashion collection, 1963

in 1953. Until well into the 1960s, Freudenberg remained the only firm in Europe "outside the fashion industry or alternatively haute couture [...] which produced collections within its own company and showed them internationally."[305]

Using the Vlieseline Studio and its own models, the company demonstrated how the interlinings should be used and processed. In this way, Freudenberg attracted the attention of fashion designers, who for example could likewise be creative in new ways using innovative Freudenberg developments like multi-directionally stretchable interlinings or novel bonding technologies. However, this meant the responsibility of Vlieseline Studio grew as well, because in every collection something really good and inspiring had to be offered for sampling and for fashion development.[306]

The success of the Vlieseline fashion show can also be measured in figures. From January to April 1965 alone, the Vlieseline trade demonstration traveled to 56 cities in West Germany and Europe and presented the Vlieseline Studio models in front of several thousand people from the tailoring, retail, vocational college and industrial sectors. The models ranged from beach and leisure wear right up to cocktail and evening dresses.[307] The fashion shows were complemented among other things by programs and application booklets, which were also available in the respective national languages – and thus for example in the languages that are particularly important in fashion: French, Italian and English.[308]

Nevertheless, despite these successes, the figures can also be utilized to show just how much the shift towards technical products had progressed already in 1970. In terms of value, the share of nonwoven sales generated by nonwoven interlinings was only 33 percent. Yet the nonwoven interlinings were still of outstanding importance: Their market share in Germany was approximately 60 percent and worldwide around 40 percent. "An impeccably running customer service" contributed to this success. In this respect, the work of the Vlieseline Studio was especially important. It gave the impetus required for the development of the right types of nonwovens and the right adhesive interfacings. In addition, customers could be shown how the nonwovens were best used, with the aid of demonstrations. The advisers in the field sales force, who constantly visited the ready-to-wear clothing companies within Germany and abroad, passed the latest insights on to their customers. Combined with a high supply readiness, market shares had been maintained despite the growth in competition – there were, meantime, approximately 25 nonwovens factories in West Germany and more than 100 around the world.[309]

One of these nonwovens factories was important partner company Japan Vilene Company, a minority shareholding of Freudenberg since its establishment in 1960, which operated independently of Freudenberg from an organizational perspective. The company's steep rise can be seen in 1970 in a market share of almost 50 percent in the Japanese nonwovens market and thus market leadership. That same year the company listed on the Tokyo stock exchange. One criterion for success was the close technological exchange between the partners in Japan and Germany. This led to a systematic diversification of the nonwovens portfolio: In 1962, the Japan Vilene Company began its own filter production; in 1969, battery separators were added to the product range; and in 1970 production of car mats started.[310] Despite the very close cooperation with Freudenberg, competitive situations also arose time and again in some markets through which the partners then became competitors as well.

Reinhart Freudenberg (1932–2017) took over responsibility for the nonwovens division as successor to Kurt Kraft on July 1, 1972. Reinhart Freudenberg had joined the company in 1961, and he was initially familiarized with the leather business. Between 1962 and 1969, he managed the Teneria Temola tannery in Mexico. In 1969, he returned to Weinheim. When he joined the Management Board as a general partner in July 1972, he took over a division which continued to grow despite the difficult situation in the clothing industry.[311] At the end of 1972, nonwovens (including the Vileda business) – based on the sales and income situation – were the largest and thus the most successful division at Freudenberg. This was also the result of the successful internationalization of production, which has been described in detail already.[312]

Because of the oil crisis and the recession that followed it, the existing sectoral problems in the clothing industry were further exacerbated. Nevertheless, the nonwovens division, including Vileda, achieved sales growth of 10 percent to 418 million deutschmarks in 1974. It was also able to maintain this level in the following year, although the Freudenberg Group's sales shrank significantly compared to the previous year.[313]

Internationalization and innovation: these were ultimately the responses that guided the nonwovens division through this crisis too. In a report about the first half of 1977, the Management Board summarized the success of the strategic direction: "It can be seen from the example of Viledon how important it is to diversify at an early stage. For years, the Vlieseline interlinings were the pillar of nonwoven sales, which they largely still are today in the foreign production sites. Through the timely development of new products for other markets, however, the Viledon business unit has succeeded in immensely reducing the excessively one-sided dependence on the clothing industry."[314] Thus the company continued to remain faithful to the combination of internationalization and innovation in the nonwovens division, as can be seen from several examples from the years that followed.

Now it is worth taking a closer look at the fashion shows: Their audiences always saw a cross-section of the fashion trends, with a focus on models which were predominantly designed in the Vlieseline Studio itself using couture styles and the latest fabrics. A key success element here were the interlinings in the Vlieseline 8000 series, made from very delicate fibers, which were developed in 1975. These novel nonwovens now enabled even very delicate haute couture and silk fabrics to be shaped into a design that did not distort the fabric. Suggestions for the collections came from the exchange of ideas with the top designers in the European fashion centers like Paris, Florence and Rome. The designs displayed by the models were shown around the world in evening and company events. The customer received a perfect presentation, comprising a mixture of "show and consultation". The aim of this consultation was to explain and illustrate the fashion and the finishing, and this promoted Vlieseline's image and sales. Direct contact with leading figures from the sector – like the designers – yielded a lively exchange of ideas. The result: Around 5,000 attendees around the world looked forward every year to the presentations of the new Vlieseline Studio collections for women's apparel.[315] These attendees also included Princess Grace of Monaco, an icon of her time who was also interested in the Freudenberg fashion collections.[316]

Following the sectoral trend in the clothing industry, Freudenberg increasingly turned its attention to Asia. Thus the Korea Vilene Co. Ltd. joint venture was established in 1973 together with Japan Vilene Company and other partners. Production of nonwovens under license began in 1974 in Korea. In the 1990s, Freudenberg and Japan Vilene Company acquired all the shares in the joint venture.[317]

Collaboration with Freudenberg's Japanese partners was further expedited in Asia – this time in Hong Kong. The reasons for this are plain to see: Hong Kong had developed into one of the most important clothing centers in the world, where German companies were increasingly outsourcing production – and they were not alone in this. Through its status as a British crown colony, Hong Kong combined the benefits of British law with significantly lower taxes and wages in Asia.[318] The Japan Vilene Company had already established a branch in Hong Kong in 1973, which supplied the local market with interlinings from its own production facility in Japan. In 1977, Freudenberg set up its first own distribution company, Freudenberg Trading Hong Kong Ltd., which began operating in October of the same year. The new company was supplied with interlinings from the Freudenberg Group's Western European and North American nonwovens factories. Apart from a correspondingly large warehouse, a technical service center was also set up, staffed with clothing engineers in order to be able to give optimum care on-site to Freudenberg customers. Nevertheless, the early years in Hong Kong were frequently exciting: At the beginning, there were customers "who could only be reached by rikshaw, by boat or by a dauntless march over the paddy field."[319] As early as 1980, the next joint venture between Freudenberg and Japan Vilene Company was founded, in which both partners hold equal shares up to the present day. This involved the merger of Freudenberg Trading Hong Kong with the local branch of Japan Vilene to form Freudenberg & Vilene International Ltd. Hong Kong.[320]

However, the internationalization was not limited to Asia. In South America, the Freudenberg Group continued to systematically expand its nonwoven activities beyond Argentina. With the acquisition of the Intece S. A. firm in Diadema near São Paulo in 1985, Brazil's largest manufacturer of nonwovens was taken over. Later, the company was renamed Freudenberg Não Tecidos Ltda.[321]

The internationalization of the spunbonded nonwovens division was also driven forward systematically. Thus, Freudenberg and US firm The Kendall Company inked an agreement in 1981 for the establishment of The Lutravil Company, later Freudenberg Spunweb, in Durham, North Carolina, USA, for the production and distribution of spunbonded nonwovens. Production of polyester spunbonded nonwovens in Durham began two years later. Kendall's share was acquired in 1987.[322] As early as 1984, the Japan Lutravil Company was established in Japan, together with Japan Vilene Company, for the distribution of spunbonded nonwovens. At that time, Freudenberg spunbonded nonwovens were predominantly used as a carrier material for car mats and as a cover fleece in baby diapers.[323] The proven cooperation with Japanese partner Japan Vilene Company was increasingly expanded. In Taiwan, the Lutravil Far East joint venture was established in 1987. Production of polyester-based spunbonded nonwovens started up in October 1990 and was thus Freudenberg's first production facility on Chinese soil. At the time, the new plant was considered to be "the most modern spunbonded nonwoven plant in Asia."[324] The company later operated under the name Freudenberg Far Eastern Spunweb Company Ltd.[325]

It is clear from international partnerships such as these that the company's strategic thinking was that "not all market segments and world regions can be exploited by Freudenberg alone. The multitude of business fields, the constantly intensifying internationalization of the markets and of competition as well as the strong increase in the capital intensity of technologies make it obvious that the company will enter into suitable alliances, if necessary, in which the partners contribute complementary skills and experiences."[326] This strategy characterized the nonwovens division right from the start.

Numerous nonwoven innovations also occured during this time. The Lutrabon-nonwoven wound compress was developed for medical applications. The

Beiersdorf company added it to its medical program in 1983 under the name Cuticell or alternatively Hansapor steril plus.[327] That same year, medical nonwoven applications were merged under the Vilmed brand name. Vilmed nonwovens were and are used as carrier materials for surgical covers and gowns, for emergency bandages and wound pads and for sticking plasters. Additionally, they are used as compresses and as plaster cast underlayers, and they are also used as components for stoma products.[328]

Likewise in 1985, Freudenberg began development of cabin air filters.[329] Four years later, and thus in 1989, the first cabin air filters were delivered to Mercedes Benz (Mercedes SL). In the same year, serial production began – for Volkswagen among others, where the filter was included in the program as an optional extra for all Golf and Jetta models.[330] Up to the end of the year, 35,000 units were produced. The novel filter protected the automobile passengers against dust, pollen and bacteria that would have otherwise found their way into the car's interior through the ventilation ducts. In addition, the new product was able to prevent pollution of downstream components like heating, cooling and air conditioning systems.[331]

The filters were named MicronAir just under a year later with the aid of an ideas competition among the employees.[332] In 1991, production of frameless, ultrasonically welded MicronAir filters began. The first standard configuration fitting occurred in the new Opel Astra.[333] Production of cabin air filters was ex-

Fig. 100 Presentation of the first MicronAir filters fitted as standard in the Opel Astra at the IAA car show in Frankfurt, 1991

panded to North America (Pellon) and Japan (Japan Vilene Company) in 1993. Production volume already reached 3.6 million filters that year, and the filters had meantime become part of the standard configuration or optional extras in most European vehicle models.[334] In 1995, production of ozone- and odor-minimizing combination filters for automobile cabins began – comprising an active carbon and a particle filter layer. The first serial fitting began in 1997 in various automobile models of the Volkswagen Group.[335]

In order to be able to drive the development of nonwovens forward systematically in the future too, the nonwoven technical center built with an investment of approximately 30 million deutschmarks was put into operation in Weinheim in 1987 – after a two-year construction period – a big thing at that time because all development activities in the nonwovens area were amalgamated here. At that point in time, it was one of Freudenberg's largest individual investments.[336] The objective: To accelerate development activity and exploit new nonwoven technologies.[337] This was also reflected in the figures: Sales for the entire nonwoven division (including Vileda) rose from 477 million deutschmarks in 1977 to 624 million deutschmarks in 1981.[338]

At that time – as already mentioned – Norbert Dahlström took over responsibility for nonwovens from Reinhart Freudenberg, who dedicated himself to other tasks on the Management Board and from 1988 on became Speaker of the Management Board as successor to his brother Hermann.[339] This heralded the beginning of a new management era at Freudenberg. Under his leadership, the organizational restructuring of the company as a group, resulting in the decentralized holding structure that would henceforth apply, was expedited and implemented. This resulted in the further development of the Group organization from a parent company character into a business group organizational form. The close market orientation that accompanied this, with clear entrepreneurial responsibility, enabled the company to adapt more flexibly and faster to changes and hold its own successfully in global competition. On June 30, 1997 Reinhart Freudenberg retired and handed over the role of Speaker of the Management Board to Peter Bettermann. Thus, for the first time, the Freudenberg Group was represented by an executive from outside the family.[340]

But back to the nonwovens, because they were likewise under new management now: On October 1, 1978 Dahlström became a member of the Management Board of Freudenberg & Co. in Weinheim and on July 1, 1980 a general partner. Until his retirement on December 31, 2000 he participated "significantly in the internationalization of the company and contributed decisively to the development of the worldwide leading role of Freudenberg nonwovens as well as Freudenberg household products."[341] The various initiatives and activities of the 1980s that have already been described lay in his remit. It was not very long before their positive effects could be felt. Hermann Freudenberg summarized the economic development of the nonwoven division in 1984 as follows: "The positive development of the nonwoven division in the past year has shown yet again to what extent Freudenberg is benefiting from its international position. Not despite, but rather because of having Freudenberg nonwoven production in eight countries outside of Germany, was Carl Freudenberg able to increase the export quota of nonwovens meantime to more than 50 percent. Supply of specialties and new developments, particularly in the countries in which Freudenberg produces nonwovens, has now taken on significant proportions. Without these foreign investments, we would have never managed to maintain our traditional business with the industries that are relocating out of Europe, like the clothing industry, and even further expand them, if the nonwovens division did not literally command a worldwide organization."[342] Thus the internationalization of the nonwoven division was a necessity within the sector, but was also in line with the trend.

Total sales of nonwovens had grown accordingly to 840 million deutschmarks in 1984[343]: Sales exceeded the one billion deutschmark level in the mid-1990s.[344] In 1995, they were already at 1,234 billion deutschmarks.[345]

Since the 1960s, the nonwovens division had been confronted with a similar situation to the war leather and shoes division because of the structural crisis in the clothing industry. In contrast, however, the nonwoven product was much more flexible in its applications and therefore equipped with much more diversified market access than leather and shoes. Thus Freudenberg succeeded in developing a broad product range for different markets and areas of application. In this way, it was able to reduce its dependence on the fashion-driven clothing industry enormously and consequently the division could continue to grow up until the mid-1990s.[346]

A new market: Freudenberg in India

Freudenberg's connections to India go back a long way. As already mentioned, initial trade relations already existed in 1867: to be precise, the procurement of raw skins and the sale of leather.[347] These trade relations intensified in the 1920s.[348] And after World War II, skin imports from India were resumed by 1949.[349] Five years later, the first Simrit agency abroad was established for India in Bombay (today Mumbai).[350] But then nothing worth mentioning happened for a long time; the Indian market for shareholdings from abroad was extremely isolated. In March 1982, Dieter Freudenberg took a long business trip to India for the first time. He attended the International Council of Tanners (ICT) meeting in Madras. On his way there, he stopped off in New Delhi, where he conducted an extensive meeting with Niranjan Ajwani, the managing director of Interconti Projects Pvt. Ltd. (IPPL) about the Indian market – particularly with regard to the leather business.[351]

That was an important meeting, because after this visit, the IPPL became an important contact for Freudenberg, initially with analyses of the Indian market pertaining to the leather and shoe industry as well as the clothing industry.[352] The efforts first led to the realization in August 1982 that IPPL should develop a proposal for a distribution concept for interlinings in India for Freudenberg.[353] Subsequently, the company, which had been established in 1973 by brothers Niranjan and Chander Ajwani, was officially commissioned in 1983 with the distribution of Vlieseline interlinings and further nonwoven products for the Indian market.[354] However, the perspective on India as a whole remained ambivalent: A market study which was conducted jointly by NOK and Freudenberg's marketing department from February to March 1983 came to the conclusion that the negative aspects that militated against investing in India still prevailed.[355]

Thus no further steps were taken initially to exploit the Indian market beyond the collaboration with IPPL. However, in 1985 and 1986, Dieter Freudenberg, who was responsible at the time for foreign relations, traveled through India once again, to check out the market and potential sites.[356] This eventually resulted in the recommendation that initial contact with the Indian automotive industry should also take place through the existing collaboration with IPPL. As an explanation, Dieter Freudenberg emphasized, alongside IPPL's reliability, particularly its influence with important business contacts as well as their connection to the Gandhi family.[357]

The result of his trips was the unequivocal recommendation to massively increase investment in India now, particularly because of the booming automobile market and general economic development. Moreover, the Indian government under Rajiv Gandhi had recently been promoting collaboration with European companies, because they feared "foreign control of Indian industry by the Japanese": "In summary, because of the far-reaching changes in India, I recommend moving away from the previous corporate policy of reticence right up to rejection of an industrial investment by the Group in India. Henceforth, the company should familiarize itself in all areas with the economic development in India and examine emerging opportunities for economic activities in India. As a first priority, in light of the start of motorization in India, it appears to me that the time has come to thoroughly examine and prepare the initiation of a production facility for automotive accessories in India," Dieter Freudenberg wrote.[358]

In light of the huge success of the Japanese automobile industry, which was becoming increasingly strong in India just then, the consideration initially arose for Dieter Freudenberg in this context to leave the production of accessories in India to NOK. "On the other hand, a significant automotive industry is to be expected in the long term on the Indian Subcontinent, which could draw level with the American and Japanese automotive industry in order of magnitude in 2 to 3 decades."[359] Leaving this immense market potential to NOK would give it a preponderance on the worldwide automotive supply market. Freudenberg would have had little to oppose it, with its roots in a European automotive market that was stagnating at the time. In order to safeguard the interests of his company in the long term, it therefore appeared to him to be essential to take over the initiative and leadership in India and secure this important market for the long term. He was convinced that even with a joint venture, for example a minority shareholding in NOK, Freudenberg's long-term interests in India would not be taken into account adequately.[360] Above and beyond this, Dieter Freudenberg advised them to exercise caution when selecting potential Indian partners:

> "When selecting a potential Indian partner, the large family enterprises are only recommendable to a limited extent, despite their financial strengths. Investments are only considered by these corporations in terms of purely capitalist aspects. There is rarely any interest or internal attitude to product and technology. For that reason, the industrial contribution in technical and commercial management is mainly low too. This contribution is to a large extent limited to the undoubtedly necessary lobbying and contact maintenance in the political context. For smaller operational units, it is more advisable to find partners from small and medium-sized industry who may be able to make a concrete contribution, or alternatively a financially strong medium-sized family as a silent partner."[361]

In the case of the automotive industry, Dieter Freudenberg believed the time had come to invest in the Indian market. In contrast to this, he believed the time to develop proprietary nonwoven production in India was not yet ripe.[362]

In June 1985 – based on Dieter Freudenberg's insights – it was recorded by the Management Board that the production and distribution of automobile parts in particular in India was promising for the future and relevant with regard to the competitive situation with NOK. Ill feeling as experienced with NOK before the agreement on a joint exploitation of the market in the United States should not be repeated in India.

In 1989, Freudenberg initially shifted its priorities in other directions, among other things because of German reunification.[363] Nevertheless, in an internal memo to his Management Board colleague Norbert Dahlström, Dieter Freudenberg came to the conclusion that they must not lose sight of the Indian market: "Alongside the PR of China, the Indian Subcontinent is undoubtedly one of the most important growth markets in the medium to long term and the Freudenberg Group cannot do without it. The liberalization process is developing steadily, albeit slowly and with occasional setbacks."[364] Two years later, the Indian market was opened decisively: Up to then, it was only possible to gain influence on the Indian market with the aid of licensing or minority shareholdings in Indian companies. Import duties were "the highest in the world."[365] This was now changing. In the wake of this Indian market liberalization, the restriction on the shareholding quota for foreign investors, who were only permitted to hold a maximum of 40 percent of the shares in a company in India, was also lifted.[366] A year later, the India project was revived: Now it was established that "it makes sense to enter the Indian market now with a proprietary production facility;" furthermore, it was recommended "to consult with NOK immediately on how to proceed and to continue the talks with the Indian partners."[367]

After further foreign trips by various representatives, an interesting discussion came about in the Management Board in its meeting on May 24, 1994 about the India investment: "A site should be earmarked especially for production under own management, to ensure far-reaching independence. – The Bangalore area is preferred. – The joint venture activity should begin at the earliest in 1995. – To the greatest possible extent, we would like to deploy used machines for the production facility that is to be built. […] Dr. Freudenberg assesses the [6 percent annual] growth [of the Indian economy] compared to other emerging industrialized countries as not overwhelming and asks the question of whether we should not wait to set up a joint venture until growth has solidified. Mr. Dahlström objects, saying the time is ripe to become active in India. We should not hope to be able to still jump onto the train when it is already moving, but instead we should invest significantly now. […] The companies TVS and Fenner [come into question] as potential joint venture partners […] (of lesser interest: Super Seals and Walchand). It will end up being a triple joint venture, since we do not want to forgo the collaboration with NOK. […] The Management Board resolves: The division is authorized to open a sales office in India for general industry. Site probably Bombay. The sales office should be set up in collaboration with NOK, which must put its previous India turnover into the office. This should be coordinated immediately with NOK. The division is tasked with […] intensifying the investigation of potential partnerships with Indian companies."³⁶⁸

Subsequently, in 1995, NOK and Freudenberg established NOK-Freudenberg Asia Holding C. Pte. Ltd. in Singapore for the administration of joint sealing and vibration control activities in India and China.³⁶⁹ Furthermore, Fenner is meantime favored as the Indian partner. But negotiations about a joint venture failed in the same year. The reason for this was mainly disagreements regarding majority shareholdings in the partnership (NOK-Freudenberg insisted on a majority, while Fenner wanted 50:50).³⁷⁰

Ultimately, NOK-Freudenberg's long-lasting joint venture negotiations with Sundaram Industries Group and the TVS Group also foundered on the question of the majority shareholding.³⁷¹ In 1998, Freudenberg nonwovens KG established a distribution company in India.³⁷² A year later, Klüber followed with the Klüber Lubrication India Pvt. branch. This was a joint venture with entrepreneur Niranjan Ajwani, who was of course already familiar from a collaboration agreement in the area of the nonwovens business.³⁷³

The real breakthrough was not achieved until 2000, when Freudenberg Dichtungs- und Schwingungstechnik formed a joint venture with Sigma and NOK in Mohali (Sigma Freudenberg-NOK PVT. Ltd.).³⁷⁴ In their meeting on May 16, 2000 the Management Board had approved the project "Setup of a Simmerring partner production facility in India together with NOK and the Sigma company with a total investment of 11 million deutschmarks and capitalization of 3.5 million deutschmarks."³⁷⁵ This time a provision on share distribution was also achieved: According to this agreement, shares and investments worth 55 percent were transferred from the respective interim Freudenberg holding company and the same worth 45 percent from Sigma. This ratio was likewise reflected in the dividend entitlement.³⁷⁶ There had been initial contact with family enter-

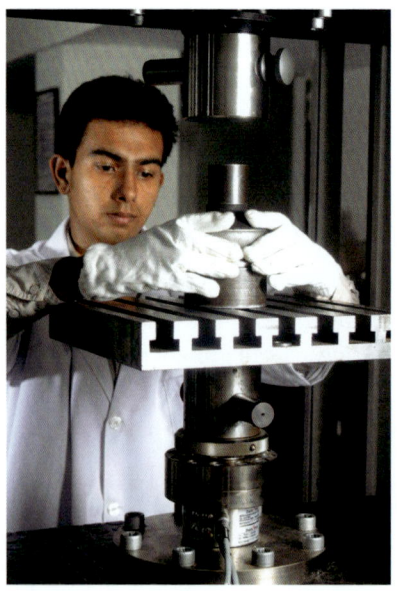

Fig. 101 Seal production in Mohali, India, around 2003

prise Sigma, which was established in 1964 with headquarters in Delhi, back in 1995, when Sigma proposed a "joint manufacturing collaboration" in the area of rubber seals to Freudenberg. However, since Freudenberg was in negotiations with other potential partners at that time, this plan was not pursued any further for the moment.[377]

The joint venture that was finally established after all by the three partners, Freudenberg, NOK and Sigma, grew fast after its establishment.[378] Then the first Indian production facility for seals was put into operation in 2003 in Mohali. In the years to come, India developed, alongside China, into an important growth market for Freudenberg.[379]

Vileda takes households by storm

The further development of Vileda must also be seen in connection with the economic situation in the 1960s in Germany, where consumer goods were produced and sold in their millions for the first time. Against this backdrop, the household cloths business, and increasingly more related products, enjoyed outstanding development, which is why a dedicated sales organization was launched at the beginning of the 1960s. For this reason, Vileda GmbH was established in Weinheim in 1962 within the nonwoven division, for the distribution of household cloths. This could be seen on the street too: Forty professionally trained sales representatives with blue company cars – this was always a blue Ford Taunus estate – which all bore the registration MA-RY alongside a number,[380] were sent on their way by Kurt Kraft, the responsible member of the Management Board, from the yard of the Old Lacquering Shop in Weinheim to the sound of a brass band, to take over and promote the sale of cleaning cloths in all of West Germany and West Berlin.[381] That was something totally new for Freudenberg. There had previously been no direct sales through a network of sales representatives – it was ultimately the adoption of the "traveling salesman" concept from the United States. At the beginning, it was certainly accompanied by considerable skepticism within the Management Board, but the results spoke for themselves.

This first "blue wave" was followed by many others, such that in 1968, 100 sales representatives were already looking after their districts in their blue vehicles.[382] In addition, the people responsible for Vileda at Freudenberg began thinking about the expansion of the product range at an early stage, and got started on the development of scourer materials in the factory in Augsburg. This was intended

Fig. 102 The first Vileda "blue wave" begins, 1962

to complement the existing household products portfolio, which was comprised of cloths. The first scourers bearing the new brand name Glitzi[383], consisting of a black scouring fleece, went on sale on November 1, 1962.[384] The Glitzi was rapidly developed further: A sponge was added to the scouring fleece in 1965, which in future ensured the cleaning of more delicate surfaces on pots and pans. The grip groove, which is still typical today, followed in 1968.[385] When the sponge was introduced, the Glitzi became a success: Sales of Glitzi scourers rose more than thirteenfold within a year. The establishment of Vileda GmbH, combined with the new products, paid off: As a result, total sales of Vileda household products

Fig. 103 The Vileda cleaning regimen helps with the cleaning in its first TV commercial, 1968

were increased more than sixfold between 1962 and 1969 – and thus within seven years.[386] The sales offensive on the consumer goods market did not balk at television advertising at that time either: Thus the first Vileda TV commercial was broadcast in 1963:[387] Using an advertising mix of radio and television advertising ("The Vileda cleaning regimen"), print advertisements and posters, Vileda's brand awareness level was systematically increased. During this time, Vileda developed from being a product name to a brand name. In 1969, there was a special cleaning cloth available from Vileda for virtually every possible use in the household: household cloth, sponge cloth, washing-up cloth, wiping-up cloth, window cloth, glass cloth, car cloth.[388] In this way, a broadly-based consumer brand had developed in the 1960s which enjoyed immense popularity among consumers – an enormous success for Freudenberg.

However, at the beginning of the 1970s, considerable difficulties had to be overcome. A worrisome stocktaking by the Vileda Management Board in the midst of changing consumer behavior – towards investments in consumer durables and in foreign trips – and of the oil crisis can be found in a document on planning for the years 1975 to 1979 dating from August 1974: More and more competitors had entered the market, which were generally offering products at lower prices – and in a quality which the customers did not perceive as worse, and in some cases even as better. "It must be expected that if the existing competitive situation continues, the Vileda market share will continue to shrink slightly," the document says. In the area of cheaper nonwoven cloths, Vileda could not compete on price. The conclusion drawn from this sounds like a wake-up call: "If something decisive does not happen in the area of our development, we will have to suffer bitter sales slumps in a few years." A marked low-cost trend was evident among traders and consumers. Customers were unsettled, so price increases were not really enforceable.[389]

In 1973, the difficult market situation caused Freudenberg to acquire Lady Esther Kosmetik GmbH, which distributed cosmetic articles produced by external manufacturers using their own recipes. The main reason for the acquisition was the distribution network for specialist retailers at Lady Esther. The cosmetic products were sold in approximately 400 depots (drugstores) in Germany. Through an affiliation to Vileda, it was hoped that a strong position could be built up in the drugstore business for the cleaning products too. An additional side-effect of the acquisition was that a better opportunity for the further utilization of Freudenberg's own collagen products was set to emerge from it.[390]

Since the mid-1970s, Freudenberg had spent time on collagen research in the cosmetics sector. The "mass" – meaning collagen fibers, a waste product from leather manufacturing – had previously been used among other things for the production of sausage skins for the Naturin joint venture. Now the organic products division was developing products for cosmetic and dermatological use using, among other things, Collapur, a soluble collagen, and collagen sponges.[391] With this prior knowledge in the cosmetics sector, the company had great hopes for the acquisition of Lady Esther Kosmetik GmbH.[392]

Lady Esther operated as an independent business. However, it was supported by affiliate Vileda, particularly in the areas of advertising and personnel. The brand itself was created in 1913 in the United States and became very well-known there. Following the death of the last company owner in the 1950s, the company was broken up. Freudenberg then took over the German Lady Esther GmbH in 1973, from Margaret Astor AG, along with the trademark rights outside of the United States. As early as 1975, Freudenberg had adapted some of the recipes in such a way that the most important Lady Esther products could be produced with Collapur, the collagen from Freudenberg's organic products range.[393] In 1982, the product range comprised approximately 190 articles in the upmarket price category, particularly care cosmetics, decorative preparations and perfumes, and also including the men's product line Yacht Man.[394] However, no notable commercial success was visible in the following years. Finally, Freudenberg divested the cosmetics firm

Fig. 104 Lady Esther advertisement for Yacht Man brand men's shower gel, 1978

for this reason. It therefore was set to only have a short period of affiliation to Freudenberg. At the beginning of the 1980s, the division suffered under the generally weak sector economy, on top of which came a low level of recognition and a small market share. In addition, production costs were much too high.[395] Therefore, Lady Esther Kosmetik GmbH was sold to businessman Horst Figaj in 1984. At the time of the sale, 13 employees were working at Lady Esther.[396]

However, Freudenberg was also working on product improvements within the scope of the Vileda product range. In this context, the Vileda Management Board struggled with the innovative performance in the factories outside Weinheim: "Since we currently cannot expect much from Augsburg and Kaiserslautern, we picked up new developments from our Weinheim development area all the more willingly."[397] The Vileda business lived off new stimuli, it said. Since Freudenberg had not gotten sufficient new developments out of its own development efforts, it was forced to buy these in: The new "Quick + Chic" product range, which was predominantly comprised of brooms and brushes, was only populated with bought-in products. Development, expertise and production were all owned by Coronet-Werke in Waldmichelbach.[398]

In light of this situation, the Vileda management came to the following conclusion in 1974: "The setbacks in the area of development are jeopardizing our business to an extent that was neither foreseeable, nor can it be justified." For years, Frema in Augsburg had been made aware of the need for focused development projects. "But here we have suffered setbacks time and again. Our development lead over the competition has shrunk in many areas." The Vileda management had reacted to these developments at an early stage and pushed through cost savings forcefully. As a result, the household division was better prepared for the unexpected cost increases from the oil crisis than many competitors: "The lion's share of the cost increases could not be passed on in the sales prices, but instead had to be compensated for by constant rationalization, greater work efficiency and sales expansion."[399] Success was already evident in the following year: "Despite the difficult situation, Vileda was able to increase sales and earnings in the consumer sector, and – contrary to the prevailing trend – especially in exports." [400]

The positive development prevailed and thus the difficulties were – initially – overcome. By 1979, and therefore within ten years, Vileda's turnover had increased by more than two and a half times to 130.7 million deutschmarks.[401] After that, however, Vileda's result no longer developed in the right direction.[402]

At the Management Board meeting on July 24, 1980 the Vileda management described the initial situation for Vileda as follows: "All three strategic units: Household Cleaning, Commercial Cleaning, Tablecloths, are at a mature state or alternatively are stagnating. [...] Activities must therefore be found that complement the existing business in a meaningful way and utilize existing capacities with profitable business."[403]

In the domestic and export business, Vileda managed to defend its own market position for most article groups. However, there were only "minimal opportunities for growth in individual product groups, for example in commercial cleaning" as well as "in brooms and brushes because of a new contract with Coronet." Gaining entry into new foreign markets also required extreme effort and high expenditure on advertising programs. "Thus, together with our new sales partner in France, Benckiser France, an advertising program worth 2 million deutschmarks per year is planned for two years, half of which will be borne by Carl Freudenberg and half by Benckiser. In Australia, Canada and the USA too, which are considered to have expansion potential, a market launch can only be achieved with high advertising expenditure."[404]

Operating results declined by more than half between 1978 and 1981, and stagnated up to 1985.[405] Another reason for this: Freudenberg lost an important customer in the form of a market-leading chain of discount retailers, because competitor products came onto the market at considerably lower prices. From 1984 onward, there was no more discount retailer business at all initially.

In 1986, Freudenberg discontinued the brush and broom range completely.[406] Thus it was immensely important that a product innovation would be able to give Vileda a totally fresh impetus. This was achieved with the introduction of the Vileda mop on the German market from June 1985 onward. In order to understand the background, we must take a leap into the past – to be precise, to the year 1956 – and to another country, Spain. As has so often been the case in Freudenberg's company history, the powers of observation and creativity of others played a role in the development of a decisive further evolution of the mop into a system: Spanish aeronautical engineer Manuel Jalón Corominas was inspired by aircraft, or rather by the cleaning equipment used to clean American military aircraft and aircraft hangars.[407]

In 1956, Corominas invented a broom-like tool with a wooden handle at one end and cotton strips at the other. A mop was born which at last made it possible to mop the floor without having to bend down or get one's hands wet.[408] In mechanic Emilio Bellvis' garage, the idea was taken to its logical conclusion: A bucket with two clamping rollers attached to it was developed for wringing out the mop – anyone who pulled the mop through it would be pleased to see that the water dripped off into the bucket automatically, so to speak. The two inventors founded the Manufacturas Rodex company in Zaragoza, Spain, and set up the first production facility for the "Fregona" mop in 1958.[409]

However, the Fregona was relatively expensive, mainly because of the manufacturing costs, which were very high due to the manual production, the expensive wooden handles and the long-fiber cotton that had to be specially produced. For that reason, only around 45,000 units could be sold in the first three years.[410] Completely independently of the original Fregona product, Vileda eventually developed a more mature version of the mop: The mop head was further developed technically by cutting the Vileda nonwoven floor cloth – which was on the market in Spain under the name Mocho[411] – into strips and then attaching them to the handle as a mop head. That was how the first strip mop made of nonwoven fabric was created; it was launched on the Spanish market in September 1973 by the Vileda sales company Comercial Rojas. Accompanied by a clever marketing strategy that focused primarily on marketing the product benefit of convenient and easy cleaning, it quickly became a popular product. And so began the Vileda mop's success story.[412] A successful market launch took place in 1977 in Italy, which had a similar tradition of cleaning floors with a wet cloth to Spain. The mop – now known under the brand name Mocio – was sold there with great success by Italian distribution company Commerciale RG.[413]

The concept was developed even further for the German market after some delay and finally launched on the market in 1985, right from the start in this improved form as a system comprising a mop, bucket and wringer. It was a sensational success: With the help of this three-component system design, the mop became one of Freudenberg's most successful household products ever.[414] Since no comparable products had previously been available on the German market, the market launch was accompanied by a correspondingly large-scale marketing campaign. "Vileda's great thing" quickly became a "sales rocket" and brought Vileda significant growth in earnings and sales.[415]

Of course, as a consumer brand, Vileda also had to adapt to changing consumer attitudes. At a time when cleaning was increasingly perceived as a burden at some stage, it was important to position the brand with a focus on "convenience" in particular, meaning particularly as a prac-

Fig. 105 The Vileda mop with bucket and wringer system, 1985

tical and convenient solution for household or daily life, in which the most essential cleaning, wiping and mopping jobs could be finished quickly.[416]

This approach included products like "Vileda Klare Scheibe" – a wiping "cushion" with a Vileda cover adapted to the size of a human hand, which immediately provided a clear view, especially in cars – as well as household gloves.[417]

The market launch of Vileda household gloves took place in June 1989 and was a great success: "Vileda had risen to become one of the most important suppliers [of household gloves in Germany] with a market share of almost 23 percent [at the end of 1989]. The tills were ringing out in the shops selling Vileda: Sales of gloves had almost doubled there within six months; over half of the household gloves sold in November and December came from the Vileda range." During the development of the household glove range, particular attention was paid to fulfilling consumer wishes: Durability, a good fit, no sweating, good tactile sensation and sensitivity, excellent grip and slip resistance, as well as durability and long arm cuffs. In the mid-1990s, Vileda was already the second largest supplier of household gloves in Germany with a market share of 25 percent.[418]

Moreover, the company acquired a shareholding – in order to expand its portfolio of viscose-based sponges and sponge cloths – in the household products division of Dutch chemicals group Akzo. The investment was conducted by establishing a 50:50 joint venture, Enka Household Products, in the Netherlands. Enka began production and distribution of viscose sponges and viscose sponge cloths with approximately 140 employees in Arnhem and Ede.[419] In 1991, all shares in Enka Household Products were acquired by Freudenberg.[420] The cleaning products division grew strongly in 1989. The new household gloves had already made a significant contribution to the overall growth of 14.4 percent to sales of 336 million deutschmarks as well.[421]

A year later the Wettex AB company headquartered in Norrköping in Sweden was acquired by Freudenberg. Wettex, the inventor of the sponge cloth, produced approximately 120 million sponge cloths per year with 220 employees. Wettex was market leader in Sweden and had a strong market position in Austria and in Italy.[422] The acquisition of Wettex AB was part of Vileda's long-term growth strategy, which among other things foresaw the "acquisition of several high-performing producers of sponge cloths and sponges."[423] [424] From 1992, Wettex AB traded under the name Freudenberg Household Products AB. This takeover was also significant for regionally adapted brand management: In Scandinavia, Vileda is called Wettex.

At the end of 1991, the management of Freudenberg Household Products formulated the strategic objective for the next five years at a Management Board meeting: "Expansion of the current business to sales of at least 700 million deutschmarks within the next five years. This economic size is considered to be necessary in order to be able to hold our own successfully against retailing."[425] And indeed the target was almost achieved: Freudenberg Household Products' sales in 1996 were just under 675 million deutschmarks.[426]

The rise to become a global player: The development of the Klüber Group after being taken over by Freudenberg

The development of subsidiary Klüber Lubrication after being taken over by Freudenberg in 1966 was initially characterized by ongoing internationalization and constant growth. Branches were established in Spain (1969), Brazil (1971), Argentina (1978) and Australia (1981). Japan – also partly because of the outstanding significance of the industry there – played a special role in this: Joint venture NOK Klüber Co. Ltd., headquartered in Tokyo, was established there in 1976. NOK held a 51 percent share in the joint venture, Klüber the rest.[427]

The reasons for the lubricant specialist's rapid economic growth lay primarily in the company's sales strategy. In contrast to Freudenberg's usual sales force strategy, Klüber did not negotiate with the purchasing department; instead, the sales representative asked the customer directly about his problem. Then the Klüber technicians inspected the problem on-site at the customer's plant and developed an optimum solution specifically tailored to the customer's needs. Advisory services and product were and are inseparably linked at Klüber. Customers appreciated this service orientation as it enabled them to save production costs. In return, Klüber generated correspondingly high income and continuous growth.[428]

However, the internationally expanding business, which had appeared to be very promising due to a constant increase in unit sales in numerous countries, was then hit by the oil crisis. The Klüber Group was still able to achieve a sales increase of more than 20 percent in 1974, with sales of 35 million deutschmarks in Germany and abroad. But the income situation weakened, even though it was still satisfactory. A year later, the picture changed: while sales only declined slightly, customer reticence and increasing competition from large petroleum companies led to price pressure that had a considerable impact on earnings.[429]

Ultimately, however, the oil crisis turned out to be only a brief episode and the situation quickly improved. As early as 1976, the Klüber Group was again able to achieve a significant increase in sales of almost 40 percent to 46 million deutschmarks, which was reflected in a satisfactory return. The distribution companies abroad were of particular importance in this respect, as they were allocated to their own production facilities where appropriate. The upward trend continued in the following years: in 1979, the Klüber Group's sales had already reached 67 million deutschmarks – with returns sustained at a satisfactory level.[430] The company continued to grow: With the foundation of Klüber Lubrication (Pty.) Ltd. South Africa, Klüber Lubrication has been able to serve customers on all continents with its own companies since 1983.[431] The figures were positive too. In 1984, the Klüber Group's sales exceeded the 100 million deutschmark level for the first time at 109 million deutschmarks. In 1986, sales had already grown to 135.9 million deutschmarks.[432] The company remained on this successful course in the following years, not least thanks to excellent growth abroad.[433]

The products also achieved publicly recognizable successes: In 1983, Briton Richard Noble set a new world speed record for land vehicles of more than 1,000 kilometers per hour in the American Black Rock salt desert in Nevada with the Thrust 2 turbine vehicle. An innovative wheel bearing lubricant developed by Klüber Lubrication that could withstand the extremely high loads made this possible. The product had already been successfully used in the landing gear of the Concorde supersonic passenger aircraft. When touching down on the runway, the wheels of the landing gear are accelerated to several thousand

Fig. 106 Working on innovative lubricant solutions in the Klüber laboratory, 1985

revolutions per minute within fractions of a second – an extreme load for the lubricant. Similar acceleration forces also had to be mastered in Richard Noble's world speed record.[434] In the world's toughest rally, between Paris and Dakar, the German Capito team achieved first and third place in the overall truck classification in 1985 – using a Mercedes Unimog. Karl Friedrich Capito, at the time sports president of the German Motorsport Association, and his two sons had put their driving skills to the test over more than 10,000 kilometers. And Klüber was there too: Not only with financial support, but also during the planning and testing phase when selecting the right specialty lubricants to meet the extreme demands of the desert race.[435]

From April 1987 to March 1993, Ernst Schön was Chairman of the Management Board of the Freudenberg subsidiary Klüber Lubrication München KG, where he expedited the development of application technology. In April 1993, he became a member of the Management Board of Freudenberg & Co. with responsibility for Klüber, building systems and shoe components, research and development as well as for the service companies, environmental protection and occupational safety and investments.[436] Under his leadership, the company turned its attention to countries such as Indonesia, Venezuela and Syria. However, the company also expanded by entering new product markets. At the end of 1988, Klüber acquired Codal Chemie GmbH in Munich, a manufacturer of plastic release agents – a business with development potential. A year later, Codal Chemie GmbH merged with release agent specialist Lange & Seidel of Nuremberg to form the new company Klüber Chemie KG in Maisach near Munich.[437]

In 1990, sales exceeded the 200 million deutschmark level for the first time. The research and development department began to increasingly develop new products with environmental protection in mind,[438] and these development efforts, which were also the result of close cooperation with the research and development department in Weinheim, produced a wealth of successes. On the one hand, Klüber's specialty lubricants have led to the use of increasingly small quantities of lubricants right up to today, while at the same time saving energy and minimizing material wear and tear because of their high efficiency. In addition, a whole range of biologically harmless and safe products was developed, like for example those required in the food industry. The result was the Klüber Bio range, which was launched in 1993.

These lubricants for the food industry had their origins in a beer tap grease that was developed and sold as early as the 1950s. This was Klüber's first organic product, because the grease was food-safe, tasteless, had no effect on the foam produced during dispensing and did not contaminate the water during cleaning. With the growing importance of the food industry – due to the increase in the industrial processing of food – the importance of lubricants also grew, as the processing machines used have numerous moving parts that require lubrication. Contact between the foodstuffs and the lubricants is therefore unavoidable. At the end of the 1970s, Klüber already had a wide range of specialty lubricants that were used in the processing of bread, pasta, chocolate, meat, fish, coffee, milk, juices, soft drinks and much more. By the early 1990s, the company had grown to become the market leader for lubricants in the food industry. In addition to the abovementioned flavor neutrality, strict international standards must still be adhered to today – including halal and kosher certifications – and the products always require official approval.[439]

There are numerous other concrete examples of this. For example, a new Klüber organic rust remover, which, unlike conventional products, is rapidly degradable and not hazardous to water because it uses completely new raw materials: From then on, by simply spraying it on without the use of greenhouse gases, any rusted screw could be loosened – with no effort, no damage to the material and no toxic residues. The products in the Klüber Bio range also include high-performance specialty lubricating oils and greases for the marine industry, which are rapidly degradable and therefore not hazardous to water.[440]

At the beginning of the 1990s, the Klüber Group continued to set record after record with these products, and the corresponding reports from these years read similarly to the balance sheet for 1995, selected here as an example:

> "Another record year for Klüber. The Klüber Group significantly increased its sales yet again [to 266.8 million deutschmarks] and gained additional market share, although the economy slowed down during the year. [...] In 1995, important steps were taken for the continued success of this company: 1. Klüber acquired North American Summit Industrial Products, Inc., Texas, a company with a high level of expertise in synthetic compressor oils. This will enable the Group to expand its product range and furthermore gain additional market share in the United States. 2. A company was established in Singapore to improve market development in the Southeast Asian economic region. 3. A new research building is under construction in Munich to open up even greater opportunities for research and development."[441]

In 1996, Klüber was the first Munich-based company ever to have completed the European Union's voluntary eco-audit. The company came up with innovative ideas encompassing environmental considerations: In order to prevent alcohol vapors from being released into the exhaust air during the production of lubricating grease, Klüber simply replaced the raw material responsible for their formation. This also brought with it clear economic advantages. Costly thermal afterburning of the exhaust air and the associated increase in carbon dioxide emissions could be avoided from then on.[442]

Klüber's development is an example of the success a company can achieve if it is completely focused on the customer, their needs and wishes from the outset. In fact, high returns can always be achieved if you are recognized by the customer as a true problem solver: With regard to Klüber and its products, this is the case. The aim is not to compete with large oil companies with mass-produced goods, but to solve very specialized customer problems. Against the backdrop of a globalizing world, Klüber's progressive internationalization is just as logical a consequence of this problem-solving strategy as its early involvement with environmental protection aspects was.

Further development and farewell to Nora

The story of Nora, whose origins lay in the production of shoe soles, is linked after 1970 to the decline of the domestic shoe industry, which had to be counteracted time and again with innovations, efficiency programs and new structures. On the other hand, remarkable successes could be chalked up in the development of floor coverings on the basis of the core business – which, for better or worse, rose and fell in tandem with the construction industry. However, operating in the construction industry was a discrete market from the rest of Freudenberg's business. This was because the other business areas had nothing to do with the construction industry. The sales organization was faced with a completely different group of target customers from the construction sector (architects, civil engineers and so on). This allowed Freudenberg to experience how the construction boom following German reunification in particular provided a boost, but also how cyclical influences can lead the other way in a very cyclical business.

At the beginning of the 1970s, the business with the Nora and Robus brand leather fiber products, which had since been merged, was now flourishing and recording considerable sales growth. Thus, by 1973, sales had risen to 49 million deutschmarks. However, the general business climate soon darkened due to the poor situation in the German and foreign shoe industry: sales declined within two years to just 34 million deutschmarks in 1975.[443]

And once again, Freudenberg tried to counteract this development with innovations – for example, the trials on polyurethane boots that had begun in 1970 led to the production of Nora safety boots four years later.[444] An important milestone in the development of the product portfolio in 1977 was the market launch of the two-colored *Norament duo* studded floor covering, in which the studs were a different shade of color to the base.[445] Then, a year later, a sales organization for Nora floor coverings was also established under the name Nora Flooring in the United States, an increasingly important export market for this business.[446] Despite product innovations, business development remained volatile, with one year of rising sales followed by another with a loss. The earnings situation mostly remained unsatisfactory, sometimes losses even had to be reported.[447]

However, there have always been real highlights in connection with product development, even in the truest sense of the word in sport: on May 8, 1978, Reinhold Messner reached the summit of Mount Everest together with Peter Habeler. They were the first people to succeed in climbing the highest mountain on earth at 8,848 meters without the use of additional oxygen. One component of his high-performance mountaineering boot was a Frelen insole made by Freudenberg. Frelen is a polyethylene foam that was developed and patented by Freudenberg in 1973. The insole was located between the inner shoe and the shell and provided effective protection against the cold to protect the feet from frostbite.[448]

Likewise, the shoes that Boris Becker wore playing tennis were also custom-made especially for him: his Frelen insole was optimized at great expense. For this purpose, impressions of Boris Becker's feet were taken, on the basis of which a detailed and perfectly molded pressing tool was then produced in collaboration with orthopedists. The result was an insole made from highly cross-linked polyethylene foam that was molded exactly to Boris Becker's feet. Becker also wore them during his 1986 Wimbledon victory against the then world number one, Ivan Lendl.[449]

However, the development of the floorcovering business became increasingly important during these years: In 1983, this already accounted for over 50 percent of Nora's production, and the trend continued to rise. In 1984, the Nora floorcovering division further secured its position as the world market leader for rubber floor coverings, primarily by expanding its international distribution network, such that sales exceeded the 100 million deutschmark level for the first time,[450] and the business continued to develop in this direction. From 1985, new electrically conductive floorcoverings once again opened up new submarkets for the company, particularly in the electrical engineering industry: These coverings protect workspaces and workplaces from electrostatic charge.[451]

Organizational changes also took place time and again though. Since 1989, the American floorcovering business had been operating under the name Freudenberg Building Systems.[452] After undergoing several phases of reorganization, the Nora division therefore focused on the production of floorcoverings, molded stairs and roofing membranes for the construction and electrical engineering industries, as well as special soling materials for the shoe industry and the shoe repair business. For this reason, the name was changed. From then on, the division was called "Building Systems and Shoe Components", which was intended to emphasize its concentration on the core business of floorcoverings as well as the small rubber sole production business.[453]

Nevertheless, even in light of the favorable construction sector, the shadow of developments on the shoe market remained. There was no longer any future for the production of Nora boots in Weinheim: in 1992, a licensing agreement was signed with the Rontani in Monsagrati di Pescaglia company in Italy to manufacture the boots. Their production was then relocated completely to Italy. In addition, the new Italian partners took over distribution in their home country and in France. The entire division was then sold to Rontani in 1998.[454]

In Germany, there was a strong upturn in the construction industry following the reunification of East and West Germany which lasted until 1994 thanks to the momentum from the new federal states.[455] Freudenberg Bausysteme KG, which became independent in mid-1994, defied the subsequent "construction crisis"[456] and continued its growth in floorcoverings. The reason for this lay in innovative products. Smooth Noraplan floorcoverings with a new scatter design and marbled look were launched on the market as early as 1993. They were followed a year later by studded Norament floorcoverings with an artificial stone look. Further product innovations were added in 1995: Noraplan Mega had a multi-colored scatter design, which made it possible to achieve a unique look. The Norament floor with a hammered surface made it possible to break up the luster of the floor while ensuring a safe tread. In addition, Noraplan Elastic, a floorcovering with a foam coating on the underside that acted as footfall sound insulation was developed, and new colors were added in line with fashion trends.[457] All of these innovations were in line with current trends and quickly achieved high sales volumes. As a result, new market segments were opened up and income was maintained at a good level in 1995 despite rising raw material prices and currency-related negative effects. Sales even increased to 208 million deutschmarks in 1996. Thus it exceeded the long-term target of "Nora 200" set in 1989.[458]

And then, just five years later, came the next external shock – this time of a profoundly negative nature: In 2001, the economic repercussions of the terror attacks of September 11 led to a turning point that called into question the long-term future of this business within the Freudenberg Group and ultimately led to its sale. The effects of the terror attacks were directly reflected in the figures: The operating result of Freudenberg Bausysteme KG in 2001 was significantly below that of the previous year due to the poor business development from September onward. In August, Freudenberg Bausysteme KG was still on course towards a record: cumulative sales were approximately 12 percent above the previous year. Then business literally collapsed in September, particularly in the United States, and did not recover until the end of the year. As a result, the operating result slumped sharply.[459]

Economic conditions remained difficult in the following two years as well. Sales and operating results shrank continuously.[460] A plethora of reasons contributed to this negative earnings trend, and even a combination of just a few of these influences would generally cause a management board to worry: stagnating or declining main customer sectors, namely the electrical engineering and construction industries, loss of contribution margins because of lower revenues and currency-related price pressures in Asia, rising raw material prices, higher personnel costs, other cost increases and unexpected quality problems with some products.[461]

At the Management Board meeting on December 11, 2003, Peter Bettermann assessed the situation at Freudenberg Bausysteme as follows – and the concluding point, number four, is decisive:

> "1. BS ["] manufactures a first-class product for the highest quality requirements. 2. the processes have been continuously improved over the last few years. The reject rates are now at a very reasonable level. 3. The sales department is very well organized and does a first-class job, as does the management. 4. Nevertheless, it should be noted that a subgroup which in the mid-1990s still achieved the highest total return on capital invested in the Group is continually approaching break-even due to external factors beyond its control."[462]

This meant that Freudenberg Bausysteme was heading into the red, and that actually happened two years later. In 2005, sales of the Freudenberg Bausysteme Business Group rose by 3.8 percent to 151.5 million euros. However, the earnings trend remained unsatisfactory: the result was minus 0.8 million euros – the first loss in 15 years. The figures were burdened by further increases in raw material and energy prices, which could be only partially passed on in price increases on the market.[463]

Despite the prevailing difficult economic environment in many markets, Freudenberg Bausysteme returned to profitability in 2006: The operating result rose to 7.1 million euros. The main stimuli for this came from the United States and Germany.[464] Further new product developments such as inlays, which have been marketed since 2005, also contributed to this development. Inlays comprised floor images worked into the floor, giving architects and building planners another creative option for room design. These were produced using an ultrasonic cutting system, which made it possible to produce inlay motifs measuring 1.5 by 3 meters – there were no limits to the choice of motif.[465] The following section from the Partners' Report on the Business for the 2006 financial year illustrates why the Management Board felt it was necessary to strategically reorganize the Freudenberg Bausysteme Business Group: "The Business Group is currently in a phase of strategic reorientation. The necessity for this resulted, among other things, from market developments: cost increases for synthetic and natural rubber, which have to be purchased for the production of BS floorcoverings, were accompanied by considerable price reductions for alternative floor coverings such as laminate or natural stone. In addition, there were rapidly growing competitors with several alternative floorcoverings in their product ranges."[466]

For this reason, "in the interest of securing the long-term future of the [...] subgroup, which focuses entirely on rubber floor coverings [...]," negotiations with strategic investors were initiated in 2006.[467] The aim of the negotiations that had been initiated was for the "investor to make a long-term contractual commitment to the Weinheim site and its existing infrastructure."[468] However, the actual sales process was extremely bumpy: The Freudenberg Bausysteme employees were informed in early summer 2006 that Freudenberg was looking for a cooperation partner for Freudenberg Bausysteme (FBS) – and therefore not about the plans for a sale, a mistake that was to come back to bite them.[469] In

Fig. 107 Nora inlays at the Evelina Children's Hospital in London, 2006

mid-November 2006, the rumors of a sale of Freudenberg Bausysteme KG became public for the first time following an indiscretion, despite corresponding confidentiality agreements. The result was an open letter from the FBS works council to the Freudenberg Management Board. The works council explained that rumors about the sale of FBS had intensified, leading to insecurity among the workforce. It therefore demanded clarification from the Management Board as to whether a sale of Bausysteme was planned.[470]

Freudenberg's Management Board first commented on the sales rumors at the end of November. It wrote an open letter to the FBS works council stating that the Management Board was reviewing various forms of cooperation with other companies due to important changes in competition. One alternative to this would be massive job cuts. The aim in examining the forms of cooperation was to "continue business activities while including the Weinheim site," meaning that the Weinheim site should be retained.[471] The Management Board offered the works council the opportunity to meet at a "round table" to discuss the status of developments.[472]

The employee representatives agreed to this proposal, but demanded an open explanation of the future plans for Freudenberg Bausysteme KG.[473]

Then, in mid-December 2006, the Management Board and representatives of Freudenberg Bausysteme KG met at a round table. Two prospective buyers were also present at the meeting.[474] Nevertheless, on December 19, employees of Freudenberg Bausysteme demonstrated against the planned sale of the division.[475] They had previously been informed about the current situation by the employee representatives at an extraordinary works meeting. Around 400 employees gathered with banners and whistles in front of Gate 1 at the Zwischen Dämmen plant and then marched into the center of Weinheim.[476]

At the subsequent rally on Weinheim's market square, the IG BCE trade union grasped the opportunity to attack the Group's management for its information policy, as the workforce had been kept in the dark for so long about the plans to sell.[477] Thus this demonstration would only be the beginning of the employee protests. The Management Board responded at the beginning of 2007 with a letter to the employees of Freudenberg Bausysteme, in which it explained the reasons for the sales negotiations: "1. The result of the Bausysteme Business Group has fallen steadily and drastically since 1998 and entered the red in 2005. […] 2. An enormous consolidation process is underway in the floorcoverings industry; large groups of companies are emerging that offer a wide range of different floorcoverings (e.g., linoleum, laminates, PVC, carpets, rubber) and have production facilities in various regions of the world. Because of their size, they have significant cost advantages, particularly in distribution. 3. In contrast,

Freudenberg Bausysteme only has one production facility in the euro zone and bears the full currency risk for business in the main markets in North America and Southeast Asia, which tend to have high dollar exchange rates. We must therefore find a connection to one of these strong groups [...] However, you can rest assured that we will only accept a solution in which 1. Bausysteme has good long-term business prospects, as this is the only way to really secure jobs in the long term; 2. the contracting partner is absolutely reputable and demonstrably thinks and acts in a long-term and success-oriented manner; 3. the Weinheim site [...] remains secure in its existence."[478]

Then the situation escalated rapidly: On January 16, 2007, the Management Board informed the works council that the company was going ahead with the planned sale to a competitor despite the division's positive earnings situation. It was clear to the works council that with this behavior, "Group management was terminating the industrial peace at FBS KG and calling out the workforce." The workforce would not wait without resistance until a fait accompli had been achieved, it said.[479] On January 18, 2007, a works meeting was held for all employees at Freudenberg Bausysteme KG.[480] At this meeting, the works council and the workforce called on the Management Board to discontinue the negotiations on the sale of Bausysteme that had been ongoing for several weeks, while retaining the site.[481] At 5 a.m. on Friday, January 19, 2007, the employees of Freudenberg Bausysteme KG blocked all access roads to the Weinheim Industrial Park. Production at Freudenberg Bausysteme came to a standstill. The following article excerpt from the *Weinheimer Nachrichten* newspaper of January 20, 2007 shows the mood that prevailed that morning:

> "'We won't rest until the sale of Freudenberg Bausysteme KG is off the table permanently.' What an FBS employee said yesterday morning is what many of those who had gathered outside the factory gates were thinking. Since 5 o'clock this morning, all entrances have been blocked for trucks. While plant security is already welcoming the lorry drivers at the Weststrasse/Viernheimer Strasse junction, leaflets from the Group Works Council are being distributed outside Gate 1. They openly question the credibility of Group management and accuse the employer of having 'finally terminated the industrial peace at FBS' with its behavior."[482]

At around 3 p.m., the demonstrators broke up the blockade at the factory gates.[483] Parallel to the blockade, the FBS works meeting, which had been running since Thursday afternoon, continued, bringing production at FBS virtually to a standstill for two days. But it was not only production at Freudenberg Bausysteme KG that was at a standstill, but also a large part of the sealing and vibration control technology business, and parts of fiber fleece and Service KG were interrupted. This was particularly problematic in view of the fact that just-in-time production largely prevailed in these companies. The interruption of production and the associated truck transport meant that important customers in the automotive industry could no longer be supplied on time. Around 1,000 employees from various companies at the main plant, as well as the works councils of all Freudenberg companies, supported the demonstrators by stopping work and likewise blocking the factory gates. At least 90 percent of production was frozen. Many of the employees joined the protest in solidarity with their colleagues at Freudenberg Bausysteme KG.[484] The willingness to show solidarity was certainly also increased by the fact that a restructuring program involving job cuts had just been adopted at Freudenberg Vliesstoffe (nonwovens) at the time.[485] In addition, on Friday morning a demonstration marched from Gate 2 of the main Zwischen Dämmen plant through the neighboring residential area and later across the factory site. For the works council and the workforce, it was clear that the works meeting would continue until the management spokesman, Peter Bettermann, gave a written statement on the abandonment of the sales plans.[486]

The company commented on the plant blockade on the same day as follows:

> "In order to secure the long-term future of the Bausysteme subgroup, which is currently focused entirely on rubber floorcoverings, and to permanently strengthen and secure the industrial park at the Weinheim site and its excellent infrastructure, Freudenberg's management bodies have drawn up a strategic concept to secure the future. The sale to a reputable company, preferably one that is already internationally established in the floorcovering market, offers the best opportunity to secure jobs at Bausysteme in the long term. Against this background, negotiations were entered into under the following demanding conditions: 1. The Weinheim site must be retained for Bausysteme. 2. The contracting partner must be reputable and offer a long-term perspective so that Bausysteme and the infrastructure have good business prospects and jobs can be secured in the long term. [...] The negotiations are being conducted with a view to enforcing these conditions. We therefore ask you especially for your patience and prudence. The most recent development, which has led to a blockade of the industrial park and severely impaired the business activities of other companies at the site, including those that are not part of the Freudenberg Group, cannot be tolerated by the management bodies. This escalation is in no way useful for securing the future of Freudenberg Bausysteme."[487]

One day later, on January 20, a meeting took place with the members of the Management Board and the chairmen of the European works council, the group works council and representatives of the works council of Freudenberg Bausysteme KG. The members of the Management Board of Freudenberg Bausysteme were also present at this meeting. The Management Board's decision not to continue the sales negotiations at this time was announced and explained.[488] Then the employees of Freudenberg Bausysteme ended their five-day works meeting on Monday, January 22 – which, of course, had not had any major impact over the weekend – and resumed work.[489]

Earlier, the Management Board of the Freudenberg Group had declared that "due to the unlawful blockade of the gates of the Weinheim Industrial Park – Zwischen Dämmen plant – last Friday, it felt compelled to discontinue the long-running talks with potential partners for the floorcovering business for the present." The parties involved in the talks had been informed of this decision. The reasons given for abandoning the negotiations were: "1. Restoring and maintaining industrial peace for all companies – both those of the Freudenberg Group and third parties – in the Weinheim Industrial Park. 2. Ensuring the supply of customers whose plants depend in part on punctual delivery and who rely on this service. 3. Facilitating discussions between potential strategic buyers and employee representatives of Freudenberg Bausysteme KG."[490] Point 2 referred to just-in-time delivery, which was already very important at the time.

Jörg Sost, the member of the Management Board who had been responsible for Bausysteme since 2005, also recalled the dramatic situation in an interview in 2019: "I've never experienced that here before, [...] it was really like a little revolution had broken out [...]. It was [...] difficult to control, it had developed an extreme momentum of its own." The works councils subsequently showed solidarity and "the trade unions [came] on the scene." Then, when the camera crews arrived and the news was reported on the *Tagesschau* and *Abendschau* TV news shows, "the whole situation" had become "extremely dangerous," Sost recalls.

"We were only able to pacify the whole thing by saying that we would stop the entire sales process, [...] we had to consolidate first and [...] then possibly enter into a new round of discussions with the employees, the works councils and the trade unions. The plant here was [...] blocked, there was a full strike, you couldn't get in and you couldn't get out, [...] no more trucks could get in, no more trucks could get out, [...] it was uncompromising, it was a very, very difficult situation." When asked about the learning effects, Sost said: "Confidentiality agreements are confidentiality agreements, and if you go through the process, you have to set it up in such a way to make sure that the decision-makers know about it, that you get them on board. So there were some things we didn't do well, I have to say that self-critically too."[491]

The process regarding the sale of the floorcovering division was resumed with a little cooling-off time – and this time the employee representatives were involved at an early stage. At the beginning of April 2007, the Management Board informed the Bausysteme Management Board as well as the works council and the workforce of Freudenberg Bausysteme KG about the resumption of the negotiation process and the search for qualified potential buyers for the business group.[492]

Sost, the responsible member of the Management Board, explained in the spring of 2007:

> "We are convinced that the business has potential. However, it is significantly different from the other areas of the Group and is not part of our core business. The further development of the floorcovering segment requires high investments continuously, which can be guaranteed by a strategically interested investor. […] It is clear that the division is to be sold. However, it is very important to us that the parties involved are convinced that the new owner represents solid future prospects for the employees and the business."[493]

In the months that followed, the Management Board of Freudenberg Bausysteme KG and the works council were involved in the selection of potential buyers and kept informed of the negotiations.[494] These negotiations were finally concluded on September 25, 2007. On that day, the purchase agreement was signed by the Freudenberg Management Board, financial investor Capiton AG from Berlin and Landesbank-Eigenkapital Agentur, a subsidiary of Landeskreditbank Baden-Württemberg.[495] [496] This was a management buy-out. One of the investors' declared aims was to expand the Weinheim site. A long-term commitment was achieved through a ten-year rental and service agreement There would be no compulsory redundancies for Freudenberg Bausysteme KG employees until the end of 2010.[497]

The Nora brand became part of the company name, which changed from Freudenberg Bausysteme KG to Nora Systems GmbH. All company activities were now to be concentrated on the Nora brand. The solution that had now been found was also welcomed by the works council. Karl-Heinz Kuschel, chairman of the works council, summarized as follows: "We are satisfied with this solution. […] The financial investors have made it credibly clear that they are not among the locusts in their sector, but are interested in the long-term growth of our company – and thus in preserving our jobs here in Weinheim."[498] The collective bargaining agreements with IG Bergbau Chemie Energie [the mining, chemical and energy workers' union – ed.] and the works agreements, as well as individual contractual provisions, were also adopted."[499]

The strategic reasons for the sale were the cyclical, barely controllable construction industry business, and the trend towards concentration in the industry, meaning the tendency to purchase all floorcoverings from a single source – a development that could only have been counteracted by taking over unfamiliar technologies. In addition, the Nora technology itself no longer matched Freudenberg's technology concept. What remains is that Freudenberg opened up this new product area in 1950 – and exploited it for a long time with remarkable success: That year, the Nora brand rubber floorcoverings were launched on the market as a further development of shoe soles. By the time Freudenberg Bausysteme was sold, the company had become the market leader in rubber floorcoverings with the Noraplan and Norament brands.[500]

> **EXCURSUS:** SOCIAL RESPONSIBILITY – PART 4: UP TO THE MID-1990S
>
> **1984** Some of the partners established the Freudenberg Foundation with capital of around 3 million deutschmarks. As a non-profit limited liability company, the foundation is a limited partner, i.e. a general partner of Freudenberg & Co. KG. Its purpose is to support the integration and promotion of disadvantaged groups and cultural projects.[501] With its programs, the Freudenberg Foundation promotes long-term, effective structural changes in order to contribute to greater inclusion, education and democracy. All projects focus primarily on children and young people and their social, linguistic, educational and vocational integration.[502]
>
> **1987** The new pension scheme regulating the company pension granted by the company comes into effect.[503]
>
> **1989** The partners donate the capital of 10 million deutschmarks for the establishment of Unterstützungskasse Carl Freudenberg e.V., a relief fund for employees in need (illness, invalidity, old age, etc.). The provident fund also pays death benefits in the event of the death of a (former) employee or the death of a spouse, irrespective of the health insurance death benefit and the company death benefit. By 2006, the provident fund had supported employees in almost 1,500 cases with a total of 1.3 million euros and paid out 2.7 million euros in death benefits.[504] By the end of 2022, approximately 7.7 million euros had been paid out on emergency and death benefits.[505]

Managing complexity through organization: From division organization to "**F**reudenberg **O**rganization for **Cu**stomer-Oriented Corporate **S**tructure" (Focus)

We recall: that company founder Carl Johann Freudenberg and later his sons were initially general partners (owners) and simultaneously managing directors of the company. This did not change fundamentally until 1921, as at that time the majority of the 14 former general partners were no longer active in the company at all. Therefore, Freudenberg & Co. GmbH was founded that year to manage the family shares. The management of the ownership structure was separated from the operational business. This is still the case today.

Therefore, at the beginning of its history, Freudenberg was a company that was managed by first and second generation owner-entrepreneurs[506] and initially restricted to the leather business area. At the beginning of the 1920s, the growing company then saw an expanded collegial management with an initially more or less informal organization of the four managing directors from the third generation of the family.[507] Diversification and the internationalization of production that began in the 1950s made the company increasingly complex in its structure and thus in its organizational requirements. Ultimately, this development made it increasingly clear that a more flexible, professional and autonomous organization was required.

The expansion of the Management Board to eight members[508] in 1959 initially took account of the situation that Carl Freudenberg KG did not have any independently managed business units and the Management Board was therefore heavily involved in the business operations. Responsibilities for the divisions or business units and overarching central functions, like for example the personnel department, were distributed among individual general partners.

Then, in 1968, a discussion paper on the organizational structure at Carl Freudenberg came to the conclusion that the increasingly fast pace of change in market conditions and the "expansion of technological and business knowledge" also required more frequent "operational adjustment processes." In order to successfully keep pace with this dynamic development, the company's organization needed to be structured in such a way that appropriate processes would be established which could be used to manage change.[509]

The diversity and complexity of the company also led not only to a discussion about the organization of the company, but also to a revision of the partnership agreement, which was to be adapted to the "economic growth"[510] of the company. The amended partnership agreement of 1970 also created the possibility of electing members of the Board of Partners from outside the family for the first time. This made it possible to appoint external experts to the supervisory and advisory boards and to adapt and professionalize the body to the requirements of the growing international company.[511]

Thus the necessity to make the organizational structure understandable and predictable in line with the company dynamic was becoming increasingly clear. This triggered an extensive discussion within the Management Board about the future structural organization of the Freudenberg Group. It was Hans Erich Freudenberg who made the first concrete proposal for the future structure of the company in a letter to his Management Board colleagues on November 20, 1970. In it, he remarked that "risky political, fiscal and economic developments" would prompt large companies to "exploit their opportunities worldwide with new organizational forms and structures." Thus Freudenberg too would have to work with foresight on its own organization and corporate strategy.[512] In January 1971, Hermann Freudenberg developed "Basic Considerations on the Organization of Freudenberg & Co. and Carl Freudenberg" from the intensified discussions of the Management Board at the end of 1970.[513] Building on this and promoted by Hermann Freudenberg, the first formal organizational chart of the Group was drawn up in 1971. It did not bring about any fundamental changes, but the normative effect of the terms and definitions it contained, which divided the company organizationally into corporate and central divisions, was considerable. They shaped the understanding of roles within the organization for two decades.[514]

Hans Erich Freudenberg, however, remained dissatisfied with the state of affairs. In December 1975, he urgently called for the company to become truly customer-oriented. The old idea had been adopted that "we are primarily German, indeed Weinheim producers […]. We go so far as to expect the sales facilities to fulfill their task in the 'service of production.'" He asked whether this was really the best way to "serve the customers" or whether they would ultimately turn away from Freudenberg because the competition offered more. He recommended setting up a wide variety of sales organizations that would have to serve customers in clearly defined markets.[515]

Due to the partial divergence of the corporate and central divisions in the years that followed, a matrix and divisional organization was created in 1979. An overview of what emerged can be found in the company's organizational brochure from 1979:[516] "Within the Freudenberg Group, Freudenberg & Co. amalgamates its subsidiaries, including Carl Freudenberg, into an entrepreneurial unit. […] In order to be able to manage the diverse business with decentralized autonomy and at the same time ensure the cohesion and exploitation of the potential of the company as a whole, the organization is divided into four corporate and four central divisions which work together in matrix form. They are headed by members of the Management Board,"[517] it said.

The divisions were responsible for the product and market activities of the units assigned to them. For the first time, divisions now appeared as organizational units within the corporate divisions, in which business units and subsidiaries with the same or similar product and market activities were combined. The divisions and subsidiaries managed the business with profit responsibility. The central divisions carried out centralized tasks for the company as a whole and – with a focus on Carl Freudenberg – business activities that were not assigned to the divisions. They formed the horizontal framework of the entire company and developed systems and guidelines for the Group on their own initiative and on request and monitored compliance with them. The Management Board continued to be the highest executive body of the Group. Its members were jointly responsible for the company and at the same time were also the heads of the corporate and central divisions.[518]

The role of the Management Board also becomes clear when one looks at the relevant passages in Hermann Freudenberg's speech at the 1980 general meeting. The following aspects were very important to him:

"1) The responsibility of the members of the Management Board is indivisible. We do not have a chairman. Everyone represents their own area internally and externally,

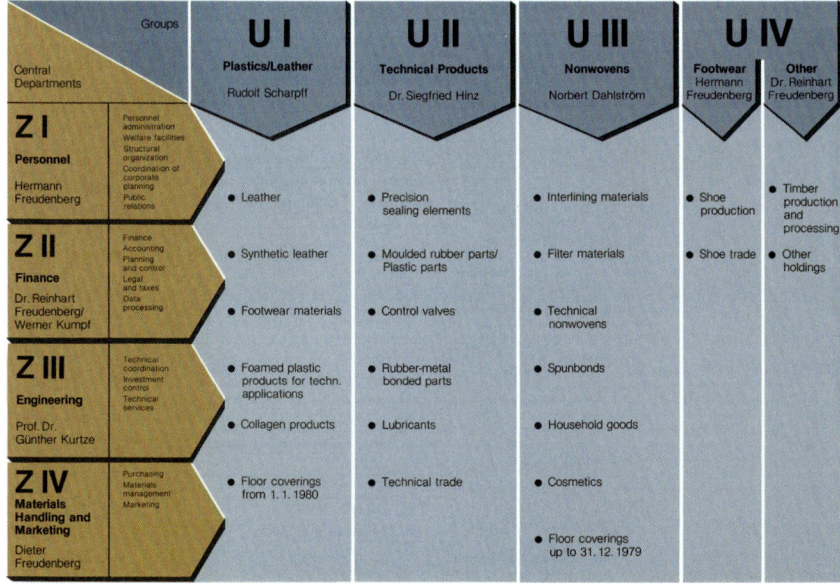

Fig. 108 The Freudenberg matrix organization, 1979

but at the same time bears full responsibility for the company as a whole. 2) There is no weighting between corporate and central divisions, as both are equally important for the successful management of the company. [...] 3) Many management and coordination tasks that used to be performed exclusively by the Management Board have been passed over to the second tier, the divisional and functional managers."[519]

In his speech in April 1980, Hermann Freudenberg also emphasized the importance he attached to the family business in its current form:

"The Management Board [...] regards it as a key task to maintain Freudenberg as a family enterprise. Tax considerations are not the only aspects to play a role in this context, but also the conviction that a family enterprise enables an individual working style and a special corporate style that is attractive to employees and appears to us to be worth preserving. From the employees' point of view, the continuity of top management, the certainty that a change of ownership through the sale of shares will not easily leave them faced with a new situation, and the stronger personal ties and relationships are positive aspects. [...] The relationship between the partners and the company differs from the relationship between the shareholders of a listed company, as they are linked by kinship and wealth inherited from common ancestors."[520]

In 1986, the divisions were abandoned as organizational units. Instead, the business units were now increasingly composed of divisions. These were supplemented by business units reporting directly to the Management Board for business that was economically less critical. The concept of central divisions was also abandoned. These were now managed as central functions. However, the original functional areas and functional departments of the former central divisions were retained. The problem with the business units was that although they were independent in terms of the development, production and distribution of their products, they lacked key functions such as HR, tax/legal and IT, which were performed jointly for them by Carl Freudenberg. Furthermore, the divisions were unable to take responsibility for a large portion of their own business because the Management Board was still very heavily involved in business operations.[521]

For this reason, in his essay dated October 22, 1991 and addressed to the Management Board, Reinhart Freudenberg stated very clearly the problems he saw to be arising from the company structure, but also at the organizational level of Carl Freudenberg for the work of the Management Board: "The Management Board [MB] is disproportionately occupied with Carl Freudenberg. I estimate that, between them all, the MB members spend well over 70 percent of their time on CF [Carl Freudenberg] (with 40 percent of sales and a much smaller

Fig. 109 The Management Board reviewing the further strategic development, 1983: Norbert Dahlström, Dieter Freudenberg, Hermann Freudenberg, Siegfried Hinz, Rudolf Scharpff, Reinhart Freudenberg, Günther Kurtze (from left)

proportion of income). The Weinheim site probably receives a disproportionate share of this." That means the Management Board was largely involved in business operations of Carl Freudenberg KG and had relatively little time to devote to its actual strategic management tasks.[522]

Based on his analysis of the problem, Reinhart Freudenberg proposed a change in the structural organization: "To achieve organizational change that could solve the problems outlined above, only a vertical division of the Group into independent and fully integrated companies would therefore work, whereby the CF Group would be dissolved and its parts allocated to these companies. The Management Board as Group management would no longer manage operational units with combined responsibility." Hence the divisions that had previously been managed as part of Carl Freudenberg would be transferred to independent companies. From Reinhart Freudenberg's point of view, the only thing that would make sense was to combine those businesses that had more commonalities than differences in terms of their markets or technology. Otherwise, too many different entities would be created, which in turn would necessitate different organizational requirements.[523]

Freudenberg & Co., which would act as the Group management company in the future, "would have as its most important task the management of this portfolio as an active, but non-operational supervisory board of the subsidiaries." That means that henceforth the Freudenberg & Co. management company would only conduct the actual Group functions. Potential functions could include: human resources, finance, tax, legal, insurance, general partners' affairs, corporate audit, investments, public relations and corporate identity.[524] In May of the following year, the Board of Partners approved the restructuring proposed by the entire Management Board, particularly that the division heads should be given more authority and responsibility. A newly created Organizing Committee of the Board of Partners, comprising Board of Partners Chairman Hermann Freudenberg and Board of Partners members Helmut Sihler, Walter Sigle (1930–2021) and Michael Rogowski (1939–2021), was to support the Management Board in the decision-making process.[525]

Thus, although plans to restructure Carl Freudenberg had been drawn up and discussed extensively with the Board of Partners at this time, it was decided to postpone the project "in view of the looming crisis."[526] "At the time, it seemed like a step too far,"[527] because after the boom years of reunification, the recession described above was looming in 1992, which would have made such a large organizational project difficult to implement. The economic situation – also a result of the López effect – led to a "crisis in the automotive industry"[528] in 1993, which had impacted the seals and vibration control technology division at Freudenberg in particular.[529]

In 1994, since there were indications of an impending business recovery at Freudenberg, the Board of Partners finally approved the planned organizational changes in the Group, and within Carl Freudenberg in particular, at its meeting on November 9, 1994.[530]

The project was restarted under the aegis of Peter Bettermann. Following intensive preparation and approval from the Board of Partners, the "Organizational Development of Carl Freudenberg – Business Units and Central Service Divisions to Become Independent Companies" statement was adopted by the Management Board in November 1994. This was based on the concept drawn up by Reinhart Freudenberg at the beginning of the 1990s.[531] In December 1994, Dirk Mahler, Head of the Legal Department at Freudenberg & Co., won a survey in which Freudenberg executives were asked to come up with catchy and apt short titles for the somewhat unwieldy name of the organizational project with his proposal, "Focus".[532] The project name is an acronym and stands for: **F**reudenberg **O**rganization for **Cu**stomer-Oriented Corporate **S**tructure.[533]

At that time, the Freudenberg Group comprised a total of 174 companies in 34 countries – including 48 production and 46 distribution companies. The largest company was the parent company, Carl Freudenberg. As described above,

Fig. 110 The Management Board responsible for the Focus organization, 1995: Peter Stehle, Ernst Schön, Peter Bettermann, Reinhart Freudenberg, Norbert Dahlström, Hans-Jochen Hüchting (from left)

Carl Freudenberg KG was subdivided into business units and central service units (known as central functions). Alongside these there were already legally independent subsidiaries which were assigned to Freudenberg & Co. as the parent and management company.[534]

The new legally independent companies (business groups) created by Focus were to be put in a position to be able to react even faster and more flexibly to their customers' special requirements and to changes in markets and technologies. Because of the broad diversification that had evolved at the company, the individual business units were very different in terms of their markets, technologies and internationality. This necessitated special working methods and structures to ensure the long-term success of the Freudenberg Group.[535]

The business and service companies were to be established by January 1, 1996 and given full responsibility for their tasks at that time. Carl Freudenberg's business units were transferred to business companies without any significant changes to their business content. The management company assumed the Group-wide business functions as well as all tasks "that serve the management and control of the Group."[536]

Reinhart Freudenberg described this process in his recollection as follows: "The Management Board still made it obvious that it came from the leather era, in which one member of the Management Board was responsible for purchasing, another for production, a third for distribution and a fourth for finance and accounting, so it had a top-down structure functionally. And part of this was that all foreign companies still reported directly to some member of the Management Board too, so there wasn't a sealing rings division, but there was the Simmer plant, and the Simrit plant, in Weinheim, and foreign companies that also did this, but which reported directly to a member of the Management Board. That could not continue any longer, it was easy to see that, and then we developed this model of a management holding company. It was also a bit fashionable at the time; there were other companies that had organized themselves as management holding companies as opposed to financial holding companies. A management holding company is one that really manages the business, and a financial holding company is one that trades in business. We wanted to be a management holding company, but that required very independent management in the divisions."[537]

This new structure became legally binding as of January 1, 1996, meaning that the business and service companies were established as planned as of January 1, 1996:

Parent Company	Business Groups	Divisions
Freudenberg & Co.	Seals and Vibration Control Technology Europe	Flexible PCBs
		Leather
		Shoe Retailing
	Seals and Vibration Control Technology North America (Freudenberg-NOK GP)	*Service Companies:*
		Systems and Tool Engineering
	Staple-Fiber Nonwovens	Informatics
	Spunbonded Nonwovens	Commercial Services
		Technical Services
	Special-Purpose Lubricants	
	Building Systems	
	Household Products	
	Footwear	
	Technical Distributors	

Fig. 111 The Freudenberg Group's new Focus structural organization, 1996

From that time onward, the new holding structure created in this way shaped the organization of the Freudenberg Group, as all further Group-wide structural changes to the organization must be regarded as a successor to Focus. With Focus, Freudenberg succeeded in overcoming the traditional parent company mentality for the first time. With the new structure, the company became significantly more agile in increasingly globalized markets. The Management Board – now that it had been largely freed from operational tasks – increasingly concentrated on the strategic management and further development of the complex Freudenberg Group.

With the slowdown in growth momentum from the late 1960s onward, and ultimately under the altered conditions in global economic competition during the 1970s, Freudenberg's organizational development is a prime example of how many German companies were faced with the question of whether their organizational structures were adequate for their own complexity and whether they would be internationally competitive. However, this was by no means just a German problem, but affected all large companies in Western countries, which "suddenly" found themselves literally at the mercy of Japanese competition in the 1970s. This was because the latter was producing much more cost-effectively with more efficient organizational structures. The question that arose now was: What could be learned from foreign competition in this respect?[538]

This challenge led to complex reactions at many companies. The focus increasingly shifted to the Far East. Business trips to Japan were commonplace now, and many companies, and hence also Freudenberg, exploited opportunities for cooperation specifically to benefit from Japanese examples.[539] Moreover, the hour of the management consultant was now approaching, which had already been heralded in the 1960s with the work of Marvin Bower on corporate organization.[540] Bower was one of the most important men behind consulting firm McKinsey, which, alongside others, was now also gaining a foothold in the West German corporate landscape and was specifically advocating here for modern matrix organization in companies.[541]

Many companies sought the advice of such experts for their reorganization projects.[542] Others – like Freudenberg – did not do this, but instead mobilized the knowledge for the necessary organizational changes in-house, whether through practical experience with organizational problems, through further training of employees or through targeted recruitment of expertise for their company. Freudenberg had already practiced this successfully in the case of environmental protection and the introduction of IT. It was likely the positive experience gained there that also permitted Freudenberg to rely on the expertise of the relevant employees in the case of the company organization and its updating. The company obviously had the confidence to take the appropriate steps towards reform. The result, the new Focus organization, lived up to these expectations too. What many other companies mobilized external consultants for, Freudenberg's top management did on their own. This is also a sure sign that the company's top management was fully aware of the simultaneous developments at the competition in Germany and abroad.

CHAPTER 7
SUSTAINABILITY, MOBILITY, DIGITALIZATION
THE COMPANY SINCE THE TURN OF THE MILLENNIUM

Euro, terrorist attacks, financial crisis, conflicts, pandemic – Freudenberg in a changing world

At the turn of the millennium, banks, financial markets, companies and people – in that order – had to adapt to a new currency. The banks had already been using the euro as an accounting currency since 1999, i.e., before its introduction as a physical currency in Europe. The launch of the euro as a currency in people's pockets was the culmination of the economic and monetary union agreed by the EU member states in the 1992 Treaty of Maastricht. The euro as a currency in their wallet was a new experience for people in Germany and 11 other member states of the European Union on January 1, 2002.[1] It is almost impossible to describe the significance of this change. From one day to the next, about 300 million people in Europe started to use the same coins and banknotes irrespective of where they were traveling and working within the "common currency area". The euro also proved to be attractive for other countries: "Six further countries joined the monetary union by 2014, by which time the eurozone already included 18 countries. They were joined one year later by Lithuania. The 20th country, the latest to become part of the monetary union, was Croatia at the beginning of 2023.[2]

However, Germans were skeptical about the introduction of the new currency and many retain this skepticism to this day. The background to Euro-skepticism is easy to explain. Following the disaster which was national socialism, the deutschmark became the symbol of economic recovery and mass prosperity. Germany's experience with the Bundesbank and its monetary policy firmly committed to a stable currency had been good. Whether the euro would remain equally stable was an open question despite all the assurances that the European Central Bank (ECB) would be a sort of European Bundesbank. This was especially so as Germany did not exactly set a good example following the introduction of the euro. There were times when the German government under Chancellor Gerhard Schröder (SPD) exceeded the deficit limit laid down in the Stability and Growth Pact. Under certain circumstances, infringements of the new rules appeared to be a matter of political legitimacy. Initially, these infringements were exceptions. However, a period of fundamental crisis in the eurozone started in the wake of the global financial crisis and its impact on national economies in 2009. At the start, the crisis focused on Greek debt but there was also severe negative impact on countries such as Portugal and Ireland. The ECB was only able to safeguard the cohesion of the monetary union by taking unconventional action, at the price of continuously rising debt and explosive growth in money supply. These consequences all seemed to be acceptable as long as inflation remained insignificant, especially since it was possible to safeguard the everyday functioning of the currency. The euro proved itself in day-to-day shopping, and exchange rate risks and fees for currency exchange became a thing of the past. As it was no longer necessary to convert currencies, price comparisons became much more convenient. Since then, exporters have found it far easier than before to handle cross-border transactions, at least in the eurozone.[3]

However, times were becoming increasingly troubled after the turn of the millennium even without these politically intended changes. In the year before the introduction of the euro as a physical currency, the world was shaken by the dramatic terrorist attacks of September 11, 2001. These caused uproar throughout the world, not only on financial markets, and led to military conflicts lasting for many years, especially in Iraq and Afghanistan. At 8:45 a. m. on September 11, 2001, when an airliner flew into one of the World Trade Center towers in New York, the world seemed to stand still. Less than 20 minutes later, a second aircraft flew into the second tower and shortly afterwards both towers collapsed as a result of the tremendous heat developed. Yet that was not the end of the attack on America. The Pentagon, the American Ministry of Defense, was also the target of an attack using a civilian aircraft. On the same morning, a fourth aircraft crashed on a field in Pennsylvania. It is suspected that the intention had been to attack the White House with this aircraft, but this attempt had been foiled by courageous passengers who fought the terrorists, resulting in the crash. Final estimates put the number of people who died as a result of these attacks at more than 3,000.

One day after these attacks, the North Atlantic Treaty Organization (NATO) invoked Article 5 of the North Atlantic Treaty (the "mutual defense" case) for the first time in its history.[4] This was followed by the wars in Afghanistan and Iraq. It was not until 2021 that the last troops of the US and its allies were withdrawn from Afghanistan.

America's economic policy response to the crisis following the terrorist attacks of September 11 was one reason for the global financial crisis of 2008/2009, which started as a real estate crisis in the United States and gradually engulfed other countries. Since the 1990s, the central banks had developed a strategy of offensive intervention in financial markets in case of doubt. Following the terrorist attacks, these interventions were used in a targeted way to stimulate the economy and to ensure that as many people as possible benefited from the stimulation. The real estate market and associated financial markets became overblown to an unprecedented extent with "sub-prime" loans, and the fragility of the market became evident when real estate prices started to fall. The first bankruptcy of a major bank sent shock waves throughout the world and effectively starved financial markets of funds. Without further intervention by governments and central banks, there was a general apprehension that there would be a total collapse of financial markets. As a consequence of the financial crisis, global economic output slumped. "For the first time since the Second World War, the real gross domestic product (GDP) of developed economies shrank. In the developing economies there was a significant reduction in GDP growth. As a result of the problems of a large number of banks and a general loss of confidence, the crisis also affected the non-financial sector, for example leading to a significant reduction in global trading."[5]

At the beginning of 2008, the Management Board in Weinheim had been pleased to report that the company had completed the 2007 financial year with record sales. The 2007 annual report states: "Sales by the Freudenberg Group rose year-on-year by 288.4 million to 5.34 billion euros, the highest ever in the company's history." Automotive original equipment manufacturers (OEMs) accounted for 42 percent of sales and mechanical and plant engineering for a further 14 percent. Consolidated profit also grew by about 25 percent to 275 million euros.[6] Despite the good development in business, a glance at the United States with its potentially dangerous developments in the real estate and finance sectors significantly dampened prospects. However, at that time, it was scarcely possible to imagine how fast the bursting of the real estate bubble in the United States would spread throughout the internationally linked financial sector to become "the most serious financial and global economic crisis since the end of the Second World War."[7]

In the early summer of 2008, Peter Bettermann, Speaker of the Freudenberg Management Board, already recognized the ominous signs of an impending spread of the financial crisis in the form of a general shortage of liquidity on capital markets. He rapidly initiated preventive action much earlier than other decision-makers in politics and industry. One of the key steps was to significantly expand the company's credit lines at an early stage at favorable conditions and for long terms. This way, Freudenberg's strategic liquidity reserve was increased by several hundred million euros.[8] This process had been completed by the fall of 2008, before the crisis in the US financial sector had started to affect the real economy.[9]

From then onward, banks faced a considerable loss of confidence and there were significant disturbances in the lending system. In addition, consumer restraint intensified and this soon had a negative impact on the automotive industry in North America, Europe and Japan, which was already struggling. The financial crisis revealed the latent structural problems that for many years had already affected the American automotive sector in particular, but also many European automakers: Scarce liquidity, misguided model policies and systematic overcapacities.[10] Bettermann recognized and correctly interpreted the alarm signals from the United States, especially for the "big three" US automakers – General Motors, Ford and Chrysler – at an early stage and lowered the profit expectations of the Freudenberg Group. He explained his predictions for the crisis in the automotive industry in July 2008 in an interview with the *Financial Times*, summing up the situation as follows: "Times are becoming harder."[11]

As a component supplier, Freudenberg was hit hard by the first effects of the financial crisis on the US automotive industry in October 2008. There were signs that the big three would default on payments as a result of the crisis.[12] In November, it was clear that General Motors especially, which had already suffered severe losses in 2007 and at the beginning of 2008,[13] would be unable to survive without support from the US administration. Chrysler was also in crisis mode. This posed challenges, especially for the automotive components business of the Freudenberg-NOK General Partnership (FNGP) Business Group and Japan Vilene (North America). For FNGP in particular, Mohsen Sohi (at that time CEO of FNGP) and Ralf Krieger (at that time CFO of FNGP) established an efficient crisis management system based on ensuring adequate liquidity at all times and steered FNGP well through the crisis.[14] The uncertainty in connection with impending payment defaults or even insolvencies in the automotive sector spread like wildfire throughout the components industry.[15]

Freudenberg networked with other companies affected, collected information and took various measures, including adjusting its cash management to the changed situation under the calm but assertive leadership of Bettermann: Investments were cut back to the absolute minimum, costs were reduced and strict price and receivables management was applied to customers and suppliers.[16] Research and development activities were deliberately excluded from the savings measures.[17] At weekly intervals, the bad news from the automotive industry was collected and discussed by the Business Groups affected in conference calls.[18] At the same time, the Management Board used its best efforts to calm the Business Groups: "As regards equity ratio, firmly committed credit lines and actual liquidity, we are better positioned than ever before at the beginning of the crisis. The same applies to the performance situation of most of our Business Groups. The prospects that we will emerge from this crisis with renewed strength are excellent."[19]

In December 2008, General Motors announced that vehicle production would be reduced by a further 250,000 vehicles in the first quarter of 2009; in the same period, additional plants in North America were to be closed.[20] The decline in automobile production, in Europe and Japan too, led to extreme slumps in orders received by Freudenberg. In the first half of 2009, the Group recorded a fall in orders of 30 percent in the passenger car segment and as much as 50 percent in the commercial vehicle segment.[21]

In the crisis, Bettermann also focused his attention on solutions adopted by the company during the global economic crisis of 1929, with a view to learning "from his predecessors". As in 1929, the consistent application of short-time working proved to be an effective solution in the 2009 crisis. According to Bettermann: "Especially in Germany, short-time working helped significantly in avoiding large numbers of permanent layoffs among the workforce. And we also applied very similar methods in other countries. We used the possibilities allowed by labor law to the greatest extent feasible. Following the crisis, we made a very impressive recovery, which would hardly have been possible if we had not retained our skilled workers."[22] The objective was also to boost employees' motivation and to offer them prospects for the future. One example is the "My Factory" campaign of the Freudenberg Seals and Vibration Control Technology (FDS) Business Group. The basic objective of this program was to ensure that workplaces were available for the time after the crisis. For example, employees tidied up and maintained factory halls and machinery. In addition to such renovation and maintenance work, Freudenberg also offered further training for employees and processes were optimized. The desired results of the campaign were summarized by Arman Barimani (at that time Member of the Management Board of FDS) as follows: "Our objective is to emerge from the crisis with renewed strength, with a modern factory, well-designed processes and motivated employees."[23]

However, the Board of Management was well aware that short-time working would not be sufficient to absorb the effects of the crisis. Forecasts consistently predicted that production figures for the automotive industry would only return to the 2007 level in five years' time. In addition, the crisis had accelerated the trend, already evident, for automobile production to be relocated to the growth regions of China, India and Brazil.[24] Capacity adjustments at the Freudenberg Business Groups were therefore unavoidable, even more so in view of the fact that products which did not offer any short-term or long-term prospect of positive development were removed from the portfolio in connection with the restructuring measures initiated in 2008. In total, eight production plants had to be closed: four in the USA and four in Europe.[25]

The bailouts provided by the US administration for Chrysler and General Motors were linked to tough restructuring programs. In the first half of 2009, both these automakers with their long traditions had to apply for Chapter 11 bankruptcy, submitting themselves to government-monitored restructuring programs. The greater part of amounts receivable by Freudenberg companies from the two US automakers was secured by the US Treasury program to aid suppliers and was collected despite the bankruptcy procedures.[26] The scrappage incentives offered by the US and German governments, which were also intended to provide support for automakers, had almost no effect on the Freudenberg companies, as dealers mainly sold vehicles that they already had in stock.[27]

The mechanical engineering sector, which was initially buoyed by its full order books, was hit by the crisis with a certain delay. In the second half of 2009, Freudenberg recorded a fall of more than 50 percent in orders from the mechanical and plant engineering sector.[28] There was also a pronounced decline in investments in the construction industry. Given the erratic ordering behavior of many customers as a result of market turbulence, Freudenberg developed greater flexibility in its production and logistics activities.[29] At the end of 2009, Bettermann did not mince his words during an interview: "In my opinion, this is no longer a recession; we already have a depression. We are preparing for a long crisis."[30]

In the eurozone as a whole, gross domestic product (GDP) fell by 4.5 percent in 2009 compared with the previous year. In export-oriented Germany, GDP was even down 5 percent, referred to by Deutsche Bundesbank as the most severe fall since the Second World War.[31] Global GDP in 2009 declined by 2.2 percent compared with 2008. Freudenberg's financial performance in 2009 reflected the massive economic downturn and the resulting costs of restructuring measures: For the first time since the 1950s, Freudenberg had to report a loss. The figure was about 250 million euros.[32]

However, the markets recovered from the economic downturn just as fast as the crisis had impacted the real economy. The decisive factors in the turnaround were massive interventions by national governments and central banks and economic developments in the emerging economies, especially China, which was the motor of growth, with GDP still growing at rates between 9 and 10 percent.[33]

At Freudenberg too, the technological modernization and restructuring measures implemented, the retention of the core workforce and the continuation of intensive research and development activities, had an immediate effect. In the first half of 2010, orders picked up again and sales grew by 645 million euros or 32 percent compared with the first half of 2009. At the end of 2010, the Group reported record sales of 5.48 billion and a record consolidated profit of about 322 million euros.³⁴ Following the catastrophic year of 2009, all the affected Business Groups attempted to learn from the way the crisis had developed.³⁵ One lesson learned by the Group from the crisis was that dependence on the automotive industry, in terms of the share in overall sales, needed to be reduced.³⁶ Significantly larger sums were therefore invested in the future-oriented markets of oil and gas, medical technology, renewable energies, civil aviation and the heavy hydraulic sector.³⁷ This was in line with the strategic growth areas defined by Freudenberg: the "Green Areas".

There was a further unpleasant surprise in 2011 as a result of a natural catastrophe. An earthquake followed by a tsunami led to a disaster at Fukushima nuclear power plant in Japan. Following this event, the future of nuclear power in Germany was hotly debated. A complete turnaround in energy policy was rapidly accomplished. On June 6, 2011, the Federal German cabinet decided that eight nuclear power plants should be closed down immediately and that the country should exit nuclear power step-by-step by the end of 2022. This decision was confirmed by majorities in the Bundestag and Bundesrat, the two chambers of the German parliament.³⁸ Of course, exiting nuclear power and the simultaneous expansion of renewable energies could only be achieved through a massive effort: Baseload gas-fired power generation capacities had to be developed in order to be prepared in the event that power was not available from renewable sources, which could happen at any time. De facto, the result of this development, although it was disputed by the German government at the time, was the dependence of Germany on Russian natural gas, which was available at relatively low prices based on a simple technical solution via pipelines. When the war in Ukraine broke out in 2022, it was precisely this energy dependency that became a problem. The end of energy links to Russia became a political priority without it being entirely clear how it would be possible to compensate for the loss of Russian fuels, or what the cost would be.

There was a long historic background to the Russian attack on Ukraine. At the beginning of March 2014, Russian troops had already occupied the Crimean peninsula, part of Ukraine. Despite the sanctions rapidly imposed by the EU and the United States, the Russian parliament, the Duma, ratified a law on March 21, 2014, concerning the annexation of Crimea, including the port of

Sevastopol, as part of the Russian Federation. This annexation was and still is a contravention of international law. In February 2022, the conflict entered a new stage with a further attack by Russian troops, in this case against the whole of Ukraine. The sanctions were drastically tightened, energy supplies from Russia were swiftly run down, and the result was a sharp hike in energy prices. It was at least possible to avoid a drastic shortage of electric power and a recession in Germany in the first instance by finding other delivery routes and temporarily extending the operation of the remaining nuclear power plants.[39]

The financial crisis, the energy transition, the conflict in eastern Europe and the conflicts between the USA and China, which have become increasingly evident since the presidency of Donald Trump and which focus mainly on the significance of China for the global economy, are all developments that have threatened globalization, which had previously been welcomed, and which had drastically changed the conditions and opportunities for action by many companies. However, the withdrawal of German companies from Russia is currently being accompanied by massive calls for a review and, where appropriate, a reduction of commitments in China, as the political influence of the People's Republic of China is considered to be increasingly dangerous and is seen as a destabilizing factor in many regions of the world. At the same time, there are trends towards further fragmentation as a result of the fact that climate change has given rise to very different responses in different regions of the world. In some cases, these will have grave consequences for the quality and cost structure of the relevant locations.

As a result, the decades following the turn of the millennium have been dominated by issues such as protectionism, nationalism, trade disputes, climate change and the global Covid pandemic – this process of change has given rise to additional unease in Europe as a result of the region's fragile institutional structures. Not only did the stabilization of the eurozone call for an expansion of the measures available to the ECB, which were scarcely compatible with the legal situation; cracks also started to appear in the European Union itself. "On June 23, 2016, a majority of British voters voted in a referendum to leave the European Union (EU). With an electoral turnout of 72.2 percent, almost 52 percent voted to leave the EU and 48 percent to remain. This referendum was followed by difficult negotiations concerning the modalities for the British departure from the EU, which was finally completed after several delays on January 31, 2020."[40]

And, in late 2019/early 2020, the world was confronted by the outbreak of a pandemic. The crisis caused by the Covid-19 virus "led to consequences and effects that changed the realities of life for communities in large parts of Europe and the world as a whole. Some of these changes will be reversed over the course of time, others will continue to have an effect and still others will only become apparent in the years to come."[41] Two years later, by the beginning of February 2022, about 397 million people in more than 190 countries had been infected and a total of 5.7 million had died in connection with the virus.[42] As the spread of the Covid pandemic rapidly gathered pace in February and March 2020, there was also a dramatic leap in the use of information services. The first televised address of the British premier Boris Johnson on the Covid pandemic, on March 23, 2020, was one of the most widely viewed live broadcasts in British television history, with some 27 million viewers.[43] German Chancellor Angela Merkel's speech on the same topic a few days before, with the urgent warning: "This is serious. Please take it seriously", had been viewed by about the same number of people on March 18.[44] Even though the response to Covid varied from country to country, the pandemic had dramatic economic consequences. The widely adopted lockdown strategies drastically affected everyday business and forced many countries to invest large sums in stabilizing their economies to a certain extent. The stringent zero-Covid strategy adopted by China adversely impacted the entire global economy, as a very large number of international supply chains were disrupted and China was effectively no longer available as a supplier of many essential products for several months. These disruptions had all ended by the beginning of 2023, but the consequences of the Covid pandemic will probably continue to be felt for many years.

The pandemic, of course, also affected business developments within the Freudenberg Group. However, following a drastic slump in sales in April and May 2020, the situation continually improved for the rest of the year. At the beginning of the pandemic, there were two priorities for the Management Board: "We wanted to guide the company safely through the crisis – and protect the health of our employees at the workplace." The company rapidly provided face masks for its employees throughout the world. Initially, these were distributed via Japan Vilene Company and then via the Chinese locations; Freudenberg ramped up production of masks at its locations in Kaiserslautern and Durham, United States.[45] Health and hygiene rules, the "10 Golden Rules", were also issued to the workforce in eight languages. These rules were intended to limit the spread of infection among employees.[46] At Freudenberg headquarters in Weinheim, the site was divided into four different zones in mid-March 2020. These zones were separated by barriers and each zone had a separate entrance via the factory gates. These measures were taken to avoid the risk that the authorities would close the entire industrial park. In the event of infections, the objective was to ensure that only one section of a building, one building, one building complex or, in the worst possible case, one zone would need to be shut down.[47]

Wherever possible, employees were instructed to work from their homes to minimize the infection risk for the workforce. Thanks to home working by thousands of employees, it was possible for Freudenberg to continue business even under lockdown conditions.[48]

At the beginning of June 2021, Freudenberg also launched its own Covid-19 vaccination program for employees and their families.[49] Despite all the measures adopted, almost 12,000 Freudenberg employees contracted Covid by the end of March 2022 and 19 of them died as a result of the disease.[50]

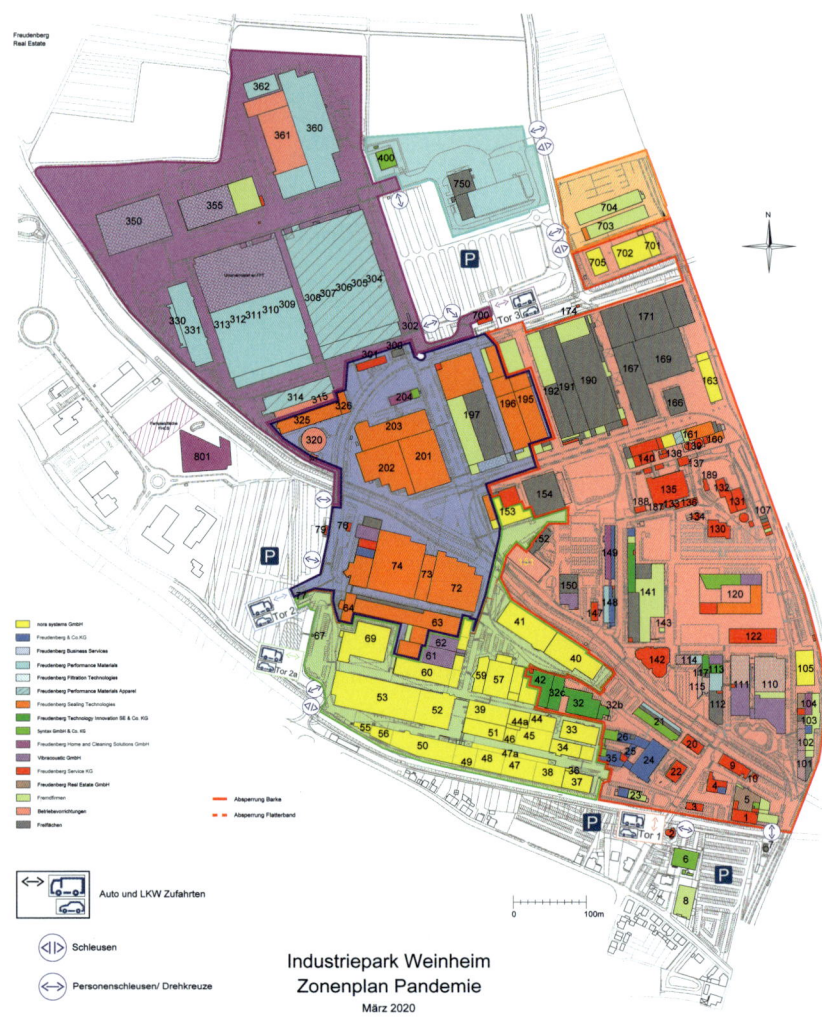

Fig. 112 Zoning plan for the Weinheim site as part of the pandemic measures, March 2020

The report given by the board of management at the end of the first year of the pandemic struck a note of subdued optimism despite the dramatic situation: "2020 was one of the toughest years in Freudenberg's 171-year history and no one can predict the course of the pandemic in 2021. We have navigated the crisis well so far, better than most comparable companies. Our control mechanisms are good, and we mostly have experienced managers who worked together during the 2008/2009 financial crisis. Building on this experience, our Business Groups could quickly take the right decisions." This is also reflected by the figures posted by the Group. On the one hand, sales fell by 6.6 percent to 8.8 billion euros as a result of the recession caused by the pandemic. On the other hand, consolidated profit, at 366 million euros, was extremely positive compared with the losses recorded during the financial crisis.[51]

For Freudenberg, the following year was also dominated to a large extent by the effects of the Covid-19 pandemic. However, the Group benefited from the general economic recovery and from post-Covid catch-up effects. Sales grew by 13.5 percent, exceeding 10 billion for the first time, and consolidated profit also rose by about 60 percent to 587 million euros.[52]

It is clear that a company like Freudenberg, with almost unparalleled post-war internationalization and a global presence that is nevertheless firmly rooted in the southwest of Germany, could not be immune to the effects of these developments and disruptions. For the company itself, there could be no question of an end to globalization, or even steps towards deglobalization, but such developments could not simply be accepted as a given. They called for far-reaching organizational and strategic decisions. The changes in the political and social environment over the past two decades have been key factors in Freudenberg's further development.

The organizational and strategic evolution: Focus 1 and its successor, Focus 2.0

Freudenberg's organization became increasingly complex as internationalization took hold and the product portfolio expanded. Time and again, the Management Board faced the challenge of maintaining the strategic guidance of the Group and its regional, technological and process-related growth in accordance with the prevailing rules and values. The tension generated by the evolving size, structure and organizational differentiation posed a permanent challenge. Globalized companies such as Freudenberg constantly adjust and realign complexity management and strategic guidance. Moreover, the backdrop to this adjustment process was extremely volatile, given increasing turbulence in the global economy in the context of the global financial crisis and in light of growing signs of political tensions. In essence, the Management Board was aware that globalization would not make the perennial task of constantly balancing expansion and risk structuring any easier.

In respect of risk distribution, Freudenberg always aimed to avoid too great a dependence on specific markets, customers, products and suppliers, and to balance out trends. In any company, an evolution of this kind results in a high level of organizational complexity. However, that brings disadvantages as regards business economics: the competitive position in the individual markets comes under pressure. As complexity increases, so do risks and costs. Consequently, Freudenberg must always stay as close to customers and their needs as possible, while at the same time keeping track of efficiency and ensuring a certain degree of conformity in its business processes. The Focus 1 and Focus 2.0 organizational programs were designed to function between these two poles.

According to Peter Bettermann, at that time Speaker of the Management Board, it would take between five and ten years to structure and execute change on the fundamental scale envisaged by the Focus 1 project. Consequently, the Management Board had to constantly realign and recalibrate: No one was of the opinion that the Focus 1 program and its execution would be the definitive solution to all problems.[53] And indeed, that turned out to be the case: For example, Freudenberg Regional Corporate Centers (FRCC) were set up beginning in 2003 to boost the Group's presence in world regions and enable the regional coordination of the Business Groups: The first was the FRCC for North America located in the USA, and was followed by FRCCs in China, India and South America.[54] In addition, 2008 saw the appointment of the first Regional Representatives – senior managers from the Business Groups – whose role was to support headquarters' strategy in the individual regions. The purpose was to keep any divergences from the Group standard in the individual regions as small as possible. At the same time, this generated synergies: Regional expert knowledge, for example in the field of the relevant (fiscal) legal system, thus interacted with know-how from Group headquarters.[55]

The Group's improved regional structure was, however, only one response to the growing corporate steering challenges faced by the Management Board. In parallel, Bettermann introduced a cyclical strategic process in 1997, initially covering planning periods of three years and underpinned by progress reports designed to steer the Group's steady evolution.[56]

Peter Bettermann, who held doctorates in law and in mineralogy, moved from the multinational energy company British Petroleum (BP) to join the

Freudenberg Management Board in 1994. He was the first person from outside the Freudenberg family to serve as Speaker of the Management Board, taking over this role from Reinhart Freudenberg. From the outset, he worked closely together with his predecessor, thus gaining a first-hand insight into the family owners' corporate management practices. Both men developed a shared understanding that was reflected in Bettermann's leadership. His style of management was not only shaped by these close ties to the family owners, but also by his strong links to German industry and to science. This was demonstrated by the numerous mandates he held in many fields, as well as an openness to ideas and suggestions from both outside and inside the Freudenberg organization. He harnessed this ability on many occasions to challenge the company and take it further forward, as illustrated, for example, by the development of the strategic process.[57]

Initially, the cyclical strategic process was very fragmented, with complex sets of data collected under a time-consuming procedure. Conversely, too little attention was devoted to precisely those strategic measures necessary to shape the process. At first, the result bore a greater resemblance to financial budgeting than strategic planning.[58] Bettermann quickly recognized that this approach was inefficient and, from 2002, sought the advice of external experts[59] for critical analysis and fresh perspectives on the strategic orientation.[60]

The strategic process was based on the three most important objectives anchored in the Partners' Agreement and the Business Principles: To safeguard the existence of the company, to preserve the status as a family-owned enterprise and to enable growth and adequate profitability. These objectives affect all aspects of corporate governance. More specifically, they mean maintaining a moderate risk-opportunity level, targeting an equity ratio of 40 percent, and using diversification as a tool to spread risk. The framework is set by the equity ratio, long-term objectives, market leadership, context, ethical principles (such as a ban on manufacturing weapons) and environmental protection, together with social responsibility and occupational health and safety. The goals developed within this framework generally have a timeline of three years.[61]

For Bettermann it was important to ensure there was more to the strategy than mere number crunching, i.e., that it was not purely devoted to quantitative planning. A solid financial foundation was a given, but only of secondary importance for the strategy identification process.[62] He therefore introduced a paradigm shift in the strategic process in 2004, whereby the process was to take its orientation from scientifically substantiated megatrends and the recommended actions for portfolio development derived from these trends. The goal was to achieve "greater creativity and out-of-the-box thinking, dialogue with each other and with the Management Board, a greater focus on execution, and less paperwork."[63]

One outcome of this new approach was to establish a supply chain management system throughout the Group to address logistics processes along global supply chains and, with effect from 2004, the definition of growth areas – known as Green Areas – not to be confused with environmental aspects despite the choice of color. These Green Areas were areas derived from the megatrend analyses and fast-tracked; they were all technologically highly challenging and offered greater scope for investments in terms of allocating financial resources. Initially, there were four Green Areas: expanding the mechanical seal business in North America, expanding the filter business, establishing a fourth pillar in the chemical business, and expanding the industrial seals business in North America with the focus on medical technology, the oil and gas industry, and aviation.[64]

These four Green Areas were realigned in 2011 when the strategic process was consolidated.[65] This consolidation was also derived from megatrends: Urbanization triggered growing demand for consumer goods and durables, opening up a broad range of specialty applications in chemical surface treatment processes used in the manufacture of many of these products. Moreover, the population was getting older and older, resulting in increased demand for medical services. This was attributable to a higher incidence of age-related chronic diseases and the fact that many older people wanted a higher quality of life. Growth forecasts for the medical technology market were correspondingly high. In addition, demand for energy was increasing: Conditions for producing fossil fuels became more difficult as demand increased, because easily accessible reserves were already largely depleted. The greater demands placed on the machinery and material used for the production of these reserves presented an opportunity for Freudenberg's innovative and high-quality sealing technology, particularly in the oil and gas industry. The desire for clean air became stronger as cities grew and motorization increased, along with an ever-greater awareness of health issues: Filters that improve air quality became increasingly relevant. And finally, growing urbanization and mobility worldwide called for traffic infrastructure expansion in and around conurbations. As a result, a boost in demand for vibration control technology in rail vehicles and construction and agricultural machinery was expected.[66] This strategic ambition led to the founding of three new Business Groups in 2011: Freudenberg Oil and Gas Technologies, Helix Medical and Freudenberg Schwab Vibration Control – all three were spin-offs from either Freudenberg Seals and Vibration Control Technology or FNGP in North America.[67] Strategic acquisitions strengthened the two Business Groups of Freudenberg Chemical Specialities (founded 2004) and Freudenberg Filtration Technologies (founded 2009) in order to drive forward the two growth fields of filtration and surface treatment.[68]

In the fourth strategic period post-2008, attention focused more closely on the strategy in Asia. Following a comparison of the planning systems in Japan and Germany, the exchange with Japanese partner NOK was intensified. For the sealing business – particularly with reference to the joint venture activities and the global customers served by the joint venture – there was a growing need to harmonize strategy and presence.[69]

Lastly, a communication process across the Business Groups was called for: Aside from the Regional Corporate Centers and the strategic process, this also included "Dialog", the senior management conference introduced in 1997, and the creation of new corporate committees, such as the Global Executive Team (GET) in 2008.[70] Initially, GET only consisted of the Management Board and the Regional Representatives and was tasked with channeling information from the world regions more effectively into corporate decisions. With the advent of Focus 2.0, the successor program to Focus 1, GET was expanded in 2013 to include Business Group Board Members and Corporate Functions Heads in addition to the Management Board and Regional Representatives. A new advisory committee, the Executive Council (ExCo), was set up at the same time. The ExCo comprises the Management Board and the CEOs of the four – later five – largest Business Groups and aims to take stronger account of the perspectives of the Business Groups in the Management Board's strategic decisions, thereby supporting the Management Board's decision-making process.[71]

In the context of this communication process, the multi-day Dialog events held at regular intervals since 1997 and attended by Freudenberg senior management from all over the world are of particular interest. "The objective of these events is to discuss key topics of relevance throughout the Group and develop specific actions."[72] In 2015, *Freudenberg Magazine* described the significance, and thus also the objective, of the Dialog events as follows: "The company has been organizing this senior management conference at regular intervals since 1997 to provide a discussion platform for key Group-wide issues and to jointly lay the foundations for the future. These events have a strategic significance and a strong internal dynamic that has the potential to drive the Group powerfully forward."[73] A total of eight Dialog events were held between 1997 and 2021. The table below presents an overview of the key issues and the respective Dialog events:

Innovation	HR management	Process optimization & efficiency	Values, identity & brand	Customer & market orientation
1997: Innovation culture	1999: Leadership development	1999: Process optimization	1997: Culture of cooperation (impulse for Guiding Principles)	2002: Customer orientation
2018: Innovating together		2006: Supply chain management	2002: Environmental protection, occupational health & safety	2006: Global market leadership
		2015: Entrepreneurship and efficiency	2011: Corporate values	2011: Profitable growth
		2018: Digitalization	2015: New positioning global Freudenberg brand	2021: Customer and market-oriented corporate culture
		2021: Digitalization 1.5		

Fig. 113 Key issues and the respective Dialog events, 1997–2021

In his speech at the first international senior management meeting held in Weinheim in July 1997, Reinhart Freudenberg underlined why he believed the event was so important: "We want […] all employees, and in particular our senior managers, to identify not only with their respective business units, but also with the Group as a whole." Citing a further reason for the event, Reinhart Freudenberg called for a new "culture of innovation and cooperation […], something that is vitally important not only for our future success in the markets, but also for internal order in the Group and its business units, and for satisfaction among our employees with the tasks they perform." He emphasized that "we can only achieve a vibrant innovation culture if we have the culture of cooperation that goes with it; these two cultures are inseparable, like the two sides of a coin."[74] However, in light of the autonomy with which the Business Groups operated and their orientation to customer satisfaction, growth and entrepreneurship, the latter aspect lost some of its focus in the following years.

In his closing speech at this particular Dialog event, Peter Bettermann explained the important role played by the quality of leadership, and thus of senior management, in corporate success. He made it clear that the senior managers present at Dialog should build on their existing individual strengths in employee leadership and underscored that the managers should also delegate more responsibility to employees, placing greater trust and confidence in their abilities. This would improve cooperation and foster innovation.[75] Addressing senior managers at Dialog 1999, Management Board member Hans-Jochen Hüchting (1942–2024) explained that the new leadership development program "Freudenberg Unfolds Entrepreneurial Leadership" (FUEL) would set the framework for achieving this objective. "In other words, FUEL is designed to assist in executing the ambitious leadership expectation set out in its own chapter of the Guiding Principles, and help ensure that leadership positions at Freudenberg are largely filled from the Group's own ranks. Four binding elements form the cornerstones of this framework":[76] An annual performance assessment of every employee, the identification of potential leadership talents, individual plans for the development of these talents, and substitute and successor planning for all key posts.[77] Through the implementation of these management development measures, the Management Board was able to gradually withdraw from operational business. As a result, membership of the Management Board was trimmed from eight to four executives between 1996 and 2006, and the corporate body increasingly focused on the Group's strategic development.[78]

As part of Focus 2.0, the FUEL leadership development program was developed further on the initiative of Mohsen Sohi to become a systematic talent management process, accompanied by the launch of IT-supported HR management tools and the introduction of an intranet learning platform.[79] The objective of the new talent management process was to ensure "the professional development of all Group employees, in particular senior management, through uniform programs and standards, and to ensure that they have the right skills."[80] To this end, Group-wide leadership development programs were set up.[81]

Subsequent Dialog events focused on issues such as value for customers, and environmental protection and occupational health and safety. The "We all take care" environmental protection and occupational health and safety initiative was launched at the 2002 Dialog conference in Weinheim.[82] The initiative encourages the entire workforce to personally engage with an improvement process in the fields of environmental protection, occupational safety and health protection: All senior managers and all employees. That is why the word "all" in the "We all take care" motto is underlined. The prime objective of the initiative was to reduce the number of accidents at Freudenberg sites worldwide – based on objective performance indicators.[83]

Later events addressed topics such as supply chain optimization, or global market leadership in the markets served by Freudenberg. Over 300 senior managers from all over the world met up in Chicago July 9–12, 2006. In an interview with *Freudenberg Magazine*, Bettermann explained the significance of this event for the company: "So far, it has been almost taken for granted that Dialog would center on Weinheim, where our Group is headquartered. On the other hand, however, we are today a highly international company, our employees, our business, our growth are all international. So we felt that, going forward, it was right and proper for Dialog to be held not only in Weinheim, but to alternate the venue between our headquarters and one of our international locations."[84] Corporate values and profitable growth were key topics at one of the events held in later years.[85]

All of these Dialog topics delivered on aspects of the new Focus 1 structure. Focus 1 shaped the Group as a transnational company whose organization was characterized by a combination of central strategic steering and divisions or Business Groups with a great deal of local autonomy and the ability to respond swiftly and flexibly to the specific demands of their markets. The result was greater entrepreneurship within the Group; this was accompanied by significant success as regards value for customers and growth. Profitability also improved: The return on sales rose from 5.5 percent in 1995 to 8 percent in 2011.[86]

The divisions and Business Groups were now operating autonomously in the market as flexible "speedboats". However, this meant that Business Group activities were "not always fully aligned with the interests of the Group as a whole".[87] In 2011, Bettermann likened the organizational changes already executed – but in his view by no means completed – to a pendulum: "When you set change in motion it gathers momentum pretty quickly. But if you don't intervene in time to contain this momentum, the pendulum could swing too far."[88] That was the case for Freudenberg.

Consequently, the main objective for Bettermann and the Management Board for the period 2011 to 2014 was to find and stabilize a better balance between centralization and decentralization.[89] A benchmark study, known internally as the "Compass" project, was commissioned in 2012 with this objective in mind. The study was confirmation for the Management Board that administration and transaction costs in the Freudenberg Group were too high, while investment in innovation, strategic HR and information technology was insufficient to be able to "rank among the best".[90]

2012 also saw the founding of Freudenberg SE, a public limited liability company under European law, as the parent company for managing business operations, with a view to making the Group's corporate law structures simpler and more transparent and to improve the Group's position in terms of international tax law. Freudenberg SE also allowed the Group to establish a uniform legal framework for all of Freudenberg's European companies, thereby dissolving numerous national companies throughout Europe that had only been set up for formal or tax reasons. Almost all Freudenberg subsidiaries – above all, the Business Groups – were brought together under the roof of the new Freudenberg SE. As a result, the Group now had two parent companies: Freudenberg & Co. KG, the strategic holding company, and Freudenberg SE, the operations holding company. There is one noteworthy feature: The composition of the corporate bodies of both holding companies is identical; membership of the Management Board and the Board of Partners of Freudenberg & Co and the Board of Management and the Supervisory Board of Freudenberg SE is identical.[91]

The high administrative costs were attributable to the duplication of various support units such as HR, purchasing, accounting and information technology in the organizational structure of the holding company and each Business Group or company. This led to significant fragmentation that complicated cross-Group processes. As Bettermann had already noted at an early stage, the pendulum of entrepreneurial independence had in some respects swung too far. For the Business Groups, the advantages of belonging to the Group as a whole had at times taken a back seat; in other words, their activities were not always fully aligned to the interests of the Freudenberg Group.[92]

Another problem of the Focus 1 structure was that the various Management Board members continued to hold personal responsibility for different Business Groups. As a result, they were still too closely involved in operative business – for example, through participation at Board meetings of their Business Groups.[93] The result: "The complexity thus generated restricts entrepreneurial action."[94]

Progression to Focus 2.0

Mohsen Sohi, who succeeded Bettermann as Management Board Speaker in 2012, therefore introduced a further organizational reform under the name of Focus 2.0; implementation got underway in 2013. Sohi, an American citizen who was born in Iran and holds a PhD in mechanical engineering and an MBA in business administration, joined Freudenberg in 2003 as CEO of Freudenberg-NOK General Partnership in the United States. He was appointed as a member of the Management Board in Weinheim in 2010. In 2012, he became the first Speaker of the Management Board to come from a different region of the world and to have acquired his managerial experience in American corporations.[95]

The notion of further organizational reform – a topic the Management Board had already considered in previous years – initially took the form of a discussion about the Group's organizational culture started by Sohi back in summer 2012. The Management Board began by getting to grips with how to shape cooperation between the Board and the downstream organizational levels – such as the Business Groups and the Corporate Functions. These deliberations culminated in the launch of the Focus 2.0 project in May 2013, with Boston Consulting Group commissioned to provide support with project execution.[96]

Sohi described the objective of Focus 2.0 as follows: "We must coordinate entrepreneurship, value for customers and growth so as to ensure that the Group is always more than the sum of its parts."[97] This latest realignment was to enable Freudenberg to leverage its full potential as a Group – and to do so with the greatest possible efficiency. Despite all the plans and adjustments to previous processes and structures, it was clear from an early stage that the overall outcome of the processes introduced under Focus 2.0 was to achieve "an evolution not a revolution."[98]

The "Lighthouse" project was one element of Focus 2.0. Based on the Compass benchmark study, Lighthouse was designed to optimize all administrative processes in the Group.[99]

Group structures required further development in order to implement process optimization under the Lighthouse project. A new governance concept, the "Strategic Guide" model, was designed. This concept marked a culture change at executive

Fig. 114 Mohsen Sohi describes the structure of Focus 2.0, 2013

management level: For the first time, the individual Management Board members no longer held operational responsibility for the Business Groups. Under the Strategic Guide model, the Board members assumed functional responsibility as CEO (Chief Executive Officer), CFO (Chief Financial Officer) or CTO (Chief Technology Officer) and concentrated on coordinating and developing the Group's strategic orientation. Under this new corporate governance structure, the Business Groups reported direct to the entire Management Board from January 2014. The existing Business Group Boards were dissolved and replaced by Business Review Meetings.[100]

A further objective was to strengthen "the Business Groups' entrepreneurship in the market and with customers" and to increase the Group's innovation strength (based on the motto: "Less administration – more innovation").[101] Many of the measures introduced by the Management Board under Focus 2.0 relieved the Business Groups of administrative tasks in particular, with these tasks returning to central steering. It was clear to everyone that the relationship between the parent company Freudenberg & Co. and the Business Groups would not only require redefinition, but also be made transparent.[102] A "Role Charter" realigning the interaction between the Corporate Functions and the Business Groups was drawn up in 2014. This policy document defined the role of the Corporate Functions as the strategic guide for the Business Groups and clearly distinguished the responsibilities of the holding companies from those of the Business Groups.[103]

The new division of tasks helped the Group to master the major thematic challenges facing Freudenberg in the early years of the new millennium: Strengthening Business Group customer and market orientation while executing process optimization and efficiency programs across the Group, accompanied by innovation and HR management, together with a stronger sense of identity, values and brand awareness.[104] One outcome was a more profitable company: The return on sales increased from 7.7 percent in 2013 to 9.1 percent in the following year[105] – and continued its upward trend in the following years.[106]

The Group's new self-perception derived from Focus 2.0 – the vision of acting as one company – is depicted by the "House of Excellence". Sohi described the significance of the new House of Excellence for the company as follows: "For Freudenberg to stay successful, we believe the eight elements that form the framework for our management and operating system (the House of Excellence) must interact with one another [...]: The foundation of our company is the first element: 'Family Ownership': The stability brought by family ownership guarantees our long-term orientation. The second element is the 'Guiding and Business Principles'. They lay the groundwork and give orientation for corporate

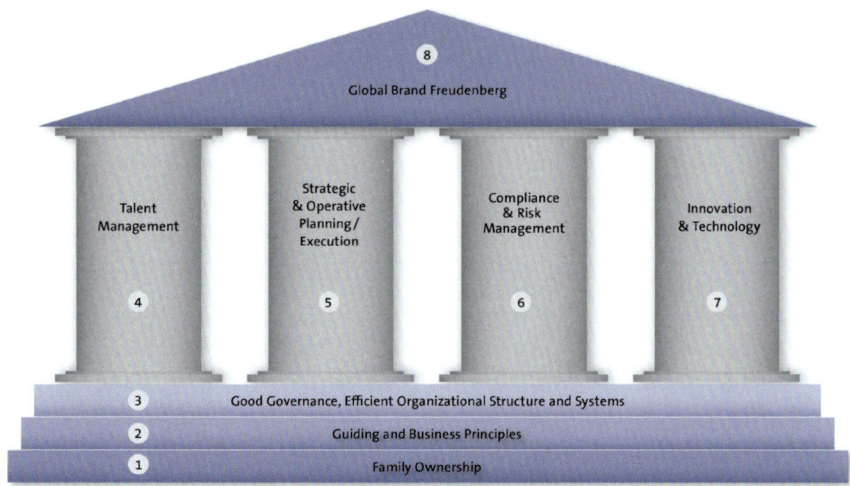

Fig. 115 The House of Excellence presents the key elements of success for Freudenberg.

leadership, our dealings with one another and our relationships with customers and partners. The third element of this foundation is 'Good Governance, Efficient Organizational Structure and Systems'. This is the crucial component for implementing our motto 'More innovation, less administration'. The fourth element in Freudenberg's 'House of Excellence' is 'Talent Management'. In a nutshell, we must become even more diverse and integrative. The fifth element is 'Strategic & Operative Planning/Execution'. All really big companies have one thing in common: They plan well – and they systematically execute their strategic and operative plans. The sixth element is 'Compliance & Risk Management'. We must comply with all laws, regulations and internal guidelines. The seventh element – and this is the lifeblood of our business – is 'Innovation & Technology'. And finally, the eighth element of the Freudenberg Management und Operating System – the roof of our house – is the 'Freudenberg Global Brand'. It epitomizes and communicates what the company stands for."[107]

Coinciding with the launch of Focus 2.0, the decision was taken to rebrand the Freudenberg corporate brand with a view to strengthening it and enhancing the visibility and attractiveness of the Group.[108]

A project team, together with the Business Group management boards and various corporate committees, spent some two years working on a complex process to position the newly created global brand.¹⁰⁹ The starting point for designing the content of the positioning was based on the question of the contribution Freudenberg as a values-oriented company could make to society "to improve present living standards and give future generations the possibility to satisfy their needs."¹¹⁰ This work culminated in the following positioning: "Freudenberg is a values-based technology group that best serves its customers and society."

Sohi was also convinced by the outcome of the search for the right positioning: "That is why our contribution as a technology group must be to develop innovations for sustainable solutions for our customers."¹¹¹ This firmly anchored the purpose of the company in the global brand of: "Freudenberg. Innovating Together". A survey was carried out among over 1,000 market managers, leaders and customers to establish whether this purpose tallied with stakeholder perceptions. Around 95 percent of the respondents confirmed that "the new positioning reflected their future expectations of Freudenberg."¹¹²

From the outset, the corporate slogan "Innovating Together" has always been not only an external promise but also internal motivation for employees across all Business Groups to constantly develop new ideas and continuously improve together.¹¹³

The new global brand and its positioning, together with the new corporate logo, were presented at the Dialog event in Detroit. The new logo adds the brand slogan "Innovating Together" to the name of Freudenberg.¹¹⁴ But that was not all: As Cornelia Buchta-Noack and Klaus Peter Meier, the brand project's dual leads, pointed out: "Now, it is up to all of us to bring the brand to life and to deliver on the promise behind the corporate slogan 'INNOVATING TOGETHER' [...]. That involves kicking off a complex change process to win all 40,000 employees as brand ambassadors."¹¹⁵

The new brand architecture was also part of this change. Surveys conducted among Freudenberg customers showed that the majority of customers buying from Freudenberg rarely made a distinction between different Business Groups or product brands. Consequently, the new global brand gave the Business Groups the opportunity to reduce the number of individual brands, thereby leveraging synergies. At the same time, strong brands such as Vileda or Klüber could designate themselves "a brand of Freudenberg". As affiliated brands, they underscored their connection to the Group more clearly, thus strengthening the new global brand.¹¹⁶

EXCURSUS: THE HISTORY OF THE FREUDENBERG LOGO[117]

The tanning era
The first logo of the newly-founded company named Carl Freudenberg, introduced in 1874, was a tanner's coat of arms. This coat of arms dates from the Middle Ages and shows the tools of a tanner: The shaving iron used to ensure uniform thickness at the center, with a crossed flesh scraper for removing flesh and fat from the underside of the hide (right) and a hair scraper for removing hair from the hide (left). The tools are flanked by two lions symbolizing the company's claim to leadership.

Diversification
Once diversification began in 1929, bringing with it an expanded product range, the medieval coat of arms became outdated. In the search for a more modern logo, Freudenberg decided to combine the initials of the company's founder Carl Freudenberg with the first letter of Weinheim where the company was headquartered. The CFW logo was introduced in 1933 and redesigned in 1950. Twenty years later, the color was adapted and the words "Carl Freudenberg" were added. This marked the debut of two of the elements typical of the present-day Freudenberg logo: The name lettering and the blue color.

Internationalization
As Freudenberg became increasingly international the "W" for Weinheim in the logo no longer adequately reflected the nature of the Group. The Freudenberg name was incorporated in an integrated logo in 1983. The wave at the bottom edge of the logo reflects the sine curve shown on the instruments for measuring the quality of Freudenberg's technical products. The logo was slightly adapted in 1990.

Planning the future: The Odyssey project

In the meantime, Freudenberg employees set out to search for future themes that would determine the Group's development in the coming decades under two projects named Odyssey 1.0 and 2.0. The task they were given by Sohi ran as follows: "Assuming the world has to manage with 80 percent fewer fossil fuels in 2050 – what does that mean for Freudenberg's portfolio and what investments, acquisitions or other measures would safeguard the Group's survival?"[118]

In a first step, a total of 70 growth fields for Freudenberg were identified with the support of foresight researchers.[119] The Odyssey 1.0 team then prioritized the 20 most important fields and drew up three business potentials for each one.

New positioning of the Freudenberg Group and rebranding with a newly designed logo

The capitals represent the strength of Freudenberg as a global player, the sine curve symbolizes Freudenberg's technical expertise. The curve acquires wings through the new positioning. These wings stand for openness and increased dynamism. At the same time, the new visual element of the logo can also be seen as a bridge representing good cooperation as well as reliability and stability.

Fig. 116-122 Historical development of the Freudenberg logo

These 60 topics were then weighted once again – according to their market relevance and the extent to which Freudenberg already had the relevant expertise. The question the team asked was: "Where must the company invest today – either in building up know-how internally or through targeted acquisitions – in order to offer the right solutions in 2050?"[120] Based on the project findings, a team led by Sohi then defined six top topics to be given priority consideration in the successor project named Odyssey 2.0: In addition to the health and energy sectors, they also included the cross-sector topics of energy storage, sensor technology and pumps. Six specific projects were prioritized: Surface treatment, advanced wound care, functional films, specialty pumps, batteries and storage, and sensors.[121]

Odyssey 2.0 faced a complex task. What was required was understanding the technologies, the underlying business models and the corresponding markets. What was also needed was to gain a feeling for the profitability of the solution and for potential regional limitations. These analyses culminated in a decision whether or not to continue with a topic. The fields of application were subsequently defined and the final step involved reassessing the attractiveness of the topic for the Freudenberg Group. The issue was whether the necessary know-how was available internally or could be developed, or whether it should be acquired externally – in line with Freudenberg's existing buy-and-build strategy that was transitioned into a bolt-on acquisition strategy.[122]

The end of the 2020 financial year marked the end of the seventh strategic period from 2018 to 2020. In keeping with the strategic megatrend orientation, there were three key topics for the Freudenberg Group during this period: Mobility, digitalization and sustainability. The Supervisory Board approved the new strategic planning in January 2021. The analysis focused on more than 40 strategic business units, each with its own highly detailed strategy tailored to the respective customer, market and technological environment. The outcome: At Group level, sustainability, electro mobility and digitalization – alongside customer orientation – remained key issues for the subsequent strategic period to 2023. Being the central innovation unit, the Freudenberg Technology Innovation (FTI) Corporate Function was tasked with advancing medium- and long-term innovation activities under some ten different technology platforms. FTI prioritizes future growth fields in close cooperation with the Business Groups under Janus, the Odyssey follow-up program.[123]

Freudenberg's development shows that the Group's strategic leadership and organizational orientation require constant realignment as business becomes increasingly complex. Handling this challenge is one of the strengths of Freudenberg's leadership, but it is also undoubtedly one of the central tasks for the future, because corporate transformation in the context of global development and competitive processes will continue to necessitate organizational and strategic solutions on which the company's success depends.

The digitalization of Freudenberg

Since 2015, there has been a paradigm shift in the utilization of information technology in industry. Until 2015, the main focus had been on the optimization of IT infrastructure.[124] Since then, the emphasis, under the heading of "digitalization," has shifted to strategic questions not only concerning work organization, but also the business model.

Ultimately, the objective is to grasp the opportunities offered by digitalization.[125] This also affects the working environment of employees, firstly with regard to the tools used and secondly with regard to the possibilities of remote working from customers' facilities or employees' own homes. The growing importance of this topic for Freudenberg, too, has been evident from the number of times the term "digitalization" has been mentioned in Partners' Reports and Annual Reports since 2015. Unsurprisingly, the frequency has significantly increased.

In particular, the development of IT at Freudenberg offers a glimpse of markets that are changing at an ever-faster pace. In view of these developments, the company and its employees must embrace change and demonstrate flexibility; digitalization not only enables, but also demands greater flexibility.

From the purely technical perspective, there has also been another change. Up to 2015, Moore's law was still widely accepted – roughly speaking, this refers to the observation that the performance of computer chips is doubled every 18 to 24 months on average. This "law" has since been called into question, although the extent has been a source of controversy among specialists.[126] Furthermore, even if the performance of chips does not increase, the storage of data is becoming increasingly simple, cheap and decentralized (in the "cloud") and data can therefore be accessed from anywhere in the world. Even if the computing power of individual chips grows at a less dynamic pace, the performance of computer systems as a whole will nevertheless continue to improve. Such disruptive changes are – and always have been – a characteristic feature of information technology and they are occurring at a faster and faster pace. A look at the time spans for changes in the past, which were considered to be breathtaking at the time, confirms this. Transformation could initially be described over the course of decades, but innovations have seemed to occur at shorter and shorter intervals since the millennium – with a corresponding impact on the digitalization strategies of all companies.

Sweeping changes also occurred in connection with the company's new data processing structures created under the Focus 1 project. The objective was to establish an independent IT service company that would also sell its services to third parties independently in the marketplace. There was a sense of optimism when the company was founded on July 1, 1995. The general conviction was that the company would "with high probability" assert its position in the marketplace in the long term. The service company, founded as Freudenberg Informatik KG – and later renamed Freudenberg IT (unfortunately, the acronym FIT thought up by the company itself was rather unpopular within Freudenberg) – was not to have any advantage in dealings with Freudenberg companies apart from its know-how on the procedures and data processing systems of the departments which had previously been its clients. For example, Freudenberg IT was not to be given priority for contract award by Freudenberg units.[127]

A crucial factor for the success of Freudenberg IT was to be the development of the long-term partnership with SAP. The main challenge was to generate any external sales at all. Because the 90 employees were working to the limit in the years that followed as a result of the Focus project and the roll-out of SAP within the Group, it was very difficult to offer competitive services and software via the sales network that had been established in the meantime. At any rate, the company reported sales of 61 million DM for the 1998 financial year. Personnel service and consultancy business grew as a result of the increased use of SAP R/2 and R/3 systems and through inquiries from customers who wanted to safeguard their data in view of the changeover to the euro and the "year 2000 problem."[128] The workforce was boosted to 210 employees and the company's first in-house software products, for example for inventory management and accounting tasks, were also sold successfully to external customers.[129]

To strengthen the position of FIT as a service provider for the mid-market, Freudenberg acquired Adicom AG, a service provider and software supplier focusing on logistics and production processes, in 2001. Together with Adicom, FIT generated sales totaling about 50 million euros in 2001.[130] To make technical procedures more efficient, Adicom developed products tailored to production facilities together with customers and attempted to exploit this niche as a competitive advantage over key market players. In 2004, FIT was even able to establish a subsidiary on the highly competitive American market.[131]

However, the pressure on prices in the IT sector became increasingly severe from 2003 onward, and a fall in demand for personnel and hosting services had a negative impact on the sales and operating profit of FIT. Within the Freudenberg Group, FIT received no orders for IT project support. Demand for hosting center capacity also fell and FIT was forced to enter new customer segments. For example, the company developed management software for the sports and events sector, which was used by customers such as the SAP Arena in Mannheim and Bayern Munich.[132] At the same time, internal structures were adapted and FIT's local hosting centers were networked in an international hosting structure. The company's management continued to opt for targeted marketing and expansive internationalization, with the development of new locations in eastern Europe (Budapest) and China (Suzhou).[133] This two-pronged strategy adopted by the FIT management was initially successful and the company reached greater awareness levels, with a significant boost in sales in the 2007 financial year, when FIT management was proud to report that "Freudenberg IT now earns 2/3 of its sales outside the Freudenberg Group".[134]

However, this phase of growth, during which FIT was even described as the "most successful German IT spin-off", came to an abrupt end in 2008 in the wake of the financial crisis.[135] As a result of drastically falling sales and the uncertain economic situation, customers were reluctant to embark on new IT projects. FIT recorded a fall in orders received at all locations. While the American market recovered relatively fast, the mood in Asia and Europe remained subdued for longer. It was only the demand for outsourcing services that brought a turnaround and new customers for FIT in 2009.[136] The company expanded its international presence with four new locations (in China, Singapore, Ukraine and the United States) and a further hosting center was installed at Weinheim. A groundbreaking event was SAP certification of FIT in the first half of 2010; FIT was one of the first companies certified to act as a global supplier of SAP cloud services. This provided key impetus, especially for the expansion of business in North America.[137]

In 2009 and 2010, FIT recorded sales growth in the double-digit percentage range. However, the above-average expansion of the company through large, complex IT outsourcing projects, where cost calculation was difficult, led to significant losses. A restructuring of FIT was essential in order to return to a positive operating result.[138] A new positioning was developed for FIT on the basis of a radical analysis considering the aspects of profitability, implementation costs and strategic relevance. The intention was that FIT should offer its SAP expertise in consulting, integration and hosting as an enabling partner of manufacturing industry and shape manufacturing processes more efficiently together with customers. This reshaping marked the cautious entry into what was later to be called "Industry 4.0". In addition, the company discontinued services with lower earnings potential; a newly installed risk management system was used to review the viability of possible new customer contracts. Thanks to these measures, FIT succeeded in putting an end to its losses in 2012 and recording a slight operating profit.[139] The close partnership with SAP also paid dividends as this market grew disproportionately compared with the overall IT market. A new office in Mexico was opened in 2013 to provide support for customers in South America.[140]

The three-year transformation program brought FIT back on track for success, mainly due to its focus on SAP hosting business.[141] From 2015 onward, FIT was consistently more profitable than the industry benchmark.[142] A lean holding company ensured that the regional companies FIT Americas, FIT Asia and

FIT Europe, which were independent in their business operations, focused on shared targets. With its market-ready product "FIT Shop Floor Suite", FIT also developed technical know-how relevant for the megatrend of Industry 4.0.[143] SAP continued to be the foundation of the company's consulting concept, but FIT also worked on its first projects related to the Internet of Things (IOT). Sales grew from slightly less than 153 million in 2015 to 173 million euros in 2017. A new location in Slovakia was developed for customers in eastern Europe.

Despite the good development in FIT business, gross margins were falling and the company's focus on business outside the Freudenberg Group meant that FIT was moving ever farther away from the requirements of Freudenberg's manufacturing companies with respect to digitalization topics. By 2018, FIT was a leading SAP cloud services and SAP consulting provider, earning 85 percent of sales from external customers. However, applications management and digitalization services such as the FIT Shop Floor Suite only accounted for about 10 percent of sales. The company earned almost two-thirds of its sales with cloud or hosting services. An in-depth strategic analysis of FIT showed that the company was becoming less and less relevant to Freudenberg's core business; at the same time, it would be necessary to make major investments in the future, especially for the expansion of FIT cloud services. The amounts required were considerable: Several million euros would have been needed. In addition, investments would have risen continuously in the future as a new hardware stack would have been required for each new customer. In each case, investments in the (low) double-digit million range would have been needed for a major new customer. The Management Board had to consider these investments in the context of other investments required within the Freudenberg Group, as the hosting services of FIT were not part of the Group's core business. With its own core hosting business, FIT increasingly faced competition from the major players in the sector: Cloud service providers such as Microsoft, leading German companies such as T-Systems or Arvato and Indian companies such as Tata or Wipro. Furthermore, hosting in Germany offered no added value for FIT's German customers, which were mainly mid-market companies. The trend towards cloud storage with major providers had an increasing impact on FIT. In view of this situation, the Management Board decided to dispose of FIT in summer 2018.[144]

Freudenberg searched for a purchaser which could successfully expand the business of Freudenberg IT and contribute additional know-how to the company. In 2019, the Canadian company Novocap, with its IT subsidiary Syntax, was finally selected. Freudenberg IT was integrated into Syntax. The newly expanded company Syntax then had an opportunity to develop into a globally active full-service provider offering leading technology for the most important

ERP system producers, SAP and Oracle.¹⁴⁵ At first glance, it may seem strange that Freudenberg should have disposed of this IT company in an environment in which digitalization was a strategic focus of the Group. However, at that time, the limited services offered by Freudenberg IT no longer played a significant role for Freudenberg Group companies. There were two main reasons: Firstly, the Freudenberg companies had developed their own digitalization know-how. Secondly, the area of Data Sciences had been developed within the Technology & Innovation Corporate Function since 2018. This area will be dealt with in more detail later.

As regards the digitalization activities of Freudenberg, it is quite clear that these are driven either by striving for customer benefits and growth or by efficiency and quality improvements in internal processes.¹⁴⁶

At the Dialog 2018 senior management conference, delegates considered the type of digitalization best suited to Freudenberg. While public discussions at that time were already focusing on topics such as artificial intelligence (AI) or blockchain (decentralized networks), the main emphasis in everyday operations was initially to lay the foundations for such innovations within the companies.¹⁴⁷ For Freudenberg, it was also always clear that personal dialogue would remain indispensable despite digitalization. Customer requirements needed to be understood faster and cycle times reduced; product development had to continue and at the same time new products needed to be brought to the market faster.¹⁴⁸

Digitalization in training, research and development

It was against this backdrop that the new Training Center in Weinheim opened in 2018.¹⁴⁹ The company invested 8.5 million euros in the new building and the equipment installed. With a floorspace of 2,600 square meters, the new facility was to train apprentices for the digital working environment of the future. In future, skilled workers will face more complex tasks in connection with Industry 4.0: They will have to tackle the coordination of smart production lines and industrial robots and the control of processes with highly complex machines, as well as solving IT problems in this production environment.¹⁵⁰ For this interdisciplinary training, which is becoming increasingly multifaceted, a Learning Factory 4.0 – a completely networked miniature Industry 4.0 factory – is crucially important. Using the Learning Factory, the apprentices can try out advanced production processes in practice, understand the various interactions, and learn to control these processes. The Learning Factory consists of

Fig. 123 Since 2018, apprentices at Freudenberg in Weinheim have been able to learn about the principles of Industry 4.0 using a miniature factory.

several modules, ranging from production (drilling station and robot assembly) through quality control to interim and high-shelf storage.[151] "Using sensors that collect data from the entire production process, processing this data and initiating appropriate production steps, products can be made up and processed in different ways."[152] This approach allows trainees to experience the digitalization of production.[153] In this manner, the Learning Factory 4.0 combines the real world of production with the virtual world of information and communication technology by showing how classical industrial processes can be supplemented and optimized by processes from the digital world.[154]

A competition analysis commissioned by Freudenberg in 2019 from the Handelsblatt Research Institute found that the company was in the global mid-field with respect to the digital evolution of operations and the digital transformation of the company and its business. According to the report, the broad-based and often technology-based product portfolio of Freudenberg made the company an ideal candidate for a comprehensive digitalization process. This was already evident in the many approaches that had been adopted in the various Business Groups to digitalization in production and business development, which had already reached an advanced stage.[155]

At the time of the study, digital transformation was already one of the top management priorities and part of Group strategy. In 2018, Martin Wentzler,

Chairman of the Board of Partners, was asked what the company could learn from the history of Freudenberg, with respect to digitalization and innovation. Part of his answer was:

> "Nevertheless, we need to be reasonable and not get caught up in the zeitgeist. The proper handling of digitalization includes realizing and mastering the risks associated with it. As in the past, innovation will be vital to our survival. We must wholeheartedly commit to this and try to establish first-class processes to act decisively and swiftly. To do so, the open exchange of information among Business Groups will become even more important and necessary."[156]

At that time, the digital transformation coordinated by top management and affecting all parts of the Group, employees, customers and partners, was already well underway. It was and still is especially important to share ideas, to learn together, to share best practices and to forge ahead with the innovation process.[157]

The FTI Corporate Function plays a key role in this context. Its task is to systematically strengthen the innovative power of the Freudenberg Group. Together with the Business Groups, FTI defines the long-term technology portfolio of the Group and acts as a competence center for leading-edge technologies. FTI is very well-networked, both within the Group and in the world of science. The broad-based material and process expertise available not only covers the physical world, but also the utilization of the digital data heritage. Within Freudenberg Technology Innovation, the new area of Data Sciences was developed from 2018 onward, with about 40 employees. Christopher Klatt, the first head of this unit, describes the task of Data Sciences as follows: "Our expertise consists of generating added value from data-based knowledge. For this purpose, we collect, analyze and assess data, making decisions on the basis of the results obtained." The objective is to produce a virtual model of the complete product life cycle, from the initial idea through to utilization and possible optimization. However, problems arise because the information is often scattered across different systems. This is why one of the key tasks of Data Sciences is to enable unified access to data via data ecosystems. It is important for the existing data silos to communicate with each other, both within individual Business Groups and throughout the global Freudenberg Group.[158] The goal is clear: Data-based knowledge is to be processed efficiently and made available. The available information can thus be put to use in algorithms – as a data product with economic value added. This leverages the potential to revolutionize standard processes such as material or product development, "for example with regard to the automated design of products and processes or by AI-assisted (artificial intelligence) materials development." In 2021,

FTI also launched the Digitalization Hub@Weinheim – a network of experts and specialists from Freudenberg, universities and start-ups. Freudenberg added important digitalization know-how to its network with the participation of Campus Heilbronn of the Technical University Munich, and the Industrial Science Group from Darmstadt.[159]

The systematic approach of the new Data Sciences unit is driven by four sections: Digital Systems gives products such as components a certain intelligence in the form of sensors (the Internet of Things). By smart integration in the Internet, customers and developers can learn more about wear on a seal and can start maintenance work at the right time. The team provides advice on the most effective way of collecting and storing data, for example in a cloud. This is where the next section, Data Analytics, takes over. This team uses a variety of methods to manage, structure and analyze the data collected. In contrast, the members of the Digital Modeling team are concerned mainly with predicting the behavior of a material, process or component. The behavior of the object considered is simulated using considerable computing power and a virtual model is created. Finally, the fourth section, Digital Technologies, ensures that the expertise developed is made available digitally to a large number of users. The Freudenberg digitalization platform also creates a permanent link to customer projects.[160]

An example of this type of customer project is located in Bolzano, capital of the South Tyrol province of Italy. This project demonstrates the digital added value offered to its customers by Klüber Lubrication. The Rittner funicular railway links the city with the mountain village of Oberbozen, some 1,000 meters higher. For up to 18 hours per day, the large cabins with a capacity of up to 30 passengers travel between the stations at four-minute intervals, placing considerable strain on the system. All maintenance and repair work must be carried out during the few hours available during the night and this work must be planned precisely. This is where the digitalization project developed by Klüber and its customer Leitner, the manufacturer of the funicular railway, comes into its own. In the digital era, "predictive maintenance" refers to the proactive supervision of a system by sensors and online monitoring, providing data on lubrication management and possible wear on a real-time basis. Work on-site such as oil sampling is no longer needed. The data collected are visualized at one point on Klüber's digital maintenance platform and analyzed to derive recommendations for action. This way, the early detection of any problems allows the proactive planning of maintenance work, preventing machine shutdowns and downtimes. Work that has been scheduled in the optimum way and is based on actual requirements saves time, effort and money. If a fully functional lubricant were replaced prematurely, that would be inefficient and not ecologically sustainable. On the other hand, if the lubricant were replaced too late, the results could include material damage and defects. Klüber calls the program, which can be adapted flexibly for a variety of machines and maintenance-relevant components, "Total Productive Management".[161] This approach gives customers an indication of the condition of their machine, their lubricants and their lubrication system. Klüber has developed the entire technology required, from sensors, via the processing of data in the cloud and data analysis to the efficiency manager for the presentation of the results. Klüber also supplies customers with the hardware needed for these services, especially sensors and gateways for data transmission. This way, the company offers an entire digital ecosystem of a type which had not previously been available in the marketplace.[162]

Smart Seal sensors for mechanical seals are a further example of the added benefits available to customers in the digital era. These seals are produced by EagleBurgmann, a company that has formed part of the Freudenberg Group since 2004. This technology developed in 2020 enables "comprehensive monitoring of the mechanical seals used, allowing not only better understanding of the process but also predictive, condition-based maintenance concepts."[163] This led to the development of "mechanical seals 4.0" with sturdy, durable three-in-one sensors for temperature, pressure and vibration measurement that can be integrated in a seal system relatively easily thanks to wireless data transmission. This system had faced a number of design challenges: On one hand, the sensors needed to be sufficiently small for integration in the seal. On the other hand, the seal design needed to be adapted and the new unit of seal and sensor had to withstand aggressive media, high temperatures, high pressures and severe vibration. The three-in-one sensor continuously measures the pressure, temperature and vibrations at the seal and in the surrounding fluid. These physical values are then converted into digital data by an integrated industrial computer, the "edge". The data evaluation provides an overview of the current performance of the seal, giving an indication of its condition. The measured data are automatically encrypted and transmitted to the EagleBurgmann Cloud, enabling the operator to monitor the seals. The data are visualized in a web-based portal that allows the operator to keep a close eye on the condition of every seal using real-time and historical data. Users can also directly initiate service or material orders via the customer portal. The combination of Smart Seal sensor and EagleBurgmann Cloud analysis developed in the EagleBurgmann digital lab provides an "out-of-the-box Industry 4.0 solution for monitoring, analyzing and identifying operating conditions, malfunctions and wear on the seal components installed."[164] The Smart Seal sensor with automated data evaluation moves the mechanical seal from analog operation straight into the digital era.[165]

Fig. 124 The monitoring data for the mechanical seal collected by the Smart Seal sensor can be read directly using a QR code

Such developments by the EagleBurgmann Business Group are the result of work at the digital lab established at EagleBurgmann headquarters in Wolfratshausen in 2019. All of the digitalization activities of the Business Group were bundled at this facility with a view to meeting specific customer wishes and resolving customers' complex problems using digital solutions. Work at the lab is always interdisciplinary, involving experts from other technical departments in the projects. For example, the lab cooperates intensively with the Sales, Engineering, R&D, Operations and IT departments.[166] The digital lab has always aimed to understand customers' issues connected with its core activities and to develop and bring to the market digital products and services designed to resolve these critical customer issues.[167]

Sensors also play a key role in the digital products of Freudenberg Sealing Technologies and have a long tradition at the Business Group. The first Simmerring with integrated sensor had been launched in 1997. Equipped with this encoder technology, the seal ring could also perform other functions in addition to sealing. For example, the sensor could measure engine speed for use in anti-lock braking systems (ABS) or engine management system control functions.[168] The first condition monitoring Simmerring was developed in 2006. This unit was equipped with an optical sensor to detect leakage at the end of the seal's service life or as a result of damage. These units prevented damage to the equipment connected and optimized maintenance costs.[169] Freudenberg Sealing Technologies has continually optimized its sensor systems. One example of this development work is the LeaCo monitoring system. This was originally based on condition monitoring systems for seals, but it now has nothing to do with seals. LeaCo "detects whether liquids are leaking from points where they should not be released, for example at a weld, a flange or valve, irrespective of whether the liquid concerned is water, an oil or chemical, or lemonade in a bottling plant. The optical sensor is installed directly at the possible danger point and no retrofitting or modification of production plant is needed. A Freudenberg nonwoven is installed on the top of the sensor. Any liquid escaping is absorbed and distributed by the nonwoven. The infrared laser unit on the sensor detects the liquid and transmits a wireless signal to a mobile unit similar to a tablet, which was also developed by Freudenberg.[170]

The spectrum of new digital applications and products at Freudenberg became wider and wider. It ranged from "intelligent filter systems that are activated exactly when the air must be purified" through to optical error identification, such as the detection of unwanted accumulations of molten plastic in nonwoven production. In this case, efficiency was improved further through the use of artificial intelligence (AI). Furthermore, internal business processes are optimized by robotics process automation.[171]

The automated, computer-controlled dosing unit for elastomer compounds commissioned in 2021 shows that the raw mixing plant of Freudenberg Sealing Technologies in Weinheim has also opted for optimized Industry 4.0 processes. In addition to rubber, Freudenberg uses a total of 120 other chemicals for seal compounds. These are all stored in the new dosing unit. The mixtures no longer need to be made up manually. The computer-controlled unit weighs the ingredients required precisely, down to the last gram, and bags them automatically. Weighing and filling the substances into the bags with a capacity of up to 35 liters is not only faster, but this process also avoids the errors which occur in manual operation as a result of incorrect or missing labels. The unit provides special foil bags of the correct sizes automatically at the beginning of the mixing process and prints a barcode on them. This ensures full transparency as to what chemicals in what quantities are filled into a bag. In addition to improved efficiency, the new dosing unit makes a key contribution to occupational health and safety. First, it is no longer necessary for employees to lift, handle and carry the bags of chemicals, some of which are heavy. Secondly, employees are no longer exposed to fine chemical particles, calling for them to wear face masks, during manual weighing.[172]

Fig. 125 The automated chemicals dosing unit for elastomer production at the raw mixing plant of Freudenberg Sealing Technologies in Weinheim

As always in the case of Industry 4.0 applications, "data" is the key word here. Data are not only important for Internet giants such as Google or Facebook, but are also an essential resource for industrial companies. Data-driven business models became a reality some time ago. In future, the ability to derive the correct conclusions from comprehensive data provided on a real-time basis will be a crucial factor in deciding the future viability of a company. Optimized processes, better products and new methods can be derived from the process, operating, material, component and quality data collected. "The trick is to convert the countless data records collected over the long path from incoming raw materials to a finished product into information. These data simply lie fallow, like oil in the ground. They need to be brought to the surface, purified and processed. Only then can they unfold their full potential." The first stage is data processing and analysis. The next stage is to model the data using mathematical algorithms in order to produce a simulation. In the final stage, this simulation is then used to develop a process optimization, for example in production.[173]

One application is rapid prototyping by 3D printing. If a 3D printer is linked to the data analysis and computer simulation system, a prototype can rapidly be produced, allowing the collection of practical experience with material behavior. In the early stages of product development, prototypes play a key role because they can be used to collect considerably more information on properties and problems than with design simulations on the computer screen. Another major advantage of 3D printing is that parts can be produced directly from the computer without costly, time-consuming toolmaking. Rapid prototyping by 3D printing therefore accelerates the development process, as changes in the virtual geometry or shape of a part shown by the computer can be transferred direct to the printed object. This way, the perfect shape for a part can be determined rapidly. Furthermore, for example in seal development, the elastomeric materials to be used later in series production can also be used for printing. Even high-performance thermoplastic materials with a high melting point can be processed.[174]

It is clear that digitalization at Freudenberg must always have specific benefits. The tradition of the company means that defined goals must always be pursued and that the objective must be the benefit to the customer, growth that would otherwise not be possible, higher efficiency or improved quality. A culture of entrepreneurial thinking must not be neglected – neither must an objective view of the trends in the industry. It is important not just to follow the latest hyped-up trend, but to decide, from an entrepreneurial point of view and based on commercial prudence, what is and is not necessary given the dynamic changes continuously taking place in the IT sector. The specific results obtained from this approach are illustrated by the examples already described. In addition, it should be noted that mobile digital communication has become more important than ever before in the era of the Covid-19 pandemic. Home working, video conferences and collaborative project work via Internet links have made working methods more flexible and opened up new types of cooperation that will remain important in the future.

> **EXCURSUS:** SOCIAL RESPONSIBILITY – PART 5: SINCE THE MID-1990S
>
> **1999** In celebration of the company's 150th anniversary, the TANNER program was launched for children and grandchildren of employees, enabling them to travel to Freudenberg sites all over the world as the guests of Freudenberg employees and their families. The goal was to expose young people to other cultures, expand their horizons and learn life lessons. Since the program was launched, over 1,300 young people have traveled the globe with TANNER. In 2022, the company decided to discontinue the program for safety reasons. In light of the Covid pandemic and the growing number of crisis situations worldwide it was felt that the young people should not be exposed to incalculable risks.[175]

1999	Following the severe earthquake in Turkey, employees showed their solidarity with Turkish colleagues and pensioners by swiftly launching a donation campaign. The campaign collected 40,000 DM, and the Freudenberg Management Board increased this sum to 110,000 DM, handing over the donation to the Médecins Sans Frontières (MSF) international aid organization.[176]
2002	The Group-wide "We all take care" initiative was launched at the end of Dialog 2002. The initiative is based on the Group's Guiding Principles. Its aim is to promote the health and safety of all employees, environmental protection, social responsibility and site safety. The driving force behind the initiative is an annual competition with awards honoring the winners.[177] The initiative has brought a significant reduction in the number of accidents at Freudenberg: The accident rate decreased from 16 accidents per 1,000 employees in 2001 to 3 in 2013, making Freudenberg a first-class employer in terms of occupational safety at production companies. Since 2015, the non-financial performance indicator used to measure the accident rate has been the LDIFR (Lost Day Incident Frequency Rate), i.e. the number of workplace accidents with at least one day of work lost per million hours, and this metric has continued to decrease since then: From 1.9 in 2013 to 1.3 in 2021.[178]
2005	Freudenberg launched a sustainable aid project in India, aimed at mitigating the aftermath of the catastrophic tsunami in 2004. A training center built in Nagapattinam south of Chennai in the province of Tamil Nadu gives young people there the prospect of a better future. The training center has since been awarded "State Level Recognition" by the province of Tamil Nadu.[179] Since 2009, Freudenberg has offered young people the opportunity to qualify as electricians, welders, pipe fitters, engine mechanics and machinists under dual training programs at the non-profit training center.[180]
2006	Freudenberg set up the "Wir tun was" project fund to promote tolerance, charity and public spirit. Each year, all denominational and non-denominational charitable groups could apply for funding. This support focused on Weinheim and the surrounding communities in the Bergstraße and Odenwald regions. The funds were earmarked for specific projects. Freudenberg provided 20,000 euros each year for projects, with a maximum of 5,000 euros for each individual project.[181] The initiative was discontinued in 2019 and the company focused on supporting various regional projects.

2009 Freudenberg opened a new primary school in the village of Haijin near the city of Jiangyou, China. The company rebuilt the village school that was completely destroyed by the devastating earthquake in the Sichuan region on May 12, 2008.[182] The building has enough space to give some 300 students a good start to their schooling. Every year, Freudenberg employees visit the elementary school and organize various activities such as the summer school project, tutoring and a Christmas party.[183]

2011 In the wake of the natural disasters in Japan on March 11, 2011, the Freudenberg Management Board launched an appeal among employees for donations to help the colleagues at the Japanese company NOK Corporation affected by the disaster. The response was overwhelming. A donation totaling 438,000 euros was handed over in early June. Some 219,000 euros had been donated by the workforce and this sum was doubled by the management.[184]

2015 The global "e²" (education and environment) initiative was introduced at the Dialog event in Detroit in 2015. The program's goal is to provide access to qualified education and to support environmental protection. Funding of 10 million euros was made available for aid projects at sites all over the world, initially until 2020, to help people access education and work and to promote environmental protection. The main focus is on activities outside Germany, but inquiries from German projects are not excluded.[185] The initiative complements existing individual initiatives that meet an established list of criteria. In 2021, Freudenberg decided to provide e² with another 4 million euros, raising total funding to 18 million euros and supporting some 170 projects.[186]

2015 Up to the end of 2015, employees, partners and retired former employees were invited to donate to the Freudenberg refugee aid initiative. The company then raised the final amount to a total 1.6 million euros. In addition, Freudenberg made a special annual donation of 250,000 euros, meaning that 2.6 million euros was available for refugee aid up to the end of 2019. The Freudenberg Group uses these funds to support various projects in Germany and other countries.[187]

2016 Freudenberg supported the initiative launched by German industry to promote the integration of refugees, called "Wir zusammen" (Us together). The initiative began with just over 30 companies, with this figure rising to over 120 by the end of 2016.[188]

2016 Under the Freudenberg refugee aid initiative, the Freudenberg training center in Weinheim and the Hans Freudenberg School in Weinheim jointly developed a one-year curriculum to prepare young refugees for an apprenticeship program in metalworking skills. The curriculum consisted of a combination of theoretical instruction and practical training in Freudenberg's training workshop.[189] Once this program was up and running, a fixed number of training places for refugees at Freudenberg sites in Germany was introduced in 2017.[190]

2020 During the Covid-19 pandemic, Freudenberg donated significantly more than 2 million euros to about 130 organizations in 28 countries through the end of 2021. These funds were used, for example, to distribute food and protective face masks to those in need.[191]

2022 Freudenberg donated 3 million euros as immediate humanitarian aid for the victims of the war in Ukraine. In addition, well over 700,000 euros was forthcoming from the company's partners and employees. These funds were made available to various aid organizations as well as local projects in Ukraine. Other relief operations complemented major donations. For example, food and clothing were donated to food banks and charitable organizations to support refugees from Ukraine. Furthermore, medical products such as compresses and dressings were delivered direct to Ukraine, and in addition there was financial support for other relief efforts, e.g. in the field of education via Mannheim and Frankfurt universities. There was also local support for Ukrainian refugees in Weinheim. In spring 2022, Freudenberg Real Estate made a total of 11 vacant company-owned apartments and bedsits in Weinheim and Muckensturm available to house 49 Ukrainian refugees.[192]

2023 In the wake of the severe earthquake in Turkey and Syria in February 2023 where the death toll exceeded 50,000, the Freudenberg Group donated 250,000 euros in immediate aid to the disaster region. Various Business Groups also helped with further aid and donations. These activities ranged from collecting urgently-needed goods that were then transported by convoy to the disaster area, to further fundraising campaigns for local aid organizations such as the Turkish Red Crescent.[193]

Freudenberg and mobility in the 21st century

When we talk about the megatrend of mobility, the main focus is usually on the fundamental transformation in progress in this sector. Climate change, scarce resources and traffic problems in the world's urban regions demand a shift away from conventional drive systems, the improvement of public transport infrastructure and entirely new creative concepts for mobility. The future of individual mobility and the transformation that the automotive industry needs to accomplish at the beginning of the 21st century in order to achieve this are at the center of discussions. The American manufacturer Tesla is often cited as an example of the successful market introduction of the electric car and the fundamental rethinking of the automobile as a digitally controlled product. The key words in this context range from autonomous driving and new connectivity to the updating of automobile software via mobile phone networks without visiting a workshop (over-the-air updates).[194]

As an established supplier to the automobile industry, Freudenberg is determined to and indeed must play its part in shaping these changes. The company is involved with all types of drive systems and is improving the mobility of a wide variety of vehicles, from passenger cars to commercial vehicles, aircraft, ships and rail vehicles. Freudenberg technology reduces the pollutant emissions of internal combustion engines and Freudenberg products are also to be found in hybrid drives, all-electric propulsion systems and fuel cells. For some time now, fuel cells in particular have been considered to offer especially promising prospects for the future. If fuel cells covered a significant share in the mobility market, vehicles equipped with these systems could be refueled in only a few minutes instead of hours in the case of all-electric vehicles. As a result of these systems in trucks, buses and also passenger cars, the air in cities would be filled not with nitrogen oxides but only with fine droplets of water. "Wind turbines in the North Sea could supply energy for electrolysis plants instead of simply operating to no avail because there was no demand for electric power at a particular time. This approach would produce "green hydrogen".[195] This is a technology with a promising future, but also with an extremely long development time in a tough competitive environment.

Freudenberg's decision to become involved in the megatrend of (new) mobility provided strong impetus for growth, especially in the Seals and Vibration Technology Business Area. After the López crisis had been mastered and restructuring had been successfully completed in the course of Focus 1, the Business Area took its first steps towards new fields of activity. A favorable opportunity arose in 1997, when Freudenberg was able to acquire Merkel Dichtelemente GmbH of Hamburg, a company with a long tradition, together with its subsidiaries, from the ailing Economs Industrie-Beteiligungs AG.[196] The acquisition of this company provided long-term security for employees working in Hamburg and added hydraulic, pneumatic and large seals for shipbuilding, steel structures and mining to the Freudenberg portfolio. Growth potential was expected, particularly in shipbuilding, as a result of new propulsion systems for ships that were more environmentally compatible and efficient.[197]

The company was integrated into the Seals and Vibration Technology Business Area under the new name of Merkel-Freudenberg Fluidtechnik GmbH with effect from January 1, 1998[198] and was to supply its traditional export markets in Italy, France, Scandinavia, the UK, Eastern Europe, the USA and Southeast Asia with its full range of seals from six locations in Europe.[199] In the hydraulic sector alone, the company offered as many as 60,000 different seals.[200] The Hydraulic Lead Center in Hamburg claimed that one of its strengths was "that we produce many seals to special order by customers. In some cases, only a few units of these special seals are produced."[201] The recipe for success is in-depth communication between customers, designers and production. One of the special features of the production facility in Hamburg was and still is that it can manufacture large seal rings with diameters up to 20 meters. These are mainly used for tunneling and aerospace projects, but also for maritime applications. For example, the gigantic tunnel boring machines with their cutting heads used for the construction of the 57-kilometer-long Gotthard Base Tunnel were protected by large-diameter seals from Freudenberg. A Freudenberg O-ring with a diameter of three meters featured in the European Ariane rocket. The drive systems of giant ships such as the cruise liners Radiance of the Seas and Oasis of the Seas are also equipped with Freudenberg seals with diameters of about three meters.[202]

Following the years of crisis in the early 1990s, the Management Board also decided on a strategic reorientation in the field of vibration control technology. The management was well aware that the company had a strong market position in the field of engine acoustics (for example, with hydro mounts for engines), but that it would be unable to build on this position from its own resources. In order to achieve a leading position in the field of vibration control systems, it would be necessary to acquire additional technical know-how. More and more customers from the automotive industry were looking for suppliers who could provide complete solutions. However, Freudenberg did not have the expertise required in the fields of conventional mounts and bushings, or air spring technology, which was becoming increasingly important in the truck sector. The Freudenberg management was therefore interested in cooperation with a partner company with a view to "establishing joint development and sales activities in the field of vibration control technology products and acoustic solutions." The objective was to achieve technology, market and cost leadership for vibration control systems in the automotive industry. It was soon found that Phoenix AG in Hamburg would be "the best of the possible partners or even the only possible partner".[203]

In April 1995, the two companies then concluded a cooperation agreement in the field of vibration control technology and acoustics, initially with a term of five years. Cooperation was intended to round off the portfolio and to create an opportunity of presenting an identical product offering to customers at all key locations throughout the world. "Freudenberg and Phoenix complement each other in an ideal way in this area. While Freudenberg has a strong position in the field of hydro mounts and vibration dampers, Phoenix's strength is in conventional engine mounts and bushings. In development and production, the two companies will concentrate on their core areas and purchase the supplementary products required from the other partner when the need arises."[204] This meant that Phoenix was responsible for conventional rubber-metal mounts, air springs and acoustics in the vehicle interior while Freudenberg dealt with hydro mounts, rotational vibration dampers and engine acoustics.[205]

At that time, Phoenix had already become one of the leading suppliers of sound damping systems for the automotive industry through the acquisition of Stankiewicz. Freudenberg had know-how in the field of engine acoustics, while Stankiewicz covered acoustics in other parts of the vehicle. Each of the partners therefore benefited from the other's know-how.[206] The companies' international networks also complemented each other: Phoenix had locations in France, Italy, Spain and a cooperation arrangement in Turkey.[207] Freudenberg operated its own subsidiaries in the United States and, through its relationship with NOK, the company also had production and sales facilities in Asia.[208] The partners were therefore in a position to "develop complete motor mounting or suspension mounting systems together in cooperation with vehicle manufacturers and to manufacture these systems at the two companies' plants throughout the world."[209]

In order to deepen the partnership, discussions between Peter Stehle, Member of the Freudenberg Management Board, and the Management Board of Phoenix AG, started in 1997 with a view to exploring the possibilities of a joint venture.[210] Two years later, the establishment of a joint venture company, to be named Vibracoustic, was announced. Freudenberg and Phoenix were to contribute their vibration control systems for the automotive industry to the new company. The two companies were reacting to increasing pressure from the automotive industry, which not only expected its suppliers to have a global presence, but also to be able to develop and manufacture entire vehicle systems in addition to individual parts.[211]

The company finally commenced operations on January 1, 2001. The claim of Vibracoustic, in which the two companies held equal shares, was "we convert noise and vibration into sound and comfort". "The product portfolios of the two partners complemented each other and covered the entire vibration control spectrum. Phoenix contributed its strengths in chassis and air spring technology, Freudenberg rounded off the range with engine mounts and torsional vibration dampers. As a result, there were four Divisions – Suspension, Chassis,

Powertrain and Drivetrain – each focusing on development, production and marketing in its specialist field."[212]

The establishment of Vibracoustic proved to be a resounding success. One example was the air spring sector. The newly established company had a product that was both innovative and ready for use in premium-segment passenger cars – axial bellow technology. However, profitability needed to be improved. Vibracoustic soon succeeded in broadening its customer base and reducing production costs. Within the first few years of operation, air spring sales grew sixfold.[213]

However, the partnership between Phoenix and Freudenberg ended in 2004. When the parent company, Phoenix AG, was acquired by Freudenberg's competitor Continental of Hanover, Freudenberg was able to invoke a clause of the joint venture contract and to acquire the Phoenix shares in the previous joint venture company Vibracoustic with effect from the end of 2004. Freudenberg thus became the sole shareholder.[214]

Since the mid-2000s, the development of new vibration control systems had been increasingly dominated by the major trends in the automotive industry. At the beginning, the key trend was the development of lower-consumption drive systems. The objective of downsizing was to develop smaller, lighter internal combustion engines with a lower fuel consumption, combined with the same or higher power outputs and reduced space requirements. The challenge faced by vibration control technology was to ensure improved acoustic properties and greater ride comfort despite the smaller space available. In 2009, the management of Vibracoustic had still assumed that this would be the key trend for the next 10 years.[215] This development led to numerous product innovations that strengthened the market leadership of Vibracoustic. Early examples included new developments for optimized fuel-saving start-stop control.[216] Further patented innovations were soon launched on the market: In 2010, the mounting brackets used for engine mounts, which had previously consisted of metal, were completely replaced by plastic parts, resulting in corresponding weight savings. These lighter mounting brackets were fitted to the BMW 1-series and 3-series models from 2012 onward.[217] CO_2 emissions were also reduced by the lightweight torsional vibration dampers introduced in 2011. The development team at Vibracoustic was also active in reducing the carbon dioxide emissions of commercial vehicles. For this purpose, they developed the innovative bionic air spring in 2011. This unit "eliminates the need for customers to produce and install complex body parts weighing up to several hundred kilograms". It also enabled manufacturers to increase vehicle payloads.[218]

As regards Freudenberg Sealing Technology, the main focus had been on development trends in the automotive sector since the early 2000s: Energy saving and emission reduction. An early example of product innovation was the "ESS" that Simmerring presented in 2005. ESS stands for "energy saving seal"; these seals allowed a 40 percent reduction in friction compared with a conventional PTFE seal lip, also reducing energy consumption.[219]

With a view to achieving lower energy consumption and emissions, development work focused on making vehicles lighter. However, it was found that there was a limit to the weight reduction that was feasible in view of technical and safety requirements. One solution adopted by the industry in the field of internal combustion engines was downsizing. Freudenberg responded to this development in 2009 with its "LESS" initiative. LESS is an abbreviation of "low emission sealing solutions" and includes a complete package of seals for all vehicle components affecting fuel consumption and pollutant emissions. The high-tech seals and specially developed moldings perform functions from the engine through to the exhaust system and brakes. They are combined with smart sensor technology, allowing more precise engine control and combustion.[220]

This way, Freudenberg supported automakers in their efforts to obtain higher outputs from engines with lower capacities and reduced fuel consumption. However, downsizing posed new challenges in terms of friction reduction as well as heat and pressure resistance. Freudenberg was called upon to demonstrate its materials expertise. To meet the emission targets set by regulators, improvements in the decimal place range became important. For example, the Levitex gas-lubricated mechanical seal alone allows reductions of between 0.5 and 1 gram per kilometer in CO_2 emissions. The crankshaft seal, developed in 2012, is almost friction-free.[221]

With a view to curbing greenhouse gas emissions in road traffic, the automotive industry had already been focusing on the use of synthetic and renewable fuels in conventional internal combustion engines in 2009. These are liquid or gaseous fuels not based on crude oil, but on carbon and hydrogen produced using solar and wind power. The seals in the LESS program are made from materials that are fit for service and ensure reliable engine functioning with such fuels.[222]

To meet the demands of automotive industry customers for greater global presence on the part of their suppliers, the activities of Freudenberg Seals and Vibration Control Europe and Freudenberg-NOK General Partnership were brought together under the umbrella of the new Freudenberg Sealing Technologies (FST) Business Group with effect from January 1, 2011.[223]

As plastic products were becoming increasingly important for lightweight vehicle design, Freudenberg Sealing Technologies made efforts to expand its expertise in this field. For this reason, FST acquired 50 percent of the shares in the Schneegans Group of Emmerich am Rhein in 2012.[224] With the know-how in the field of multi-component injection molding technology gained through this acquisition, Freudenberg Sealing Technologies was able to add high-quality thermoplastic moldings to its product portfolio for the automotive industry. For example, a pump housing presented in 2013, which was produced from such high-tech thermoplastic materials, was 500 grams lighter than a comparable metal component.[225]

At Freudenberg too, the technological transformation in the automotive industry soon not only related to the internal combustion engine. Efforts focused increasingly on developments for vehicles with electric and hybrid drive systems. With respect to vibration control, the damping of high-frequency noise and vibration posed new challenges. Such noise and vibrations were much more perceptible to vehicle occupants, as they were no longer masked by the sounds produced by the internal combustion engine. One solution to this problem offered by Vibracoustic was the "space-, weight- and cost-saving double insulation mount patented in 2012 that eliminates a broad range of high-frequency vibrations even before they can be transmitted as annoying noise to the occupants via the chassis."[226]

2012 also saw the establishment of a further joint venture company in the automotive sector – in this case for vibration control technology. On January 31, 2012, Freudenberg and the Swedish company Trelleborg AB signed a memorandum of understanding concerning the establishment of a "50:50 joint venture

Fig. 126 Production of vibration control elements at Morganfield, United States, 2023. These elements are used in electric vehicles, among other applications

between Vibracoustic and the automotive antivibration business of Trelleborg AB."²²⁷ The operations of the joint venture company, in which the two partners initially held equal shares, commenced on July 1, 2012.²²⁸ The partners' vibration control portfolios complemented each other very well. While Vibracoustic products were mainly used in mid-range and premium vehicles, Trelleborg had a strong market position in the mid-range and compact segments. In terms of their regional operations, the two companies also complemented each other. Vibracoustic was well-positioned in Europe, and Trelleborg in Asia and North America. Thanks to the cooperation, the joint venture could supply air springs and suspension parts for all manufacturers and all vehicle classes in the key regions of the world for the automotive industry.²²⁹

TrelleborgVibracoustic reverted to the name Vibracoustic in 2016. At the beginning of 2016, the two companies agreed on the future shareholding structure of Vibracoustic. Initially, a joint IPO was planned, but this was not realized in view of the unfavorable conditions on the capital market at the time. The two companies therefore decided to go their separate ways. Freudenberg acquired the 50 percent stake of Trelleborg in the joint venture company and Trelleborg-Vibracoustic GmbH was renamed Vibracoustic GmbH. The transaction was completed on July 5, 2016, following approval by the anti-trust authorities.²³⁰

In connection with the acquisition of Vibracoustic, Freudenberg also reviewed its vibration control activities for rail vehicles. How had Freudenberg acquired this business in the first place? While negotiations with Phoenix AG were underway in 1998, discussions with the Schwab Group, a specialist in vibration control components for rail vehicles, had started.²³¹ This business had appeared to the Freudenberg management to be especially promising for the future: "The relevant market in Europe for vibration control products for rail vehicles is 140 million DM. In this sector, GB ST-I [the Business Group Vibration Control Technology – Industry] has a market share of 8 %. [...] In view of the steady growth in rail traffic, in Europe and especially in the USA, Australia and the Far East, as well as increasing demands with regard to vehicle behavior and comfort, we expect good growth prospects in this market."²³² However, the European rail vehicle market in particular was becoming more and more demanding and, like the automotive industry, was "transferring services to suppliers to a growing extent and calling for complete solutions and system design competence. Currently, none of our competitors can meet these requirements in Europe. Only Schwab, which is to be part of this cooperation arrangement, has system design competence. The air spring is a key component of a modern bogie. GB ST-I currently cannot offer a product of this type."²³³

In January 1999, agreement was reached with Schwab on the establishment of a joint company, in Velten near Berlin. Freudenberg held a stake of 51 percent in the new company, Freudenberg Schwab GmbH, and Schwab Schwingungstechnik AG of Adliswil held a stake of 49 percent.[234] Freudenberg also acquired shares in Schwab Schwingungstechnik AG in Switzerland, representing a stake of 20 percent, with an option to purchase further shares.[235]

As had been planned, Freudenberg Schwab GmbH successfully reinforced its market position in the years that followed. The management board therefore decided to integrate the entire rail business in the Freudenberg Group and acquired the remaining shares in the joint venture company and in Schwab Schwingungstechnik AG in Switzerland in July 2010.[236] The two companies laid the foundation for the Freudenberg Schwab Business Group, established with effect from January 1, 2011, in the course of the Green Areas realignment. In 2011, the first series-produced hydraulic axle-guide bearings (HALL), which optimize driving performance and reduce wear on bogies in rail vehicles, were delivered to customers in the UK.[237] The subsequent development of this product with respect to environmental aspects and energy savings was revolutionary. HALL 2.0, presented in 2014, receives its control information from cameras, GPS data and programmed maps or from built-in sensors for power control. Using these signals, the axles are automatically adjusted to the correct angle. The result is less wear on the wheels and rails, as well as less noise and lower resource and energy consumption.[238] This environmentally compatible technology is also suitable for industrial vehicles, excavators and agricultural machinery in all applications where bearings need to absorb considerable impact energy.

In organizational terms, the Business Group expanded as a result of the integration of the Vibration Control Technology – Industry Business Group and the relocation of the various facilities to Velten. The new Freudenberg Schwab Vibration Control recorded sales of 56 million euros, with 252 employees, in 2012.[239] In addition to units in France, England, Sweden and Russia, the workforce was boosted especially in China, one of the key markets for the rail and construction industries. In 2013, the length of the rapidly growing Chinese railway network already exceeded that of all the comparable systems in the world, with more than 10,000 kilometers. The Harbin-Dalian line in the northeast of China posed special challenges for vibration control, as speeds of 200 km per hour were to be reached even at temperatures as low as –40 degrees Celsius. At such low temperatures, normal components manufactured from natural rubber become extremely brittle and can shatter like glass if they are knocked. At the request of the customer, Freudenberg developed a special elastomer rubber compound that remains fully functional at temperatures down to −50 degrees Celsius and has the same service life as a natural rubber compound.[240]

Within the framework of the organizational realignment following Focus 2.0, Schwab Vibration Control was transferred to the umbrella of Freudenberg Sealing Technologies in 2014. Subsequently, the Freudenberg-Schwab vibration control business was sold to Trelleborg AB in Sweden with effect from October 1, 2016, as it had been decided that Freudenberg Sealing Technologies would focus on its core business.[241]

In the automotive engineering sector, Freudenberg continued to follow the major trends that had gathered further momentum from the Paris Climate Agreement of December 2015, especially with regard to e-mobility. Two years before, Freudenberg Sealing Technologies had already developed an innovative transmission seal for hybrid and all-electric vehicles: The Simmerring equipped with an electrically conductive nonwoven. In an electric drive system, the motor transfers a voltage to the drive shaft which can damage the shaft bearings. The nonwoven in the Simmerring absorbs this electric charge and conducts it away from the motor. The series production of this Simmerring with conductive nonwoven, marketed under the name of eCON, started two years later, in 2015.[242]

Air spring business provides an example of how Vibracoustic grasped the new market opportunities offered by this trend towards e-mobility from 2017 onward. Air spring systems not only improve passenger comfort and driving dynamics: in all-electric vehicles, they can also contribute to reducing air resistance and improving the passive cooling of the battery.[243]

Also in 2017, Freudenberg Sealing Technologies launched its patented pressure compensation element, DIAvent, for electric vehicle traction batteries. These batteries, which run on voltages of several hundred volts, must be well protected. Electrical components are packed into a thin-walled yet stable metal housing so that splashing water and fallen rocks cannot damage them. But the housing cannot be fully hermetically sealed because it would deform, for example, due to fluctuations in the external air pressure or the temperature. That is why housings of this kind are equipped with at least one pressure compensation valve. A second valve is a safety measure: it only opens if damage to battery cells results from a malfunction and it is imperative to drain off all the gas emitted by a damaged cell in just a few seconds. DIAvent is a smart pressure compensation element which combines both functions in a single component. The DIAvent element permits engineers to make electric vehicles more reliable and economical.[244]

Other safety-relevant innovations from Freudenberg for electric vehicles include heat shields and fireproof seals for batteries. Heat shields can be integrated between individual cells with almost no impact on the installation space required. In the event that an individual cell overheats, they prevent a chain reaction, which could lead to an explosion of the entire battery system in the worst possible case. The Freudenberg heat shield ensures that the heat remains isolated in the faulty cell until it has been dissipated by the cooling system. Foldable, fireproof seals for the battery housing can withstand a battery fire for a significant period of time, preventing the fire from spreading. The elastomer (i.e., rubber) components required for the seals were developed in cooperation with the aviation experts at Freudenberg Sealing Technologies. They achieved the highest safety classification available and, in practical tests, ensured that the flame in the battery was extinguished in 10 seconds.[245]

Separator technology is important for the safe operation of battery systems in electric vehicles. The separator is a key component of the battery as it keeps the two poles of the battery apart, preventing short circuits and uncontrolled discharges which could cause a battery explosion in the worst possible case. As regards battery separators for nickel-metal hydride batteries of the types mainly used in hybrid vehicles, Japan Vilene Company had already been the leading supplier for many years, especially for Asian markets. With the growth of all-electric drive systems, lithium-ion batteries became increasingly important. These had already functioned reliably in mobile phones and laptop computers since the early 2000s. However, the larger batteries needed for hybrid and electric vehicles initially posed technical challenges. With a maximum thickness measured in micrometers, the separator had to withstand high temperatures and continuous loads on the electric drive system. The material must "neither shrink nor melt nor become permeable." Nonwoven separators meeting these requirements had been the object of research work by the nonwoven experts at Freudenberg in cooperation with Japan Vilene Company since 2010. The two partners further developed their separator technology with a view to improving the range of electric vehicles, while at the same time boosting their energy efficiency. Separator business with the automotive industry was subsequently mainly continued by Japan Vilene Company.[246]

In the years that followed, manufacturers began systematically aligning their portfolios to electric vehicles, either adapting existing vehicle platforms to e-mobility or introducing new ones. Freudenberg supported this process with a large number of innovations for automakers. These included "NVH" solutions optimized for electric vehicles. NVH stands for "noise, vibration, harshness" and refers to all the vibrations that can be heard and felt in a vehicle.[247]

Weight reduction remained a key topic, as lighter weight also means higher efficiency for electric vehicles. One example is an innovative textile underbody from Freudenberg Performance Materials, where development work

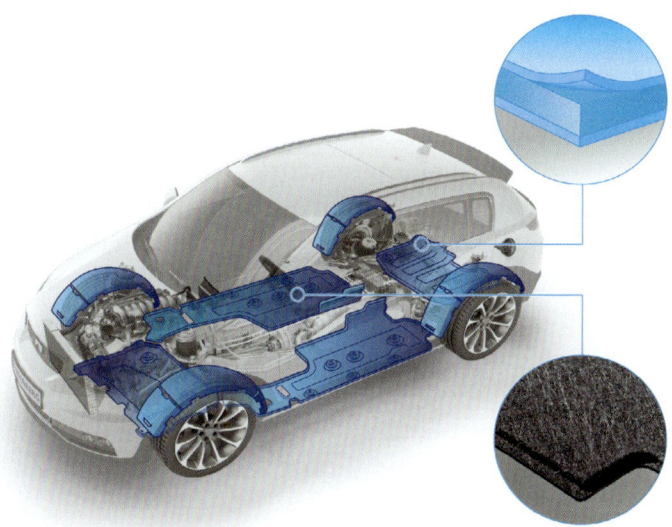

Fig. 127 The textile underbody from Freudenberg Performance Materials is not only especially light, it also has noise-absorbing properties

started in 2014. This is significantly lighter than a comparable injection-molded product – on average 700 grams per square meter lighter. In comparison with glass-fiber-reinforced textiles, the saving is still about 400 grams. Although it is manufactured from a polyester nonwoven, the underbody element is almost rock hard and meets all the relevant safety requirements, including protection against stone chips. The material is also recyclable, opening up new possibilities of sustainable production.[248]

This also applies to another innovation in lightweight design from Freudenberg's nonwoven experts: Acoustic pads. Freudenberg acoustic pads replace the relatively heavy insulating barrier layers of the conventional type used to block noise. These pads are installed inside various vehicle areas: in doors, trunk liners, roof liners, and A, B and C pillars, as well as the wheel-arch liners. The multi-layer nonwoven mixture, consisting of microfibers and needlepunch materials, absorbs noise and is much lighter. Furthermore, the acoustic pads absorb high-frequency sound highly effectively and are therefore especially well-suited for use in electric vehicles in which tire and wind noise are significantly more perceptible. The industrialization of acoustic nonwovens was implemented through Filc, a Slovenian company acquired in 2019. Filc, a specialist manufacturer of needlepunch nonwoven textiles for the automotive industry, contributed its series production expertise, which was then adapted by the Freudenberg experts for industrial-scale production of the acoustic pads.[249]

Further key innovations for e-mobility came from the Freudenberg Chemical Specialities Business Group. For example, specialty lubricants from Klüber also support the new drive systems developed by the automotive industry. Hydro lubricants for electric vehicle transmissions ensure lower wear and high heat dissipation. These high-performance lubricants have been adapted to the high torque values of electric motors and can also conduct electric charges away from the drive system to ground. This way, they improve the service life and efficiency of electric drive systems.[250] Chem-Trend also supports the production of lightweight body and drivetrain components with zinc and magnesium alloys.[251]

The fuel cell – a technology for the future

On the other hand, Freudenberg also invested in the systematic development of its own expertise in the manufacture of battery and fuel cell systems, especially for heavy commercial vehicles. The electrification solutions already implemented were not suitable for such vehicles.

> In the fuel cell, electric power is generated from a fuel – hydrogen – with oxygen as the oxidizing agent. The hydrogen reacts with oxygen from the air. A nonwoven gas diffusion layer is installed on each side of the electrolyte membrane in a fuel cell. This layer distributes hydrogen and oxygen evenly to the membrane and guides the products of the zero-emission chemical reaction – electric power, heat and water – away from the membrane. In an electric vehicle, the electric power generated is fed directly to the electric motor, which converts it into motion.[252]

Freudenberg had already started in-house development work on the fuel cell in the 1990s, initially concentrating on individual fuel cell components. Following a first market survey in 1994, the main focus was on sealing solutions. The technical development center of Freudenberg Seals and Vibration Control Technology then started to develop seals for bipolar plates for the Siemens group. Two years later, the first fuel cell products were manufactured and supplied to customers.[253] In addition to developing fuel cell components, "the possibility of using methanol as a fuel instead of pure hydrogen" was investigated. This question was to become important for marine drive systems at a much later stage. In 1996, the Freudenberg specialists also considered the question of whether nonwovens could be used as a base or reinforcement material for the electrolyte

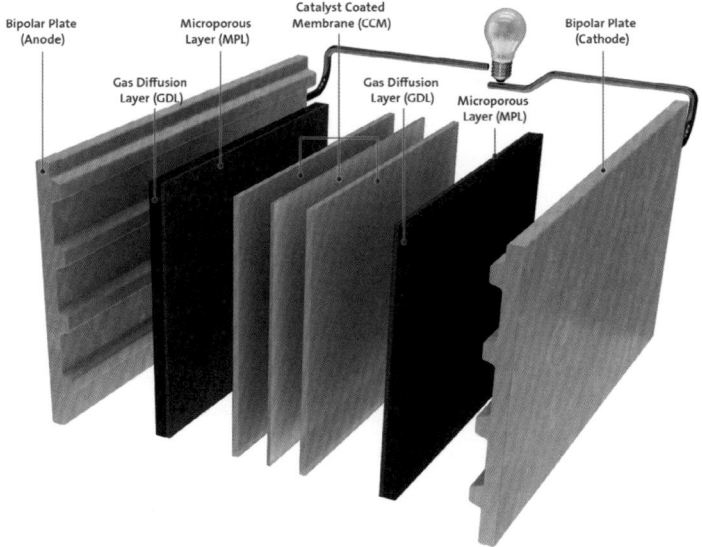

Fig. 128 Structure of a fuel cell

membrane.[254] Two years later, work started on the development of gas diffusion layers (GDLs) based on treated carbon fiber nonwovens.[255] The function of the GDL within the fuel cell "is to distribute the gases – hydrogen on the one side and oxygen on the other side – as evenly as possible. The better this function is performed, the higher the energy density at the catalyst in the center of the cell, and the more efficient the drive system in the final resort. The quality of the GDL is crucially important for the service life of the cell."[256]

From 1998 onward, the independent fuel cell projects of the seal technology and nonwovens segments were coordinated by Freudenberg Research Services. Through this approach, a regular exchange of information between the project teams of the individual Business Groups was established. Freudenberg Research Services was a predecessor of the present Freudenberg Technology Innovation Corporate Function, FTI. The following year, Freudenberg started work on the development of filters and humidifiers for purifying and conditioning the intake air of fuel cells.[257]

Freudenberg Fuel Cell Components Technology (FFCCT) was then founded on December 31, 2001.[258] This new company bundled the entire fuel cell know-how available throughout the Freudenberg Group into a systematic form and was intended to continue the development of Freudenberg fuel cell components. The overall objective was to bring fuel sector technology considerably closer to industrial use. Freudenberg therefore continued to work mainly on the production of fuel cell components. The development strategy focused on two key areas – stationary applications for power generation and mobile applications in the automotive market.[259]

Development work in the field of fuel cell technology had a very long-term perspective right from the start. In 2002, it was expected that it would be more than 10 years before fuel cells were used in series production. Initially, sales were entirely negligible. The combination of a variety of specialist disciplines at FFCCT proved to be very useful as the experts could carry out their development work together. This is how, for example, a GDL with an integrated seal was developed:[260] "For the operation of a fuel cell, the reaction zones must be sealed off not only against each other but also against their surroundings. This way, efficiency losses caused by external leakage are prevented and the destruction of the fuel cell by direct reaction of hydrogen with oxygen is avoided. From the technical point of view, this sealing task may be solved in a variety of different ways."[261]

In 2004, loose flat seals still represented the state of the art, "because they can be manufactured by stamping or cutting and are easy to adapt to different designs. However, they are difficult to assemble [...]. Seals on backing foils which can also be coated with adhesive are an alternative to flat seals. This variant is technically more complex, but is easier to install." With a view to reaping the benefits of this high-quality design at the same time as reducing production costs, the Freudenberg experts succeeded in developing an injection molding process that allowed the seal to be applied directly to the membrane electrode assembly (MEA). The MEA is a multi-layer composite consisting of a gas diffusion layer and membrane. It is the key component in any polymer electrolyte membrane (PEM) fuel cell for the conversion of chemical energy into electric power. Using this technology, it was possible to save the cost of backing film and adhesive, as well as the cost of fitting the seal. In addition, this was a process fit for mass production, which would allow the low-cost, reproducible manufacture of large volumes in the future.[262] FFCCT then began to develop small-series production of stack seals to meet orders placed by customers such as EFC, Viessman and Nuvera, and was integrated into the newly established Freudenberg New Technologies Business Group in 2005.[263] "At the same time, our first competitors were already exiting their development activities – this once again confirms the long-term approach adopted by Freudenberg."[264] In an interview, Martin Stark, who was a Member of the Management Board from 2005 to 2013 and responsible for Research Services, explained the investment opportunities in the field of fuel cell development: "The real entrepreneurial challenge in connection with this technology is to invest at the right time, not too late, but also not too soon."[265]

Freudenberg also became a development partner and supplier for the small series of Mercedes B-Class cars produced with fuel cell drive systems. Freudenberg supplied the entire humidifier module.[266] And in 2011, on the "F-CELL World Drive" motoring challenge, three Mercedes B-Class vehicles equipped with an electric propulsion system powered by fuel cells with no local emissions drove round the world in 125 days. The Freudenberg humidifier module consists of an aluminum housing with optimized flow mechanics, containing hollow-fiber membranes. The humidifier module was also a cooperation product, as the hollow-fiber membranes were supplied by partner company NOK.[267]

In 2009, FFCCT also developed (together with Freudenberg Filtration Technologies) a standard air intake filter for a wide range of fuel cell systems. The innovative filter combined high-efficiency filter media with a housing featuring optimized flow mechanics – without a leakage risk. This product from Freudenberg offered a solution for fuel cell applications in domestic power, telecommunications and forklift trucks.[268] A year later, FFCCT developed the innovative FAST (flip and seal technology) seal for fuel cells to maturity for series production.[269] With FAST, the nonwoven material of the gas diffusion layer is surrounded by a seal edge. The seal can be opened and closed like a sandwich. This way, two components were combined to form one assembly manufactured in its entirety by Freudenberg. "This led to a simpler, more reliable production process for fuel cells combined to form a stack."[270] By 2014, the development of fuel cell components by FFCCT had laid the foundation for the products developed to be handed over to the Business Groups.[271]

By 2016, Freudenberg Performance Materials was one of the leading global manufacturers of gas diffusion layers for fuel cells. At that time, products were supplied to customers in Europe, North America and Asia who used them in applications for vehicle drive systems, domestic energy supplies and forklift trucks.[272] According to information provided by the company, gas diffusion layer nonwovens from Freudenberg Performance Materials were characterized by "high thermal and electric conductivity, optimum protection of the membrane against damage and very easy processing."[273] They are a key element of efficient hydrogen fuel cell technology. The three-dimensional fiber structure of the carbon in the nonwoven plays a key role in power generation. It ensures that the "hydrogen as the fuel and the oxygen as the oxidizing agent are distributed across the polymer electrolyte membrane (PEM) as evenly as possible. The more homogeneously the gases flow to the membrane, the more electric power is generated" by the fuel cell. "Thanks to a chemically stable coating with conductive carbon particles such as carbon black or graphite, water simply drips off the surface. Products from FPM have already put their high functionality to the test successfully in a variety of applications and vehicle types."[274]

Systematic further development work also continued on Freudenberg filtration technology for fuel cells. A multi-stage filtration process that removed salts, large particles, gas and fine particulate matter ensured optimized intake air.[275]

The following year, Freudenberg Sealing Technologies went one step further and moved from being a component producer to a system supplier. With the acquisition of Elcore and its affiliate Elcomax in Munich (specializing in the development of stationary fuel cell systems for single- and two-family homes), Freudenberg Sealing Technologies was able to integrate system expertise for stationary fuel cell units into its own portfolio. In 2018, Freudenberg Sealing Technologies also established a Battery & Fuel Cell Systems Division. "The objective is the combination of battery and fuel cell technology for the supreme discipline of drive system electrification. Initially, this hybrid technology combining fuel cells and batteries focused on heavy duty vehicles such as trucks, ships, heavy agricultural machinery and vehicles used in mining."[276] The division coordinated the activities of Elcore and XALT Energy, a US company with headquarters in Midland, Michigan, which had been acquired by Freudenberg.[277] XALT produced large lithium-ion battery cells, battery modules and systems. In addition, the objective was to integrate the know-how of other Freudenberg Business Groups for battery and fuel cell components[278] into newly developed hybrid systems.[279]

XALT had specialized in lithium-ion technologies for high energy/high-performance storage applications in the logistics, railroads, maritime, general industry and automotive sectors. At its automated cleanroom production facilities in Midland, with an area of more than 40,000 square meters, the company produces lithium-ion battery cells, packs and modules, along with associated controls and software.[280] An innovation developed at the XALT research and development laboratory in Pontiac, Michigan, in 2019 was a low-profile lithium-ion battery pack for commercial vehicles. This product is especially well-suited for buses, trucks and rail vehicles where batteries need to be installed in spaces with restricted heights and depths. The battery packs are designed so that manufacturers do not need to change the design of their vehicles.[281] As a result of these efforts, XALT presented the first all-electric long-distance passenger coach together with bus manufacturer New Flyer Industries in November 2019.[282]

Also in 2019, Freudenberg Sealing Technologies became part of the Pa-X-ell2 project.[283] The objective is to optimize fuel cells for use on seagoing passenger vessels. The project is being publicly funded by the Federal Ministry of Transport and Digital Infrastructure (BMVI) as part of the "National Innovation Program Hydrogen and Fuel Cell Technology" (NIP).[284]

Fig. 129 Production of lithium-ion battery packs for commercial vehicles at Midland, United States, 2023

Freudenberg also started a strategic partnership with Lürssen Werft to develop fuel cell systems for mega yachts. Together, the two companies defined a technology roadmap for yachts without internal combustion engines. This roadmap is based on the methanol-operated maritime fuel cell system with integrated fuel reforming developed by Freudenberg. The integration of this system is to be simulated in the new innovation laboratory operated by Lürssen.[285]

The objective of another research project focusing on fuel cell technology, launched in 2021, is to investigate hybrid powertrains consisting of hydrogen-powered fuel cells combined with an electric drive and complementary battery storage. For this purpose, Freudenberg, ZF Friedrichshafen, FlixBus and a major European bus manufacturer joined forces to develop a high-performance fuel cell system for long-distance coaches under a project named HyFleet. Within the project, Freudenberg is developing a long-range fuel cell system that will be tested directly in a demonstrator long-range bus. Claus Möhlenkamp, CEO of Freudenberg Sealing Technologies, explained the goal of the project: "We aim to significantly advance the long-term durability and efficiency of the technology and set standards" for the viability of the fuel cell. The project will also focus on optimizing the interaction of fuel cell and battery within the powertrain.[286]

Fig. 130 Production of fuel cell components at Freudenberg e-Power Systems in Munich, Germany, 2023

At the same time, development work continued on XALT battery systems for maritime applications: On New Zealand's first all-electric ferry, lithium-ion batteries from XALT Energy have ensured that passengers experience a clean, quiet voyage since January 2022. The batteries were integrated in the ship's design together with the McKay Group, an electro-technology company that is focused on sustainable transportation solutions. The 19-meter, 135-passenger ship will complete nine trips around the New Zealand capital Wellington every day. A total of 72 high-performance battery packs from XALT with a capacity of about 550 kWh provide energy free from fumes and emissions. The battery system on the ferry powers two twin electric motors that enable the ferry to reach speeds of 20 knots and allow continuous operation for one hour between charges.[287]

The new Freudenberg e-Power Systems Business Group (FEPS) was established with effect from April 1, 2022. The previous activities of the FST Battery & Fuel Cell Systems Division and the XALT Energy joint venture were combined under the umbrella of this Business Group.[288] Furthermore, Freudenberg acquired the remaining shares in XALT Energy with effect from January 1, 2023.[289]

In 2022, Freudenberg e-Power Systems was the first manufacturer to receive type approval for a methanol-powered fuel cell system for oceangoing vessels from the international classification society RINA. This represented a "milestone in the development of sustainable technologies in the maritime sector."

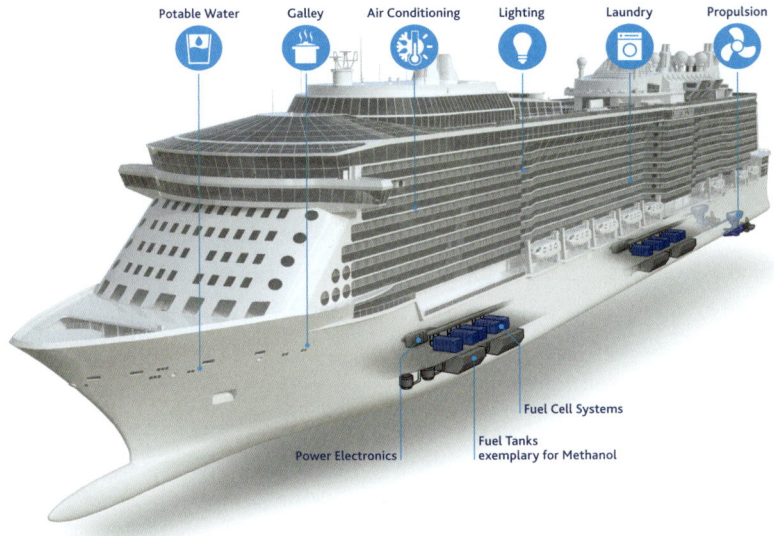

Fig. 131 Use of a methanol-powered fuel cell system on oceangoing vessels

For the first time, RINA confirmed that a methanol fuel cell system met all the relevant maritime standards and regulations. A first Freudenberg fuel cell system has already been installed on the AIDAnova cruise ship.[290] Especially efficient hybrid drive solutions can be produced by combining methanol fuel cell systems and the maritime battery systems of Freudenberg e-Power Systems. "In this context, the use of climate-neutral methanol represents a turning point on the road to maritime sustainability and the achievement of IMO [International Maritime Organization] emission reduction targets"[291]: Compared with the reference year 2008, the carbon dioxide emissions of international shipping are to be reduced by 40 percent by 2030 and 70 percent by 2050.[292]

To use methanol for powering ships, Freudenberg e-Power Systems has developed an innovative approach. This technology generates hydrogen via steam reforming. The hydrogen then reacts with oxygen from the air in the fuel cell. The heat required for the reformer can be taken from the waste heat of the fuel cells. This creates an energy cycle for low-emission ship propulsion systems.[293]

Furthermore, Freudenberg and ZF Friedrichshafen AG entered into a long-term strategic agreement in 2022. The objective is "the development of a hybrid fuel cell/battery drive system for trucks and coaches that is sustainable and emission-free."[294] Long-term trials of the new hybrid drive system are currently in progress on stationary test rigs. The first prototypes are expected to take to the roads by the beginning of 2025, with series production to start by the end of 2026. These efforts will supplement and expand the HyFleet project launched in 2021.[295]

Initially, the main focus will be on truck and bus applications. Later, the cooperation can be extended to "rail and special vehicle systems – such as construction and agricultural vehicles – as well as to marine applications." As in the case of marine propulsion systems, the focus of development is on a long service life and high efficiency for individual components and subsystems. "With its fuel cell system, Freudenberg e-Power Systems relies on a modular approach that can accommodate different performance categories depending on customer and application requirements while also offering simple vehicle integration (plug&play)." For heavy-duty applications, fuel cell systems needed to be redesigned, as most of the systems available on the market were originally developed for use in passenger cars. "For heavy-duty applications, however, all aspects of the system must be designed for a long service life and the highest possible system efficiency. While passenger cars run for about 8,000 hours during the vehicle lifetime, trucks spend at least 35,000 hours on the road. In addition, it is particularly important to achieve the highest possible overall system efficiency – at nominal load and taking into account the energy requirement of the components, Freudenberg's fuel cell experts are striving for an overall efficiency of an industry-leading 50 percent. After all, high efficiency of the entire powertrain leads to less fuel consumption, which in turn reduces the Total Cost of Ownership."[296]

In heavy-duty applications, customers benefit from sustainable, emission-free solutions that remain highly economical over their entire lifetime.[297]

By concentrating on fuel cell drive systems for heavy trucks and ships, Freudenberg and its FEPS Business Group are aligning themselves with the changing requirements of the mobility sector.

Demographic change – a great opportunity for Freudenberg

Birth rates in almost all industrialized countries have been decreasing – in some cases quite significantly – since the 1960s, while life expectancy has continued to increase as the standard of living improves. At the same time, the decline in the population – also in some cases quite significant – has encouraged a willingness to support immigration in these countries.

An aging population is a universal trend that, while it differs tremendously from world region to world region, nevertheless impacts all societies and their social systems. The statistics in Germany speak for themselves: "While only 15 percent of the population was aged 65 or older in 1990, this figure had already risen to 22 percent in 2020, and is expected to come in at just short of 30 percent in 2040. As a result, the share of the elderly population in German society is set to double within the space of just five decades." Politicians are discussing further pension reforms, minimum pensions and life benefits. "Similarly, an aging population presents a challenge to the health system and care services. The shortage of care workers is an issue that had already been raised by those concerned prior to the corona pandemic, and it is an issue that will worsen going forward."

Moreover, population growth in many world regions has weakened significantly. While immigration has mitigated this phenomenon in Germany, not all regions have benefited. And, in the short term at least, immigration cannot compensate for the obvious shortage of skilled workers also faced by Freudenberg on the German labor market.[298]

The demographic trend towards an aging society will bring further growth in the market for medical products. Freudenberg has been systematically developing this market since 2004 through acquisitions and the expansion of traditional applications (wound care and filters).[299] Independent of demographic development, there is growing global demand for hygiene and convenience products. This is a trend that had already led to expansion of the Household Products Business Area outside Europe. Moreover, digitalization was already making inroads into the household product lines with the development of smart household appliances such as the Vileda cleaning robots that use algorithms to navigate round the home. These products derive from the company's evolution prior to the systematic development of a medical products division from 2004.

The Nonwovens Business Area, for example, already touched on medical applications in the 1950s and 1960s through the development of microfilters and wound dressings.[300] In 1985, the various medical applications such as wound pads, nonwovens for adhesive plasters, compresses and backing materials for surgical drapes and gowns were brought together under the Vilmed brand.[301] From these beginnings Freudenberg developed the medical business further as an additional counterweight to the Group's predominant interdependence on the automotive sector. Furthermore, the Seals and Vibration Control Technology Business Area looked into long-term options for acquiring more know-how on liquid silicone products in light of the fact that above-average growth of up to 10 percent had been forecast for this as yet modest niche market up to the end of the century.[302] Initially, the direct application of this technology in the health sector was only of secondary importance; the decisive factor for Freudenberg was the gains in material and tooling competence. The phased acquisition of Lederer GmbH, a company headquartered in Öhringen near Heilbronn, began in 2002; the company was the ideal fit for Freudenberg's entry into this future technology.[303]

The Management Board took the view that the regional focus for setting up the medical division was first and foremost North America, where business activities were in urgent need of diversification. Given the enormous significance of the market for medical products in the United States, FNGP was tasked with building this business as an alternative to the automotive sector.[304]

With annual growth forecasts for the global medical technology market averaging 7.5 percent,[305] FNGP therefore concentrated on expanding business in this area, taking the first steps on this road with the acquisition of Jenline Industries in 2004. This American company, founded in 1989, manufactured liquid elastomers, in particular medical silicone rubber products.[306] In October 2006, this was followed by the acquisition of Helix Medical LLC based in Carpinteria, California, that later became the core of the medical business. Launched as a start-up in 1984, Helix Medical had grown into a leading supplier of silicone products for surgical applications.[307] With the Helix product portfolio of precision-molded components, implants, catheter and tubing applications for cardiology, endoscopy, dental medicine and diagnostic applications, Freudenberg decided to take the courageous step of entering the highly regulated medical technology business. The products, such as implants, had to be produced in cleanrooms and many of them were required to perform very complex tasks. Gastric bands reduce the gastric volume of obese patients, and laryngeal prostheses inserted following a laryngectomy enable patients to swallow and breathe while preserving natural sounding speech. In medical ophthalmology, Helix Medical's silicone punctal plugs are tiny devices that can be inserted into tear ducts.

With Jenline and Helix, FNGP climbed into second place in the modest market for silicone components.[308] With the approval of the Management Board, FNGP set up an independent medical division in California in early 2008. To move forward with developing business in medical technology applications, the next steps in strategic planning targeted the attractive market for advanced thermoplastic elements.[309] Freudenberg built up this material competence by acquiring Anura Plastic Engineering Corporation (APEC), headquartered in Baldwin Park, California, in 2008. At the time of the acquisition, APEC's thermoplastic portfolio did not include ready-for-use devices, but rather focused primarily on components for medical systems and were often disposable products.[310]

In 2007, Freudenberg New Technologies KG (FNT) began research into medical nonwoven fabrics to produce biological, bioresorbable materials for use

Fig. 132 Extrusion of tubing for medical applications at Freudenberg Medical in Kaiserslautern, Germany, 2019

in wound care and surgery. Under cleanroom conditions and using a specially developed rotary spinning process, researchers successfully manufactured these bioresorbable nonwovens that can also incorporate drugs such as antibiotics or enzymes. As the fabric is absorbed by the body, the drugs are released and delivered precisely where they are needed. Named "scaffolene", this special technology was brought to market maturity by 2011. The business was sold in 2020.[311]

The three companies acquired in the medical division – Jenline, Helix and Anura – initially only generated 3 percent[312] of the Freudenberg Group's total sales in 2008, but from the outset the buy-and-build strategy for the medical division had a long-term orientation: Acquiring the specialist materials and medical know-how took time, as did putting together a sales team. In agreement with FNGP, the name of Helix was to form the anchor brand for the medical technology market.[313]

Helix Medical Europe KG was established in July 2009 to develop the European market; one year later, the new company commenced production of silicone seal rings in Kaiserslautern, having first commissioned an injection molding line and a cleanroom. Via the European subsidiary, Freudenberg acquired one-half of the shares in VistaMed Ltd., a company based in Carrick-on-Shannon, Ireland, and set up in 1997, in April 2010. VistaMed had a workforce of 85 at two manufacturing locations in Ireland and produced complex tubing systems and precision components for medical devices under cleanroom conditions. Applications included components used in endoscopy and catheters for minimally invasive surgery.[314] Freudenberg increased its stake in the catheter specialist to 90 percent in 2017.[315]

At that time, seals were an issue in the pharmaceutical industry: Ordinary black seals, whose color was attributable to their carbon black filler, were not suitable for many applications. Transparent silicone was an option for some areas of the pharmaceutical industry, but it cannot be sterilized because it disintegrates at temperatures above 120 degrees Celsius. In 2010, Freudenberg Seals and Vibration Control Technology achieved a breakthrough in meeting the long-cherished dream of the pharmaceutical industry for white EPDM seals. In terms of efficiency, these seals perform as well as their carbon black counterparts and they also meet all the hygiene criteria of customers in the pharmaceutical industry and medical technology sector.[316]

Systematic and strategic development was called for to cater to the growing significance of this market segment, as documented by the new production areas described above. To plan further steps in the medical sector, the Management Board therefore tasked FNT with a systematic analysis of the Group's opportunities in this new business area and a review of the potential. A project team was formed in collaboration with Heinz Nixdorf Institut of Paderborn University. The team was made up of representatives from the university, FNT, Simrit, Research Services and Nonwovens. The final report, entitled "Opportu-

Fig. 133 Stress test of a catheter shaft at Freudenberg Medical in Carrick-on-Shannon, Ireland, 2023

nities for Freudenberg in Medical Technology," was presented in 2010. With reference to Freudenberg's positioning and the strategic thrust, the report says that "Freudenberg should position itself vis-à-vis the key players in the medical technology sector as the technology specialist with proven problem-solving competence as a component supplier."[317]

Outlining the consequences for the orientation of the Group as a whole, the project team wrote: "Given that Freudenberg currently focuses on supplying companies in the automotive technology and mechanical and plant engineering sectors, it will moreover be necessary to build up expertise in the field of those materials used in medical technology. This includes biodegradable and bioresorbable materials. Surface technology is also a relevant area – expertise in microbiological and chemical analysis must also be developed. Furthermore, deep functional integration with regard to medical technology is required. Examples in this context include sensors for consumables and auxiliaries as well as with reference to implants and prostheses. Know-how in the field of sensor technology is therefore indispensable."[318]

Apart from these long-term requirements, the team also searched for new conceptual fields and relevant technologies for Freudenberg's future engagement in the medical device sector. The project team's 250-page report outlines several areas of action to be borne in mind by the Business Groups. The preliminary conclusion was "that the greatest opportunities for Freudenberg are to be found in the product groups of catheters, cannulas, etc., as well as in wound care and filtration. These opportunities could be realized by building up and expanding expertise in the Business Areas of Freudenberg Sealing and Vibration Control Technology, respectively Helix Medical and Freudenberg Nonwovens."[319]

Based on this study, Freudenberg New Technologies drafted a strategy to establish Freudenberg in the field of regenerative medicine. The goal was for the Group to make a name for itself among medical device manufacturers as a development and production partner for bioresorbable or biocompatible polymer-based products. Furthermore, this goal should be borne in mind when considering future acquisitions.[320]

It was not long before the portfolio was expanded in this direction. The acquisition in 2012 of the American company MedVenture Technology Corporation headquartered in Jeffersonville, Indiana, expanded know-how for technological solutions in minimally invasive surgery. In the following year, Helix Medical acquired a 50 percent stake in Cambus Teoranta based in Galway, Ireland, adding this company's high-quality precision catheter elements and systems to the specialty portfolio offered by the VistaMed Ltd. joint venture.[321]

Freudenberg acquired a total of 94.9 percent of the shares in Cambus Teoranta in the period to March 2022.[322]

The Helix Medical Business Group was renamed Freudenberg Medical under the Group's 2015 global brand strategy. This measure was also designed to support positioning as a global technology partner for the medical and pharmaceutical industry. The buy-and-build strategy to expand this business continued: 2015 was also the year when Freudenberg Medical acquired 75 percent of Hemoteq AG based in Würselen, Germany. This company developed interesting combination products such as drug-eluting stents – tiny devices coated with drugs used to keep arteries open – or balloon catheters also available with drug coatings.[323] These products are used, for example, in voice prostheses. Just three years later, the stake in Hemoteq was increased to 87.5 percent.[324]

Freudenberg Medical's global headquarters in the USA relocated from Gloucester to Beverly, Massachusetts, in November 2018. Some of the manufacturing capabilities, housed in buildings with a total floor space of 3,500 square meters, were also moved to Beverly. The factory began operating in the second half of 2019.

It is not only the elderly who benefit from avoiding serious surgical risks through the use of less risky minimally invasive techniques. Heart diseases that would once have required the use of heart-lung machines can now be treated by specialists on an outpatient basis using local anesthetic. They do this by inserting a small catheter into an artery in the patient's groin and then guiding it through the blood vessels to the part of the patient's body where treatment is required. Irregular heart rhythm (atrial fibrillation), for example, can be treated using electrode catheters to ablate (cauterize) certain points on the inner wall of the heart. After two years of development, Freudenberg launched the Composer Steerable Introducer used to control various types of catheters in 2019. This patented catheter handle technology opens up numerous new avenues for diagnostic tests, therapeutic procedures and positioning heart implants. "Compared with existing products, this design is unique because it can be easily

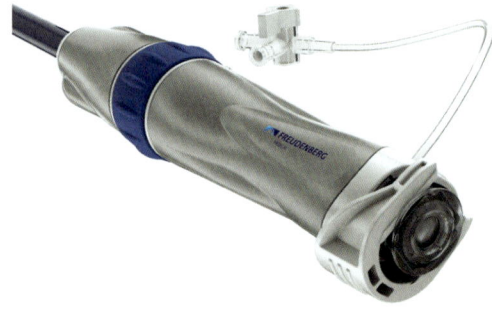

Fig. 134 Using the Composer Steerable Introducer, various types of catheter tubing can be controlled precisely during minimally invasive operations

adapted to suit different catheter architectures and sizes", is how the Jeffersonville site described the handle's distinctive features.[325]

Know-how about skin-friendly silicone mixtures brought Freudenberg Medical into contact with the Eindhoven-based start-up company Bambi Medical, established in 2016. Its founder, pediatrician Sidarto Bambang Oetomo, was working on systems to monitor the vital signs of newborn babies, especially preterm babies. Monitoring these signs is important because the organ systems of premature babies are often not sufficiently developed and mature. As a result, these babies spend an average of 42 days under medical supervision in intensive care units. The monitoring cables and separation from the mother make this a stressful experience. The start-up's founder designed a wireless, skin-friendly monitoring belt that records the vital functions and transmits them to a mobile device. Freudenberg Medical's materials expertise and medical technology process and production knowledge helped design the belt. The Bambi Belt allows the parents of preterm babies to take their children out of the incubator and bond with them through intense skin-to-skin contact. Prototypes were successfully tested under two studies at Dutch hospitals. The next step was certification, which was completed in May 2023. This was followed by the start of (pre-) series production for five hospitals.[326]

Sales figures for the 2022 financial year highlight the success of the medical business – across all Business Groups – in the challenging environment of differing healthcare systems around the world. At over 500 million euros, the share of medical and pharmaceutical products in Group sales has already climbed to 4.3 percent. The wisdom of establishing the medical business as part of the strategy, and therefore of Freudenberg's overall positioning, was also obvious during Covid. Many medical facilities postponed medical procedures during the Covid-19 pandemic. As a result, production in the medical technology sector, normally immune to economic developments, dipped. The decrease was 3 percent in Germany, 11 percent in Japan, and 9 percent in the USA. In contrast, China recorded an increase of 5 percent. At Freudenberg Medical, this triggered a downturn in sales of medical technology products that was particularly noticeable in the second and third quarters of 2020. On the other hand, though, sales of Covid-19-related products such as diagnostic consumables rose significantly, clearly offsetting the Business Group's sales losses due to the lower number of medical procedures. Overall, sales by Freudenberg Medical grew almost 10 percent in 2020. In the two years that followed, the Business Group also benefited as the level of medical procedures gradually returned to normal and demand for Freudenberg's medical products rebounded. Freudenberg Medical sales followed this trend, with an increase of some 23 percent to 232 million in 2021 and a further rise of 41 percent to some 328 million euros in the following year.[327]

Household Products, demographic change and globalization

Demographic change, changes in society, and even shifts in consumer behavior such as the trend towards convenience products for cleaning, have always had a direct impact on the Freudenberg Household Products (FHP) Business Group. The Business Group's response can be traced back to the mid-1990s, both in terms of geographic expansion of business and with regard to product innovations, extending as far as cleaning robots. At that time, geographic expansion to Eastern Europe, South America and Asia was already well underway, and Household Products set out to make further progress: Sales companies began operating in Hungary, the Czech Republic and Slovenia in 1997. In South America, the Business Group already generated additional sales of 15 million DM with new companies in Argentina, Chile and Mexico in 1996. A new sales company in Brazil was founded in April 1997. And lastly, a sales company was established in Hong Kong in 1996.[328]

As business became more international, one important market – the United States – was missing until 1998. The Management Board had already discussed the possibility of entering the North American market for household products back in 1993. Initially, this was to be realized together with American partners because the Management Board agreed that "we can't start from scratch with Vileda in the USA." Discussions on setting up a joint venture with the household products manufacturer O'Cedar commenced.[329] Talks progressed to the stage where the specifics of an acquisition were on the table, but broke down in March 1996 due to the excessive price expectations of O'Cedar's owners.[330]

This was followed by discussions between Freudenberg and M. B. Walton of River Grove (Illinois), that reached a conclusion at the end of 1997. Freudenberg acquired Walton's floor cleaning equipment business at the beginning of 1998 and integrated this business into the newly-founded Freudenberg Household Products LP. Needless to say, the new company was also tasked with convincing US consumers of the benefits of Vileda products.[331]

However, success in the North American business did not come automatically. On the contrary: This business needed significant promotional support. Responsibility for Household Products on the Management Board had meantime changed hands: Norbert Dahlström retired in 2000 and was succeeded by Albert W. Pürzer. Pürzer, who was a member of the Management Board from 2000 to 2008, also held responsibility for the Nonwovens Business Group, Politex and – at a later stage – Chemical Specialities. Under his leadership, a nationwide TV campaign was launched in the United States in March 2002 to

Fig. 135–136 Historic advertisements for O'Cedar household products, about 1920

gradually raise awareness of the Vileda brand to the level the brand had already achieved in Europe.[332] Despite these marketing efforts, sales development in the United States remained disappointing.[333] In parallel, the takeover of O'Cedar again came up for discussion to help accelerate expansion of American business. The American company, however, had become a case for restructuring and, as a result, takeover talks were temporarily shelved.[334]

This changed in the following year. Another major TV advertising campaign was launched in 2003 to expand Vileda business in the United States. But the campaign was ill-fated because the prices for TV spots had risen by 30 percent. To make matters worse, many viewers were following reports on the war in Iraq and had switched from the family channels where the Vileda spots were booked to news stations, thus diluting any broad-ranging impact of the ads. However, the biggest obstacle to expanding Vileda business was a very aggressive campaign by competitors Procter & Gamble, Clorox and S. C. Johnson in the market for ready-to-use systems. The competition not only invested some 100 million dollars in TV campaigns, but also massively restricted the opportunities for Vileda product placements in retail business through their "aggressive promotional activities". Given its competitors' high marketing expenditure that was way beyond Freudenberg's advertising budget, Vileda focused on expanding the distribution of household products through existing business channels.[335] In this situation, taking over O'Cedar brands provided an opportunity to expand business in North America swiftly and on a broad scale. Founded in Chicago/Illinois in 1906, O'Cedar initially sold wax and oil goods, later adding mechanical household cleaning products to its portfolio. Freudenberg grasped the opportunity when the company, now registered in Springfield/Ohio, filed for bankruptcy in August 2003. O'Cedar was integrated into Freudenberg Household Products LP in Northlake/Illinois, USA.[336] Freudenberg was finally able to significantly expand its distribution and market position in the United States through the O'Cedar takeover. The fact that O'Cedar was listed with Walmart, America's largest supermarket chain, was crucial. FHP management estimated that creating a comparable business volume through its own efforts would have taken at least five years. In December 2003, management expected sales in North America to double as a result of the O'Cedar deal.[337]

They were proved right as early as 2004: With sales in excess of 100 million dollars, business in the United States had in fact more than doubled. And Freudenberg had become the market leader in the USA for classic handle mops for floor cleaning.[338]

North America was not the only white spot on the Freudenberg Household Products' map that the Business Group had set its sights on conquering. While business was being built up in America, the company had already turned its attention to expansion in Australia in 1998, setting up its own sales company there in the same year to develop the market for Vileda and Wettex articles. At the same time, business in China saw low-level positive development; Freudenberg Household Products (Suzhou) was established in Suzhou and commenced assembling Vileda products for the Chinese market at the turn of the year.[339]

In 2006, a production joint venture began operating in Jordan to supply the Middle East. The major step to expand on the Indian growth market was taken three years later, in 2009, when the Freudenberg Gala Household Products joint venture with Indian partner Gala Brush Limited was established. At that time the family-owned company had already been in existence for 50 years and was being run by the third generation of family members. Freudenberg acquired a 60 percent stake in the new Freudenberg Gala Household Products Pvt. Limited joint venture headquartered in Mumbai.[340]

And Freudenberg Household Products continued to expand: The operative business of Trade & Investment in Asia Limited (TIA) was taken over in 2011. The acquisition added the second-largest manufacturing facility for mechanical cleaning equipment in China, additional established sales companies in Thailand, Malaysia, Indonesia and Taiwan, the Swash brand, and some 20 million euros in sales to the Business Group's portfolio. In Australia, Freudenberg signed an agreement to acquire E. D. Oates Pty Ltd. in 2017. Oates was Australia's market leader in the professional cleaning business and had a broad range of household and cleaning products in the consumer sector. The transaction expanded the Business Group's presence in the Asia-Pacific market. To reflect this global presence, Freudenberg Haushaltsprodukte SE & Co. KG was renamed Freudenberg Home and Cleaning Solutions GmbH in 2013.[341]

This international expansion was accompanied by further additions to Freudenberg's product portfolio. The first step focused on mechanical laundry care, for example ironing boards and clothes driers. Entry into the laundry care market began in Germany in 2003 through a strategic partnership with Hailo, a company based in Haiger. Freudenberg took over the production and marketing of Hailo ironing boards and ironing board covers, clothes driers and laundry sorters, as well as ironing board accessories. One year later, Vileda launched its own laundry care range.[342] In 2016, Freudenberg Home and Cleaning Solutions successfully acquired Gimi S. p. A. registered in Monselice, Italy. Gimi was already the market leader in Italy for laundry care, and in particular ironing boards and clothes driers.[343]

In a second step, Freudenberg significantly expanded its household gloves business, especially at international level. 2014 marked the beginning of this process, with the acquisition of the Marigold business from the Australian-based Ansell Group. Marigold was already the market leader for household gloves in England and Ireland, and also operated in Italy, the Netherlands, Hong Kong and Japan.[344] Three years later, the next coup came in North America, with the acquisition of Playtex, the market leader for household gloves in the United States. The company had successfully established its Living and Handsaver brands on the market over a period of more than 65 years.[345]

In-house innovations of course also featured in the expansion of the product range. The impact of demographic change was one focal point of research and development work. Innovations in the traditional floor cleaning segment increasingly focused on making housework easier. The Ultramat, a flat mop system with patented wringing mechanism, was successfully launched worldwide in 2004. A further development of this design is the Ultramax, with an electric wringing system developed in cooperation with Kärcher and featuring a bucket with an electrically operated wringer.[346]

Further innovations followed in rapid succession: 2007, for example, saw the large-scale launch of cleaning cloths made from an innovative nonwoven called Novolon. Novolon has a three-dimensional structure that absorbs dirt more effectively for easier cleaning. A new industrial-scale production line for Novolon was commissioned at the Augsburg site.[347] The green "Vileda Natural Line" was introduced one year later. These products are manufactured exclusively from renewable or recycled materials and comply with strict sustainability criteria. Furthermore, wringer systems based on bionic principles and more lightweight products were launched in almost all categories – with positive effects in terms of the company's cost efficiency on the one hand, and convenience for customers when doing household chores on the other.[348]

The first cleaning robot was presented in 2011.[349] The innovative dry dusting robot called ViRobi was commercialized one year later. The Vileda Relax robotic vacuum cleaner with an intelligent navigation system followed in 2013.[350]

The Steam mop debuted the following year. It is designed for the hygienic cleaning of all types of floor surfaces using only water and no chemicals. It can kill up to 99.9 percent of bacteria and the microfiber mop pad ensures a thorough steam clean. Thanks to its low weight, the elderly find it easy to use, because the steam can be applied to cleaning floors with only a minimum of effort. The Windomatic, a rechargeable window vacuum cleaner, debuted in 2015.[351]

Business development, however, was not uniformly positive, and the Business Group's presence on several regional markets was reevaluated: Freudenberg exited the Chinese and Korean consumer markets back in 2018. Since then, the company has focused on business with commercial customers in China, while the office in Seoul, Korea, was closed.[352]

A review of Freudenberg's various activities related to demographic development confirms that the entire Group does in fact see this megatrend as an opportunity – in medical technology; for household products where the trend towards convenience also plays a role; or in other areas of the Group. The trend towards digitalization is clearly visible in many product lines, and in many homes today it is already difficult to imagine doing the housework without some help from

Fig. 137 The Vileda Steam mop uses steam instead of chemicals for cleaning

robots. The impact of artificial intelligence will be immense and at the time this book goes to press it is almost impossible to describe this impact in any detail.

International expansion and continuous product development have proved their worth – in the context of an aging population too. Overall, the headcount and sales at Household Products rose from 1,544 employees and 675 million DM (today's equivalent: 344.9 million euros) in 1996 to 3,300 employees and sales of around 1.3 billion euros in 2022. In other words, the workforce has more than doubled, while sales have increased almost fourfold during this period.[353]

Commitment to sustainability for future generations

Reconciling ever-rising raw material prices in the medium and long term on the one hand and dwindling resources on the other presents a major challenge. At the same time, though, it opens up new growth markets for Freudenberg, and the pressure for change this dilemma brings accelerates the pace of the development and acquisition of innovative technologies. Society's ever-growing awareness of environmental issues reflects this. The impact on the environment, particularly with reference to leather production and processing, was always a major concern. This trend, then, is not new, but has gathered increasing momentum since the Club of Rome's report in 1972 and the numerous environmental scandals that hit the headlines. The issue then, as now, was not restricted to individual phenomena, but rather to the consequences of modern industrial life for ecological balances, whereby climate change is a symbolic blanket term to describe changes that are increasingly seen as a threat. Since then, the Kyoto Protocol (1997) and the Paris Climate Agreement (2015) have been key political milestones in the fight against global warming: The voluntary undertakings of many countries to mitigate climate change by reducing CO_2 emissions will shift legislative frameworks in favor of sustainable products. The inevitable consequence is that Freudenberg is impelled to rethink its production processes in the knowledge that resources are limited and drastic reductions in CO_2 emissions are imperative. That is no mean challenge, given that it compels the Group to redesign products to be environmentally compatible with regard to conserving materials and avoiding waste and even to introduce new filter elements for water and air treatment to its portfolio.

Lieselotte Feikes could be considered to be the first environmental officer, taking up this post in 1972: Her successor in 1987 was Ditmar Flothmann. At that time, expenditure on environmental protection averaged an annual 11 million DM.[354] Three years later, a character called "Uli Umwelt" (an English approximation would be "Eric Environment") became Freudenberg's first environmental symbol.³⁵⁵ Symbolism aside, it is the content of this decision that is most relevant. The Management Board was clearly stating that environmental protection ranked equally with market position, profitability and social justice as a corporate goal. Every employee was called on to be vigilant in avoiding waste.³⁵⁶ The Group's maxim was: "Avoidance is better than recovery – recovery is better than disposal." This was factored into investment planning in the following five years, with a swift rise in expenditure on environmental protection – initially to 80 million DM.³⁵⁷

Fig. 138 Freudenberg's environmental symbol in the 1990s: Uli Umwelt ("Umwelt" is the German word for "environment")

In 1992, Freudenberg was an early signatory to the "Business Charter for Sustainable Development" of the International Chamber of Commerce.³⁵⁸ The Group's first Health, Safety and Environment Guideline was approved in 1993.³⁵⁹ Furthermore, from 1996, the Health, Safety and Environment Corporate Function coordinated and steered occupational health and safety and environmental protection throughout the entire Group, as part of the Focus organization.³⁶⁰ In the same year, the Management Board approved the concept for environmental management systems pursuant to ISO 14001 that was to be applied Group-wide. Under this concept, all Freudenberg sites worldwide are certified under an audit process according to this ISO standard. This ensures that all Freudenberg sites operate in compliance with the Group's environmental protection principles and guidelines.³⁶¹ The first manual on health, safety and environmental protection with binding rules for the entire Freudenberg Group was published in 1998.³⁶²

As a result of these developments, the customer offering became increasingly focused on the concept of sustainability and environmental protection – as is still the case today. Freudenberg joined forces with a firm called Politex to establish a company manufacturing polyester nonwovens. Based in Italy, this company took an ecological approach to the manufacturing process, using recycled PET bottles as the raw material.³⁶³ Politex had been using this technology since 1989 and its factories in Italy, the United States and Poland specialized in the production of roof membranes. Today, these nonwoven insulation products made from recycled material are still used all over the world to insulate houses and reduce energy consumption. For the Politex founder and owner who could not find a successor among his own relations, support from family-owned Freudenberg was the preferred option, and indeed paved the way for the complete takeover of Politex in 2004.[364] Since then, the factories in Italy and France have been turning shredded PET bottles into polyester fibers for Freudenberg. Describing the ecological effect of this business, Tilman Krauch, Chief Technology Officer and a member of the Management Board since 2014, said in 2020: "To us, PET bottles are not waste: By recycling five billion plastic bottles each year, we save 155 kilotons of CO_2."[365]

The polyester fibers provide thermal insulation, they are lightweight, weatherproof and retain their shape, making them well-suited to use in apparel. Freudenberg developed a special thermal insulation for the booming sport and outdoor sector in 2017. The developers at Freudenberg Performance Materials discovered that a combination of binder fibers and fiber balls made an excellent padding. The eco version of "comfortemp Fiberball Padding" is made of 100 percent recycled fiber balls.[366]

In the interlinings segment, Freudenberg kept in step with the global shifts and changes in the apparel industry at the end of the 1990s, adding woven and knitted interlinings to the portfolio. To that end, Freudenberg acquired the Italian company Marelli & Berta in 1998. One year earlier, a joint venture had been formed to distribute Italian-made woven and knitted interlinings worldwide.[367]

The global expansion of the nonwovens business also put the spotlight back on Japan Vilene Company, a listed joint venture. Freudenberg had just become the largest shareholder with a stake of 25.1 percent when Japan Vilene Company's sales fell sharply as a result of the financial crisis.[368] Sales and profitability continued to underperform in the years that

Fig. 139 "Comfortemp Fiberball Padding" - the padding made from fiber balls provides especially lightweight, breathable thermal insulation for sport and outdoor clothing

followed, and the Management Board pursued the notion of making a friendly approach to acquiring the majority shareholding in Japan Vilene Company. The objective was to be in a position to exert direct influence on the Japanese management in order to speed up the global expansion of the nonwovens business while driving forward the Group's own filter and nonwoven activities in the Asia-Pacific region. In 2015, the shareholders accepted Freudenberg's takeover offer. Freudenberg acquired 75 percent of the shares; the founding partner, Toray Industries Inc., retained a 25 percent stake in the joint venture. Integration of Japan Vilene Company into the Freudenberg Group as a new independent Business Group began one year later. This process called for a degree of cultural sensitivity and tact, as there were plenty of cautionary examples from other sectors warning of the dangers involved in transitioning a Japanese company to European-German management structures. Freudenberg handled this difficult task with aplomb, not least thanks to decades-long experience of cooperating with Japanese partners. Since then, Japan Vilene Company has been an important pillar in the Technical Textiles and Filtration Business Area and supports the further development of e-mobility through its long-standing experience in the field of battery separators.[369] Japan Vilene Company's portfolio was extended in 2018 with the acquisition of Hanns Glass GmbH registered in Grafing near Munich, another family-owned company. Its floor mats, floor trims and luggage compartment trims for the automotive industry bring significant weight savings and thus help reduce energy consumption.[370]

To expand its own nonwovens know-how, Freudenberg set its sights on acquiring London-based Low & Bonar PLC, a listed heavyweight with a workforce of 1,900, production facilities in Europe, Asia and North America, and sales in excess of 390 million euros. With its multi-stage production process, Low & Bonar was to expand Freudenberg's competence in spunlaid nonwovens and open up new fields for Freudenberg with its proprietary technological applications.[371] The takeover was approved by the shareholders in November 2019 and authorized by the European Commission the following April.[372] Low & Bonar and the Filc Group, the other new acquisition, accounted for roughly one-third of sales by the Freudenberg Performance Materials Business Group in the 2021 financial year.[373]

Technically mature nonwovens for filter media are extremely important in terms of the sustainable management of our natural resources such as clean air and water. Patented materials with the corresponding filtration properties were developed by Freudenberg using microfilaments such as Evolon.[374] The Filtration Technologies Business Group has come a long way from its origins of solely producing filter mats, and now manufactures complete systems such as cas-

Fig. 140 Aquabio filter system for wastewater treatment, 2014

sette, pocket or HEPA filters, all tailored to customers' individual wishes. The spectrum ranges from mass-produced products such as MicronAir cabin air filters, to be found in two out of every three automobiles throughout the world, to special filter solutions for heavy industry. Viledon filter bags remove dust from heavily loaded systems in steelworks or foundries; apart from keeping the air clean, they also improve energy efficiency.[375] In addition to air filtration, progress has also been made in gas phase filtration. Solvent vapors or fuel vapors are avoidable risks to health. Ventilation systems at data centers must filter contaminant gases to prevent corrosion and the loss of data caused by corrosion damage.[376]

From an ecological perspective, the acquisition of the relatively small company called Aquabio Ltd. in 2013 was a visionary move. Established in 1997, Aquabio made a name for itself in the fast-growing market for industrial water filtration as a leading provider of water treatment and waste water filtration systems. Based in Hallow, England, the team develops and plans multi-stage membrane filtration plants that can purify up to 70 percent of waste water to drinking water quality. This enables industry to comply with environmental protection requirements and conserve water, a resource that is essential to life. In 2016, cooperation in the generally risk-averse food industry was particularly successful. The Aquabio system installed at a producer of ready meals enabled more than 80 percent of the water used to be returned to the factory for food production, in the canteen and as drinking water.[377]

Demand for filter solutions has also risen in Chinese industrialized society in recent decades, primarily as a result of more stringent regulations and increased environmental awareness. In December 2018, Freudenberg submitted an offer to purchase the majority shareholding in Apollo Air-cleaner Co. Ltd., registered in Shunde, Guangdong Province, in order to tap into the significant growth potential of this market. The provider of high-quality air and water filtration solutions with a headcount of some 1,000 and sales of 96 million euros was only established in July 2000.[378] The former sole proprietor, Apollo Trading Group from Japan, continued to hold 25 percent of the joint venture alongside the majority shareholder, Freudenberg. The takeover brings mutual benefits for Apollo and Freudenberg, in both production and research as well as market coverage. Chinese customers can now also benefit from Freudenberg's filtration technology with its high environmental standards.[379]

Sustainability in the chemical sector

Freudenberg's chemical sector is also committed to sustainability. Knowledge of lubricants and friction between two interacting surfaces is part of the science known as "tribology." This discipline is named after the ancient Greek word for "rub and wear." Tribology has a positive effect on energy and resource consumption through the reduction of friction. For example, in large factory halls, the durable, customized lubricants produced by Klüber help save energy and reduce CO_2 emissions.[380]

In February 2004, the entire chemical sector of Freudenberg was restructured when the Klüber Group was joined by the newly acquired companies OKS and Chem-Trend. This development called for organizational and management changes that led to the establishment of the Freudenberg Chemical Specialities (FCS) Business Group.[381] Hanno D. Wentzler, a member of the Freudenberg family and a long-standing managing director of Klüber Lubrication, was appointed as CEO of the new Business Group.[382] Klüber had already acquired all the shares in OKS GmbH of Munich, a producer of high-performance lubricants, in 2003. With its sales channels via industrial distributors and oil dealers, OKS ideally complemented Klüber's own direct sales organization. Furthermore, OKS had an outstanding position on the Indian market, which made the small company with sales of 9.1 million euros particularly attractive.[383]

Through the acquisition of the American Chem-Trend Group in 2004, Freudenberg entered the chemical release agent market. These products prevent "stickers" and are used in molding and mold release processes, for example, for releasing the rubber compounds of car tires from their molds. At the time of the acquisition, Chem-Trend, with headquarters in Howell, Michigan, had 400 employees and was the world's leading producer of special release agents for rubber, plastic and polyurethane molded parts and for high-pressure metal injection molding.[384]

Thanks to the newly acquired companies, Freudenberg Chemical Specialities initially had three companies forming solid pillars (Klüber, OKS, Chem-Trend). However, the strategic development of this Business Group was far from being completed. Under the project name of Urania, led by Wentzler, Freudenberg Chemical Specialities investigated further opportunities for expanding its portfolio.[385] Over the course of the five-year project, certain segments such as water chemicals and plastics additives were considered and rejected; of the 128 companies assessed, only a few proved to be viable options.[386] The conclusion stated in the application to the Board of Partners submitted in June 2010 was: "As a result of in-depth analyses and discussions with industry experts, FCS has identified 'special chemicals for surface technology' as a target market." The candidate selected for acquisition was SurTec International, a company established in 1993 and located in Zwingenberg, not far from Freudenberg's headquarters in Weinheim. In the long term, Freudenberg Chemical Specialities intended to offer the closely related functions of "separation, protection and lubrication" from a single source.[387]

The buy and build strategy pursued in this case is a good example of Freudenberg's prudent approach to the development of new business areas: "In order to reduce risks, it is proposed to acquire a relatively small but highly specialized group of companies, thus forming a 'platform' for further acquisitions. This will allow FCS to develop and prepare its internal management structures as well as familiarizing itself with market mechanisms and taking a look at market players. Following the integration of this group of companies, it is planned to implement 'build' acquisitions of smaller, technologically leading market players to round off the product portfolio and to reinforce our global presence. In the medium term, the business area of surface treatment is to be built up to a sales figure of between 180 million and 220 million euros."[388]

Surface treatment technology from SurTec was to be the key to a new market segment. The company produced chemical specialities for surface pre-treatment, cleaning and finishing. Freudenberg was especially interested in the company's experience in electroplating, i.e., know-how in processes for the application of metallic coatings to components.[389] An impressive example of environmentally compatible, sustainable development is the technology developed by SurTec allowing the use of trivalent chromium (chromium (III)) to replace hexavalent chromium (chromium (VI)), a toxic, carcinogenic material that had been used for many years for electroplating zinc and aluminum surfaces.[390] At the time of the acquisition, the SurTec Group had a workforce of about 460 people and operated companies in 25 countries on all five continents.[391]

Once again, Freudenberg's next acquisition opened the door on an entirely new market segment of chemical specialities. Capol, a company acquired in 2013, has a portfolio of release agents, glazes and sealing agents that ensure that confectionery products do not stick or absorb moisture. The products are shipped to about 50 countries from three locations in Germany, the UK and the USA and prevent chocolate drops from melting or jelly babies from sticking together. Hanno D. Wentzler gave the following reason for the strategic decision in favor of Capol: "Additives for the food industry are an attractive market segment in the long term. Capol fits in very well with Freudenberg Chemical Specialities. Our business models match each other well. […] Finally, it makes sense for us to enter this market in terms of the diversification of risks."[392]

Freudenberg Chemical Specialities therefore has four independent pillars: Lubricants, release agents, surface treatment and additives for the food industry. All Freudenberg chemical companies in Germany and other countries are called upon to minimize their environmental footprint.

Sustainable solutions for the oil and gas industry

Despite all the efforts being made in connection with the energy transition, fossil fuels will remain indispensable over the next few decades. Increasingly, oil and gas production is being developed in areas which had previously been considered to be non-viable. Production calls for capital-intensive machinery and equipment, in order to meet increasingly stringent safety and environmental standards too. These developments offer a variety of opportunities for Freudenberg's innovative, high-quality sealing technology – especially in the oil and gas industry. Freudenberg's entry into this business area dates back to deliberations made in 2001 when the mechanical seals business was to be expanded by the acquisition of Burgmann.[393] In 2000, Freudenberg had already entered into a 50:50 joint venture with Burgmann via Merkel Freudenberg Fluidtechnik – for cooperation in the field of packing seals. The portfolio was now to be expanded to include mechanical seals, i. e., seals for turbines or pumps which could be operated at high pressures and temperatures as well as with contaminated fluids. Mechanical seals for many applications are produced from high-strength steels and both production and fine machining call for considerable know-how. Between 1966 and 1971, Freudenberg had already taken its first steps into this product area, but these efforts, connected with the acquisition of the Johann Schmengler GmbH mechanical seal plant, had failed in the marketplace.[394] In 1972, when the plant near Hanover closed down, Freudenberg initially discontinued production of steel mechanical seals. However, a small production line for the automotive and domestic appliance industries remained in operation in Schwalmstadt, producing seals under the brand name Simrax.[395]

For Freudenberg's second attempt to assert itself against established competitors, the Management Board relied on the long-term experience of its Japanese partners. NOK had been producing mechanical seals since 1956[396] and Freudenberg already marketed cast steel counter seal rings produced by NOK subsidiary Eagle Industry.[397] On the basis of the agreement concluded in 1960, Freudenberg and NOK decided in 1976 to establish a mechanical seal production company in Weinheim which would focus on the European market. The joint venture, in which NOK held a stake of 40 percent, started operations under the established name of Simrax GmbH with Japanese production managers.[398] Simrax received additional technical support under a distribution and consultancy contract with Eagle Industry, which had become the largest manufacturer of mechanical seals in Japan. However, the transfer of Japanese know-how to Germany failed in practice as a result of European standards and the higher demands of German customers who called for mechanical seals developed specially for their applications. For this reason, Simrax recorded losses, was transformed into a sales company[399] and only developed in a positive direction under new management from 1983 onward.[400] In the new Focus organization, Simrax became the European lead center for mechanical seals within Freudenberg Dichtungs- und Schwingungstechnik KG in 1996 and was further strengthened by the acquisition of a Dutch manufacturer of mechanical seals for automobile water pumps. Following the acquisition, sales of mechanical seals reached 44.4 million DM in 1998.[401]

Freudenberg's own mechanical seal business had therefore already been placed on a firm footing when Freudenberg considered a takeover of its former competitor Burgmann in 2001. The company, founded by Feodor Burgmann in Dresden in 1884, impressed specialists at the time with the first mechanically woven self-lubricating stuffing box packings.[402] In the third generation, the family company had to make an entirely new start in West Germany in 1945. Production at the new location in Wolfratshausen grew at a breathtaking pace. In 1997, Burgmann established subsidiaries in the United States, Brazil and Switzerland. The company also held participations in international groups in Scandinavia and Italy from the 1990s onward.[403] However, the future of the group had been rather uncertain since the death of CEO Feodor Burgmann in 1988. In his will, he had placed his heirs, company management and the administrative board under an obligation to safeguard the location and the jobs of the workforce in the long term and to reach solutions by consensus up to 2008.[404] It therefore became very difficult for many competitors and investors to gain a foothold with the company, which was represented throughout the world and operated more than 50 subsidiaries and joint ventures, employing about 3,300 people in 2002. The sales figure of 292 million euros was also attractive.[405]

Nevertheless, only Freudenberg's overtures to Burgmann were successful, leading to an exclusive negotiation and review process. On Freudenberg's side, the company's Japanese partners were also involved in the background, as international expansion in the mechanical seals segment called for the participation of NOK and its affiliate Eagle Industry.[406] Following almost one and a half years of intensive discussions, the parties reached a satisfactory agreement in 2003 and obtained approval from the German antitrust authorities in February 2004. Talking to the press, Burgmann CEO Elmar Baur used a rather romantic metaphor: "The two partners in this dream wedding, Burgmann and Freudenberg, have 120 or, in the case of Freudenberg, 150 years of experience. We are not looking for a fleeting affair but for a long-term relationship. We had several years to get to know each other and we have found that we go together well. [...] I remain convinced that Freudenberg is our dream partner."[407] Freudenberg Management Board member Peter Stehle stated the specific benefits for the partners in a more down-to-earth way: "As a result of the acquisition, we can grow outside the automotive industry and become a supplier for the export-oriented German plant and mechanical engineering industry. Our aim is to become a strong development and service partner for this group of customers with a technologically demanding profile. Outside Germany, we have held a stake in Eagle Industry, Japan's leading mechanical seals supplier, for many years. Burgmann will be developing a strong alliance with Eagle Industry in foreign markets. As globalization continues for our customers, Burgmann will benefit from new opportunities on the Asian and American markets."[408] Furthermore, in 1996, Burgmann was the first German seal manufacturer to have its locations audited and certified in accordance with the EU Eco-Management and Audit Scheme (EMAS) Regulation. In 1999, a further audit of the company's environmental management system was conducted in accordance with EMAS and ISO 14001.[409]

Burgmann's alliance with Eagle Industry (EKK) rapidly took shape. The first global conference of Eagle Industry and Burgmann, attended by the manage-

Fig. 141 Assembly of an EagleBurgmann mechanical seal on a test rig at Eurasburg, Germany, 2022

ment and board members of all affiliates, took place in Niigata, Japan, in April 2005. The topics of the conference were: The integration of various activities, especially in the Asia-Pacific region; the harmonization of sales, production and development; and a joint strategy. These were to lay the foundations for a global sealing technology alliance under the name of Eagle Burgmann Industries (EBI).[410] Initially, one strategic emphasis of EBI was to expand business in North America. With a volume of about 600 million dollars, North America was the largest market for mechanical seals. In this region, EBI's modest market share of 2.5 percent was to be boosted by emphasizing service business for final customers.[411] In connection with this growth strategy, EagleBurgmann succeeded in acquiring the American company Expansion Joint Systems in mid-2009. Expansion Joint Systems was highly successful in producing metal expansion joints for sectors including oil and gas, and petrochemicals. In these sectors of industry, these flexible expansion joints are used for handling highly aggressive media.[412]

Despite a slump in sales in the United States, the EBI Group mastered the financial and economic crisis in 2008 and 2009 relatively well, with sales figures already returning to pre-crisis levels in 2010.[413] In view of the success of cooperation and the close links between subsidiaries, it was only logical that Burgmann should assume the well-known double name of its many joint ventures and the company was renamed EagleBurgmann Germany GmbH & Co KG with effect from January 1, 2010. In 2009, many crossover shareholdings had already allowed Burgmann to participate in Japanese business and Eagle to participate in German business.[414]

The products and services of EagleBurgmann for the oil and gas industry concerned the midstream (transport and storage) and downstream (further processing of crude oil, for example in refineries) segments. In the exploration and production field itself (the upstream segment) on the other hand, there was a need for action. On the basis of its megatrend analyses, this segment had been identified by Freudenberg as a strong growth factor, and Freudenberg intended to grasp this opportunity. Initially, the strategy developed for the upstream segment was based on smaller acquisitions. From 2004 onward, Freudenberg Sealing Technologies and the American FNGP therefore took over appropriate partner companies. The Freudenberg Oil & Gas (FOG) Business Group was created from these companies with effect from January 1, 2011.[415] Christoph Mosmann, Managing Director of EagleBurgmann for many years and Member of the Management Board from 2010 to 2014, was responsible for the development of FOG. He emphasized: "Freudenberg Oil & Gas is not part of the EagleBurgmann partnership and focuses mainly on oil and gas exploration and production (upstream applications). While the two companies share the same success factors in their market segments, their products, customers and applications are different."[416]

While EagleBurgmann reported sales of 815 million euros and had more than 5,800 employees in the 2012 financial year, the new Freudenberg Oil & Gas Business Group, with 350 employees, only recorded sales of 52 million euros in 2012. The two business units broadened their area of activities through acquisitions. EagleBurgmann expanded in the United States through the acquisition of Seal Pots Inc., a manufacturer of supply systems for the oil and gas industry. In 2012, the FOG Business Group made two acquisitions: In August, Scott Matrix Ltd., Newcastle, UK, a company specializing in elastomer seals for the oil and gas sector, and in December, the Norwegian Vector Technology Group, one of the leading manufacturers of seal solutions for offshore production, with 280 employees.[417] Vector's patented metal-to-metal seal technology and connectors are used in floating production, storage and offloading facilities as well as refineries and petrochemical plants at pressures up to more than 15,000 psi (1,000 bar).[418] The international production locations of the Vector Group in Norway, the UK, Malaysia and the USA, as well as sales offices in Australia and Brazil, reinforced the global presence of FOG in the upstream segment of the oil and gas industry. In 2013, the word "Technologies" was added to the name of the Business Group, which then traded as Freudenberg Oil & Gas Technologies

(FOGT) and relocated its headquarters to the newly constructed North American headquarters of EagleBurgmann in Houston, Texas.[419]

On the product side, the Freudenberg Group also worked on a large number of seal innovations focusing on sustainability, including seals for blow-out preventers (BOP). The importance of a high-quality BOP seal is highlighted by the Deepwater Horizon catastrophe in the Gulf of Mexico in April 2010, which was caused by a malfunction in a competitor's product.[420] In 2007, EagleBurgmann had already presented an innovative type of wear protection for mechanical seals in the form of a specially developed microcrystalline diamond coating. This coating reduces friction by more than 20 percent, offering improved dry running properties and lower heat development, in turn resulting in a longer service life for the seals and greater energy efficiency in plant operation. The electrical conductivity of the diamond coating also helps in preventing electrochemical corrosion.[421]

In 2010, FST used sustainable SUL[422] technology for the first time. This technology replaced the conventional process for producing metal rings for Simmerrings. It had been normal practice to stamp these rings out of large steel sheets. As in the case of cookies produced from a sheet of dough, a large amount of material that could not be used remained after stamping. In contrast, SUL technology involves making rings from long, narrow steel strips by laser cutting and welding. There is virtually no waste and it becomes easier to produce the many different shapes required for Simmerring models. Compared with stamping, this process uses up to 70 percent less steel sheet, meaning that fewer truckloads are needed and CO_2 emissions are reduced. In 2011, Freudenberg received the Deutscher Innovationspreis (German Innovation Award)[423] and the Deutscher Innovationspreis für Klima und Umwelt (IKU – German Innovation Award for Climate and Environment) of the Federal Environment Ministry and BDI for its SUL technology.[424]

Apart from CO_2, methane is one of the most harmful greenhouse gases. In 2020, EagleBurgmann succeeded in completely eliminating methane emissions from compressors for the first time. This is possible thanks to an innovative gas-lubricated mechanical seal (dry gas seal) which prevents any methane from escaping from equipment such as pipelines, gas storage facilities, turbines and pumps, even at high operating pressures. This enables the energy industry, and especially the oil and gas industry, to significantly reduce methane emissions.[425]

Recently, Freudenberg took a further strategic step in this area. With effect from January 1, 2024, the two Business Groups EagleBurgmann and Freudenberg Oil & Gas Technologies were combined to form the new Business Group Freudenberg Flow Technologies with headquarters in Wolfratshausen. One objective is to leverage synergy effects in sales more effectively, especially with respect to sustainable products for flow technologies. Furthermore, the Management Board hopes to identify even better growth opportunities through the organizational change.[426]

A systematic sustainability strategy

These product innovations with ecological benefits are examples of Freudenberg's sustainability strategy that has its origins in the 2002 "We all take care!" initiative. This initiative was the trigger for numerous projects to improve environmental protection. Freudenberg strengthened its commitment to sustainability even further by signing the Global Compact in 2014. This step was the beginning of the gradual development towards the present approach to sustainability.

By becoming a signatory to the UN Global Compact, Freudenberg affirmed its support for the Global Compact's ten basic principles on human rights, labor standards, anti-corruption and environmental protection, to which the United Nations agreed in 1987. Freudenberg thus expressed its commitment to the 17 Sustainable Development Goals that were proclaimed as a global framework in 2016, shortly after the Paris climate conference. Since 2019, Freudenberg has prioritized eight of the 17 goals to which it can make an important contribution. These eight goals are: good health and wellbeing; quality education; affordable and clean energy; decent work and economic growth; industry, innovation and infrastructure; reduced inequalities; responsible consumption and production; and climate action. This covers, for example, healthy nutrition and the mental health of employees, vaccination campaigns, the provision of masks, reductions in the use of critical substances, lifelong learning for employees with many training and continuing education courses, sustainable industrialization with ongoing investment in existing and new plants, the use of recyclates and recyclable raw materials, and the elimination of plastic packaging.[427]

Progress must be always be quantifiable and documented. To that end, Freudenberg introduced an electronic sustainability reporting system. Each Business Group defines its own path to climate neutrality. Production processes vary in terms of their energy intensity, and different technological hurdles require overcoming.[428]

Under the leadership of Tilman Krauch, the first Group-wide sustainability strategy firmly anchoring sustainability in the Freudenberg Group's strategic process was drawn up in 2016. Sustainability has two dimensions for the

Fig. 142 The current structure of Freudenberg's sustainability strategy

Freudenberg Group, and aims to save resources in order to conserve them for future generations.[429] The first dimension is the way the Freudenberg Group shapes its processes and uses its systems to reduce the consumption of raw materials and natural resources to minimize its own ecological footprint (footprint). Experience to date shows that it is possible to achieve up to 25 percent in savings, on average, after improvements have been made. Going forward, the facility in Oberwihl in southern Germany, for example, will meet its own heating and warm water demand in a unique climate-neutral way by using woodchips from the Black Forest to replace the fossil fuel-based heating oil.[430] With the second dimension Freudenberg offers many products and solutions that allow customers to manufacture more efficiently and sustainably or to make their products more resource-efficient (handprint).[431] The footprint is to be kept as small as possible by continuously improving processes and plant. There are Group-wide key performance indicators for material efficiency, energy efficiency and CO_2 emission reductions. In terms of the handprint, on the other hand, the effect for customers should be as large as possible.

Based on this sustainability strategy Freudenberg launched the "Sustainability drives Climate Action" project at the end of 2019. The aim was to reduce CO_2 emissions by 25 percent by 2025.[432] Furthermore, the company intends to be climate-neutral by 2045. Freudenberg has turned to a multi-step strategy: Energy efficiency is to be maximized and energy consumption reduced. Energy supply is to be electrified and green electricity to be used. The share of green power used at Freudenberg in 2021 already stood at more than 346 gigawatt hours, or some 21 percent, and had reached 30 percent by 2022. It is expected to rise to up to 50 percent by 2025. Where processes cannot be electrified or green electricity is not available, Freudenberg will initially achieve climate neutrality by means of compensation programs.[433]

The company is constantly intensifying its efforts to expand the share of electricity sourced from green power in order to achieve its climate targets. To accelerate the pace of this process even further, a long-term supply contract – a power purchase agreement – was concluded with the operator of the Nordsee Ost offshore wind farm. Located off the island of Helgoland, this wind farm with its 48 turbines is one of the largest commercial wind power projects off the German coast. The agreement secures a firm amount of this climate-friendly electricity for Freudenberg.[434]

Freudenberg is also expanding its self-generation capabilities for green power in order to meet its climate targets. The Freudenberg Filtration Technologies site in Shunde, China, commissioned one of Freudenberg's largest photovoltaic arrays in the fall of 2022. Covering over 9,500 square meters, the array has a

Fig. 143 Photovoltaic array on the roof of the Freudenberg Filtration Technologies factory building in Shunde, China, 2022

generating capability of some 2 million kilowatt hours per year, meeting up to 20 percent of the site's electricity demand, thus saving more than 1,500 tons of CO_2 emissions at the Shunde plant per year.[435]

One example of the scale of handprint support is Freudenberg's participation in Sorek II. This is the world's largest and most advanced seawater desalination plant, south of Tel Aviv, still under construction at the beginning of 2023. Once completed, the plant will desalinate an annual 100 billion liters of water and convert it into potable and industrial process water for over 1.5 million people, thus meeting 20 percent of Israel's water needs. A reverse osmosis process is used to purify the water. Under this process, seawater is separated from drinking water through pressure and membrane filtration. Freudenberg's EagleBurgmann Business Group supplied mechanical seals specially developed for the extremely high pressure of this water treatment technology. They enable reliable and smooth operation and thanks to their durability also help make the desalination plant more sustainable.[436]

Looking at all the activities in the field of sustainability it is very clear that Freudenberg makes a considerable effort to address the challenges of rising raw material prices and ever-scarcer resources. This trend has led to a greater environmental awareness among society – and presented Freudenberg with new growth opportunities. The mechanical seals business, for example, has almost trebled since 2004.[437] An important factor is that the company committed to environmental protection very early, and established environmental protection on an equal footing with market position, profitability and social equality.

Cooperation with, and the acquisition of, various companies have helped Freudenberg to expand the product portfolio in line with environmental protection and to broaden the present sustainability strategy. Examples include the manufacture of polyester nonwovens from recycled PET bottles, the development of eco-friendly thermal insulation for sports and outdoor wear and the production of nonwovens for filter media used in air and water treatment. New approaches in sealing technology and specialty chemicals conserve existing resources, make their extraction safer for the environment or minimize harmful emissions. Freudenberg sets great store by sustainability, energy efficiency and the protection of natural resources, including with regard to present and future activities relating to fossil fuels – in harmony with the tradition of sustainability that has been one of Freudenberg's tenets for many decades.

Leadership, family, values

Back in 1914, Hermann Ernst Freudenberg was already convinced that the company would not necessarily always be led by family members: "I most certainly do not believe that the management should always come from the family; the business is too large and the family too extensive for this enterprise to be seen purely as a family business. What is important is that management comprises experienced, hardworking specialists, and only if such persons are to be found within the family should they be chosen – otherwise they should come from outside the family."[438] Guided by this basic concept put forward by Hermann Ernst, 1971 saw an important innovation in the composition of the Management Board. For the first time, two senior managers who did not come from the Freudenberg family were appointed to the Management Board as general representatives: Rudolf Wassermann and Werner Kumpf.[439] The Freudenberg family took a further step towards professionalizing the management body in 1976 with the appointment of the first members of the Board of Partners who did not come from the company's owners.[440] Even though the majority of seats on the Board of Partners are still held by family members today, it had nevertheless become necessary to add further expert knowledge only found outside the family to the supervisory body of this increasingly complex company.

The appointment of the first non-family managers at executive management level in 1971 raised two questions for the family members who served on the Management Board, that required urgent attention: What principles should govern the employment of family members in the company in the future? And how should non-family managers engage with the traditional family values as practiced by the owners? These discussions soon came to the conclusion that rules for the employment of family members in the company were required. As a result, the "Guidelines for the employment of family members" were drafted in June 1974; these guidelines were to be taken into account when making appointments. The introduction to the guidelines sets out the situation prevailing at that time:

> "In the past it was usual procedure to only employ those family members in the company who were considered to be potential candidates for a position as general partners at a later date. Given that personal disappointment would be unavoidable should a family member selected on this basis not be appointed to top management, and in light of the fact that early decisions on such a course would have to be taken at an age when reliable knowledge of the applicant's skills was not yet possible, recent years have seen a change in this procedure whereby members of the family are employed in

our company whose prospects of advancement to serve on the management board have either not been raised or where this has been left entirely open."[441]

With the introduction of the guidelines, the following principles governing the employment of family members in the company were to apply:

"a) Every partner must be aware from the first day of employment with the company that neither the fact that said partner holds a financial participation in the company nor the size of that participation constitutes any right to employment by the company or to serve in a senior management position. Partners and persons outside the family, such as the children of senior managers and other employees, must all be treated according to the same standards. […] b) On no account may preference be given to family members over more suitable non-family employees nor may family members be appointed to supervise employees who are better qualified than those family members. The company may not appoint any family member to a senior management position unless said family member has at least the same qualifications as the employees under that person's supervision. […] c) On no account may near relatives (father, father-in-law or siblings) be involved in decisions relating to the qualifications of partners. Furthermore, as a general rule, family members who are new to the company should not be employed in departments managed by close relatives. d) The company benefits from having the largest possible number of employees with a sense of loyalty fostered by tradition, upbringing and financial interest such as that which may be assumed to exist among family members. Notwithstanding, in the own interests of the company and its partners, and for reasons of personnel policy, there must be strict standards governing the employment of family members, particularly with regard to senior management positions. e) The Management Board must keep the Board of Partners regularly informed of successor problems among family members and report on negative experience and qualifications. f) Every family member must accept that personnel policy must be guided solely by the principle of finding the best possible candidates to fill senior management positions in the company."[442]

However, these rules, clearly oriented to the principle of performance, only lasted for a few years in this form. At the Partners' Meeting on April 26, 1980, Hermann Freudenberg explained why, in his view, the 1974 version of the guidelines for the employment of family members should be reviewed:

"The bond between the partners and the company is to some extent of a personal nature. Family members serving on the Management Board have a special function as regards relations with the partners. For the partners, they are the link. That calls first and foremost for trust, an adequate exchange of information, and as much contact as possible. Having family members serving on the Management Board in future, too, is desirable. You may rest assured that is our firm conviction. In particular the relationship between the younger partners and the Management Board should become less constrained and less complicated. An element of tension has arisen in some cases. For our part, we will do all we can to relieve this tension."[443]

The following was therefore to be added to the guidelines for the employment of family members:

"1. The Management Board welcomes applications from partners interested in employment with the company. Partners do not need to wait until they are contacted in this regard. 2. On the other hand, the Management Board will become more active in conducting talks with partners who have commenced or are about to complete their training in subjects that make them eligible for employment in industry. These efforts may include temporary employment with the company, e. g., internships in Germany or another country."[444]

As a result, the Management Board and the Board of Partners revised the guidelines for the employment of family members and approved the amended version on March 4, 1981. The requested addition to the guidelines was worded as follows: "The Management Board will take the initiative to contact family members who, based on their past performance and qualifications, the Management Board considers qualified to perform tasks in the company. This applies in par-

Fig. 144-146 Hermann Freudenberg (1924-2010) – Member of the Management Board 1959-1988 (Speaker 1962-1988), 1988-1997 Chairman of the Board of Partners 1988-1997 ▪ Werner Kumpf (1915-2009) – Member of the Management Board 1971-1980 ▪ Rudolf Wassermann (1913-1976) – Member of the Management Board 1971-1976

ticular to new appointments in middle and senior management."⁴⁴⁵ With this addition, the qualifications of a general partner were of vital importance for the family member's possible career in the company.

This was reflected by appointments to the relevant corporate bodies. When family member Peter Wentzler departed in 1972, he was succeeded by Siegfried Hinz, who moved from the Klöckner Group. Kurt Kraft, also a member of the owner family, was succeeded by Reinhart Freudenberg and Günther Kurtze, who came from Grünzweig & Hartmann and also held a teaching post at Karlsruhe University. When Rudolf Wassermann died in 1976, he was succeeded by Otto Klötzer, who served with Elefanten-Schuh GmbH. The Management Board was subsequently streamlined. When family members Helmut Fabricius, Hans Erich Freudenberg and Otto Schildhauer retired in 1976, their responsibilities were redistributed. In 1978, Hermann Norbert Dahlström, who had made a career for himself at Monsanto and Conti Gummi, was elected, followed by Rudolf Scharpff from Robert Bosch in 1979. The only member of the owner family to join the Management Board as a new member in the 1970s was Reinhart Freudenberg. And subsequently, only one further member of the family, Hans-Jochen Hüchting, who served from 1994 to 2004, joined the Management Board.

The Board of Partners and the Management Board addressed the issue of employing family members in the company once again in early 2012. This discussion was based on interviews conducted by external consultants commissioned for this purpose. The interviewees were family members serving on the Board of Partners as well as current or former family members and senior managers from

Fig. 147-149 Reinhart Freudenberg (1932-2017) – Member of the Management Board 1972-1997 (Speaker 1988-1997), 1997-2005 Chairman of the Board of Partners ▪ Günther Kurtze (1921-1986) – Member of the Management Board 1972-1985 ▪ Siegfried Hinz (1927-2001) – Member of the Management Board 1974-1990

the company. The key questions were "how those concerned experienced or had experienced the work of family members within the company and what needed to be done to make this work a success for everyone concerned."[446]

Based on the findings of the interviews, a benchmark study comparing Freudenberg with similar family companies in Europe and the USA was conducted. The interviews and the study crystallized out various key points for re-aligning the guidelines. As before, the requirements and interests of the company "continue to take priority over those of the family and individual family members. Management positions will continue to be filled solely on the basis of the performance principle, irrespective of the applicant's origin. [...] The Board of Partners and the Management Board regard the employment of family members in operational functions as one of several important links between the company and the family and also consider such employment to be desirable in the future. In order to avoid potential conflicts between performance assessment and the suitability of family members from the outset, family members who are interested and eligible will have to demonstrate that their performance is suitable for management positions outside the company before being appointed to a management position within the company. Like all other internal and external applicants, family members will in future first have to complete an independent assessment."[447]

In the guidelines that followed these considerations, family members were excluded from working at any level below the top management level (with the exception of internships, work on dissertations and vacation work), a very big step for the owner family: "Family members may only be appointed after successfully proving themselves for several years outside the company in man-

Fig. 150–152 Otto Klötzer (1927–1998) – Member of the Management Board 1976–1979 ▪ Hermann Norbert Dahlström (1936–2014) – Member of the Management Board 1978–2000 ▪ Rudolf Scharpff (1929–2019) – Member of the Management Board 1980–1993

agement positions reporting directly to the Management Board (management board members of Business Groups, managers in Corporate Functions of the holding company) insofar as a suitable position is available and an independent assessment which is mandatory for all candidates at this level has been successfully completed."[448]

The guidelines for the employment of family members were revised a further time and approved by the Management Board and the Board of Partners on April 10, 2013. In his letter to the partners of the same date, Wolfram Freudenberg, Chairman of the Board of Partners from 2005 to 2014, explained the reasons for the new version: "Family members pursuing a successful career in their own company are often generally suspected, both by colleagues and by other family members, of receiving preferential treatment. On the other hand, the family members themselves frequently have the subjective impression that they are placed at a disadvantage because of their family membership. This is one of the most frequent and most serious causes of conflicts between the companies concerned and family members as well as within the families concerned. [...] The guidelines laid down for Freudenberg, which date from 1981, are very open. They rightly give priority to the interests of the company over the interests of the family and family members, stating that management positions should be filled by the best possible candidates, irrespective of their origin, and expressly deny any claim to a specific position in the company. They advocate equal treatment for candidates outside the family and set out certain governance rules for decisions. However, in practice these open rules have not prevented repeated doubts on the part of managers and family members concerning the implementation of equal treatment. The lack of transparent performance assessment and talent

Fig. 153-155 Wilhelm Schmitt – Member of the Management Board 1983–1993 ▪ Rudolf Fischer (1933–1997) – Member of the Management Board 1987–1995 ▪ Peter Stehle – Member of the Management Board 1990–2005

development processes at the level of the company has certainly played a part in this development. However, both within the company and within the family itself, people are uncertain as to whether it is even desired that family members should work for the company and, if so, under what conditions and with what expectations."[449]

At the same time as the guidelines for the employment of family members were being drawn up in the early 1970s, a discussion on corporate values began within the Management Board. A form was to be found to express the traditional family values that would also be binding on those managers who did not have family ties. The Management Board wished to set down the character of the family company and the values-based orientation of business policy for the future. The first results of these early discussions are to be found in various information manuals for managers published from 1972 onward. They represent the first guidelines for cooperation between supervisors and employees.[450] The first broader discussion on this topic within Freudenberg management and also including downstream management levels took place in 1983, led by Hermann Freudenberg. There were brainstorming and discussion sessions as well as concept papers on the formulation of corporate principles. It is interesting to note that all of these contributions referred in one way or another to the long tradition of Carl Johann Freudenberg's value basis. However, no principles valid across the Group were formulated yet.[451]

In the early 1990s the issue of values returned to the Management Board's agenda. As a result of these deliberations – and under an initiative spearheaded by the two brothers Reinhart, as Speaker of the Management Board, and Hermann Freudenberg, as Chairman of the Board of Partners – business principles

Fig. 156-158 Ernst Schön – Member of the Management Board 1993-2005 ▪ Hans-Jochen Hüchting (1942-2024) – Member of the Management Board 1994-2004 ▪ Peter Bettermann (1947-2021) – Member of the Management Board 1994-2012 (Speaker 1997-2012)

valid throughout the Group were set out in writing for the first time in 1994. Before that, however, the Management Board turned its attention to a statement on restrictions regarding business with arms issued in August 1991: "Freudenberg's products should not be used for war or the oppression of people. Our business policy therefore not only rules out the manufacture and supply of weapons, warfare agents and other armaments, but also, as a general principle, bars indirect participation in the production, distribution and use of such items. We are, however, conscious of the fact that numerous products can be used to apply violence as well as to defend against it, and that many products have both military and non-military applications." For this reason, the manufacture and supply of weapons, warfare agents and weapon components was explicitly banned. The same applied to products "specifically destined (i.e., particularly designed for this purpose) to enable the use of violence against people or objects, especially through the use of weapons." Freudenberg products suitable for both civilian and military applications – such as seals that can be installed in tanks as well as civilian vehicles – were subject to monitoring by the Management Board "if there are indications of their intended use for military purposes".[452] This position was later directly incorporated in the Business Principles, which state: "We will not manufacture any products intended for harming people (e.g., weapons)."[453]

In the early 1990s, coinciding with the political discussion on the right to asylum in Germany, right-wing extremists committed a series of arson attacks on homes for asylum seekers and apartment blocks that were home to people with migrant backgrounds. These pogroms came to a climax in Rostock-Lichtenhagen in August 1992.[454] On the evening of August 22, several thousand people

Fig. 159–161 Albert W. Pürzer – Member of the Management Board 2000–2008 ▪ Martin Stark – Member of the Management Board/Board of Management 2005–2013 ▪ Jörg Sost – Member of the Management Board 2005–2010

gathered outside the home for asylum seekers and attacked the eleven-storey building and the neighboring hostel for Vietnamese contract workers, initially throwing stones and subsequently incendiary devices. The overstretched police force was attacked and the emergency services were prevented from accessing the buildings. Once the home for asylum seekers had been evacuated on August 24, the attackers turned their attention to the hostel for Vietnamese contract workers. The crowd stormed the building, ran riot and subsequently set fire to the hostel. Some 150 people were trapped inside it, including a TV team and some German supporters, as well as the Vietnamese workers. Quite by chance they were able to scramble to the roof and flee to the neighboring building. The riots caused outrage all over the world and are described as "the most massive racist attacks or possibly even the largest pogrom in German post-war history".[455] Alarmed by these xenophobic attacks, the Management Board and the Works Council issued a joint statement condemning xenophobia in December 1992:

> "We will not and cannot stand by and watch the brutal actions and words of some citizens as they attack asylum seekers, foreigners and German nationals of foreign origin, and indeed who do not even shy away from a new antisemitism. We unreservedly condemn these crimes, and we support and welcome the fact that all the means available under our country's rule of law are being determinedly and unrelentingly directed against the perpetrators and instigators. [...] At Freudenberg, employees from Germany and other nations have been working together peacefully and industriously for many years. [...] We therefore feel we have a special duty and accept this obliga-

Fig. 162-164 Wolfram Freudenberg - Member of the Board of Partners 1975-1988 and 1991-2014 (Chairman 2005-2014) ▪ Christoph Mosmann - Member of the Management Board/Board of Management 2010-2014 ▪ Mohsen Sohi - Member of the Management Board/Board of Management since 2010 (Speaker/CEO since 2012). Photo: martinjoppen.de

tion to defend ourselves against all forms of xenophobia and not allow them in our company. Moral outrage alone is not sufficient, we must raise our voices and visibly demonstrate our condemnation. We therefore call on all our employees to respond peacefully and resolutely to all forms of xenophobia and violations of tolerance and mutual respect, not only within the company, but also outside the factory gates. Show your strong opposition to all comments – even the thoughtless ones – that demand or support hate and violence against people. There is no place in our company for employees who fan the flames of xenophobia or act violently."[456]

This position, too, was later incorporated in the Business Principles and is reflected by the Guiding Principles.[457]

Reinhart and Hermann Freudenberg now launched the discussion about values among the partners, in other words, with the owner family. In his speech at the Partners' Meeting on June 22, 1993, Reinhart came to the conclusion that the "sense of belonging between the family and the company" has a special value for the Group: "For the company, its employees and its customers, this tradition is the bedrock of trust and it defines the character and thus the identity of the company in a special way." For him, this went hand in hand with the visible presence of the Business Principles founded on the family tradition: "Everyone in the Management Board – and likewise in the Board of Partners – identifies with the tradition of our family company and unanimously agrees that this tradition should be continued." In order to "preserve the necessary sense of belonging between the partners and the company, there has to be a mutual affinity. This affinity must be founded on the understanding that each side accords with

Fig. 165–167 Ralf Krieger – Member of the Management Board/Board of Management 2011–2024. Photo: martinjoppen.de ▪ Martin Wentzler – Member of the Board of Partners 1993–2024 (Chairman 2014–2024). Photo: martinjoppen.de ▪ Tilman Krauch – Member of the Management Board/Board of Management 2014–2024. Photo: martinjoppen.de

the actions of the other and with the manner in which the other side acts." For Reinhart, this meant "ensuring a corporate style that sits well with the partners", in other words, "the partners must be able to identify with the company – with its actions and with its style." In so doing the company should "take social demands seriously; that is not only an ethical imperative, it is also good business policy." The very nature of entrepreneurial activity means that it "does not float in a value-neutral space. It is possible, for example, to treat the environment irresponsibly and hope not be caught in the act, or it is possible to proactively engage in protecting the environment, putting this on an equal footing with economic and social issues. We seek to do the latter. It is possible to treat employees coldly and inconsiderately, or to be strict but understanding; it is possible to play cat and mouse with the Works Council, or to strive for a fair partnership; it is possible to manufacture products such as weapons that cause human misery or to deliberately refrain from doing so. It is also possible to do business through wheeling and dealing with politicians, or to confront competition full-on without seeking help from such quarters […] I believe, however, that it is very important for all partners to know that the company – not just the Management Board, but the entire organization – has a clear standpoint on all these issues […] Another stylistic characteristic that is important to us is significant liberalism within the company. We aim to give our senior managers broad scope for exercising responsibility and not to cast them, or any other of our employees, in stereotype roles. In fact, we do indeed have different corporate cultures in our company, oftentimes in line with the idiosyncrasies of different businesses […]. A further feature that has been in evidence since the first generation is that trust

Fig. 168–170 Esther Maria Loidl – Member of the Management Board/Board of Management since 2021. Photo: Johannes Vogt ▪ Frank Heislitz – Member of the Management Board/Board of Management since 2024. Photo: Johannes Vogt ▪ Thomas Herr – Member of the Management Board/Board of Management since 2024. Photo: martinjoppen.de

takes precedence over control. Our actions are to a very large degree based on this principle and that possibly sets us apart from many other companies of our size [...]."[458] The family values Reinhart Freudenberg set out in this speech were incorporated in the Business Principles of the Freudenberg Group approved in December 1994.[459]

From the outset, Carl Johann Freudenberg's principles and values played a key role in the genesis of the Business Principles. He wrote down his personal business principles for his sons in 1887.[460] Written for his sons Friedrich Carl and Hermann Ernst Freudenberg, who were each to hold one-third of the company, they were intended to serve as guidelines for the successful continuation of the company. Modesty, honesty, a solid financial foundation and the ability to adapt to change were Carl Johann Freudenberg's most important principles for successful entrepreneurship. Carl Johann also set great store by trust as the foundation of every business and working relationship. Two quotations on his principle of trust have been handed down through the generations:[461] "Better to trust a hundred times and run the risk of being taken in once – that is preferable to one single case of erroneous mistrust" and "If the trust between me and my workers breaks down, I shall shut up shop!"[462]

However, putting these ideas to paper in 1994 did not put an end to the discussion on corporate values and on how these values should be addressed at Freudenberg. Reinhart Freudenberg took up the subject again at the 1997 Dialog senior management meeting. He believed it was necessary to reiterate the need for a value orientation in order to create a "culture of innovation and cooperation".

> "To be able to identify with the Group, all business units need shared values. [...] If we search for what our businesses have in common, the answer lies in a customer orientation characterized by customer service and practical benefit. In terms of a shared business mentality, that is no mean achievement. [...] However, very different types of business also have shared values with regard to business conduct, operating principles, the way of working together and with others. In our company, the special emphasis we place on trust is a particularly essential factor. [...] Among the values that we take seriously and that are highlighted in the Business Principles are a sense of responsibility towards the environment, the rejection of irregular business practices and the refusal to participate in the manufacture of weapons."[463]

The desire to communicate this code of values and conduct, so deeply rooted in the family, led to the preparation and presentation of what became known as the Freudenberg Group's Guiding Principles at the next Dialog meeting in 1999.[464]

The Guiding Principles are a condensed version of the Business Principles. They define and explain the value basis of the Freudenberg Group for all employees: Conduct vis-à-vis employees, business partners, other stakeholders and third parties.[465] Some additions were made in 2011 to reflect the constant evolution of the Group and the growing cultural diversity, in order to foster a better understanding and ensure consistent interpretation in an international context.[466]

In keeping with this value orientation, Freudenberg signed the United Nations Global Compact in 2014. The Global Compact was launched by Kofi Annan, then UN Secretary General, in 2000.[467] It is described as the "world's largest and most important initiative for sustainable and responsible corporate governance".[468] By signing the Global Compact, Freudenberg committed to values-based and sustainable action in the fields of human rights, labor standards, environmental protection and anti-corruption (compliance). The Global Compact principles were already to be found in Freudenberg's Business Principles and Guiding Principles and were put into practice accordingly. This voluntary commitment is the external manifestation of the Freudenberg Group's values base for the wider public, because joining the Global Compact required Freudenberg to publish an annual Communication on Progress detailing its progress in activities to embed the Compact's principles, thereby objectivizing the Group's own values-based governance. In the words of Management Board Speaker Mohsen Sohi: "We joined the Global Compact because it represents an internationally acknowledged positioning."[469]

Unlike many other family companies in Germany run in a similar manner, those responsible at Freudenberg recognized the importance of safeguarding the company for coming generations very early. Such foresight prevented the "Buddenbrooks effect", by which a dynasty begins to crumble in the third generation. And in the period that followed, timely foundations were laid to master the challenges of leading a steadily growing, ever-more diversified and international company – while at the same time keeping a watchful eye on internal requirements as well as external demands. That was not always an easy role to play, but the guidance was successful, even when times were difficult. It is precisely this ability to facilitate on the part of the entrepreneurial players that has always given Freudenberg modern corporate governance and a values structure that can hold its own in comparison with others.

"FREUDENBERG WILL REMAIN A FAMILY-OWNED ENTERPRISE"

INTERVIEWS WITH MOHSEN SOHI AND MARTIN WENTZLER

During interviews in the spring and summer of 2023, Martin Wentzler and Mohsen Sohi look at Freudenberg's past, but particularly at its future. It becomes a discussion about the company's culture, and about how Freudenberg, buoyed by its values, remains flexible enough for new things. It is therefore also about internationalization and innovation, about politics and pandemics, about the world of work of the future – and the question of how a company can make a meaningful contribution to protecting the planet and its climate: "Freudenberg has invariably demonstrated great willingness to change, the family has always adapted to new circumstances, and politically, it was Carl Johann Freudenberg's guiding principle that one should always conform to the prevailing conditions," is how Wentzler opens the discussion.

Particularly in the past ten to fifteen years, the company has undergone an enormous transformation to meet the challenges of the future, he says. The company has been completely reorganized, processes in many areas professionalized and digitized, a talent management system introduced, innovation management installed, technology platforms created, excellent technologies developed and the Freudenberg brand has been repositioned. Furthermore, corporate social responsibility has been developed to give access to work and education to people worldwide and to promote environmental protection, he states. And then there is long-term thinking, he adds.

Mr. Wentzler, as a family-owned enterprise with a 175-year history, is Freudenberg an example of long-term thinking and action?

Wentzler: "If we take a look at the portfolio today, and at divisions like Vibracoustic or Freudenberg Medical, then we really had to have great staying power there during development until they were as successful as we see them today. During all these changes, one always acted according to the value system that can be traced back strongly to Carl Johann: The company comes first, then the family

Fig. 171 Martin Wentzler, 2024

interests. Dividends or disbursements were subordinate. And one always made sure that the shares were passed on to the next generation with increased value.

These are the key points that from my perspective have always applied during the entire 175 years and continue to apply, up to today – and for the future too." *Will that stay that way?* "Yes, everything we do is geared to that. Preservation of the company is our number one. Number two is its preservation as a family-owned enterprise, if that does not collide with one. Thirdly, long-term profitability, and fourthly, short-term profitability."

However, Freudenberg will only be able to achieve this, Sohi interjects, if a constant willingness to change is retained at the same time: "The fact that Freudenberg is family-owned is what makes the prioritization mentioned by Martin Wentzler possible, meaning putting long-term goals before a dividend. That is a distinctive feature which I believe to be very important. The second characteristic is the fact that the company has succeeded in changing constantly." *And, particularly important to Sohi:* "Of course, the speed of change has changed: A hundred years ago, fifty years ago, today, the pace is by no means comparable. We are experiencing what is known as technological compression. Many countries in Africa, for example, are simply leapfrogging the development of telephone lines and are relying completely on mobile telephony right from the start. Because there are developments such as these in very many areas, we have to change increasingly fast."

Fig. 172 Mohsen Sohi, 2024

Mr. Sohi, you took over the position of Speaker of the Management Board of Freudenberg & Co. and that of CEO of the newly established Freudenberg SE from Peter Bettermann in mid-2012 and initiated cultural change just a few months later through Project Focus 2.0. Although deliberations on this had been the subject of discussions in previous years, you were the one who kicked off the process. What were your motives?

Sohi: "As you know, before my time as CEO in Weinheim, I was President and CEO of Freudenberg-NOK General Partnership in Plymouth. That was a significant advantage, because I did not have to get involved in local corporate politics in Weinheim and at the same time I was able to recognize the weaknesses in the organization. Naturally, I did not know back then that I would one day be managing the company. But I did say: If I ever assume this position, there are certain things that I will change. The family representatives gave me great support right from the start. I was asked: 'If your heart tells you it's a good idea, then why don't you want to do it?' Even Peter Bettermann himself completely agreed with the ideas for further changes. Sometimes you just need a change of personnel to make progress on certain tracks again. At that time, the issue was more a lack of assertiveness into the organization and its inertial forces, but not the concept. It is therefore important to know: The most valuable time, that is the first 12 to 18 months after taking on a position. After that, you become part of the system. Hence, I decided to implement Focus 2.0 very quickly."

Just as a reminder: From then on, the Management Board members took on functional responsibilities as CEO (Chief Executive Officer), CFO (Chief Financial Officer) or CTO (Chief Technology Officer) and concentrated on the coordination and development of the Group's strategic direction. When this new corporate governance structure was implemented, the Business Groups reported directly to the entire Management Board from January 2014 onward. The existing boards were dissolved and replaced with what are known as business review meetings. Many of the measures relieved the Business Groups, particularly from administrative tasks.

Sohi too recalls: "One of the challenges back then was that Freudenberg was always regarded as a solid company, but never as a high-performance company. Thus there was a gap between what we said and reality. What I mean is: We talked a lot about innovation, but we did not invest enough in it. We spoke a lot about social responsibility. But our programs in that area were not systematic enough." *Ultimately, many good ideas were killed off under the guise of supposed entrepreneurship, he says. The feeling of operating in particularly close proximity to the market within the old structure had been an illusion, he states. The flow of information between the management levels is now much better; there had previously been deficits there too, he says. However, it is also true that not all managers had initially been convinced about the new structure: two of them had left the company as a result, Sohi says.*

Indeed, the Focus 2.0 approach of strengthening the business groups' entrepreneurship in the direction of market and customers and developing innovativeness ("less administration – more innovation") has paid off: The Group's administration expenses have decreased significantly, the share of R&D investments in sales has risen to around 5 percent – sales and operating results post record figures year after year ...

Sohi: "The slogan 'less administration, more innovation' really did resonate, it was obviously the right move. The most recent developments showed that too." *Sohi says today. On the basis of this organizational structure, Freudenberg did not merely handle the Covid-19 pandemic well, but also came out of it stronger than it had gone into it, he says. And Freudenberg is also coping brilliantly with the various changes in the automotive industry, where manufacturers' production volumes are declining sharply in some areas, he states.*

Focus 2.0 illustrated the new "act as one company" self-image in the "House of Excellence." The House comprises eight elements which have been continuously revised and developed since then. Will this ecosystem bear up to the challenges of the future?

Sohi: "Yes. We have created a solid foundation with this, including for what is to come. When we conceived this structure, one of our concerns was that we will overextend the organization and the employees, that we will have too many initiatives running at the same time. But it proved to be a highly efficient communication instrument. A company that wants to be successful in a world that is changing increasingly rapidly has to be good in all aspects that the House of Excellence portrays. After all, the question of whether we need the brain or the heart or the lungs to a greater extent to survive is not valid. We need them all, and they all have to be healthy. That also applies in the figurative sense to a company too. But this is important too: The future generation of management naturally has the right and even the responsibility to question everything."

Mr. Sohi, you already postulated ten years ago that Freudenberg must become more diverse and inclusive. Systematic personnel management was introduced across the entire Group, periodic talent management conferences set up, new top management training programs were established ...

Sohi: "Yes, we have improved greatly in this respect since then. Particularly the aspect of thinking in internal networks has made significant progress along this track. Let me give you an example: As late as 2008, when the CEOs of the business groups were invited to a conference on a Group-wide initiative, the enthusiasm to attend was not great. That has changed immensely. In the meantime, such opportunities to come together are utilized intensively to talk about the concepts that have an effect on all Freudenberg business areas. The competence training that is conducted as part of our management development is functioning wonderfully, and the programs are really good, it is one of the best management development programs in the world. It comprises an entire cascade of development options on diverse management levels, and we invest a lot more into this training than we did 15 years ago, ten thousand euros in each participant."

A technology group thrives on innovations that are always driven by well educated people – you organize your innovation activities around the Odyssey and Janus projects and the technology platforms aligned with them. Is that flexible enough, given the pace in the market?

Sohi: "Whether it is the Odyssey Project or the Janus Project – we use our strategic planning to look three to five years ahead, and sometimes ten years. What was missing from our planning were some of the longer-term trends that will change the world in 20, 30, 40 years. Let me give you an example here too: In 2015, we imagined a world that will be 80 percent less dependent on fossil fuels in 2050. Only something like this can provide the right impetus. Thus you start to invest in fuel cells or in lithium-ion battery technology. And this means creating a culture in which mistakes are tolerated. We have to do our homework, be ready to accept a calculated risk: You can't succeed if you don't tolerate mistakes here and there."

Digitalization is a huge challenge in this respect. How satisfied are you with the level of implementation?

Sohi: "Highly satisfied. In the years between 2015 and 2017, the discussion about digitalization increased exponentially. And we had to draw up a very pragmatic and yet effective concept: Whenever we talk about digitalization at Freudenberg, it is very clear that these activities are driven either with regard to customer benefit and growth or by increases in efficiency and quality in internal processes. This clarity really helped us to concentrate our efforts on projects which we knew were really valuable. Compared to the progress of other companies in this area, I would say that I feel very good."

Success never means financial success alone to Freudenberg, but also accepting social responsibility. Was the company's commitment focused too much on Germany, in your view?

Sohi: "I would say it was not just Germany, we also had projects outside of Germany, one example of this would be India. But that was not systematic, we had to change that. The same thing applies here too: We talked about it more than we did anything about it, and we constantly dealt with the same projects. Now we work more systematically and more globally in this respect too."

Your aspiration was and is to make Freudenberg "one of the most innovative and most strongly diversified global companies." How far do you think you have gotten towards this goal?

Sohi: "If you look back precisely ten years, we have grown by an average annual rate of 7 percent during this timeframe. And our expenditure on research and development actually rose by 12 percent on average, operating profit in its turn increased by 8 percent. And all of that despite the high investments, for example in fuel cell or lithium-ion technology. To be honest, I could not be more proud. We used the past decade to align the company integrally – in an ecosystem, so to speak – towards willingness to change and flexibility. On the one hand with the variety of our products and markets, the diversity and competence of our employees from 146 nations and our broad global positioning. On the other hand, we have pressed ahead with digitalization within the company to offer customers added value and to markedly improve our internal efficiency. It is part of our self-image to permanently question what we do and to want to improve."

Wentzler shares this impression: "That will stay with us, and not just within the company, but also within the family. We will prepare to keep up with this pace of change that is required in the company. That is not always easy, because it also means that old habits become obsolete. For example, this Weinheim-centricity: The family and the company in Weinheim – that created an extremely close connection. That is becoming increasingly obsolete. And those of us at top management level have to become even more international and more diverse. For a few years now, we have consciously sought and also gained international members on the Board of Partners. That is a development that can be intensified even further."

Employees from almost 150 countries around the world now work at Freudenberg. That is a challenge for the company's management, but equally a great opportunity too: How can you manage to harness the strengths of the various cultures and nonetheless achieve a common value system?

Wentzler: "We were still really a German company up until 2010: very German in character, including in terms of our structures. And in the past 15 years, we have experienced an incredible transformation – with modern, transparent processes. For many years now, we have had a talent management process which encompasses the lion's share of employees worldwide. This standardized procedure in the entire Group, together with an entire raft of further training opportunities on an international level, generates on the one hand a deep understanding for the company and its values and on the other hand networks the employees together. English is our corporate language. In the factories, our 'Guiding Principles' are posted on the walls everywhere."

"It is about openness to change," *Sohi adds. But at the same time it must be ensured that the changes being made are the right ones, otherwise one is on the wrong track, he says:* "In this context, it is also about the fact that we are actually no longer being driven by a patriarch, but by the collective search for the right decision – and not just by the Management Board. We do not immediately call in one of the big, renowned management consultancies whenever there is a problem. We rely on the expertise of our management executives and employees: well educated, talented people who can combine their knowledge and competence with entrepreneurial thinking and action."

Then comes another sentence to which Sohi attaches great significance: "What is decisive is that we draw first and foremost on the organization's collective knowledge, something which works very well for most of the really difficult questions. Irrespective of how brilliant an individual is, collective wisdom is always stronger, much stronger. And when you go through the process, then all employees are on board in the end."

The idea of entrepreneurial freedom is equally important to Wentzler, particularly with an eye to the future: "Peter Bettermann already realized that the Business Groups must be given entrepreneurial freedom, but that was only really implemented for the first time in Focus 2.0. This entrepreneurial freedom is extremely important. Earlier, the Management Board also had operational responsibility, but this model does not work anymore because of the size of the company. Freudenberg should be an enterprise of entrepreneurs. And that only works when the Management Board takes a step back so that this entrepreneurial freedom really exists. That was then truly implemented in the new structure as well."

In this context, Sohi points out that in life, just like in a company, everything is always a question of balance, something which ultimately also applies to important policy issues, he says: "On the surface it can appear to be a contradiction in terms, but it is not: We want the organization to be agile and to adapt very rapidly, and at the same time we cannot overreact when it is a matter of current events. Let us take the Covid-19 pandemic: In the first three months, the decision makers in politics reacted well, however, the next 21 months were more of an overreaction. You have to be able to live with both, be very flexible, but at the same time not overreact to the emotions of the moment. We have to be very disciplined here."

As to the question of whether the world of work has also changed for the better because of the effect of the Covid-19 pandemic, Sohi gives an ambivalent answer: "In many areas, the digital tools make work easier because we can get together fast. In an emergency, Microsoft Teams is always an option, also for example to send a spontaneous invitation to management executives of an evening, in some cases you can work very efficiently with it. But from my perspective, personal contact is essential. I believe that organizations must be more flexible in this respect. But for a company like Freudenberg, this also applies: We are a production company, two-thirds of our employees had no choice during the Covid-19 pandemic. They had to go to the factory. In that sense, although we want to work more flexibly, the focus of our work lies in the factories, the laboratories and the offices."

Freudenberg's business model was subjected to several disruptive changes in 175 years. Does Freudenberg possibly have a competitive advantage from its own experiences for that reason?

Wentzler: "Compared to younger companies, which have not had this experience at all up to now, that is certainly an advantage, but of course there are definitely companies who have experienced comparable upheavals."

The topic of joint innovation in particular at Freudenberg has been derived from the company's history, in which an idea from one business has led time and again to a totally new business field – from the Simmerring right up to the very topical area of fuel cells …

However, a company's long-term orientation can never be confused with forbearance, Sohi warns emphatically: "We have a long-term orientation, but that cannot be a reason for management to exercise forbearance, for example in the development of the fuel cell too. We may not necessarily want to be the most profitable company among our competitors, but we work very hard to be among the best 25 percent. Because if you are not successful, you cannot afford the luxury of increasing your expenditure for research twice as fast as your income. Thus it is important to ensure that this long-term orientation is not used as an excuse to say that everything that comes takes time."

Earlier, developments were a little bit random too; ideas emerged from external circumstances, for example the Simmerring or the air filter. How is that today, Mr. Sohi?

Sohi: "We approach that much more systematically today. To do this, we have amalgamated our research topics into four overarching areas of competence. The individual topics are developed further within more than ten different technology platforms. The solutions that emerge are then handed over to the Business Groups for industrial implementation. We definitely have the advantage of this broad field of technologies here which we can constantly fall back on."

This point will be of decisive importance with regard to the climate debate. Which brings up the question of whether the goal of being carbon-neutral in 2045 is still ambitious enough?

Sohi: "Sustainability takes high priority at Freudenberg. However, we have to do what makes sense for Freudenberg. In that respect, we are relying on a multi-stage strategy comprising energy savings, electrification, the procurement and in-house production of green energy, and compensating CO_2 emissions. However, the initial situation of our Business Groups varies greatly, depending on how much energy is required for production processes. To that extent, some Freudenberg companies will be producing carbon-neutrally earlier than others. What is important is that we measure and document our progress verifiably. By 2025, relative CO_2 emissions should have been reduced by 25 percent, Freudenberg wants to be carbon-neutral by 2045 at the latest."

However, he adds one important aspect to his comments on the climate: "If you have big factories in India, for example, and if the majority of the energy is derived from coal there, you can either purchase a certificate or you simply won't achieve your goals. Unrealistic goals which you know you cannot achieve just make no sense. Moreover, I have not yet seen one supplier either who said: 'What are your sustainability goals?' We have never had one customer who said: 'You won't be carbon-neutral until 2045? That is too late!' Naturally, Freudenberg is confronted by customer demands, but interests can normally be balanced."

Which brings up the question of how Sohi assesses the future prospects for fuel cells against this background: "1,000 days after Germany declared it had a hydrogen strategy, very little had happened that was tangible by way of infrastructure, by way of vehicles. More was said than done there. But it is true: We believe that the hydrogen industry will come, but maybe not as soon as some of the so-called experts are predicting. We believe that it is a technology that will not be used for passenger cars, but for example for ships and for long-haul trucks, and that is why we are investing in this business. In addition, however, we are also ensuring that we will have the right technology available for every customer, whether it is a purely battery-operated vehicle, a plug-in hybrid, a mild hybrid or an ICE."

The meeting with Sohi and Wentzler takes place at the end of a long Covid-19 pandemic and in the middle of a war in Europe. Will such unforeseeable critical mega-events tend to become the norm? What does that mean for the company's flexibility and how it deals with its employees?

Sohi: "I do not believe that we can take anything for granted anymore. And it is incredible that whenever we think we have overcome a crisis and achieved a certain level of stability, something else comes up that no one had on their radar," *Sohi replies. And Wentzler is also of the opinion that uncertainty will stay with the company for a very long time to come:* "We have to prepare the employees for the new situation by talking with them even more, by explaining even more."

Freudenberg operates in around 60 countries. How do you steer the group and its strong code of values through the different political, and in some cases nationalist, systems of the various countries?

Sohi: "We always look for possibilities to hold onto our values under the respective conditions. However, as a comparatively small company, we do not necessarily have the option; sometimes we cannot simply withdraw from the market." "Implementing this is extremely difficult. We only ever undertake measures to the extent that we do not endanger our employees," *Wentzler adds.*

At the end of the interview, we ask which episode out of Freudenberg's 175-year history inspired Sohi and Wentzler the most – and why.

Wentzler responds first: "For me personally, it is the era of the 1930s and during World War II, in which the company was kept going and even developed further under great economic and personal pressure. To me, that is the most impressive time. Also considering how family members who had to sell their shares back then overcame this time." *And Sohi adds from his perspective:* "I would say, one of the cleverest things that the company has done was that the family realized that it had to transition to an external management that did not just comprise members of the family."

Mr. Wentzler, will Freudenberg remain a family-owned enterprise?

Wentzler: "Yes."

How do you keep a family-owned enterprise with increasingly more partners together? How do you achieve this continuity and identification with the company?

Wentzler: "You have to put in a lot of effort. We have just had our five regional meetings in England, in the United States, and three in Germany, and discussed the topic of communication with our partners. This is becoming increasingly challenging. The young American partners reported to us: We do not read emails anymore, only WhatsApp messages. You have to be extremely open in communication. You have to convey appreciation, you have to listen and take suggestions on board. We have always done that. And the fact that we extended the partnership agreement by 30 years in 2015 with 100 percent approval definitely sends a strong message."

Are the values of the next generation of partners the same?

Wentzler: "In the past ten years, the values at the core of the partners' circle have remained stable. We would have huge problems if we wanted to make changes to their core today."

Does the word "change" still have sufficiently positive connotations in Western societies? Or are we going to have problems because people do not really want to be disturbed by a new train station anymore, for example in Stuttgart?

Wentzler: "On the contrary, the young generation definitely sees the necessity to react to climate change. And on the board of partners, everyone is always prepared to work with us to implement the necessary changes. Sometimes it is not fast enough and not radical enough for them, but on the whole, we have a good common basis there."

Sohi: "In the end, it is up to us to keep the organization agile and prepare it for changes."

A SUSTAINABLE CORPORATE CULTURE
FREUDENBERG AS A GENERATIONAL MODEL

Every generation faces its own challenges. In the here and now, technological or political changes often appear to be a question of survival. They are hotly debated from the management board right down to the canteen. A company, and particularly a family-owned enterprise, which has endured and been successful for many generations, has two major advantages in this situation: It has a memory and a corporate culture that enables it to draw the right conclusions from the past – if its own history has not fallen into oblivion. At Freudenberg, professionally organized Corporate Archives work day after day to preserve memories. And in the year of the company's 175th anniversary, taking a look far back into the past is just as worthwhile as looking through a telescope at the challenges of the future.

Whoever dares to do both will discover that the tasks that the founders' generation had to overcome, long before the legal foundation of the company, were enormous: The fact that, for example, on the one hand, the long tradition of leather manufacturing at the Weinheim headquarters was helpful, but on the other hand that guild rules existed which took a skeptical, or even dismissive view of new things. Ultimately, the founders won out, and later Freudenberg and its employees modernized and internationalized production and sales. That did not always go smoothly either; even the fiercest arguments with one of the most important employees from the age of the founders (*Gründerzeit*) have been handed down. This episode of company history is about skill, it is about vanity, loyalty and rigidity. It helps one of the founders' sons to achieve a decisive profile and shows that great things can emerge from bitter conflicts if they are recognized on time and solved correctly.

A company and its management are always a subject of politics too – whether this is because of war, whether because of regulatory interventions, right up to today's development of electro mobility, which is equally not free from political influences. Above and beyond this, a company is also a factor of politics, a company behaves in a political climate in a way that makes sense from the management board's perspective, but in Freudenberg's case has behavioral principles which ordain that they must keep out of wielding political influence themselves.

World War I, for example, which no longer plays a major role in people's memories today, was a turning point for a company which back then was already an integral part of an economy that had experienced what we now call globalization. On the other hand, the Nazi era constituted a particular turning point, and Bonn-based historian Joachim Scholtyseck produced a comprehensive work on this with the support of the company and the Freudenberg family, which enables this dark epoch in Germany's history to be followed in this book in brief and critical form.

Here, the focus of attention is on the product ideas, the creativity that was born from the scarcity of raw materials, from the elastomers through the synthetic leather right up to the nonwovens.

The company and its owners followed the young Federal Republic of Germany, in its turn, with enthusiasm into the foundation of the state and the economic upturn. Freudenberg was well prepared for the world of the economic miracle. It was familiar with globalization from earlier times, now old and new bonds were being forged in the international business world. The company became global (again), but remained true to its local home town of Weinheim. This combination even impressed its most important international partner to date too: The relationship with the Japanese NOK company is based on the five principles of friendship, trust, harmony, respect and peace. The fact that these are not empty words to Freudenberg in other partnerships too is demonstrated through this book as well.

Freudenberg has long since become a group that is led by the family's time-honored values but managed by entrepreneurs from outside the family, even if they are general partners. They face new challenges. And yet not much is changing: Technology is changing, politics sometimes provides a tailwind, other times a headwind. Time and again, good ideas are needed, that lead to innovations, to manage the transition to new forms of mobility or even the digital transformation of entire business models – together with external partners, but of course especially from the think tanks within the company itself.

Above and beyond that, the aim is to operate increasingly sustainably, which in turn reflects the company's social responsibility which it traditionally put into practice. Sustainable processes and products also require innovations; the power to create new things must also be maintained and boosted day by day, even in a company like Freudenberg. The right way of dealing with one another and further training of employees are the keys to achieving this – and there are many positive examples of this in Freudenberg's history too.

It always becomes particularly exciting whenever a company succeeds in combining external stimuli, whether from another department, whether from customers or external partners, in such a way with one another that together with its own thoughts, truly brilliant, surprising ideas emerge – particularly in team collaborations that interconnect across business groups, regions, customers and other institutions (like, for example, science).

Anyone who dedicates time to this will gain the confidence to become successful in the future too and be proud of the past.

Thus special thanks go to the employees in Freudenberg's Corporate Archives, Achim Korres, Katharina Sattler and particularly Julia Schneider, who contributed significantly to the compilation of this book for six years through comprehensive research and guidance in formulation. This book ends almost six years of regular visits to the archives in Weinheim. And although every project must come to a close some time, there is also a sense of melancholy in this farewell. Because I always feel welcome in this wonderful team.

Michael Horchler, Head of Corporate Archives in Weinheim, held all the threads together and set the manuscript on the right path time and again when it risked getting bogged down in the complexities of the company's development. No one knows Freudenberg's history as well as he does; without him, it would not have been possible to complete this project alongside my main job in Frankfurt.

My thanks also go to Werner Plumpe from Goethe University Frankfurt, who supported the entire emergence of the book with his academic expertise and contributed an essay in his own name.

I also owe my gratitude to Cornelia Buchta-Noack for coordinating the project within the Group and for building a bridge to Martin Wentzler and Mohsen Sohi. Her emotional connection to the company is impressive and a compliment to Freudenberg in itself.

This demonstrates: Many people are involved in a major project. That applies particularly to the work in and about a company. For reasons of narrative, not all management executives who played a major part in the success of the whole have been acknowledged at such length. However, that does not mean that their work should be particularly upvalued or devalued: Without the dovetailing of everyone and everything, it would not work. That will stay that way too, that much is certain.

Fig. 173 Wardrobe trunk of Richard Freudenberg

HOW ARCHIVE TREASURES ARE REVEALED

THE STORY OF A TRAVELING COMPANY AND R. F.'S WARDROBE TRUNK

Past and yet present, memory and yet motivation for what is to come. Not just texts can build this bridge, but also objects that tell us a story. The Corporate Archives in Weinheim has a wardrobe trunk from the 1930s in its repository. It can be opened and closed like a book. The wardrobe trunk bears the marks of the work it has done. You can see central locks that no longer work, worn leather handles and partially torn-off shipping labels. It was used for the purpose for which it was conceived. Because its owner traveled a lot.

He traveled to lead his company in Weinheim more securely into a good future. On the black and meantime desiccated leather, which is stretched across a wooden frame, "R. F." can be read in large, faded lettering. "R. F.", that stands for the trunk's owner: Richard Freudenberg (1892–1975), Speaker of the Management Board from 1923 to 1962. What a time span!

As the shipping labels prove, Richard Freudenberg often traveled on the Hamburg-America line operated by Hapag, a German shipping company. Back then, such trips required totally different foresight and planning from nowadays, but Richard Freudenberg had these. He was traveling in an international business world, long before the word globalization was invented. Foresight here too: Such historical exhibits are contemporary witnesses which literally make history tangible. For this reason, archives have the important task here of collecting and preserving such objects, and documents too, for posterity. Archives are institutions that give a sense of identity, the memory, in this case, of a company.

This book would not exist without the Corporate Archives in Weinheim. Drawing the right conclusions from what is learned from the past for the present and the future is the task of all employees. "R. F." has set the example.

ANNOTATIONS

Preface

1 Cf. Berghoff/Köhler, 2000, p. 15–20.

Chapter 1: Foundation of the company

1 Cf. transcript of co-ownership agreement dated February 5, 1849, in: Corporate Archives 3/01001.
2 Wollstein, 2010, p. 15.
3 Cf. website of the State of Baden-Württemberg, Restauration und Revolution, at: https://www.baden-wuerttemberg.de/de/unser-land/geschichte/der-suedwesten-bis-1945, accessed April 17, 2023.
4 The German Confederation was a federation of various powers as well as medium-sized and small states, with the "Federal Convention", a congress of envoys appointed by the individual governments, acting as the only common government body. It convened up to 1848 in Frankfurt am Main. Cf. Wollstein, 2010, p. 6.
5 Cf. memoirs of Sophie Freudenberg, née Martenstein, 1894, in: Familienschriften, Vol. 1, p. 77 f.
6 Cf. Horchler, 2011, p. 33.
7 Cf. transcript of co-ownership agreement dated February 5, 1849, in: Corporate Archives 3/01001.
8 Cf. MARCHIVUM, Member list IHK Mannheim 1831–1846, under item number 51 Heinze [sic], Heinrich, in: entry 35/1966 (IHK), No. 3. A business guild (*Handlungs-Innung*) was the precursor of today's IHK, a chamber of industry and commerce.
9 Cf. Schlottau, 1993, p. 13 and 36 f.
10 Cf. ibid, p. 35–36. In 1849 there were almost 7,000 leather-manufacturing businesses in Prussia and Saxony alone (see Schlottau, 1993, p. 36). Thus, it can be assumed that there were far more than 10,000 leather businesses in Germany overall at this time.
11 Cf. letter from businessmen Heintze and Sammet to the Grand Duchy Office in Weinheim dated July 12, 1828, in: Corporate Archives 3/01001.
12 Cf. Pflästerer, 1949, p. 23 ff.
13 Cf. transcript of Baden's Interior Ministry dated November 20, 1828, on the application of businessmen Heinrich Christian Heintze and Johann Baptist Sammet to set up a leather factory in Weinheim in this regard, in: Generallandesarchiv Karlsruhe 236 No. 6883. Furthermore, the 1833 list of guilds and guild masters in Mannheim attests to the fact that there were no tanners in Mannheim. Cf. Mannheimer Geschichtsblätter 34 (1933), No. 3, Column 61–62.
14 Cf. website of the State of Baden-Württemberg, Restauration und Revolution, at: https://www.baden-wuerttemberg.de/de/unser-land/geschichte/der-suedwesten-bis-1945, accessed on April 17, 2023.
15 The small-state mentality that prevailed in Germany at the time led to customs and trade barriers, smuggling, as well as a rise in the cost of goods because of the customs duties. In this situation, regional customs alliances were initially formed, and subsequently the first trade associations and customs unions emerged in 1828: Particularly manufacturers were very interested in unifying

customs. The major solution finally came in 1834: on Prussia's initiative, most German states joined forces to form the German Customs Union. The customs union enabled the abolition of internal customs duties, tariff-free movement of goods between states, joint defense against smuggling, common customs laws based on the Prussian model and finally the gradual creation of a unified coinage, weights and measures system. Cf. Ausführungen zur Zollgeschichte, in: www.zoll.de, https://www.zoll.de/DE/Der-Zoll/Zollmuseum/Ausstellung/Historische-Abteilung/Deutscher-Zollverein/deutscher-zollverein_node.html, accessed on April 28, 2019.

16 Cf. Statistisches Landesamt Baden-Württemberg, population of Rhein-Neckar-Kreis administrative district on June 30, 2018, at: https://www.rhein-neckar-kreis.de/site/Rhein-Neckar-Kreis-2016/get/documents_E1366781392/rhein-neckar-kreis/Daten/Infomaterial/Bevölkerungsfortschreibung.pdf, accessed on December 7, 2018.
17 Cf. Horchler, 2011, p. 30 ff.
18 Ibid, p. 31 f.
19 Pflästerer, 1949, p. 27.
20 Cf. transcript of the contract of sale dated May 8, 1828, transcript from the land register of the City of Weinheim, Vol. 18, p. 880, in: Corporate Archives 3/01001.
21 Cf. Pflästerer, 1949, p. 67.
22 Cf. Gorka, 2006, p. 12.
23 Cf. letter from businessmen Heintze and Sammet to the Grand Duchy Office in Weinheim dated July 12, 1828, in: Corporate Archives 3/01001 and Pflästerer, 1949, p. 67.
24 "Foreign" in this context does not just mean countries like France, England or the Netherlands, but also the other German states – thus in this case the states outside the Grand Duchy of Baden.
25 Cf. letter from businessmen Heintze and Sammet to the Grand Duchy Office in Weinheim dated July 12, 1828, in: Corporate Archives 3/01001.
26 A guild charter meticulously documented the rules of a craft guild. Among other things, it regulated the master craftsman's examination, how apprenticeships were organized, the role of the guild master, and also what should happen in the event of the death of a master craftsman or his wife. Cf. Fresin, 1962, p. 128–133.
27 Roth, 1981, p. 7.
28 Cf. Stürmer, 1985, p. 13.
29 Roth, 1981, p.7.
30 Cf. ibid, p. 26 and p. 30.
31 Roth, 1981, p. 30.
32 Pflästerer, 1949, p. 65.
33 Cf. Stürmer, 1985, p. 13.
34 Cf. transcript of the resolution of the district authority dated August 1, 1828, in: Corporate Archives 3/01001.
35 In the southern German region, the *Conventionsthaler* (a silver coin with a troy weight of 23.385 g) was the standard coinage at this time; minting ceased in southern Germany in 1838. It was originally equivalent to two guilders, but later in southern Germany, however, it became worth 2 guilders 12 kreutzers. At this time (1816–1861), a simple Bavarian soldier earned 2 ¼ guilders a month. Cf. "Löhne und Preise im Königreich Bayern im 19. Jhdt.", in: https://www.pressglas-korrespondenz.de/aktuelles/pdf/pk-2011-3w-klose-preise-1800-1900.pdf, accessed on February 28, 2019.
36 Cf. transcript of the resolution of the district authority dated August 7, 1828, in: Corporate Archives 3/01001.
37 Cf. transcript of the resolution of the district authority dated August 13, 1828, in: Corporate Archives 3/01001.
38 Cf. transcript of the most obedient justification against the official resolution dated August 21, 1828, in: Corporate Archives 3/01001.
39 Cf. transcript of the resolution dated March 26, 1829, in respect of March 7, 1829, in: Corporate Archives 3/01001. Whether Heintze & Sammet nonetheless – and particularly under which legal regulation, for example purchase or leasehold – already began manufacturing leather in Weinheim in 1829 cannot be definitively proven based on the surviving sources. The first verifiable acquisition of a tannery in Weinheim's Müllheimer Tal did not take place according to the land registers until October 10, 1835. Cf. excerpt from the land register of the City of Weinheim, Vol. 19, Land Register 23, contract of sale between Freiherr von Babo, Emilie von Babo and Heintze and

Sammet dated October 10, 1835, as well as the transcript of the contract of sale, both in: Corporate Archives 3/01001.
40 Cf. Horchler, 2019, p. 63.
41 Cf. memoirs of Friedrich Carl Freudenberg, in: Familienschriften, Vol. 1, p. 93.
42 Cf. Mitterauer, 1986, p. 62 f. and p. 77 f.
43 Cf. memoirs of Sophie Freudenberg, née Martenstein, 1894, in: Familienschriften, Vol. 1, p. 76.
44 Ibid, p. 74 ff.
45 Cf. ibid, p. 76.
46 Cf. Horchler, 2011, p. 33.
47 Memoirs of Friedrich Carl Freudenberg, 1938, in: Familienschriften, Vol. 1, p. 93 f.
48 Memoirs of Sophie Freudenberg, née Martenstein, 1867, in: Familienschriften, Vol. 1, p. 79 f. There is no evidence of the 30,000 guilders mentioned by Sophie Freudenberg up to 1855 in the capital account of the general ledger. The first evidence of incoming capital listed in the equity capital is 9,000 guilders from the Martenstein family in May 1850. A further capital increase of 4,2000 guilders from the Martenstein family follows in July 1855. The advances from her father mentioned by Sophie Freudenberg were booked through a separate account, the Martenstein loan account.
49 Cf. 1848 general ledger, in: Corporate Archives 3/06207 as well as Purchasing power equivalents of historical amounts in German currencies (Last updated: March 2019), in: https://www.bundesbank.de/resource/blob/615162/7ca8c81bb5b80fb993be76b79adbdee5/mL/kaufkraftaequivalente-historischer-betraege-in-deutschen-waehrungen-data.pdf, accessed on May 15, 2019. This would mean: 12,000 guilders (1844) – ca. 220,000 euros; 15,000 guilders (1844) – ca. 275,000 euros; 14,300 guilders (1848) – ca. 318,000 euros; 20,876.44 guilders (1849) – ca. 495.000 euros; 30,000 guilders (1849) – ca. 711,000 euros.
50 Cf. 1849 general ledger, in: Corporate Archives 3/06207.
51 Memoirs of Sophie Freudenberg, née Martenstein, 1894, in: Familienschriften, Vol. 1, p. 82.
52 Cf. Scholtyseck, 2016, p. 21.
53 Cf. Heintze & Freudenberg general ledgers from 1849–1867, in: Corporate Archives 3/06207.
54 Memoirs of Sophie Freudenberg, née Martenstein, 1894, in: Familienschriften, Vol. 1, p. 78.
55 Cf. Fresin, 1962, p. 201–203.
56 Cf. website of the State of Baden-Württemberg, Restauration und Revolution, at: https://www.baden-wuerttemberg.de/de/unser-land/geschichte/der-suedwesten-bis-1945, accessed on April 17, 2023.
57 Ibid.
58 Cf. Fresin, 1962, p. 203–205.
59 Memoirs of Sophie Freudenberg, née Martenstein, 1894, in: Familienschriften, Vol. 1, p. 78.

Chapter 2: Formative years, innovations and growth

1 Cf. excerpt from the 1895 death register of the City of Weinheim for the biographical data and names, in: StA Weinheim: main death register of the City of Weinheim 1895, No. 13.
2 Memoirs of Sophie Freudenberg, née Martenstein, 1894, in: Familienschriften, Vol. 1, p. 78.
3 Cf. Scholtyseck, 2016, p. 22 as well as Freudenberg Corporate Archives, Employee and sales statistics.
4 According to the memoirs of Sophie Freudenberg, née Martenstein, Leopold Heintze became the third general partner in the "Heintze & Freudenberg" company on July 1, 1850. "She also writes in her memoirs: To save on many expenses, he remained unnamed in the firm and all sales and income were attributed to the old gentleman and my husband." Cf. Freudenberg, 1867, p. 4. However, from general ledger for the years from 1848 to 1858, it appears that Leopold Heintze was only assigned his own capital account from July 1, 1851. According to the general ledger, he did not previously have such an account, and this was necessary for a shareholding in a company, even at this time. Cf. general ledger 1848–1858, p. 196, in: Corporate Archives 3/06207–1848–58.
5 Cf. Horchler, 2018, p. 129.
6 Cf. History Brochure, 2019, p. 4 as well as general ledger 1867–1874, p. 851, in: Corporate Archives 3/06207–1867–74.

7 Cf. Freudenberg, 1938, p. 13.
8 Friedrich Carl Freudenberg: Patent leather and the business situation between 1865 and 1880, in: Familienschriften, Vol. 3, p. 38.
9 At the first Expo, or Great Exhibition, in London, the "Exhibition of the Works of Industry of All Nations", a total of 14,000 exhibitors from 25 countries and 15 British Colonies displayed their products in 30 different industry classes. As one of 14 attendees from the then Grand Duchy of Baden, Heintze & Sammet presented its innovative black patent calf leather for boots and shoes. Cf. in this regard: Horchler, 2019a, p. 58.
10 "They marked their own leather with what were known as leather tags, which were used in various ways. In the form of paper labels, they were enclosed in leather packages that were ready for shipment or stamped onto the undersides of the leathers using an embossed stamp." Horchler, 2019a, p. 58 f.
11 Cf. Horchler, 2018, p. 130; Horchler, 2019a, p. 58 f. as well as Freudenberg Corporate Archives, Employee and sales statistics Employee and sales statistics. 1850: employees 50; sales 87,000 fl.; 1856: employees 320 (up 640 percent), sales 791,278 fl. (up 910 percent). After 1865, employee numbers remained more or less unchanged. They did not rise again significantly until after Eduard Michel was let go in 1884 (1885: 450, 1886: 522).
12 Cf. memoirs of Hermann Ernst Freudenberg, Hermann's own account, 1913, in: Familienschriften, Vol. 3, p. 135.
13 The German war of 1866 describes the military conflicts of the German Confederation led by Austria against Prussia and its allies for supremacy in Germany. When Prussia emerged victorious over Austria, the war came to an end. The war also led to the dissolution of the German Confederation. Thus, Prussia gained supremacy in Germany and subsequently founded the North German Confederation, in which it bound the German small and medium-sized states and city-states north of the Main River to Prussia. Cf. Schulz, 2011, p. 181–186.
14 Cf. memoirs of Friedrich Carl Freudenberg on "Patent leather and the business situation between 1865 and 1880", in: Familienschriften, Vol. 3, p. 40–42.
15 Cf. also report from a former tanner from Brombach, who together with Friedrich Carl Freudenberg had worked as a trainee in a tannery in Barr in Alsace in the summer of 1867, in: Corporate Archives 1/00431.
16 Cf. Freudenberg, 1938, p. 6–7, p. 14–20 as well as p. 23–31.
17 Cf. Scholtyseck, 2016, p. 22.
18 The sources also refer to the terms "iron plant" or "hammer plant".
19 Cf. Letter from Carl Johann Freudenberg to his eldest son, Friedrich Carl Freudenberg, on December 29, 1868, in: Familienschriften, Vol. 2, p. 56–57. Comment: Previously, Schönau's mainstay had long been broadcloth fabrication; however, this industry was in decline at this time. Cf. City of Schönau, special excerpt from "Die Stadt- und die Landkreise Heidelberg und Mannheim," Vol. II, Staatliche Archivverwaltung Baden-Württemberg (Publ.), 1968, in: Corporate Archives 3/01227.
20 Cf. Comments from Karl Johann Freudenberg to Friedrich Carl Freudenberg: Patent leather and the business situation between 1865 and 1880, in: Familienschriften, Vol. 3, p. 41.
21 Cf. "Hundert Jahre Werk Schönau" ("100 Years of the Schönau factory"), in: Der Freudenberger, 3/1969, p. 1–14; memoirs of Friedrich Carl Freudenberg dated 1938, in: Familienschriften, Vol. 1, p. 103 and List of the establishment of the various stand-alone plants, including Schönau, in: Corporate Archives 3/07239.
22 Cf. "Hundert Jahre Werk Schönau" ("100 Years of the Schönau factory"), in: Der Freudenberger, 3/1969, p. 7.
23 Cf. Friedrich Carl Freudenberg: Patent leather and the business situation between 1865 and 1880, in: Familienschriften, Vol. 3, p. 41.
24 Cf. 1869 partnership agreement, in: Corporate Archives 3/03490 as well as Freudenberg, 1938, p. 37 f. as well as p. 44 ff.
25 Cf. Freudenberg, 1938, p. 47.
26 Cf. 1869 partnership agreement, in: Corporate Archives 3/03490.
27 Cf. "Hundert Jahre Werk Schönau" ("100 Years of the Schönau factory"), in: Der Freudenberger, 3/1969, p. 1.
28 Cf. Friedrich Carl Freudenberg: Patent leather and the business situation between 1865 and 1880, in: Familienschriften, Vol. 3, p. 41–43.

29 Ibid, p. 41. The stamp for Schönau leather was still F. W. B., while leathers from Weinheim were stamped with "Carl Freudenberg".
30 Comments from Karl Johann Freudenberg to Friedrich Carl Freudenberg: Patent leather and the business situation between 1865 and 1880, in: Familienschriften, Vol. 3, p. 39.
31 Ibid.
32 Ibid, p. 38 f.
33 Cf. also Leicht, 2015.
34 Cf. Scholtyseck, 2016, p. 22 f.
35 Friedrich Carl Freudenberg: Patent leather and the business situation between 1865 and 1880, in: Familienschriften, Vol. 3, p. 39.
36 Cf. memoirs of Friedrich Carl Freudenberg to his brother Hermann Ernst Freudenberg (n. d.), in: Corporate Archives 3/01110/05. On the background of the document: A history of the development of the firm instigated by Walter Freudenberg for his father Friedrich Carl Freudenberg's 90th birthday in 1938. After a short description of a confrontation between Hermann Ernst and Michel about sick employees, it portrays that Friedrich Carl himself had regarded his role of initiator of Hermann Ernst's return from America and the resulting reorganization of the firm as his greatest achievement in running the company.
37 Cf. also "Friedrich Carl's comments on Hermann Ernst's activities," in: Familienschriften, Vol. 3, p. 122–134.
38 Memoirs of Hermann Ernst Freudenberg, 1913, in: Familienschriften, Vol. 3, p. 135 ff. Cf. also Friedrich Carl Freudenberg's memories of his brother Hermann Ernst Freudenberg (n. d.), in: Corporate Archives 3/01110/05.
39 There is evidence in the general ledgers of significant loans from Eduard Michel, which are shown in a business partner account as credit. Between 1867 and 1874, the credit volume ranges between 8,000 guilders and 4,000 marks (around 2,300 guilders). Up to 1878, the credit volume rises to ca. 21,000 marks (12,300 guilders). Cf. general ledgers 1867–1878, in: Corporate Archives 3/06207. There is a fundamental problem that the figures in the memoirs in the Familienschriften (family writings) frequently diverge markedly from the verifiable figures in the general ledgers. Note on conversion: 1 guilder was 1.71 marks. Cf. Theurl, 1998.
40 Cf. Scholtyseck, 2016, p. 24.
41 Excerpt from Weinheimer Anzeiger [newspaper – ed.], published March 1, 1894, in: Familienschriften, Vol. 2, p. 276 f.
42 Cf. 1867–1882 general ledgers, in: Corporate Archives 3/06207.
43 Cf. History Brochure, 2019, p. 5.
44 Cf. Transcript of Carl Johann Freudenberg's Business Principles entitled "General observations!" dated 1887, in: Corporate Archives 3/05163.
45 Horchler, 2018, p. 131.
46 Unfortunately, the date of origin of the attached quotation cannot be precisely determined. However, it is likely that it dates from the 1870s, when Carl Johann's sons (Friedrich Carl and Hermann Ernst) joined the company.
47 Pinnow, 1949, p. 96.
48 Ibid.
49 Cf. Reden zum Dialog 99, in: Corporate Archives 3/05307.
50 The first entry containing the term "health insurance scheme" can be found in the 1875–1882 general ledger under "workers health insurance scheme". Cf. general ledger, in: Corporate Archives 3/06207-1875–82, p. 94. In the 1867–1874 general ledger, the workers' relief fund can be found from 1874, which was used to cover the expenses of the health insurance scheme. The penalties account, which was kept up to 1873, was paid into this. The penalties, which were charged for violating the factory regulations, were therefore used as a capital base for the health insurance scheme. Cf. general ledger, in: Corporate Archives 3/06207-1867–74, p. 248 f.
51 Cf. Documents on the Schönau nursing care association, in: Corporate Archives 3/05636. Comment: In a historical retrospective of the nursing care association, a meeting of "respected and influential, in some cases wealthy citizens" is described as a founding event. Friedrich Carl Freudenberg is named as first chairman of the committee. His wife Johanna is not mentioned here. However, in a speech given by Richard Freudenberg on Friedrich Carl Freudenberg's 90th birthday in 1938, the foundation of a social care center by Johanna Freudenberg is mentioned in one sentence – but incorrectly dated 1899 here. Cf. History of the Schönau factory, in: Corporate Ar-

chives 3/01224. In a letter from the Schönau church parish to Friedrich Carl Freudenberg dated October 19, 1892, Sophie Freudenberg is described as the "foundress of our social care center". Cf. in this regard, documents pertaining to the donation, in: Corporate Archives 3/10805.

52 Cf. documents pertaining to the donation, in: Corporate Archives 3/10805 as well as Richard Freudenberg's ceremonial address to mark 100 years of Schönau on July 4, 1969, p. 13 and Richard Freudenberg's speech marking Friedrich Carl Freudenberg's 90th birthday in 1938, p. 4, in: Corporate Archives 3/01224. The esteem enjoyed by the Freudenberg family in Schönau is expressed as follows in a letter from the church parish dated October 19, 1892: "With this resolution [to build the kindergarten] the parish council joins in renewed expression of our heartfelt gratitude for the most excellent family of Mr. [Friedrich Carl] Freudenberg, who, as the father of our workers, and for whose most esteemed parents, particularly his mother, who as foundress of our social care center and benefactress to our poor, have become a bounteous blessing to our parish." Cf. documents pertaining to the donation, in: Corporate Archives 3/10805.

53 Cf. transcript of the deed dated February 24, 1894, in: Corporate Archives 3/03055. In addition, the source details the conditions related to the donation. Cf. letter: "To mark their golden wedding anniversary, Mr. Kommerzienrath [honorary title conferred during the German Empire on distinguished personages in industry – ed.] Carl Freudenberg and his spouse Sophie, née Martenstein, for public notarization [...]" (n. d.), in: Corporate Archives 3/03055. A further pointer to the motivations behind the relief fund is provided in Carl Johann Freudenberg's speech to the workforce to mark his golden wedding anniversary on February 27, 1894. Cf. excerpt from Weinheimer Anzeiger [newspaper – ed.] dated March 1, 1894, in: Familienschriften, Vol. 2, p. 276 f.)

54 Cf. Richard Freudenberg's ceremonial address to mark 100 years of Schönau on July 4, 1969, p. 13 and Richard Freudenberg's speech marking Friedrich Carl Freudenberg's 90th birthday in 1938, p. 4, in: Corporate Archives 3/01224.

55 Cf. foundation documents, in: Corporate Archives 3/01005a. Comment: The original announcement document dated March 15, 1903 is an extremely faded, hardly legible reprint. A transcript on file.

56 Cf. Deed of foundation of the widow and orphan fund dated September 20, 1904, in: Corporate Archives 3/03055.

57 Cf. documents in: Corporate Archives 3/03743 and the 1901 general ledger, in: Corporate Archives 3/06207–1901, p. 237–239. Comment: The entries in the general ledger only begin in 1906.

58 Cf. "Apprenticeship in Weinheim. The sons. Hermann's apprenticeship from the fall of 1871 to May 1874," in: Familienschriften, Vol. 3, p. 49–51, here, p. 50 f.

59 Ibid.

60 Ibid.

61 Cf. Friedrich Carl Freudenberg: Patent leather and the business situation between 1865 and 1880, in: Familienschriften, Vol. 3, p. 40–44.

62 Cf. Letter from Hermann Ernst to Auguste Freudenberg dated August 22, 1875, in: Corporate Archives 3/01035.

63 Cf. "Apprenticeship in Weinheim. The sons. Hermann's apprenticeship from the fall of 1871 to May 1874," in: Familienschriften, Vol. 3, p. 49–51, here, p. 51.

64 Cf. the approval certificate for the installation of a steam boiler dated June 27, 1888, issued by the Grand Duchy of Baden's District Authority, in: Corporate Archives 3/06575. However, the first 20 HP steam engine had already been installed at Freudenberg between 1850 and 1860 in the Müll factory. Cf. Freudenberg, 1938, p. 13.

65 Although Bevington & Sons was the most important sales partner in Britain, it was by no means the only one. For London alone, evidence of more than 30 customers for Freudenberg leather can be found in the general ledgers in the 1860s to 1870s (the same applies to the 1880s). Thus, there can be no exclusivity claims on the part of Bevington & Sons or later on the part of Georg Morris, even though the trade conducted with these partners was the most extensive based on volume. Cf. general ledgers, in: Corporate Archives 3/06207.

66 This likely occurred in 1879. There is evidence of a takeover account for George Morris & Son in the general ledger. From this point onwards Freudenberg also conducted business with the firm George Morris & Son. According to the general ledgers, the business relationship with Bevington & Sons ended in 1882. Cf. general ledgers, in: Corporate Archives 3/06207.

67 Cf. "Friedrich Carl's comments on Hermann Ernst's activities," in: Familienschriften, Vol. 3, p. 122–123.

68 Cf. Archive documentation on the works of August Friedrich Siegert owned by the Freudenberg Group dated November 20, 2017.
69 "Friedrich Carl's comments on Hermann Ernst's activities," in: Familienschriften, Vol. 3, p. 126. However, trade literature from the early 20th century shows that selling by surface area initially only became the standard practice for fine leather, i.e., selling by area and selling by weight were still conducted alongside one another for a long time. Cf. in this regard Zeidler, 1914, p. 191. Whether Hermann Ernst indeed initiated the transition to selling by area, as described in the memoirs of Friedrich Carl Freudenberg, cannot be determined conclusively based on the available sources.
70 Cf. Horchler, 2009 as well as the documents in: Corporate Archives 3/01210 and Corporate Archives 3/01110.
71 Cf. "Friedrich Carl's comments on Hermann Ernst's activities," in: Familienschriften, Vol. 3, p. 126.
72 "Friedrich Carl Freudenberg's memories of his brother Hermann Ernst Freudenberg" (n.d.), in: Corporate Archives 3/01110/05.
73 Cf. "Friedrich Carl's comments on Hermann Ernst's activities," in: Familienschriften, Vol. 3, p. 126.
74 Horchler, 2015, p. 46.
75 Cf. also Hermann Ernst Freudenberg's Depiction of the development of chrome tanning, in Corporate Archives 3/00841.
76 Cf. History Brochure, 2019, p. 6.
77 Horchler, 2015, p. 46.
78 Ibid. At that time, 12 million marks corresponded to around 83 million euros, 54 million marks to around 288 million euros. Cf.: Purchasing power equivalents of historical amounts in German currencies (Last updated: March 2019), in: https://www.bundesbank.de/resource/blob/615162/7ca8c81bb5b80fb993be76b79adbdee5/mL/kaufkraftaequivalente-historischer-betraege-in-deutschen-waehrungen-data.pdf, (Purchasing power equivalents of historical amounts in German currencies) accessed on May 15, 2019.
79 Cf. Freudenberg Corporate Archives, Employee and sales statistics.
80 Horchler, 2015, p. 46.
81 Cf. municipal council minutes of the City of Weinheim, in: Corporate Archives 3/01001; memoirs of Philipp Schäfer, 1937, in: Corporate Archives 3/01157 as well as memoirs of Peter Trautmann, 1948, in: Corporate Archives 3/01157.
82 Cf. Compilation of 100 years of Freudenberg, 1961, in: Corporate Archives 3/01110.
83 "Friedrich Carl's comments on Hermann Ernst's activities," in: Familienschriften, Vol. 3, p. 127. "Grain-lacquered chrome patent leather" is a chrome tanned patent leather in which the grain side (the fell side of the hide) is tanned as the upper side of the leather.
84 Cf. ibid. as well as the tannery's 1899–1912 cost book, in: Corporate Archives 3/00855.
85 Cf. Announcement of the partnership of Friedrich Carl and Hermann Ernst Freudenberg dated April 20, 1887, in: Corporate Archives 3/01005/02.
86 Scholtyseck, 2016, p. 27 and p. 466.
87 Ibid, p. 27.
88 Cf. 1896 Carl Freudenberg GmbH partnership agreement, in: Corporate Archives 3/03062.
89 Horchler, 2019.
90 Cf. Scholtyseck, 2016, p. 27.
91 Cf. Jakob Schuhmann: "The relationship of the two brothers Friedrich Carl and Hermann Ernst Freudenberg among themselves," (n.d.), in: Corporate Archives 3/01157; Valentin Dielmann to Hempfing, dated March 21, 1936, in: Corporate Archives 3/01157.
92 Valentin Dielmann to Hempfing, dated March 21, 1936, in: Corporate Archives 3/01157.
93 Cf. Hütter, 2009, p. 120.
94 Cf. Freudenberg, 1938, p. 42f.
95 Cf. Documents on Bahder family history in Corporate Archives 1/00211, 1/00588, 1/00614, 1/00818 as well as resume of Eduard von Bahder, in: Freudenberg Familienzeitung, 2/1997, p. 2.
96 Cf. Scholtyseck, 2016, p. 27 as well as Freudenberg, 1938, p. 80 ff.
97 Cf. Freudenberg, 1938, p. 80 ff. Friedrich Carl describes the situation on p. 81 from memory as follows: "My brother felt it was necessary to take away any influence I had on management when the G.m.b.H. agreement was renewed at the end of 1902."

98 Hütter, 2009, p. 121.
99 Cf. ibid.
100 The path to this agreement is documented in extensive legal correspondence supported by lawyers of the two brothers, which is located in Corporate Archives 3/01005a. Cf. also regarding partnership agreement of the Carl Freudenberg GmbH firm dated February 24, 1905: Corporate Archives 3/03062 and 3/03558.
101 Cf. documents – among other things the statutes – on the building cooperative, in: Corporate Archives 3/07838. The building cooperative was founded in 1911 with the collaboration of Carl Freudenberg GmbH, its first chairperson was Friedrich Carl Freudenberg, later chairpersons were Hans and Dieter Freudenberg as well as Hans-Jochen Hüchting.
102 Cf. Documents on the construction of Freudenberg & Co. GmbH Frankfurt am Main, in: Corporate Archives 3/03463.
103 Cf. partnership agreement of the Carl Freudenberg GmbH firm dated February 24, 1905, in: Corporate Archives 3/03558 as well as 3/03062, along with the documents on the payout to the sisters, in: Corporate Archives 3/03063.
104 Cf. partnership agreement of the Carl Freudenberg GmbH firm dated February 24, 1905, in: Corporate Archives 3/03558 as well as 3/03062.
105 "Friedrich Carl's comments on Hermann Ernst's activities," in: Familienschriften, Vol. 3, S 134.
106 The notarized certificate of appointment dated December 11, 1908 verifies the appointment of Walter and Hermann Ernst jun. as managing directors as of December 12, 1908. Cf. official record of general meeting of the Karl Freudenberg, G. m. b. H. firm in Weinheim issued by the Weinheim notary's office dated December 11,1908, in this regard, in: Corporate Archives 3/03061.
107 He died on March 14, 1920. Cf. Documents on the biography of Hermann Ernst Freudenberg jun., in: Corporate Archives 1/00307.
108 Familienschriften, Vol. 3, p. 246.
109 Cf. Resume of Hermann Ernst Freudenberg jun., in: Corporate Archives 1/00307 as well as 3/10744.
110 Cf. Ernstes und Heiteres aus unserem Firmen-Archiv (Serious and amusing items in our Corporate Archives), in: Der Freudenberger, t 5/1965, p. 21.
111 Cf. memoirs of Philipp Glaser (n. d.), in: Corporate Archives 3/01157.
112 Cf. Scholtyseck, 2016, p. 29 f.
113 Letter from Hermann Ernst to Friedrich Carl dated March 14, 1914, in: Familienschriften, Vol. 2, p. 341.
114 Cf. Resumes of the third generation of family members on the Management Board, in: Corporate Archives 3/10744.
115 Cf. Abstammungstafeln der Familie Freudenberg (Family Trees of the Freudenberg Family), 2018, Vol. 2, p. 19 ff. and Resume of Hermann Ernst Freudenberg jun., in: Corporate Archives 1/00307.
116 Cf. Resume of Hermann Ernst Freudenberg jun., in: Corporate Archives 1/00307 as well as 3/10744.
117 Hermann Ernst jun. served for one year between 1903 and 1904 in the 14th Field Artillery Regiment in Karlsruhe. Cf. Resume of Hermann Ernst Freudenberg jun., in: Corporate Archives 1/00307. It is interesting to note that he served in the same regiment as his cousin Walter.
118 Cf. Resume of Hermann Ernst Freudenberg jun., in: Corporate Archives 1/00307 as well as 3/10744.
119 Cf. History Brochure, 2019, p. 6.
120 In 1829, brothers Heinrich Bender (1801–1870) and Karl Friedrich Bender (1806–1869) established a private educational institution, the Bendersches Institut, in Weinheim. The educational reform movements of the end of the 18th century and thus the educational principles of e. g., Jean-Jacques Rousseau and Johann Heinrich Pestalozzi formed the basis for the scholars' education. Thus, movement also played an important role. In the subsequent period, the establishment developed into an institution for "elite bourgeois education" with scholars who did not just come from Weinheim, but also from abroad, in some cases from England or the USA. However, competitive pressure arose from the improved state-maintained schools in Weinheim. Subsequently, between 1876 and 1899, the Bendersches Institut was merged with the Höhere Bürgerschule in Weinheim. Finally, in 1918, this educational institution was dissolved. Cf. Grau/Guttmann, 2008, p. 286 ff.
121 Cf. memoirs of Walter Freudenberg (1948), in: Corporate Archives 1/00719. In his memoirs, Walter Freudenberg describes his schooldays in Frankfurt am Main as follows: "My time in Frankfurt

caused me to form a close relationship with my father's two brothers-in-law, the then director of the Goethe-Gymnasium Karl Reinhard and Director Baier of the Lessing-Gymnasium [a *Gymnasium* is a high school – ed.], whose kindly solicitude I fondly remember. I myself lived with the director of the third *Gymnasium* in Frankfurt and was thus very looked after and through this accommodation of mine with the Hartwig family, our family's connection to the Hartwig family came about, to be precise the marriage between my friend Wilhelm Hartwig, former president of the Reichsbahn [German National Railway – ed.] but now retired, and Hans and Richard's elder sister, Auguste."
122 Memoirs of Walter Freudenberg (1948), in: Corporate Archives 1/00719.
123 Ibid.
124 Cf. ibid.
125 Cf. memoirs of Walter Freudenberg (n. d.), in: Corporate Archives 3/01158.
126 He served in the 14th Field Artillery Regiment in Karlsruhe like his cousin Hermann Ernst Freudenberg jun. Cf. Resume of Hermann Ernst Freudenberg jun., in: Corporate Archives 1/00307.
127 Walter Freudenberg writes about the trip to the USA and Canada with Philipp Baer in his memoirs: "Despite the difference in ages, we became friends on this shared journey, since the industrious salesman saw that even the boss's son had made use of his apprenticeship period in America. The trip was a pleasant experience for us both, full of amusing incidences which will be appreciated at another opportunity." Cf. memoirs of Walter Freudenberg (n. d.), in: Corporate Archives 3/01158.
128 Cf. memoirs of Walter Freudenberg (n. d.), in: Corporate Archives 3/01158.
129 Cf. Speech given by Richard Freudenberg at the funeral of Hans Freudenberg, in: Sonderheft der Werkzeitschrift der Firma Carl Freudenberg, Weinheim/Bergstr. 1966.
130 Cf. Goethe-Gymnasium certificate commemorating the 50th anniversary of the day of the *Reifeprüfung* [school leaving certificate – ed.], in: Corporate Archives 1/00204.
131 Cf. Certificate of good conduct No. 8 of the troop muster roll for 1907, in: Corporate Archives 1/00413.
132 Cf. Speech given by Richard Freudenberg at the funeral of Hans Freudenberg, in: Sonderheft der Werkzeitschrift der Firma Carl Freudenberg, Weinheim/Bergstr. 1966.
133 Ibid.
134 Cf. Scholtyseck, 2016, p. 54.
135 Cf. Personnel file for Otto Freudenberg, compiled by the Königliches Bezirkskommando Heidelberg (Imperial Municipal Draft Office) between 1911 and 1920, in: Corporate Archives 3/09295.
136 Among other things, he was awarded the Iron Cross (*Eisernes Kreuz*) Grade I and II as well as the Knight's Cross (*Ritterkreuz*) 2nd Class. Cf. Compilation of personal information on Otto Freudenberg (n. d.), in: Corporate Archives 1/00242.
137 Cf. ibid.
138 Cf. Personnel file for Otto Freudenberg, compiled by the Königliches Bezirkskommando Heidelberg (Imperial Municipal Draft Office) between 1911 and 1920, in: Corporate Archives 3/09295.
139 Cf. Resume of Otto Freudenberg, in: Corporate Archives 3/10744.
140 Cf. Resume of Richard Freudenberg, in: Corporate Archives 3/02128.
141 Speech given by Hermann Ernst Freudenberg at the wedding of Richard Freudenberg and Sibille Sternberg on September 12, 1922, in: Corporate Archives 1/00274.
142 Letter from Richard Freudenberg to Helene Freudenberg dated February 8, 1916, in: Freudenberg, 1974, p. 114.
143 Cf. Resume of Richard Freudenberg, in: Corporate Archives 3/02128.
144 Cf. Familienschriften, Vol. 3, p. 298. As early as November 1915, Hermann Ernst Freudenberg was fulsome in his praise of his son, Richard, who had apparently familiarized himself very quickly with this unfamiliar area of expertise: "Things are going very well thanks to Richard's excellent assistance." Cf. letter from Hermann Erst Freudenberg to Hans Freudenberg dated November 16, 1915, in: Familienschriften, Vol. 3, p. 301. This is also expressed by his brother, Karl Johann Freudenberg, in a letter dated December 1918: "It is always especially reassuring to know that Hans [Freudenberg] is there with us at work, because he has ideas. These and technical knowledge are the best insurance against setbacks. What makes Richard stand out on the commercial side, Hans has in the field of technology." Cf. Letter from Karl Johann Freudenberg to Hermann Ernst and Helene Freudenberg dated December 17, 1918, in: Familienschriften, Vol. 3, p. 309.

145 Cf. Archive compilation: The Freudenberg Management Moard – chronological sequence.

Chapter 3: From World War I to Great Depression

1 Ansprache Richard Freudenbergs vom 16. April 1948, p. 8, in: Corporate Archives 1/00274.
2 Cf. Münkler, 2013, p. 25–82 as well as Mayer, 2014, p. 3.
3 Cf. Freudenberg Corporate Archives, Mitarbeiter- und Umsatzstatistik.
4 Cf. Horchler, 2018, p. 132.
5 Cf. Mayer, 2014, p. 3.
6 Cf. Freudenberg Corporate Archives, Mitarbeiter- und Umsatzstatistik.
7 Cf. namentliche Verzeichnisse der Gefallenen, in: Corporate Archives 3/01110.
8 Cf. Lebensläufe der Geschäftsführer der dritten Familiengeneration, in: Corporate Archives 3/10744.
9 Hermann Ernst Freudenberg jun., the eldest son of Hermann Ernst Freudenberg, had been in charge of the cost estimation books since 1907. In 1908, he was appointed as a managing director of the Carl Freudenberg firm together with his cousin, Walter Freudenberg. Even before war broke out, Hermann jun. had shown symptoms of a grave illness. It increasingly prevented him from working and led to his early death in 1920. Cf. Documents on the biography of Hermann Ernst Freudenberg, in: Corporate Archives 1/00307.
10 Cf. Documents on the biography of Hermann Ernst Freudenberg, in: Corporate Archives 1/00307. Hermann Ernst Freudenberg jun. left the company already in 1917 because of health reasons.
11 Cf. Vita von Richard Freudenberg, in: Corporate Archives 3/02128.
12 Freudenberg, 1945, p. 3.
13 Cf. Scholtyseck, 2016, p. 36.
14 Cf. ibid, p. 36f.
15 Secondary source: Scholtyseck, 2016, p. 37.
16 Cf. Freudenberg Corporate Archives, Mitarbeiter- und Umsatzstatistik: Compared to 1913, the last peacetime year, sales fall by almost 24 percent by 1915 and by more than 60 percent by 1917. Cf. also Asmuss, 2011.
17 Cf. Baupläne der geplanten Hauptverwaltung von 1914, in: Corporate Archives 5/00041.
18 Cf. Brief von Richard Freudenberg an Hans Freudenberg vom 2. November 1916, in: Corporate Archives 3/01110.
19 Cf. Brief von Richard Freudenberg an Hans Freudenberg vom 28. Dezember 1916, in: Corporate Archives 3/01110, as well as Geschäftsbericht, 1917, in: Corporate Archives 3/01110.
20 "Neradol" was one of the first synthetic tanning agents to come on the market, but it was a failure and disappeared from production processes again very quickly. Cf. Freudenberg, 1945, p. 3. Comment: At the beginning of the 20th century, Freudenberg procured its tanning chemicals predominantly from the firms BASF, E. de Haën and Röhm. It is not clear where the chromium salts were procured, but there is much to suggest that it was from BASF (Cf. also Corporate Archives 3/00841). However, it must be noted that chromium naturally occurs almost exclusively in mineral form and is quarried in open-cast mining as chromite or as chrome iron ore. In Germany, there are no known deposits. The best-known countries for mining chromium are currently South Africa, India, Kazakhstan, Brazil, Zimbabwe, Turkey and Finland. Cf. Chrom, in: https://www.chemie.de/lexikon/chrom.html#Vorkommen, accessed on July 11, 2019. Thus, it cannot be determined from the documents in the Corporate Archives where the chromium salts were imported from by suppliers. It is certain, however, that they had to have been imported.
21 Cf. Brief von Hermann Ernst Freudenberg an Hans Freudenberg vom 13. September 1917, in: Corporate Archives 3/01110.
22 Freudenberg, 1945, p. 10.
23 Cf. Bericht von Richard Freudenberg, in: Familienschriften, Vol. 3, p. 302.
24 Ansprache Richard Freudenbergs vom 16. April 1948, p. 8, in: Corporate Archives 1/00274.
25 Freudenberg, 1945, p. 10.
26 Cf. Erinnerungen von Friedrich Carl Freudenberg an seinen Bruder Hermann Ernst Freudenberg, in: Familienschriften, Vol. 3, p. 134.

27 Cf. Erinnerungen von Friedrich Carl Freudenberg an seinen Bruder Hermann Ernst Freudenberg (n. d.), in: Corporate Archives 3/01110/05 as well as Erinnerungen des ehemaligen Prokuristen Peter Trautmann vom 26.08.1948, in: Corporate Archives 3/01157.
28 Cf. Unterstützungsfonds, in: Corporate Archives 3/00846, Geschäftsbericht, 1914, p. 9, in: Corporate Archives 3/07282 as well as Erinnerungen von Friedrich Carl Freudenberg an seinen Bruder Hermann Ernst Freudenberg, in: Familienschriften, Vol. 3, p. 134. Comment: The voluntary staff contributions amounted to 10 percent of married people's salaries and 15 percent of single people's salaries.
29 Cf. The Carl Freudenberg firm's leaflet entitled "An die Frauen unserer zum Heeresdienst einberufenen Arbeiter"[To the wives of our workers who have been drafted into military service – ed.] dated July 31, 1915., in: Corporate Archives 3/01069.
30 Cf. Erinnerungen von Friedrich Carl Freudenberg an seinen Bruder Hermann Ernst Freudenberg (n. d.), in: Corporate Archives 3/01110/05
31 Of the 1,206 employees at the end of 1918, 413 women were employed at the company at the end of the war, meaning that the share of women in the workforce at the end of the war was probably significantly higher in reality. Cf. Freudenberg Corporate Archives, Mitarbeiter- und Umsatzstatistik, as well as Pinnow, 1949, p. 110.
32 Hermann Ernst Freudenberg an Hans Freudenberg vom 13. September 1917, in: Corporate Archives 3/01110. Comment: The figures reflect the status in September 1917. Hermann Ernst Freudenberg also states his opinion in the quoted letter that the French were "quite unpleasant chaps". Furthermore, employing prisoners of war was legitimate under the law of war that was valid at the time. Cf. also Scholtyseck, 2016, p. 38 regarding the latter point.
33 Cf. Freudenberg Corporate Archives, Mitarbeiter- und Umsatzstatistik.
34 Cf. Erinnerungen des ehemaligen Prokuristen Peter Trautmann vom 26.08.1948, in: Corporate Archives 3/01157 and cf. on food rationing: Michaelis, 2014. Comment: As soon as the war broke out, disruptions already began to occur in Weinheim citizens' food supply and led to so-called "hamster purchases" – panic buying – which the government sought to regulate through state intervention. From the beginning of 1915, the first ration cards for bread were distributed in several cities – and this was the official start of food rationing. Further rationing measures followed later, on milk, fats and oils, eggs, and other foodstuffs. The regulation of rationing was in the purview of the municipal authorities, meaning that there were deviations in the amounts of food distributed from region to region. Cf. Michaelis, 2014.
35 Cf. Freudenberg/Schuster, 1999, p. 45.
36 Cf. Erinnerungen des ehemaligen Prokuristen Peter Trautmann vom 26.08.1948, in: Corporate Archives 3/01157.
37 Cf. Dankesschreiben von Mitarbeitern an der Front an die Firma Carl Freudenberg, in: Corporate Archives 3/01110.
38 At the end of the war, it can be assumed that a total of more than 8.5 million soldiers had been killed. Cf. Hochschild, 2013, p.439.
39 Cf. Jürgs, 2005.
40 This person is probably the later authorized signatory, Valentin Dielmann, who held general power of attorney between 1938 and 1944. Cf. also Prokura-Anzeigen, in: Corporate Archives 3/01005.
41 Brief von V. Dielmann an Carl Freudenberg vom 10. Mai 1915, in: Corporate Archives: 3/01110.
42 Cf. Schreiben der Firma Carl Freudenberg an die Mitarbeiter mit dem Titel "An unsere zum Kriegsdienst einberufenen Arbeiter!" im August 1918 [Letter from the Carl Freudenberg company to employees entitled "To our employees who have been called up to military service!" in August 1918], especially the section on the introduction of the *"Dienstprämienvertrag"* (service bonus agreement), in: Corporate Archives 3/01110.
43 In 1930, the amount of capital in the service bonus agreements totaled 1,177,022 RM [Reichsmarks – ed.]. Cf Unterlagen zum Dienstprämienvertrag, in: Corporate Archives 3/04800.
44 Cf. Unterlagen zum Dienstprämienvertrag, in: Corporate Archives 3/00812 and Corporate Archives 3/03440. The letter to the employees on the battlefield with the offer of a "service bonus agreement" can also be found in: Corporate Archives 3/01110.
45 Cf. Unterstützungsfonds, in: Corporate Archives 3/00846, Geschäftsbericht, 1914, p.9, in: Corporate Archives 3/07282 as well as Erinnerungen von Friedrich Carl Freudenberg an seinen Bruder Hermann Ernst Freudenberg, in: Familienschriften, Vol. 3, p. 134.

46 Cf. Unterlagen zum Dienstprämienvertrag, in: Corporate Archives 3/00812 and Corporate Archives 3/03440.
47 Cf. Stiftungsunterlagen, in: Corporate Archives 3/04787.
48 Cf. Stiftungsunterlagen, in: Corporate Archives 3/01153.
49 The Treaty of Versailles was signed in June 1919 by 26 Allied and associated powers as well as Germany. It came into effect in January 1920. Cf. Henssler, 2007.
50 Cf. Kunzel, 2014 as well as Sturm, 2018a, p. 90.
51 Cf. Wagner, 1924.
52 Cf. Kunzel, 2014 as well as Sturm, 2018a, p. 90.
53 The highest nominal value of a Reichsbank banknote was ultimately 100 trillion marks (100,000,000,000,000 M). Cf. Kunzel, 2014.
54 Cf. Freudenberg, 1945, p. 11 as well as Pinnow, 1949, p. 115.
55 Cf. samples of these "Freudenberg vouchers" worth 1 and 2 million marks dating from 1923, in: Corporate Archives 3/01092.
56 Cf. Carl Freudenberg company voucher for 1 dollar, in: Corporate Archives 3/01091 as well as Scholtyseck, 2016, p. 50.
57 Cf. The partial debentures of a gold loan dating from 1923 with maturity by 1933, in: Corporate Archives 3/01092 as well as Scholtyseck, 2016, p. 50f.
58 Cf. Familienschriften, Vol. 3, p. 303.
59 Cf. Lindenlaub, 1985.
60 The Bally company had been a purchaser of Freudenberg leathers since 1851 and was one of the company's longest-standing customers. Cf. also Hauptbuch von 1851, in: Corporate Archives 3/06207–1848–58.
61 Cf. Familienschriften, Vol. 3, p. 302f. as well as Scholtyseck, 2016, p. 51.
62 Scholtyseck, 2016, p. 49. A minority share in the company was held by Alfred Morris. He was the main purchaser of Freudenberg leathers in Great Britain and owner of the firm George Morris & Son. Cf. also Geschäftsbericht, 1921, in: Corporate Archives 3/07282.
63 Scholtyseck, 2016, p. 49 as well as Geschäftsbericht, 1924, in: Corporate Archives 3/07282. "Carl Freudenberg paid 84,200 Swiss francs for a share in the Tannerie de Lausanne, which had capital of 631,500 Swiss francs, through Externa SA. In 1929, the capital was reduced at a ratio of 5:1; when the subsequent recapitalization to 500,000 Swiss francs occurred, Externa acquired a majority shareholding – thus the extent of the influence Carl Freudenberg had previously held remained unchanged." Secondary source Scholtyseck, 2016, p. 473.
64 Scholtyseck, 2016, p. 49. "Walter Baer was the first director, then from 1930 Ernest Suter, who was simultaneously also a director of Externa; there was also the technical director of the tannery, Paul Recht." [Editor's translation] Cf. also the Swiss Clearing Office's "Audit report on SA de Tannerie" dated December 31, 1951, BAR E7160–07#1968/54#2381.
65 Scholtyseck, 2016, p. 49. "The method was not discovered at the time and functioned despite Polish customs checks until Gebr. Krafft, which had been used as a transfer firm, went bankrupt in 1930. It had been deeply in debt because of the global economic crisis. From then on, Vienna-based leather factory Gerhardus GmbH, of which 51 percent was held by Carl Freudenberg, assumed the function of agent." [Editor's translation] Secondary source: Scholtyseck, 2016, p. 49. Cf. also Rudolf Reiman, "Mein vorläufiger Kurzbericht" (1971), in: Corporate Archives 3/01599 as well as note "Josef Reiman, Wien, II., Große Mohrengasse 5", in: Corporate Archives 3/02961.
66 Cf. Scriba, 2011 as well as Feldman, 1998, p. 522–529, here in particular p. 524.
67 Cf. Sturm, 2018, p. 67.
68 Scholtyseck, 2016, p. 43. Cf. also Carl Freudenberg an I. Kavallerie-Brigade (Krozingen) vom 28. November 1918, in: Corporate Archives 3/01110 as well as Carl Freudenberg an Ersatz-Bataillon des Württembergischen Landwehr-Infanterieregiments 124 vom 16. November 1918, in: Corporate Archives 3/01110.
69 Cf. Plumpe, 1999, p. 47f.
70 Scholtyseck, 2016, p. 44.
71 Cf. Protokolle des Betriebsrates, des Arbeiterrates und des Vertrauensrates der Firma Carl Freudenberg, in: Corporate Archives 3/01510.
72 Scholtyseck, 2016, p. 45. See also Geschäftsbericht, 1921, in: Corporate Archives 3/07282.
73 Scholtyseck, 2016, p. 45.

74 Hermann Ernst Freudenberg an Karl Freudenberg vom 2. Februar 1919, in: Familienschriften, Vol. 3, p. 312.
75 Ibid, p. 313.
76 Cf. Scholtyseck, 2016, p. 43.
77 Cf. Palmer, 2018.
78 Cf. Vgl. Hermann Ernst Freudenberg an Karl Freudenberg vom 20. Juli 1919, in: Familienschriften, Vol. 3, p. 316 as well as Scholtyseck, 2016, p. 48.
79 When a company is divided into a holding company and an operating company as occurred in this case, the holding company (Freudenberg & Co.) acts as the owner, and the operating company (Carl Freudenberg) assumes responsibility for business operations. A holding company can also be the owner of several subsidiaries. Cf. also Finanzlexikon online under the heading: Besitzgesellschaft, in: http://www.finanzlexikon-online.de/besitzgesellschaft.html, accessed on June 2, 2020.
80 Scholtyseck, 2016, p. 48. Freudenberg & Co. GmbH had equity capital of 500,000 marks; profits were generated from the dividends of Carl Freudenberg GmbH. Cf. also Freudenberg/Schuster, 1999, p. 257 as well as Hütter, 2009, p. 145 f.
81 Scholtyseck, 2016, p. 48.
82 Ibid. However, there were already regulations on the withdrawal of stakeholdings in the 1917 partnership agreement and its adjustments from the years 1920 to 1921. Cf. the relevant Gesellschaftsverträge [partnership agreements], in: Corporate Archives 3/03075.
83 Scholtyseck, 2016, p. 48.
84 Cf. Sturm, 2018a, p. 90.
85 Cf. Geyer, 1988, p. 384.
86 Cf. Scholtyseck, 2016, p. 52.
87 Scholtyseck, 2016, p. 52. Cf. also Hermann Ernst Freudenberg an seine Frau vom 8. November 1921, in: Familienschriften, Vol. 3, p. 319.
88 Cf. Notiz von Hermann Ernst Freudenberg in der Chronik des Hauses Champex vom 2. September 1922, in: Familienschriften, Vol. 3, p. 320.
89 Cf. Hermann Ernst Freudenberg an Adolf Freudenberg vom 1. April 1923, in: Familienschriften, Vol. 3, p. 321.
90 Cf. Scholtyseck, 2016, p. 52; Freudenberg, 1962, p. 70 as well as Hermann Ernst Freudenberg an Karl Freudenberg vom 19. August 1919, in: Familienschriften, Vol. 3, p. 317.
91 1 Rentenmark corresponded to 1 trillion paper marks. Cf. Braun, 2006.
92 Sturm 2018a, p. 92.
93 Scholtyseck, 2016, p. 55. Cf. also "150 Jahre Freudenberg – Die Belegschaften im Wandel der Zeit" [150 years of Freudenberg – the workforce down the years] (1999), p. 8, in: Corporate Archives 3/08920.
94 Scholtyseck, 2016, p. 55. Cf. also Freudenberg Corporate Archives, Mitarbeiter- und Umsatzstatistik.
95 Erinnerungen von Walter Freudenberg, um 1947, in: Familienschriften, Vol. 3, p. 321.
96 Scholtyseck, 2016, p. 53.
97 Ibid. Cf. also Siegrist, 1981, p. 145.
98 Cf. Scholtyseck, 2016, p. 55.
99 Cf. Freudenberg/Schuster, 1999, p. 54.
100 Scholtyseck, 2016, p. 55. What are known as "Kruppschlepper" were the first motorized towing vehicles or trucks manufactured by the Krupp company. Cf. also "Erinnerungen des Betriebsleiters Philipp Schäfer" (1937), in: Corporate Archives 3/01157.
101 Cf. Scholtyseck, 2016, p. 54.
102 Freudenberg/Schuster, 1999, p. 54. Cf. also Trauerrede von Richard Freudenberg für Hans Freudenberg, in: Corporate Archives 3/10742.
103 Scholtyseck, 2016, p. 55. Cf. also Geschäftsbericht, 1924, in: Corporate Archives 3/07282.
104 Scholtyseck, 2016, p. 55. Cf. also Erinnerungen von Richard Freudenberg, in: Familienschriften, Vol. 3, p. 327.
105 Scholtyseck, 2016, p. 55. Cf. also Freudenberg, 1945, p. 12 f.
106 Cf. Scholtyseck, 2016, p. 55 f. Cf. also Richard Freudenberg an Joseph Bernfeld vom 6. November 1945, in: NA Washington, OMGUS, Finance, Box 188.
107 Scholtyseck, 2016, p. 56.

108 Cf. Reisebericht der USA-Reise von Hermann Ernst und seinem Sohn Otto Freudenberg aus dem Jahre 1914, in: Corporate Archives 3/01030 as well as Tagebuch der Amerika-Reise von Hermann Ernst Freudenberg von 1914, in: Corporate Archives 1/00226.
109 Cf. Reiseberichte von Otto Freudenberg aus den Jahren 1925, 1929 und 1932, in: Corporate Archives 3/01053.
110 Scholtyseck, 2016, p. 54. Cf. also Freudenberg, 1948.
111 Scholtyseck, 2016, p. 56. Cf. also some anecdotal mentions by Richard Freudenberg in: Der Freudenberger, Sonderheft/1962, Richard Freudenberg 70 Jahre, p. 24–26 as well as Reisebericht der Amerika-Reise von Richard Freudenberg 1928, in: Corporate Archives 3/01032. The Carl Freudenberg Inc. Boston company was dissolved in 1935 in accordance with the laws of the Third Reich and the capital delivered to the Reichsbank. Cf. Unterlagen zur Liquidation und den Bilanzen der Carl Freudenberg Inc. Boston, in: Corporate Archives 3/01856 and Corporate Archives 3/01468.
112 Scholtyseck, 2016, p. 56. The Freudenberg shares were held in trust by long-standing business acquaintances Enrico Rollier and Philippe Galbiati. The company, which received production patents and brand rights through a licensing agreement, still operated satisfactorily even during World War II, because it received enough calfskins from domestic production. The "Industria Lombarda Pelli al Cromo" company achieved a turnover equivalent to around 2 million RM in 1944. Cf. also documents in: Corporate Archives 3/01385 and Corporate Archives 3/03808.
113 Scholtyseck, 2016, p. 49. The original purpose became irrelevant after the outbreak of World War II. The company was restructured in 1941 and relocated to Berlin. Of the 50,000 RM in capital shares, Freudenberg & Co. took over 20,000 RM; Richard Freudenberg became Vice-Chairman of the Advisory Council. From then on, the company's purpose was to process orders for the manufacture of civilian shoes, for example in Switzerland. Cf. Geschäftsbericht, 1927, in: Corporate Archives 3/07282; the documents in Corporate Archives 3/03102 and Corporate Archives 3/03103 as well as Freudenberg an das Amt für Vermögenskontrolle vom 12. November 1947, in: Corporate Archives 3/09133.
114 Scholtyseck, 2016, p. 50. Cf. also the documents in: Corporate Archives 3/03107 and Corporate Archives 3/07541.
115 Cf. Scholtyseck, 2016, p. 50. Cf. also the documents in: Corporate Archives 3/03080 and Corporate Archives 3/03081.
116 Cf. Scholtyseck, 2016, p. 50. The two best ships had to be written off at the beginning of World War II. One was destroyed by the British in Narvik, the other scuppered itself off the coast of the Azores. Cf. "Scholtyseck, 2016, p. 50. Cf. also the documents in: Corporate Archives 3/03107 and Corporate Archives 3/07541", in: Corporate Archives 1/00343. All the other ships were lost as well because of wartime events or the capitulation.
117 Cf. Schulze, 1994, p. 350–356. Cf. on the interim crisis of 1925/26 also Hesse/Köster/Plumpe, 2014, p. 54 as well as Spoerer/Streb, 2013, p. 85 f.
118 Cf. Winkler, 2018, p. 408–444.
119 Cf. Scholtyseck, 2016, p. 59; Borchardt, 1982, p.178 f.; Weber, 2010; Zahn, 1996 as well as Buchheim/Hutter/James, 1994.
120 Cf. Sturm 2018b, p. 99–101.
121 Scholtyseck, 2016, p. 47. Cf. also Kleinschmidt, 2007, p. 35; Breisig, 1990, p. 57 f.; Mai, 1997, p. 312 as well as Freyberg, 1989.
122 Scholtyseck, 2016, p. 47. Cf. also Sudrow, 2010, p. 220–228.
123 Freudenberg/Schuster, 1999, p. 50 f.
124 Scholtyseck, 2016, p. 47. Cf. also Stellungnahme von Walter Freudenberg, in: Ausschuss zur Untersuchung der Erzeugungs- und Absatzbedingungen der deutschen Wirtschaft. Die Deutsche Lederindustrie, S. 147.
125 Scholtyseck, 2016, p. 47 f.
126 Scholtyseck, 2016, p. 59. Cf. also Plumpe, 2013, p. 81 as well as James, 1988; Cf. also on the European dimension overall: Feinstein/Temin/Toniolo, 2008.
127 Cf. Scholtyseck, 2016, p. 59 as well as Hesse/Köster/Plumpe, 2014, p. 202 f.
128 Cf. Hesse/Köster/Plumpe, 2014, p. 71 ff. as well as Scriba, 2014.
129 Scholtyseck, 2016, p. 60.
130 Cf. Hesse/Köster/Plumpe, 2014, p. 71.
131 Cf. Scholtyseck, 2016, p. 60 as well as Geschäftsbericht, 1928, in: Corporate Archives 3/07282.

132 Cf. Scholtyseck, 2016, p. 60 f.
133 Scholtyseck, 2016, p. 62. Cf. also "Rede des Herrn Richard Freudenberg anlässlich der Feier des 50. Geburtstags von Herrn Hans Freudenberg am 31:3.38", in: Corporate Archives 1/00272 as well as the "Bericht" (August 1936), in: Corporate Archives 3/01363. Ultimately, production of patent leather was discontinued entirely in 1941.
134 Scholtyseck, 2016, p. 62 f. Cf. also Freudenberg, 1945.
135 Scholtyseck, 2016, p. 63. Cf. also "Bericht" (August 1936), in: Corporate Archives 3/01363 as well as Richard Freudenberg an Karl Möll vom 11. September 1930, in: Corporate Archives 3/02961.
136 Cf. Scholtyseck, 2016, p. 63. Cf. also "Betriebsratssitzung 29. Dezember 1931 nachmittags 2 Uhr in der Gerberei", in: Corporate Archives 3/01510; "Richard Freudenberg sprach zu seiner Gefolgschaft. Betriebsappell der Lederwerke Carl Freudenberg", in: Weinheimer Nachrichten dated April 17, 1937 as well as the "Bericht" (August 1936), in: Corporate Archives 3/01363.
137 Cf. Scholtyseck, 2016, p. 61, Erinnerungen von Richard Freudenberg, in: Familienschriften, Vol. 3, p. 327 as well as Freudenberg, 1945, p. 13.
138 Scholtyseck, 2016, p. 61. Cf. also Born, 1983, p. 126–128.
139 Scholtyseck, 2016, p. 61. Cf. also "Bericht" (August 1936), in: Corporate Archives 3/01363.
140 Scholtyseck, 2016, p. 61 f. Cf. also Erinnerungen von Richard Freudenberg, in: Familienschriften, Vol. 3, p. 327.
141 Scholtyseck, 2016, p. 62. Cf. also "Rede des Herrn Richard Freudenberg über den Hauptpunkt der Tagesordnung der außerordentl. Generalversammlung am Sonnabend, den 28. November 1936", in: Corporate Archives 3/01064.
142 Cf. Scholtyseck, 2016, p. 62 as well as Freudenberg, 1945, p. 14.
143 Cf. History brochure, 2019, p. 8 as well as "Rede des Herrn Richard Freudenberg über den Hauptpunkt der Tagesordnung der außerordentl. Generalversammlung am Sonnabend, den 28. November 1936", in: Corporate Archives 3/01064, here p. 5.
144 Cf. Horchler, 2018, p. 134.
145 Cf. Merz, 2000, p. 93 f.
146 Cf. ibid, p. 95 as well as Horchler, 2011, p. 34.
147 Cf. Merz, 2000, p. 96.
148 Cf. ibid.
149 Cf. History brochure, 2019, p. 8.
150 From 1932 onward, the development team led by Walther Simmer comprised engineer Alexander von Löwis of Menar and master craftsman Wilhelm (Willy) Röder. Later, Fritz Hartmann, Ernst von Veh and others also joined the team. Cf. also the documents in: Corporate Archives 3/01250 and Corporate Archives 3/05944.
151 Cf. History brochure, 2019, p. 8.
152 Cf. Merz, 2000, p. 96.
153 There are two reasons for the choice of name: 1. The sealing ring was named after the lead developer, Walther Simmer, and 2. The name was chosen because it was easy to remember and because of the advertising impact due to its linguistic similarity to the motor race on the Semmerring in Austria, which was popular at the time. Cf. Merz, 2000, p. 96 f.
154 Cf. Merz, 2000, p. 96 f. as well as the documents, in: Corporate Archives 3/01250 and Corporate Archives 3/05944.
155 Brief von Walther Simmer an Georg Boysen vom 30. April 1951, p. 3, in: Corporate Archives 3/05657. Comment: Georg Boysen (1890–1964) was sales manager of the Simrit seals department from 1937–1954. Cf. the documents, in: Corporate Archives 3/01694.
156 Cf. Merz, 2000, p. 101.
157 Scholtyseck, 2016, p. 207.
158 Cf. History brochure, 2019, p. 11.
159 The terms "leather substitute materials" and "leather replacement materials" are used interchangeably
160 Cf. History brochure, 2019, p. 10 as well as "Von der Ersatzstoff-Forschung zu Corporate Innovation", in: Corporate Archives 3/10890.
161 Cf. History brochure, 2019, p.10.
162 Horchler, 2018, p. 135.
163 Cf. Schreiben von E. Angus an Richard Freudenberg vom 11.11.1947, in: Corporate Archives

3/05339 as well as Antwortschreiben von Richard Freudenberg an E. Angus vom 26.11.1947, in: Corporate Archives 3/05196.
164 Cf. Brief des britischen Luftfahrtministeriums zur Freigabe der Angus-Dichtungen vom 17.12.1936 [letter from the British Air Ministry on the approval of Angus seals dated December 17, 1936], in: Corporate Archives 3/04822.
165 Cf. documents on the partnership between Freudenberg the Corte & Cosso company, in: Corporate Archives 3/08520.
166 Apart from the *Nora* soles, other leather replacement materials were also developed at Freudenberg for use in shoes. One of these were "Iganil" shoe heels made of synthetic resin, which the company began producing in 1941 and on which it initially held a monopoly. At the beginning of 1945, production of "Iganil" heels was discontinued because of a lack of raw materials. Cf. Unterlagen zur Geschichte des Kunststoffwerkes, in: Corporate Archives 3/01340 as well as Richard Freudenberg an Gustav Rheinberger vom 31. Januar 1945, in: Corporate Archives 3/03088. Above and beyond this, Igelit, a polyvinylchloride manufactured by I.G. Farben, had been used at Freudenberg since 1938 as a leather substitute material for shoes and bags. Cf. also Unterlagen zur Geschichte des Kunststoffwerkes, in: Corporate Archives 3/01340. As early as 1932, development of leather fiber sheets made of defibrated leather offcuts began, which were marketed under the brand names *Robus*, *Ledergon* or *Cefa* and were used among other things to make heel counters for shoes. Cf. also Unterlagen zur Entwicklung der Lederfaserprodukte, in: Corporate Archives 3/01247 and Corporate Archives 3/01267.
167 Cf. Scholtyseck, 2016, p. 219.
168 Cf. Scholtyseck, 2016, p. 229.
169 Bericht für die Geschäftsführermappe vom 21. Februar 1938, in: Corporate Archives 3/01247.
170 Cf. Hofmann, 1978.
171 Cf. History brochure, 2019, p.11 as well as Aktennotiz vom 7. Juli 1938, in: Corporate Archives 3/05138.
172 Cf. Hans Erich Freudenberg an Bischoff vom 11. April 1975, in: Corporate Archives 3/01247.
173 Cf. Hofmann, 1978.
174 Cf. Unterlagen zur *Nora*-Sohle, in: Corporate Archives 3/01620 and Corporate Archives 3/03083.
175 Horchler, 2018a, p. 78.
176 Ibid.
177 Frequently, the fibers were initially boiled in a 1.5-percent sodium hydroxide solution under pressure at a temperature of 125 °C and subsequently washed and dried, before they were further processed into the actual fiber web of the nonwoven. This facilitated the impregnation with latex. Cf. also Patentschrift für Kunstleder von 1936, in: Corporate Archives 3/03086.
178 Cf. Patentschrift für Kunstleder von 1936, in: Corporate Archives 3/03086 as well as Nottebohm, 1985, p. 9 ff.
179 During the initial meetings in Weinheim, the following demonstration of the quality of the *Naturin* artificial skins on the part of Becker & Cie partner Robert Ahrens is reported to have occurred: "He [Robert Ahrens] asked for a bucket of water, moistened the collagen tube he had brought with him in it, blew it up, stood on it with his considerable body weight and – the tube withstood it. This impressive event marked the start of a […] successful collaboration." Cf. "Abteilung Collan – Neue Produkte aus Hauteiweiß", in: CF-intern, 8/1978, p. 4–5, here p. 4.
180 In what was known as the "*Masse-Bau*" [mass building] the untanned glue stock, also known as lime fleshings, obtained during leather production – waste products of parts of the hide unsuitable for leather production which occur after the liming process or after the hides have been split (e.g., low quality flesh split, which has deep butchers' cuts) – are processed chemically and mechanically. In the process, the hide-fiber fabric is cleaned and loosened further in a chemical process without altering the structure of the fibers. Afterwards, further mechanical processing occurs: The hide-fiber fabric that is still wet is cut up and then pressed through sieve plates while preserving the fiber lengths and structures. The resulting mixture is known as "mass" (*Masse*) a sterile, plastic collagen fiber paste. Cf. "Masse + Naturin", in: Der Freudenberger, 4/1954, p. 6–14, here: p. 13 as well as "Abteilung COLLAN – Neue Produkte aus Hauteiweiß", in: CF-intern, 8/1978, p. 4f., here: p. 4.
181 For the young enterprise Becker & Cie, this also had the advantage that they could procure the main raw material (collagen mass based on glue stock) directly on-site for the *Naturin* skins and

benefit from the Freudenberg company's long-standing raw material expertise. Cf. "Masse + Naturin", in: Der Freudenberger, 4/1954, p. 6–14, here: p. 8 f.
182 Cf. 75 Jahre Naturin, in: Corporate Archives 013/1230, p. 11.
183 The artificial skin is based on the "mass" produced at Freudenberg (a paste made of collagen fibers. This is processed again and shaped into a continuous tube of skin, which is completed in a dry channel. Subsequently, the skin goes through more departments: rinsing and inspection department, steam room, winding room and finally the bundling room, from which the final product, the *Naturin* skin, is delivered in fixed bundle sizes. Cf. "Masse + Naturin", in: Der Freudenberger, 4/1954, p. 6–14, here: p. 10.
184 Cf. "25 Jahre Naturin", in: Der Freudenberger, 1/1958, p. 53.
185 Cf. "Veränderung bei Naturin", in: Der Freudenberger, 6/1990, p. 1. The Naturin company continued to procure the mass for production from Freudenberg right up to 1997. Afterwards, Naturin took over production of the collagen mass itself.
186 Cf. Patentschrift Nr. 652874 zur Herstellung von künstlichem Roßhaar, in: Corporate Archives 3/01307 as well as Armin Abel: Bauchronik, in: Corporate Archives 3/01194.
187 Cf. Scholtyseck, 2016, p. 203 ff.

Chapter 4: Freudenberg in the Nazi era

1 The information that will follow about Freudenberg during the Nazi era draws largely on Joachim Scholtyseck's academic study, "Freudenberg. Ein Familienunternehmen in Kaiserreich, Demokratie und Diktatur" published in 2016.
2 Cf. Kershaw, 2009, p. 270–289.
3 Cf. ibid, p. 296 ff. Cf. also Hett, 2016 on the Reichstag fire. [The decree "for the Protection of People and State" became commonly known as the "Reichstag Fire Decree". – ed.]
4 Cf. Frei, 2013, p. 49 and 281.
5 Cf. Asmuss, 2015.
6 Cf. Kershaw, 2009, p. 299 f.
7 Cf. Frei, 2013, p. 30–37, p. 62–79, p. 80–96 as well as p. 282. (The SA was the *Sturmabteilung*, the original paramilitary wing of the Nazi party during the Weimar Republic – ed.)
8 The Supervisory Board Chairman of I. G. Farbenindustrie AG, Carl Duisberg, is a typical example of this attitude. Cf. Plumpe, 2016, p. 784–793.
9 The remaining distribution of votes for Weinheim was as follows: (Baden) German Centre Party, a Christian Democratic and Catholic party, 9.72 %, Kampffront Schwarz-Weiss-Rot, an electoral alliance of DNVP and Stahlhelm, a soldiers' party, 4.09 %, Deutsche Volkspartei, a conservative-liberal party, 1.41 %, Evangelischer Volksdienst, a conservative Protestant party, 1.98 %, and Deutsche Bauernpartei, a farmers' party, 0.02 %. Cf. also Keller, 2000, p. 13.
10 Cf. Keller, 2000, p. 13 f.
11 Cf. Scholtyseck, 2016, p. 90 f.
12 Keller, 2000, p. 16. [The SA were the Sturmabteilung (Assault Division), a paramilitary organization founded by Hitler in 1921 and also known as the Storm Troopers or Brownshirts. – ed.]
13 Cf. Keller, 2000, p. 61–64.
14 Cf. Scholtyseck, 2016, p. 94 and Keller, 2000, p. 88 f.
15 Cf. Scholtyseck, 2016, p. 451 f. as well as Lebenslauf von Richard Freudenberg, in: Corporate Archives 3/02128.
16 Cf. Wilderotter, 1992, p. 21 ff. as well as Lebenslauf von Richard Freudenberg, in: Corporate Archives 3/02128.
17 Scholtyseck, 2016, p. 440.
18 Secondary source: Scholtyseck, 2016, p. 77. Cf. also Auszug aus der *Volksstimme* vom 18. Februar 1933 mit Richard Freudenbergs Zitat über Hitler als Zirkusdirektor, in: Corporate Archives 3/02992/05.
19 Cf. Scholtyseck, 2016, p. 77 f. The dispute in the press, from which Richard and Walter Freudenberg's attitude to Nazi politics can be determined, can be read in detail in: Scholtyseck, 2016, p. 77–78.

20 Scholtyseck, 2016, p. 440.
21 At the end of June 1937, Ernst Freudenberg was sent into compulsory retirement "because of § 6 of the Law for the Restoration of the Professional Civil Service dated April 7, 1933." The reason was, as Ernst von Hülsen, a trustee of the University of Marburg, formulated, "that his wife, although she is of the Protestant confession, is 100 % Jewish by race." Thus, according to the Nazi guidelines, Ernst Freudenberg was no longer permitted to practice his profession as a pediatrician in Germany. Cf. Urkunde über Versetzung Ernst Freudenbergs in den Ruhestand vom 27. Juni 1937, in: Personalakte Prof. Dr. Ernst Freudenberg 1922–1953, Stadtarchiv Marburg, StAM 310, Acc. 1978/15, No. 2581 as well as Schreiben von Ernst von Hülsen vom 26. April 1938, in: Personalakte Prof. Dr. Ernst Freudenberg 1922–1938, Stadtarchiv Marburg, StAM 305a, Acc. 1978/15, No. 4036. Cf. also: Bernhard, 2001, p. 43.
22 Beschlussbegründung des Landgerichts Kassel vom 25. September 1952, Kopie der Entschädigungsakte des Regierungspräsidiums Darmstadt No. 13775 (HHStA-W-Best. 518), in: Corporate Archives 1/00978.
23 The Reich flight tax (*Reichsfluchtsteuer*) is not a Nazi invention. It had already been introduced on December 8, 1931 as part of the "[Not-]Verordnungen des Reichspräsidenten zur Sicherung von Wirtschaft und Finanzen" ([Emergency] Decrees of the Reich President to Safeguard the Economy and Finance) enacted under the pressure of the Great Depression. The main objective pursued by Heinrich Brüning in introducing the tax was to stem the flight of capital out of Germany. Then, under the Nazi regime, the Reich flight tax was tightened significantly and utilized for discriminatory purposes. Cf. also Banken, 2018 as well as Leicht, 2015a.
24 Cf. Abschrift des Veräußerungsvertrages zwischen Ernst Freudenberg und den persönlich haftenden Gesellschaftern vom 16. November 1937, in: Corporate Archives 1/00539, as well as Schreiben der Süddeutschen Revisions- und Treuhand AG an Ernst Freudenberg vom 29. Juni 1951, in: Corporate Archives 1/00410.
25 The available sources documenting Adolf Freudenberg's job at the Foreign Office do not state clearly whether he gave up his profession as a diplomat in 1934 or 1935.
26 Cf. Lebenslauf von Adolf Freudenberg aus dem Heft zur Trauerfeier von 1977 in Bad Vilbel, in: Corporate Archives 1/00950.
27 Cf. Schreiben des Finanzamtes Zehlendorf/Berlin-Lichterfelde mit der Pfändungsverfügung vom 21. Oktober 1938, in: Corporate Archives 1/00552.
28 Schreiben von Adolf Freudenberg an Richard Freudenberg vom 10. November 1938, in: Corporate Archives 1/00552.
29 Aufzeichnungen von Elsa Freudenberg, geb. Liefmann, über die Zeit 1919–1939, verfasst 1980–1982, p. 80 ff., in: Corporate Archives 1/00976.
30 Schreiben von Adolf Freudenberg an Dr. Ernst Boesebeck vom 15. November 1938, in: Corporate Archives 1/00552.
31 Cf. Angebotsschreiben von Adolf Freudenberg an die persönlich haftenden Gesellschafter der Freudenberg & Co. vom 29. Dezember 1938, in: Corporate Archives 1/00690, as well as Schreiben von Richard Freudenberg an Adolf Freudenberg vom 31.12.1938, in: Corporate Archives 1/00690.
32 Cf. Unterlagen zur Anteilsübertragung von Adolf Freudenberg, in: Corporate Archives 1/00690.
33 Cf. Lebenslauf von Adolf Freudenberg vom 14. August 1952, in: Kopie der Entschädigungsakte (Entschädigungsamt Berlin, RegNr 006.340), in: Corporate Archives 1/00977, as well as Schreiben von Professor D. Albertz an Adolf Freudenberg vom 7. August 1952, Kopie der Entschädigungsakte (Entschädigungsamt Berlin, RegNr 006.340), in: Corporate Archives 1/00977.
34 Cf. Scholtyseck, 2016, p. 390 f. Cf. also for further information Freudenberg, 1969, p. p. 38 f., as well as Freudenberg, 1964, p. 132; Freudenberg-Hübner/Wiehn, 1993; Freudenberg, 1989, here Vorwort von Helmut Gollwitzer; Stöhr/Würmell, 1994 as well as Brief von Adolf Freudenberg an Hans Freudenberg vom 22. August 1946 on the work of the Ökumenische Flüchtlingskommission after the end of World War II, in: Corporate Archives 1/00387.
35 Abschrift der Vereinbarung zwischen Adolf Freudenberg, Ernst Freudenberg und der Firma Freudenberg vom 24. Juni 1951 über Wiedereinräumung von Kommanditeinlagen, in: Corporate Archives 3/01860/04.
36 Cf. ibid. as well as the correspondence of the Freudenberg company and the law firm with the authorities as well as Abschrift der Vereinbarung, Vollmachten und Briefe, in: Corporate Archives 1/00477.

37 Cf. Konten der Gesellschafter zum 30. Juni 1950 und 30. Juni 1951, in: Corporate Archives 3/04384 as well as Rückerstattungsunterlagen, in: Corporate Archives 3/01860.
38 Cf. Hockerts, 2013.
39 Cf. Unterlagen zur Treuhänderschaft, in: Corporate Archives 3/09133.
40 Cf. Niederschrift über die Sitzung der Gesellschafter am 25. September 1948 in Weinheim, in: Corporate Archives 3/04378.
41 Cf. Informationen zur Gesellschafterversammlung im Zeitraum 1945–1951, in: Corporate Archives 3/04378, as well as Abschrift der Vereinbarung zwischen Adolf Freudenberg, Ernst Freudenberg und der Firma Freudenberg vom 24. Juni 1951 über Wiedereinräumung von Kommanditeinlagen, in: Corporate Archives 3/01860/04.
42 The restitution took place on the basis of the *"Bundesergänzungsgesetz zur Entschädigung für Opfer der nationalsozialistischen Verfolgung"* (BEG) of 1956/57 [an amendment to the original German Restitution Law of 1953 regulating restitution for private individuals who were victims of Nazi persecution – ed.]. Cf. Schreiben des Regierungspräsidiums Kassel an Ernst Freudenberg vom 10. Juli 1956, Kopie der Entschädigungsakte des Regierungspräsidiums Darmstadt Nr. 13775 (HHStA-W-Best. 518), in: Corporate Archives 1/00978 as well as Entschädigungsbescheid für Adolf Freudenberg vom 24. April 1958, Kopie der Entschädigungsakte (Entschädigungsamt Berlin, RegNr 006.340), in: Corporate Archives 1/00977. Cf. also Mussgnug, 1993, p. 65.
43 The most recent adjustment under German company law occurred in 2012 with the establishment of Freudenberg SE. Cf. History Brochure, 2019, p. 26.
44 Cf. Scholtyseck, 2016, p. 448.
45 Furthermore, the Management Board had the entirely justifiable fear of being removed from office by the Nazi authorities. A management board would then have been appointed to replace them that was identified as being ideologically in line with Nazism, something which the three directors felt they must avoid at all costs. Cf. Scholtyseck, 2016, p. 316 ff.
46 Scholtyseck, 2016, p. 442.
47 Cf. ibid, p.102–109. This can be concluded, among other things, from the letter from shop steward Peter Wolf to the German Labor Front (DAF) district chairman dated November 26, 1942: "Signs of a German salute from the directors can only be seen towards me personally and towards political personages." Cf. documents in: Corporate Archives 1/00805.
48 Cf. also the unemployment figures in Weinheim and its hinterland in the first half of 1933: "In June 1933, 1,796 Weinheim citizens were registered with the employment office as unemployed. If this figure is juxtaposed with the district's annual average (1933 = 4,357), it becomes clear that around 40 % of the unemployed of the district came from Weinheim, although Weinheim only accounted for 24 % of the inhabitants of the unemployment office district. Thus Weinheim was disproportionately heavily affected by unemployment. The unemployment rate in the municipalities in the hinterland, which tended to be more rural in structure, was far lower than in the heavily industrialized city of Weinheim." Cf. Lang, 2000, p. 180. The unemployment office district of Weinheim comprised 34 municipalities in Hessen and 13 in Baden, with a total residential population of 73,768 people (as of: July 16, 1933). Cf. Statistisches Jahrbuch für das Land Baden 1938, p. 213.
49 Cf. "Betriebsratssitzung am 10. Januar 1933 nachmittags 2 Uhr in der Gerberei [Müll]", in: Corporate Archives 3/01510. For comparison: Regular working hours – referring to 1928 – in the German leather industry were 48 hours per week. Cf. Wirtschaftsausschuss, 1930, p. 165.
50 "Betriebsratssitzung am 10. Januar 1933 nachmittags 2 Uhr in der Gerberei [Müll]", in: Corporate Archives 3/01510.
51 Scholtyseck, 2016, p. 97.
52 Cf. Scholtyseck, 2016, p.98–100.
53 Cf. Bestätigung von Philipp Vetter, in: Corporate Archives 1/00805.
54 Cf. Brief von Rudolf Reiman an Helmut Fabricius vom 29. Januar 1965 (Richard Freudenberg's statement is reproduced in this letter), in: Corporate Archives 3/01599.
55 Cf. Scholtyseck, 2016, p. 102. [The act was called the *"Gesetz zur Ordnung der nationalen Arbeit"* in German – ed.]
56 Cf. ibid, p. 107.
57 Cf. ibid, p. 109 and p. 442.
58 Cf. ibid, p. 181 f. Cf. also Bähr on the Loan Fund Act, 2006, p. 56 ff.
59 Cf. Boesebeck, 1962, p. 35.

60 Scholtyseck, 2016, p. 182.
61 Cf. Hütter, 2009, p. 153 f.
62 Cf. in detail Freudenberg/Schuster, 1999, p. 258–263; Hütter, 2009, p. 149–159.
63 Cf. Biographie von Richard Freudenberg, in: Corporate Archives 3/10744.
64 Cf. Geschichte der Rechtsform von Freudenberg, in: Corporate Archives 3/11071.
65 Cf. Boesebeck, 1962, p. 36.
66 Cf. Kommanditvertrag der Freudenberg & Co. KG vom 28. November 1936, § 44, in: Corporate Archives 3/07422.
67 Ibid.
68 Ibid.
69 Ibid.
70 Ibid.
71 Cf. Scholtyseck, 2016, p. 183.
72 Ibid, p. 182.
73 Rede des Herrn Richard Freudenberg über den Hauptpunkt der Tagesordnung der ausserordentl. Generalversammlung am Sonnabend, den 28. November 1936, in: Corporate Archives 3/01064, here: p. 9 f.
74 Cf. Scholtyseck, 2016, p. 183.
75 Cf. Wöhe/Döring, 2013, p. 219.
76 The term "Aryanization" originates from Nazi vocabulary. It has been the subject of discussions in historical scholarship right up to the present day and still has not been clearly defined. Thus it was attributed different meanings during the Nazi era. Cf. Fritsche, 2013, p. 14.
77 Cf. Hönecke, 2005, p. 13.
78 Cf. Scholtyseck, 2016, p. 113–119. Cf. also the documents on the general manager of the Freudenberg branch in Berlin, Hubert Schuhmann, who had essentially conducted the negotiations, in: Corporate Archives 3/01791.
79 Cf. "Gleichschaltungsurkunde" vom 20. Mai 1933, "Gleichschaltung certificate" (- ed.) which is unique in this form, printed in: Scholtyseck, 2016, p. 120. "Gleichschaltung" was a term coined by the Nazis to signify their policy of enforced conformity in all aspects of life, beginning with the media – ed.
80 Cf. Scholtyseck, 2016, p. 118 ff. and p. 442–443. Cf. also Correspondence documents of Carl Freudenberg and Richard Freudenberg with Tack and Hermann Krojanker's lawyers, in: Corporate Archives 3/02959 as well as a letter from Wilhelm Keppler, dem "Beauftragten für Wirtschaftsfragen beim Führer", about the "Aryanization" of Tack by Freudenberg, dated November 20, 1933, printed in: "Tack-Chronik", in: Corporate Archives 3/01237.
81 Cf. Scholtyseck, 2016, p. 443.
82 Cf. ibid, p. 176, as well as the documents, in: Corporate Archives 3/02363: "The former Tack shareholders and heirs of Hermann Krojanker received in total deutschmark sums equivalent to around 10 percent of the original nominal share capital in Reichsmarks in a restitution settlement, which was paid out in instalments. The amount corresponded approximately to the restitution amounts which were customary at the time. An out-of-court restitution settlement was concluded with Gertrude Krojanker, the […] widow of Hermann Krojanker, and her daughter, which came into force on December 21, 1950 and made provisions for a pension for life; likewise, the entitlements of the employees who were laid off in 1933 were regulated by granting pensions."
83 Heel counters reinforce the heel area of the shoe.
84 Cf. "Übernahme und Eingliederung von J. Kern & Co., Pirmasens" vom 15. September 1945, in: Corporate Archives 3/02959 as well as Kommanditvertrag vom 24. Juni 1938, in: Corporate Archives 3/05326. According to statements in the Denazification Court file on Richard Freudenberg (Paul Vogler and Jakob Schwab, the latter an employee of the Kern firm), good relations prevailed between the Jewish owners of the Kern firm (Messrs. Kern, Bendel and Wolf) and Freudenberg during the takeover negotiations. Cf. Ausführung der Firma Carl Freudenberg im Spruchkammerprozess von Richard Freudenberg 1946–1947, in: Corporate Archives 3/04223.
85 Cf. Scholtyseck, 2016, p. 167 and p. 444. Cf. also the following documents: Alfons Bendel, Arthur Wolff, Isidor Kern, "Erklärung" vom 2. Juni 1938, as well as Unterlagen des Finanzamtes Pirmasens, "Kaufpreisabtretung der Firma I. Kern & Co." vom 1. Dezember 1937, in: Corporate Archives 3/02113.

86 Cf. Ausführungen der Firma Carl Freudenberg im Spruchkammerprozess von Richard Freudenberg von 1946–1947, in: Corporate Archives 3/04223.
87 The former owners received 600,000 deutschmarks, after Carl Freudenberg had initially been prepared to pay 150,000 deutschmarks. Cf. Scholtyseck, 2016, p. 177.
88 Scholtyseck, 2016, p. 177. Cf. also Unterlagen zum Rückerstattungsvergleich bzgl. Kern, in: Corporate Archives 3/01577 and 3/04384.
89 From 1933 onwards, Freudenberg gradually took over the Gustav Hoffmann children's shoe factory in Kleve, which had been established in 1908 and had the "elefanten" brand, but this was not an "Aryanization". Freudenberg was already the largest shareholder at that time with a 31 percent stake. Back then, Gustav Hoffmann was one of the major manufacturers of shoes for children and adolescents in Germany. As a result of the Great Depression, the company was in financial difficulties which forced it to stop making payments to its financiers. These financiers included the Freudenberg company, which wanted to use the possibility of vertical product expansion by having a shareholding in a shoe factory. In the years that followed, Freudenberg succeeded in acquiring more and more of the Hoffmann company's shares. From 1937 onwards, Freudenberg held about 70 percent, and from 1941 it already held 98 percent of the shares in Gustav Hoffmann AG, which was thus fully integrated into the Freudenberg sales organization. Cf. Scholtyseck, 2016, p. 199–201 as well as Unterlagen zu Gustav Hoffmann AG, in: Corporate Archives 3/02971, 3/02973 and 3/08530.
90 The former owners of the Fisch company received a restitution payment of 350,000 deutschmarks in 1950. Cf. Scholtyseck, 2016, p. 176 as well as documents on "Wiedergutmachung Fisch", in: Corporate Archives 3/09130 and 3/09131.
91 The "Lederwerke Sigmund Hirsch GmbH" firm, which had been established by Sigmund Hirsch in Weinheim in 1868, was one of the long-standing companies in Baden's tannery trade. The company manufactured horse hide leather with around 400 employees. The horse hide leather tannery's products were used worldwide. Cf. Scholtyseck, 2016, p. 149.
92 The Carl Freudenberg company purchased the land, buildings, machinery and equipment of the Hirsch firm for a price of around 1.2 million RM. A breakdown of the individual prices, for e. g. the buildings and machinery, can be found in the "Bericht der Süddeutschen Revisions- und Treuhand-Aktien-Gesellschaft Mannheim betreffend die im Juni/Juli 1939 14:40 ausgeführte Prüfung der Bilanz- und Gewinn- und Verlustrechnung zum 31. Dezember 1938." Cf. documents in: Corporate Archives 3/08509.
93 Cf. Scholtyseck, 2016, p. 149 and p. 443.
94 Cf. Unterlagen von Helmut Fabricius vom 26. April 1949, in: Corporate Archives 3/09129.
95 Scholtyseck, 2016, p. 443.
96 Hirsch, 1940, p. 185 f. (The "blocked marks" were known as "Sperrmark" in German. – ed.)
97 Cf. Scholtyseck, 2016, p. 156 as well as Hirsch, 1940, p. 178 ff.
98 Secondary source: Scholtyseck, 2016, p. 157. The statement made by Arthur Hirsch to the FBI in 1944 is documented in: National Archives Washington, RG 65, Stack Area 250, Row 86, Compartment 15, Shelf 6, Box 112.
99 Ibid.
100 Scholtyseck, 2016, p. 177. Cf. hierzu auch die Unterlagen zum Rückerstattungsvergleich im Fall Hirsch, in: Corporate Archives 3/01608 as well as further documents, in: Corporate Archives 3/09129. As part of the restitution of the horse hide leather plant to the Hirsch family, the horse hide leather factory was incorporated into the newly established Rosslederwerk KG a. A. in 1948. Freudenberg leased the Rossrederwerk KG a. A. factory from June 1949. Cf. also documents, in: Corporate Archives 3/09077. In 1957, Rossleder KG a. A. was liquidated. Freudenberg re-acquired all the properties of the former horse hide leather factory in this context. Cf. Bescheinigung zur Gewerbeabmeldung der Stadt Weinheim vom 6. Mai 1957, in: Corporate Archives 3/01845 as well as Eintragungsbekanntmachung des Grundbuchamtes Weinheim über die Eigentumsübertragung der Liegenschaften an Carl Freudenberg vom 8. Mai 1957, in: Corporate Archives 3/01478.
101 Cf. Scholtyseck, 2016, p. 310 f.
102 Cf. Richard Freudenberg's memorandum on the takeover of the Del-Ka branches: Richard Freudenberg, "Aktennotiz über eine Besprechung mit Herrn Ministerialdirigent Dr. Ruelberg (Reichswirtschaftsministerium) am 28.06.1938" vom 30. Juni 1938, in: Corporate Archives 3/01235.
103 The Creditanstalt bank, which was based in Vienna, was owned by the Austrian state. It held

shareholdings in many, frequently indebted, shoe factories, and independently pursued its own "de-Judaization" plan. Cf. Scholtyseck, 2016, p. 245.
104 Cf. Scholtyseck, 2016, p. 246 ff.
105 Del-Ka was merged with the ailing Aeterna shoe factory in the summer of 1938. Aeterna Schuhfabriks AG, which had around 750 employees, was based in Vienna and under Jewish ownership. It was one of the largest shoe manufacturers in Austria. Cf. Scholtyseck, 2016, p. 245.
106 Cf. Scholtyseck, 2016, p. 251.
107 Cf. Scholtyseck, 2016, p. 446 f. as well as Richard Freudenberg's correspondence with Jens Heinz Peters (General Manager of Tack) among others on the takeover of Chaussures André, in: Corporate Archives 3/02960 and 3/08978.
108 In 1934, Jacques Keller, a Swiss banker, had acquired the licensing rights for several manufacturing processes for Freudenberg seals and had awarded these to Chromex in France, a company which had been established for this purpose. Frenchman Gustave Maire and Swiss engineer Paul Geissman then founded the Société Chromex company in May 1934. Of the share capital totaling 250,000 French francs, 62,500 French franc shares were held by Geissman, the remaining 75 percent (187,500 French franc shares) were held by Maire. However, Maire administered his shares in trust for Jacques Keller and thus for Carl Freudenberg. Freudenberg had reached an agreement with Keller that this latter would surrender the shares in his possession on request to Freudenberg. Hence: In reality, the majority shareholding in Chromex was held by Freudenberg. The shareholding ratio changed up to 1941, since Keller sold on a portion of his shares. Cf. Scholtyseck, 2016, p. 295 ff. as well as Berichte, Korrespondenzen zwischen der Firma Carl Freudenberg und Jacques Keller, in: Corporate Archives 3/01347.
109 Cf. Scholtyseck, 2016, p. 446.
110 Scholtyseck, 2016, p. 444–447.
111 Cf. Scholtyseck, 2016, p. 314 as well as Schreiben von Rudolf Brinkmann an Richard Freudenberg vom 7. November 1938 zum Titel "Wehrwirtschaftsführer", in: Corporate Archives 3/02992.
112 Secondary source: Scholtyseck, 2016, p. 277. On the categorization of Walter Freudenberg's job in the service of the "authorized representative for recording raw materials" in Poland cf. Scholtyseck, 2016, p. 273–282. The WiFi (Economic Research Company) was a Nazi company tasked with constructing and operating solid fuel storage depots. – ed.
113 Scholtyseck, 2016, p. 265; Freudenberg & Co., Geschäftsbericht für den Gesellschafterausschuss vom 4. Mai 1940, in: Corporate Archives 3/03637 as well as Rundbrief von Richard und Hans Freudenberg vom 8. Mai 1940, in: Corporate Archives 3/09041.
114 Cf. Bericht der Süddeutschen Revisions- und Treuhand-Aktien-Gesellschaft Mannheim über die im Juni/August 1944 ausgeführte Prüfung des Jahresabschlusses zum 31. Dezember 1943, in: Corporate Archives 3/08509. The "Simmerwerk" was under "drastic deadline pressure" with regard to the demands of the armaments industry. Cf. Hoffmann, 1978. At the start of World War II, daily production figures were 23,500 units. There were the following types of seal: around 6,000 units of crawler track seals, around 4,000 units of hydraulic seals, around 500 units of special u-ring seals as well as around 12,000 units of Simmerrings and a few thousand cup seals for the Reichsbahn air brakes, as well as axle bearing seals "for the Reichsbahn's plain bearings" and seals for the pumps on the V1 and V2 rockets. Cf. memorandum "SIMRIT-Produktion während des 2. Weltkrieges" vom 16. Januar 1978, in: Corporate Archives 3/01250.
115 Cf. Scholtyseck, 2016, p. 265–271.
116 Cf. Hoffmann, 1978.
117 Cf. Scholtyseck, 2016, p. 268 as well as Hoffmann, 1978.
118 Scholtyseck, 2016, p. 448. The Simmerwerk is the seal production facility at the Freudenberg headquarters in Weinheim.
119 Cf. "Das Geschäftsjahr 1952", in: Der Freudenberger, 1/1953, p. 5–6. Even in December 1952, it was said that: "We will never forget the 548 company employees who fell or were declared dead, the 210 prisoners and the missing, the two who are still interned, even when the noise- and worry-filled daily grind often conceals our view of their images." Cf., "Die unzerstörbare Gemeinschaft", in: Der Freudenberger 6/1952, p. 40.
120 It is not clear who exactly is meant by "war dead".
121 Cf. Unterlagen zur Jubilarrede 1955, in: Corporate Archives 3/04788.
122 Cf. Mitarbeiterstatistik des Freudenberg Unternehmensarchivs (Employee statistics in the

Freudenberg Corporate Archives). These refer to the employees in the Carl Freudenberg company's factories in Weinheim, Schönau, Neckarsteinach and Schopfheim.
123 Cf. Scholtyseck, 2016, p. 396 f. as well as Berichte über den Schanzeinsatz in Buc, in: Corporate Archives 3/01132 and 3/03113.
124 Cf. Vita von Otto Freudenberg, in: Corporate Archives 3/10744.
125 Gedenkrede (Tischrede) von Richard Freudenberg für Otto Freudenberg vom 27. Dezember 1940, in: Corporate Archives 1/00242.
126 Otto Freudenberg was appointed as a reserve lieutenant in the service of the *Wehrmacht* on the orders of the army reserve recruitment inspectorate in Mannheim, effective February 1, 1937. While he remained out of commission, this nonetheless caused him to be reactivated as an officer. On March 1, 1938 Otto Freudenberg was promoted to reserve lieutenant and on August 27, 1939 to reserve captain. Cf. Schreiben des Wehrbezirks-Kommando Mannheim II an Otto Freudenberg von Februar 1937 bis Oktober 1939, in: Corporate Archives 1/00979. Richard Freudenberg had already been rejected as unfit for military service in World War I because of a congenital mispositioned arm. Walter Freudenberg lost an arm in World War I and was therefore no longer fit for military service. Hans Freudenberg was indispensable to the company because of his function as technical head on the Management Board. Cf. also Lebensläufe, in: Corporate Archives 3/10744.
127 Scholtyseck, 2016, p. 107. Cf. also: Bestimmungen für die Unterstützungszahlungen an die Familienangehörigen der zum Wehrdienst einberufenen Arbeiter der Firma Carl Freudenberg, Weinheim 15. Februar 1940, in: Corporate Archives 3/03036.
128 Cf. Beschluss der Geschäftsführung der Firma Carl Freudenberg (gez. Walter, Hans und Richard Freudenberg) vom 24. Januar 1945, in: Corporate Archives 3/07254. The conditions were that the children had not yet reached the age of 18 at the time of their father's death, that the father had been employed at the company for at least four full years before being called up and that the child was at least one year old. In the event that the father had a shorter period of service at the company, the amount transferred to the savings book was 100 RM for each year of service commenced. The resolution was expanded in July 1947. A savings book was then also to be issued to those children whose fathers had died as prisoners of war while they were employees, had been released from imprisonment as a result of illness, had lain at home ill for a protracted period and had died without having returned to work. Cf. Erweiterung des Beschlusses der Geschäftsführung der Firma Carl Freudenberg vom 16. Juli 1947, in: Corporate Archives 3/07254. It is not evident from these sources how long these savings books were issued. It can be assumed that this was the case up to the mid-1950s, since the last reports on lists of the fallen exist up to this time.
129 Cf. Keller, 2000, p. 91 and p. 108 f. Reports of the air strikes on Weinheim at the beginning and end of August 1941 can be read here (including an air raid on the Freudenberg company's factory premises) as well as two further bomb attacks in February 1945, in which several people died.
130 Cf. Scholtyseck, 2016, p. 399 f. After the *Wehrmacht* had withdrawn thanks to the mediation of Hans and Richard Freudenberg, there were small skirmishes around the Müll factory and in Lützelsachsen with scattered *Wehrmacht* units. Cf. also Tagebuchaufzeichnungen von Julius Hempfing, in: Corporate Archives 3/05796.
131 Bericht von Hans Freudenberg und Paul Vogler vom 8. August 1941 über den Luftangriff vom 6./7. August 1941, in: Corporate Archives 3/01096. The summary "Fliegerschaden – Gebäude" (vermutlich von 1941), in: Corporate Archives 3/01096 describes which buildings on the Zwischen Dämmen plant premises were damaged to what extent during the 1941 air raid: Building 1a – boilerhouse (entrance door and external wooden components completely destroyed), Building 3 – warehouse and production hall, waste sorting room, Cefa and Ledergon, adjoining bike shed, canopy for private sidings (completely destroyed), Building 3b – telephone exchange, waiting room and break room (partially destroyed), Building 4 – central warehouse and Ledergon facility (partially destroyed), Building 5 and 5a – dispatch and lavatory facilities (partially destroyed), Building 17c – warehouse for stretching frames (partially destroyed), Building 18 – storage shed for lime (completely destroyed), Building 18a – bike shed (completely destroyed), Building 19a – break room, office, storage shed and vehicle shed (completely destroyed).
132 Cf. Documentation on the 1941 air raid, in: Corporate Archives 3/01096.
133 Cf. Scholtyseck, 2016, p. 395 and p. 430. The Gustav Hoffmann shoe factory in Kleve was able to manufacture children's and adolescents' shoes again in 1945 after the end of World War II because of deliveries from Weinheim and Heidelberg (Fisch shoe factory).

134 Cf. Scholtyseck, 2016, p. 395. This was the beginning of what was to become the Vital-Schuhgesellschaft Hartwig & Co. KG shoe company in 1949 in the plant in Müll. Cf. Unterlagen zur Gründung der Vital Schuhgesellschaft, in: Corporate Archives 3/01858.
135 Cf. Scholtyseck, 2016, p. 429 f. The remaining machines in the shoe factory in Burg near Magdeburg were dismantled in 1946 and transported to the Soviet Union. The branches in the Soviet occupation zone were requisitioned.
136 Cf. Unterlagen zur Organisation des Luftschutzes im Zweiten Weltkrieg, in: Corporate Archives 3/01108 as well as Unterlagen zum Stollenbau im Zweiten Weltkrieg, in: Corporate Archives 3/03601.
137 Cf. Unterlagen zum Thema Zwangsarbeiter, in: Corporate Archives 3/08976. Incidentally, the figures for the subsidiaries are not available (particularly on Tack and Gustav Hoffmann).
138 Cf. Kriegsgefangenenstatistik, in: Corporate Archives 3/01099, Arbeiterbuch, Vol. 3, in: Corporate Archives 3/05956–3 as well as Versicherungskarten der ausländischen Zivilarbeiter (1942–45), in: Corporate Archives 3/06607.
139 From September 1943, the remaining 104 prisoners of war are listed as civilian workers and insured, these are recorded in the table with the French civilian workers. Cf. also Kriegsgefangenenstatistik, in: Corporate Archives 3/01099.
140 In May 1941, Richard Freudenberg talks about 1,657 employees who had been called up. This corresponds to around 40 % of the total workforce – based on 1939 – who had been called up to active duty. Cf. Rede von Richard Freudenberg anlässlich der Feier zum 1. Mai 1941, in: Corporate Archives 1/00274.
141 Cf. Scholtyseck, 2016, p. 366 ff.
142 Cf. Documents on the topic of forced laborers, in: Corporate Archives 3/08976 as well as the workers' records for detailed analysis, in: Corporate Archives 3/05956–3.
143 Cf. Employee statistics in the Corporate Archives. CF is an acronym for the Carl Freudenberg firm – ed.
144 Scholtyseck, 2016, p. 449. Secondary source: Freudenberg, 1974, p. 305.
145 Cf. for example Freudenberg, 1974, p. 305.
146 Cf. Scholtyseck, 2016, p. 374–380.
147 Bestätigung von Adam Becker vom 26. November 1946 für den Spruchkammerprozess von Richard Freudenberg, in: Corporate Archives 1/00805.
148 Cf. Scholtyseck, 2016, p. 377–379.
149 Cf. Notification of deaths relating to foreign workers at Freudenberg, dated February 11, 1947, in: Corporate Archives 3/01099. However, the countries of origin of two of the deceased (Belgium and Poland) in the documents on the forced laborers in the workers' records (Corporate Archives 3/05956–3) as well as the insurance cards (Corporate Archives 3/06607). In both of these, each of the deceased is recorded as Italian.
150 Scholtyseck, 2016, p. 379.
151 Bescheinigung von Guy W. Wharton vom 15. Juni 1946 bzgl. Behandlung der Zwangsarbeiter bei der Firma Freudenberg, in: Corporate Archives 3/04221.
152 Scholtyseck, 2016, p. 449. Cf. additionally in Scholtyseck's academic study: the remarks on the conditions of the forced laborers at Freudenberg – particularly on the topics of accommodation, rations and medical care, free time and daily life, payment as well as sanctions and punishments – on pages 369–387.
153 Cf. Correspondence on "participation" in the foundation initiative, in: Corporate Archives 3/08976 as well as Scholtyseck, 2016, p. 387.
154 Cf. Scholtyseck, 2016, p. 329.
155 Cf. 30 Jahre Nora-Werk, in: Der Freudenberger, 4/1964, p. 6.
156 Cf. Richard Freudenberg, "Akten-Notiz über meine Besprechung mit Herrn Dir. Häusermann, Leiter der Schuhmacherschule in Pirmasens" vom 13.11.1939 ("Memorandum on my meeting with Director Häusermann, Head of the cobblers' school in Pirmasens," dated Nov. 13, 1939), in: Corporate Archives 3/01103. The memorandum states on p. 10: "Over and above all theoretical tests of the outsole – the same applies to the theoretical testing of the leather fiber materials – it must in my opinion be required that checks are continuously conducted through practical wearing trials in a neutral location by taking samples in the shoe factories and the cobbler's craft business or the sole manufacturing factories. For that reason, I have demonstrated precisely to you too once again today the great diligence with which we have conducted such wearing trials. You have had the

opportunity to inspect the test track yourselves. I strongly urge you to spare no expense – even if it [the cost] has to be split within the shoe and rubber industry – to conduct these wearing trials on a large scale under the strictest and most objective conditions. I would like to take this opportunity to make the suggestion that these wearing trials should be conducted in consultation with an office of the fatigue duty that is responsible for providing the marching columns. To ensure objectivity, I suggest that an advisory board is assembled under governmental chairmanship comprising two representatives each from the rubber manufacturing industry, the shoe industry, the leather fiber materials manufacturing industry and the cobbler's craft." Initially young men were engaged by the *Reichsarbeitsdienst* (RAD, Reich labor service) for six months before their military service. The fatigue duty was predominantly concentrated on activities in agriculture. With the outbreak of World War II, the RAD was extended to include young women as well.

157 The "Head of the Shoe Testing Facility", an employee of the "Reich Office for Economic Expansion" (*Reichsamt für Wirtschaftsausbau*) in the Sachsenhausen concentration camp, was responsible for conducting the trials on-site. As the implementing body, the "Reich Office for Economic Expansion" transferred 6 RM per day and per prisoner to the SS *Wirtschaftsverwaltungshauptamt* (the Nazi office that ran the concentration and extermination camps – ed.). The SS (in its role as "landlord" of the concentration camp) was responsible for monitoring the "shoe tester commando". Cf. Scholtyseck, 2016, p. 338 f.
158 Cf. Scholtyseck, 2016, p. 343–348.
159 Cf. Scholtyseck, 2016, p. 337–339. Cf. also the list of companies whose products were tested on the "shoe test track" in the Sachsenhausen concentration camp, in: Sudrow, 2010, p. 791–792. For information on how the "shoe test track" was organized in the Sachsenhausen concentration camp and on the working and living conditions of the "shoe testers" cf. Scholtyseck, 2016, p. 339–348 as well as Sudrow, 2010, p. 511–591.
160 Cf. Scholtyseck, 2016, p. 330–332 and p. 340.
161 Cf. Scholtyseck, 2016, p. 334–336. For companies that did not participate in these joint tests, this meant that they would be excluded from future production contracts. Thus, from a commercial perspective, there were good reasons to participate in the joint tests. Cf. Scholtyseck, 2016, p. 334.
162 The "*Gemeinschaft Schuhe*" (a collective of institutions and producers related to the shoe manufacturing industry – ed.) was established in November 1942 and operated under the auspices of the Reich Economics Ministry. Its members included companies, factories and individuals who manufactured all types of footwear. "Thus it was now responsible for the procurement of raw materials, assigned 'production orders' to the firms, dictated production, ran the rationalization of production processes, the typification and standardization of the footwear, and ordered business closures and mergers. Likewise, the efforts to produce shoes using replacement materials also came within the area of competence of the *Gemeinschaft Schuhe*." Cf. Bräutigam, 1997, p. 77.
163 Cf. Scholtyseck, 2016, p. 352 f.
164 Cf. Unterlagen der Spruchkammerakte von Wilhelm Braunss (Documents from the Denazification Panel files on Wilhem Braunss, in: Corporate Archives 3/10981. The first legal investigation proceedings specifically targeting the "shoe test track" began in 1947 in the Soviet occupation zone, and not until much later in West Germany, in the 1950s. However, these pertained to the direct mistreatments and crimes of the SS men and the managers of the "shoe test track" in the concentration camp. The connection to representatives of participating companies was not investigated in these proceedings. Cf. Scholtyseck, 2016, p. 348 as well as Sudrow, 2010, p. 540–544.
165 Bescheinigung von Guy W. Wharton vom 15. Juni 1946 bzgl. Behandlung der Zwangsarbeiter bei der Firma Freudenberg, in: Corporate Archives 3/04221.

Chapter 5: New beginning and economic miracle: Internationalization and diversification

1 Cf. Scholtyseck, 2016, p. 398–399. Cf. also the diary entry of Julius Hempfing, manager of Freudenberg's leather factory in Weinheim on the Americans' march into Weinheim, in: Corporate Archives 3/05796.

2 Cf. Wilderotter, 1992, p. 39 as well as Lebenslauf von Richard Freudenberg, in: Corporate Archives 3/02128.
3 Cf. Scholtyseck, 2016, Scholtyseck, 2016, p. 399.
4 Flugblatt "An die Einwohner der Stadt Weinheim" von Richard Freudenberg vom 03.04.1945, in: Corporate Archives 4/0009/13.
5 Cf. Scholtyseck, 2016, Scholtyseck, 2016, p. 400.
6 Cf. Freudenberg, 1974, p. 355 f. as well as Barney Barnes, "Application für reinstatement of Richard Freudenberg" vom 7. Juli 1945, in: Corporate Archives 1/00758. An *"Abwehrbeauftragter"* was a security officer in a company who decided whether to hand workers over to the Gestapo following breaches of conduct. The honorary title of *"Wehrwirtschaftsführer"* was bestowed by the Nazis on the executives of companies vital to rearmament.
7 Brief von Richard Freudenberg an Sibille Freudenberg vom 2. Juli 1945, in: Freudenberg, 1974, p. 366.
8 Cf. Brief von Hans und Adolf Freudenberg an Richard Freudenberg vom 3. Juli 1945, in: Freudenberg, 1974, p. 367.
9 Brief von Richard Freudenberg an den Weinheimer Pfarrer Hermann Brecht vom 4. Juli 1945, in: Corporate Archives 3/02992.
10 Beurteilungsschreiben von Hermann Brecht als Vertreter der evangelischen Kirchengemeinde Weinheim vom 1. Juli 1945, in: Corporate Archives 3/02992.
11 Cf. Scholtyseck, 2016, p. 405–407.
12 Cf. Brief von Joseph H. Bernfeld an Richard Freudenberg vom 13. Januar 1948 (Letter from Joseph H. Bernfeld to Richard Freudenberg dated January 13, 1948), in: Corporate Archives 1/00758. Bernfeld and Freudenberg stayed in contact by letter even after the hearings had concluded, since a "personal mutual trust" had developed between the two men. Cf. also Scholtyseck, 2016, p. 407 f.
13 Cf. Scholtyseck, 2016, p. 401–402 and p. 409–417.
14 Cf. ibid.
15 Cf. Scholtyseck, 2016, p. 404 ff. and p. 420 as well as Freudenberg, 1974, p. 375.
16 Cf. Entnazifizierungsbescheid zu Walter Freudenberg, in: Corporate Archives 3/09287.
17 Cf. Vita von Walter Freudenberg, in: Corporate Archives 3/10744.
18 Cf. Spruchkammerakte von Hans Freudenberg, in: Corporate Archives 3/09290.
19 Cf. Schreiben von Joseph Bernfeld an das Office of Military Government vom 28.11.1945, in: Corporate Archives 3/09133 as well as Schreiben der Freudenberg & Co. an ihre Tochtergesellschaften von November/Dezember 1945, in: Corporate Archives 3/09133.
20 Cf. Entnazifizierungsbescheid für Hans Freudenberg, in: Corporate Archives 3/09287.
21 Scholtyseck, 2016, p. 421 f.
22 Cf. "Dr. Ing. Ernst Demme verstorben," in: Freudenberg-Intern, 6/1984, p. 8.
23 Cf. Unterlagen der Spruchkammer Weinheim zum Verfahren gegen Ernst Demme, in: Corporate Archives 3/09293.
24 Cf. Staff list of senior executives and master craftsmen by place of residence with details on Nazi memberships, dated 1946, in: Corporate Archives 3/02918.
25 Cf. Meldebogen auf Grund des Gesetzes zur Befreiung von Nationalsozialismus und Militarismus vom 5. März 1946 für Carl Ludwig Nottebohm, in: Corporate Archives 3/10976.
26 Cf. Staff list of senior executives and master craftsmen by place of residence with details on Nazi memberships, dated 1946, in: Corporate Archives 3/02918.
27 Cf. Unterlagen der Spruchkammerakte von Georg Boysen, in: Corporate Archives 3/10980.
28 Cf. Unterlagen zum Arbeitsvertrag von Wilhelm Braunss, in: Corporate Archives 3/09311. The *"Gemeinschaft Schuhe"* was a collective of institutions and producers related to the shoe manufacturing industry established by the Nazis in 1942. – ed.)
29 Cf. Unterlagen der Spruchkammerakte von Wilhelm Braunss, in: UA 3/10981. Cf. also comments on Wilhelm Braunss after 1945, in: Scholtyseck, 2016, p. 421 f.
30 Cf. Professor Walther Simmer verstorben, in: Der Freudenberger, 3/1986, p. 8.
31 Cf. Notiz für Herrn Hans Freudenberg vom 3. Februar 1947, in: Corporate Archives 3/03104.
32 Cf. Vertragsentwurf vom 28. Oktober 1946, in: Corporate Archives 3/03104.
33 Cf. Spruch der Spruchkammer Weinheim vom 9. August 1947, in: Corporate Archives 3/09192.
34 Cf. Schreiben des Präsidenten des Landesbezirks Baden, Abteilung Wirtschaft und Verkehr des Landeswirtschaftsamtes vom 22. Juni 1948 and Schreiben des Finanzministeriums in Stuttgart an

das Amt für Vermögenskontrolle Mannheim vom 07. Juli 1948, in: Corporate Archives 3/03104 as well as Bonfert, 1999.
35 Cf. Gesellschaftsvertrag der Simmerwerke W. Simmer GmbH & Co. KG Kufstein, in: Corporate Archives 3/08571.
36 Cf. "Simmerwerke Kufstein. Alle Anteile übernommen," in: Der Freudenberger, 11/1992, p. 1. The title of *Kommerzienrat* is an honorary title bestowed on businesspeople for service to the Republic of Austria. – ed.
37 Cf. Fath, 1998, p. 3.
38 Cf. Spruchkammerunterlagen zu Paul Vogler und Carl Gustav Müller, in: Corporate Archives 3/09133, 3/10976 and 3/10982.
39 Richard Freudenberg, "Einige persönliche Erinnerungen von vor zwanzig Jahren" von 1965, p. 7, in: Corporate Archives 3/01158/01.
40 Cf. Geschäftsführungsunterlagen, in: Corporate Archives 3/09133.
41 Cf. Scholtyseck, 2016, p. 422.
42 Cf. das "Appointment of Custodian" des "Office of Military Government Stadt- And Landkreis Mannheim Detachment F-16 Property Control Section" vom 26. Februar 1946, in: Corporate Archives 3/09133. "Although the Schönau plant was confiscated by the American Military Government on October 27, 1945 and placed under trusteeship, this was lifted again on November 8 following negotiations." Scholtyseck, 2016, p. 424.
43 Schreiben der Firma Carl Freudenberg an das Werk in Schopfheim vom 18. März 1946, in: Corporate Archives 3/09133.
44 Cf. das Schreiben des Office of Military Government – Stadtkreis and Landkreis Mannheim an Carl Gustav Müller vom 10. Dezember 1945, in: Corporate Archives 3/09133.
45 Cf. also the American Military Government letter dated October vom 31, 1945 with the subject line "Appointment of Custodian of Property" for a description of the function of a trustee, in: Corporate Archives 3/09133. In this letter, the tasks of the trustees, which they term "custodians," are described as follows: "1. C. Gustav Müller, Weinheim, Friedrichstr., Paul Vogler, Weinheim, Hauptstr., are hereby appointed as Military Government Custodian of the property described hereafter, Property: Freudenberg & Co., Address: Weinheim, Höhnerweg 4. 2. The Custodian shall a) administer the property in accordance with the instructions of the Military Government and in anticipation of such instructions, he will not transfer it, surrender it or otherwise dispose of it. b) shall preserve, maintain and secure the property and shall permit no action which will deteriorate the value or the usefulness of the property. c) keep precise records and accounting in relation to the property and the income from it. 3) No person should undertake any action or inaction, or permit the implementation thereof, which involves damage or misappropriation of the property."
46 It occurred time and again that less heavily incriminated members – like Hans Freudenberg – of the previous management were tolerated in the company. However, formal participation in the management board is probably unlikely to have been permitted. Cf. also Woller, 1986, p. 245–256.
47 Cf. Gantert, 1955, p. 34.
48 Cf. Personalunterlagen von Paul Vogler, in: Corporate Archives 3/03126. (The Handelshochschule Mannheim was the municipal commercial college, the forerunner of today's University of Mannheim – ed.)
49 Cf. "Ansprache von Herrn Richard Freudenberg bei der Trauerfeier für Herrn C.G. Müller am 17.7.1968," in: Der Freudenberger, 4/1968, p. 28–29 as well as "Ansprache von Herrn Richard Freudenberg bei der Trauerfeier für Herrn Direktor i.R. Paul Vogler am 30. Dezember 1968," in: Der Freudenberger, 1/1969, p. 38–39. (The Technische Hochschule was Karlsruhe's technical university at the time, and is now called KIT – ed.)
50 "Ansprache von Herrn Richard Freudenberg bei der Trauerfeier für Herrn Direktor i.R. Paul Vogler am 30. Dezember 1968," in: Der Freudenberger, 1/1969, p. 38–39, here p. 38.
51 Cf. ibid. as well as "Ansprache von Herrn Richard Freudenberg bei der Trauerfeier für Herrn C.G. Müller am 17.7.1968," in: Der Freudenberger, 4/1968, p. 28–29, here p. 29.
52 Lagebericht von Hans Freudenberg, in: Corporate Archives 3/03131.
53 Cf. Freudenberg & Co., "Die Lage der Firma 6 Monate nach der Besetzung" vom 29. September 1945, in: Corporate Archives 3/04378.
54 Cf. Scholtyseck, 2016, p. 422.
55 Cf. Deutsches Branchenhandbuch für Industrie und Handel, Lieferung 10: Leder und Schuhe – Gummi und Asbest. Bearbeitet vom IFO Institut für Wirtschaftsforschung, München 1954.

56 Scholtyseck, 2016, p. 425. The breakdown of production in September 1945 was as follows: 66 % leather, 13 % *Nora*, 5 % heel stiffeners, 5 % heels, 5 % Robus, 7 % other (Viledon, Simmerwerk, Marena, mass, drive belts and P soles). Cf. also Freudenberg & Co., "Die Lage der Firma 6 Monate nach der Besetzung" vom 29. September 1945, in: Corporate Archives 3/04378.
57 Cf. Freudenberg & Co., "Die Lage der Firma 6 Monate nach der Besetzung" vom 29. September 1945, in: Corporate Archives 3/04378.
58 Cf. "Richard Freudenberg schreibt uns," in: Der Freudenberger, 1/1953, p. 3.
59 Cf. Erinnerungen von Hans Freudenberg (o. D.) zur Lage im Unternehmen in den Monaten nach dem Einmarsch der Amerikaner, in: Corporate Archives 3/01094; Freudenberg und die Leder- und Schuhwirtschaft, 2. Teil, in: Der Freudenberger, 2/1970, p. 16–22. as well as Bericht über die Demontage und Enteignung der Schuhfabrik in Burg, in: Corporate Archives 3/05535.
60 Scholtyseck, 2016, p. 425.
61 Cf. ibid. as well as Freudenberg & Co., "Die Lage der Firma 6 Monate nach der Besetzung" vom 29. September 1945, in: Corporate Archives 3/04378.
62 Cf. Scholtyseck, 2016, p. 426 as well as Barney Barnes, "Application for reinstatement of Richard Freudenberg" vom 7. Juli 1945, in: Corporate Archives 1/00758.
63 Cf. Scholtyseck, 2016, p. 425 f.
64 Erinnerungen von Hans Freudenberg (o. D.) zur Lage im Unternehmen in den Monaten nach dem Einmarsch der Amerikaner, in: Corporate Archives 3/01094.
65 Brief von Hans Freudenberg an Dr. Schubert/Eisendrath B. D. Tanning Co. vom 21. Mai 1946, in: Corporate Archives 3/06726.
66 Scholtyseck, 2016, p. 427.
67 Cf. Bericht über die Demontage und Enteignung der Schuhfabrik in Burg, in: Corporate Archives 3/05535.
68 Cf. 25 Jahre Curator Schuhfabrik, in: Corporate Archives 3/01234.
69 Cf. Scholtyseck, 2016, p. 427.
70 Ibid, p. 428.
71 Cf. ibid, p. 432.
72 Cf. Klageschrift der Spruchkammer Weinheim vom 15. Januar 1947, in: Corporate Archives 3/09292.
73 Schreiben von Hans Erich Freudenberg an den öffentlichen Kläger, die Spruchkammer Weinheim, vom 24. Januar 1947, in: Corporate Archives 3/09292.
74 Cf. Unterlagen der Spruchkammerakte von Dr. Hans Erich Freudenberg, in: Corporate Archives 3/09292.
75 Cf. "Dr. Hans Erich Freudenberg verstorben," in: CF-Intern, 8/1981, p. 2 as well as Planungsüberlegungen von Hans Erich Freudenberg aus dem Jahre 1948, in: Corporate Archives 3/01488.
76 Cf. Berichte und Korrespondenz des Vital-Schuhvertriebs, in: Corporate Archives 3/01650.
77 Cf. die Berichte über die Japanreisen von Hans Erich Freudenberg, in: Corporate Archives 3/01079, Corporate Archives 3/09008, Corporate Archives 3/06240, Corporate Archives 3/01038 and Corporate Archives 3/01049.
78 Cf. "Dr. Hans Erich Freudenberg verstorben," in: CF-Intern, 8/1981, p. 2; Horchler, 2020 as well as Horchler, 2020a.
79 "Dr. Hans Erich Freudenberg verstorben," in: CF-Intern, 8/1981, p. 2.
80 Cf. Unterlagen zum Lebenslauf von Helmut Fabricius, in: Corporate Archives 1/00738.
81 Cf. Schreiben von Helmut Fabricius an den öffentlichen Kläger Weinheim (Spruchkammer Weinheim) vom 18. Oktober 1946 mit Betreff "Anzeige gegen mich selbst," in: Corporate Archives 1/00940 as well as die Unterlagen zu Helmut Fabricius und seinen beruflichen Tätigkeiten in der NS-Zeit, in: Corporate Archives 3/09318.
82 Cf. Lebenslauf von Helmut Fabricius, in: Corporate Archives 3/08760 as well as die Zusammenstellung zu Helmut Fabricius' Tätigkeiten im Unternehmen Freudenberg, in: Corporate Archives 3/02123.
83 Cf. Unterlagen zum Lebenslauf von Helmut Fabricius, in: Corporate Archives 1/00738.
84 Cf. Scholtyseck, 2016, p. 428.
85 Cf. Berichte über die Amerika-Reise von Richard Freudenberg, in: Corporate Archives 3/01659.
86 Schreiben von Richard Freudenberg an Hans Freudenberg vom 15. Juni 1948, in: Corporate Archives 3/01659.
87 Scholtyseck, 2016, p. 432.

88 Cf. Ansprache von Hans Freudenberg am 22. Juni 1948 bei einer Zusammenkunft sämtlicher Betriebsleiter von Weinheim, Schönau, Neckarsteinach und Schopfheim, in: Corporate Archives 3/01094.
89 Cf. Abelshauser, 2011, p. 124 as well as Benz, 2005, p. 49–50.
90 Benz, 2005, p. 49–50.
91 Cf. Paragraph 3 des Kommanditvertrags der Freudenberg & Co. Kommanditgesellschaft vom 7. April 1956, in: Corporate Archives 3/07422.
92 Cf. Wilderotter, 1992, p. 13 f. and p. 21 ff.
93 Richard Freudenberg's job in the DDP ended when it was dissolved in 1933. Cf. Wilderotter, 1992, p. 25 f.
94 Cf. Bildungswerk für Kommunalpolitik e. V., Die Freien Wähler in Baden-Württemberg. Eine Dokumentation. Schwäbisch Hall 1982, p. 5 and p. 25 f.
95 Cf. Brief von Theodor Heuss an Lewtanant-Colonel [sic.] Winning vom 19. Juni 1945, in: Corporate Archives 3/02992.
96 Alongside Richard Freudenberg, Eduard Edert (Flensburg constituency) was also elected to the first *Bundestag* as an independent member of parliament in 1949. However, because he was urged to stand for election as a candidate by a party alliance of CDU, DP, FDP, Zentrum (the German Centre Party, Germany's oldest political party – ed.) and DkonP, which nominated him for electoral reasons to prevent the election of the candidate of the Südschleswigscher Wählerverband voters' association, Richard Freudenberg can be called the only truly independent member of parliament in the first *Bundestag*. Cf. Wilderotter, 1992, p. 61.
97 Cf. Wilderotter, 1992, p. 69 ff. as well as correspondence and minutes of meeting on the "southwestern state" question during Richard Freudenberg's political activities in the FDP, in: Corporate Archives 3/09357.
98 Cf. Wirsching, 2018, p. 88–89.
99 Cf. Thränhardt, 2013.
100 Cf. Wirsching, 2018, p. 90–91.
101 Cf. Benz, 2005a, p. 57.
102 Cf. Wirsching, 2018, p. 86–92.
103 Cf. Abelshauser, 2011, p. 87 ff. and p. 163 ff.
104 Cf. Thränhardt, 2013.
105 Cf. Abelshauser, 2011, p. 129–152.
106 Cf. Thränhardt, 2013.
107 Cf. Abelshauser, 2011, p. 243–245 and p. 426.
108 Schadt, 2002, p. 30.
109 Cf. Wilderotter, 1992, p. 72 ff. and Vita zu Richard Freudenberg, in: Corporate Archives 3/10744 and 3/02128.
110 Cf. Wilderotter, 1992, p. 78 ff. and Vita zu Richard Freudenberg, in: Corporate Archives 3/10744 and 3/02128.
111 Cf. on the European Defence Community (EDC): Wirsching, 2018, p. 92.
112 Cf. Transcript of Richard Freudenberg's speech in the German *Bundestag* on December 5, 1952, based on the audio recording, in: Corporate Archives: 1D/0011 and Corporate Archives 8/0081 respectively.
113 Cf. Wilderotter, 1992, p. 89 ff.
114 Cf. Schildt, 2012, p. 15–16.
115 Cf. Wirsching, 2018, p. 92 as well as Grau/Würz, 2014.
116 Cf. Schildt, 2012, p. 19.
117 Cf. Wilderotter, 1992, p. 102 ff.
118 Cf. Vita zu Richard Freudenberg, in: Corporate Archives 3/10744 and Corporate Archives 3/02128. (The Association of German Chambers of Commerce and Industry (*Deutscher Industrie- und Handelskammertag*, DIHT), was renamed Deutsche Industrie- und Handelskammer, or German Chamber of Commerce and Industry (DIHK) as of Jan 1, 2023. – ed.)
119 Cf. Abelshauser, 2011, p. 126–129.
120 Herrmann, 2019, p. 47 f.
121 Cf. die Vereinbarung zur Gründung der Vital-Schuh-Gesellschaft Hartwig & Co. vom 22. Oktober 1949 as well as Gesellschaftsvertrag der Vital-Schuh-Gesellschaft Hartwig & Co. vom 22. Oktober 1949, in: Corporate Archives 3/01858. Production at the Vital Schuhfabrik in Weinheim was

stopped in 1964. However, the liquidation of the Vital-Schuh-Gesellschaft Hartwig & Co. company did not officially take place until the deletion of the company from the commercial register, which was completed on October 29, 1971. Cf. Freudenberg, 1964a, p. 1 as well as Löschungsbestätigung, in: Corporate Archives 3/01858.
122 Rede von Richard Freudenberg an die Belegschaft anlässlich der Schließung der Vital-Schuhproduktion in Weinheim am 27. August 1964, in: Corporate Archives 3/01236.
123 Cf. Rede von Hermann Freudenberg zum 60. Geburtstag von Dr. Hans Erich Freudenberg am 21. Mai 1971, in: Corporate Archives 3/01236.
124 Gespräch mit Werner Kumpf über die Entwicklung der Firma vom 17. Februar 1987 (Interview with Werner Kumpf on the development of the company on February 17, 1987), in: Corporate Archives 6/00016, from minute 36:55 here.
125 Cf. Schreiben der Vital-Schuhgesellschaft an Jakob Brohl vom 7. Juli 1950, in: Corporate Archives 3/07430.
126 Cf. Brief von Richard Freudenberg an Ludwig Erhard vom 8. November 1948, in: Corporate Archives 3/02658.
127 Cf. ibid. Cf. also on the general situation of the German leather industry in 1947/48: Wirtschaftsbericht der Verwaltung für die Wirtschaft der Bizone, in: Corporate Archives 3/01666.
128 Cf. Brief von Theodor Siebel an Friedrich Holzapfel, Vorsitzender der C.D.U. Fraktion des Wirtschaftsrats Frankfurt vom 27. November 1948, in: Corporate Archives 3/02658.
129 Cf. Brief von Richard Freudenberg an Ludwig Erhard vom 8. November 1948, in: Corporate Archives 3/02658.
130 Cf. ibid. as well as Vereinbarung über den Kauf inländischer Rohware, in: Corporate Archives 3/02658.
131 Brief von Ludwig Erhard an Richard Freudenberg vom 12. August 1949, in: Corporate Archives 3/02658.
132 Cf. Schreiben von Richard Freudenberg an Ludwig Erhard, Direktor der Verwaltung für Wirtschaft des Vereinigten Wirtschaftsgebietes vom 24. Dezember 1948, in: Corporate Archives 3/02658.
133 Cf. Brief von Richard Freudenberg an Ludwig Erhard vom 12. Februar 1949, in: Corporate Archives 3/02658.
134 Cf. Brief von Richard Freudenberg an Ludwig Erhard vom 22. März 1949, in: Corporate Archives 3/02658.
135 Cf. also Korrespondenzen zwischen Richard Freudenberg und Ludwig Erhard, in: Corporate Archives 3/02658.
136 Cf. Brief von Richard Freudenberg an Ludwig Erhard vom 18. August 1949, in: Corporate Archives 3/02658.
137 Brief von Richard Freudenberg an Bundeswirtschaftsminister Ludwig Erhard vom 22. Dezember 1949, in: Corporate Archives 3/02658.
138 The German leather industry's dependence on imports had been further exacerbated by the loss of the heavily agrarian eastern German regions and by the separation of the Soviet occupation zone, which was likewise more heavily agrarian, after 1945. Cf. Die wirtschaftliche Lage der ledererzeugenden Industrie in der Bundesrepublik Deutschland 1955/56 (Leder-Enquête), 1959, in: Corporate Archives 3/01842.
139 Cf. Entwicklung der durchschnittlichen Häutepreise, in: Corporate Archives 3/03560.
140 Cf. "Entwicklung des Lederimports bereitet größte Sorgen," in: Leder- und Häutemarkt, 26/1960, p. 278, in: Corporate Archives 3/06505.
141 Cf. Rede von Hermann Freudenberg an die Gesellschafter vom 4. März 1961, in: Corporate Archives 3/00893.
142 Cf. "Aktive Selbsthilfe," in: Leder- und Häutemarkt, 26/1960, p. 278, in: Corporate Archives 3/06505 as well as Die wirtschaftliche Lage der ledererzeugenden Industrie in der Bundesrepublik Deutschland 1955/56 (Leder-Enquête), 1959, in: Corporate Archives 3/01842.
143 Cf. Bührer, 2012, p. 34.
144 Cf. Berlinghoff, 2018.
145 Cf. Die wirtschaftliche Lage der ledererzeugenden Industrie in der Bundesrepublik Deutschland 1955/56 (Leder-Enquête), 1959, in: Corporate Archives 3/01842.
146 Cf. "Freudenberg und die Leder- und Schuhwirtschaft," in: Der Freudenberger, 1/1970, p. 28–34.
147 Cf. Umsatzkennzahlen, in: Corporate Archives 3/00893, Corporate Archives 3/01006, Corporate

Archives 3/03912 and Corporate Archives 3/05018 as well as turnover statistics (Umsatzstatistik) in the Corporate Archives.
148 Cf. Lebenslauf von Hermann Freudenberg, in: Corporate Archives 3/08760.
149 Brief von Hermann Freudenberg an seinen Onkel Hans Freudenberg vom 24. August 1948, in: Corporate Archives 1/00355.
150 Cf. "Hermann Freudenberg – 60 Jahre," in: Freudenberg Intern, 7/1984, p. 1–2.
151 Cf. Aktennotizen von Hermann Freudenberg, in: Corporate Archives 3/00893.
152 Cf. Lebenslauf von Hermann Freudenberg, in: Corporate Archives 3/08760. In 1959, further general partners – apart from Hermann Freudenberg – were also appointed: Kurt Kraft, Otto Schildhauer, Peter Wentzler and Dieter Freudenberg.
153 Cf. Rede von Hermann Freudenberg zur 60. Geburtstagsfeier von Dieter Freudenberg vom 28. Februar 1986, in: Corporate Archives 3/04851.
154 Cf. "Dieter Freudenberg – 60 Jahre" (o. A.), published in Leder und Häutemarkt am 21. Februar 1986, in: Corporate Archives 3/03757. Dieter Freudenberg completed the following training placements from October 1947 to the fall of 1952: 1. Deutsche Bank in Esslingen (1947–1948), 2. International haulage company in Bremen (1948–1949), 3. Hide wholesaler Blum in Paris, France and attended the Alliance Française cultural institute (1949–1950), 4. Shoe and leather wholesaler J. H. Carter in London, England, and attended the London College (1950–1951), 5. Shoe factory in Cape Town, South Africa (1951) and 6. Import-/export wholesaler Staudt & Co. in Argentina (1951–1952).
155 Cf. die Berichte der Südamerika-Reise von Dieter Freudenberg von 1951–1953, in: Corporate Archives 3/01059, Corporate Archives 3/01050 and Corporate Archives 3/01051. Cf. also "Dieter Freudenberg – 60 Jahre" (o. A.), published in Leder und Häutemarkt am 21. Februar 1986, in: Corporate Archives 3/03757, as well as "Dieter Freudenberg gestorben," in: Freudenberg Magazin, 3/2010, p. 44.
156 "Dieter Freudenberg gestorben," in: Freudenberg Magazin, 3/2010, p. 44.
157 Rede von Hermann Freudenberg zur 60. Geburtstagsfeier von Dieter Freudenberg vom 28. Februar 1986, in: Corporate Archives 3/04851.
158 Cf. "Dieter Freudenberg gestorben," in: Freudenberg Magazin, 3/2010, p. 44.
159 Cf. "Richard schreibt uns," in: Der Freudenberger, 2/1959, p. 3.
160 Cf. "Dieter Freudenberg – 60 Jahre" (o. A.), published in Leder und Häutemarkt am 21. Februar 1986, in: Corporate Archives 3/03757.
161 Cf. "Freudenberg und die Leder- und Schuhwirtschaft, 2. Teil," in: Der Freudenberger, 2/1970, p. 16–22. Turnover reached 48.2 million deutschmarks in 1949. Production volume at Gustav Hoffmann reached 4.6 million pairs of shoes in 1938.
162 Cf. 25 Jahre Curator Schuhfabrik, in: Corporate Archives 3/01234.
163 Cf. Umsatzwerte für die konsolidierte Bilanz 1951, in: Corporate Archives 3/05018. According to the turnover figures for the consolidated balance sheet in 1951, group turnover was 218.9 million deutschmarks. This is comprised of turnover for leather: 94.6 million deutschmarks, shoes: 75.9 million deutschmarks (Tack: 9.8 million deutschmarks, Gustav Hoffmann: 45 million deutschmarks, Vital: 21.1 million deutschmarks) and all other business areas 48.4 million deutschmarks.
164 Cf. 25 Jahre Curator Schuhfabrik, in: Corporate Archives 3/01234.
165 Cf. Aufbau und derzeitige Lage bei "Curator", Bericht von Dr. Hans Erich Freudenberg vom 9. Dezember 1960, in: Corporate Archives 3/01234.
166 Cf. Hans Erich Freudenberg: Unsere Aufgaben der kommenden Jahre, Studie vom Juni 1968, in: Corporate Archives 3/02269.
167 Cf. "Freudenberg und die Leder- und Schuhwirtschaft, 2. Teil," in: Der Freudenberger, 2/1970, p. 16–22.
168 Cf. "Wir arbeiten für den Schuh," in: Der Freudenberger, 1/1953, p. 7–12. The poster portrays the components of a *Nora* shoe.
169 Cf. "Blick über den eigenen Zaun," in: Der Freudenberger, 1/1954, p. 12. According to this, more than 90 % of the West German shoe factories in 1954 are considered to be "small and medium-sized businesses," since they have a workforce of fewer than 200 employees.
170 At the beginning of 1953, around 1,200 workers were employed in Vital Schuhgesellschaft shoe manufacturing at Freudenberg in Weinheim. At Gustav Hoffmann some 3,300 workers were employed. Of these, 2,000 alone were working in production at the main factory in Kleve. Cf.

"Richard Freudenberg schreibt uns," in: Der Freudenberger, 1/1953, p. 3 as well as Berichte über die Geschäftsentwicklung Elefanten, 1953, in: Corporate Archives 3/02350.
171 Cf. Umsatzwerte für die konsolidierte Bilanz 1954, in: Corporate Archives 3/05018. According to the turnover figures for the consolidated balance sheet in 1954, group turnover were 286 million deutschmarks. This is comprised of turnover for leather: 106 million deutschmarks, shoes: 81 million deutschmarks (Tack: 13 million deutschmarks, Gustav Hoffmann: 44 million deutschmarks, Vital: 24 million deutschmarks) and all other business areas 99 million deutschmarks.
172 Cf. "D-Mark wurde zur Weltwährung," in Der Freudenberger, 1/1957, p. 18.
173 Cf. Schreiben von Richard Freudenberg, "Gedanken, ausgelöst durch die Schließung der Vital," vom 18. September 1964, in: Corporate Archives 3/06754.
174 Cf. 25 Jahre Curator Schuhfabrik, in: Corporate Archives 3/01234 as well as Werk Offenbach, Kurzinformation 56 vom 20. Dezember 1973, in: Corporate Archives 3/01234.
175 Cf. Schreiben von Richard Freudenberg, "Gedanken, ausgelöst durch die Schließung der Vital," vom 18. September 1964, in: Corporate Archives 3/06754.
176 Cf. Hermann Freudenberg: Zur Geschäftslage, in: Der Freudenberger, 6/1964, p. 1.
177 Cf. Hans Erich Freudenberg: Unsere Aufgaben der kommenden Jahre, Studie vom Juni 1968, in: Corporate Archives 3/02269.
178 Cf. "C. F. Versehrtenwerkstatt in Bayern," in: Der Freudenberger, 2/1951, p. 14. The foundation of a workshop for disabled war veterans was considered in early 1948 after a meeting with a doctor from the disabled veterans' home in Rottach-Egern on the Tegernsee lake. After Werneck Castle is selected as the central heavily disabled hospital, a manufacturing workshop is set up there for the Simrit-Werk plant. Disabled veterans are employed there from December 1949. After moving to Würzburg in 1958, the workshop is closed in 1975 after rationalization measures had been introduced. Cf. "Unsere Wernecker ziehen um," in: Der Freudenberger, 1/1958, p. 37–39 as well as Monatsbericht ZI [ZI = Zentraler Informationsdienst bei Carl Freudenberg] März/1975, in: Corporate Archives 3/01269.
179 Cf. Einladungsschreiben des Vereins vom 9. Januar 1995 and Vereinbarung zwischen Carl Freudenberg und dem Verein für Gemeindediakonie und Rehabilitation e. V. vom 10. Oktober 1988, in: Corporate Archives 3/08047. After the closure of the Müllheimer Tal factory, the workshop moved into the Zwischen Dämmen plant in 1994.
180 Cf. "Landespreis für den Einbezug Schwerbehinderter," in: Marktplatz, 1/2017, p. 11.
181 Cf. Unterlagen zur Gründung der Freudenberg Wohnbauhilfe, in: Corporate Archives 3/04512.
182 Cf. "Freitisch," in: Der Freudenberger, 1/1952, p. 15. In 1951, 800 deutschmarks were donated by the workforce to serve a free lunch to 30 needy people from Weinheim over the age at Christmas for 12 weeks in the canteen kitchen. From 1957 the timeframe is extended to six months, while the company pays for the other six months of the year. Thus the free meal system (*Freitisch*) takes place throughout the year. In 2017, a total of 10,111.19 EUR was collected for 20 needy people. Cf. "Mittagstisch für 40 alte Leute," in: Der Freudenberger, 1/1957, p. 6 as well as "Spendenrekord für den Freitisch," in: Marktplatz, 1/2018, p. 1.
183 Georg Böhler was a master coppersmith (*April 28, 1857) and lived to 103 years old. He worked at Freudenberg from July 26, 1886 to November 1, 1925 and was thus at the company for almost 40 years. Cf. Personal-Datenbank des Unternehmensarchivs).
184 Cf. documents, in: Corporate Archives 3/01861 as well as "Georg-Böhler-Stiftung," in: Der Freudenberger, Sonderausgabe Mai 1957, p. 3.
185 Cf. documents, in: Corporate Archives 3/01654. The foundation's residual assets of 42,051.77 deutschmarks is given as a donation to the City of Weinheim in 1978.
186 Cf. Nottebohm, 1985, p. 7. Prof. Mechels was one of Freudenberg's technical advisors at this time.
187 Cf. Patentschrift für Kunstleder von 1936, in: Corporate Archives 3/03086 as well as Nottebohm, 1985, p. 9 ff.
188 Cf. Lauppe, 1978.
189 How *Vlieseline* is made: "The fibrous material in "*Vlieseline*" is a mixture of wool, spun rayon, camel hairs, regenerated wool and women's hair; cotton is predominantly used for household items. After the coarse impurities have been removed from the fibers, they are put through the "shredder", the well-known textile machine, which combines them into a rough fiber mixture. This fiber mixture then goes through a carding line and is processed into a fine staple fiber. [...] The nonwoven is then impregnated with a binding agent, which is mainly comprised of high-quality synthetic rubbers, and [...] dried. In this way, a textile fabric is produced that is mainly only

connected to the fibers that are overlying in orientation at the points of intersection and thus retains its specific characteristics, like stability, porosity and elasticity. After impregnation and drying, the material is washed and finished; finally, the material is smoothed in calenders and vulcanized thoroughly in large drying chambers," Cf. "Viledon. Ein Kind der CF-Familie," in: Der Freudenberger, 1/1952, p. 5–7.
190 Cf. "Selbstschneidern leicht gemacht. The wonder under. Weiches Vlies – schicke Linie. Fachlehrschauen um Vlieseline," in: Der Freudenberger, 2/1954, p. 23–25, here p. 24 f. as well as "Dasselfliegen im Viledon-Werk?," in: Der Freudenberger, 1/1955, p. 16–17.
191 Cf. "Selbstschneidern leicht gemacht. The wonder under. Weiches Vlies – schicke Linie. Fachlehrschauen um Vlieseline," in: Der Freudenberger, 2/1954, p. 23–25, here p. 24 f. as well as "Zehn Jahre Vlieseline Studio," in: Der Freudenberger, 4/1963, p. 5–7. Cf. also: Fath, 2016; Hasenhüttl, 2018 as well as "Mode und Kreativität, das ist Mailand! Freudenberg in Italien," in: Freudenberg Magazin, 3/2012, p. 10–13.
192 Cf. Brief und Berichte as well as Gesellschaftsvertrag, in: Corporate Archives 3/04891.
193 Cf. Handelsregisterauszug des Amtsgerichts Heidelberg, in: Corporate Archives 3/04749 as well as die Zusammenstellung zum Gespräch mit Herrn Pfaff am 30. Dezember 1974 zum Übergang seiner Firma auf Vlieseline Vertrieb GmbH ab 1. April 1975, in: Corporate Archives 3/01931. Cf. also: "Vlieseline-Vertrieb Südwest," in: CF-Intern, 2/1975, p. 2.
194 Cf. Geschichtsbroschüre, 2019, p. 13 as well as Nottebohm, 1985.
195 Ibid.
196 Cf. Nottebohm, 1985.
197 Cf. History brochure, 2019, p. 13 as well as Nottebohm, 1985.
198 Cf. Lauppe, 1978.
199 Vileda, 2008, p. 8.
200 Cf. Nottebohm, 1985.
201 Cf. Lauppe, 1978.
202 Ibid.
203 Ibid.
204 Cf. Schiller, 1955, p. 10.
205 Cf. Lauppe, 1978 as well as Bilanzbuch des Frema-Werkes, in: Corporate Archives 3/11106.
206 Cf. Geschichte des Fremawerks Augsburg, in: Corporate Archives 3/10960 as well as 25 Jahre Fremawerk, in: Corporate Archives: 3/00310.
207 Cf. Geschichte des Fremawerks Augsburg, in: Corporate Archives 3/10960.
208 Cf. Lizenzvertrag zwischen Freudenberg und der Downing Trading Corporation (New York, USA) vom 30. Dezember 1950, in: Corporate Archives 3/01333 as well as Korrespondenzunterlagen von Carl-Ludwig Nottebohm, Wilhelm Lauppe und David Morgenstern zur Einrichtung der ersten Pellon-Strecke in Amerika, in: Corporate Archives 3/03164. New York businessman David Morgenstern had already had business relations with Freudenberg before 1935, when he was a skin trader in Krakow. He had emigrated to America. In the spring of 1950, he visited Freudenberg and was shown around the *Viledon* department. Cf. Korrespondenz mit David Morgenstern von der Downing Trading Corporation zwischen 1950 und 1951, in: Corporate Archives 3/02297.
209 Cf. the excerpt from Richard Freudenberg's eulogy on Carl Ludwig Nottebohm on the latter's resignation from the company on October 31, 1970 regarding the problems of procuring foreign currency, in: Corporate Archives 3/01333.
210 Cf. Freudenberg/Schuster 1999, p. 227 as well as Lauppe, 1978.
211 Cf. Unterlagen zur Auszahlung der Partner Morgenstern und Westreich, in: Corporate Archives 3/00845.
212 The name "Bondina" is derived from the English word for nonwovens: "bonded fabrics". Cf. Lauppe, 1978.
213 Cf. Lauppe, 1978 as well as Verträge zur Gründung der Bondina, in: Corporate Archives 3/07107.
214 The driver was probably Peter Bormuth, who celebrated 50 years of working at Freudenberg in 1960. Cf. Listen der Werkmeister, Handwerker, Wachleute und Chauffeure / Kutscher, in: Corporate Archives 3/07251 A 3.
215 Cf. "Viledon Filtermatten helfen gegen Staub und Ruß," in: Der Freudenberger, 5/1959, p.11 as well as "50 Jahre bei CF," in: Der Freudenberger, 2/1960, p. 47–48.
216 Cf. Deutsches Patentamt, Auslegeschrift 1 154 999, in: Corporate Archives 3/07088. The inventors are named as: Dr. Carl-Ludwig Nottebohm, Dr. Wilhelm Lauppe and Dr. Robert Schabert.

217 Cf. Deutsches Patentamt, Patentschrift 1 719 006, in: Corporate Archives 3/07088. The inventors are named as: Dr. Carl-Ludwig Nottebohm, Dr. Robert Schabert and Albrecht Burk. Cf. also: Lauppe, 1978.
218 Cf. Huber, 1959.
219 Cf. Filter-Informationsmaterial, in: Corporate Archives 3/00404 as well as Nottebohm, 1985.
220 Cf. Huber, 1959 as well as Lauppe, 1978.
221 Cf. Kraft, 1963, p. 3 as well as Gärtner, 1968, p. 33.
222 Cf. Personalrundschreiben U III vom 20. November 1980, in: Corporate Archives 3/07038
223 Cf. Huber, 1964; Freudenberg Bauchronik, in: Corporate Archives 3/01194 as well as Gärtner, 1968, p. 3.
224 Cf. Bührer, 2012, p. 36.
225 Cf. Bonfert, 1999.
226 West German automotive production reached a new record high in June 1953: 46,425 vehicles in one month. Total production for the first six months of 1953 was 222,804 vehicles – 20,000 more than in the first six months of 1952, which corresponds to a production increase of around 10 percent. Cf. "Blick über den eigenen Zaun," in: Der Freudenberger, 4/1953, p. 24–25, here p. 25.
227 Cf. "Wohlstand für alle, 1945–1966," in: Bundesministerium für Wirtschaft und Klimaschutz, can be accessed online at: https://www.bmwk.de/Redaktion/DE/Artikel/Ministerium/Geschichte/1945-1966.html, accessed on August 7, 2023.
228 Cf. Bonfert, 1999.
229 Cf. "100 Millionen Simmerringe," in: Der Freudenberger, 1/1953, p. 4–5 and 100-Millionster Simmerring, in: Corporate Archives 2/0005.
230 Cf. Bonfert, 1999. Georg Boysen had been dismissed from Freudenberg on October 5, 1945 on the basis of Law No. 8 of the Military Government in the American Occupation Zone and had only been reemployed as after his Denazification Panel hearings were over (end of 1947) in 1948 as Head of Sales for the Simrit-Werk plant. Cf. Unterlagen zum Spruchkammerverfahren von Georg Boysen, in: Corporate Archives 3/10980.
231 Cf. "Georg Boysen 65 Jahre," in: Der Freudenberger, 4/1954, p. 4–5 as well as Umsatz- und Personalentwicklung, in: Corporate Archives 3/04403.
232 Group turnover in 1954 was 286 million deutschmarks. Cf. Konzernumsatzstatistik im Freudenberg-Archiv.
233 Cf. Bonfert, 1999. The "*Vulkollan*" polyurethane was made of the diisocyanates Desmophen® and Desmodur®.
234 Cf. Technische Korrespondenz zu den Greer-Patenten von Jean Mercier, in: Corporate Archives 3/01896 and Bonfert, 1999.
235 Cf. Raymond Sprey: Disogrin Historical Review, in: Corporate Archives 3/03596. The name "*Disogrin*" is derived from **Diiso**cyanate of **Gr**eer **In**dustries. Diisocyanates were basic chemical components in the manufacture of polyurethane.
236 Cf. Bonfert, 1999.
237 Cf. Raymond Sprey: Disogrin Historical Review, in: Corporate Archives 3/03596; Bonfert, 1999 as well as Analysen für geplante Disogrin-Standorte, in: Corporate Archives 3/07075.
238 Cf. Bonfert, 1999.
239 Cf. "Vertrag von Rom (EWG)," in: EUR-Lex, can be accessed online at: https://eur-lex.europa.eu/legal-content/DE/TXT/?uri=LEGISSUM:xy0023, accessed on November 13, 2020.
240 Corte & Cosso were granted a license to manufacture Simmerrings under Italian patent no. 319.529. Production was moved from Turin to Pinerolo (outside Turin) in 1941.
241 Cf. Unterlagen zur Geschichte der Corcos, in: Corporate Archives 3/05739 as well as Bonfert, 2008.
242 Cf. Verträge zur Gründung der Corcos Industriale, in: Corporate Archives 3/01867 and Corporate Archives 3/06906. The shareholder structure of the joint venture was as follows on its establishment: Freudenberg 50 %, Corte & Cosso 49.3 % and Ludovico Cosso 0.7 %.
243 Cf. Jahresabschlüsse der Corcos Industriale, in: Corporate Archives 3/08377 as well as Personal- und Umsatzstatistiken der Corcos, in: Corporate Archives 3/05739.
244 Cf. Nachruf auf Giuseppe Corte, in: Corporate Archives 3/01700 as well as Bonfert, 2008.
245 Cf. Hoch, 2008, p. 40.
246 Bonfert, 2008.
247 Cf. ibid.

248 Cf. Jahresabschlüsse der Corcos Industriale, in: Corporate Archives 3/08377 as well as Personal- und Umsatzstatistiken der Corcos, in: Corporate Archives 3/05739.
249 Cf. Stober, 1957.
250 Cf. Korrespondenzen und Aktennotizen zu den Besuchen der Firma Freudenberg bei Metalastik Limited zwischen 1955 und 1957, in: Corporate Archives 3/02743; Aktennotiz zum Besuch von Helmut Fabricius und Heinz Stober von 1956 bei Metalastik as well as Unterlagen zum Gegenbesuch der Firma Metalastik Limited bei Freudenberg von 1956, in: Corporate Archives 3/02738.
251 Cf. Bonfert, 1999.
252 Schreiben von Hr. Goldsmith von der Firma Metalastik Limited an Hans Freudenberg vom 01. September 1955, in: Corporate Archives 3/02743.
253 Cf. den Lizenzvertrag zwischen Metalastik Limited und Carl Freudenberg vom 17. Januar 1957, in: Corporate Archives 3/02716 as well as Bonfert, 1999, p. 230.
254 Development of the brand: In 1957, Freudenberg acquires the license for vibration control technology with the brand name "Metalastik". In 1973, when the licensing agreement expires, the name is changed to "Megulastik". Then, in 1976, "Megulastik" becomes "Freudenberg Megulastik". In 1993, the *Vibration Control* Segment is merged with the *Seals and Precision Moldings* Segment to become the *Seals and Vibration Control* Segment. The "Megulastik" brand name disappears. In 2001, the *Vibracoustic* Segment is established and thus Vibration Control Automotive is hived off from the Freudenberg *Seals and Vibration Control* Segment. In 2011, Vibration Control Industry is merged with Vibration Control for Rail. The new brand name is: Freudenberg Schwab Vibration Control. In 2012, the brand name is renamed TrelleborgVibracoustic and in 2016 Vibracoustic. Cf. Entwicklung der schwingungstechnischen Marken von Freudenberg, in: Corporate Archives 3/11172.
255 Cf. "Hans-Peter Wentzler gestorben," in: Freudenberg Magazin, 1/2002, p. 35 as well as Bonfert, 1999, p. 230.
256 The date of birth is uncertain, since all that can be found in the sources is that Heinz Stober died in 2003 aged 90. Cf. "Heinz Stober verstorben," in: Marktplatz, 4/2003, p. 10.
257 Cf. "Personalnachrichten," in: CF-intern, 1/1977, p.4 as well as "Im Ruhestand," in: CF-intern, 10/1977, p. 9.
258 Bonfert, 1999.
259 Cf. ibid.
260 Cf. Bericht von Heinz Stober zur Entwicklung von Metalastik, in: Corporate Archives 3/05945 as well as Bonfert, 1999.
261 Cf. Hoppe, 1952, p. 5.
262 Cf. Scholtyseck, 2016, p. 224.
263 Cf. Berichte zur Entstehung des Kunststoffwerkes und zur Entwicklung der Kunststoff-Produktion bei Freudenberg, in: Corporate Archives 3/01340 as well as "Der Nora-Schuh," in: Der Freudenberger, 3/1951, p. 11–12. The acronym "PVC" stands for polyvinylchloride. This material is a thermoplastic, meaning "a material that softens in the heat while it is as hard as wood at room temperature."
264 Cf. "Zwei Jahre NORAPLAN," in: Der Freudenberger, 3/1952, p. 12.
265 Cf. Hoppe, 1952, p. 5. Heinz Hoppe moved from Freudenberg to Daimler-Benz shortly afterwards, where he initially successfully developed sales of the Mercedes brand in the USA and was later appointed to the Daimler-Benz management board. However, he remained involved with Freudenberg and was a member of the Board of Partners from 1982 to 1990, and was first and hitherto the only non-family member to be its chairman, from 1983 to 1988. Cf. also: Stadler, 1994.
266 Cf. Berichte zur Entstehung des Kunststoffwerkes und zur Entwicklung der Kunststoff-Produktion bei Freudenberg, in: Corporate Archives 3/01340.
267 In 1957, the sirens were still tested every month in Weinheim – a circumstance that was due to the only relatively recent end of World War II. This always occurred on the first Friday of the month around midday. Since November 1, 1957 fell on a Friday, the siren test was still carried out – despite the fact that it was a local holiday in Baden-Württemberg. Thus the alarm was sounded directly after the fire sirens were tested. Cf.: Unterlagen zum Nora-Brand von 1957, in: Corporate Archives 3/01160 as well as Corporate Archives 3/01247.
268 Cf. Aktennotiz vom 6. November 1957, in: Corporate Archives 3/01160 as well as Pressedokumentation zum Nora-Brand, in: Corporate Archives 3/01160.

269 Cf. Brandbericht von E. Klotz vom Januar 1958, in: Corporate Archives 3/01160 as well as Bericht von Hans Freudenberg vom 5. November 1957, in: Corporate Archives 3/01247.
270 Cf. documents in: Corporate Archives 3/01617 as well as Schreiben von Richard und Dieter Freudenberg an die Nora-Kunden vom 2. November 1957, in: Corporate Archives 3/01160.
271 Cf. Brandbericht von E. Klotz vom Januar 1958, in: Corporate Archives 3/01160.
272 Cf. Correspondence as well as Bericht der Staatsanwaltschaft, in: Corporate Archives 3/01617 as well as Bericht von Hans Freudenberg vom 5. November 1957, in: Corporate Archives 3/01247.
273 For biographical data on Helmut Stepf, cf. "Helmut Stepf verstorben," in: Der Freudenberger, 4/1962, p. 50.
274 Aktennotiz vom 7. Februar 1958, in: Corporate Archives 3/01617.
275 Cf. Correspondence as well as Bericht der Staatsanwaltschaft, in: Corporate Archives 3/01617.
276 Cf. Aktennotiz vom 6. November 1957, in: Corporate Archives 3/01160; Bericht von Hans Freudenberg vom 5. November 1957, in: Corporate Archives 3/01247 as well as Kaufkraftäquivalente historischer Beträge in deutschen Währungen (Stand März 2023), in: Deutsche Bundesbank, can be accessed online at: https://www.bundesbank.de/resource/blob/615162/7ca8c81bb5b80fb993be76b79adbdee5/mL/kaufkraftaequivalente-historischer-betraege-in-deutschen-waehrungen-data.pdf, accessed on August 7, 2023.
277 Cf. Berichte zur Entstehung des Kunststoffwerkes und zur Entwicklung der Kunststoff-Produktion bei Freudenberg, in: Corporate Archives 3/01340.
278 Cf. Fußbodenzeitung 1982, in: Corporate Archives 3/03569.
279 Cf. "Norament – Karriere eines Bodenbelages," in: CF-intern, 10/1977, p. 3.
280 Cf. "Freudenberg und die Leder- und Schuhwirtschaft, 2. Teil," in: Der Freudenberger, 2/1970, p. 16–22. Total production of sole materials in the Federal Republic of Germany was: 1952 – 61,900 t, of which rubber soles made up 33,700 t; 1960 – 74,200 t, of which rubber soles made up 57,600 t; 1968 – 79,700 t, of which rubber soles made up 64.200 t. Total sales volumes of rubber soles were: 1954 – 28,640 t, of which *Nora* soles made up 5,865 t; 1960 – 30,275 t, of which *Nora* soles made up 9,175 t; 1968 – 42,575 t, of which *Nora* soles made up 15,945 t.
281 Cf. Brief Richard Freudenbergs an Joachim Rehbock in São Paulo, Weinheim, den 9. Mai 1957, in: Corporate Archives 3/01166.
282 Cf. Bericht von Richard Freudenberg vom 2. April 1966, in: Corporate Archives 3/02175.
283 Ibid.
284 Cf. Exemplare der Werkzeitung "Cafmanchete" der Holzbetriebe (FIM und CAFMA), in: Corporate Archives 3/00418.
285 Cf. Aktennotiz von Richard Freudenberg vom 26. Februar 1965, in: Corporate Archives 3/02174.
286 Cf. Testergebnisse vom 23. Dezember 1965, in: Corporate Archives 3/02174.
287 Cf. also photographic records, in: Corporate Archives 4/0067 and Corporate Archives 4/03555.
288 "Männer mit dem Geist der Bandeirantes," in: Der Freudenberger, 1/1989, p. 2.
289 Cf. ibid.
290 Mitteilung an die Führungskräfte, Weinheim 19. September 1988, in: Corporate Archives 3/03271.
291 Hütter, 2009, p. 168.
292 Freudenberg, 1970, p. 2.
293 Hütter, 2009, p. 168.
294 Ibid.
295 Cf. Freudenberg, 1970, p. 2.
296 Cf. Hütter, 2009, p. 168.
297 Cf. "Dieter Freudenberg – 60 Jahre" (o. A.), veröffentlicht in Leder und Häutemarkt am 21. Februar 1986, in: Corporate Archives 3/03757.
298 In 1959, the following were also appointed – alongside Hermann Freudenberg – as general partners: Kurt Kraft, Otto Schildhauer, Peter Wentzler and Dieter Freudenberg.
299 Cf. Ansprache von Hermann Freudenberg bei der Trauerfeier für Otto Schildhauer, in: Corporate Archives 1/00428.
300 Cf. Lebenslauf von Otto Schildhauer, in: Corporate Archives 1/00303 and Corporate Archives 3/02127 as well as Hütter, 2009, p. 171.
301 Hütter, 2009, p. 171.
302 Cf. ibid, p. 172.
303 Cf. "Hans-Peter Wentzler gestorben," in: Der Freudenberger, 1/2002, p. 35.
304 Cf. Hütter, 2009, p. 173.

305 Cf. Vita von Kurt Kraft, in: Corporate Archives 3/08760.
306 Cf. Hütter, 2009, p. 173.
307 Cf. Handelsregisterauszug, in: Corporate Archives 3/03483.
308 Hütter, 2009, p. 173.
309 Hoppe, 1991, p. 47.
310 Cf. ibid. as well as Stadler, 1994.
311 Cf. Hoppe, 1991, p. 48 ff. as well as Besuchsberichte und Briefe aus den USA von Heinz Hoppe aus dem Jahr 1951, in: Corporate Archives 3/01057.
312 Stadler, 1994.
313 Cf. Hoppe, 1991, p. 57 ff.
314 Cf. for example Korrespondenz zwischen Hermann Freudenberg und Heinz Hoppe 1977–1982, in: Corporate Archives 3/04733. This correspondence contains an exchange of information about new technologies alongside personal correspondence.
315 Brief von Dieter und Hermann Freudenberg an Heinz Hoppe vom 15. Februar 1982, in: Corporate Archives 3/04733.
316 Brief von Heinz Hoppe an Hermann Freudenberg vom 19. März 1982, in: Corporate Archives 3/04733.
317 Stadler 1994. Cf. on the election of the Board of Partners also: Dankesschreiben von Heinz Hoppe an Hermann Freudenberg vom 3. Mai 1982, in: Corporate Archives 3/04733.
318 Cf. Stadler, 1994 as well as Hoppe, 1991, p. 58 f. Cf. also on the transition of the chairmanship of the Board of Partners from Helmut Fabricius to Heinz Hoppe: Aktennotiz von Reinhart Freudenberg vom 14. April 1983, in: Corporate Archives 3/04733.
319 Cf. Brief von Hermann Freudenberg an Heinz Hoppe vom 29. November 1988, in: Corporate Archives: 3/04733.
320 Cf. Unterlagen zur Übergangsschule, in: Corporate Archives 3/01439. The first "transition school" was held on the initiative of the Badisches Gewerbeamt office of trade and industry in Karlsruhe in 1950 in Königsfeld in the Black Forest. One trainer and six teenagers from Freudenberg also attended. The result convinced Hans Freudenberg, who initiated Freudenberg's first own transition school in the same year, which was held in the rooms of the Odenwaldschule school in Oberhambach. Cf. Bericht von Manfred Hocke über Sinn und Zweck der Übergangsschule aus dem Jahr 1958, in: Corporate Archives 3/01439. The first transition school for girls was set up in 1963. Cf. Burkhardt, 1963.
321 Cf. on gifted youth support: "Ein großes Werk und junge Menschen," in: Corporate Archives 3/01439.
322 Secondary source: Hellmut Becker's speech at the funeral of Hans Freudenberg on October 6, 1966, in: Corporate Archives 3/10742.
323 The foundation was named after Hans Freudenberg's two sons, who had fallen in World War II. Cf. Unterlagen zur Heiner und Walter Freudenberg Stiftung, in: Corporate Archives 3/01654.
324 Cf. Horchler, 2017.
325 Cf. documents on the Heiner and Walter Freudenberg Foundation, in: Corporate Archives 3/01654. The following schools were integrated into Freudenberg's gifted youth support program: Odenwaldschule in Oberhambach, Martin-Luther-Schule in Rimbach, Albertus-Magnus-Schule in Viernheim, Gymnasium Wald-Michelbach, Goethe Gymnasium in Bensheim, Altes Kurfürstliches Gymnasium in Bensheim, Wirtschaftsgymnasium Weinheim and Wirtschaftsgymnasium Bensheim.
326 Cf. Horchler, 2017. The residual assets from the Heiner and Walter Freudenberg Foundation is donated to the City of Weinheim for "use for charitable purposes, preferably supporting gifted people." Cf. Schreiben der Heiner- und Walter Freudenberg Stiftung an die Stadt Weinheim vom 20. März 1978, in: Corporate Archives 3/01639.
327 Cf. Unterlagen zur Heiner und Walter Freudenberg Stiftung, in: Corporate Archives 3/01654 und Stipendiatenlisten der Heiner und Walter Freudenberg Stiftung, in: Corporate Archives 3/01652, Corporate Archives 3/01653 und Corporate Archives 3/01656. Insofar as can be ascertained from the surviving sources, around half the scholarship recipients completed a course of study.
328 Hans Freudenberg was the driving force behind the formation of the *Ettlingen Circle*. He was involved in the group as a founding member and organizer up to 1964. Afterwards, his functions in the *Ettlingen Circle* passed over to Hermann Freudenberg, who was a member until it was dissolved in 1977.

329 Further personages who regularly attended the meetings were, for example, Carl Wurster, CEO of BASF, later German President Richard von Weizäcker as well as Alfred Herrhausen, a member of the Deutsche Bank management board, who was later assassinated by German militant group RAF. Cf. Hütter, 2013, p. 161.
330 Cf. Unterlagen zum Ettlinger Kreis, in: Corporate Archives 3/01438 und Corporate Archives 3/08644–62
331 Cf. Vorschläge zur Linderung von Notständen im Erziehungs- und Bildungswesen vom Mai 1957, in: Corporate Archives 3/08644–62.
332 Cf. Horchler, 2017.
333 Cf. Hütter, 2013, p. 171 and p. 175. The Stifterverband is a joint initiative of companies and foundations promoting improvements in education, science and innovation. – ed.
334 Cf. ibid, p. 163–165 as well as 171–175.
335 Cf. Unterlagen zum Thema "Gastarbeiter," in: Corporate Archives 3/00813. The word "*Gastarbeiter*" (guest workers) was frequently used to denote the foreign workers recruited in the 1960s (and acquired a very negative connotation – ed.). Today, the term is no longer considered politically correct. The standard expression today is "*Arbeitsmigration*" (labor migration), but this is strictly speaking only a replacement word. Nevertheless, the term is used in some cases throughout this text to ensure a clear reference to the subject matter.
336 Cf. Unterlagen zum Thema "Gastarbeiter," in: Corporate Archives 3/00813. The Cornelius-Heim building, (which was formerly a rest home for workers and then for children) was used from August 1963 up to the fall of 1974 as a hostel for "*Gastarbeiter*." The Turkish workers who still lived there moved into the hostel on Langmaasweg in Weinheim.
337 Cf. Unterlagen zum Thema "Gastarbeiter," in: Corporate Archives 3/00813.
338 Cf. Unterlagen zum Sprachlabor, in: Corporate Archives 3/01437. The lessons can only be verified from 1961 from the Freudenberg archive documents; however, German lessons for the "*Gastarbeiter*" had probably already begun in 1960.
339 Cf. Statistiken der ausländischen Arbeitnehmer, in: Corporate Archives 3/01953.
340 Cf. Unterlagen zum Thema "Gastarbeiter," in: Corporate Archives 3/00813 and Statistiken der ausländischen Arbeitnehmer, in: Corporate Archives 3/01953.
341 Cf. Horchler, 2020.
342 Cf. hereto in general Kleinschmidt, 2002.
343 Later the Central Marketing Department, cf. documents, in: Corporate Archives 3/09008.
344 Cf. Horchler, 2020a. Dr. Hans Erich Freudenberg's first trip to Japan took place in May/June 1959. Accompanying him in Japan was Dr. Kurt Brasch, who was half Japanese and very knowledgeable about Japan and its culture. All contact to the Japanese leather and shoe industry had already been conducted through him and his company. He ultimately forged the relationship between the Freudenberg and Tsuru families.
345 Cf. also Bericht von Shozo Iwakuma zu den Anfängen der Japan Vilene Company, in: Corporate Archives 3/00964.
346 The name was derived from the English-language brand name "Vilene".
347 Cf. Verträge zur Gründung der Japan Vilene Company, in: Corporate Archives 3/07110 and Corporate Archives 3/07113.
348 Cf. Horchler, 2020.
349 Cf. ibid.
350 Cf. ibid.
351 Cf. Freudenberg, 1968, p. 2.
352 NOK was formed in 1951 through the merger of Nihon Yushi Kogyo, whose director was Shogo Tsuru, with a second rubber-processing company. The newly established company bore the name Nippon Oil Seal Kogyo (NOK), later Nippon Oil Seal Industry Co. Ltd. Cf. "Shogo Tsuru, Präsident der NOK," in: Der Freudenberger, 2/1968, p. 5 f.
353 According to Hans Erich Freudenberg, NOK was already in negotiations with an American company regarding an exchange of experience and the construction of a new factory. Cf. Freudenberg, 1968, p. 2.
354 Cf. Horchler, 2020a.
355 Cf. Freudenberg, 1968, p. 2.
356 Cf. Hans Erich Freudenberg: Bericht von Japanreise (15.11.-02.12.1961), in: Corporate Archives 3/06256.

357 It is often described how the two addressed each other as "my father" / "my son". Cf. "NOK und Freudenberg: 20 Jahre Partnerschaft und internationale Zusammenarbeit," in: CF-intern, 4/1980, p. 1–2.
358 Vertrag vom 15. März 1960, in: Corporate Archives 3/05719 and Corporate Archives 3/10966.
359 Cf. Freudenberg, 1968, p. 2.
360 Cf. Horchler, 2020a.
361 Relationships with foreign companies were strictly monitored and controlled by the Japanese authorities.
362 Vertrag vom 15. März 1960, in: Corporate Archives 3/05719 and Corporate Archives 3/10966.
363 Cf. Hans Erich Freudenberg: Bericht von Japanreise (15.11.-02.12.1961), in: Corporate Archives 3/06256.
364 Cf. "NOK und Freudenberg: Eine Partnerschaft in Fakten," in: CF-intern, 4/1980, p. 2.
365 Cf. Horchler, 2020.
366 Cf. ibid.
367 Rede von Hans Freudenberg anlässlich des Festaktes zum 70. Geburtstag Richard Freudenbergs am 9. Februar 1962, in: Der Freudenberger, 2/1962, p. 63–64, here p. 64.
368 Cf. Kommanditvertrag der Kommanditgesellschaft i. Fa. Freudenberg & Co. (Februar 1959), in: Corporate Archives 3/07218.
369 Alongside Richard Freudenberg, the general partners at this time (1961/62) were: Peter Wentzler, Otto Schildhauer, Kurt Kraft, Hermann Freudenberg, Dieter Freudenberg, Helmut Fabricius and Hans Erich Freudenberg.
370 The following members of the Freudenberg family were on the Board of Partners in 1961/62: Hans Freudenberg (Chairman), Werner Disko, Lilli Freudenberg, Rudolf Freudenberg, Adolf Freudenberg, Wilhelm Hartwig.
371 Richard Freudenberg attended a Management Board meeting for the last time at the end of May 1975 teil. He died on November 21, 1975. Cf.: Protokolle der Sitzungen der Geschäftsleitung für die Zeit von 1967 bis 1975, in: Corporate Archives 3/04561 and Corporate Archives 3/04568 as well as Vita von Richard Freudenberg, in: Corporate Archives 3/02128.
372 Minutes of the Management Board meetings only exist in the form of a report and summary of proceedings since 1973 (with lists of attendees). Previously, one member of the Management Board used to write a summary report in the form of a letter directly addressed to those members, who for example, had been unable to attend the meeting because of a business trip. There were no lists of attendees. Cf.: Protokolle der Sitzungen der Geschäftsleitung für die Zeit von 1967 bis 1975, in: Corporate Archives 3/04561 and Corporate Archives 3/04568.
373 Cf. Protokolle der Sitzungen der Geschäftsleitung für die Zeit von 1967 bis 1975, in: Corporate Archives 3/04561 and Corporate Archives 3/04568.
374 Cf. Lebenslauf von Hermann Freudenberg (1924–2010), in: Corporate Archives 3/08760.
375 Cf. Richard Freudenberg, Gedanken, ausgelöst durch die Schließung der Vital, 18. September 1964, in: Corporate Archives 3/06754.
376 Cf. Schreiben von Hermann Freudenberg an Kurt Freudenberg vom 20. Juni 1972, in: Corporate Archives 3/04561.
377 Richard Freudenberg, Rede zur Gesellschafterversammlung am 16. Juni 1962 in Heidelberg, in: Corporate Archives 3/03387.
378 Cf. Carl Freudenberg – Informationen über das Unternehmen, 1969, p. 58–59, in: Corporate Archives 3/07059. (Carl Freudenberg – Information about the company – ed.)
379 Cf. "Hermann Freudenberg verstorben," in: Freudenberg Magazin, 4/2010, p. 41.
380 Cf. Protokoll über die außerordentliche Sitzung des Gesellschafterausschusses der Freudenberg & Co. am 15. April 1972 in Weinheim, in: Corporate Archives 3/07319. Cf. also: Personalnachrichten, in: Der Freudenberger, 4/1972, p. 34 as well as Kommanditvertrag der Kommanditgesellschaft i. Fa. Freudenberg & Co. (Juli 1970), in: Corporate Archives 3/07218.
381 Cf. Protokolle der Sitzungen des Gesellschafterausschusses der Freudenberg & Co. für die Zeit von 1966 bis 1975, in: Corporate Archives 3/07319 as well as Kommanditvertrag der Kommanditgesellschaft i. Fa. Freudenberg & Co. (Juli 1970), in: Corporate Archives 3/07218.
382 Cf. Carl Freudenberg – Informationen über das Unternehmen, 1969, p. 58, in: Corporate Archives 3/07059. (Richard Freudenberg is named on the page by his photo as Chairman of the Board of Partners. – ed.)

383 Rede von Kurt Kraft bei der Gesellschafterversammlung am 15. April 1972, Tonbandaufnahme, in: Corporate Archives 6/00069.
384 Rede von Richard Freudenberg bei der Gesellschafterversammlung am 15. April 1972, Tonbandaufnahme, in: Corporate Archives 6/00069.
385 Cf. on the introduction of the first punch card systems: Brief von Heinrich Karrer an Günter Bischoff vom September 1976, wiedergegeben in: Sinz, 2008, p. 15 f. as well as die ungekürzte Fassung des Referats von Heinrich Karrer zum Stand der EDV vom 16. September 1967, p. 4 f., in: Corporate Archives 3/08754.
386 Cf. Sinz, 2008, p. 12. The correspondence with Dehomag can be found in: Corporate Archives 3/04938.
387 Cf. ibid, p. 18.
388 Cf. ibid, p. 19.
389 Ungekürzte Fassung des Referats von Heinrich Karrer zum Stand der EDV vom 16. September 1967, p. 4 f., in: Corporate Archives 3/08754.
390 Ibid, p. 5 f.
391 Cf. "Im Ruhestand. Heinrich Karrer," in: CF-intern, 1/1978, p. 10.
392 Cf. Sinz, 2008, p. 21.
393 Cf. ibid, p. 25.
394 Cf. Binarium: Röhren und Röhrencomputer, can be accessed online at: https://binarium.de/vakuumroehre_roehrenrechner, accessed on January 13, 2021; Betschon, 2019 as well as Borchers, 2001.
395 Cf. "Transistorrechner," can be accessed online at: https://www.frauen-informatik-geschichte.uni-bremen.de/index.php-id=128.htm, accessed on January 15, 2021.
396 Ibid.
397 Cf. Sinz 2008, p. 41 and p. 49.
398 "IBM schrieb vor 50 Jahren IT-Geschichte," in: Computerwoche. Can be accessed online at: https://www.computerwoche.de/a/ibm-schrieb-vor-50-jahren-it-geschichte,2553799, accessed on January 27, 2021
399 Cf. ibid.
400 Cf. Sinz, 2008, p. 49.
401 Cf. ibid, p. 59.
402 Cf. Firmenportrait zur Klüber-Gruppe, in: Corporate Archives 3/02383.
403 Cf. Rede von Dr. Ernst Schön anlässlich der 75-Jahrfeier der Klüber-Gruppe am 10. September 2004, in: Corporate Archives 3/06999.
404 Schreiben von Theodor Klüber an Geschäftsfreunde vom 31. März 1959, in: Corporate Archives 3/06999.
405 Cf. Rede von Dr. Ernst Schön anlässlich der 75-Jahrfeier der Klüber-Gruppe am 10. September 2004, in: Corporate Archives 3/06999 as well as Firmenportrait zur Klüber-Gruppe, in: Corporate Archives 3/02383. Cf. also: Schreiben von Theodor Klüber an Geschäftsfreunde vom 31. März 1959, in: Corporate Archives 3/06999.
406 Cf. Aktennotiz von Richard Freudenberg, Betr.: "Klüber Lubrication München GmbH," 24. Januar 1966, in: Corporate Archives 3/04567.
407 Schreiben von Theodor Klüber an Richard Freudenberg vom 2. Dezember 1965, in: Corporate Archives 3/11005.
408 Transcript of Richard Freudenberg's speech in the German *Bundestag* on December 5, 1952, based on the audio recording, in: Corporate Archives: 1D/0011 or Corporate Archives 8/0081. Cf. also: abgedruckte Rede von Richard Freudenberg vom 5. Dezember 1952, in: Richard Freudenberg. 80 Jahre, 1972, p. 28 ff., in: Corporate Archives 3/07061.
409 Cf. politisches Testament der Stifter Theodor und Helen Klüber von 1976, in: Corporate Archives 3/02382.
410 Rede von Dr. Ernst Schön anlässlich der 75-Jahrfeier der Klüber-Gruppe am 10. September 2004, in: Corporate Archives 3/06999.
411 Schreiben von Theodor Klüber an Richard Freudenberg vom 2. Dezember 1965, in: Corporate Archives 3/11005.
412 Cf. Aktennotiz von Richard Freudenberg für die Unternehmensleitung, "Betr.: Klüber Lubrication München GmbH" vom 5. Januar 1966, in: Corporate Archives 3/04567 and Corporate Archives 3/11006.

413 Cf. Richard Freudenberg, Aktennotiz "Betr.: Klüber Lubrication München GmbH" vom 5. Januar 1966, in: Corporate Archives 3/11007.
414 Cf. Günter Balbach, Kurzbericht über die Firma Klüber vom 29. Juni 1966, in: Corporate Archives 3/11009 as well as Klüber-Unterlagen zu Erwerb und Integration, in: Corporate Archives 3/11003.
415 Dr. Ernst Demme had been in retirement since the end of 1965. He had retired at the end of 1965 after working for 31 years as the first head of the Central Laboratory. The fact that Demme nonetheless had traveled to visit the company with Richard Freudenberg during his retirement shows that Richard Freudenberg regarded him as an important advisor. Cf. "Dr. Ing. Ernst Demme verstorben," in: Freudenberg-Intern, 6/1984, p. 8.
416 Cf. Aktennotiz von Richard Freudenberg an Hermann Freudenberg vom 24. Januar 1966, in: Corporate Archives 3/04567.
417 Cf. verschiedene Firmenauskünfte, in: Corporate Archives 3/11003.
418 Cf. Günter Balbach, Kurzbericht über die Firma Klüber vom 29. Juni 1966, in: Corporate Archives 3/11009.
419 Bericht von Hans Erich Freudenberg und Helmut Fabricius, "Betr.: Firma Klüber, München," 11. Juli 1966, in: Corporate Archives 3/03496.
420 Ibid.
421 Bericht von Hermann Freudenberg an Dieter Freudenberg vom 1. Juli 1966, in: Corporate Archives 3/04587 as well as Bericht von Helmut Fabricius zu den Entwicklungen in der Übernahme von Klüber Lubrication für die Geschäftsführerbesprechung am 1. Juli 1966, in: Corporate Archives 3/04587.
422 Cf. Schreiben des Rechtsanwaltes Wolfgang Fricke an die Freudenberg & Co. in Weinheim vom 10. August 1966 über die Gründung der Firma "Klüber Lubrication Verwaltungsgesellschaft Kommanditgesellschaft" in München, in: Corporate Archives 3/06064. August 9, 1966 is mentioned in various publication formats as the date of the Freudenberg acquisition.
423 Cf. Kopien der beglaubigten Abschriften der Urkunden zur Abtretung der Geschäftsanteile der Eheleute Klüber an die Freudenberg & Co. vom 12. August 1966, in: Corporate Archives 3/11007 as well as diverse Zusatzverträge zwischen den Eheleuten Klüber und Freudenberg, in: Corporate Archives 3/11007 and Corporate Archives 3/11008.
424 Cf. Beratungsvertrag zwischen Theodor Klüber und der Firma Carl Freudenberg vom 12. August 1966, in: Corporate Archives 3/11007.
425 Cf. Unterlagen zur Tätigkeit von Peter Wentzler als persönlich haftender Gesellschafter, in: Corporate Archives 3/04032.
426 Cf. Notiz von Günter Balbach vom 2. Mai 1979, in: Corporate Archives 3/11007.
427 Cf. ibid.

Chapter 6: Freudenberg under the influence of economic crises, growing complexity and innovations

1 Hinz-Wessels, 2003.
2 Cf. ibid.
3 Cf. Borowsky, 2002 as well as Wirsching, 2018, p. 104–106.
4 Cf. Wirsching, 2018, p. 105 f.
5 Cf. "Stabilitätsgesetz, Gesetz zur Förderung der Stabilität und des Wachstums," in: Bundeszentrale für politische Bildung (Publ.): Das Lexikon der Wirtschaft, Bonn 2016. Can be accessed online at: https://www.bpb.de/nachschlagen/lexika/lexikon-der-wirtschaft/20711/stabilitaetsgesetz, accessed on April 5, 2021.
6 Cf. Hinz-Wessels, 2003a as well as Bührer, 2001, p. 14.
7 Cf. "60 Jahre BRD: Die Wirtschaft der 70er, Grenzen des Wachstums," in: Süddeutsche Zeitung vom 17. Mai 2010. Can be accessed online at: https://www.sueddeutsche.de/politik/60-jahre-brd-die-wirtschaft-der-70er-grenzen-des-wachstums-1.387327, accessed on April 5, 2021 as well as Hinz-Wessels, 2003a.
8 "60 Jahre BRD: Die Wirtschaft der 70er, Grenzen des Wachstums," in: Süddeutsche Zeitung vom

17. Mai 2010. Can be accessed online at: https://www.sueddeutsche.de/politik/60-jahre-brd-die-wirtschaft-der-70er-grenzen-des-wachstums-1.387327, accessed on April 5, 2021.
9 Cf. ibid.
10 Elkhofer, 2014.
11 Cf. ibid.
12 Cf. Hinz-Wessels, 2003a as well as Bührer, 2001, p. 14 as well as information on the figures: Registrierte Arbeitslose und Arbeitslosenquote nach Gebietsstand, in: Statistisches Bundesamt, can be accessed online at: https://www.destatis.de/DE/Themen/Wirtschaft/Konjunkturindikatoren/Lange-Reihen/Arbeitsmarkt/lrarb003ga.html, accessed on April 5, 2021.
13 Cf. Bruttoinlandsprodukt (BIP) in Deutschland von 1950 bis 2020, in: Statista, can be accessed online at: https://de.statista.com/statistik/daten/studie/4878/umfrage/bruttoinlandsprodukt-von-deutschland-seit-dem-jahr-1950/, accessed on April 5, 2021.
14 Cf. "Anwerbestopp 1973," in: Bundeszentrale für politische Bildung (Publ.): Dossier: 1961: Anwerbeabkommen mit der Türkei, Bonn 2011. Can be accessed online at: https://www.bpb.de/geschichte/deutsche-geschichte/anwerbeabkommen/43270/anwerbestopp-1973, accessed on April 5, 2021.
15 Cf. Bührer, 2001, p. 15.
16 Cf. "Aus dem Jahresbericht 1974," in: Der Freudenberger, 4/1974, p. 6–7.
17 Cf. Gesellschafterbrief, 1975, in: Corporate Archives 3/02275.
18 Cf. Dispan/Stieler, 2015, p. 20; Schnaus 2017, p. 22; Donath/Szegfü, 2021, p. 23; Haid/Wessels, 1997, p. 514 as well as Rede von Hermann Freudenberg an die Belegschaft vom 14. Juli 1972, in: Corporate Archives 3/00893.
19 Cf. Gesellschafterbrief, 1975, in: Corporate Archives 3/02275.
20 Cf. "Kurzmeldungen," in: CF-intern, 2/1975, p. 2.
21 Gesellschafterbrief, 1975, in: Corporate Archives 3/02275.
22 Ibid.
23 Cf. Bührer, 2001, p. 15.
24 Cf. Schlupp, 1980, p. 33 ff. as well as Statz, 1984.
25 Cf. Registrierte Arbeitslose und Arbeitslosenquote nach Gebietsstand, in: Statistisches Bundesamt, can be accessed online at: https://www.destatis.de/DE/Themen/Wirtschaft/Konjunkturindikatoren/Lange-Reihen/Arbeitsmarkt/lrarb003ga.html, accessed on April 5, 2021.
26 Cf. Inflationsrate in Deutschland seit 1948–2020, in: Statista, can be accessed online at: https://de.statista.com/statistik/daten/studie/4917/umfrage/inflationsrate-in-deutschland-seit-1948/, accessed on April 5, 2021.
27 Cf. Wohltmann, 2018.
28 Gesellschafterbrief, 1976, in: Corporate Archives 3/02275.
29 Cf. Mergel, 2005, p. 179–201; Gutermann, 1985, p. 69–96 as well as Wirsching, 2006.
30 Cf. Martens, 2020.
31 Cf. Die wirtschaftspolitische Entwicklung von 1949 bis heute, Wirtschaft im wiedervereinigten Deutschland (1990–1998), in: Bundesministerium für Wirtschaft und Klimaschutz, can be accessed online at: https://www.bmwi.de/Redaktion/DE/Textsammlungen/Ministerium/wirtschaftspolitik-seit-1949.html, accessed on February 12, 2022 as well as Vertrag über die Schaffung einer Währungs-, Wirtschafts- und Sozialunion zwischen der Bundesrepublik Deutschland und der Deutschen Demokratischen Republik, can be accessed online at: https://www.gesetze-im-internet.de/wwsuvtr/WWSUVtr.pdf, accessed on February 12, 2022.
32 Cf. Arbeitslose und Arbeitslosenquote, in: Bundeszentrale für politische Bildung (Publ.): Soziale Situation in Deutschland, Bonn 2020. Can be accessed online at: https://www.bpb.de/nachschlagen/zahlen-und-fakten/soziale-situation-in-deutschland/61718/arbeitslose-und-arbeitslosenquote, accessed on February 12, 2022.
33 Cf. Die wirtschaftspolitische Entwicklung von 1949 bis heute, Wirtschaft im wiedervereinigten Deutschland (1990–1998), in: Bundesministerium für Wirtschaft und Klimaschutz, can be accessed online at: https://www.bmwi.de/Redaktion/DE/Textsammlungen/Ministerium/wirtschaftspolitik-seit-1949.html, accessed on February 12, 2022 as well as Treusch, 2016.
34 Cf. Gesellschafterbrief, 1990, in: Corporate Archives 3/05393.
35 Cf. Gesellschafterbriefe, 1995 und 1996, in: Corporate Archives 3/05393. Production began at the first sites in Czechia in 1996.
36 Cf. Statistische Jahrbücher 1962 bis 1965, Produktion ausgewählter Erzeugnisse: Leder insgesamt,

in: Statistisches Bundesamt, can be accessed online at: https://www.destatis.de/DE/Themen/Querschnitt/Jahrbuch/_inhalt.html, here: Statistisches Jahrbuch für die Bundesrepublik Deutschland, Vol. 1952 to 1990, accessed on March 31, 2022.
37 Cf. for general information Haid/Wessels, 1996.
38 Cf. Dispan/Stieler 2015, p. 20 as well as Haid/Wessels, 1997, p. 513 f.
39 Dispan/Stieler, 2015, p. 20.
40 Cf. Haid/Wessels, 1997, p. 512 f.
41 Ibid, p. 514.
42 Cf. ibid.
43 Cf. "Entwicklungstendenzen in der Lederindustrie. Ein Bericht von Dieter Freudenberg," in: Der Freudenberger, 2/1973, p. 4–6.
44 Cf. Rede von Hermann Freudenberg an die Belegschaft vom 14. Juli 1972, in: Corporate Archives 3/00893.
45 Cf. Bundesministerium für Wirtschaft und Energie: Branchenskizze Lederindustrie, can be accessed online at: https://www.bmwi.de/Redaktion/DE/Artikel/Branchenfokus/Industrie/branchenfokus-lederindustrie.html, accessed on: March 16, 2021.
46 Cf. Haid/Wessels, 1997, p. 512.
47 Cf. Freudenberg, 1966.
48 Freudenberg, 1964b, p. 1.
49 Cf. ibid. as well as Freudenberg, 1965, p. 1.
50 Cf. "Entwicklungstendenzen in der Lederindustrie. Ein Bericht von Dieter Freudenberg," in: Der Freudenberger, 2/1973, p. 4–6.
51 Cf. ibid.; Freudenberg, 1973; Gesellschafterbrief, 1982, in: Corporate Archives 3/06697; Haid/Wessels, 1997, p. 509 as well as Bundesministerium für Wirtschaft und Energie: Branchenskizze Lederindustrie, can be accessed online at: https://www.bmwi.de/Redaktion/DE/Artikel/Branchenfokus/Industrie/branchenfokus-lederindustrie.html, accessed on March 16, 2021.
52 Cf. Information der Geschäftsleitung der Firma Carl Freudenberg vom Juli 1965, in: Corporate Archives 3/01006; Freudenberg, 1964b, p. 1 as well as Freudenberg,1965, p. 1.
53 Cf. Umsatzentwicklung Leder 1960–1966, in: Corporate Archives 3/00893; Entwicklung des Betriebsergebnisses Leder 1960–1969, in: Corporate Archives 3/03190 as well as Freudenberg Corporate Archives, Employee and turnover statistics. According to these, group turnover is 866.3 million deutschmarks and turnover for leather is 186 million deutschmarks; net income is 42.1 million deutschmarks and operating result for leather is 2.2 million deutschmarks.
54 Freudenberg, 1967.
55 Cf. "Ein neues Freudenberg-Erzeugnis," in: Der Freudenberger, 2/1963, p. 11–14; "Das Helia-Werk," in: Der Freudenberger, 4/1968, p. 3–4 as well as "Abschied von Rolf Wassermann," in: CF-intern, 6/1976, p. 1–2.
56 Cf. "Ein neues Freudenberg-Erzeugnis," in: Der Freudenberger, 2/1963, p. 11–14 as well as the letter from Rolf Merton dated December 8, 1961 on the Syntilon synthetic leather, in: Corporate Archives 3/01319.
57 Cf. "Die Produktion von Helia-Schaumkunstleder," in: Corporate Archives 3/01320; a more up-to-date description on production in 1995 can be found in: Corporate Archives 3/05506. **Reverse process** production involved applying the PVC film or surface made of PVC onto a paper carrier material, which is later removed, and letting it dry. The foamed PVC – later polyurethane too – was then applied onto it. Finally, a fabric carrier made of jersey or Freudenberg nonwoven, later also made of an innovative spunbond nonwoven, ensured stability on the inside.
58 Cf. "Die Produktion von Helia-Schaumkunstleder," in: Corporate Archives 3/01320.
59 Cf. "10 Jahre Helia," in: Der Freudenberger, 5/1973, p. 30–31 as well as Freudenberg Corporate Archives, Employee and turnover statistics.
60 Cf. Freudenberg, 1968a.
61 Cf. Entwicklung des Betriebsergebnisses Leder 1960–1969, in: Corporate Archives 3/03190 as well as Freudenberg Corporate Archives, Employee and turnover statistics. According to these, group turnover was 1,029 million deutschmarks and turnover for leather is 205.5 million deutschmarks in 1968.
62 Cf. "Leder drängt aus der Verlustzone," in: Der Freudenberger, 2/1973, p. 3.
63 Cf. "Rückblick und Vorschau zur Jahreswende," in: Der Freudenberger, 1/1970, p. 2–8.
64 Cf. "Freudenberg und die Leder- und Schuhwirtschaft, 1. Teil," in: Der Freudenberger, 1/1970,

p. 28–34. The German leather industry's total production was 221 million square feet (sq. ft.) and 1.8 sq. ft. of upper leather was required for a pair of shoes.
65 Cf. Freudenberg Corporate Archives, Employee and turnover statistics. Turnover in 1966 was 866.3 million deutschmarks, in 1968 1,029 million deutschmarks and in 1970 1,260 million deutschmarks. Profits fluctuated: In 1966, they were at 42.1 million deutschmarks, in 1968 they leaped to 73 million deutschmarks. In 1970, net income was only 56.6 million deutschmarks.
66 Cf. "Jahresbericht 1970," in: Der Freudenberger, 1/1971, p. 2–8 as well as "Zur Lage in unseren Lederwerken," in: Der Freudenberger, 1/1971, p. 13–14.
67 Cf. Freudenberg Corporate Archives, Employee and turnover statistics as well as Gesellschafterbrief, 1972, in: Corporate Archives 3/02275.
68 The shortage predominantly stemmed from the fact that Argentina had imposed an export ban on raw hides and slaughtering volumes had declined sharply in Europe because of rising meat prices. Cf. Rede von Hermann Freudenberg an die Belegschaft vom 14. Juli 1972, in: Corporate Archives 3/00893.
69 Cf. ibid.
70 Cf. Kurzreferat von Hans Erich Freudenberg für die Gesellschafterversammlung vom 24. April 1971, in: Corporate Archives 3/03190.
71 Cf. Freudenberg Corporate Archives, Employee and turnover statistics. According to these, group turnover was 1,390.2 million deutschmarks and turnover for leather is 185 million deutschmarks.
72 Cf. Gesellschafterbrief, 1972, in: Corporate Archives 3/02275. Teneria Temola in Mexico still achieved profits of 1.7 million deutschmarks in 1972. Cf. Turnover and profit development of Teneria Temola 1972–1980, in: Corporate Archives 3/02440.
73 Cf. Rede von Hermann Freudenberg an die Belegschaft vom 14. Juli 1972, in: Corporate Archives 3/00893.
74 Cf. ibid.
75 Cf. "Rationalisierungsschutzvertrag," in: Der Freudenberger, 1/1973, p. 11.
76 Cf. "Entwicklungstendenzen in der Lederindustrie. Ein Bericht von Dieter Freudenberg," in: Der Freudenberger, 2/1973, p. 4–6.
77 Cf. "Bericht der Geschäftsleitung," in: Der Freudenberger, 3/1973, p. 45.
78 Cf. Protokolle der Sitzungen der Unternehmensleitung vom 30. April 1973 und 3. Oktober 1973, in: Corporate Archives 3/04561.
79 Cf. Langfristige Planung des Geschäftsbereichs Leder vom 24. Juli 1974, in: Corporate Archives 3/01207.
80 Cf. Freudenberg Corporate Archives, Employee and turnover statistics.
81 Protokoll der Sitzung der Unternehmensleitung vom 3. Oktober 1973, in: Corporate Archives 3/04561.
82 Cf. Protokoll der Sitzung der Unternehmensleitung vom 16. Oktober 1973, in: Corporate Archives 3/04561.
83 Cf. "Dr. Haas-Wittmüss," in: Der Freudenberger, 1/1974, p. 45 as well as Protokoll der Sitzung der Unternehmensleitung am 22. April 1974, in: Corporate Archives 3/04572; "Die Freudenberg-Gruppe im Jahre 1973," in: Der Freudenberger, 2/1974, p. 2–4 as well as "Bericht der Geschäftsleitung über das 2. Quartal 1974," in: Der Freudenberger, 4/1974, p. 41.
84 Cf. "Lederproduktion in Schönau läuft aus," in: Der Freudenberger, 2/1974, p. 36–37. Since many employees in Schönau and its environs found new jobs, the lion's share of the workforce accepted the benefits of the social compensation plan (severance pay according to length of employment at the company, severance pay staggered according to age, retention of company pension entitlement for employees with 20 years of service and over, or over the age of 59, payment of employee savings scheme contributions for 1974, special conditions for older employees). For further information regarding reconciliation of interests social and the compensation plan see the copy of the works agreement between the Management Board of the Carl Freudenberg company and the works council of the Carl Freudenberg company in the Schönau plant dated May 13, 1974, in: Corporate Archives 3/02842 and Corporate Archives 3/01985. Regarding the number of job cuts, cf. Workforce statistics for 1973 and 1974, in: Corporate Archives 3/07263.
85 Cf. "Aus dem Jahresbericht 1974," in: Der Freudenberger, 4/1974, p. 6–7.
86 Cf. Freudenberg Corporate Archives, Employee and turnover statistics. According to these, group turnover is 1,613.3 million deutschmarks and turnover for leather is 91 million deutschmarks.
87 Cf. Protokoll der Sitzung der Unternehmensleitung vom 30. April 1974, in: Corporate Archives

3/04561; Belegschaftsstatistik 1969, in: Corporate Archives 3/00618; Belegschaftsstatistik 1974, in: Corporate Archives 3/01011 as well as "Die Freudenberg-Gruppe im Jahre 1973," in: Der Freudenberger, 2/1974, p. 2–4.
88 Cf. Freudenberg, 1973 as well as Freudenberg Corporate Archives, Employee and turnover statistics.
89 Cf. as an example Protokoll der Sitzung der Unternehmensleitung vom 30. April 1974, in: Corporate Archives 3/04561.
90 Cf. "Bericht der Geschäftsleitung über das IV. Quartal 1975," in: CF-intern, 2/1976, p. 5.
91 Cf. Gesellschafterbrief vom March 31, 1982, in: Corporate Archives 3/06697. This enabled the Freudenberg building department to save 25 million deutschmarks in investment costs.
92 Cf. Freudenberg, 1976.
93 Freudenberg, 1973.
94 Ibid.
95 Cf. Protokoll der Sitzung der Unternehmensleitung vom 1. Juni 1976, in: Corporate Archives 3/04561.
96 Cf. Umsatz- und Ergebnisentwicklung des Geschäftsbereichs Leder 1975–1985, in: Corporate Archives 3/03277. The leather division posted a loss of 1.5 million deutschmarks in 1977.
97 Cf. "Lederbetrieb stellt die Weichen für die Zukunft," in: CF-intern, 3/1979, p. 1–2 as well as Belegschaftsstatistik 1978, in: Corporate Archives 3/01011.
98 Cf. Protokoll der Sitzung der Unternehmensleitung vom 10. April 1981, in: Corporate Archives 3/05913.
99 Cf. Protokoll der Sitzung der Unternehmensleitung vom 28. Oktober 1980, in: Corporate Archives 3/03293 as well as Turnover and profit development of Teneria Temola 1972–1980, in: Corporate Archives 3/02440.
100 Cf. Vertrag über den Verkauf der Anteile an der Teneria Temola vom 30. November 1992, in: Corporate Archives 3/08608.
101 Cf. Unterlage zur Sitzung der Unternehmensleitung am 30. August 1983 zum Thema "Spezialisierung GB-Leder," in: Corporate Archives 3/04901 as well as Protokolle der Sitzungen der Unternehmensleitung vom 26. Mai 1983 und 30. August 1983, in: Corporate Archives 3/04606.
102 Cf. Umsatz- und Ergebnisentwicklung des Geschäftsbereichs Leder 1978–1988, in: Corporate Archives 3/03195. The losses in detail: 1978 – 6.2 million deutschmarks, 1979 – 4.6 million deutschmarks, 1980 – 8.8 million deutschmarks, 1981 – 1.8 million deutschmarks, 1982 – 5.2 million deutschmarks, 1983 – 6.3 million deutschmarks, 1984 – 1.7 million deutschmarks, 1985 – 3.1 million deutschmarks, 1986 – 4.6 million deutschmarks.
103 Cf. Rentabilitätsuntersuchung des Geschäftsbereichs Leder, in: Corporate Archives 3/03277.
104 Cf. Unterlagen zur Prüfung der Schließung des Geschäftsbereichs Leder, in: Corporate Archives 3/03277 as well as letter from the Management Board dating from 1986 which was not sent to the Limited Partners, in: Corporate Archives 3/02756.
105 Cf. Unterlagen zur Prüfung der Schließung des Geschäftsbereichs Leder, in: Corporate Archives 3/03277 as well as Gesellschafterbrief, 1986, in: Corporate Archives 3/06764.
106 Cf. Umsatz- und Ergebnisentwicklung des Geschäftsbereichs Leder 1978–1988, in: Corporate Archives 3/03195 as well as Gesellschafterbrief, 1. Halbjahr 1987, in: Corporate Archives 3/06764.
107 Profits of the leather division were approximately 1.4 million deutschmarks in 1987. Cf. Umsatz- und Ergebnisentwicklung des Geschäftsbereichs Leder 1987–1996, in: Corporate Archives 3/06395.
108 Cf. Lagebericht der Unternehmensleitung im Geschäftsbericht 1988, in: Corporate Archives 3/10996
109 Cf. Umsatz- und Ergebnisentwicklung des Geschäftsbereichs Leder 1987–1996, in: Corporate Archives 3/06395.
110 Cf. "Präsident Bush," in: Der Freudenberger, 6/1989, p. 8.
111 Cf. Geschäftsbericht, 1997, in: Corporate Archives 3/10983; Geschäftsbericht, 2000, in: Corporate Archives 3/07909; Protokoll der Sitzung der Unternehmensleitung am 12. November 2001, in: Corporate Archives 3/10514 as well as Schreiben der Unternehmensleitung an die Gesellschafter vom 1. Februar 2002, in: Corporate Archives 3/07809.
112 Cf. Schreiben der Unternehmensleitung an den Konzernbetriebsrat 4. Februar 2002, in: Corporate Archives 3/07809.

113 Cf. Schreiben der Unternehmensleitung an die Gesellschafter vom 1. Februar 2002, in: Corporate Archives 3/07809.
114 Cf. Vorwort der Unternehmensleitung im Geschäftsbericht 2002, in: Corporate Archives 3/07910.
115 Cf. Gesellschafterbrief von Peter Bettermann vom March 17, 2002, in: Corporate Archives 3/07809.
116 Cf. Documents on the biography of Dr. Dr. Peter Bettermann for the period 1994–1997, in: Corporate Archives 3/05385. Cf. also: "Dr. Peter Bettermann. Von BP in die Unternehmensleitung," in: Der Freudenberger, 3/1994, p. 1 as well as "Verabschiedung Dr. Peter Bettermann. Mit Leidenschaft und Wissensdurst," in: Freudenberg Magazin, 2/2012, p. 4–7.
117 Cf. Vita von Rudolf Fischer, in: Corporate Archives 3/11107.
118 Cf. Nutzungsvertrag zwischen der Weinheimer Leder GmbH und der Freudenberg & Co. Kommanditgesellschaft vom November 2002, in: Corporate Archives 3/07809.
119 Cf. Transcript of the interview with Reinhart Freudenberg on November 26, 2013, p. 5, in: Corporate Archives 3/11147.
120 Cf. Zusammenstellung der Gesuche, Genehmigungen, Verfügungen etc. hinsichtlich Wasser und Abwasser 1859–1920, Protokolle des Bezirksamts, Gemeinderat etc. Weinheim, in: Corporate Archives 3/01433. Germany's first wastewater treatment plant began operating in 1887 in Frankfurt/Main. Cf. Historie der Stadtentwässerung Frankfurt am Main, can be accessed online at: https://www.stadtentwaesserung-frankfurt.de/anlagen/historie/geschichte-der-alten-klaerbeckenanlage-vor-1900.html, accessed on September 27, 2023.
121 Schreiben der Unternehmensleitung (Hermann Freudenberg und Prof. Dr. Günther Kurtze) an den Ministerpräsidenten des Landes Baden-Württemberg, Lothar Späth, vom 15. Februar 1985, in: Corporate Archives 3/11015. Cf. also: Schreiben von Lieselotte Feikes an Hans Freudenberg vom 23. September 1953, in: Corporate Archives 3/11015.
122 In the C. F. process, the sulfides that are dissolved in the water are first precipitated as solids in order to be subsequently converted into non-critical sulphate by air introduction, which completes the decontamination process.
123 Cf. Documents on the Schönau wastewater treatment plant, in: Corporate Archives 3/04885 and Corporate Archives 3/04886.
124 Schreiben der Unternehmensleitung (Hermann Freudenberg und Prof. Dr. Günther Kurtze) an den Ministerpräsidenten des Landes Baden-Württemberg, Lothar Späth, vom 15. Februar 1985, in: Corporate Archives 3/11015.
125 Cf. Freudenberg Construction History, Section 4. Wastewater disposal, in: Corporate Archives 3/01194 as well as press releases on the opening of the chemical stage of the wastewater treatment plant in 1975, in: Corporate Archives 3/02699.
126 Cf. Informationen zur Inbetriebnahme der neuen Klärstufe zur Stickstoffelimination im Mai 1993, in: Corporate Archives 3/02914.
127 Cf. Klärwerk Carl Freudenberg Weinheim im Jahr 1976, in: Corporate Archives 3/00890.
128 Cf. Documents on the press invitation to the wastewater treatment plant in 1967, in: Corporate Archives 3/02869.
129 According to a statement in Freudenberg's employee newspaper, Freudenberg was the first company in the world to achieve perfect chemical-biological purification of tannery wastewater. Cf. "Japanische Wissenschaftler besuchen CF-Klärwerk," in: CF-intern, 10/1976, p. 5.
130 Cf. Schreiben der Unternehmensleitung (Hermann Freudenberg und Prof. Dr. Günther Kurtze) an den Ministerpräsidenten des Landes Baden-Württemberg, Lothar Späth, vom 15. Februar 1985, in: Corporate Archives 3/11015.
131 Cf. "Zentralbereich Technik," in: Der Freudenberger, 1/1973, p. 24.
132 Cf. Schreiben von Dr. Dietmar Flothmann an Herrn Floss vom 10. Januar 1992, in: Corporate Archives 3/11015.
133 Her successor in both positions was Dr. Dietmar Flothmann. Cf. "Personalnachrichten," in: Der Freudenberger, 3/1987, p. 7 as well as "Entsorgung wird schwieriger. 22. Sitzung des Umweltausschusses," in: Der Freudenberger, 10/1987, p. 2.
134 Cf. Rede von Hermann Freudenberg vor den Angestellten am 15. Juli 1972, in: Corporate Archives 3/01320.
135 Cf. Pressenotiz Helia vom 5. Oktober 1973, in: Corporate Archives 3/01320.
136 Cf. "Helia: Der Kunstleder-Markt bleibt schwierig," in: CF-intern, 5/1976, p. 1; "Helia-Werk: Wie-

der Großinvestition für den Umweltschutz," in: Der Freudenberger, 3/1973, p. 18 as well as "Weitere Anlage zur Nachverbrennung," in: Der Freudenberger, 2/1974, p. 24–25.
137 Cf. Geschäftsbericht Helia – Planung 1975–1979, in: Corporate Archives 3/01320.
138 Cf. "Helia-Material jetzt auch in der Bekleidungsindustrie," in: Freudenberger, 1/1970, p. 34–35.
139 Cf. Gesellschafterbrief, 1978, in: Corporate Archives 3/02275.
140 In 1979, there were still 663 employees working at Helia, this figure was adjusted to 285 employees by the end of 1985, while avoiding the use of social compensation plans. Cf. Rückschau zur Entwicklung des ehemaligen Unternehmensbereiches I im Zeitraum 1979–1989, in: Corporate Archives 3/05128.
141 Cf. Protokolle der Sitzungen der Unternehmensleitung am 2. Juli 1980, 10. September 1982, 1. Oktober 1982, 5. Dezember 1983 und 29. Mai 1984, in: Corporate Archives 3/03358.
142 Cf. Gesellschafterbriefe, 1979–1985, in: Corporate Archives 3/02275. According to these documents, Helia's turnover shrank to 89.6 million deutschmarks up to1985, and thus accounted for only approximately 2.7 % of group turnover at that time. Cf. Gesellschafterbrief, 1985, in: Corporate Archives 3/02275 as well as Freudenberg Corporate Archives, Employee and turnover statistics.
143 Cf. Gesellschafterbrief, 1. Halbjahr 2000, in: Corporate Archives 3/07208 as well as the notice: "Information über die Entscheidung zur Schließung HELIA" vom 3. April 2000, in: Corporate Archives 3/07370.
144 Cf. "Hornschuch mit Helia-Kunstleder" aus Lederwaren Report, 4/2001, in: Corporate Archives 3/07964.
145 Cf. "Freudenberg und die Leder- und Schuhwirtschaft, 2. Teil," in: Der Freudenberger 2/1970, p. 16–22 as well as Freudenberg Corporate Archives, Employee and turnover statistics.
146 At 72.8 million deutschmarks, turnover was approximately 51 percent higher than turnover in 1958. Cf. "Freudenberg und die Leder- und Schuhwirtschaft, 2. Teil," in: Der Freudenberger 2/1970, p. 16–22.
147 Cf. Freudenberg und die Leder- und Schuhwirtschaft, 2. Teil, in: Der Freudenberger 2/1970, p. 16–22.
148 Cf. "Und 1970 hängen wir unsere Werbung an die große Glocke", in: Der Freudenberger 2/1970, p. 22.
149 Cf. documents on the development of Elefanten-Schuh GmbH, in: Corporate Archives 3/01244.
150 Turnover was 297.1 mill. deutschmarks, which corresponded to a 9.2 percent share of group turnover (3.2 Mrd. deutschmarks). Cf. Freudenberg Corporate Archives, Employee and turnover statistics.
151 Cf. Geschäftsbericht 1987, in: Corporate Archives 3/01524; Geschäftsbericht 1988, in: Corporate Archives 3/10996 as well as Freudenberg Corporate Archives, Employee and turnover statistics.
152 Cf. Lagebericht der Unternehmensleitung im Geschäftsbericht 1989, in: Corporate Archives 3/02110.
153 Cf. Protokoll der Sitzung der Unternehmensleitung vom 25.10.1990, in: Corporate Archives 3/04628.
154 Cf. Geschäftsbericht 1992, in: Corporate Archives 3/10989.
155 Cf. Geschäftsbericht 1995, in: Corporate Archives 3/10991 as well as Geschäftsbericht 1996, in: Corporate Archives 3/10992.
156 Cf. Lagebericht der Unternehmensleitung im Geschäftsbericht 1997, in: Corporate Archives 3/10993.
157 Cf. Lagebericht der Unternehmensleitung im Geschäftsbericht 2000, in: Corporate Archives 3/07909.
158 Cf. Geschäftsbericht 1999, in: Corporate Archives 3/10985.
159 Cf. Geschäftsbericht 2000, in: Corporate Archives 3/07909.
160 The Jela organization and brand, which were spun off in 1971, were sold to the Austrian Kapsch AG's "Young Footwear" group. Production of Elefanten shoes in Kleve was closed down by Clarks at the end of 2004. However, Deichmann acquired and revived the "Elefanten" brand as early as 2005.
161 Cf. Siegle/Zepelin, 2008, p. 21.
162 Cf. Sinz, 2008, p. 88.
163 Cf. Sinz, 2008, p. 89. Sinz had studied electrical engineering, specializing in telecommunications. Cf. also: Interview with Karl Sinz in February 2003, in: Corporate Archives 3/11027.

164 Interview with Karl Sinz in February 2003, in: Corporate Archives 3/11027.
165 Cf. "Er programmierte noch mit bunten Lochkarten," in: Freudenberg Magazin, 3/2009, p. 29.
166 Cf. Siegle/Zepelin, 2008, p. 21.
167 Cf. Sinz, 2008, p. 89.
168 Cf. Siegle/Zepelin, 2008, p. 21–23 as well as Sinz, 2008, p. 89–90.
169 Sinz, 2008, p. 90. The name SAP is an abbreviation of "**S**ystem**a**nalyse **P**rogrammentwicklung". – ed.
170 Ibid.
171 Siegle/Zepelin, p. 22–23.
172 Cf. ibid, p. 23.
173 Ibid, p. 24
174 Cf. Sinz, 2008, p. 91.
175 Ibid.
176 Cf. "Informationen zum Einsatz des IBM Systems /370, Modell 165 im Hause Carl Freudenberg, Weinheim," Mannheim, Oktober 1971, in: Corporate Archives 3/08805.
177 Cf. Sinz, 2008, p. 94.
178 Ibid, p. 100–101.
179 Cf. Sinz, 2008, p. 95, p. 100 and p. 199 f.; Interview with Karl Sinz in February 2003, in: Corporate Archives 3/11027; "Personalnachrichten," in: CF-intern, 1/1978, p. 12 as well as "Karl Sinz geht in Ruhestand," in: Freudenberg Magazin, 1/2003, p. 40.
180 Cf. Vorlage für die Sitzung der Unternehmensleitung am 26. Januar 1993 zum Thema SAP-Standardsoftware bei Freudenberg vom 22. Januar 1993, in: Corporate Archives 3/08719.
181 Cf. Sinz, 2008, p. 105 f. and p. 119.
182 Ibid, p. 120.
183 Ibid, p. 120 as well as p. 139 ff.
184 Ibid, p. 1020 and p. 175.
185 Cf. Umsatz- und Personalentwicklung Simrit, in: Corporate Archives 3/04403.
186 Cf. "Simrit S. A. Mâcon," in: CF-intern, 6/1976, p. 3.
187 Cf. Bonfert, 1999, p. 51.
188 Ibid, p. 52–56.
189 Ibid, p. 57 as well as p. 148aI.
190 Cf. Edelmann, 1966, p. 5–8 as well as "Im Ruhestand: Fritz Edelmann," in: CF-Intern, 3/1978, p. 9. In the run-up to the establishment of the plant on the site of the former railway station in Reichelsheim, there was a discussion within the company about whether to leave production in Weinheim or to shift it to another location. Then, when the site of the former railway station in Reichelsheim was offered at a reasonable price, the Management Board in Reichelsheim decided to build a new plant for PTFE and membrane production and thereby solve the lack of space in the "Teflon Department" for the long term.
191 Cf. Bonfert, 1999, p. 60–63, p. 80 and p. 148aI.
192 Ibid, p. 61.
193 Cf. Transcript of the interview with Wilhelm Schmitt on March 11, 2014, p. 5, in: Corporate Archives 3/11150.
194 Wentzler, 1972, p. 11.
195 Cf. Firmen-Chronologie Unternehmensbereich II, IPC Limited Partnership, in: Corporate Archives 3/00843.
196 David S. Williams was also a family member of the owners. His father had transferred approximately 65 % of the shares which he owned to a foundation, which administered these shares in trust for the family. Cf. International Packings Corporation History vom 29. September 1966, in: Corporate Archives 3/04414.
197 Cf. Visit reports and correspondence on IPC, in: Corporate Archives 3/04414.
198 Cf. Vorlage zu den NOK-Beziehungen für die Unternehmensleitungssitzung vom 25. Juli 1986, in: Corporate Archives 3/06226 sowie Bonfert, 1999, p. 65 f., p. 449 and p. 510–512.
199 Cf. Bonfert, 1999.
200 Cf. Fehrle, 1970, p. 12–14.
201 Cf."Megulastik" compilation in: Corporate Archives 3/01281 as well as "Blickpunkt Werk Neuenburg. Blick ins Werk," in: Der Freudenberger, 1/1974, p. 21.
202 Cf. Zusammenstellung "Gummi-Metall-Werk" vom 1. Juli 1975, in: Corporate Archives 3/01281.

203 The change of name to Freudenberg-Megulastik took place in 1976.
204 Cf. Bonfert, 1999, p. 238.
205 The sealing business at Simrit was particularly hard hit by the oil price crisis because of its heavy dependence on the automotive industry and the sales crisis in that industry. Cf. "Aus dem Jahresbericht 1974," in: Der Freudenberger, 4/1974, p. 6–7 as well as "Auftragsrückgang zwingt zu Entlassungen," in: Der Freudenberger, 4/1974, p. 5.
206 Cf. "Going West," in: Freudenberger Magazin, 1/2000, p. 26–30, here p. 27; Illius, 2004, p. 14 as well as Cuautla Site Profile, in: Freudenberg Portal, accessed on February 10, 2017.
207 Cf. "Simrit S. A. Mâcon," in: CF-intern, 6/1976, p. 3 as well as Gesellschafterbrief, 1976, in: Corporate Archives 3/02275.
208 Cf. takeover documents, in: 3/06848.
209 Cf. Parets del Vallés site profile, in: Freudenberg Portal, accessed on February 16, 2017.
210 Cf. 10 Jahre Qualitätsverbesserungs-Programm "Q76," in: Corporate Archives 3/06127.
211 Cf. Bonfert, 1999, p. 55.
212 Cf. Gesellschafterbrief, 1977, in: Corporate Archives 3/02275.
213 Cf. documents on Simflex GmbH & Co. KG, in: Corporate Archives 3/06921.
214 Cf. "Freudenberg übergibt Mektec-Anteile," in: Freudenberg Magazin, 2/2010, p. 5.
215 Cf. Joint Venture Agreement zur Gründung der NOK-Megulastik Co. Ltd. vom 5. Oktober 1978, in: Corporate Archives 3/06923.
216 Cf. Gesellschafterbrief, 1982, in: Corporate Archives 3/02275.
217 Cf. Simmerring® Radial-Wellendichtring mit PTFE-Dichtlippe, in: Corporate Archives 3/02424 as well as "Es läuft rund – seit 85 Jahren. Von Lederresten bis 'Levitex'," in: Freudenberg Magazin 4/2017, p. 58–59, here p. 58.
218 Cf. "Größte Investition in der Simrit-Geschichte. Der Simrit-3-Jahresplan," in: Freudenberg intern, 5a/1985, p. 1.
219 Ibid.
220 Cf. Documents on the preparation for IZ production, in: Corporate Archives 3/06226.
221 Cf. Kanban, in: Ionos Digital Guide, can be accessed online at: https://www.ionos.de/digitalguide/websites/web-entwicklung/kanban/, accessed on February 1, 2022.
222 Cf. Transcript of interview with Reinhart Freudenberg on November 26, 2013, p. 7, in: Corporate Archives 3/11147.
223 Cf. Gesellschafterbrief, 1988, in: Corporate Archives 3/02546.
224 Cf. ibid.
225 Cf. Horchler, 2014, p. 50.
226 Cf. Identity Proposal Freudenberg North America Inc. of August 1987, in: Corporate Archives 3/02222; Memorandum "Future company and product nomination in the North American technical companies" dated October 5, 1987, in: Corporate Archives 3/03843 as well as Bonfert, 1999, p. 508.
227 Cf. Vorlage zu den NOK-Beziehungen für die Unternehmensleitungssitzung vom 25. Juli 1986, in: Corporate Archives 3/06226; Gesellschafterbrief, 1988, in: Corporate Archives 3/02546; correspondence and minutes of Freudenberg-NOK meetings, in: Corporate Archives 3/06823; documents on NOK Inc., in: Corporate Archives 3/05664 as well as Bonfert, 1999, p. 510–513.
228 Cf. Joint Venture Agreement vom 23. März 1989, in: Corporate Archives 3/10966; General Partnership Agreement vom 1. Juli 1989, in: Corporate Archives 3/10966 as well as "Gemeinschaftsfirma unter Dach und Fach," in: Der Freudenberger, 6/1989, S. 1.
229 Cf. General Partnership Agreement vom 1. Juli 1989, in: Corporate Archives 3/10966; Notiz der F&Co.-Beteiligungsverwaltung zur Joint-Venture-Gründung vom 30. März 1989, in: Corporate Archives 3/06824 as well as Gegenüberstellung der Vermögenswerte von IPC und NOK Inc. durch die Firma Ernst & Whinney vom 23. März 1989, in: Corporate Archives 3/06824. The combined turnover of all merged companies amounted to 247.7 mill. US dollars in 1988. The Freudenberg companies accounted for 207.6 mill. US dollars (IPC: 140.8; Escan: 37; Disogrin: 23; Simrit Corp.: 3.6; Simrit de Mexico: 3.2) and NOK Inc. 67.1 mill. US dollars. Cf. Bonfert, 1999, p. 512.
230 Cf. "Neue Bundesländer. Übernahme von drei Werken," in: Der Freudenberger, 7/8 1991, p. 1 as well as Vertrag zum Erwerb der Polymant Kautschuk- und Kunststoffverarbeitung GmbH von 1991, in: Corporate Archives 3/06832. From then on, the plants traded under the names Freudenberg Dichtungs- und Schwingungstechnik GmbH, Freudenberg Schwingungstechnik Industrie GmbH & Co. KG and Freudenberg Formenbau und Kunststofftechnik GmbH. The Triptis plant in

Thüringen had already been sold to former senior executives in 1994, who continued operating it as an independent plant. Thus products for the Seals and Molded Parts division (rubber molded parts) were predominantly manufactured in the Berlin plant, vibration control technology products in Velten, north of Berlin, and forming tools in Triptis. Cf. also Pressemitteilung "Mitarbeiter übernahmen Freudenberg-Tochterunternehmen in Thüringen" vom 7. Juli 1994, in: Corporate Archives 3/05396.
231 Cf. Gesellschafterbrief, 1991, in: Corporate Archives 3/05393.
232 In addition, he took over responsibility for the flexible printed circuit boards from Wilhelm Schmitt in 1994 and for technical distributors from Hans-Jochen Hüchting in 1998. On December 31, 2005 Peter Stehle retired from the company. Cf. Vita Peter Stehle, in: Corporate Archives 3/11038.
233 Cf. Gesellschafterbrief, 1992, in: Corporate Archives 3/05393.
234 Cf. Bonfert, 1999, p. 258.
235 Gesellschafterbrief, 1992, in: Corporate Archives 3/05393.
236 Cf. "Freudenberg als Automobilzulieferer weltweit," Kurzbericht für die erste Sitzung des Gesellschafter-Informationskreises am 15. Oktober 1993, in: Corporate Archives 3/04907.
237 "'Würger' und 'Krieger' – die rauen Sitten der VW-Kostensenker," in: Manager Magazin, can be accessed online at: https://www.manager-magazin.de/fotostrecke/kostendruecker-wie-vws-ein kaufschefs-bei-zulieferern-sparen-fotostrecke-140420.html, accessed on March 1, 2022.
238 Cf. ibid. as well as "22. Mai 1993 – Beginn der Lopez-Affäre bei VW," in: WDR, can be accessed online at: https://www1.wdr.de/stichtag/stichtag-beginn-lopez-affaere-100.html, accessed on January 29, 2022.
239 Protokoll der Unternehmensleitungssitzung vom 28. Mai 1993, in: Corporate Archives 3/10834.
240 Cf. Protokoll der Unternehmensleitungssitzung vom 28. Mai 1993, in: Corporate Archives 3/10834.
241 Cf. Transcript of interview with Jörg Sost in November 2019, in: Corporate Archives 3/11148.
242 Cf. Gesellschafterbrief, 1994, in: Corporate Archives 3/05393.
243 Cf. Protokoll der UL-Sitzung vom 28. Mai 1993, in: Corporate Archives 3/10834 as well as "Freudenberg als Automobilzulieferer weltweit," Kurzbericht für die erste Sitzung des Gesellschafter-Informationskreises am 15. Oktober 1993, in: Corporate Archives 3/04907.
244 Cf. Gesellschafterbrief, 1995, in: Corporate Archives 3/05393.
245 Cf. Gesellschafterbrief, 1993, in: Corporate Archives 3/03307.
246 Cf. Transcript of interview with Reinhart Freudenberg on November 26, 2013, p. 5, in: Corporate Archives 3/11147.
247 Cf. Gesellschafterbrief, 1992, in: Corporate Archives 3/05393.
248 Cf. Franz, 2008.
249 Cf. Vertretungsvertrag, in: Corporate Archives 3/06498. Specifically, the exclusive agency agreement comprised the Helia, Nora, Robus, Frelen, Viledon and leather divisions.
250 Cf. correspondence to this effect by post and telex, in: Corporate Archives 3/06498.
251 Cf. Reisebericht China 11. bis 23. September 1979 vom 11. Oktober 1979, in: Corporate Archives 3/06498 as well as Treffen mit NOK hinsichtlich Projektes in "Rotchina," in: Corporate Archives 3/06499. The participants in the first trip to China in 1979 were Freudenberg employees Dr. Wilhelm Schmitt, Dr. Werner Wolz and Otto Hohenadel.
252 Cf. Bericht über Austausch mit der NOK in Tokio 20.-27. Oktober 1979 vom 30. November 1979, in: Corporate Archives 3/06499.
253 Cf. Correspondence with the First Ministry of Machine Building of the People's Republic of China in January and February 1980, in: Corporate Archives 3/06498.
254 Cf. Memorandum on Dieter Freudenberg's meeting with the First Ministry of Machine Building of the People's Republic of China in Peking on October 3, 1980 dated October 27, 1980, in: Corporate Archives 3/06498.
255 Schreiben der Simrit Spartenleitung an das Erste Maschinenbauministerium der Volksrepublik China vom 1. Dezember 1980, in: Corporate Archives 3/06498.
256 Cf. Schreiben von Masato Tsuru an Siegfried Hinz vom 26. April 1982, in: Corporate Archives 3/06498.
257 Cf. Correspondence between the Simrit division management and the First Ministry of Machine Building of the People's Republic of China between December 1980 and February 1981, in: Corporate Archives 3/06498.

258 Cf. Basic Agreement zwischen Carl Freudenberg und NOK hinsichtlich China Project vom 7. März 1980, in: Corporate Archives 3/05411 and Corporate Archives 3/06499.
259 Contrary to the procedure stipulated in Tokyo in October 1979, NOK had begun operating independently in China. In order to resolve the disputes, personal mediation by Shogo Tsuru was required. Cf. minutes of meetings between NOK and Freudenberg as well as correspondence to this effect from the time from February to March 1980, in: Corporate Archives 3/06499.
260 Cf. Schreiben von Dieter Freudenberg an Siegfried Hinz vom 26. Mai 1982, in: Corporate Archives 3/06498.
261 Cf. "Abschied von Norbert Dahlström," in: Freudenberg Magazin, 3/2014, p. 44 as well as "Neu in der Geschäftsleitung: Norbert Dahlström," in: CF-intern, 8/1978, p. 8.
262 Cf. Eindrücke einer Chinareise im Juni 1985, in: Corporate Archives 3/03224; Kostenkalkulation für die Fabrik in Nantong, in: Corporate Archives 3/02198 as well as Notiz zum Gespräch von Dieter Freudenberg mit dem Ersten Maschinenbauministerium der Volksrepublik China in Peking am 3. Oktober 1980 vom 27. Oktober 1980, in: Corporate Archives 3/06498.
263 Cf. "China-Projekt Nantong Factory" feasibility study vom 29. August 1985, in: Corporate Archives 3/02198 as well as on the necessity of the feasibility study: Bericht von Dieter Freudenberg zum EMF-China Meeting am 8. Juni 1984 in Genf vom 14. Juni 1984, in: Corporate Archives 3/02211.
264 Cf. Schreiben von Matthias Risler an Dieter und Hermann Freudenberg vom 8. November 1985, in: Corporate Archives 3/04731 as well as Notiz an Hermann Freudenberg vom 6. Juli 1987 über Vlieseline Aktivitäten in der Jiangsu Provinz, in: Corporate Archives 3/04731.
265 Schreiben von Norbert Dahlström zu den Eindrücken seiner Chinareise im Juni 1985 an seine Unternehmensleitungskollegen vom 27. Juni 1985, in: Corporate Archives 3/03224.
266 Cf. Bericht über die deutsch-chinesische Kooperationsveranstaltung des Ostausschusses der deutschen Wirtschaft am 11. März 1986 an der IHK Frankfurt, in: Corporate Archives 3/06498.
267 Cf. documents, in: Corporate Archives 3/06499.
268 After the violent "suppression of the liberalization policy" during what became known as the Tian'anmen Square massacre at the Gate of Heavenly Peace in Peking in June 1989, political sanctions against China and a recession in the Chinese economy followed. Then, in the 1990s under Deng Xiaoping, the "fundamental conditions for a market economy" were created, which dramatically increased the attractiveness of the Chinese market. Cf. Gesprächsnotiz Dieter Freudenbergs mit Wirtschaftsvertretern der deutschen Botschaft in China vom 29. Juni 1990, in: Corporate Archives 3/02781 as well as Spakowski, 2022.
269 Cf. Protokoll der Sitzung der Unternehmensleitung vom 9. November 1992, in: Corporate Archives 3/04635 as well as "Überlegungen zum chinesischen Markt," Vorlage für die Sitzung der Unternehmensleitung am 9. November 1992, in: Corporate Archives 3/04635.
270 Protokoll der Sitzung der Unternehmensleitung vom 9. November 1992, in: Corporate Archives 3/04635.
271 Cf. ibid. as well as Press information on the shareholding in Elring and takeover of Procal dated January 13, 1993, in: Corporate Archives 3/05394. However, the acquisition of Procal could only be achieved in tandem with a minority 20 percent shareholding in er Elring GmbH (from 1994: Elring Klinger). The shareholding in Elring Klinger, which was ultimately 37 percent, was sold to ZWL Grundbesitz- und Beteiligungs-AG Ludwigshafen in 1998.
272 Cf. Press information on the shareholding in Elring and takeover of Procal dated January 13, 1993, in: Corporate Archives 3/05394.
273 Cf. Protokoll der Sitzung der Unternehmensleitung am 25 Mai 1993, in: Corporate Archives 3/10834. The date of foundation of the joint venture in Changchun is October 25, 1992. Cf. Changchun NOK-Freudenberg Oilseal Co., Ltd., in: Freudenberg Corporate Database, accessed on August 24, 2022.
274 The shares were held by the newly established NOK-Freudenberg Asia Holding in Singapore from 1995 onward. Cf. Changchun NOK-Freudenberg Oilseal Co., Ltd., in: Freudenberg Corporate Database, accessed on August 24, 2022.
275 Cf. Notiz zum Gespräch beim UL-Mittagessen am 9. September 1994, in: Corporate Archives 3/10924. Wuxi NOK-Freudenberg Oilseal Co. Ltd. was officially founded on June 28, 1995. Cf. Wuxi NOK-Freudenberg Oilseal Co., Ltd., in: Freudenberg Corporate Database, accessed on August 11, 2022.

276 Cf. Wuxi NOK-Freudenberg Oilseal Co., Ltd. company brochure dated 1996, in: Corporate Archives 3/05359.
277 Cf. Vorlage zur Gesellschafterausschuss-Sitzung am 31. August 1994, in: Corporate Archives 3/03878; Pressemitteilung zur Gründung der Freudenberg & Vilene Nonwovens in China vom 20. April 1995, in: Corporate Archives 3/05398; Gesellschafterbriefe, 1995 und 1996, in: Corporate Archives 3/05393 as well as Fath, 1996, p. 1 and p. 6. The date of foundation of Freudenberg & Vilene Nonwovens (Suzhou) Co. Ltd. is February 28, 1995. Cf. Freudenberg & Vilene Nonwovens (Suzhou) Co. Ltd., in: Freudenberg Corporate Database, accessed on August 11, 2022.
278 Cf. Press release on activities in China and India dated February 15, 1995, in: Corporate Archives 3/05398 as well as "Freudenberg und NOK: Holding in China," in: Der Freudenberger, 3/1995, p. 1.
279 Cf. "Professor Dr. Kurt Kraft: Vliesstoffbereich zur Weltgeltung geführt," in: Der Freudenberger, 5/1972, p. 18–20, here p. 20.
280 Cf. Schnaus, 2017, p. 9–33.
281 Donath/Szegfü, 2021, p. 23.
282 Cf. Schnaus, 2017, p. 17–18.
283 Ibid, p. 21
284 Cf. ibid, p. 22 as well as Donath/Szegfü, 2021, p. 23.
285 Cf. Lauppe, 1968, p. 10.
286 In the sources, the spelling "Géza Tolnay" is also used.
287 Cf. Contract between Nontex S. A., the shareholders of Nontex S. A., and Freudenberg dated September 21, 1962, in: Corporate Archives 3/07109 as well as Lauppe, 1968, p. 10.
288 Cf. "Freudenberg Vliesstoffgesellschaften im Ausland ändern Namen," in: Der Freudenberger, 1/1987, p. 1.
289 Cf. Protokoll zur Sitzung der Unternehmensleitung am 29. Juni 1993 zum Erwerb der Minderheitsanteile, in: Corporate Archives 3/04637 as well as documents on the preparation of the acquisition of the Nontex shares dating from 1991, in: Corporate Archives 3/10779.
290 Cf. on the development of the sector: Schnaus 2017, p. 22.
291 Documents on the establishment of Vilene Argentina, in: Corporate Archives 3/01596 as well as Röhrs1998, p. 4.
292 Cf. Kraft, 1963, p. 2 f.
293 Cf. Docke, 1973, p. 18.
294 Cf. Kraft, 1963, p. 2 f.
295 Cf. Gärtner, 1968, p. 3 as well as Huber, 1966, p. 4.
296 Cf. Lauppe, 1978, S 18; Viledon-Jahresbericht 1957, in: Corporate Archives 3/09082 as well as Aufträge Separatoren Viledon I, in: Corporate Archives 3/09075.
297 Cf. Hett, 1967, p. 4–5.
298 Cf. Horchler, 2006, p. 31.
299 Cf. Anlage 1 von Juli 1969 zum Generalvertrag zwischen den Firmen Freudenberg & Co. und Carl Freudenberg sowie der BASF vom 2. Januar 1970 bzw. 27. Januar 1970, in: Corporate Archives 3/06611.
300 Cf. ibid.
301 Generalvertrag zwischen den Firmen Freudenberg & Co. und Carl Freudenberg sowie der BASF vom 2. Januar 1970 bzw. 27. Januar 1970, in: Corporate Archives 3/06611.
302 Cf. ibid. as well as Appendices 2a and 2b of the General Agreement: Gesellschaftsverträge der Lutravil Spinnvlies GmbH & Co. (bzgl. Änderung der Rechtsform (Gesellschaftsvertrag 2a vom 3. Februar 1970, Gesellschaftsvertrag 2b o. D.), in: Corporate Archives 3/06611.
303 Cf. Horchler, 2006, p. 31.
304 Cf. "Vlieseline: Neues Technikum für die Konfektionsindustrie," in: Der Freudenberger, 5/1970, p. 29.
305 Cf. Lehmann, 1963, p. 5–7.
306 Cf. ibid. as well as "Du und Dein Werkstück," in: Der Freudenberger, 5/1959, p. 5–9.
307 Cf. "VLIESELINE-Fachlehrschau unterwegs," in: Der Freudenberger, 2/1965, p. 28.
308 Cf. Programm- und Anwendungshefte, in: Corporate Archives 3/10224.
309 Cf. Kraft, 1970, p. 5.
310 Cf. Kraft, 1970a, p. 18 as well as 60 Years of Japan Vilene, p. 15 and p. 30–33, in: Corporate Archives 3/11022.
311 Cf. "Personalnachrichten," in: Der Freudenberger, 4/1972, p. 34; Schreiben von Reinhart Freuden-

berg an Herrn Bischoff (Werksarchiv) über seinen Lebenslauf vom 29. Oktober 1975, in: Corporate Archives 1/00304; correspondence on the operation of Teneria Temola in Mexico City for the time span from 1961 to 1969, in: Corporate Archives 3/08128 as well as Gesellschafterbrief, 1972, in: Corporate Archives 3/02275.
312 Cf. Gesellschafterbriefe, 1972 und 1974, in: Corporate Archives 3/02275.
313 Cf. Donath/Szegfü, 2021, p. 30 as well as Gesellschafterbriefe, 1974 und 1975, in: Corporate Archives 3/02275.
314 "Bericht der Geschäftsleitung über das erste Halbjahr 1977," in: CF-intern, 6/1977, p. 5.
315 Cf. "Neue Generation von Vlieseline®-Einlagen," in: CF-intern, 8/1975, p. 2; "Vlieseline Formsystem 8000," in: CF-intern, 4/1976, p. 2 as well as "Vlieseline im Dienst der Mode," in: CF-intern, 3/1979, p. 3.
316 Cf. "In Monaco: VLIESELINE auf der 'Intersew'," in: CF-intern, 10/1979, p. 3.
317 Cf. Schuster, 2002, p. 13; "Freudenberg investiert in Korea," in: der Freudenberger, 1/2/1999, p. 6; Fath, 1999, p. 4 as well as 60 Years of Japan Vilene, p. 34–37, in: Corporate Archives 3/11022.
318 Cf. Schnaus, 2017, p. 22.
319 "Mit der Rikscha zu den Kunden in Fernost," in: Der Freudenberger, 10/1989, p. 6.
320 Cf. ibid.; "Vertriebsgesellschaft in Hongkong," in: CF-intern, 10/1977, p. 2 as well as 60 Years of Japan Vilene, p. 33–34, in: Corporate Archives 3/11022.
321 Cf. "Vliesstoff-Gesellschaft in Brasilien," in: Freudenberg intern, 5/1985, p. 2.
322 Cf. "Spinnvliesgesellschaft in USA gegründet," in: CF-intern, 8/1981, p. 2; "The Lutravil Company: Freudenberg wird Alleineigentümer," in: Der Freudenberger, 9/1987, p. 2 as well as Horchler, 2006, p. 31.
323 Cf. Geschäftsbericht, 1984, in: Corporate Archives 3/00834.
324 Pressemitteilung "Modernstes Spinnvliesstoffwerk Asiens startet Produktion" vom 22. Oktober 1990, in: Corporate Archives 3/04264.
325 Cf. "Spinnvliesstoffe aus Taiwan," in: Der Freudenberger, 7/1987, p. 1; "Die erste Fabrik steht," in: Der Freudenberger, 10/1987, p. 3, "Gemeinsam zum Erfolg," in: Der Freudenberger, 11/1990, p. 4–5; Pressemitteilung "Vliesstoffe von Freudenberg" vom Mai 1991, in: Corporate Archives 3/04264; Pressemitteilung "Modernstes Spinnvliesstoffwerk Asiens startet Produktion" vom 22. Oktober 1990, in: Corporate Archives 3/04264 as well as 60 Years of Japan Vilene, p. 36, in: Corporate Archives 3/11022.
326 "Freudenberg konsolidiert und wächst," in: Freudenberger, 2/2000, p. 8–11, here p. 9.
327 Cf. "Wundkompresse für klinische Anwendung," in: CF-intern, 6/1983, p. 3.
328 Cf. documents on Vilmed, in: Corporate Archives 3/05087, Corporate Archives 3/05477 and Corporate Archives 10/000764-0.
329 Previously, Freudenberg had delivered simple filter mats which the automotive manufacturers fitted individually.
330 Cf. "Technik für das Auto von morgen," in: Der Freudenberger, 8/1989, p. 6.
331 Cf. "Hier dreht sich alles um reine Luft," in: Der Freudenberger, 3/1993, p. 4.
332 Cf. "Mitarbeiter tauften Autozuluftfilter 'MicronAir'. Gewinner gehen in die Luft," in: Der Freudenberger, 5/1990, p. 6.
333 After the MicronAir was initially only fitted in the standard configuration of the Mercedes SL Class and a few BMW models, the Opel Astra was the first mid-range car to have the MicronAir fitted as standard. The VW Golf III followed shortly afterwards. Cf. "Für frische Luft beim Autofahren," in: Der Freudenberger, 11/1993, p. 4.
334 Cf. "Für frische Luft beim Autofahren," in: Der Freudenberger, 11/1993, p. 4.
335 Cf. Illius, 1997, p. 4.
336 Cf. "Neues Faservliesstoff-Technikum nahm seinen Betrieb auf: Mit großer Investition einen großen Schritt in die Zukunft," in: Der Freudenberger, 7/1988, p. 1–2.
337 Cf. Gesellschafterbrief, 1988, in: Corporate Archives 3/02546.
338 Cf. Gesellschafterbriefe, 1977 und 1981, in: Corporate Archives 3/02275.
339 Reinhart Freudenberg then assumed the following tasks until he stepped down from the Management Board in 1997: limited partner affairs, finance, legal and taxes, central business administration and human resources. Cf. Vita von Reinhart Freudenberg, in: Corporate Archives 3/11040.
340 Cf. Vita von Reinhart Freudenberg, in: Corporate Archives 3/11040.
341 "Abschied von Norbert Dahlström," in: Freudenberg Magazin, 3/2014, p. 44. Cf. also "Neu in der Geschäftsleitung: Norbert Dahlström," in: CF-intern, 8/1978, p. 8.

342 "Hermann Freudenberg auf der traditionellen Jubilarfeier. 'Carl Freudenberg wieder auf gesundem Fundament'," in: Freudenberg intern, 2/1984, p. 2–3, here p. 2.
343 Cf. Geschäftsbericht, 1984, in: Corporate Archives 3/00834 as well as Gesellschafterbrief, 1984, in: Corporate Archives 3/02275.
344 Cf. Geschäftsbericht, 1989, in: Corporate Archives 3/02110.
345 Cf. Geschäftsbericht, 1995, in: Corporate Archives 3/10991.
346 Cf. "Viledon-Vertrieb vereint stärker," in: CF-intern, 9/1981, p. 5.
347 The first Indian business partner is Hasonally Fezhyder in Bombay (now known as Mumbai). Cf. Hauptbuch 1867–1874, p. 644, in: Corporate Archives 3/06207–1867–74.
348 Raw materials, particularly hides, came from Amritsar via Rotterdam to Weinheim with the help of Mohamed Hussein Allahibusc from 1924 onward. From 1926, trade relations with India were conducted primarily through German trading companies. From 1927 particularly through Jewish trading offices in Stuttgart (Gebrüder Levi Import; Elias Moos). The reason for this was probably the poor quality of the hides up to that time Grund. Now procurement was also coming from other parts of India, for example "Farther India" (Burma). Cf. Kalkulationen Afrika und Asien, J, 2, Skontro, p. 860 and p. 1010 f., in: Corporate Archives 3/03965.
349 After the establishment of the Federal Republic of Germany in May, Freudenberg resumed hide imports from India again in October. Cf. Kalkulationen Polen, Rußland, Asien, Afrika 1941, in: Corporate Archives 3/03964.
350 Die Alleinvertretung für Simrit-Produkte in India wird an B. Chowdhury in Bombay übertragen. Cf. Simrit Auslandvertretungen, in: Corporate Archives 3/06158 as well as Vertrag mit Chowdhury, in: Corporate Archives 3/06904.
351 Cf. correspondence between Dieter Freudenberg and Niranjan Ajwani, in: Corporate Archives 3/02764. When talks began between Dieter Freudenberg and Niranjan Ajwani, the personal acquaintance between the two men, which originated many years beforehand, was also revived. Cf. also the earlier correspondence between Dieter Freudenberg and Niranjan Ajwani from the 1970s, in: Corporate Archives 3/02764.
352 Cf. correspondence between Dieter Freudenberg and Niranjan Ajwani, in: Corporate Archives 3/02764.
353 Cf. Schreiben von Dieter Freudenberg an Niranjan Ajwani vom 17. August 1982, in: Corporate Archives 3/02764
354 Cf. Vertrag zwischen Carl Freudenberg und Interconti Projects (IPPL) vom 7. Juni 1983, in: Corporate Archives 3/02764. IPPL was founded in 1973 by brothers Niranjan and Chander Ajwani. Freudenberg still has partnerships in India with the Ajwani family today. IPPL was solely responsible for the sale of nonwovens. Cf. Bericht von Dieter Freudenberg für die Unternehmensleitung zur Marktsituation in Indien vom 22. November 1985, in: Corporate Archives 3/02780.
355 Cf. Marktuntersuchung Indien der Herren Kohl und Yamaguchi vom 21. Februar bis 5. März 1983, in: Corporate Archives 3/05471.
356 Dieter Freudenberg traveled to India for the first time in March 1982. In various exchanges of correspondence, he refers to an International Council of Tanners (ICT) Meeting he attended in Madras as well as a sojourn in Neu-Delhi. Subsequently, he initiated research into the potential of some of the markets that would be relevant to Freudenberg in India. For example for leather production. Cf. correspondence with Dharmsee Parpia dated May 5, 1982, with Helmut Haarhaus from Elefanten-Schuh GmbH with April 1, 1982 as well as with the Indo-German Chamber of Commerce in Madras in February/March 1982, in: Corporate Archives 3/02765.
357 Cf. Protokoll der Sitzung der Unternehmensleitung vom 25. Juni 1985 as well as Bericht über die Indien-Reise im April, Dieter Freudenberg an die Geschäftsleitung, vom 9. Mai 1985, in: Corporate Archives 3/04610; Berichte über die Indienreise, Berichte der IPPL as well as Reiseunterlagen, in: Corporate Archives 3/02780 as well as NOK-Strategie, in: Corporate Archives 3/04895.
358 Cf. Bericht über die Indien-Reise im April 1985, Dieter Freudenberg an die Geschäftsleitung, vom 9. Mai 1985, in: Corporate Archives 3/02780.
359 Ibid.
360 Cf. ibid.
361 Bericht über die Indien-Reise im April 1985, Wirtschaftspolitische Rahmenbedingungen für Auslandsinvestitionen, vom 9. Mai 1985, in: Corporate Archives 3/02780.
362 Cf. Bericht von Dieter Freudenberg für die Unternehmensleitung zur Marktsituation in Indien vom 22. November 1985, in: Corporate Archives 3/02780.

363 Cf. Brief von Niranjam Ajwani von Interconti Projects vom 10. April 1996, in: Corporate Archives 3/07524.
364 Schreiben von Dieter Freudenberg an Nobert Dahlström und Willi Hasselbrink vom 3. Mai 1989, in: Corporate Archives 3/02765.
365 UL-Vorlage im Umlaufverfahren hinsichtlich Klüber Gründung in Indien vom 1. Dezember 1997, in: Corporate Archives 3/08852.
366 Cf. ibid.; Bericht von Dieter Freudenberg zur Indienreise im November 1985 vom 18. November 1985, in: Corporate Archives 3/02780 as well as Matter, 1999.
367 Cf. Reisebericht vom 25. September 1992, in: Corporate Archives 3/07729.
368 Protokoll der Sitzung der Unternehmensleitung vom 24. Mai 1994, in: Corporate Archives 3/07643, Corporate Archives 3/10869 and Corporate Archives 3/10895.
369 Cf. Press release on activities in China and India dated February 15, 1995, in: Corporate Archives 3/05398 as well as "Freudenberg und NOK: Holding in China," in: Der Freudenberger, 3/1995, p. 1.
370 Cf. Unterlagen zur Unternehmensleitungssitzung am 2. Juni 1995, in: Corporate Archives 3/04646 as well as documents on the negotiations with Fenner, in: Corporate Archives 3/07524.
371 Cf. documents, in: Corporate Archives 3/07524; Auszug aus dem Protokoll der UL-Sitzung am 19. November 1997, in: Corporate Archives 3/07624 as well as description of the majority shareholding problem, in: Corporate Archives 3/07524. In September 1997, the Management Board assumed that the joint venture with TVS would happen, since it approved "the establishment of a joint venture with NOK and TVS Group in India for the production of radial shaft sealing rings and similar products as well as the sale of NOK and Freudenberg products (and those of the joint venture) with a total investment of 13,1 mill. deutschmarks up to 2002 and capitalization of 4 mill. deutschmarks" under certain conditions in the meeting on September 19, 1997. Cf. Protokoll der Sitzung der Unternehmensleitung vom 19. September 1997, in: Corporate Archives 3/07646 and Corporate Archives 3/11025–11.
372 Cf. Fath, 1998a, p. 4 as well as Freudenberg Performance Materials India Pvt. Ltd., in: Freudenberg Corporate Database, accessed on May 6, 2022. The company was established on March 30, 1998 – without any shareholding on the part of the Ajwani family. Freudenberg Nonwovens India Private Ltd. was renamed Freudenberg Performance Materials India Pvt. Ltd. on April 1, 2016.
373 Longstanding business partner Niranjan Ajwani holds a 10 % share. Cf. "Going East. Die Erfolgsgeschichte beginnt in Japan," in: Freudenberg Magazin, 2/1999, p. 32–35, here p. 34 as well as Hoch, 2007, p. 17. Planning to establish the joint venture had begun as early as 1997. The reason behind this was that "the Klüber objectives" were not achievable with the previous Indian representative (loss of trust). The site that was foreseen from the start was the Mumbai (Bombay) industrial hub. Cf. UL-Vorlage im Umlaufverfahren hinsichtlich Klüber Gründung in Indien vom 1. Dezember 1997, in: Corporate Archives 3/08852.
374 Simmerrings, damper seals and valve stem seals were jointly produced and sold, particularly in the domestic market. The sales office for sealing and vibration control technology was integrated into it. Cf. Verträge and Joint Venture Agreement, in: Corporate Archives 3/06876 as well as "Freudenberg-NOK und Sigma gründen Joint Venture in Indien," in: Freudenberg Magazin, 2/2000, p. 30.
375 Protokoll der Sitzung der Unternehmensleitung vom 16. Mai 2000, in: Corporate Archives 3/07649 and Corporate Archives 3/10485.
376 Cf. Joint Venture Agreement, in: Corporate Archives 3/06876 as well as Protokoll der Sitzung der Unternehmensleitung vom 16. Mai 2000, in: Corporate Archives 3/07649 and Corporate Archives 3/10485. The distribution of shares was regulated as follows: equity shares, which comprised 90 % of total equity: 50 % Sigma, 50 % NOK-Freudenberg Asia Holding (NFAH), shares with limited voting rights, which comprised 10 % of total equity: 100 % NFAH. This resulted in a share ratio of 55:45.
377 Cf. Fax von Sigma mit Unternehmensvorstellung vom 24. April 1995, in: Corporate Archives 3/07624 as well as "Freudenberg-NOK und Sigma gründen Joint Venture in Indien," in: Freudenberg Magazin, 2/2000, p. 30.
378 Cf. Hoch, 2007, p. 16.
379 Cf. "Neue Produktionsstandorte: Indien," in: Freudenberg Magazin, 1/2003, p. 8.
380 Cf. "Die 'Blaue Vileda-Welle'," in: Der Freudenberger, 2/1962, p. 9; Tagebuch der Vileda GmbH, 1966, p. 6 and p. 8, in: Corporate Archives 3/00930; Praet/Horchler, 2012, p. 38 as well as Vileda, 2008, p. 16–17.

381 Cf. "Vileda, Vlieser, Vlik, Vlextil," in: Der Freudenberger, 1/1963, p. 8–15, here p. 8.
382 Cf. Willaredt, 1964, p. 31 as well as "Sechs Jahre 'Vileda'," in: Der Freudenberger, 2/1968, p. 11–13, here p. 11.
383 The "Glitzi" brand was registered with the German Patent and Trade Mark Office on February 19, 1962. Cf. Kopie der Urkunde des Deutschen Patentamts, in: Corporate Archives 3/08108.
384 Cf. 5 Jahre Vileda GmbH, p. 34, in: Corporate Archives 3/00930.
385 Cf. Vileda, 2008, p. 20; Offenlegungsschrift Nr. 1703721 zur Patentanmeldung vom 3. Juli 1968, in: Corporate Archives 3/07086 as well as Werbematerial zum Vileda-Glitzi, in: Corporate Archives 4/06207, Corporate Archives 7/00174 and Corporate Archives 7/00808.
386 Cf. 5 Jahre Vileda GmbH, p. 1 and p. 36, in: Corporate Archives 3/00930. Turnover rose from almost 7 million deutschmarks in 1962 through 21.5 million deutschmarks in 1966 to 43.1 million deutschmarks in 1969.
387 Cf. Tagebuch der Vileda GmbH, 1966, p. 10, in: Corporate Archives 3/00930.
388 Cf. Vileda-Produktinformationen, in: Corporate Archives 3/03590.
389 Cf. Bericht der Vileda GmbH zur Planung 1975–1979 Vileda, Odewa, Lady Esther vom 15. August 1974, p. 3, in: Corporate Archives 3/00929.
390 Cf. "Neuer Vertriebszweig für Vileda: Lady Esther," in: Der Freudenberger, 3/1973, p. 16 as well as Notiz an Dr. Balbach vom 11. Mai 1973, in: Corporate Archives 3/06173.
391 Cf. "Neue Produkte bei Markenartikeln," in: CF-intern, 6/1975, p. 2.
392 Cf. "Neuer Vertriebszweig für Vileda: Lady Esther," in: Der Freudenberger, 3/1973, p. 16 as well as Notiz an Dr. Balbach vom 11. Mai 1973, in: Corporate Archives 3/06173.
393 Cf. "Neue Produkte bei Markenartikeln," in: CF-intern, 6/1975, p. 2.
394 Cf. Auskunft über Lady Esther durch FB Beteiligungen vom 21. Oktober 1982; in: Corporate Archives 3/06173.
395 Cf. Notiz Herrn Dr. Balbach – Bilanzbesprechung 1982 vom 30. Juni 1983; in: Corporate Archives 3/06173 as well as Gesellschafterbrief, 1982, in: Corporate Archives 3/02275.
396 Cf. Kauf- und Übertragungsvertrag vom 26. April 1984; in: Corporate Archives 3/05943.
397 Cf. Bericht der Vileda GmbH zur Planung 1975–1979 Vileda, Odewa, Lady Esther vom 15. August 1974, p. 3, in: Corporate Archives 3/00929.
398 Cf. ibid, p. 12; "Am größten Arbeitsplatz der Welt macht es jetzt mehr Spaß, morgens zu beginnen," in: Der Freudenberger, 1/1974, p. 24–25 as well as documents on the collaboration with the Coronet plants, in: Corporate Archives 3/08079.
399 Cf. Bericht der Vileda GmbH zur Planung 1975–1979 Vileda, Odewa, Lady Esther vom 15. August 1974, p. 12, in: Corporate Archives 3/00929.
400 Gesellschafterbrief, 1975, in: Corporate Archives 3/02275.
401 Cf. documents on Vileda GmbH's strategy, with analysis, objective, measures and funds in 1987, here Vileda turnover for 1977–1986, in UA: 3/07990.
402 Cf. Protokoll der Sitzung der Unternehmensleitung am 24. Juli 1980, in: Corporate Archives 3/03293.
403 Ibid.
404 Cf. ibid.
405 Cf. Vileda-Betriebsergebnis (in Mio. D-Mark) für die Jahre von 1977 bis 1986, in: Corporate Archives 3/04044.
406 Cf. documents on Vileda GmbH's strategy, with analysis, objective, measures and funds in 1987, here Vileda turnover for 1987, p. 33–37, in UA: 3/07990.
407 Cf. Sabria/Rahola, 2001, p. 14 and Wolf, 2005, p. 42.
408 Cf. ibid.
409 Cf. Esteva 2006, p. 44–45 as well as Vileda, 2008, p. 26.
410 Cf. Sabria/Rahola, 2001, p. 14 as well as Esteva, 2006, p. 44–45.
411 Cf. Konsolidierte Wertschöpfungsanalyse für Frema-/Vileda-Produkte vom 9. September 1981, in: Corporate Archives 3/05812.
412 Cf. Sabria/Rahola, 2001, p. 14; Kurzbericht über die Freudenberg Haushaltsprodukte für die Tagung des Gesellschafterinformationskreises am 26. April 1996, in: Corporate Archives 3/05178 as well as Wolf, 2005, p. 42.
413 Cf. Sabria/Rahola, 2001, p. 15.
414 Cf. Vileda, 2008, p. 26–27.
415 Cf. Gesellschafterbriefe, 1985 und 2. Halbjahr 1986, in: Corporate Archives 3/02275; Market-

ing-Plan Vileda Wischmop, 21. Mai 1985; in: Corporate Archives 3/08100 as well as Vileda, 2008, p. 27.
416 Cf. documents on Vileda GmbH's strategy, with analysis, objective, measures and funds in 1987, here Vileda turnover for 1987, p. 131, in UA: 3/07990 as well as Marketing-Plan Vileda Wischmop, in: Corporate Archives 3/08100.
417 Cf. Vileda, 2008, p. 30–31.
418 Cf. "Dem Erfolg auf die Finger geschaut," in: Der Freudenberger, 5/1990, p. 3.
419 Cf. "Markenware aus Holland," in: Der Freudenberger, 3/1991, p. 5; Presseinformation zur Beteiligung von Freudenberg an Akzo-Haushaltsprodukten vom 16. Januar 1989, in: Corporate Archives 3/02194; Presseinformation zur Übernahme der Wettex vom 27. Februar 1990, in: Corporate Archives 3/02052 as well as Gesellschafterbrief, 1990, in: Corporate Archives 3/05393.
420 Cf. Protokoll zur Sitzung der Unternehmensleitung vom 9. Dezember 1991, in: Corporate Archives 3/10774.
421 Gesellschafterbrief, 1989, in: Corporate Archives 3/02546.
422 Cf. Presseinformation zur Übernahme der Wettex vom 27. Februar 1990, in: Corporate Archives 3/02052 as well as "Wettex," in: Der Freudenberger, 3/1991, p. 5.
423 Vorlage zur UL-Sitzung vom 24. April 1989 zum Akquisitionsprojekt Wettex, in: Corporate Archives 3/03319.
424 Cf. Presseinformation zur Übernahme der Wettex vom 27. Februar 1990, in: Corporate Archives 3/02052.
425 Protokoll zur Sitzung der Unternehmensleitung am 9. Dezember 1991, in: Corporate Archives 3/10774.
426 Cf. Geschäftsbericht, 1996, in: Corporate Archives 3/10992.
427 Cf. Gesellschaftsverträge und Gründungsunterlagen der Klüber-Auslandstöchter, in: Corporate Archives 3/03498 and Corporate Archives 3/06063; "Ernst Umhöfer im Ruhestand. Die Klüber-Firmengruppe: Sein Lebenswerk," in: Der Freudenberger, 4/1987, p. 10 as well as "Klüber Lubrication: Wechsel in der Geschäftsleitung," in: Der Freudenberger, 4/1987, p. 10.
428 Cf. Stadler, 1992, p. 4.
429 Cf. Gesellschafterbriefe, 1972, 1974 und 1975, in: Corporate Archives 3/02275.
430 Cf. Gesellschafterbriefe, 1976, 1977, 1978 und 1979, in: Corporate Archives 3/02275.
431 Cf. Pioniergeist seit 1929: die Geschichte von Klüber Lubrication, can be accessed online at: https://www.klueber.com/de/de/unternehmen/die-geschichte-von-klueber-lubrication, accessed on October 10, 2023.
432 Cf. Gesellschafterbriefe, 1984 und 1986, in: Corporate Archives 3/02275.
433 Cf. "Veränderungen in der UL," in: Der Freudenberger, 4/1993, p. 1. as well as Orians, 2005, p. 36–37.
434 Cf. "Weltrekord in Sicht," in: CF-intern, 5/1983, p. 4 as well as Brunner, 2020.
435 Cf. "Rallye Paris-Dakar: Klüber Schmierstoffe siegten mit," in: Freudenberg intern, 1/1985, p. 3.
436 Under his aegis, there was a drastic reduction in the number of accidents at Freudenberg. As of June 30, 2005 Schön stepped down from the Management Board and retired. Cf. Vita von Ernst Schön, in Corporate Archives 3/11039.
437 Cf. Gesellschafterbriefe, 1988 und 1989, in: Corporate Archives 3/02546.
438 Cf. Gesellschafterbrief, 1990, in: Corporate Archives 3/05393.
439 Cf. "Spezialschmierstoffe für viele Einsatzbereiche," in: Der Freudenberger, 5/1979, p. 2; "Am Anfang stand das Bierhahn-Fett. Marktführer im Bereich Lebensmittel-Industrie," in: Der Freudenberger, 10/1992, p. 5; "Klüber und der Umweltschutz," in: Der Freudenberger, 10/1992, p. 5; "Hier wird Umweltschutz großgeschrieben," in: Der Freudenberger, 5/1993, p. 3 as well as brochure: "Mehr als Lebensmittelsicherheit. Spezialschmierstoffe für die Getränkeindustrie," in: Corporate Archives 3/11037.
440 Cf. "Bio-Rostlöser mit neuen Rohstoffen," in: Der Freudenberger, 6/1994, p. 8 as well as brochure "EAL: The next generation. Lubricant innovations for the shipping industry," in: Corporate Archives 3/11037.
441 Gesellschafterbrief, 1995, in: Corporate Archives 3/05393.
442 Cf. Fath, 1996a, p. 4.
443 Cf. Gesellschafterbriefe, 1975 und 1976, in: Corporate Archives 3/02275.
444 Cf. Berichte zur Entstehung des Kunststoffwerkes und zur Entwicklung der Kunststoff-Produktion bei Freudenberg, in: Corporate Archives 3/01340.
445 Cf. "Norament – Karriere eines Bodenbelages," in: CF-intern, 10/1977, p. 3.

446 Cf. "Auch Amerikaner 'stehen auf Freudenberg'," in: Der Freudenberger, 5/1986, p. 3 as well as "Going West," in: Freudenberg Magazin, 1/2000, p. 26–30, here p. 27. It has operated under the name Freudenberg Building Systems since 1989. Cf. minutes of the Management Board meetings from January 15, 1988 to June 20, 1988 on Nora Flooring, in: Corporate Archives 3/04616.
447 Cf. Gesellschafterbrief, 1980, in: Corporate Archives 3/02275.
448 Cf. Horchler, 2014, p. 50.
449 Cf. ibid.
450 Cf. Geschäftsbericht, 1984, in: Corporate Archives 3/00687 as well as Gesellschafterbriefe, 1983 und 1984, in: Corporate Archives 3/02275.
451 Cf. Geschäftsbericht, 1985, in: Corporate Archives 3/00744.
452 Cf. minutes of the Management Board meetings from January 15, 1988 to June 20, 1988 on Nora Flooring, in: Corporate Archives 3/04616. Leather fiber production ("Robus") was sold in 1987. Cf. documents on the sale of the Robus Product Corp. shares, in: Corporate Archives 3/08602 and Corporate Archives 3/06260 as well as "Rückschau zur Entwicklung des ehemaligen Unternehmensbereichs I im Zeitraum 1979–1989" vom Oktober 1989, in: Corporate Archives 3/05128.
453 Cf. Gesellschafterbriefe, 1987 und 1989, in: Corporate Archives 3/02275 and Corporate Archives 3/02546.
454 Cf. Korrespondenzen von Freudenberg mit der Firma bzw. Familie Rontani in Lucca, in: Corporate Archives 3/06403.
455 Cf. Gesellschafterbrief, 1991, in: Corporate Archives 3/05393.
456 Gesellschafterbrief, 1995, in: Corporate Archives 3/05393.
457 Cf. "Aus den Arbeitsgebieten," in: Der Freudenberger, 6/1993, p. 3, "Per Schiff zum Flughafen bei Osaka," in: Der Freudenberger, 11/1993, p. 1; "Dem Ziel Nora 200 rückt BS immer näher," in: Der Freudenberger, 4/1994, p. 2 as well as "Aktuellen Trends vielfältig entsprochen," in: Der Freudenberger, 4/1995, p. 1–2.
458 Cf. Gesellschafterbriefe, 1995 und 1996, in: Corporate Archives 3/05393 as well as "Sturm auf den Gipfel 'NORA 200'," in: Der Freudenberger, 4/1989, p. 4.
459 Unterlage zur Sitzung der Unternehmensleitung am 13. Dezember 2002 [sic! gemeint ist 2001], TOP 6: Geschäftsgruppe Bausysteme – Vorschau 2002, in: Corporate Archives 3/10523.
460 Cf. Unterlage zur Sitzung der Unternehmensleitung am 11. Dezember 2002, Vorschau 2003, in: Corporate Archives 3/10542 as well as Protokoll zur Vorschausitzung der Unternehmensleitung am 11. Dezember 2003, in: Corporate Archives 3/10558.
461 Cf. Unterlage zur Vorschausitzung der Unternehmensleitung am 11. Dezember 2003, in: Corporate Archives 3/10558.
462 Cf. Protokoll zur Vorschausitzung der Unternehmensleitung am 11. Dezember 2003, in: Corporate Archives 3/10558.
463 Cf. Protokoll zur Vorschausitzung der Unternehmensleitung am 6. Dezember 2005, in: Corporate Archives 3/10586.
464 Cf. Protokoll zur Vorschausitzung der Unternehmensleitung am 6. Dezember 2006, in: Corporate Archives 3/10603.
465 Cf. Gesellschafterbrief, 2005, in: Corporate Archives 3/07892 as well as Röhrs, 2005, p. 25.
466 Gesellschafterbrief, 2006, in: Corporate Archives 3/07928.
467 Ibid.
468 Ibid.
469 Cf. "Verkaufsgerüchte über Bausysteme KG. Betriebsrat fordert in einem offenen Brief Aufklärung, doch der Freudenberg-Konzern schweigt," in: Weinheimer Nachrichten, 14. November 2006, in: Corporate Archives 3/08623.
470 Cf. "Freudenberg: Sorge in der Belegschaft," in: Mannheimer Morgen, 14. November 2006, in: Corporate Archives 3/08623 as well as Transcript of interview with Jörg Sost in November 2019, in: Corporate Archives 3/11148.
471 Cf. "Freudenberg prüft Verkauf der Bausysteme KG," in: Rhein-Neckar-Web, 23. November 2006, in: Corporate Archives 3/08623.
472 Cf. "Freudenberg-Vorstand bietet runden Tisch an," in: SWR.de, 21. November 2006, in: Corporate Archives 3/08623.
473 Cf. "Verkauf ist eine der Optionen. Freudenberg reagiert auf Gerüchte über die Bausysteme KG," in: Mannheimer Morgen, 23. November 2006, in: Corporate Archives 3/08623.

474 Vgl. "Entscheidung über Verkauf der 'Bausysteme' steht bevor", in: SWR 4, 11. Dezember 2006, in: Corporate Archives 3/08623.
475 Cf. "Demo bei Freudenberg," in: Mannheimer Morgen, 20. Dezember 2006, in: Corporate Archives 3/08623.
476 Cf. "400 Mitarbeiter von Freudenberg kämpfen gegen Werksverkauf," in: BILD, 20. Dezember 2006, in: Corporate Archives 3/08623.
477 Cf. "Belegschaft will 'ehrliche Antworten'. Bausysteme KG der Firma Freudenberg will Verkauf verhindern – Kundgebung auf dem Marktplatz – Noch mehr KGs gefährdet?," in: Rhein-Neckar-Zeitung, 20. Dezember 2006, in: Corporate Archives 3/08623.
478 Schreiben der Unternehmensleitung an die Mitarbeiterinnen und Mitarbeiter der Freudenberg Bausysteme KG vom 2. Januar 2007, in: Corporate Archives 3/11149.
479 Secondary source: "Betriebsversammlung bei FBS," in: Weinheimer Nachrichten, 18. Januar 2007, in: Corporate Archives 3/08623.
480 Cf. "Freudenberg verhandelt mit Interessenten," in: Darmstädter Echo, 18. Januar 2007, in: Corporate Archives 3/08623.
481 Cf. Pressemeldung der Freudenberg & Co. Unternehmenskommunikation vom 19. Januar 2007, in: Corporate Archives 3/08623.
482 "Zehn Stunden lang die Freudenberg-Werkstore blockiert. Betriebsversammlung bei Bausysteme KG ging gestern weiter / Konzernleitung rückt von Verkaufsplänen nicht ab," in: Weinheimer Nachrichten, 20. Januar 2007, in: Corporate Archives 3/08623.
483 Cf. ibid.
484 Cf. "Blockade mit System errichtet. Freudenberger riegelten aus Protest gegen den Verkauf der Bausysteme das Werksgelände ab," in: Rhein-Neckar-Zeitung, 20. Januar 2007, in: Corporate Archives 3/08623.
485 The "*Fit für die Zukunft*" or "Fit for the Future" restructuring program initiated in 2005, which foresaw the cutting of approximately 400 jobs at Freudenberg's German nonwovens sites, was also met with fierce protests on the part of the workforce in Weinheim and IG BCE, the trade union for the mining, chemical and energy industries, among others including leather, until finally an agreement was reached with the works council in the second half of 2006. Cf. Mitteilungen des Betriebsrates und der Gewerkschaft IG BCE, in: Corporate Archives 3/08000; Hoch, 2005, p. 14; "Einigung bei Freudenberg Vliesstoffe," in: Freudenberg Magazin, 3/2006, p. 7 as well as Röhrs, 2007, p. 2.
486 Cf. "Stürmische Zeiten bei Freudenberg. Demo der Mitarbeiter der Bausysteme KG / OB Bernhard spricht auf Betriebsversammlung," in: Weinheimer Nachrichten, 19. Januar 2007, in: Corporate Archives 3/08623 as well as "Weiter Proteste bei Freudenberg," in: Mannheimer Morgen, 19. Januar 2007, in: Corporate Archives 3/08623.
487 Mitarbeiter-Information zur Blockade des Industrieparks der Freudenberg & Co. Unternehmenskommunikation vom 19. Januar 2007, in: Corporate Archives 3/08623.
488 Cf. Protokoll der Sonder-Sitzung der Unternehmensleitung vom 22. Januar 2007 in Weinheim, in: Corporate Archives 3/10610.
489 Cf. "Betriebsversammlung beendet – Mitarbeiter von Bausysteme nehmen Arbeit wieder auf," in: Marktplatz Aktuell, 1/2007, in: Corporate Archives 3/08623.
490 Cf. ibid.
491 Cf. Transcript of interview with Jörg Sost in November 2019, in: Corporate Archives 3/11148.
492 Cf. Hoch, 2007a, p. 9.
493 Secondary source: Hoch, 2007a, p. 9.
494 Cf. Orians, 2007, p. 7.
495 "Majority shareholder capiton AG is an owner-managed financial investment company, which gets involved as an investor and growth financier in profitable, established small and medium sized enterprises with turnover of between 50 and 500 million euros. Its portfolio currently includes for example the Borsig Group and energy company Ensys. L-Eigenkapital Agentur (L-EA) will acquire shares in nora systems GmbH as a minority shareholder. It is a business area of Landeskreditbank Baden-Württemberg and finances established small and medium sized enterprises (SMEs) through its SME fund. As part of the management buyout (MBO), the management executives of nora systems GmbH are also financially bound to the company. A management buyout – basically – means the takeover of a company by its previous management, generally with the

support of further investors. In the case of nora systems GmbH, these are capiton AG and L-EA." Röhrs, 2007b, p. 1.

496 Cf. "Viel Glück nora! Verkauf der Bausysteme an Finanzinvestoren," in: KBR-Netz 45, Oktober 2007, in: Corporate Archives 3/08000 as well as Orians, 2007, p. 7.

497 Cf. Orians, 2007, p. 7.

498 Secondary source: Röhrs, 2007a, p. 1.

499 Cf. Röhrs, 2007c, p. 2.

500 Cf. "Verkaufsgerüchte über Bausysteme KG. Betriebsrat fordert in einem offenen Brief Aufklärung, doch der Freudenberg-Konzern schweigt," in: Weinheimer Nachrichten, 14. November 2006, in: Corporate Archives 3/08623.

501 Cf. documents on the Freudenberg Foundation, in: Corporate Archives 3/04734.

502 Cf. Verantwortung für die Gesellschaft (UN-Global-Compact-Fortschrittsbericht 2019), p. 31, in: Geschäftsbericht, 2018, in: Corporate Archives 3/10709.

503 Cf. documents on the reform of the company pension, in: Corporate Archives 3/04117 and Corporate Archives 3/04118 as well as special edition of employee magazine "Der Freudenberger" dated October 1986, p. 1–4. The works agreement on the new pension scheme was signed on September 18, 1986 by the Management Board and General Works Council and came into effect on January 1, 1987.

504 Cf. Gründungsunterlagen, in: Corporate Archives 3/07335; Jahresbericht der Unterstützungskasse, 2008, in: Corporate Archives 3/08937 as well as Fath, 2006, p. 11. The inaugural meeting took place on December 4, 1989, the scheme was registered in the associations register on December 15, 1989. In the notification letter about the foundation of the welfare assistance (scheme) dated 1990, 15 years of service at the company is stated as a condition of eligibility for an employee (or former employee). In a welfare assistance information brochure (as of December 2008) five years of service is stated for active employees and 10 years of service for pensioners. The change in the conditions for eligibility can be found in the Regulations for Granting Benefits dated November 29, 2001. Cf. Satzung und Richtlinien der Unterstützungskasse, in: Corporate Archives 3/06156. Richtlinien zur Gewährung von Unterstützungsleistungen

505 Cf. Jahresbericht der Unterstützungskasse Freudenberg e. V. 2022, p. 3, in: Corporate Archives 3/11145. According to this annual report, the welfare assistance scheme began its activities in March 1990.

506 This refers to Carl Johann Freudenberg and his sons Friedrich Carl and Hermann Ernst.

507 The Management Board comprised Walter, Hans, Otto and Richard Freudenberg. Richard Freudenberg assumed the role of Speaker.

508 The Management Board members were: Richard Freudenberg (Speaker), Hans Erich Freudenberg, Helmut Fabricius, Otto Schildhauer, Peter Wentzler, Hermann Freudenberg, Kurt Kraft and Dieter Freudenberg.

509 Cf. Diskussionsbeitrag zur Aufbauorganisation von Carl Freudenberg vom 5. Juli 1968, in: Corporate Archives 3/04600.

510 Schreiben der Unternehmensleitung an die Gesellschafter zur "Neuordnung der Rechtsverhältnisse in unserer Gesellschaft" vom Dezember 1969, in: Corporate Archives 3/08097.

511 Cf. ibid. as well as Gesellschaftsvertrag von 1970, in: Corporate Archives 3/01076.

512 Cf. Freudenberg 1970a.

513 Cf. Freudenberg, 1971.

514 Cf. Interne Informationsschrift über die Organisation der Freudenberg Group (Freudenberg & Co., insbesondere Carl Freudenberg) vom November 1971, in: Corporate Archives 3/03918.

515 Cf. Memo von Hans Erich Freudenberg vom Dezember 1975, in: Corporate Archives 3/04218.

516 Cf. "Weitere Überlegungen zur Verbesserung der F. u. Co.-Organisation" vom 22. Juni 1978, in: Corporate Archives 3/03918 as well as Informationsschrift über die Organisation der Freudenberg Group (August 1979), in: Corporate Archives 3/03918.

517 Informationsschrift über die Organisation der Freudenberg Group (August 1979), in: Corporate Archives 3/03918.

518 Cf. ibid.

519 Rede von Hermann Freudenberg bei der Gesellschafterversammlung am 26. April 1980, p. 5, in: Corporate Archives 3/02178.

520 Ibid, p. 6–7.

521 Cf. "Organisation der Freudenberg Group vom 1. Oktober 1986, in: Corporate Archives 3/01832.

522 Cf. Reinhart Freudenberg an Rudolf Scharpff, Rudolf Fischer und Hermann Norbert Dahlström, Unternehmensstruktur, 22. Oktober 1991, in: Corporate Archives 3/07340.
523 Cf. ibid.
524 Cf. ibid.
525 Cf. ibid.
526 Cf. Protokoll der Sitzung des Gesellschafterausschusses der Freudenberg & Co. am 21. Mai 1992 in Badenweiler, in: Corporate Archives 3/07321.
527 Protokoll der Sitzung des Gesellschafterausschusses der Freudenberg & Co. am 8. und 9. November 1994 in Weinheim, in: Corporate Archives 3/07321.
528 Protokoll der Sitzung des Gesellschafterausschusses der Freudenberg & Co. am 29. und 30. März 1993 in München, in: Corporate Archives 3/07321.
529 Cf. Protokolle des Gesellschafterausschusses der Freudenberg & Co. für die Jahre 1992–1993, in: Corporate Archives 3/07321.
530 Cf. Protokoll der Sitzung des Gesellschafterausschusses der Freudenberg & Co. am 8. und 9. November 1994 in Weinheim, in: Corporate Archives 3/07321.
531 Cf. Schreiben der Unternehmensleitung an den Gesellschafterausschuss "Organisatorische Weiterentwicklung von Carl Freudenberg – Geschäftseinheiten und Zentrale Dienstleistungsbereiche werden selbständige Gesellschaften" vom 2. November 1994, in: Corporate Archives 3/07321.
532 Cf. call for proposal to find a project name dated mid-December 1994, signed by Peter Bettermann and Hans Barleben, in: Corporate Archives 3/11036.
533 Cf. "Hans Barleben wird das Projekt koordinieren. Für alle Beteiligten das Beste erreichen," in: Der Freudenberger, 12/1994, p. 4 as well as Fokus, Informationen zur Organisationsentwicklung, Ausgabe 1, 27. Januar 1995, in: Corporate Archives 3/11036.
534 Cf. brochure "Organisatorische Weiterentwicklung von Carl Freudenberg. Geschäftseinheiten und zentrale Dienstleistungsbereiche werden selbständige Gesellschaften," November 1994, in: Corporate Archives 3/03667.
535 Cf. ibid.
536 Cf. Schreiben der Unternehmensleitung an den Gesellschafterausschuss "Organisatorische Weiterentwicklung von Carl Freudenberg – Geschäftseinheiten und Zentrale Dienstleistungsbereiche werden selbständige Gesellschaften" vom 2. November 1994, in: Corporate Archives 3/07321.
537 Cf. Transcript of interview with Reinhart Freudenberg on November 26, 2013, p. 7, in: Corporate Archives 3/11147.
538 Cf. Kleinschmidt, 2002.
539 Cf. ibid.
540 Cf. Bower 1967.
541 Examples of this can be found in: Reitmayer/Rosenberger, 2008.
542 Ibid.

Chapter 7: Sustainability, Mobility, Digitalization – The company since the turn of the millennium

1 Cf. Würz, 2023.
2 Cf. "Rückblick auf 20 Jahre Euro", in: Bundesministerium der Finanzen, online available at: https://www.bundesfinanzministerium.de/Content/DE/Standardartikel/Presse/Namensartikel/2022/2022-01-01-Gem-Beitrag-EU-Gruppe.html, retrieved on 2023/01/11 as well as "Währungsunion", in: Bundesministerium der Finanzen, online available at: https://www.bundesfinanzministerium.de/Web/DE/Themen/Europa/Der_Euro/Waehrungsunion/waehrungsunion.html, retrieved on 11.01.2023.
3 Cf. Würz, 2023.
4 Cf. Chmura/Haunhorst, 2014.
5 Cf. "Globale Finanz- und Wirtschaftskrise 2008/2009", in: Bundeszentrale für politische Bildung, Bonn 2017, online available at: https://www.bpb.de/kurz-knapp/zahlen-und-fakten/globalisierung/52584/globale-finanz-und-wirtschaftskrise-2008-2009, retrieved on 19.04.2022.

6 Cf. Geschäftsbericht, 2007, p. 10, in: Corporate Archives 3/07949.
7 Geschäftsbericht, 2009, p. 5, in: Corporate Archives 3/08629.
8 Syndicated credit lines were boosted by 230 million to 270 million euros, certificates of indebtedness, with a term of five years and a volume of about 270 million euros, were issued and a commercial paper program, initially with a volume of 150 million euros, was established. This program gives the company the possibility of issuing short-term fixed-interest securities to investors such as insurance companies or pension funds. Cf. Übersicht der Kreditlinien und liquiden Mittel im November/Dezember 2008, in: Corporate Archives 3/11110.
9 Cf. Geschäftsbericht, 2008, in: Corporate Archives 3/08158; Protokoll der Management-Montagsrunde vom 30. Juni 2008, in: Corporate Archives 3/11111; Weekly reports of the Finance Department on the liquidity situation of the Freudenberg Group for the year 2008, in: Corporate Archives 3/11110; Übersicht der Kreditlinien und liquiden Mittel im November/Dezember 2008, in: Corporate Archives 3/11110 as well as Transcription of the interview with Peter Bettermann from 4 December 2018, in: Corporate Archives 3/11112.
10 Cf. "Die Absatzmärkte von Freudenberg. Massive Rückgänge", in: Freudenberg Magazin, 2/2009, p. 16–17, hier p. 16.
11 Cf. Smolka, 2008, p. 3.
12 Cf. Mitteilung von Dr. H. R. Randau an Dr. Stark vom 19. Oktober 2008 betr. Forderungsmanagement gegenüber GM, Ford und Chrysler, in: Corporate Archives 3/11074.
13 As a result of falling sales figures and continuing losses, General Motors (GM) reported a loss of US$ 3.3 billion in the first quarter of 2008. It reduced its production forecast for the second quarter of 2008 by 130,000 units to 950,000 vehicles. Cf. Bericht des Finanzbereichs an Peter Bettermann per 31. März 2008 vom 23. Juni 2008, in: Corporate Archives 3/11110.
14 Cf. E-mail from Mitsuo Kanno (JVC) to Bruce Olson (F-NW), November 29, 2008, in: Corporate Archives 3/11074; E-mail from Peter Bettermann to Mohsen Sohi (FNGP) of 27 January 2009, in: Corporate Archives 3/11074 as well as Gesellschafterbrief, 2008, in: Corporate Archives 3/08667.
15 Cf. Documents on the development of the financial crisis 2008/2009, in: Corporate Archives 3/11074.
16 Cf. E-mail from Peter Bettermann to Ralf Krieger dated 11 November 2008, in: Corporate Archives 3/11074 as well as Protokoll der Sitzung der Unternehmensleitung von 24. November 2008, in: Corporate Archives 3/10642.
17 However, certain postponements had to be accepted in the case of projects developed directly with customers, especially in the automotive industry. This explains why the research and development expenditure of Freudenberg fell from 195.1 million in 2008 to 170.9 million euros in 2009. Cf. Gesellschafterbrief, 1. Halbjahr 2009, p. 7, in: Corporate Archives 3/08939; Geschäftsbericht, 2009, in: Corporate Archives 3/08629 as well as Q&A catalogue for the annual press conference on May 15, 2009, in: Corporate Archives 3/11113.
18 Cf. Documents on the development of the financial crisis 2008/2009, in: Corporate Archives 3/11074 as well as to set up the weekly watchlist, the Protokoll der Sitzung der Unternehmensleitung vom 24. November 2008, in: Corporate Archives 3/10642.
19 Vertrauliches Rundschreiben von Peter Bettermann, Jörg Sost und Martin Stark an die Geschäftsführungen der Teilkonzerne vom 23. Dezember 2008, in: Corporate Archives 3/11074.
20 Cf. E-Mail von Mohsen Sohi an Peter Bettermann betr. US-Geschäft FNGP vom 14. Dezember 2008, in: Corporate Archives 3/11074.
21 Cf. Gesellschafterbrief, 1. Halbjahr 2009, p. 3, in: Corporate Archives 3/08939.
22 Cf. Transcription of the interview with Peter Bettermann from 4. December 2018, in: Corporate Archives 3/11112 as well as Geschäftsbericht, 2009, in: Corporate Archives 3/08629.
23 Cf. Fath, 2009, p. 5.
24 Cf. Fath, 2009a, p. 13.
25 The following plants had to be closed as a result of the crisis: in the United States (FNGP) – Laconia/New Hampshire, radial seals, spring 2009 with 106 employees; Franklin/New Hampshire, transmission components, mid-2009, all 66 employees were transferred to another plant; Scottsburg/Indiana, brake components, mid-2009 with 119 employees; Ligionier/Indiana, vibration dampers, mid-2009 with 68 employees – in Europe – Mâcon/France (FST), closed in fall 2009 and relocated to Langres. 66 employees were made redundant; Ceperka/Czech Republic (FST), closed in mid-2009, with production relocated back to Kufstein (53 employees affected); Ripaberarda/Italy (nonwovens), closed in mid-2009 (24 employees affected); Loz/Poland (Freudenberg Politex),

one of the geotextile production lines was relocated to Russia at the end of 2009 (61 employees affected). Cf. Geschäftsbericht, 2009, p. 18, in: Corporate Archives 3/08629; Gesellschafterbrief, 2008, p. 3, in: Corporate Archives 3/08114; Q&A catalogue for the Annual Press Conference on April 13, 2010, in: Corporate Archives 3/11114; Protokolle der Unternehmensleitungssitzungen vom 3. und 24. November 2008, in: Corporate Archives 3/10640 und Corporate Archives 3/10642 as well as Buchta-Noack/Hoch, 2009, p. 18–23.

26 The amounts receivable by Freudenberg companies from GM alone totaled more than US$ 3 million. Cf. Notiz zur Automotive-Telefonkonferenz vom 10. Juni 2009, in: Corporate Archives 3/11074.

27 Vibracoustic also recorded no positive effects as the scrappage incentive for small cars did not result in any recovery of business for premium manufacturers. Cf. Minutes of conference calls, February 25, 2009 and March 4, 2009, in: Corporate Archives 3/11074. However, in the long term, the scrappage incentive offered in the USA (Car Allowance Rebate System) did mean that short-term working and the closure of factories for certain weeks in the USA could be brought to an end. Cf. Gesellschafterbrief, 2009, p. 19, in: Corporate Archives 3/08628.

28 Gesellschafterbrief, 1. Halbjahr 2009, p. 3, in: Corporate Archives 3/08939 as well as Geschäftsbericht, 2009, p. 9, in: Corporate Archives 3/08629. The machinery and plant engineering sector only reacted to the economic downturn with a certain delay. Following the record year of 2008, a fall of 20 percent in global production was recorded in 2009.

29 Cf. "Die Absatzmärkte von Freudenberg. Massive Rückgänge", in: Freudenberg Magazin, 2/2009, p. 16 as well as Gesellschafterbrief, 1. Halbjahr 2009, p. 3, in: Corporate Archives 3/08939

30 "Wir haben eine Depression", Interview mit Peter Bettermann, in: Die Welt, 27. März 2009, p. 16.

31 Cf. Deutsche Bundesbank, Monatsbericht Oktober 2010, Frankfurt, 15. Oktober 2010, p. 20, Online available at: https://www.bundesbank.de/resource/blob/692944/45e039b4b0d1223d05d940 c6dc14e5b0/mL/2010-10-monatsbericht-data.pdf, retrieved on 18.01.2023. Cf. zu den statistischen Angaben: "Globale Finanz- und Wirtschaftskrise 2008/2009", in: Bundeszentrale für politische Bildung, Bonn 2017, online available at: https://www.bpb.de/kurz-knapp/zahlen-und-fakten/glo balisierung/52584/globale-finanz-und-wirtschaftskrise-2008-2009, retrieved on 18.01.2023.

32 Cf. Geschäftsbericht, 2009, p. 9, in: Corporate Archives 3/08629.

33 GDP growth in China, compared with the previous year: 9.2 percent (2009) and 10.6 percent (2010). Cf. "Globale Finanz- und Wirtschaftskrise 2008/2009", in: Bundeszentrale für politische Bildung, Bonn 2017, online available at: https://www.bpb.de/kurz-knapp/zahlen-und-fakten/globalisie rung/52584/globale-finanz-und-wirtschaftskrise-2008-2009, retrieved on 18.01.2023 as well as Geschäftsbericht, 2009, p. 9, in: Corporate Archives 3/08629.

34 Cf. Gesellschafterbrief, 1. Halbjahr 2010, p. 3, in: Corporate Archives 3/08663 as well as Geschäftsbericht, 2010, in: Corporate Archives 3/08896.

35 Cf. for example, the presentation of FST: Lessons Learned from 15 March 2010, in: Corporate Archives 3/11074.

36 Cf. Gesellschafterbrief, 1. Halbjahr 2010, p. 3, in: Corporate Archives 3/08663.

37 Cf. Fath, 2009a, p. 13.

38 Cf. "Die Energiewende 2011", in: Landeszentrale für politische Bildung Baden-Württemberg, online available at: https://www.lpb-bw.de/energiewende, retrieved on 19.04.2022.

39 Cf. Marschner, 2016; Pennekamp, 2023 as well as "Bundestag stimmt für Laufzeitverlängerung von AKW", in: FAZ.NET vom 11. November 2022, online available at: https://www.faz.net/aktuell/ wirtschaft/akw-laufzeitverlaengerung-von-bundestag-beschlossen-18453371.html, retrieved on 04.02.2023.

40 "Vor 5 Jahren: Großbritannien stimmt für den EU-Austritt", in: Bundeszentrale für politische Bildung, Bonn 2021, online available at: https://www.bpb.de/kurz-knapp/hintergrund-aktuell/ 335261/vor-5-jahren-grossbritannien-stimmt-fuer-den-eu-austritt/, retrieved on 19.04.2022.

41 Hoffmann, 2022, p. 8.

42 Cf. ibid.

43 Cf. Schulz, 2022, p. 16. This speech ranks 10th amongst the most widely viewed live TV transmissions. First place is still held by the final of the soccer World Cup in 1966, with 32.3 million viewers. Cf. Goodhart, 2022.

44 Cf. Schulz, 2022, p. 16.

45 From mid-2020, about 500,000 surgical face masks were produced every day at the newly-com-

missioned face mask production facility of Freudenberg Filtration Technologies in Kaiserslautern alone. Cf. Geschäftsbericht, 2020, in: Corporate Archives 3/11046.
46 Cf. ibid.
47 Cf. Pandemic planning for the Weinheim Industrial Park, in: Corporate Archives 3/11115 as well as Freudenberg Portal News vom 17. und 18. March 2020, in: Corporate Archives 3/11116.
48 Cf. Sohi, 2020, p. 1–2 as well as Geschäftsberichte, 2020 and 2021, in: Corporate Archives 3/11046 and Corporate Archives 3/11047.
49 Cf. Jahresbericht 2021 des Arbeitsmedizinischen Dienstes, in: Corporate Archives 3/11118 as well as "In Indien, Deutschland und Österreich über 6.500 Mitarbeitende der Freudenberg Gruppe geimpft", Freudenberg Portal News from June 30, 2021, in: Corporate Archives 3/11117.
50 Cf. Statistics of Covid case numbers of the HSE department, in: Corporate Archives 3/11115
51 Cf. Geschäftsbericht, 2020, in: Corporate Archives 3/11046.
52 Cf. Geschäftsbericht, 2021, in: Corporate Archives 3/11047.
53 Cf. Gesellschafterbrief, 2011, p. 43 ff., in: Corporate Archives 3/10841.
54 The FRCC North America began operating in Manchester, New Hampshire, in 2003, and moved to Plymouth, Michigan, in 2013. The FRCC Asia opened in Shanghai in 2006, the FRCC India in Bangalore and the FRCC in Alphaville near São Paulo, Brazil, were both set up in 2013. The FRCC South America closed down in 2020. Its tasks were transferred to Freudenberg-NOK Sealing Technologies South America. Cf. "Corporate Center Nordamerika nimmt Arbeit auf", in: Freudenberg Magazin, 4/2003, p. 8; Fath, 2006a, p. 15; Freudenberg Portal News vom 25. und 26. Juni 2013, 12. Juli 2013, 21. und 24. Oktober 2013, in: Corporate Archives 3/09107; Böttcher, 2013, p. 5; Böttcher, 2013a, p. 8; Sadikovic, 2013, p. 9 as well as Freudenberg Portal News of July 23, 2020, in: Corporate Archives 3/11116.
55 Cf. Gesellschafterbrief, 2011, p. 43 ff., in: Corporate Archives 3/10841.
56 The first planning cycle covered the period 1998–2000, the second 2001–2003, the third 2004–2006; in 2007, the cycle was extended to cover a 5-year planning period due to the global financial crisis in 2008–2009.
57 Cf. Curriculum vitae of Peter Bettermann, in: Corporate Archives 3/11108 as well as Fath, 1997, p. 3.
58 Cf. Konzernhandbuch Controlling (Stand Januar 2009), in: Corporate Archives 3/11075.
59 Initially, the external experts came from business consultant Siddall & Co. and the economic research center Prognos based in Basel; later, the experts came from consultancy company Schlegel & Partner in Weinheim and the University of Mannheim.
60 Cf. Gesellschafterbrief, 2011, p. 43 ff., in: Corporate Archives 3/10841.
61 Cf. ibid.
62 Cf. ibid.
63 Cf. Strategy Review 2004 Instructions, in: Corporate Archives 3/11076 as well as Lecture by Dr. Hans J. Barth "Weltwirtschaftliche Entwicklungsperspektiven bis 2020" at the Management Board meeting on January 21, 2004, in: Corporate Archives 3/07634.
64 Cf. Gesellschafterbrief, 2011, p. 43 ff., in: Corporate Archives 3/10841; Protokoll der Sitzung der Unternehmensleitung vom 4. Oktober 2011, in: Corporate Archives 3/10750 as well as Documents for the F&Co Strategy Review 2007, in: Corporate Archives 3/11077.
65 As an interim step, an attempt was made to combine the megatrends with the Green Areas by organizing them in the five categories of Energy, Excellence, Efficiency, Esprit and Exploitation of Trends – known as the 5E strategy. Cf. Documents for the F&Co Strategy Review 2007, in: Corporate Archives 3/11077.
66 Cf. Böttcher, 2012, p. 23–25 as well as "Bei Trends ganz vorn", in: Freudenberg Magazin, 2/2012, p. 30–31.
67 Cf. Unterlagen zur Sitzung der Unternehmensleitung vom 4. Oktober 2011, in: Corporate Archives 3/10750 as well as History Brochure, 2019, p. 25. The founding of the new Business Groups was preceded by several strategic acquisitions resulting from the 2004 Green Areas. In the oil and gas segment, FNGP acquired Imperial Rubber and Urethane Corporation in Nisku, Canada, in 2002, and Tetralene, United States, in 2008. Cf. "Freudenberg-NOK GP kauft Zulieferer für Öl- und Gasindustrie", in: Freudenberg Magazin, 3/2006, p. 11 as well as Freudenberg Portal News of June 19, 2008, in: Corporate Archives 3/09102. In the medical technology sector, FNGP initially acquired Jenline Industries Ltd. in Gloucester, MA, United States, in 2004, followed by the acquisition of Helix Medical LLC in Carpinteria, California, United States, in 2006. Cf. "FNGP kauft

Flüssigelastomerhersteller Jenline Industries", in: Freudenberg Magazin, 4/2004, p. 8 as well as "Verstärkung bei Medizintechnik", in: Freudenberg Magazin, 24/2006, p. 9. In the vibration technology sector, Freudenberg Seals and Vibration Control Technology acquired all the shares in Schwab Schwingungstechnik and in Freudenberg Schwab GmbH from its long-standing joint venture partner Schwab Holding AG in 2010. Cf. "Schienenfahrzeugbereich wird ausgebaut", in: Freudenberg Magazin, 3/2010, p. 6.
68 In the chemical sector, Capol GmbH in Elmshorn was acquired in 2013. In the same year, Freudenberg Filtration Technologies acquired the British filter manufacturer Aquabio Limited registered in Worcestershire, England. Cf. Freudenberg Portal News of March 12, 2013 and August 8, 2013, in: Corporate Archives 3/09107.
69 Cf. Documents for the F&Co Strategy Review 2010, in: Corporate Archives 3/11078.
70 Cf. Hoch, 2008a, p. 18–19 as well as "Organisation, Strategie, Initiativen. Die Aufgaben des GET", in: Freudenberg Magazin, 4/2008, p. 20–21.
71 Cf. Buchta-Noack, 2013, p. 25; Protokoll der UL-Klausur von 25.-26. September 2013, in: Corporate Archives 3/11128 as well as Letter from the Management Board to the management of the Business Groups on the roll-out of Focus 2.0 from November 2013, in: Corporate Archives 3/11124.
72 "DIALOG 2006: Die Vorbereitungen haben begonnen", in: Freudenberg Magazin, 1/2006, p. 43.
73 Schnoklake, 2015, p. 15.
74 Cf. Eröffnungsrede von Dr. Reinhart Freudenberg beim DIALOG 97 am 1. Juli 1997, in: Corporate Archives 3/04676.
75 Cf. Illius, 1997a, p. 3 as well as Abschlussrede von Peter Bettermann beim Dialog 97 am 2. Juli 1997, in: Corporate Archives 3/04676.
76 Zitiert nach: Fath, 1999a, p. 3.
77 Cf. ibid.
78 Cf. Diskussionspapier der Unternehmensleitung zum Strategy Review 2011 vom 15. Oktober 2010, in: Corporate Archives 3/11078.
79 This development was supported by organizational measures such as periodic Talent Management Conferences at all levels to present potential talents.
80 Greeting by Dr. Wolfram Freudenberg and Dr. Mohsen Sohi, in: Freudenberg Magazin, 4/2013, p. 3.
81 Cf. Baldauf, 2013, p. 12–13 as well as Leadership Development Program Documents, in: Corporate Archives 3/10803. The cascading leadership development program comprises the following trainings: Freudenberg Leadership Foundation (FLF), Freudenberg Leadership Development Program (FLDP), Individual Leadership Development Program (ILDP), Leading Leaders Development Program (LLDP), Operations Leadership Program (OLP), Business Leadership Program (BLP), Strategic Leadership Program (SLP). The SLP is for top management (Business Group Management Board members, Corporate Function Heads and Regional Representatives), the BLP is for the next level downstream.
82 Cf. Illius, 2002, p. 16–17. as well as Important developments in the Bettermann era on 1 March 2012, in: Corporate Archives 3/09011.
83 Cf. Important developments in the Bettermann era on 1 March 2012, in: Corporate Archives 3/09011; Letter from the Management Board to the management of the Business Groups, dated February 26, 2003, in: Corporate Archives 3/08618 as well as Orians, 2002, p. 11. The yardstick selected was the number of reported accidents per 1,000 employees.
84 Zitiert nach: Hoch/Orians, 2006, p. 5.
85 Cf. Hoch, 2011, p. 18–25.
86 Cf. Gesellschafterbrief, 2011, p. 45, in: Corporate Archives 3/10841.
87 Quoted from: Buchta-Noack, 2013a, p. 14.
88 Cf. Gesellschafterbrief, 2011, p. 43 ff., in: Corporate Archives 3/10841.
89 Cf. ibid.
90 Cf. Buchta-Noack, 2013a, p. 14 as well as to the Compass benchmark study: Documents on the Compass project for the closed-door meeting of the Management Board from January 22-23, 2013, in: Corporate Archives 3/11154.
91 Cf. Protokoll der Sitzung des Gesellschafterausschusses vom 11. Januar 2011, in: Corporate Archives 3/11122; Protokoll und Unterlagen zur Sitzung der Unternehmensleitung vom 16. März 2011, in: Corporate Archives 3/11123 as well as Baldauf, 2012, p. 12.

92 Cf. Gesellschafterbrief, 2011, p. 43 ff., in: Corporate Archives 3/10841; Buchta-Noack, 2013a, p. 14 as well as letter from the Management Board to the management of the Business Groups on the roll-out of Focus 2.0 from November 2013, in: Corporate Archives 3/11124.
93 Cf. Documents on the work and composition of the boards of the Business Groups as well as on the responsibilities of the Management Board according to Focus, in: Corporate Archives 3/07639; Buchta-Noack, 2013, p. 25 as well as Communication documents for the roll-out of Focus 2.0 in the Business Groups, in: Corporate Archives 3/11124.
94 Letter from the Management Board to the management of the Business Groups on the roll-out of Focus 2.0 from November 2013, in: Corporate Archives 3/11124.
95 Cf. Curriculum vitae of Mohsen Sohi, in: Corporate Archives 3/11125.
96 Cf. Protokoll der UL-Klausur von 4.-5. Juli 2012, in: Corporate Archives 3/11126 as well as Protokoll der Sitzung der Unternehmensleitung vom 13. Mai 2013, in: Corporate Archives 3/11127.
97 Quoted from: Buchta-Noack, 2013a, p. 14.
98 Cf. ibid, p. 14–15.
99 Cf. Buchta-Noack, 2013, p. 23.
100 Cf. Documents on the work and composition of the boards of the Business Groups as well as on the responsibilities of the Management Board according to Focus, in: Corporate Archives 3/07639; Buchta-Noack, 2013, p. 25; Communication documents for the roll-out of Focus 2.0 in the Business Groups, in: Corporate Archives 3/11124 as well as Protokoll der UL-Klausur von 25.-26. September 2013, in: Corporate Archives 3/11128.
101 Cf. Documents on the Focus 2.0 project, in: 3/11129.
102 Cf. Buchta-Noack, 2013, p. 23.
103 Cf. Buchta-Noack, 2013a, p. 15; Baldauf, 2014, p. 20 as well as Documents on the Focus 2.0 project, Subproject: Functional Responibilities, 7/2013–4/2014, in: Corporate Archives 3/11129.
104 Cf. ibid.
105 Cf. Gesellschafterbrief, 2014, in: Corporate Archives 3/09520.
106 The return on sales continue on an upward trend, reaching 9.8 percent in 2016. Cf. Gesellschafterbrief, 2016, in: Corporate Archives 3/09522.
107 Mohsen Sohi quoted in: Schnoklake, 2015, p. 17.
108 Cf. Buchta-Noack, 2013a, p. 15.
109 Cf. Böttcher, 2015, p. 19–21.
110 Quoted in: Böttcher, 2015a, p. 18.
111 Ibid.
112 Cf. Böttcher, 2015, p. 20.
113 Cf. "Die neue Positionierung von Freudenberg auf einem Blick", in: Freudenberg Magazin, 2/2015, p. 22–23.
114 "Das Look & Feel der globalen Marke", in: Freudenberg Magazin, 2/2015, p. 26–28, hier p. 26.
115 Schnoklake, 2015, p. 22–23.
116 Cf. Böttcher, 2015, p. 21.
117 Cf. History of the Freudenberg Logo: History Brochure, 2019, p. 30–31 as well as Horchler, 2015a, p. 46.
118 Schnoklake, 2017, p. 19.
119 Some 30 employees from various Business Groups, organizations and world regions were supported by trend and foresight specialists from Z_punkt The Foresight Company. Cf. hereto "Zukunft im Expertenblick", in: Freudenberg Magazin, 1/2017, p. 18 as well as Schnoklake, 2017, p. 19.
120 "Das Ergebnis von Odyssey 1.0", in: Freudenberg Magazin, 1/2017, p. 23.
121 Cf. ibid. as well as "Von der Science Fiction zur konkreten Umsetzung", in: Freudenberg Magazin, 1/2017, p. 24.
122 Cf. Schnoklake, 2017, p. 23. Similar to the buy-and-build strategy, the bolt-on acquisition strategy in essence relates to the further development of existing business. In terms of the bolt-on strategy, "this is achieved by expanding the portfolio through selective, targeted acquisitions in order to close identified technology gaps and develop access to new markets." Cf. Geschäftsbericht, 2018, in: Corporate Archives 3/10709.
123 Cf. Geschäftsberichte, 2020–2022, in: Corporate Archives 3/11046, Corporate Archives 3/11046 und Corporate Archives 3/11070.
124 Cf. Sinz, 2008, p. 120 ff.

125 Cf. as regards the definition of digitalization, also Müller-Brehm/Otto/Puntschuh, 2020, pp. 4–5.
126 According to the website nature.com, the semiconductor industry will recognize in March 2016 that Moore's Law can no longer be met. On this basis, chips will not necessarily become faster, but there will continue to be progress and efficiency will continue to be maximized. Cf. Schanze, 2016. – In contrast: "Intel CEO Pat Gelsinger believes that Moore's Law is by no means obsolete. Thanks to innovative production technology, the rule that the number of transistors will double every two years will continue to apply – especially, of course, for Intel chips." Cf. Quandt, 2021.
127 Cf. Sinz, 2008, p. 195–197.
128 The "year 2000 problem," describes the problems arising in connection with the changeover to the date of January 1, 2000 at the turn of the millennium. At that time, computer systems only processed the last two digits of the year and the "19" was added by the system automatically in the background in the course of processing. As a result of the "millennium bug" there was therefore a risk that computer systems would indicate the year 2000 as the year 1900. This could have resulted in many systems crashing. Cf. also Patalong, 2007.
129 For example, the products "inoway" and "EasyWork". Cf. Gesellschafterbrief, 1998, p. 9 f., in: Corporate Archives 3/05478.
130 Cf. Gesellschafterbrief, 2001, in: Corporate Archives 3/07208 as well as "Freudenberg IT übernimmt 75 Prozent an Systemhaus ADICOM", in: Marktplatz, 6/2001, p. 4.
131 Cf. Gesellschafterbrief, 1. Halbjahr 2004, p. 15, in: Corporate Archives 3/07208.
132 Cf. Gesellschafterbriefe, 2002–2004, in: Corporate Archives 3/07208.
133 Cf. Gesellschafterbrief, 1. Halbjahr 2005, p. 26, in: Corporate Archives 3/07892.
134 Cf. Gesellschafterbrief, 2007, p. 26 f., in: Corporate Archives 3/08977.
135 Recognized as the "most successful German IT spin-off" by Pierre Audoin Consultants (PAC), the market analysis company for the software and IT services industry. Cf. Gesellschafterbrief, 1. Halbjahr 2008, p. 25, in: Corporate Archives 3/08008.
136 Cf. Gesellschafterbrief, 2009, p. 30, in: Corporate Archives 3/08628.
137 Cf. Gesellschafterbrief, 1. Halbjahr 2010, p. 29, in: Corporate Archives 3/08663.
138 Cf. Gesellschafterbrief, 2011, p. 32, in: Corporate Archives 3/10841. The losses, which were certainly dramatic for FIT, were mainly the result of a major outsourcing product for DWP Bank. As a result of inadequate contract management and process deficiencies, suppliers were not included or not adequately included in the supply chain. This resulted in considerable additional cost to FIT. Cf. Protokoll der Sitzung der Unternehmensleitung vom 17. Februar 2011, in: Corporate Archives 3/10694.
139 Cf. Gesellschafterbrief, 1. Halbjahr 2012, p. 22, in: Corporate Archives 3/11130. The low margin services which were discontinued were the operation of workplace systems and the operation of telecommunication networks.
140 Cf. Gesellschafterbrief, 2012, p. 54, in: Corporate Archives 3/11130.
141 One of the core competences of FIT concerns Manufacturing Execution Systems, i.e. the computerization of manufacturing technology and logistics in machine-to-machine communication. Cf. Gesellschafterbrief, 1. Halbjahr 2013, p. 39, in: Corporate Archives 3/10942.
142 Cf. Gesellschafterbrief, 1. Halbjahr 2015, p. 35, in: Corporate Archives 3/09521.
143 Cf. Gesellschafterbrief, 2014, p. 48 f., in: Corporate Archives 3/09520.
144 Cf. Gartner-Studie "Future Market Strategy and Opportunities for Freudenberg IT" vom 16. Dezember 2016, in: Corporate Archives 3/11045 as well as Documents on the sale of the FIT, in: Corporate Archives 3/11045.
145 Cf. Genehmigungsantrag des Vorstands beim Aufsichtsrat zum Verkauf der Freudenberg IT vom 11. Januar 2019, in: Corporate Archives 3/11045 as well as Press release and press review on the sale of Freudenberg IT, in: Corporate Archives 3/0088 und Corporate Archives 3/11053
146 Cf. Handelsblatt Research Institute Benchmarking Study vom 28. Oktober 2020, in: Corporate Archives 3/11044.
147 Cf. Gesellschafterbrief, 1. Halbjahr 2017, p. 3 und p. 40, in: Corporate Archives 3/10132.
148 Cf. Gesellschafterbriefe, 1. Halbjahr 2018, p. 3 und 2018, p. 9, in: Corporate Archives 3/10734.
149 Cf. "2.600 m² Zukunft: Bau eines neuen Ausbildungszentrums in Weinheim", in: Freudenberg Magazin, 2/2016, p. 8 as well as Fath, 2018, p. 3.
150 Cf. Muschelknautz, 2018, p. 6.
151 Cf. "2.600 m² Zukunft: Bau eines neuen Ausbildungszentrums in Weinheim", in: Freudenberg Magazin, 2/2016, p. 8; Muschelknautz, 2018, p. 6 as well as Propp, 2018, p. 9.

152 Illius, 2018, p. 2.
153 Cf. "Fit für die Arbeitswelt der Zukunft", Presseinformation vom 22. März 2018, in: Corporate Archives 3/11131.
154 Cf. Ausbildungsbroschüre "Industrie 4.0 – Qualifizierung für die Fabrik der Zukunft", in: Corporate Archives 3/11131.
155 Cf. Handelsblatt Research Institute, Digital Strength Report 2019 – The digital maturity matrix & individual company assessments vom 1. März 2019, in: Corporate Archives 3/11043.
156 "Mit der Familie gemeinsam die Zukunft gestalten", Speech by Martin Wentzler at DIALOG 2018, in: Freudenberg Magazin, 3/2018, p. 26–27, here p. 27.
157 Cf. Baldauf, 2020, p. 29 as well as Handelsblatt Research Institute Benchmarking Study vom 28. Oktober 2020, in: Corporate Archives 3/11044.
158 Cf. Schultens/Wagener, 2020, p. 42.
159 Cf. Geschäftsbericht, 2021, p. 66, in: Corporate Archives 3/11047.
160 Cf. Schultens/Wagener, 2020, p. 43.
161 Cf. Fath, 2020, p. 52–53.
162 Cf. Internal paper on the status of digitalization at Freudenberg Chemical Specialities in 2020, in: Corporate Archives 3/11044.
163 "So kommen Dichtungen ins Industrie-4.0-Zeitalter", in: Process 11–12/2022, p. 15.
164 Ibid.
165 Cf. ibid; Fath, 2019, p. 53; "Mehr als dicht: Dichtungsexperte mit Lust auf Zukunft", in: Process 11–12/2022, p. 10–13, here p. 11–12; "Wartungskonzepte aus dem digitalen Labor", in: cav. Chemie-Anlagen + Verfahren, 17. August 2021, p. 12 as well as Müller, 2022, p. 84.
166 Cf. Fath, 2019, p. 52–53 as well as "Mehr als dicht: Dichtungsexperte mit Lust auf Zukunft", in: Process 11–12/2022, p. 10–13, here p. 12.
167 Cf. "Wartungskonzepte aus dem digitalen Labor", in: cav. Chemie-Anlagen + Verfahren, 17. August 2021, p. 12 as well as "Mehr als dicht: Dichtungsexperte mit Lust auf Zukunft", in: Process 11–12/2022, p. 10–13, here p. 11–12.
168 Cf. Geschichtsbroschüre, 2019, p. 20.
169 Cf. "Neuartiger Simmerring schlägt bei Undichtigkeiten Alarm", in: Maschinen Markt – Das Industriemagazin, 16/2005, p. 16, in: Corporate Archives 3/07434.
170 Cf. Fath, 2022, p. 6.
171 Cf. Geschäftsbericht, 2020, p. 88, in: Corporate Archives 3/11046.
172 Cf. Fath, 2022a, p. 6.
173 Cf. Rzepka/Wagener, 2019, p. 33–35.
174 Cf. Fath, 2019a, p. 48–49.
175 Cf. Documents on the TANNER program, in: Corporate Archives 3/07082 und Corporate Archives 3/07765; Illius, 1999, p. 1 as well as Geschäftsbericht, 2020, p. 33, in: Corporate Archives 311046.
176 Cf. Burkhardt, 1999, p. 9.
177 Cf. Management Newsletter on the initiative We all take care of 20 March 2003, in: Corporate Archives 3/08618 as well as Illius, 2002, p. 16–17.
178 Cf. Geschäftsberichte, 2002, 2014 und 2021, in: Corporate Archives 3/07910, Corporate Archives 3/10715 und Corporate Archives 3/11047.
179 Cf. Hoch, 2005, p. 10.
180 Cf. Geschäftsbericht, 2018, p. 30, in: Corporate Archives 3/10710.
181 Cf. Press release of 13 December 2006 as well as Information brochures from 2006 and 2007, in: Corporate Archives 3/08055 as well as Fath, 2006b, p. 5.
182 Cf. Documents on Ke De Bao primary school, in: Corporate Archives 3/08943 as well as Mao, 2009, p. 6. Since Ke De Bao primary school reopened, numerous Freudenberg employees have taken part in the "Love Beyond Donation" activities to support the pupils. Freudenberg has been recognized with several awards for this commitment, including the "Best Responsible Brand Award" from the China Charity Festival, one of the top charity events in China. Cf. Schnoklake, 2015a, p. 43.
183 Cf. Geschäftsbericht, 2018, p. 30, in: Corporate Archives 3/10710.
184 Cf. Hoch, 2011a, p. 6.
185 Cf. Schnoklake/Zins, 2015, p. 26–27 as well as "Bildung und Umweltschutz", in: Marktplatz, 6/2015, p. 1 und p. 7. Two of the first projects to be given support were "The Greening of Detroit"

for a greener and healthier city, and "Beyond Basics", also in Detroit, a project to further the literacy of children in under-resourced communities. Five further e2 initiatives were launched one year later, four in the United States and one in Brazil. Cf. Baumann, 2016, p. 48–49.
186 Cf. Geschäftsbericht, 2018, p. 29, in: Corporate Archives 3/10710 as well as Geschäftsbericht, 2021, p. 53, in: Corporate Archives 3/11047.
187 Cf. "Freudenberg: Unternehmen und Mitarbeiter spenden Millionen", in: Rhein-Neckar-Zeitung, 15. April 2016, p. 4.
188 Cf. Press release "Freudenberg unterstützt 'Wir zusammen'-die Integrations-Initiative der deutschen Wirtschaft für Flüchtlinge" of 12 February 2016, in: Corporate Archives 3/11051 as well as Reporting in the Mannheimer Morgen of 14 September 2016, in: Corporate Archives 3/0085.
189 Cf. "Junge Geflüchtete starten Praktikum", in: Marktplatz, 6/2016, p. 11.
190 Cf. Illius, 2017, p. 1 und p. 9; Illius, 2019, p. 1 und p. 6 as well as "Vom Gewürzhändler zum Maschinen- und Anlagenführer", in: Marktplatz, 3/2022, p. 16.
191 Cf. Geschäftsbericht, 2021, in: Corporate Archives 3/11047.
192 Cf. Freudenberg Portal News zur Ukraine-Hilfe, in: Corporate Archives 3/11132 as well as Fath, 2022b, p. 15.
193 Cf. "Hilfe für die Türkei und Syrien", in: Freudenberg Magazin online 2023, in: Corporate Archives 3/11049 as well as "Beben in Türkei und Syrien: Zahl der Toten steigt auf mehr als 50.000", in: Tagesschau.de, February 24, 2023, https://www.tagesschau.de/ausland/asien/erdbeben-tote-tuerkei-syrien-101.html, retrieved on 02.03.2023.
194 Cf. Müller, 2021.
195 Cf. Niemann, 2019, p. 44–46.
196 Merkel was established in Hanover in 1899 by Heinrich Martin Merkel, who had completed an apprenticeship with Burgmann of Dresden (stuffing box packings). The company relocated to Hamburg in 1903, as a result of its international orientation and 10 years later it became an "asbestos and rubber plant". Cf. Newspaper reports on the sale, in: Corporate Archives 3/04792.
197 Cf. Merkel Freudenberg Fluidtechnik Leadcenter Hydraulik, Strategic orientation up to 2004 from February 1999, in: Corporate Archives 3/07629.
198 For the 1998 financial year, the Hamburg company recorded a profit of 77 million DM. Cf. Jahresabschluß zum 31. Dezember 1998 Merkel Freudenberg Fluidtechnik GmbH Hamburg, in: Corporate Archives 3/09831.
199 The European locations were: Hamburg (Lead Center Hydraulics), Schwalmstadt (Lead Center Mobile and Standard Hydraulics, Moldings), Reichelsheim (PTFE Automobile), Dublin, Ireland (Lead Center Packings), Kvistgard, Denmark (Lead Center PTFE) and Auray, France (partner production hydraulics). cf. Fath, 1998b, p. 1–2.
200 Cf. Fath, 1998b, p. 1.
201 Friedrich Nuttelmann of the Hydraulics Lead Center Hydraulik Hamburg quoted after: ibid, p. 2.
202 Cf. Geschäftsbericht, 2010, p. 16, in: Corporate Archives 3/08896; Fath, 1998b, p. 2; "Maritimes Luxushotel kreuzt auf hoher See", in: Freudenberg Magazin, 2/2001, p. 11 as well as Hoch, 2009, p. 4.
203 Cf. Unterlagen und Protokoll der Sitzung der Unternehmensleitung am 28. April 1995; in: Corporate Archives 3/07582 und Corporate Archives 3/10905.
204 Press release of 6 April 1995, in: Corporate Archives 3/07582. Peter Bettermann had already established contact with Phoenix AG in 1994 with a view to exploring "possible cooperation in the field of engine mounts, the combination of small series and processes and purchasing cooperation." Cf. Besuchsbericht Phoenix AG vom 20. April 1994 von Peter Bettermann, in: Corporate Archives 3/07582.
205 Cf. Kooperationsvertrag zwischen Phoenix und Freudenberg vom 17. April 1995; in: Corporate Archives 3/07582.
206 Cf. ibid; Press release of 6 April 1995; in: Corporate Archives 3/07582 as well as Unterlagen zur Sitzung der Unternehmensleitung am 28. April 1995; in: Corporate Archives 3/07582.
207 Protokoll zur Sitzung der Unternehmensleitung am 28. April 1995; in: Corporate Archives 3/07582. Phoenix products were manufactured under licence in Turkey, and Phoenix intended to acquire a stake in the production company.
208 UL-Vorlage zur Sitzung am 28. April 1995; in: Corporate Archives 3/07582.
209 "Freudenberg und Phoenix – Zusammenarbeit vereinbart", in: Der Freudenberger, 6/1995, p. 1.

210 Cf. Entwurf eines Rahmenvertrags für ein Gemeinschaftsunternehmen zwischen Phoenix und Freudenberg vom 17. April 1997, in: Corporate Archives 3/07582.
211 Cf. "Zulieferer unter Fusionsdruck", in: Hamburger Abendblatt, 30. April 1999, in: Corporate Archives 3/05362; "Joint Venture mit Freudenberg", in: Handelsblatt, 30. April 1999, in: Corporate Archives 3/05362 as well as Geschäftsbericht, 1999, in: Corporate Archives 3/10985.
212 "10 Jahre Vibracoustic", in: Corporate Archives 3/08913. Initially, the Vibration Control Industry Business Group was part of the Freudenberg Seals and Vibration Technology Business Area. Later, it was integrated in the Freudenberg Schwab Vibration Control Business Group. Cf. Geschäftsbericht, 2012, p. 7, in: Corporate Archives 3/10711.
213 Cf. "10 Jahre Vibracoustic"; in: Corporate Archives 3/08913.
214 Cf. Unterlagen der Sitzung der Unternehmensleitung vom 18. Oktober 2004, in: Corporate Archives 3/10565; Geschäftsbericht, 2004, in: Corporate Archives 3/07911; Gesellschafterbrief, 2004, in: Corporate Archives 3/07208 as well as on the foreign invasion clause, § 14 of the framework agreement for the establishment of the joint venture Vibracoustic, in: Corporate Archives 3/06884.
215 Cf. Geschäftsberichte, 2005 und 2008, in: Corporate Archives 3/07912 und Corporate Archives 3/08158 as well as Gesellschafterbriefe, 2008 und 1. Halbjahr 2009, in: Corporate Archives 3/08114 und Corporate Archives 3/08939.
216 Cf. Geschäftsbericht, 2005, in: Corporate Archives 3/07912.
217 Cf. Geschäftsberichte, 2010 und 2012, in: Corporate Archives 3/08896 und Corporate Archives 3/10711.
218 Cf. Geschäftsbericht, 2011, in: Corporate Archives 3/08950 as well as Gesellschafterbrief, 2012, in: Corporate Archives 3/11130.
219 Cf. Geschäftsbericht, 2005, in: Corporate Archives 3/07912; Brochure "LESS: Low Emission Sealing Solutions, June 2009, in: Corporate Archives 3/11133 as well as "LESS ist das neue More", in: 85 Jahre Simmerring, online available at: https://www.fst.com/simmerring/, retrieved on 28.02.2023. In technical terms, ESS is a springless Simmerring combining the sturdy seal mechanism of a PTFE sleeve with the reduced friction of an elastomeric seal.
220 Cf. "Kleiner, aber stärker", in: Sealing World, Dezember 2009, p. 4; "LESS: Weniger ist mehr", in: Sealing World, December 2009, p. 4 as well as Geschäftsbericht, 2008, in: Corporate Archives 3/08158.
221 Cf. Geschäftsbericht, 2013, in: Corporate Archives 3/10713 as well as brochure "Low Emission Sealing Solutions. LESS is more. More Responsibility", August 2016, in: Corporate Archives 3/11133. The Levitex seal has a slide ring interacting with a counter-ring to form a cushion of air, resulting in up to 90 percent less frictional loss than with a conventional crankshaft seal ring. Because there is less wear, the service life of the seal is also extended. Cf. Geschäftsbericht, 2013, in: Corporate Archives 3/10713.
222 Cf. Geschäftsbericht, 2019, in: Corporate Archives 3/10984; brochure "LESS: Low Emission Sealing Solutions", June 2009, in: Corporate Archives 3/11133 as well as Corporate Archives "Low Emission Sealing Solutions. LESS is more. More Responsibility", August 2016, in: Corporate Archives 3/11133.
223 Cf. Geschäftsbericht, 2010, in: Corporate Archives 3/08896 as well as Geschäftsbericht, 2011, in: Corporate Archives 3/08950.
224 The company was then renamed Schneegans Freudenberg GmbH.
225 Cf. Geschäftsbericht, 2012, in: Corporate Archives 3/10711 as well as Fath, 2013, p. 8.
226 Cf. Geschäftsbericht, 2012, in: Corporate Archives 3/10711.
227 Cf. Geschäftsbericht, 2011, in: Corporate Archives 3/08950.
228 Cf. Geschäftsbericht, 2012, in: Corporate Archives 3/10711.
229 Cf. Press releases on the planned cooperation of January 18, 2011, in: Corporate Archives 3/0080 as well as Press Releases February 1 and 2, 2012, in: Corporate Archives 3/0081.
230 Cf. Geschäftsbericht, 2016, in: Corporate Archives 3/10719.
231 Cf. Protokoll der UL-Sitzung vom 22. Januar 1998, in: Corporate Archives 3/11028–2.
232 Vorlage für die UL-Sitzung am 22. Januar 1998: Kooperation des Geschäftsbereichs Schwingungstechnik Industrie mit der Phoenix AG unter Einbeziehung der Firma Schwab, p. 1, in: Corporate Archives 3/08853.
233 Ibid, p. 2.
234 Cf. signed Memorandum of Understanding between Schwab Holding AG and Freudenberg Dichtungs- und Schwingungstechnik KG dated January 27/28, 1999, in: Corporate Archives 3/06878.

235 Cf. Protokoll der UL-Sitzung vom 23. März 1999, in: Corporate Archives 3/11029–5.
236 Cf. Freudenberg Press Release, January 1, 2012, in: Corporate Archives 3/11155.
237 Cf. Geschäftsbericht, 2011, in: Corporate Archives 3/08950.
238 Cf. Press release Freudenberg Sealing Technologies from September 23, 2014, in: Corporate Archives 3/11155 as well as Geschäftsbericht, 2014, in: Corporate Archives 3/10715.
239 Cf. Gesellschafterbrief, 2011, p. 21, in: Corporate Archives 3/10841.
240 The elastomer compound was marketed under the name of POLAR-FLEX 215. Cf. Li, 2015, p. 25.
241 Cf. Geschäftsberichte, 2014 und 2016, in: Corporate Archives 3/10715 und Corporate Archives 3/10719 as well as Press releases on the sale of Schwab Vibration Control, in: Corporate Archives 3/11050.
242 Cf. FNST press release dated October 17, 2013, in: Corporate Archives 3/0082; Geschäftsbericht, 2015, in: Corporate Archives 3/10717; "Im Elektromotor funkt's nicht mehr", in: Fokusthema E-Mobilität, online available at: https://www.fst.com/de/corporate/magazin/e-mobilitaet/interview-bock-morgenstern/, retrieved on 15.03.2023 as well as "Getriebedichtung mit integriertem Blitzableiter", in: 85 Jahre Simmerring, online available at: https://www.fst.com/simmerring/, retrieved on 28.02.2023.
243 Cf. Geschäftsbericht, 2018, in: Corporate Archives 3/10709.
244 Cf. Geschäftsbericht, 2017, in: Corporate Archives 3/10721; "DIAvent® – robust, wiederverschließbar, sicher", in: "DIAvent® – das vielseitige Druckausgleichselement für Lithium-Ionen-Batterien", online available at: https://www.fst.com/de/sealing/produkte/spezialdichtungen/diavent/#ProductDetails, retrieved on 22.02.2023 as well as Fath, 2021, p. 8.
245 Cf. Geschäftsbericht, 2018, in: Corporate Archives 3/10709.
246 Cf. Hoch, 2010, p. 27 as well as Geschäftsberichte, 2014 und 2019–2021, in: Corporate Archives 3/10715, Corporate Archives 3/10984, Corporate Archives 3/11046 und Corporate Archives 3/11047.
247 Cf. Geschäftsbericht, 2021, in: Corporate Archives 3/11047.
248 Cf. "Abspeckplan für Autos: Wie können Vliesstoffe dem Leichtbau Flügel verleihen?", in: Performance Materials News & Storys, online available at: https://www.freudenberg-pm.com/Storys/Lightweight_construction, retrieved on 15.03.2023 as well as "Leichtbau-Spezial: die Unterbodenkonstruktion", in: "Zukunftsweisende technische Textilien", online available at: https://www.freudenberg-pm.com/Innovationen/Leichtbau-Spezial-Unterbodenkonstruktion, retrieved on 15.03.2023.
249 Cf. "Leichtbau-Spezial: Unsichtbare Lärmschlucker", in: "Zukunftsweisende technische Textilien", online available at: https://www.freudenberg-pm.com/Innovationen/Leichtbau-Spezial-Unsichtbare-Laermschlucker, retrieved on 15.03.2023 as well as "Transaktion abgeschlossen: Filc ist Teil der Freudenberg Gruppe", Freudenberg Portal News from January 14, 2020, in: Corporate Archives 3/11116.
250 Cf. "Was Schmierstoffe im Antriebsstrang leisten", online available at: https://www.klueber.com/de/de/industrie-loesungen/industrie/schmierstoffe-automobilindustrie-1, retrieved on 30.03.2023 as well as "Spezialschmierstoffe für neue Antriebskonzepte", online available at: https://www.klueber.com/de/de/industrie-loesungen/industrie/automotive/spezialschmierstoffe-fuer-das-automobil-rund-um-den-antriebsstrang/, retrieved on 30.03.2023.
251 Cf. "Automobilindustrie / Transportwesen", online available at: https://chemtrend.com/industry/automobilindustrie-transportwesen/?lang=de, retrieved on 30.03.2023.
252 Cf. Horchler, 2021, p. 71.
253 Cf. Horchler, 2021, p. 69–71; "Was hat Freudenberg mit der Brennstoffzelle zu tun?", in: Freudenberg Forschungsdienste im Dialog, 2/1996, p. 8–9, hier p. 9 as well as Fuel Cell activities at Freudenberg & FNGP, Presentation for the Management Board Meeting on 13 March 2001, in: Corporate Archives 3/10502.
254 Cf. "Was hat Freudenberg mit der Brennstoffzelle zu tun?", in: Freudenberg Forschungsdienste im Dialog, 2/1996, p. 8–9, hier p. 9.
255 Cf. Horchler, 2021, p. 69 as well as Hasenhütl, 2016, p. 16.
256 Niemann, 2019.
257 Cf. "Freudenberg Forschungsdienste werden 1998 selbständige KG", in: Freudenberg Forschungsdienste im Dialog, 3/1997, p. 1; Zillmann, 2011, p. 5 as well as Horchler, 2021, p. 69.
258 Cf. Protokoll der UL-Sitzung vom 11. Dezember 2001, in: Corporate Archives 3/10519.
259 Cf. Illius, 2002a, p. 18; "Die F&E-Förderung durch die EU", in: FNT Info, 2/2007, p. 8–15, here

p. 13; Protokoll der Unternehmensleitungssitzung vom 9. Dezember 2002, in: Corporate Archives 3/10538 as well as Horchler, 2021, p. 70.
260 Cf. Horchler, 2021, p. 70; "Neue Brennstoffzellen-Dichtungen", in: Freudenberg Magazin, 1/2004, p. 32 as well as Protokoll der Unternehmensleitungssitzung vom 9. Dezember 2002, in: Corporate Archives 3/10538.
261 "Dichtungen für PEM-Brennstoffzellen", in: FFD im Dialog, 3/2004, p. 8–9, here p. 9.
262 Cf. ibid.
263 Cf. Hoch, 2005b, p. 10.
264 Horchler, 2021, p. 70.
265 "Interview mit Herrn Dr. Martin Stark", in: FFD im Dialog, 2/2005, p. 4–5, hier p. 5.
266 Cf. Hoch, 2008b, p. 37. Only a small series of Mercedes f-cell vehicles was produced and the model was discontinued in 2020.
267 Cf. Baldauf, 2011, p. 8. The F-CELL World Drive was one of the events celebrating the 125th anniversary of the invention of the motor car.
268 Cf. Hoch, 2009a, p. 7.
269 The lead center liquid elastomers for special seal products had been part of Lederer of Öhringen, a company specializing in liquid silicone seals, which had become a wholly-owned subsidiary of Freudenberg in 2002 – 2003.
270 Horchler, 2021, p. 70. See also: Fath, 2010, p. 38.
271 Cf. Faas, 2017, p. 46–47.
272 Cf. Hasenhütl, 2016, p. 7.
273 Cf. Factsheet Innovations at the Annual Press Conference on April 10, 2019, in: Corporate Archives 3/10708.
274 Cf. Illius, 2018a, S 7 as well as Illius, 2020, p. 5.
275 Cf. Faas, 2017, p. 46–47 as well as Illius, 2018b, p. 7.
276 Cf. Horchler, 2021, p. 71; Questions and Answers for the Annual Press Conference 2018, in: Corporate Archives 3/11134 as well as Fath, 2018a, p. 54.
277 Freudenberg initially acquired 31.8 percent of the shares in XALT Energy in March 2018. At the beginning of 2019, the Freudenberg Sealing Technologies Business Group increased its stake to 50.1 percent. As the majority shareholder, Freudenberg acquired industrial control over XALT. Cf. "Freudenberg stärkt Kompetenz in Lithium-Ionen-Technologie", Press release of 4 February 2019, in: Corporate Archives 3/11053.
278 . These included battery components such as separators, EMI nonwovens for electromagnetic shielding, connectors, housing seals and heat shields, as well as fuel cell components and materials such as gas diffusion layers, seals, filters, humidifiers and lubricants.
279 Cf. Fath, 2018a, p. 54.
280 Cf. "Freudenberg stärkt Kompetenz in Lithium-Ionen-Technologie", Press release of 4 February 2019, in: Corporate Archives 3/11053.
281 Cf. "Neu von XALT Energy: Flacher Lithium-Ionen-Batteriepack für Nutzfahrzeuge", Press release of 17 October 2019, in: Corporate Archives 3/11068.
282 Cf. "New Partnership to Support Emission-Free Mobility in the U. p.", Press release of 26 November 2019, in: Corporate Archives 3/11068.
283 Apart from Freudenberg, the project consortium incudes Meyer Werft – the largest shipbuilder specializing in cruise ships –Lürssen Werft, the classification society DNV GL, the German Aerospace Center DLR, AIDA Cruises, represented by Carnival Maritime GmbH, besecke GmbH and EPEA GmbH.
284 Cf. "Brennstoffzellen für die Schifffahrt", Press release FST of 10 October 2019, in: Corporate Archives 3/11060.
285 Cf. "Für nachhaltiges Yachten", Press release of 15 June 2021, in: Corporate Archives 3/11062.
286 "Klimaneutral reisen", Press release of 10 November 2021, in: Corporate Archives 3/11062.
287 Cf. "Freudenberg-Batterien von XALT Energy treiben erste vollelektrische Fähre in Neuseeland an", Press release of 22 April 2021, in: Corporate Archives 3/11062 as well as "Wellington Gets the First Electric Ferry in the Southern Hemisphere", in: The Maritime Executive of 20 January 2022, online available at: https://maritime-executive.com/article/wellington-gets-the-first-electric-ferry-in-the-southern-hemisphere, retrieved on 24.03.2023.
288 FEPS was initially announced as Freudenberg Battery & Fuel Cell. Cf. "Freudenberg gründet neue

Geschäftsgruppe Battery & Fuel Cell", in: Freudenberg Magazin, 1/2022, p. 5 as well as Gesellschafterbrief, 1. Halbjahr 2022, in: Corporate Archives 3/11042.
289 Cf. Press release on the full XALT acquisition dated January 9, 2023, in: Corporate Archives 3/11068.
290 Cf. "Um Schiffslängen voraus", Press release of 8 September 2022, in: Corporate Archives 3/11056.
291 Ibid. Methanol is a simple alcohol that is liquid under normal ambient conditions and has around three times the volumetric energy density of liquefied hydrogen. As an important raw material for the chemical industry, climate-neutral methanol is characterized by proven manufacturing processes as well as good availability.
292 Cf. "Initial IMO GHG Strategy", in: International Maritime Organization, online available at: https://www.imo.org/en/MediaCentre/HotTopics/Pages/Reducing-greenhouse-gas-emissions-from-ships.aspx, retrieved on 29.09.2022.
293 Cf. "Um Schiffslängen voraus", Press release of 8 September 2022, in: Corporate Archives 3/11056.
294 "Wasserstoff statt Diesel", Press release 15 September 2022, in: Corporate Archives 3/11056.
295 Cf. ibid. as well as FEPS internal communication on the status of the HyFleet project of 24 October 2023, in: Corporate Archives 3/11152.
296 Cf. "Wasserstoff statt Diesel", Press release of 15 September 2022, in: Corporate Archives 3/11056.
297 Ibid.
298 Cf. Bujard, 2022, p. 5.
299 Cf. Böttcher, 2012, p. 22–25.
300 The polyamide spunbond nonwovens were marketed under the Lutrabon brand. Cf. Lauppe, 1978, p. 30.
301 Cf. Documents about medical products, in: Corporate Archives 3/05087, Corporate Archives 3/05477 und Corporate Archives 10/000764-0.
302 Cf. Protokoll und Unterlagen zur Sitzung der Unternehmensleitung vom 26. Juni 2001, in: Corporate Archives 3/10511.
303 The company was founded as a partnership in 1963 by its managing director Hermann Lederer. Converted into a limited liability company (GmbH) in 1975, Lederer with its workforce of 120 was one of the leading liquid silicone rubber processing companies in Europe until 2001. Cf. Protokoll und Unterlagen zur Sitzung der Unternehmensleitung vom 26. Juni 2001, in: Corporate Archives 3/10511.
304 2008 statistics: Global sales of medical products totaled 200 million euros, of which 42 % in the USA, 30 % in Europe 13 % in Japan and 15 % in the other world regions. Cf. Gausemeier, 2010, p. 39 f.
305 Annual growth of 7.5 % was forecast for the global medical technology market for the period 2005–2015, with the forecast for the USA even higher at 8 %. Cf. Langfristige Konjunkturaussichten 2007 bis 2015, Studie von Schlegel und Partner vom Januar 2007, p. 19 f., in: Corporate Archives 3/11073.
306 Cf. "FNGP kauft Flüssigelastomerhersteller Jenline Industries", in: Freudenberg Magazin, 4/2004, p. 8.
307 Cf. "Verstärkung bei Medizintechnik", in: Freudenberg Magazin, 4/2006, p. 9.
308 Cf. Unterlagen zur Sitzung der Unternehmensleitung am 26. September 2007, in: Corporate Archives 3/10618.
309 For comparison: The market for silicone components in 2006 had a volume of approx. US$ 345 million, the market for specially-designed thermoplastic components, on the other hand, had a volume of US$ 830 million. Cf. hereto Unterlagen zur Sitzung der Unternehmensleitung am 26. September 2007, in: Corporate Archives 3/10618 as well as Strategy presentation for the establishment of a medical division for the Management Board meeting on February 16, 2007, p. 191–193, in: Corporate Archives 3/11086.
310 Cf. Protokoll und Unterlagen zur Sitzung der Unternehmensleitung vom 26. September 2007, in: Corporate Archives 3/10618
311 Cf. Hoch, 2010a, p. 24; Press release "Vliesstoff mit besonderer Mission", published on Forschung-Entwicklung-online at November 12, 2014, in: Corporate Archives 3/0083 as well as Sales documents, in: Corporate Archives 3/11171.
312 Cf. Gausemeier, 2010, p. 3.
313 Cf. Protokoll der Sitzung der Unternehmensleitung vom 2. September 2008, p. 6, in: Corporate Archives 3/10635.
314 Cf. "Beteiligung an VistaMed", in: Freudenberg Magazin, 2/2010, p.4.

315 Cf. Geschäftsbericht, 2017, in: Corporate Archives 3/10721.
316 Cf. Fath, 2010a, p. 2.
317 Cf. Gausemeier, 2010, p. 3 und p. 9.
318 Cf. ibid, p.9.
319 Cf. ibid, p. 23.
320 Cf. Präsentation der Freudenberg New Technologies KG "Regenerative Medicine" vom 9. September 2011, p. 17 und p. 33, in: Corporate Archives 3/11072.
321 Cf. Geschäftsberichte, 2012–2013, in: Corporate Archives 3/10711 und Corporate Archives 3/10713.
322 From 2022, Cambus operated as Freudenberg Medical. Cf. Geschäftsbericht, 2022, in: Corporate Archives 3/11070.
323 Cf. Geschäftsbericht, 2016, in: Corporate Archives 3/10719.
324 Cf. Geschäftsbericht, 2018, in: Corporate Archives 3/10709.
325 Cf. Ganzer, 2019, p. 40–41.
326 Cf. Muschelknautz, 2021 as well as Bambi-Medical press release 23 May 2023, in: Corporate Archives 3/11156.
327 Cf. Geschäftsberichte, 2020–2022, in: Corporate Archives 3/11046, Corporate Archives 3/11047 und Corporate Archives 3/11070.
328 Cf. Protokoll der Sitzung der Unternehmensleitung vom 6. September 1996, in: Corporate Archives 3/11024-13 as well as Gesellschafterbrief, 1996, in: Corporate Archives 3/05393. Freudenberg Household Products started building up its own production capabilities in São Paulo, Brazil, in 1995. In light of poor business development in South America due to the financial crisis there (Brazilian Real crisis), sales in the country were already transferred to a local distributor in 1999 and the activities of the Business Group's own sales company were terminated. Cf. Vorlage zur Sitzung der Unternehmensleitung vom 27. Juni 1995, in: Corporate Archives 3/07511 as well as Protokoll zur Vorschausitzung der Unternehmensleitung vom 6. Dezember 1999, in: Corporate Archives 3/11029-15.
329 Cf. Protokoll der Sitzung der Sitzung der Unternehmensleitung vom 2. April 1993, in: Corporate Archives 3/07642 und Corporate Archives 3/10832.
330 For O'Cedar acquisition efforts cf. Minutes of management meetings of 24 November 1995, in: Corporate Archives 3/10917, vom 26. Januar 1996, in: Corporate Archives 3/11024-1 as well as of 29. März 1996, in: Corporate Archives 3/11024-5.
331 Cf. Protokolle der Sitzungen der Unternehmensleitung vom 19. September 1997 as well as vom 2. Dezember 1997, in: Corporate Archives 3/07646 as well as Geschäftsbericht, 1998, in: Corporate Archives 3/10983. The market presence was also expanded in neighboring Canada: A joint venture with the long-standing sales partner Atlantic Promotions was formed in 1999. The focus on the North American market therefore continued. Cf. Geschäftsbericht, 1999, in: Corporate Archives 3/10985.
332 Cf. Geschäftsberichte, 2000–2001, in: Corporate Archives 3/07909 as well as Curriculum vitae of Albert Pürzer, in: Corporate Archives 3/11157.
333 Cf. Protokoll der FHP-Borad Sitzung vom 26. November 2002, in: 3/11159.
334 Cf. Memorandum on the meeting of Albert Pürzer and Hans-Georg Franke of 22 February 2002, in: Corporate Archives 3/11158.
335 Cf. Unterlagen zur Sitzung der Unternehmensleitung am 11. Dezember 2003, in: Corporate Archives 3/11136.
336 Cf. Geschäftsbericht, 2003, in: Corporate Archives 3/07910 as well as "Haushaltsprodukte stärken US-Geschäft", in: Freudenberg Magazin, 4/2003, p. 10.
337 Cf. Unterlagen zur Sitzung der Unternehmensleitung am 11. Dezember 2003, in: Corporate Archives 3/11136 as well as Protokoll der FHP Board Sitzung vom 15. September 2003, in: Corporate Archives 3/11160.
338 Cf. Unterlagen zur Sitzung der Unternehmensleitung am 11. Dezember 2003, in: Corporate Archives 3/11136; Geschäftsbericht, 2004, in: Corporate Archives 3/07911 as well as Gesellschafterbrief, 2004, in: Corporate Archives 3/07208.
339 Cf. Geschäftsbericht, 1998, in: Corporate Archives 3/10983.
340 Cf. Geschäftsberichte, 2006 und 2009, in: Corporate Archives 3/07913 und Corporate Archives 3/08629.
341 Cf. Geschäftsberichte, 2011 und 2013, in: Corporate Archives 3/08950 und Corporate Archives

3/10713 as well as "Freudenberg stärkt Haushaltsgeschäft", Freudenberg Portal News of November 6, 2017, in: Corporate Archives 3/11162.
342 Cf. Geschäftsberichte, 2003 und 2004, in: Corporate Archives 3/07910 und Corporate Archives 3/07911.
343 Cf. "Gimi p. p. A. wird Teil der Freudenberg Gruppe", Freudenberg Portal News of September 1, 2016, in: Corporate Archives 3/11161.
344 Cf. Freudenberg Portal News of December 20, 2013, in: Corporate Archives 3/09107; "Perfekte Ergänzung", in: Freudenberg Magazin, 1/2014, p. 5 as well as Geschäftsberichte, 2013 und 2014, in: Corporate Archives 3/10713 und Corporate Archives 3/10715.
345 Cf. "Freudenberg investiert in Haushaltshandschuhe", Freudenberg Portal News of October 5, 2017, in: Corporate Archives 3/11162. The Playtex household gloves business was acquired from Edgewell Personal Care.
346 Cf. Geschäftsberichte, 2004 und 2005, in: Corporate Archives 3/07911 und Corporate Archives 3/07912.
347 Novolon's predecessor was the world's first microfiber all-purpose household cloth launched on international markets under the brand name of "vileda Microfaser Plus" from 2000. The cloth was based on the new Evolon microfiber technology developed by Freudenberg. Cf. Geschäftsberichte, 2001 and 2007, in: Corporate Archives 3/07909 and Corporate Archives 3/07949.
348 Cf. Geschäftsberichte, 2007 and 2008, in: Corporate Archives 3/07949 and Corporate Archives 3/08158.
349 Cf. Geschäftsbericht, 2011, in: Corporate Archives 3/08950.
350 Cf. "Vileda bringt Putzroboter auf den Markt", in: Presse Box Online of December 27, 2013, in: Corporate Archives 3/0083.
351 Cf. Geschäftsberichte, 2014–2015, in: Corporate Archives 3/10715 und Corporate Archives 3/10717.
352 Cf. "FHCS beendet Verbrauchergeschäft in China und Korea", Freudenberg Portal News of October 18, 2018, in: Corporate Archives 3/11163.
353 Cf. Geschäftsberichte, 1996 and 2022, in: Corporate Archives 3/05374 and Corporate Archives 3/11070.
354 Cf. Speech by Dr. Wilhelm Schmitt at the shareholders' meeting on June 30, 1990, in: Corporate Archives 3/10360.
355 Cf. "Der Sieger heißt Uli Umwelt", in: Der Freudenberger, 12/1990, p. 8.
356 Cf. "Alle Mitarbeiter sind gefordert, Umweltschutz wird zum wichtigen Unternehmensziel", in: Der Freudenberger, 7–8/1990, p. 2.
357 Cf. Speech by Dr. Wilhelm Schmitt at the shareholders' meeting on June 30, 1990, in: Corporate Archives 3/10360.
358 Cf. "Ein Blick zurück", in: Freudenberger, 2/2001, p. 28–31, hier p. 31.
359 Cf. Environmental and occupational health and safety at Freudenberg. Guidelines and Directives, version of March 1993, in: Corporate Archives 3/03403 as well as "Leitlinien zum Thema Umwelt- und Arbeitsschutz", in: Der Freudenberger, 7–8/1993, p. 5. The 1993 guideline was revised in 1996. Cf. hereto Environmental and occupational health and safety at Freudenberg. Guidelines and Directives, version of 1 January 1996, in: Corporate Archives 3/06191.
360 Cf. "Ein Blick zurück", in: Freudenberger, 2/2001, p. 28–31, hier p. 31.
361 Cf. Protokoll der Sitzung der Unternehmensleitung vom 6. September 1996, in: Corporate Archives 3/04650.
362 Cf. Handbuch Umwelt- und Arbeitsschutz vom 27. Juli 1998, in: Corporate Archives 3/06988.
363 Cf. Protokolle der UL-Sitzungen vom 29. März 1996, in: Corporate Archives 3/11024–5 as well as vom 20. September 1996, in: Corporate Archives 3/11024–14.
364 In 2004, Freudenberg acquired all the shares in Freudenberg Politex Nonwovens SpA that operated plants in Italy, Poland and Colmar, France. Cf. "Freudenberg Politex wird zur 100 Prozent-Tochter", in: Freudenberg Magazin, 1/2004, p. 7 as well as Schlegel & Partner-Study "The market for PET bottles and recycled PET in Europe, Russia, China and the US" of Oktober 14, 2010, in: Corporate Archives 3/11074–1.
365 Cf. "Wir machen Ernst beim Klimaschutz", in: Freudenberg E-Magazin Spirit, online available at: https://www.freudenberg.com/de/unternehmen/nachhaltigkeit-bei-freudenberg/wir-machen-ernst-beim-klimaschutz, retrieved on 26.03.2023.
366 Cf. Gaide, 2019, p. 42–43.

367 Cf. "Freudenberg expandiert bei Einlagestoffen", Börsenzeitung of October 7, 1997, in: Corporate Archives 3/04792.
368 Development of the shareholding in Japan Vilene Company: Freudenberg increased its share by 2.6 % between March 2007 and September 2008, becoming the largest shareholder in Japan Vilene Company with 25.1 % in September 2008. Cf. Presentation Martin Stark at the Management Board meeting from 1 to 3 April 2009, slide 6, in: Corporate Archives 3/11079.
369 Japan Vilene Company's battery know-how was contributed by the partner Toray Industries. Cf. Strategic considerations for a cooperation Toray – Freudenberg in the field of Nonwovens from March 2012, slide 3, in: Corporate Archives 3/11079.
370 Cf. "Freudenberg stärkt Fußmattengeschäft", Press release of 7 February 2018, in: Corporate Archives 3/11052 as well as Entwicklung bei Hanns Glass, online available at: https://www.hannsglass.de/entwicklung/cad-design/, retrieved on 26.03.2023.
371 Low & Bonar was founded in 1903. Cf. "Freudenberg unterbreitet Angebot für börsennotiertes Unternehmen Low & Bonar PLC", Press release of 20 September 2019, in: Corporate Archives 3/11053.
372 Cf. "Low & Bonar ist jetzt Teil der Freudenberg Gruppe", Press release of 12 May 2020, in: Corporate Archives 3/11054.
373 FPM sales in 2021: 1.32 billion euros. For Filc, please also refer to the section entitled "Freudenberg and mobility in the 21st century". Cf. Geschäftsbericht, 2021, p. 88–89, in: Corporate Archives 3/11047.
374 Cf. "60 Jahre Filterlösungen für mehr Lebensqualität", in: Viledon News, March 2017, p. 1.
375 Ventilation systems can consume 40 to 80 percent of a building's total energy requirements. This is mainly due to the flow resistance of air filters. Materials from Freudenberg, however, ensure a ow pressure drop combined with high dust holding capacity. Cf. "Die Maxime: Nachhaltig handeln", in: Viledon News, May 2017, p.1 f.
376 "Korrosionsschutz: Ein sicheres Passwort: Honeycomb, Filterlösungen sorgen für Datensicherheit in Rechenzentren", in: Viledon News, March 2017, p. 3.
377 Cf. "Aquabio wins Water Reuse Europe Innovation Award", Presseinformation vom 8. November 2017, online available at: https://aquabio.co.uk/aquabio-wins-water-reuse-europe-innovation-award/, retrieved on 18.04.2023.
378 2017 figures for headcount and sales. Cf. "Apollo jetzt Teil der Freudenberg Gruppe", Press release of 1 April 2019, in: Corporate Archives 3/11053.
379 Freudenberg Filtration Technologies brought its current consumer filtration business into the joint venture. Cf. "Apollo jetzt Teil der Freudenberg Gruppe", Press release of 1 April 2019, in: Corporate Archives 3/11053.
380 At ITMA 2019 (International Textile Machinery Association trade fair), Klüber presented its automatic lubrication systems and its service and consultancy concept for boosting energy efficiency and sustainability. Cf. "Neue tribologische Lösungen", in: Industriezeitschrift.de online of May 8, 2019, in: Corporate Archives 3/0088.
381 Cf. Gesellschafterbrief, 1. Halbjahr 2004, p. 13, in: Corporate Archives/ 3/07208
382 Hanno D. Wentzler is a member of the fifth generation of the Freudenberg family and had been CEO of Klüber Lubrication, Munich since 1995.
383 These sales were generated in 2002 with 45 employees. Cf. "Klüber und OKS agieren gemeinsam", Press documentation from October 2003, in: Corporate Archives 3/07967.
384 Cf. "Freudenberg Chemical Specialities", in: O+P Zeitschrift für Fluidtechnik, 48 (2004) Nr. 4, in: Press documentation from 2004, in: Corporate Archives 3/07968.
385 Cf. Current Business Pillar 4 – Acquisition Opportunity and General, in: Corporate Archives 3/11080 und Corporate Archives 3/11081, especially the presentation "Projekt Urania – Wachstum durch Akquisitionen – Analyse der Segmente" from December 1, 2004, in: Corporate Archives 3/11081.
386 Cf. Excerpts from the FCS Board Meeting Minutes 2004–2008 on the topic of "Urania", in: Corporate Archives 3/11081.
387 Cf. Antrag vor dem Gesellschafterausschuss zur GA-Abschlussermächtigung zum Erwerb der SurTec Gruppe vom 22. Juni 2010, p. 2, in: Corporate Archives 3/11080.
388 Ibid.
389 Cf. Böttcher, 2012a, p. 26–27.
390 Cf. Hoch, 2011b, p. 16.

391 Cf. "SurTec ist jetzt ein Bereich des Freudenberg-Konzerns", in: Bergsträßer Anzeiger from July 1, 2010, p. 9.
392 Cf. "Freudenberg übernimmt Capol GmbH", in: Presse Box Online from August 8, 2013, in: Corporate Archives 3/0082.
393 Cf. Protokoll der UL-Sitzung vom 4. September 2001, in: Corporate Archives 3/10509.
394 Cf. Bonfert, 1999, p. 377–390.
395 This brand name was a combination of SIMRit and AXial-Gleitringdichtungen (axial mechanical seals). In 1976, this peripheral operation, with a workforce of 18 people, reported sales of 962,000 DM. Cf. Bonfert, 1999, p. 380.
396 Cf. Brochure "EAGLE Outline of the Company & Main Products, Cat. No. 001–8592", p. 2. o. D. [1992], in: Corporate Archives 3/11082.
397 These products were marketed under the brand of SIRONIT. Cf. Bonfert, 1999, p. 380.
398 Cf. Joint Venture Agreement vom 1. August 1976, in: Corporate Archives 3/06922 as well as Bonfert, 1999, p. 381.
399 The production facility was acquired by Freudenberg with effect from December 31, 1981 and SIMRAX GmbH was operated as a sales company, which was supplied with products for the automotive and domestic appliance industries by Freudenberg SIMRIT or from Japan in 1982 and 1983. Cf. Bonfert, 1999, pp. 382 ff.
400 In 1983, SIMRAX passed the break-even point for the first time, with sales of 4.8 million DM and a profit of 240,000 DM. Cf. ibid, pp. 384 f.
401 Pioneer Laura Automotive B. V. in Kerkrade was acquired with effect from January 1, 1996 . Cf. ibid, p. 389.
402 Cf. Klier, 2004, p. 16.
403 In 1993, Burgmann acquired a significant stake in the Scandinavian KE Group. In 1998, all the shares in the Italian BT Group and Gustav Espey GmbH in Duisburg were acquired. Cf. ibid, p. 16.
404 Cf. "Burgmann kurz vor Hochzeit mit 'Traumpartner'", in: Münchner Merkur from July 18, 2003.
405 Cf. Klier, 2004, p. 16.
406 Cf. Hoch, 2004, p. 23–25 as well as "Das Team für alle Fälle", in: Freudenberg Magazin extra, Special Issue 2004, p. 17.
407 Orians, 2004, p. 7.
408 Ibid.
409 Umwelterklärung der Feodor Burgmann Dichtungswerke GmbH & Co. für die Standorte Wolfratshausen und Eurasburg 1999, in: Corporate Archives 3/11082.
410 Cf. Gesellschafterbrief, 1. Halbjahr 2005, p. 15, in: Corporate Archives 3/07892.
411 Cf. Presentation on the EBI US strategy for the EBI Board Meeting on 16 May 2006, in: Corporate Archives 3/11083 as well as Strategy Review Status Presentation for the EB Board Meeting on May 20, 2011, slide 26, in: Corporate Archives 3/11084.
412 Cf. Gesellschafterbrief, 2009, p. 17, in: Corporate Archives 3/08628.
413 Cf. Presentation EB Group Results September 2010 for the EB Board Meeting on November 17, 2010, slides 2–4, in: Corporate Archives 3/11085.
414 Cf. Gesellschafterbrief, 1. Halbjahr 2008, p. 15, in: Corporate Archives 3/08008.
415 Cf. Gesellschafterbrief 1. Halbjahr 2011, p. 15, in: Corporate Archives 3/10841. The companies grouped together under the umbrella of FOG included TBS of Scotland (acquired in 2005), Imperial Rubber and Urethane Corporation in Nisku, Canada (acquired in 2006), the American company Tetralene (acquired in 2008) and Petroleum Elastomers in Houston, Texas (acquired in 2008). Cf. "Freudenberg-NOK kauft Zulieferer für Öl- und Gasindustrie", in: Freudenberg Magazin, 3/2006, p. 11; Portal News of 19 June 2008, in: Corporate Archives 3/09102 as well as Portal News of 12 November 2008, in: Corporate Archives 3/09102.
416 Baldauf/Buchta-Noack/Hoch, 2011, p. 21.
417 Cf. Gesellschafterbrief, 2012, p. 34, in: Corporate Archives 3/11130.
418 Cf. "Freudenberg übernimmt Vector Technology Group", Press release of 10 December 2012, in: Corporate Archives 3/0081.
419 Cf. Gesellschafterbrief, 2013, p. 32 f. und p. 35, in: Corporate Archives 3/10942.
420 Cf. Seynsche, 2020. For the function of a BOP seal, see also Steingräber, 2013, p. 16.
421 Cf. Product catalog "EagleBurgmann DiamondFace-Technologie für Gleitringdichtungen", January 2015, in: Corporate Archives 3/09097/04; Klier, 2007, p. 35 as well as Hoch, 2010b, p. 25.

422 SUL stands for Schmalband-Umform-Laserschweißtechnologie ("narrow strip-forming laser welding technology"). Cf. History brochure, 2019, p. 25.
423 Cf. "Der Deutsche Innovationspreis 2011 geht an: Freudenberg, Carl Zeiss Meditec und HMI", in: Wirtschaftswoche from March 25, 2011, online available at: https://www.presseportal.de/pm/55137/2014743, retrieved on 25.05.2023.
424 Cf. "Preisträger des deutschen Innovationspreis für Klima und Umwelt (IKU) 2011", in: Youtube, online available at: https://www.youtube.com/watch?v=OjAsbAQ6008, retrieved on 25.05.2023.
425 Cf. Product data sheet "EagleBurgmann CobaDGS – Zero Emission Solution", May 2023, in: Corporate Archives 3/11167 as well as Gesellschafterbrief, 1. Halbjahr 2020, p. 26, in: Corporate Archives 3/10977.
426 Cf. Organizational announcement on the establishment of Freudenberg Flow Technologies dated October 25, 2023, in: Corporate Archives 3/11153.
427 Cf. UN Global-Compact-Fortschrittsbericht 2021, p. 18, in: Corporate Archives 3/11147.
428 Cf. "Wir machen Ernst beim Klimaschutz", in: Freudenberg Magazin Online, online available at: https://magazine.freudenberg.com/de/verantwortung/wir-machen-ernst-beim-klimaschutz, retrieved on 26.03.2023.
429 Cf. Horchler/Schultens, 2021, p. 27.
430 Cf. "Wir machen Ernst beim Klimaschutz", in: Freudenberg Magazin Online, online available at: https://magazine.freudenberg.com/de/verantwortung/wir-machen-ernst-beim-klimaschutz, retrieved on 26.03.2023.
431 Cf. UN-Global-Compact-Fortschrittsbericht 2020, p. 19, in: Corporate Archives 3/11046.
432 Cf. ibid, p. 20 as well as Horchler/Schultens, 2021, p. 27.
433 Cf. UN-Global-Compact-Fortschrittsbericht 2021, p. 22–26, in: Corporate Archives 3/11047; "Wir machen Ernst beim Klimaschutz", in: Freudenberg Magazin Online, online available at: https://magazine.freudenberg.com/de/verantwortung/wir-machen-ernst-beim-klimaschutz, retrieved on 26.03.2023 as well as Verantwortungsbericht der Freudenberg Gruppe 2022, p. 86–94, in: Corporate Archives 3/11070.
434 Cf. Verantwortungsbericht der Freudenberg Gruppe 2022, p. 97, in: Corporate Archives 3/11070.
435 Cf. ibid, p. 98.
436 Cf. ibid, p. 102.
437 Sales by the EagleBurgmann Business Group increased from some 315 million euros in 2004 to some 918 million euros in 2022. Cf. Geschäftsberichte, 2004 and 2022, in: Corporate Archives 3/07911 and Corporate Archives 3/11070.
438 Cf. Letter from Hermann Ernst to Friedrich Carl dated 14 March 1914, in: Familienschriften, Bd. 2, p. 341.
439 Cf. Press release Carl Freudenberg, June 27, 1980, in: Corporate Archives 3/02850. With reference to the development of the Helia division and the role played by Rudolf Wassermann, cf. Horchler, 2021a.
440 The first non-family members of the Board of Partners in 1976 were the economics expert Jörg A. Henle (1934–2019) from the Management Board of Klöckner-Werke (Board of Partners member for the period 1976–1987) and Joachim Zahn (1914–2002) from the Board of Management of Daimler-Benz (Board of Partners member for the period 1976–1982). Cf. History and composition of the Board of Partners, in: Corporate Archives 3/11169.
441 Guidelines for the Employment of Family Members in the Business Sector, June 1974, in: Corporate Archives 3/02178.
442 Ibid.
443 Speech by Hermann Freudenberg at the Partners' Meeting on April 26, 1980, in: Corporate Archives 3/02178.
444 Ibid.
445 Guidelines for the employment of family members in the business sector of 4 March 1981, in: Corporate Archives 3/02178.
446 Cf. Q&A catalogue on the introduction of the new employment policy for family members in 2013, in: Corporate Archives 3/10891.
447 Letter from Wolfram Freudenberg to the partners dated April 10, 2013, in: Corporate Archives 3/10891.
448 Cf. Policy for the employment of family members of 10 April 2013, in: Corporate Archives 3/10891.

449 Letter from Wolfram Freudenberg to the partners dated April 10, 2013, in: Corporate Archives 3/10891.
450 Cf. Information manual for senior managers from 1979, in: Corporate Archives 3/03660 as well as I Information Manual on Management Guidelines of Gustav Hoffmann GmbH, dated May 1, 1972, in: Corporate Archives 3/03660.
451 Cf. Brainstorming for the development of corporate principles of July 31, 1983, in: Corporate Archives 3/02730; Discussion papers on the topic of corporate principles at Freudenberg of August 16, 1983, in: Corporate Archives 3/04712; Information documents on the formation of corporate principles of August 25, 1983, in: Corporate Archives 3/02730 as well as Basic principles of the company – draft from Dr. Ahrend to Hermann Freudenberg from 1983, in: Corporate Archives 3/04712.
452 Cf. Declaration by the Management Board Concerning the Restriction and Monitoring of Armaments Business, dated August 27, 1991, in: Corporate Archives 3/07346.
453 Cf. Business Principles of the Freudenberg Group from December 1994, in: Corporate Archives 3/03661.
454 Cf. Hille, 2020.
455 Cf. Prenzel, 2022.
456 Cf. Joint declaration by the Management Board and the Central Works Council on xenophobia, dated December 14, 1992, in: Corporate Archives 3/07346.
457 Cf. Business Principles of the Freudenberg Group from December 1994, in: Corporate Archives 3/03661.
458 Cf. "Familie und Unternehmen", Speech by Reinhart Freudenberg at the Partners' Meeting on June 22, 1993, in: Corporate Archives 3/04662.
459 Cf. Business Principles of the Freudenberg Group from December 1994, in: Corporate Archives 3/03661.
460 Cf. Transcript of business principles of Carl Johann Freudenberg with the title "General Considerations!" from 1887, in: Corporate Archives 3/05163.
461 Unfortunately, the dates when these quotes originated cannot be accurately determined. However, they are likely to have been made in the 1870s after Carl Johann's sons had entered the business.
462 The quotes on trust can also be found in, e.g. Pinnow, 1949, p. 96.
463 Opening speech by Reinhart Freudenberg at the Dialog 97, in: Corporate Archives 3/04676.
464 Cf. Speeches at the Dialog 99, in: Corporate Archives 3/05307.
465 Cf. Opening speech by Reinhart Freudenberg at the Dialog 97, in: Corporate Archives 3/04676; "Die Identität der Freudenberggruppe", Presentation by Reinhart Freudenberg at the Partners' Meeting on June 28, 1997, in: Corporate Archives 3/04917 as well as Concept for the closing speech at the Dialog 97 by Dr. Peter Bettermann, in: Corporate Archives 3/04676.
466 Cf. Documents for the brochure "Werte & Grundsätze", in: Corporate Archives 3/08964; Guiding Principles Survey, in: Corporate Archives 3/08909 as well as Hoch/Baldauf, 2011, p. 27.
467 Cf. Letter of accession to the Global Compact from Mohsen Sohi to UN Secretary-General Ban Ki-moon of 13 January 2014, in: Corporate Archives 3/11170 as well as "United Nations Global Compact", in: Global Compact Netzwerk Deutschland, online available at: https://www.globalcompact.de/ueber-uns/united-nations-global-compact, retrieved on 07.12.2022.
468 "United Nations Global Compact", in: Global Compact Netzwerk Deutschland, online available at: https://www.globalcompact.de/ueber-uns/united-nations-global-compact, retrieved on 07.12.2022: As at December 2022, more than 20,000 companies worldwide had signed the UN Global Compact. Cf. hereto United Nations Global Compact, online available at: https://unglobalcompact.org/, retrieved on 07.12.2022.
469 Cf. Baldauf, 2013a, p. 5.

BIBLIOGRAPHY AND LIST OF REFERENCES

Abelshauser, 2011: Werner Abelshauser: Deutsche Wirtschaftsgeschichte. Von 1945 bis zur Gegenwart, Bonn 2011.

Asmuss, 2011: Burkhard Asmuss: Das Hindenburg Programm, Berlin 2011. Accessible online at: https://www.dhm.de/lemo/kapitel/erster-weltkrieg/industrie-und-wirtschaft/hindenburg-programm.html, accessed on December 3, 2019.

Asmuss, 2015: Burkhard Asmuss: Die Reichstagswahl vom 5. März 1933, Berlin 2015. Accessible online at: https://www.dhm.de/lemo/kapitel/ns-regime/etablierung-der-ns-herrschaft/reichstagswahl-1933.html, accessed on December 13, 2019.

Bähr, 2006: Johannes Bähr: Unternehmens- und Kapitalmarktrecht im "Dritten Reich": Die Aktienrechtsform und das Anleihestockgesetz, in: Johannes Bähr, Ralf Banken (Publ.): Wirtschaftssteuerung durch Recht im Nationalsozialismus. Studien zur Entwicklung des Wirtschaftsrechts im Interventionsstaat des "Dritten Reichs", Frankfurt am Main 2006, p. 35–69.

Baldauf, 2011: Andreas Baldauf: Freudenberg-Produkt bei Weltreise dabei, in: Freudenberg Magazin, 1/2011, p. 8.

Baldauf, 2012: Andreas Baldauf: Freudenberg SE nimmt konkrete Formen an, in: Freudenberg Magazin, 2/2012, p. 12.

Baldauf, 2013: Andreas Baldauf: Gruppenweite Programme für Top-Führungskräfte, in: Freudenberg Magazin, 3/2013, p. 12–13.

Baldauf, 2013a: Andreas Baldauf: Freudenberg Gruppe unterzeichnet Global Compact, in: Freudenberg Magazin, 4/2013, p. 5.

Baldauf, 2014: Andreas Baldauf: Fokus 2.0 Update. Zusammenarbeit definiert, in: Freudenberg Magazin, 3/2014, p. 20.

Baldauf, 2020: Andreas Baldauf: Strategieperiode 2018 bis 2020. Ein Überblick, in: Freudenberg Magazin, 5/2020, p. 28–30.

Baldauf/Buchta-Noack/Hoch, 2011: Andreas Baldauf, Cornelia Buchta-Noack, Thomas Hoch: Interview mit Christoph Mosmann und Dr. Mohsen Sohi: Ehrgeizige Ziele, in: Freudenberg Magazin, 1/2011, p. 19–22.

Banken, 2018: Ralf Banken: Steuerpolitik, Berlin 2018, in: Historikerkommission Reichsfinanzministerium von 1933–1945, accessible online at: http://www.reichsfinanzministerium-geschichte.de/teilprojekte/steuerpolitik, accessed on October 14, 2019.

Baumann, 2016: Charlotte Baumann: Ein Hoch auf Solidarität und gute Nachbarschaft, in: Freudenberg Magazin, 1/2016, p. 48–49.

Benz, 2005: Wolfgang Benz: Wirtschaftsentwicklung 1945 bis 1949, in: Bundeszentrale für politische Bildung (Publ.): Deutschland 1945–1949, Informationen zur politischen Bildung, 259, Bonn 2005.

Benz, 2005a: Wolfgang Benz: Zwei Staatsgründungen auf deutschen Boden, in: Bundeszentrale für politische Bildung (Publ.): Deutschland 1945–1949, Informationen zur politischen Bildung, 259, Bonn 2005.

Berghoff/Köhler, 2000: Hartmut Berghoff, Ingo Köhler: Verdienst und Vermächtnis – Familienunternehmen in Deutschland und den USA seit 1800, Frankfurt/Main, 2000.

Berlinghoff, 2018: Marcel Berlinghoff: Geschichte der Migration in Deutschland, in: Bundeszentrale für politische Bildung (Publ.): Dossier: Migration, Bonn 2018. Accessible online at: https://www.bpb.de/themen/migration-integration/dossier-migration/252241/geschichte-der-migration-in-deutschland/, accessed on July 31, 2023.

Bernhard, 2001: Michael Bernhard: Der Pädiater Ernst Freudenberg 1884–1967, Marburg 2001.

Betschon, 2019: Stefan Betschon: Wie die Elektronengehirne die Welt eroberten, in: Neue Zürcher Zeitung-Online, Zurich 2019. Accessible online at: https://www.nzz.ch/digital/computer-wie-die-elektronenhirne-die-welt-eroberten-ld.1516256#back-register, accessed on January 13, 2021.

Boesebeck, 1962: Ernst Boesebeck: Das Verhältnis zum Gesellschaftsrecht, in: Der Freudenberger, Special Edition/1962, Richard Freudenberg 70 Jahre, p. 35–37.

Bonfert, 1999: Werner Bonfert: Freudenberg. 70 Jahre Dichtungs- und Schwingungstechnik. 1929 bis 1998, Weinheim 1999, in: Corporate Archives 3/05944.

Bonfert, 2008: Werner Bonfert: Tradition und Geschichte. Corte & Cosso, Corcos, Corfina, Freudenberg & Cosso. 1936–2008, Weinheim 2008, in: Corporate Archives 3/08520.

Borchardt, 1982: Knut Borchardt: Zwangslagen und Handlungsspielräume in der grossen Weltwirtschaftskrise der frühen dreissiger Jahre. Zur Revision des überlieferten Geschichtsbildes, in: Knut Borchardt: Wachstum, Krisen, Handlungsspielräume der Wirtschaftspolitik, Göttingen 1982, p. 165–182 and p. 265–283.

Borchers, 2001: Detlef Borchers: Vor 50 Jahren fing alles an: das erste "Elektronenhirn" in Deutschland, in: Heise online, Hannover 2001. Accessible online at: https://www.heise.de/newsticker/meldung/Vor-50-Jahren-fing-alles-an-das-erste-Elektronenhirn-in-Deutschland-51722.html, accessed on January 13, 2021.

Born, 1983: Karl Erich Born: Vom Beginn des Ersten Weltkrieges bis zum Ende der Weimarer Republik (1914–1933), in: Wissenschaftlicher Beirat des Instituts für bankhistorische Forschung (Publ.): Deutsche Bankengeschichte, Vol. 3, Frankfurt am Main 1983, p. 17–146.

Borowsky, 2002: Peter Borowsky: Das Ende der "Ära Adenauer", in: Bundeszentrale für politische Bildung (Publ.): Zeiten des Wandels, Deutschland 1961–1974, Informationen zur politischen Bildung, 258, Bonn 2002. Accessible online at: https://www.bpb.de/izpb/10093/das-ende-der-aera-adenauer?p=all, accessed on April 5, 2021.

Böttcher, 2012: Katrin Böttcher: Auf Kurs. Strategische Wachstumsmärkte, in: Freudenberg Magazin, 2/2012, p. 22–25.

Böttcher, 2012a: Katrin Böttcher: Chemische Oberflächenbehandlung – Erfolg auf drei Säulen, in: Freudenberg Magazin, 2/2012, p. 26–27.

Böttcher, 2013: Katrin Böttcher: Freudenberg Regional Corporate Center Indien eröffnet, in: Freudenberg Magazin 3/2013, p. 5.

Böttcher, 2013a: Katrin Böttcher: Freudenberg Regional Corporate Center in Südamerika eröffnet, in: Freudenberg Magazin 3/2013, p. 8.

Böttcher, 2015: Katrin Böttcher: Der Weg zur neuen Positionierung, in: Freudenberg Magazin, 2/2015, p. 19–21.

Böttcher, 2015a: Katrin Böttcher: Wir brauchen 40.000 Markenbotschafter. Interview mit Mohsen Sohi, in: Freudenberg Magazin, 2/2015, p. 16–18.

Bower, 1967: Marvin Bower: Die Kunst zu führen, Düsseldorf 1967.

Braun, 2006: Helmut Braun, Währungsreform, 1923/24, in: Historisches Lexikon Bayerns. Accessible online at: https://www.historisches-lexikon-bayerns.de/Lexikon/Währungsreform,_1923/24, accessed on November 5, 2019.

Bräutigam, 1997: Petra Bräutigam: Mittelständische Unternehmer im Nationalsozialismus. Wirtschaftliche Entwicklungen und soziale Verhaltensweisen in der Schuh- und Lederindustrie Badens und Württembergs, Munich 1997.

Breisig, 1990: Thomas Breisig: Skizzen zur historischen Genese betrieblicher Führungs- und Sozialtechniken, Munich 1990.

Brunner, 2020: Mathias Brunner: Richard Noble: Der schnellste Mann der Welt, in: Speedweek, accessible online at: https://www.speedweek.com/katalog/news/159446/Richard-Noble-Der-schnellste-Mann-der-Welt.html, accessed on February 15, 2022.

Buchheim/Hutter/James, 1994: Christoph Buchheim, Michael Hutter, Harold James (Publ.): Zerrissene Zwischenkriegszeit. Wirtschaftshistorische Beiträge. Knut Borchardt zum 65. Geburtstag, Baden-Baden 1994.

Buchta-Noack, 2013: Cornelia Buchta-Noack: Veränderte Strukturen, gebündelte Kompetenzen: Die transparente Organisation, in: Freudenberg Magazin, 4/2013, p. 18–25.

Buchta-Noack, 2013a: Cornelia Buchta-Noack: Fokus 2.0. Organisatorische Weiterentwicklung von Freudenberg, Interview mit Dr. Mohsen Sohi zu FOKUS 2.0, in: Freudenberg Magazin, 4/2013, p. 14–17.

Buchta-Noack/Hoch, 2009: Cornelia Buchta-Noack, Thomas Hoch: Jetzt die Strukturen für die Zukunft schaffen. Interview mit Dr. Peter Bettermann und Lorenz Freudenberg, in: Freudenberg Magazin, 2/2009, p. 18–23.

Bührer, 2001: Werner Bührer: Wirtschaftliche Entwicklung in der Bundesrepublik, in: Bundeszentrale für politische Bildung (Publ.): Deutschland in den 70er und 80er Jahren, Informationen zur politischen Bildung, 270, Bonn 2001, p. 14–19.

Bührer, 2012: Werner Bührer: Wirtschaft in beiden deutschen Staaten. Ökonomische Entwicklung in der Bundesrepublik 1945–1961, in: Bundeszentrale für politische Bildung (Publ.): Deutschland in den fünfziger Jahren, Informationen zur politischen Bildung, 256, Bonn 2012, p. 32–39.

Bujard, 2022: Martin Bujard: Warum der demografische Wandel uns alle betrifft, in: Bundeszentrale für politische Bildung (Publ.): Demografischer Wandel, Informationen zur politischen Bildung, 350, Bonn 2022, p. 4–11.

Burkhardt, 1963: Hildegard Burkhardt: Übergangsschule für Mädchen, in: Der Freudenberger, 6/1963, p. 9–14.

Burkhardt, 1999: Benjamin Burkhardt: 110.000 Mark für Erdbebenopfer, in: Marktplatz, 1/1999, p. 9.

Chmura/Haunhorst, 2014: Nadine Chmura, Regina Haunhorst: Jahreschronik 2001, in: Lebendiges Museum Online, Stiftung Haus der Geschichte der Bundesrepublik Deutschland, Bonn 2014. Accessible online at: http://www.hdg.de/lemo/jahreschronik/2001.html, accessed on March 14, 2022.

Dispan/Stieler, 2015: Jürgen Dispan, Sylvia Stieler: Leder- und Schuhindustrie: Branchentrends und Herausforderungen, Informationsdienst des IMU Instituts, Heft 3/2015, Stuttgart 2015.

Docke, 1973: Helmut Docke: Wegweisende Vlieseline® Neuentwicklungen, in: Der Freudenberger, 5/1973, p. 18–20.

Donath/Szegfü, 2021: Peter Donath, Annette Szegfü: "Wir machen Stoff". Die Gewerkschaft Textil-Bekleidung 1949–1998, Bielefeld 2021.

Edelmann, 1966: Fritz Edelmann: Werk Reichelsheim im Odenwald, in: Der Freudenberger, 4/1966, p. 5–8.

Elkhofer, 2014: Volker Elkhofer: Rückblick auf eine folgenreiche Zeit, in: Bayerischer Rundfunk: Die Ölkrise der 1970er. Accessible online at: https://www.br.de/radio/bayern2/sendungen/radiowissen/soziale-politische-bildung/oelkrise-1970er-wirtschaft-fahrverbot-opec-100.html, accessed on April 30, 2021.

Esteva, 2006: Lola Esteva: La fregona, el invento que puso en pie a las mujeres, cumple 50 anos, in: Pronto Magazin, 2006, p. 44–45.

Faas, 2017: Darius Faas: Preisgekrönte Luftzufuhr, in: Freudenberg Magazin, 4/2017, p. 46–47.

Familienschriften, Vol. 1: Karl Johann Freudenberg (Publ.): Schriften der Familie Freudenberg in Weinheim nach alten und neuen Berichten, Vol. 1, Heidelberg 1969.

Familienschriften, Vol. 2: Karl Johann Freudenberg (Publ.): Schriften der Familie Freudenberg in Weinheim, Carl Johann Freudenberg (1819–1898) und die Seinen, Briefe und Blätter, Vol. 2, Heidelberg 1971.

Familienschriften, Vol. 3: Karl Johann Freudenberg (Publ.): Schriften der Familie Freudenberg in Weinheim, Hermann Ernst Freudenberg (1856–1923), Vol. 3, Heidelberg 1976.

Fath, 1996: Volker Fath: Drachentanz und Kung Fu, in: Der Freudenberger, 9/1996, p. 1 and p. 6.

Fath, 1996a: Volker Fath: Schadstoffen auf der Spur: "Umweltschutz Highlights" bei Klüber vorgestellt, in: Der Freudenberger, 11/1996, p. 4.

Fath, 1997: Volker Fath: Neues lernen macht mir Spass, in: Der Freudenberger, 12/1997, p. 3.

Fath, 1998: Volker Fath: Freudenberg Simrit Kufstein, in: Der Freudenberger, 8/9/1998, p. 3.

Fath, 1998a: Volker Fath: Go East! Vliesstoffe gründen Vertriebsgesellschaft in Indien, in: Der Freudenberger, 7/1998, p. 4.

Fath, 1998b: Volker Fath: Wir kombinieren unsere Stärken, in: Der Freudenberger, 4/1998, p. 1–2.

Fath, 1999: Volker Fath: Ein extrem leistungsfähiges Unternehmen, in: Der Freudenberger, 3/1999, p. 4.
Fath, 1999a: Volker Fath: FUEL wird unternehmensweit einführt, in: Der Freudenberger, 7/8/1999, p. 3.
Fath, 2006: Volker Fath: Einmischen und dranbleiben, in: Marktplatz 2/2006, p. 11.
Fath, 2006a: Volker Fath: Corporate Service Center Asia in Shanghai eröffnet, in: Freudenberg Magazin, 4/2006, p. 15.
Fath, 2006b: Volker Fath: Freudenberg fördert Ideen für guten Zweck, in: Marktplatz, 2/2006, p. 5.
Fath, 2009: Volker Fath: Wir wollen uns fit machen für die Zukunft, in: Marktplatz, 2/2009, p. 5.
Fath, 2009a: Volker Fath: Gute Voraussetzungen, um gestärkt aus der Krise hervorzugehen, in: Freudenberg Magazin, 2/2009, p. 12–13.
Fath, 2010: Volker Fath: Zwei Flügel zum Fliegen, in: Freudenberg Magazin, 1/2010, p. 38.
Fath, 2010a: Volker Fath: Türöffner in die Pharmazie, in: Marktplatz, 4/2010, p. 2.
Fath, 2013: Volker Fath: Weniger ist mehr, in: Marktplatz, 4/2013, p. 8.
Fath, 2016: Volker Fath: Kreatives für Nadel und Faden. Die Mitarbeiterinnen des Vlieseline-Studios von Freudenberg Performance Materials inspirieren mit Tipps und Tricks, in: Marktplatz, 2/2016, p. 1 and 7.
Fath, 2018: Volker Fath: Das Bildungszentrum in "neuen Kleidern", in: Marktplatz, 1/2018, p. 3.
Fath, 2018a: Volker Fath: FST macht sich fit für die Königsdisziplin, in: Freudenberg Magazin, 2/2018, p. 54.
Fath, 2019: Volker Fath: Intelligent heisst automatisiert und skaliert. Digitale Produkte und Services bei EagleBurgmann, in: Freudenberg Magazin, 4/2019, p. 52–53.
Fath, 2019a: Volker Fath: Rapid Prototyping. 3D-Druck steht für Agilität und Flexibilität, in: Freudenberg Magazin, 1/2019, p. 48–49.
Fath, 2020: Volker Fath: Oben in den Alpen die digitale Zukunft erkunden, in: Freudenberg Magazin, 5/2020, p. 52–53.
Fath, 2021: Volker Fath: Schnell raus hier: aber sicher, in: Marktplatz, 3/2021, p. 8.
Fath, 2022: Volker Fath: Früh erkannt heisst schnell gebannt, in: Marktplatz, 1/2022, p. 6.
Fath, 2022a: Volker Fath: Genauigkeit im grossen Stil, in: Marktplatz, 1/2022, p. 6.
Fath, 2022b: Volker Fath: FRE Hilft!, in: Marktplatz, 3/2022, p. 15.
Fehrle, 1970: Kurt Fehrle: Im Blickpunkt: Werk Neuenburg, in: Der Freudenberger, 4/1970, p. 12–14.
Feinstein/Temin/Toniolo, 2008: Charles H. Feinstein, Peter Temin, Gianni Toniolo: The European Economy between the Wars, Oxford 2008.
Feldman, 1998: Gerald D. Feldman: Hugo Stinnes. Biographie eines Industriellen 1870–1924, Munich 1998.
Franz, 2008: Uli Franz: Porträt: Deng Xiaoping, in: Bundeszentrale für politische Bildung (Publ.): Dossier: China, Bonn 2008. Accessible online at: https://www.bpb.de/themen/asien/china/44262/portraet-deng-xiaoping/, accessed on September 9, 2022.

Frei, 2013: Norbert Frei: Der Führerstaat. Nationalsozialistische Herrschaft 1933 bis 1945, Munich 2013.

Fresin, 1962: Josef Fresin: Die Geschichte der Stadt Weinheim, Weinheim 1962.

Freudenberg, 1867: Freudenberg, Sophie: Für meine Kinder, die Entstehung und Begründung des Geschäftes Heintze & Freudenberg im Jahr 1848 und den folgenden, November 1867, in: Corporate Archives 3/01110.

Freudenberg, 1938: Freudenberg, Friedrich Carl: Erinnerungen an unser Elternhaus und früheste Geschichte der Firma, Weinheim 1938, in: Corporate Archives 3/01154.

Freudenberg, 1945: Richard Freudenberg: Die deutsche Ledererzeugung von 1913–1945, Weinheim, 1945, in: Corporate Archives 3/01110.

Freudenberg, 1948: Walter Freudenberg: Otto Freudenberg. Aus den Erinnerungen von Walter Freudenberg anlässlich der Erstellung einer Festschrift zur Hundertjahrfeier, niedergeschrieben 1948, Weinheim, 1948, in: Corporate Archives 1/00242.

Freudenberg, 1962: Adolf Freudenberg: Der Benjamin im Badischen Landtag, in: Der Freudenberger, Special Edition/1962, Richard Freudenberg 70 Jahre, p. 70–83.

Freudenberg, 1964: Adolf Freudenberg: Besuche in Genf, in: Wolf-Dieter Zimmermann (Publ.), Begegnungen mit Dietrich Bonhoeffer. Ein Almanach, Munich 1964, p. 131–134.

Freudenberg, 1964a: Hermann Freudenberg: Zur Geschäftslage, in: Der Freudenberger, 6/1964, p. 1.

Freudenberg, 1964b: Hermann Freudenberg: Halbjahresbericht 1964, in: Der Freudenberger, 4/1964, p. 1–3.

Freudenberg, 1965: Hermann Freudenberg: Zur Geschäftslage, in: Der Freudenberger, 2/1965, p. 1.

Freudenberg, 1966: Hans Erich Freudenberg: Der heutige "Ledermarkt" – Folgerungen für Carl Freudenberg vom 20. Juni 1966, in: Corporate Archives 3/03190.

Freudenberg, 1967: Hans Erich Freudenberg: Struktur- und Konjunkturprobleme aus der Sicht von Carl Freudenberg. Referat gehalten auf der Gesellschafterversammlung der Freudenberg & Co. am 15. April 1967, in: Corporate Archives 3/03190.

Freudenberg, 1968: Hans Erich Freudenberg: Beginn einer Freundschaft zwischen der Nippon Oil Seal und Carl Freudenberg, in: Der Freudenberger, 2/1968, p. 2–4.

Freudenberg, 1968a: Hans Erich Freudenberg: Unsere Aufgaben der kommenden Jahre, Studie vom Juni 1968, in: Corporate Archives 3/02269.

Freudenberg, 1969: Adolf Freudenberg: Im freien Genf. Ökumenischer Flüchtlingsdienst 1939–1945, in: Adolf Freudenberg (Publ.), Rettet sie doch! Franzosen und die Genfer Ökumene im Dienste der Verfolgten des Dritten Reiches, Zurich 1969, p. 19–59.

Freudenberg, 1970: Hans Erich Freudenberg: Probleme der Geschäftsleitung Freudenberg & Co. (Geschäftsordnung) vom 16. Oktober 1970, Weinheim, 1970, in: Corporate Archives 3/02561.

Freudenberg, 1970a: Hans Erich Freudenberg: Überlegungen zur künftigen Firmenstruktur der Freudenberg & Co. mit Folgerungen für die Geschäftsführung (November 1970), in: Corporate Archives 3/04600.

Freudenberg, 1971: Hermann Freudenberg: Grundüberlegungen zur Organisation von Freudenberg & Co. und Carl Freudenberg vom 27. Januar 1971, in: Corporate Archives 3/04600.

Freudenberg, 1973: Hans Erich Freudenberg: Begründung der Einschränkungen im CF-Lederbereich vom 22. Oktober 1973, in: Corporate Archives 3/03190.

Freudenberg, 1974: Sibille Freudenberg: Gesammeltes Leben. Auszüge aus Tagebüchern, Briefen und Reiseberichten, Weinheim, 1974, in: Corporate Archives 1/00371.

Freudenberg, 1976: Hans Erich Freudenberg: Ist die Freudenberg & Co. für ihre Zukunft gerüstet? Referat gehalten auf der Gesellschafterversammlung der Freudenberg & Co. am 8. Mai 1976, in: Corporate Archives 3/03190.

Freudenberg, 1989: Adolf Freudenberg (Publ.), "Befreie, die zum Tode geschleppt werden!" Ökumene durch geschlossene Grenzen 1939–45, Munich 1989.

Freudenberg/Schuster, 1999: Reinhart Freudenberg, Sibylla Schuster: 150 Jahre Freudenberg. Die Entwicklung eines Familienunternehmens von der Gerberei zur internationalen Firmengruppe, Weinheim, 1999.

Freudenberg-Hübner/Wiehn, 1993: Dorothee Freudenberg-Hübner, Erhard Roy Wiehn (Publ.): Abgeschoben. Jüdische Schicksale aus Freiburg 1940–42. Briefe der Geschwister Liefmann aus Gurs und Morlaas an Adolf Freudenberg in Genf, Konstanz 1993.

Freyberg, 1989: Thomas von Freyberg: Industrielle Rationalisierung in der Weimarer Republik. Untersucht an Beispielen aus dem Maschinenbau und der Elektroindustrie, Frankfurt am Main, New York 1989.

Fritsche, 2013: Christiane Fritsche: Ausgeplündert, zurückerstattet und entschädigt. Arisierung und Wiedergutmachung in Mannheim, Ubstadt-Weiher et al. 2013.

Gaide, 2019: Peter Gaide: Nichts wie raus! Freudenberg Innovation Award Top 5, in: Freudenberg Magazin, 2/2019, p. 42–43.

Gantert, 1955: Edmund Gantert: Abschiedsabend für Direktor Paul Vogler, in: Der Freudenberger, 6/1955, p. 34–35.

Ganzer, 2019: Niko Ganzer: Mit Herz und Verstand, Freudenberg Magazin, 2/2019, p. 40–41.

Gärtner, 1968: Rudolf Gärtner: Viledon-Werk II und III Zwischen Dämmen, in: Der Freudenberger, 5/1968, p. 3–5.

Gausemeier, 2010: Jürgen Gausemeier u. a.: Chancen für Freudenberg in der Medizintechnik, written on behalf of Freudenberg at the Heinz Nixdorf Institute, University of Paderborn, publ. by Freudenberg New Technologies, Paderborn 2010, in: Corporate Archives 3/11072.

History brochure, 2019: The history of the Freudenberg Group 1849–2019, publ. by Freudenberg & Co. Kommanditgesellschaft, Corporate Communications, Weinheim 2019.

Geyer, 1988: Martin H. Geyer: Verkehrte Welt. Revolution, Inflation und Moderne, Göttingen 1988.

Goodhart, 2022: Benjie Goodhart: The ten most iconic live TV moments in British broadcasting history, in: Saga Magazine online, 17 February 2022, accessible online at: https://www.saga.co.uk/magazine/entertainment/tv/most-iconic-moments-live-tv, accessed on January 12, 2023.

Gorka, 2006: Cornelius Gorka: Die Vorgeschichte. Amtskörperschaften, Oberämter, Landkreise und ihre Interessenvertretungen bis 1945. Baden, in: 50 Jahre Landkreistag Baden-Württemberg, published by Landkreistag Baden-Württemberg, Stuttgart 2006, p. 12–18. Accessible online at: https://www.landkreistag-bw.de/fileadmin/user_upload/PDFs/Landkreistag/Geschichte/Geschichte_Baden.pdf, accessed on April 11, 2019.

Grau/Guttmann, 2008: Ute Grau, Barbara Guttmann: Weinheim. Geschichte einer Stadt, publ. by Stadt Weinheim, Weinheim 2008.

Grau/Würz, 2014: Andreas Grau, Markus Würz: Militärallianzen, in: Lebendiges Museum Online, Stiftung Haus der Geschichte der Bundesrepublik Deutschland, Bonn 2014. Accessible online at: https://www.hdg.de/lemo/kapitel/geteiltes-deutschland-gruenderjahre/weg-nach-westen/militaerallianzen.html, accessed on September 17, 2020.

Gutermann, 1985: Siegfried S. Gutermann: Geldpolitik und Reagonomics, in: Ernst Otto Czempiel u. a. (Publ.): Politik und Wirtschaft in den USA, Opladen 1985, p. 69–96.

Haid/Wessels, 1996: Alfred Haid, Hans Wessels: Entwicklung und Aussichten der deutschen Leder- und Schuhindustrie, Berlin 1996.

Haid/Wessels, 1997: Alfred Haid, Hans Wessels: Die deutsche Ledererzeugung – ein Verlierer der Globalisierung?, in: DIW-Wochenbericht, 29/1997, Berlin 1997, p. 508–516.

Hasenhütl, 2016: Anja Hasenhütl: Auf neuen Wegen zur Energiegewinnung, in: Marktplatz, 6/2016, p. 7.

Hasenhütl, 2018: Anja Hasenhütl: Ideen mit Vlieseline, in: Marktplatz, 3/2018, p. 11.

Henssler, 2007: Patrick Henssler: Versailler Vertrag, 1919/20, in: Historisches Lexikon Bayerns. Accessible online at: https://www.historisches-lexikon-bayerns.de/Lexikon/Versailler_Vertrag,_1919/20, accessed on November 6, 2019.

Herrmann, 2019: Ulrike Herrmann: Deutschland. Ein Wirtschaftsmärchen. Warum es kein Wunder ist, dass wir reich geworden sind, Frankfurt am Main 2019.

Hett, 1967: Herbert Hett: Freudenberg als Zulieferer der Automobilindustrie. Internationale Automobilausstellung 1967 in Frankfurt, in: Der Freudenberger, 5/1967, p. 1–5.

Hett, 2016: Benjamin Carter Hett: Der Reichstagsbrand. Wiederaufnahme eines Verfahrens, Reinbek bei Hamburg 2016.

Hesse/Köster/Plumpe, 2014: Jan-Otmar Hesse, Roman Köster, Werner Plumpe: Die grosse Depression. Die Weltwirtschaftskrise 1929–1939, Frankfurt am Main, New York 2014.

Hille, 2020: Peter Hille: Chronologie: Rechte Gewalt in Deutschland vom 20. Februar 2020, in: Deutsche Welle online, accessible online at: https://www.dw.com/de/chronologie-rechte-gewalt-in-deutschland/a-49251032, accessed on December 9, 2022.

Hinz-Wessels, 2003: Annette Hinz-Wessels: Bergbaukrise und Rezession, in: Lebendiges Museum Online, Stiftung Haus der Geschichte der Bundesrepublik Deutschland, Bonn 2003. Accessible online at: https://www.hdg.de/lemo/kapitel/geteiltes-deutschland-modernisierung/bundesrepublik-im-wandel/bergbaukrise-und-rezession.html, accessed on April 5, 2021.

Hinz-Wessels, 2003a: Annette Hinz-Wessels: Wirtschaftskrise, in: Lebendiges Museum Online, Stiftung Haus der Geschichte der Bundesrepublik Deutschland, Bonn 2003. Accessible online at: https://www.hdg.de/lemo/kapitel/geteiltes-deutschland-krisenmanagement/bundesrepublik-im-umbruch/wirtschaftskrise.html, accessed on April 5, 2021.

Hirsch, 1940: Max Hirsch: Lederwerke Sigmund Hirsch GmbH 1868–1938, Erinnerungen von Max Hirsch (Manuskript von 1940), Reprint Chevy Chase 1991, in: Corporate Archives 3/03186

Hoch, 2004: Thomas Hoch: Das Geheimnis um Lancelot, in: Freudenberg Magazin Spezial, Special Edition 2004, p. 22–25.

Hoch, 2005: Thomas Hoch: Restrukturierung soll deutsche Vliesstoff-Standorte sichern, in: Freudenberg Magazin, 4/2005, p. 14.

Hoch, 2005a: Thomas Hoch: Freudenberg baut Schulungszentrum in Tsunami-Region, in: Freudenberg Magazin, 4/2005, p. 10.

Hoch, 2005b: Thomas Hoch: Neue Geschäftsgruppe für neue Technologien, in: Freudenberg Magazin, 1/2005, p. 10.

Hoch, 2007: Thomas Hoch: Indien ist im Kommen, in: Freudenberg Magazin, 1/2007, p. 14–17.

Hoch, 2007a: Thomas Hoch: Zukunftsperspektive durch strategischen Investor, in: Freudenberg Magazin, 1/2007, p. 9.

Hoch, 2008: Thomas Hoch: Eine leidenschaftliche Unternehmerin. Maria Luisa Cosso im Portrait, in: Freudenberg Magazin, 1/2008, p. 40–41.

Hoch, 2008a: Thomas Hoch: Die Gründung des Global Executive Team. Mehrwert durch Zusammenarbeit, in: Freudenberg Magazin, 4/2008, p. 18–19.

Hoch, 2008b: Thomas Hoch: Forschungsdienste produzieren für Brennstoffzellen-B-Klasse, in: Freudenberg Magazin, 4/2008, p. 37.

Hoch, 2009: Thomas Hoch: Grösstes Kreuzfahrtschiff der Welt mit Freudenbergprodukten, in: Freudenberg Magazin, 3/2009, p. 4.

Hoch, 2009a: Thomas Hoch: Standardfilter für Brennstoffzelle, in: Freudenberg Magazin, 2/2009, p. 7.

Hoch, 2010: Thomas Hoch: Der Schlüssel zur Sicherheit. Batterieseparator für Elektroautos, in: Freudenberg Magazin, 4/2010, p. 27.

Hoch, 2010a: Thomas Hoch: Vliesstoffe mit heilender Wirkung in: Freudenberg Magazin, 4/2010, p. 24.

Hoch, 2010b: Thomas Hoch: Mit Diamantschicht gegen Selbstzerstörung, in: Freudenberg Magazin, 4/2010, p. 25.

Hoch, 2011: Thomas Hoch: Mitreissende Momente. Die Chronik des Dialog 2011, in: Freudenberg Magazin, 3/2011, p. 16–25.

Hoch, 2011a: Thomas Hoch: Grosse Hilfsbereitschaft. Spenden für Japan, in: Freudenberg Magazin, 2/2011, p. 6.

Hoch, 2011b: Thomas Hoch: SurTec in Zwingenberg – Chemiker mit grüner Ader, in: Freudenberg Magazin, 1/2011, p. 14–17.

Hoch/Baldauf, 2011: Thomas Hoch, Andreas Baldauf: Gemeinsames Werteverständnis weltweit vorleben. Interview mit Dr. Dirk Mahler und Jochen Strasser, in: Freudenberg Magazin, 3/2011, p. 26–27.

Hoch/Orians, 2006: Thomas Hoch, Wolfgang Orians: Interview mit Dr. Peter Bettermann zum DIALOG. 'Wir haben die Kraft, Verbesserungen umzusetzen', in: Freudenberg Magazin, 2/2006, p. 4–7.

Hochschild, 2013: Adam Hochschild: Der grosse Krieg. Der Untergang des alten Europa im Ersten Weltkrieg, Stuttgart 2013.

Hockerts, 2013: Hans Günter Hockerts: Wiedergutmachung in Deutschland 1945–1990. Ein Überblick, in: Bundeszentrale für politische Bildung (Publ.): Aus Politik und Zeitgeschichte, 63, Bonn 2013, p. 15–22. Accessible online at: https://www.bpb.de/apuz/162883/wiedergutmachung-in-deutschland-19451990-ein-ueberblick?p=all, accessed on August 18, 2020.

Hoffmann, 1978: G. Hoffmann: Das Simrit-Werk 1929–1978. Die Entwicklung seiner Produktionsstätten, Weinheim 1978, in: Corporate Archives 3/01250.

Hoffmann, 2022: Felizia Hoffmann: Im Zangengriff der Coronavirus-Pandemie – zwischen Resilienz und Illusion, in: Frankfurt University of Applied Sciences (Publ.): Die Coronavirus-Pandemie – Gesellschaftliche, ökonomische und politische Folgen für Europa, Schriftenreihe CAES, Vol. 6, Frankfurt, 2022, p. 8–15.

Hönecke, 2005: Karin Hönecke: 'Tack' – Europas ältester Schuhbetrieb. 110 Jahre Schuhindustrie in Burg, publ. by Heimatverein Burg und Umgebung e. V., Oschersleben 2005.

Hoppe, 1952: Heinz Hoppe: Das Norawerk, in: Der Freudenberger, 6/1952, p. 4–12.

Hoppe, 1991: Heinz C. Hoppe: Ein Stern für die Welt. Vom 'einfachen Leben' in Ostpreussen zum Vorstand bei Daimler-Benz. Munich, 1991.

Horchler, 2006: Michael Horchler: Die Väter der Vliesstoffe, in: Freudenberg Magazin, 4/2006, p. 30–31.

Horchler, 2009: Michael Horchler: Ein echter Krimi, in: Freudenberg Magazin, 3/2009, p. 28.

Horchler, 2011: Michael Horchler: Die Entwicklung der Lederherstellung in Weinheim – vom Handwerk zur Industrie, in: Unser Museum, Mitteilungen des Förderkreises des Museums Weinheim, No. 22/2011, Förderkreis des Museums Weinheim e. V. (Publ.), Weinheim 2011, p. 29–38.

Horchler, 2014: Michael Horchler: Sportliche Höchstleistungen dank Freudenberg, in: Freudenberg Magazin 3/2014, p. 50.

Horchler, 2015: Michael Horchler: Wie Freudenberg die Lederindustrie revolutionierte, in: Freudenberg Magazin, 1/2015, p. 46.

Horchler, 2015a: Michael Horchler: Vom mittelalterlichen Wappen zur Weltmarke, in: Freudenberg Magazin, 2/2015, p. 46.

Horchler, 2017: Michael Horchler: Eine Frage der Tradition. Hans Freudenberg, Wegbereiter der Talentförderung und -entwicklung, in: Freudenberg Magazin 2/2017, p. 55.

Horchler, 2018: Michael Horchler: Von der Gerberei zum globalen Technologiekonzern. Die Internationalisierung der Freudenberg Gruppe (1849–2002), in: Ute Engelen, Michael Matheus (Publ.): Regionale Produzenten oder Global Player? Zur Internationalisierung der Wirtschaft im 19. und 20. Jahrhundert, in: Geschichtliche Landeskunde, Vol. 74, Stuttgart 2018, p. 129–140.

Horchler, 2018a: Michael Horchler: Richtungswechsel oder langer Atem, in: Freudenberg Magazin, 4/2018, p. 78–79.

Horchler, 2019: Michael Horchler: Firmengründer mit Strahlkraft. 200. Geburtstag von Carl Johann Freudenberg, in: Freudenberg Magazin, 2/2019, p. 63.

Horchler, 2019a: Michael Horchler: Weltklasse – von Anfang an. Historische Auszeichnungen als Motor für Transformation, in: Freudenberg Magazin, 3/2019, p. 58–59.

Horchler, 2020: Michael Horchler: Geschichte der Japan Vilene Company (1958–2020), Weinheim 2020, in: Corporate Archives 3/11001.

Horchler, 2020a: Michael Horchler: Geschichte der Partnerschaft Freudenberg-NOK (1959–2020), Weinheim 2020, in: Corporate Archives 3/11002.

Horchler, 2021: Michael Horchler: Dauerbrenner Brennstoffzelle, in: Freudenberg Magazin, 1/2021, p. 69–71.

Horchler, 2021a: Michael Horchler: Das Freudenberg Schaumkunstleder Helia, Weinheim 2021, in: Corporate Archives 3/11168.

Horchler/Schultens, 2021: Michael Horchler, Leonie Schultens: Vom Umweltschutz zu "Sustainability drives Climate Action". Rückblick auf über 120 Jahre Nachhaltigkeit bei Freudenberg, in: Freudenberg Magazin, 3/2021, p. 26–27.

Huber, 1959: Kurt Huber: Viledon Filtermatten helfen gegen Staub und Russ, in: Der Freudenberger, 5/1959, p. 11.

Huber, 1964: Kurt Huber: Viledon-Filtermatten, in: Der Freudenberger, 1/1964, p. 33.

Huber, 1966: Kurt Huber: Das neue Viledon-Werk II Zwischen Dämmen, in: Der Freudenberger, 3/1966, p. 4–5.

Hütter, 2009: Daniel Hütter: Nachfolge in Familienunternehmen – Eszet Staengel & Ziller und Freudenberg GmbH & Co. KG im 19. und 20. Jahrhundert, Ostfildern 2009.

Hütter, 2013: Daniel Hütter: Der Ettlinger Kreis 1957–1977. Unternehmer als bildungs- und gesellschaftspolitische Reformelite in der jungen Bundesrepublik, in: Miriam Gebhardt, Katja Patzel-Mattern, Stefan Zahlmann: Das integrative Potential von Elitekulturen. Festschrift für Clemens Wischermann, Stuttgart 2013, p. 161–176.

Illius, 1997: Elisabeth Illius: Damit Partikel, Gase und Gerüche draussen bleiben. Neue Generation von MicronAir Kombifiltern, in: Der Freudenberger, 5/1997, p. 4.

Illius, 1997a: Elisabeth Illius: "Appell an die Führungskräfte. Rede von Dr. Dr. Peter Bettermann bei DIALOG 97", in: Der Freudenberger, 7/1997, p. 3.

Illius, 1999: Elisabeth Illius: Freudenberg startet das internationale Jugend-Programm TANNER, in: Der Freudenberger, 5/1999, p. 1.

Illius, 2002: Elisabeth Illius: We (all) take care: Vorschläge für mehr Sicherheit, in: Freudenberger, 3/2002, p. 16–17.

Illius, 2002a: Elisabeth Illius: Durch Innovation und neue Strukturen zur Marktreife, in: Freudenberger, 2/2002, p. 18.
Illius, 2004: Elisabeth Illius: Wachstumspotenzial in Nordamerika, in: Freudenberg Magazin, 3/2004, p. 12–16.
Illius, 2017: Elisabeth Illius: Offen für Neues, in: Marktplatz, 3/2017, p. 1 and p. 9.
Illius, 2018: Elisabeth Illius: Die Zukunft ist zum Greifen nah, in: Marktplatz, 3/2018, p. 2.
Illius, 2018a: Elisabeth Illius: Gasdiffusionslagen von FPM, in: Marktplatz, 1/2018, p. 7.
Illius, 2018b: Elisabeth Illius: Filter für Brennstoffzellen von FFT, in: Marktplatz, 1/2018, p. 7.
Illius, 2019: Elisabeth Illius: Beim Ankommen zur Seite stehen, in: Marktplatz, 4/2019, p. 1 and p. 6.
Illius, 2020: Elisabeth Illius: Das Projekt muss zur Strategie passen, in Marktplatz, 4/2020, p. 5.
James, 1988: Harold James: Deutschland in der Weltwirtschaftskrise 1924–1936, Stuttgart 1988.
Jürgs, 2005: Michael Jürgs: Der kleine Frieden im grossen Krieg: Westfront 1914. Als Deutsche, Franzosen und Briten gemeinsam Weihnachten feierten, Munich 2005.
Keller, 2000: Heinz Keller: Weinheim 1933–1945 – Zeitskizzen, in: Stadt Weinheim (Publ.): Die Stadt Weinheim zwischen 1933 und 1945, Weinheim 2000, p. 9–133.
Kershaw, 2009: Ian Kershaw: Hitler 1889–1945, Munich 2009.
Kleinschmidt, 2002: Christian Kleinschmidt, Der produktive Blick. Wahrnehmung amerikanischer und japanischer Management- und Produktionsmethoden durch deutsche Unternehmer 1950–1985, Berlin 2002.
Kleinschmidt, 2007: Christian Kleinschmidt: Technik und Wirtschaft im 19. und 20. Jahrhundert, Munich 2007.
Klier, 2004: Ellen Klier: Burgmann und seine Wurzeln, in: Freudenberg Magazin Spezial, Special Edition 2004, p. 14–16.
Klier, 2007: Ellen Klier: Diamantschicht sorgt für aussergewöhnlichen Verschleissschutz, in: Freudenberg Magazin, 2/2007, p. 35.
Kraft, 1963: Kurt Kraft: Freudenberg Vliesstoffe, in: Der Freudenberger, 4/1963, p. 1–4.
Kraft, 1970: Kurt Kraft: Die Vliesstoff-Gruppe bei Freudenberg, 2. Teil, in: Der Freudenberger, 3/1970, p. 2–9.
Kraft, 1970a: Kurt Kraft: Zehn Jahre Japan Vilene Company, in: Der Freudenberger, 4/1970, p. 18–19.
Kunzel, 2014: Michael Kunzel: Die Inflation, Berlin 2014. Accessible online at: https://www.dhm.de/lemo/kapitel/weimarer-republik/innenpolitik/inflation-1923.html, accessed on June 2, 2020.
Lang, 2000: Toni Lang: Nationalsozialistische Wirtschafts- und Sozialpolitik in der Stadt Weinheim, in: Stadt Weinheim (Publ.): Die Stadt Weinheim zwischen 1933 und 1945, Weinheim 2000, p. 161–312.
Lauppe, 1968: Wilhelm Lauppe: Die Nontex S. A. in Spanien, in: Der Freudenberger, 4/1968, p. 10–12.

Lauppe, 1978: Wilhelm Lauppe: Bericht zur Vliesstoffgeschichte bei Freudenberg, Weinheim 1978, in: Corporate Archives 3/00835.

Lehmann, 1963: Alfred Lehmann: Zehn Jahre Vlieseline-Studio, in: Der Freudenberger, 4/1963, p. 5–7.

Leicht, 2015: Johannes Leicht: Gründerkrach und Gründerkrise, Berlin 2015. Accessible online at: https://www.dhm.de/lemo/kapitel/kaiserreich/industrie-und-wirtschaft/gruenderkrach.html, accessed on April 24, 2019.

Leicht, 2015a: Johannes Leicht: Die "Arisierung" im NS-Regime, Berlin 2015. Accessible online at: https://www.dhm.de/lemo/kapitel/ns-regime/industrie-und-wirtschaft/arisierung.html, accessed on October 14, 2019.

Li, 2015: Roy Li: Sicher durch extreme Kälte, in: Freudenberg Magazin, 1/2015, p. 25.

Lindenlaub, 1985: Dieter Lindenlaub: Maschinenbauunternehmen in der Deutschen Inflation 1919–1923. Unternehmenshistorische Untersuchungen zu einigen Inflationstheorien, Berlin 1985.

Mai, 1997: Gunter Mai: Die Ökonomie der Zeit. Unternehmerische Rationalisierungsstrategien und industrielle Arbeitsbeziehungen (Literaturbericht), in: Geschichte und Gesellschaft, Zeitschrift für historische Sozialwissenschaften 23, Göttingen 1997, p. 311–327.

Mao, 2009: Donyan Mao: Ein Symbol des Aufbruchs – Deutsch-chinesische Zusammenarbeit beim Erdbebenhilfsprojekt in China, in: Freudenberg Magazin 3/2009, p. 6.

Marschner, 2016: Diana Marschner: Jahreschronik 2014, in: Lebendiges Museum Online, Stiftung Haus der Geschichte der Bundesrepublik Deutschland, Bonn 2016, accessible online at: http://www.hdg.de/lemo/jahreschronik/2014.html, accessed on March 14, 2022

Martens, 2020: Bernd Martens: Wirtschaftlicher Zusammenbruch und Neuanfang nach 1990, in: Bundeszentrale für politische Bildung (Publ.): Dossier: Lange Wege der Deutschen Einheit, Bonn 2020. Accessible online at: https://www.bpb.de/geschichte/deutsche-einheit/lange-wege-der-deutschen-einheit/47133/zusammenbruch, accessed on February 12, 2022.

Matter, 1999: Dirk Matter: Indien: Wirtschaftsreformen seit 1991, in: Friedrich Ebert Stiftung: Digitale Bibliothek, Bonn 1999. Accessible online at: https://library.fes.de/fulltext/stabsabteilung/00837.htm, accessed on May 20, 2022.

Mayer, 2014: Berthold Mayer: Mahnmal Erster Weltkrieg, Bundeszentrale für politische Bildung (Publ.): Themenblätter im Unterricht No. 103, Bonn 2014.

Mergel, 2005: Thomas Mergel: Grossbritannien seit 1945, Göttingen 2005.

Merz, 2000: Eberhard Merz: Die Geschichte des Simmerrings, in: Die Technikgeschichte als Vorbild moderner Technik, Vol. 25. Vom Leder zum Chemiewerkstoff, a series of publications issued by the Georg-Agricola-Gesellschaft, Bochum 2000, p. 93–105.

Michaelis, 2014: Andreas Michaelis: Die Lebensmittelrationierung, Berlin 2014. Accessible online at: https://www.dhm.de/lemo/kapitel/erster-weltkrieg/alltagsleben/lebensmittelrationierung.html, accessed on July 11, 2019.

Mitterauer, 1986: Michael Mitterauer: Sozialgeschichte der Jugend, Frankfurt/Main 1986.

Müller, 2021: Stefan Müller: (Auto)Mobile Disruption. Die Zukunft der Automobilindustrie und warum kein Stein auf dem anderen bleibt, Books on Demand, Norderstedt 2021.

Müller, 2022: Eva Müller: Die Digitalisierung der Dichtungsringe, in: Manager Magazin, 3/2022, p. 84–87.

Müller-Brehm/Otto/Puntschuh, 2020: Jaana Müller-Brehm, Philip Otto, Michael Puntschuh: Einführung und Überblick: Was bedeutet Digitalisierung?, in: Bundeszentrale für Politische Bildung (Publ.): Digitalisierung. Informationen zur politischen Bildung, Vol. 344, Bonn 2020, p. 4–5.

Münkler, 2013: Herfried Münkler: Der Grosse Krieg. Die Welt 1914–1918, Berlin 2013.

Muschelknautz, 2018: Martina Muschelknautz: Fit für die digitale Arbeitswelt der Zukunft. Freudenberg investiert 8,5 Millionen in das neue Bildungszentrum am Standort Weinheim, in: Freudenberg Magazin, 1/2018, p. 6–7.

Muschelknautz, 2021: Martina Muschelknautz: Freudenberg Medical entwickelt gemeinsam mit Partner Bambi Belt innovativen Überwachungsgürtel aus Silikon für Frühgeborene, Freudenberg-Portal Meldung vom November 2021, in: Corporate Archives 3/11117.

Mussgnug, 1993: Dorothee Mussgnug: Die Reichsfluchtsteuer 1931–1953. Schriften zur Rechtsgeschichte, Vol. 60, Berlin 1993.

Niemann, 2019: Anna-Lena Niemann: Wasserstoff, Mobilität der Zukunft?, in: Frankfurter Allgemeine Zeitung, 1. November 2019, p. 44–46.

Nottebohm, 1985: Carl Ludwig Nottebohm: Erinnerungen an die Anfänge der Kunstleder- und Vliesstoffentwicklung bei der Firma Carl Freudenberg, Weinheim 1985, in: Corporate Archives 3/01580.

Orians, 2002: Wolfgang Orians: Wir müssen der Massstab für unsere Wettbewerber werden, in: Der Freudenberger, 3/2002, p. 10–11.

Orians, 2004: Wolfgang Orians: Wir wollen weltweit die Nummer eins bei unseren Kunden werden, Interview mit Prof. Elmar Baur und Dr. Peter Stehle, in: Freudenberg Magazin Spezial, Special Edition 2004, p. 6–8.

Orians, 2005: Wolfgang Orians: Dr. Ernst Schön geht in den Ruhestand. Ein Mann für schwierige Fälle, in: Freudenberg Magazin, 2/2005, p. 36–37.

Orians, 2007: Wolfgang Orians: Vertrag über Verkauf der Bausysteme unterzeichnet. Erwerber-Konsortium übernimmt Bausysteme, in: Freudenberg Magazin, 3/2007, p. 7.

Palmer, 2018: Christoph Palmer: Reichsfinanzreform (Weimarer Republik), in: Historisches Lexikon Bayerns. Accessible online at: https://www.historisches-lexikon-bayerns.de/Lexikon/Reichsfinanzreform_(Weimarer_Republik), accessed on December 4, 2019.

Patalong, 2007: Frank Patalong: Millennium-Bug. Die Nacht, in der wir alle noch einmal davonkamen, 31. Dezember 2007, in: Spiegel online, accessible online at: https://www.spiegel.de/geschichte/millennium-bug-a-948986.html, accessed on November 30, 2022.

Pennekamp, 2023: Johannes Pennekamp: 2 Prozent Wachstum trotz Krise, in: FAZ.NET on January 13, 2023, accessible online at: https://www.faz.net/aktuell/wirtschaft/konjunktur-fast-2-prozent-wachstum-trotz-krise-18600974.html, accessed on February 4, 2023.

Pflästerer, 1949: Philipp Pflästerer: Die Weinheimer Rotgerberzunft, in: Weinheimer Geschichtsblatt No. 21, published on behalf of the City of Weinheim, Weinheim 1949.

Pinnow, 1949: Hermann Pinnow: 100 Jahre Freudenberg 1849–1949, published to mark the 100-year anniversary of the Carl Freudenberg company, Frankfurt am Main 1949.

Plumpe, 1999: Werner Plumpe: Betriebliche Mitbestimmung in der Weimarer Republik. Fallstudien zum Ruhrbergbau und zur chemischen Industrie, Munich 1999.

Plumpe, 2013: Werner Plumpe: Wirtschaftskrisen. Geschichte und Gegenwart, Munich 2013.

Plumpe, 2016: Werner Plumpe: Carl Duisberg 1861–1935. Anatomie eines Industriellen, Munich 2016.

Praet/Horchler, 2012: Philipp Praet, Michael Horchler: Die blaue Welle von Vileda, in: Freudenberg Magazin, 4/2012, p. 38.

Prenzel, 2022: Thomas Prenzel: Vor 30 Jahren: Die rassistisch motivierten Ausschreitungen von Rostock-Lichtenhagen, in: Bundeszentrale für politische Bildung (Publ.): Hintergrund aktuell, Bonn 2022, accessible online at: https://www.bpb.de/kurz-knapp/hintergrund-aktuell/254347/vor-30-jahren-die-rassistisch-motivierten-ausschreitungen-von-rostock-lichtenhagen/, accessed on December 9, 2022.

Propp, 2018: Carsten Propp: Hier wird die Digitalisierung greifbar, in: Weinheimer Nachrichten, Januar 27, 2018, p. 9.

Quandt, 2021: Roland Quandt: Intel-Chef: Mooresches Gesetz gilt weiter und lässt sich noch übertreffen, October 28, 2021, accessible online at: https://winfuture.de/news,126054.html, accessed on October 18, 2022.

Reitmayer/Rosenberger, 2008: Morten Reitmayer, Ruth Rosenberger (Publ.): Unternehmen am Ende des "Goldenen Zeitalters". Die 1970er Jahre in wirtschafts- und unternehmenshistorischer Perspektive, Essen 2008.

Röhrs, 1998: Annette Röhrs: Vliesstoffe in Südafrika, in: Der Freudenberger, 10/1998, p. 4.

Röhrs, 2005: Annette Röhrs: Ultrapräzise durch Ultraschall – Bodenbilder aus Kautschuk, in: Freudenberg Magazin, 3/2005, p. 25.

Röhrs, 2007: Annette Röhrs: Dem Fitwerden folgt das Fitbleiben, in: Marktplatz, 3/2007, p. 2.

Röhrs, 2007a: Annette Röhrs: Aus Bausysteme wird nora systems. Der Verkauf der Freudenberg Bausysteme ist abgeschlossen, in: Marktplatz, 5/2007, p. 1.

Röhrs, 2007b: Annette Röhrs: Caption AG, L-EA und MBO, in: Marktplatz 5/2007, p. 1.

Röhrs, 2007c: Annette Röhrs: Anders – und doch fast alles gleich, in: Marktplatz, 5/2007, p. 2.

Roth, 1981: Hans Roth: Von alter Zunftherrlichkeit, Rosenheim 1981.
Rzepka/Wagener, 2019: Gabriele Rzepka, Silke Wagener: Das neue Öl. Daten: kostbarer Rohstoff, in: Freudenberg Magazin, 1/2019, p. 33–35.
Sabria/Rahola, 2001: Juan Sabria, Miguel Rahola: A Passion for Mocio, in: The House of FHP, 1/2001, p. 14–16.
Sadikovic, 2013: Indira Sadikovic: Freudenberg Regional Corporate Center Nordamerika in Plymouth eingeweiht, in: Freudenberg Magazin, 4/2013, p. 9.
Schadt, 2002: Jörg Schadt: Richard Lederherz. Der Fabrikant Freudenberg war ein Wegbereiter des Landes, in: Momente, 4/2002, p. 28–30.
Schanze, 2016: Robert Schanze: Mooresches Gesetz: Definition und Ende von Moore›s Law – Einfach erklärt, February 25, 2016, online anrufbar unter: https://www.giga.de/ratgeber/specials/mooresches-gesetz-defintion-und-ende-von-moore-s-law-einfach-erklaert/, accessed on October 18, 2022.
Schildt, 2012: Axel Schildt: Politische Entscheidungen und Einstellungen, in: Bundeszentrale für politische Bildung (Publ.): Deutschland in den fünfziger Jahren, Informationen zur politischen Bildung, 256, Bonn 2012, p. 10–23.
Schiller, 1955: Günther Schiller: Eine Weltreise für CF und Vlieseline, in: Der Freudenberger, 6/1955, p. 9–10a.
Schlottau, 1993: Klaus Schlottau: Von der handwerklichen Lohgerberei zur Lederfabrik des 19. Jahrhunderts, Wiesbaden 1993.
Schlupp, 1980: Frieder Schlupp: "Modell Deutschland" and the International Division of Labour. The Federal Republic of Germany and the World Political Economy, in: Eckehard Krippendorf and Volker Rittberger (Eds.): The Foreign Policy of West Germany, London, Beverly Hills 1980, p. 33 ff.
Schnaus, 2017: Julia Schnaus: Das leise Sterben einer Branche – Der Niedergang der westdeutschen Bekleidungsindustrie in den 1960er/70er Jahren, in: Zeitschrift für Unternehmensgeschichte, herausgegeben im Auftrag der Gesellschaft für Unternehmensgeschichte von Jan-Otmar Hesse, Christian Kleinschmidt, Werner Plumpe, Berlin/Boston 2017, p. 9–33.
Schnoklake, 2015: Christina Schnoklake: Dialog 2015. Wegbereiter des Wandels, in: Freudenberg Magazin, 3/2015, p. 14–24.
Schnoklake, 2015a: Christina Schnoklake: Freudenberg wieder ausgezeichnet, in: Freudenberg Magazin, 1/2015, p. 43.
Schnoklake, 2017: Christina Schnoklake: Der Reise in die Zukunft, in: Freudenberg Magazin, 1/2017, p. 19 and p. 21–22.
Schnoklake/Zins, 2015: Christina Schnoklake, Christian Zins: Soziale Verantwortung mit Weitblick: e2 weltweit ausgerollt, in: Freudenberg Magazin, 3/2015, p. 26–27.
Scholtyseck, 2016: Joachim Scholtyseck: Freudenberg. Ein Familienunternehmen in Kaiserreich, Demokratie und Diktatur, Munich 2016.
Schultens/Wagener, 2020: Leonie Schultens, Silke Wagener: Gemeinsam Wissen durch Digitalisierung schaffen, in: Freudenberg Magazin, 5/2020, p. 42–43.
Schulz, 2011: Schulz, Matthias: Das 19. Jahrhundert (1789–1914), Stuttgart 2011.
Schulz, 2022: Anne Schulz: Populismus und die Pandemie – der Beginn einer Freundschaft?, in: Frankfurt University of Applied Sciences (Publ.): Die Coro-

navirus-Pandemie – Gesellschaftliche, ökonomische und politische Folgen für Europa, a series of publications issued by the CAES at Frankfurt University of Applied Sciences, Vol. 6, Frankfurt, 2022, p. 16–23.

Schulze, 1994: Hagen Schulze: Die Deutschen und ihre Nation. Weimar, Deutschland 1917–1933, Berlin 1994.

Schuster, 2002: Sibylla Schuster: Freudenberg in Asien, in: Freudenberg Magazin, 4/2002, p. 12–15.

Scriba, 2011: Arnulf Scriba: Das Stinnes-Legien-Abkommen, Berlin 2011. Accessible online at: https://www.dhm.de/lemo/kapitel/weimarer-republik/industrie-und-wirtschaft/stinnes-legien-abkommen-1918.html, accessed on December 4, 2019.

Scriba, 2014: Arnulf Scriba: Weimarer Republik. Aussenpolitik, Berlin 2014. Accessible online at: https://www.dhm.de/lemo/kapitel/weimarer-republik/aussenpoli tik.html, accessed on June 5, 2020.

Seynsche, 2020: Monika Seynsche: Der grösste Ölunfall der Geschichte. Deepwater-Horizon-Unglück 2010, in: Deutschlandfunk-online, April 20, 2020, accessible online at: https://www.deutschlandfunk.de/deepwater-horizon-unglueck-2010-der-groesste-oelunfall-der-100.html, accessed on June 19, 2023.

Siegle/Zepelin, 2008: Jochen Siegle, Joachim Zepelin: Matrix der Welt: SAP und der neue globale Kapitalismus, Frankfurt 2008.

Siegrist, 1981: Hannes Siegrist: Vom Familienbetrieb zum Managerunternehmen. Angestellte und industrielle Organisation am Beispiel der Georg Fischer AG in Schaffhausen 1797–1930, Göttingen 1981.

Sinz, 2008: Karl Sinz: Datenverarbeitung bei Freudenberg. Die Entwicklung der Organisation/Datenverarbeitung eines Familienunternehmens, Weinheim 2008, in: Corporate Archives 019/1123.

Smolka, 2008: Klaus Max Smolka: US-Autokrise zwingt Freudenberg zu Kurskorrektur, in: Financial Times Deutschland, July 28, 2008, p. 3.

Sohi, 2020: Mohsen Sohi: "Gesund sein" – als Mensch und als Unternehmen, in: Freudenberg Magazin, Special Edition, May 2020, p. 1–2.

Spakowski, 2022: Nicola Spakowski: China – vom Sturz der Qing-Dynastie bis zur Gegenwart, 2022, in: Bundeszentrale für politische Bildung (Publ.): Dossier: China, Bonn 2022. Accessible online at: https://www.bpb.de/themen/asien/chi na/508602/china-vom-sturz-der-qing-dynastie-bis-zur-gegenwart/, accessed on September 9, 2022.

Spoerer/Streb, 2013: Mark Spoerer, Jochen Streb: Neue deutsche Wirtschaftsgeschichte des 20. Jahrhunderts, Munich 2013.

Stadler, 1992: Gudrun Stadler: Der Spezialist löst schwere Fälle reibungslos, in: Der Freudenberger, 10/1992, p. 4.

Stadler, 1994: Gudrun Stadler: Viele Jahre eng mit Freudenberg verbunden, in: Der Freudenberger 7/8, 1994, p. 7.

Statz, 1984: Albert Statz: Die Rolle der Bundesrepublik in Westeuropa, in: Gert-Joachim Glaessner (Publ.): Die Bundesrepublik in den siebziger Jahren. Versuch einer Bilanz, Opladen 1984, p. 263–285.

Steingräber, 2013: Holger Steingräber: Houston, wir haben ein Problem, in: Freudenberg Magazin, 3/2013, p. 15–17.

Stöhr/Würmell, 1994: Martin Stöhr, Klaus Würmell (Publ.): Juden, Christen und die Ökumene. Adolf Freudenberg 1894–1994. Ein bemerkenswertes Leben, Frankfurt am Main 1994.

Stober, 1957: Heinz Stober: Metalastik. Eine neue Produktionsabteilung bei Carl Freudenberg, in: Der Freudenberger, 6/1957, p. 7–13.

Sturm, 2018: Reinhard Sturm: Vom Kaiserreich zur Republik 1918/19, in: Bundeszentrale für politische Bildung (Publ.): Dossier: Weimarer Republik, Bonn 2018, p. 56–77.

Sturm, 2018a: Reinhard Sturm: Kampf um die Republik 1919–1923, in: Bundeszentrale für politische Bildung (Publ.): Dossier: Weimarer Republik, Bonn 2018, p. 78–95.

Sturm, 2018b: Reinhard Sturm: Zwischen Festigung und Gefährdung 1924–1929, in: Bundeszentrale für politische Bildung (Publ.): Dossier: Weimarer Republik, Bonn 2018, p. 96–117.

Stürmer, 1985: Michael Stürmer: Die Zünfte und die Zukunft, Frankfurter Allgemeine Zeitung, January 11, 1985, p. 13.

Sudrow, 2010: Anne Sudrow: Der Schuh im Nationalsozialismus. Eine Produktgeschichte im deutsch-britisch-amerikanischen Vergleich, Göttingen 2010.

Theurl, 1998: Theresia Theurl: Währungsumstellungen in der deutschen Geschichte seit 1871, in: Historisch-Politische Mitteilungen. Archiv für Christlich-Demokratische Politik, Vol., 1998, p. 175–200. Accessible online at: https://www.kas.de/c/document_library/get_file?uuid=6c7279bd-0aab-0f78-34c4-c78a431706de&groupId=252038, accessed on April 24, 2019.

Thränhardt, 2013: Dietrich Thränhardt: Bundesrepublik Deutschland – Entwicklung 1949–1990, in: Uwe Andersen, Wichard Woyke (Publ.): Handwörterbuch des politischen Systems der Bundesrepublik Deutschland, Heidelberg 2013, Accessible online at: https://www.bpb.de/nachschlagen/lexika/handwoerterbuch-politisches-system/201996/bundesrepublik-deutschland-entwicklung-1949-1990, accessed on September 17, 2020.

Treusch, 2016: Wolf-Sören Treusch: Vor 25 Jahren, "Gemeinschaftswerk Aufschwung Ost" wird beschlossen, in: Deutschlandfunk, accessible online at: https://www.deutschlandfunk.de/vor-25-jahren-gemeinschaftswerk-aufschwung-ost-wird.871.de.html?dram:article_id=347378, accessed on February 12, 2022.

Vileda, 2008: Vileda GmbH (Publ.): 60 Jahre Vileda, Weinheim 2008.

Wagner, 1924: E. Wagner (Publ.), Historisches Album 1914/1923. Deutsche Zahlungsmittel, Deutsches Reichs-Gebrauchsmuster No. 866037, Mühlhausen 1924.

Weber, 2010: Petra Weber: Gescheiterte Sozialpartnerschaft – Gefährdete Republik? Industrielle Beziehungen, Arbeitskämpfe und der Sozialstaat. Deutschland und Frankreich im Vergleich (1918–1933/39), Munich 2010.

Wentzler, 1972: Peter Wentzler: Simrit heute und morgen. Vortrag vor den Gesellschaftern, Weinheim 1972, in: Corporate Archives 3/10170.

Wilderotter, 1992: Stefan D. Wilderotter: Richard Freudenberg. Liberaler Politiker und unabhängiger Bundestagsabgeordneter, Weinheim 1992.

Willaredt, 1964: H. E. Willaredt: Die dritte blaue Vileda-Welle, in: Der Freudenberger, 1/1964, p. 31.

Winkler, 2018: Heinrich August Winkler: Weimar 1918–1933. Die Geschichte der ersten deutschen Demokratie, Munich 2018.

Wirsching, 2006: Andreas Wirsching: Abschied vom Provisorium. Geschichte der Bundesrepublik Deutschland 1982–1990, Munich 2006.

Wirsching, 2018: Andreas Wirsching: Deutsche Geschichte im 20. Jahrhundert, Munich 2018.

Wirtschaftsausschuss, 1930: Ausschuss zur Untersuchung der Erzeugungs- und Absatzbedingungen der deutschen Wirtschaft (Publ.): Die Deutsche Lederindustrie. Verhandlungen und Berichte des Unterausschusses für allgemeine Wirtschaftsstruktur (I. Unterausschuss), 5. Arbeitsgruppe (Aussenhandel), Vol. 1, Berlin 1930.

Wöhe/Döring, 2013: Günter Wöhe, Ulrich Döring: Einführung in die Allgemeine Betriebswirtschaftslehre, 25th edition, Munich 2013.

Wohltmann, 2018: Hans-Werner Wohltmann: Stagflation, in: Gabler Wirtschaftslexikon Online. Accessible online at: https://wirtschaftslexikon.gabler.de/definition/stagflation-45364/version-268659, accessed on April 16, 2021.

Wolf, 2005: Claudia Wolf: Wie ein Flugzeugingenieur Hausfrauen zum aufrechten Gang verhalf, in: Freudenberg Magazin, 1/2005, p. 42.

Woller, 1986: Hans Woller, Gesellschaft und Politik in der amerikanischen Besatzungszone. Die Region Ansbach und Fürth, Munich 1986.

Wollstein, 2010: Günter Wollstein: Revolution von 1848, in: Bundeszentrale für politische Bildung (Publ.): Informationen zur politischen Bildung, 265, Bonn 2010, p. 15.

Würz, 2023: Markus Würz: Einführung des Euro, in: Lebendiges Museum Online, Stiftung Haus der Geschichte der Bundesrepublik Deutschland, Bonn 2023. Accessible online at: http://www.hdg.de/lemo/kapitel/globalisierung/internationale-herausforderungen/einfuehrung-des-euro.html, accessed on January 27, 2023.

Zahn, 1966: Clemens Zahn: Arbeitskosten und Lebenslagen zwischen Inflation und grosser Krise, St. Katharinen 1996.

Zeidler, 1914: Hermann Zeidler, Die moderne Lederfabrikation. Ein praktischer Wegweiser durch das Gesamtgebiet der Gerberei, Leipzig 1914.

Zillmann, 2011: Jens Zillmann: Das Auto wird 125 Jahre alt und Freudenberg feiert mit, in: Freudenberg Magazin, 3/2011, p. 4–5.

All images displayed in this book, if not otherwise attributed, were sourced from the Freudenberg & Co. KG Company Archives.